Economics
of Development

Pan A. Yotopoulos

Stanford University

Jeffrey B. Nugent

University of Southern California

Economics of Development
EMPIRICAL INVESTIGATIONS

Harper & Row, Publishers
New York / Hagerstown / San Francisco / London

Sponsoring Editor: John Greenman
Project Editor: Alice M. Solomon
Designer: T. R. Funderburk
Production Supervisor: Francis X. Giordano
Compositor: V & M Typographical, Inc.
Printer and Binder: Halliday Lithograph Corporation
Art Studio: Eric G. Hieber Associates, Inc.

ECONOMICS OF DEVELOPMENT: Empirical Investigations

Library of Congress Cataloging in Publication Data

Yotopoulos, Pan A
    Economics of development.

    Bibliography: p.
    Includes indexes.
    1. Economic development.   I. Nugent, Jeffrey B.,
joint author.   II. Title.
HD82.Y58   338.9   75-38733
ISBN 0-06-047329-0

To the memory of our fathers
Konstantin and John Rolf

Contents

List of Tables

List of Figures

Preface

This book was inspired by what we consider to be an imbalance in the treatment of development economics: Theoretical analysis seems to have grown entirely independently of the accumulation of empirical findings. As a result, there are development theories that have largely remained devoid of empirical content, especially of hard corroborative evidence; and on the other hand, there are bodies of empirical findings that are still in search of a theory. We attempt to bridge this gap by dealing exclusively with empirical hypotheses in the economics of development—that is, with alternative propositions among which one can discriminate by reference to the facts.

It is this focus on empirical hypotheses that most clearly differentiates this book from others in the field. The empirical content, however, is obtained at the cost of all-inclusive coverage. Excluded are some otherwise-interesting hypotheses that have yet to be

referenced to a systematic body of data; also absent are observable facts that have yet to be organized around a systematic analytical framework. In an attempt to offset the lack of balance with respect to topical coverage, we have tried for balance in some other important aspects.

First, our eclectic approach to development makes it easier to avoid some of the false dilemmas that have been featured in the literature: the primacy of capital accumulation versus the importance of increasing employment opportunities in the short run, agricultural development versus industralization, export expansion versus import substitution, and market freedom versus intervention and planning. Dilemmas are commonly fraught with the twin dangers of choosing the wrong term of an option or, even worse, mistaking the option itself. The latter peril may arise when one chooses between two approaches, neither of which is a solution to the problem involved, or both of which are complements rather than substitutes.

Second, our eclectic treatment of the subject opens up possibilities for synthesizing different approaches to development. Partial analysis has obvious applications but also severe limitations as compared to general equilibrium techniques. Macroeconomic approaches leave some important gaps that have to be filled by microanalytic techniques, and vice versa. Although aggregate demand analysis sheds light on some important questions, development evolves to a great extent around the economics of supply.

The most important area for synthesizing lies in the combination of neoclassical equilibrium analysis with structural disequilibrium approaches. This is a difficult and largely unfinished task in any field of economics, but especially in development economics, because it involves the clash of two alternative paradigms. The neoclassical paradigm envisions economic development as a process that is gradual and continuous, harmonious and cumulative, and endowed with important spread and trickle-down effects. Although the neoclassical paradigm adequately describes some aspects of development, it leaves important phenomena—like migration, dualism, income distribution, and some aspects of trade—begging for explanation. In such cases, discontinuities, conflicts of interest, cumulative departures from equilibrium, backwash effects, and growth that trickles up rather than down become the bedrock of reality, and the paradigm of development disequilibrium may be more relevant.

The book has been designed for a two-semester course at the advanced undergraduate or graduate level. It leaves much room, however, for the instructor to distill the material for use at a lower-level or in a shorter course. Experience from our classes, for example, has suggested the following outline for a basic one-semester undergraduate course in the economics of development.

1. *Introduction: Economic and Social Content of Development*
   Chapter 1, portions of Chapter 3
2. *Methodological Problems in Economic Development*
   Chapter 2
3. *Poverty and the Distribution of Income*
   Chapter 14
4. *Labor, Unemployment, and Migration*
   Chapters 12 and 13
5. *The Organization of Production: Economies of Scale and Technological Change*
   Elements of neoclassical production analysis from Chapter 5, the nontechnical portions of Chapter 6, the nontechnical portions of Chapter 9
6. *The Organization of Production: Structural Change, Balances, and Linkages*
   Elements of input-output analysis from Chapter 5, Chapter 16
7. *The Role of Agriculture*
   Portions of Chapter 15
8. *Trade Dependence*
   Chapter 17
9. *The Unfinished Business*
   Chapter 22

Other combinations of the material are possible to accomodate courses such as: Economic Development and International Trade, Planning and Economic Development, or The Role of Agriculture in Economic Development.

In the course of researching and writing this book, we have accumulated a sizable intellectual debt to numerous students, friends, and colleagues. The people who prodded us along, who served as helpful critics, and who set us straight at times are too numerous to mention. Among those who read portions of the manuscript in one or another of its many versions and made numerous comments are: G. C. Archibald, Kenneth J. Arrow, Jere R. Behrman, Henry J. Bruton, Walter P. Falcon, Moheb Ghali, Robert E. Evenson, Walter Miklius, Bertrand Renaud, John H. Power, Lance Taylor, Larry E. Westphal, and Jeffrey G. Williamson. Any rough edges and errors that remain may suggest that we have not taken full advantage of the perspicacity and helpfulness of these reviewers who are gratefully thanked and eagerly absolved from responsibility.

Even greater are our intellectual debts to our colleagues Michael DePrano, Larry Lau, and John Wise for their critically important contributions to the joint research we have drawn upon in several chapters of the book. We would also like to acknowledge the *American Economic Review*, the *Quarterly Journal of Economics*, *Econometrica*, the *Journal of Development Economics*, the *Journal of Political Economy*, the *Review of Economics and Statistics*, the Center of Planning and

Economic Research, and Johns Hopkins University Press, who have published earlier versions of some of this research. Similarly, we are indebted to the East-West Center, Technology and Development Institute, which provided to one of the authors a Senior Fellow Award and a welcome respite from his usual academic duties at a period that was most critical for finalizing the manuscript.

The process of turning ideas into a readable manuscript demands both skill and good humor that is often beyond the ability of the authors to provide. Joyce Sanders provided the former, and often the latter as well, by carefully, speedily, and cheerfully typing innumerable indecipherable drafts; Verna Abe made order out of the chaos of the bibliography. Our greatest debt, of course, goes to our wives, Mary and Patricia, for inexhaustible supplies of good humor and for forbearance, tolerance and cooperation; a final debt is to our children for their bemused understanding of their fathers' long periods of truncated aloofness.

Pan A. Yotopoulos
Jeffrey B. Nugent

Part I
Introduction

Part I introduces the reader to what this book is and is not about.

Our endeavor is largely prompted by the cynicism that has recently engulfed economic development viewed as a policy goal and by the disaffection that has afflicted the field of development economics. We discuss these factors and the scope of the book in Chapter 1.

A distinctive characteristic of our approach is that we concentrate on operational hypotheses—a relatively small subset of the literature on economic development. Our excursion into the methodology of science in Chapter 2 serves to sensitize the reader to the essential characteristics of the hypotheses we will be examining and to introduce the formal requirements of empirical testing. A substantial portion of the literature in the field has been based on introspective rationalization rather than on empirical propositions that have been or could be tested. Chapter 2 is useful in steering a course clear of the twin dangers of inappropriate generalization and empty formalism.

This book is about the economics of development, and as a result, it largely ignores noneconomic factors—at least to the extent that they cannot be readily incorporated in operational hypotheses. To help bridge this gap, we devote Chapter 3 to some higher level hypotheses that are often difficult to test. If they are not operational, we attempt to show how and why they are not. In a sense, therefore, Chapter 3 can be considered a continuation of the methodological discussion of Chapter 2.

Chapter 1

The Record of Economic Development and the Disillusionment with Development Economics

Throughout the almost three decades since World War II, development has been viewed as an important goal of economic life. Economic development has become an overriding objective of poor and rich nations alike. The new nations especially have seen development as the continuation of the political struggle that brought their independence. Thus, they have associated development with the success or failure of their attempts to gain freedom from alien domination.

The universality of the goal of economic development, along with the discovery of an array of frustrating and seemingly never ending obstacles in the quest of less developed countries (LDCs) for economic growth, have fostered an economic literature rich in general diagnoses and policy prescriptions. Development economics long ago became an active, or more appropriately an activist, subject with a vast number of recipes for "how to do it."

For years, the performance of LDCs with respect to the goal of economic development has generally been improving. Similarly, the economic development literature has also been improving—and proliferating. Nevertheless, it is not difficult to detect an almost catatonic disaffection with respect to both. The goal of development is now being questioned, and the record of achievement with respect to that goal is being criticized; concurrently, the respectability of the economics of development as an analytical discipline is being impugned.[1]

We are in accord with much of this criticism. We recognize that the price of development is frequently high. We are also disap-

---

[1] For example, Srinivasan (1972) attributes to an unnamed but highly respected economic theorist the following statement: "Those among economists who cannot make the grade as mathematical economists, statisticians, monetary or trade economists or economic historians usually end up either as labor economists or worse still as development economists."

pointed because after considerable efforts—and despite some notable successes—the LDCs, as a whole, are still falling behind the developed countries (DCs) with respect to economic development. In the same breath, we must admit that despite a voluminous literature the field of development economics remains distinctly underdeveloped in terms of systematic analysis and an empirically tested body of knowledge.

Nevertheless, the goal of development, whatever its costs, is sufficiently important—indeed, it is entwined with survival in a number of LDCs—that it will undoubtedly be retained. Furthermore, the experience of some LDCs that have managed to achieve impressively high rates of growth suggests that the record of development performance can be improved. Finally, the development literature is being revitalized by shedding its early doctrinaire approach, and this fact inspires considerable hope for development economics—at least once the field becomes firmly based on analytically sound and operationally meaningful foundations. Although much progress has been made in recent years, there still exists a substantial gap between the insights gained from development experience and the requirements of systematic analysis and empirically tested theory in this field of crucial and worldwide importance. Our desire to contribute to the closing of this gap serves as the primary motivation for this book.

The Record of Economic Development

Successes, Failures, and Some Lessons from Experience

The postwar period has been characterized by the active pursuit of economic development. In the 1950s, LDCs plunged into planning for economic development, and the DCs, apart from increasing their own growth rates, began making conscious efforts (primarily bilateral at first but eventually also multilateral) to assist LDCs in their quest for development. The 1960s opened with the United Nations General Assembly Resolution 1710 (XVI) announcing the "Development Decade"—an appellation that, for better or worse, has remained. The quantitative objective, as formulated in the United Nations resolution, was to achieve a minimum annual growth rate of aggregate national income of 5 percent in all, or most, LDCs. Although national income accounting figures for earlier periods are available for very few LDCs, the general presumption is that the 5 percent target represented a significant advance over the growth rates previously obtained by most of these countries.

Table 1.1 describes the record of achievement for DCs and LDCs over two decades, 1950–1969.[2] At first glance, the record of both DCs and LDCs would seem very creditable. Gross domestic product (GDP) in real terms increased on the average at 4.7 percent per annum during the 1950s in both DCs and LDCs. During the Development Decade of the 1960s, the average annual growth rate increased to 5.2 percent in the DCs and 5.0 percent in the LDCs. About two-thirds of the LDCs included in the table increased their growth rates during the Development Decade. The deceleration of the growth rate observed for some LDCs was largely due to exogenous factors, such as a slowdown in the rate of growth of oil exports (Venezuela and Iraq) or a significant fall in the international price of an export commodity (such as cocoa in Ghana). Indeed, during the 1960s especially, a number of LDCs performed extremely well, rivaling the outstanding performance of Japan among the DCs. For example, Taiwan, Korea, Iran, Thailand, Panama, Puerto Rico, Spain, Greece, and Nicaragua all achieved growth rates of real GDP exceeding 7 percent per annum.

The higher population growth rates of the LDCs have implied a lesser improvement in per capita GDP than that of the DCs. Nevertheless, the per capita growth rates of 2.0 and 2.3 percent per annum sustained by the LDCs over the decades of the 1950s and 1960s respectively are quite respectable. If continued, these growth rates would permit a doubling of living standards within a period of 30 years—well within the working lifetime

[2]The table does not include growth rates for the socialist countries or for a large number of LDCs in Africa and Asia for which comparable data are unavailable. It is not clear how the inclusion of these countries would affect the results. Judging from data for the socialist countries, which are defined in terms of "gross material product" (a concept not exactly comparable with the data given in terms of "gross domestic product" for Western countries), the socialist LDCs and DCs alike would appear to have been growing at 6 percent per annum or better. Some other LDCs, also missing from the table, that have struck oil in recent years have been growing rapidly, but some resource-poor countries of Africa and Asia would appear to have been doing especially poorly.

Table 1.1 *Average Annual Growth Rates of Gross Domestic Product at Constant Prices, 1950–1969 (Percent)*

	Developed Countries					Less Developed Countries			
	GDP		GDP Per Capita			GDP		GDP Per Capita	
Country	1950–1959	1960–1969	1950–1959	1960–1969	Country	1950–1959	1960–1969	1950–1959	1960–1969
Australia	3.9	5.4	2.2	3.4	Argentina	3.0	4.0	1.1	2.4
Austria	6.1	4.3	5.6	3.8	Bolivia	0.0	6.0	−2.5	3.3
Belgium	3.0	4.5	2.5	3.9	Brazil[b]	5.8	4.4	2.8	1.2
Canada	4.0	5.7	1.3	3.8	Chile	3.6	4.6	1.2	2.0
Denmark	3.4	4.5	2.8	3.7	China-Taiwan	6.6	10.3	3.3	7.1
France	4.5	5.6	3.6	4.5	Colombia[a]	4.7	4.9	1.6	1.7
Germany	7.9	4.4	6.9	3.4	Cyprus	5.0	6.3	4.0	5.2
Iceland	5.0	5.1	2.9	3.4	Dominican Republic[b]	6.1	2.9	2.5	−0.6
Italy	5.7	5.2	5.1	4.4	El Salvador[b]	4.2	6.6	1.5	2.8
Japan	9.8	10.6	8.9	9.4	Ghana	4.4	2.2	1.9	−0.5
Netherlands	4.8	5.2	3.6	3.9	Greece	5.9	7.3	5.0	6.6
Norway	3.6	5.0	2.7	4.2	Guatemala	3.8	5.3	0.8	2.1
South Africa	—	6.1	—	3.7	Honduras	3.8	5.5	0.9	2.1
Sweden	3.3	4.6	2.7	3.8	India[b]	4.1	3.1	2.0	0.5
Switzerland	4.4	4.0	3.1	2.3	Indonesia[b]	—	2.1	—	−0.3
United Kingdom	2.7	2.9	2.3	2.2	Iran	—	9.0	—	5.9
United States	3.3	4.9	1.7	3.3	Iraq	10.6	6.4	8.0	2.8
AVERAGE, unweighted	4.7	5.2	3.6	4.1	Jamaica	10.1	4.7	7.8	2.5
AVERAGE, weighted by population	4.9	5.6	3.9	4.4	Korea[a]	4.4	9.1	1.6	6.3
					Malta	—	4.9	—	5.3
					Mexico[c]	6.1	6.6	2.9	3.1
					Morocco	1.4	3.8	0.0	1.0
					Nicaragua	5.2	7.2	2.3	3.6
					Pakistan	2.7	5.4	0.7	3.2
					Panama	5.2	7.8	2.2	4.4
					Peru	5.2	4.9	2.8	1.7
					Philippines[a]	4.5	4.9	1.4	1.4
					Portugal	4.1	6.1	3.6	5.2
					Puerto Rico	—	7.5	—	5.7
					Spain	5.0	7.4	4.2	6.4
					Syria	—	5.7	—	2.8
					Thailand	4.4	8.2	1.4	4.9
					Tunisia	2.8	4.1	0.0	1.0
					Turkey	5.7	6.4	2.9	3.8
					Uruguay[a]	−0.1	0.3	−1.5	−1.0
					Venezuela	8.2	5.9	4.2	2.3
					AVERAGE, unweighted	4.7	5.0	2.0	2.3
					AVERAGE, weighted by population	4.4	4.3	1.8	1.9

Notes: Two biases must be kept in mind in interpreting Table 1.1. First, in a number of LDCs, the actual rate of growth in the level of income must be lower than that indicated by the GDP rate of growth because the GDP exceeds GNP by the amount of net factor payments abroad (wage payments, profit dividends, and interest), which are often significant. Second, the rate of growth registered for DCs is most likely biased upward, by conceivably as much as 100 percent at times, for the reasons analyzed by Kuznets (1972).

[a]Years 1955–1960.
[b]Years 1960–1968.
[c]Years 1961–1969.
Sources:
Income Data:
U.N. (1972), *Yearbook of National Accounts Statistics, 1970,* Vol. 2. New York: U.N., Tables 4A, 4B.
Agency for International Development (1968), "Gross National Product: Growth Rates and Trend Data by Region and Country." Washington, D.C. (July).
O.E.C.D. (1968), *National Accounts of Less Developed Countries, 1950–1966.* Paris: OECD, Tables C, E.
Population Data:
U.N. (1972), *Statistical Yearbook, 1970.* New York: U.N., Table 18.

of the average citizen. Thus, the first lesson learned from the Development Decade is that the poverty of nations is not immutable. Development can be attained.

On the other hand, since some of the larger and more populous LDCs, such as India, Indonesia, and to a lesser extent Brazil, were growing at below average rates and one of the larger DCs, Japan, was growing at well above the average rate, the unweighted averages may somewhat overstate the development performance of the LDCs and understate that of the DCs. This can be seen by comparison with the population-weighted averages, also given in Table 1.1. More importantly, because growth of per capita income in the LDCs has been lagging noticeably behind that of the DCs, the gap between them has been increasing. In addition, the growth rates of some of the poorer LDCs, such as India, Indonesia, Pakistan, and Egypt (not shown in the table), have been considerably lower than those of some of the wealthier LDCs, such as Greece, Cyprus, Spain, and Portugal. This fact suggests the second lesson of the Development Decade: that the distribution of income, both between DCs and LDCs as a whole and among LDCs themselves, has become more rather than less unequal.

While the growth in per capita income in the LDCs has been lagging in comparison to the DCs, employment growth has fallen even farther behind. The agricultural sectors of LDCs have been less able than in the past to hold on to the rural population.[3] As a result, the lagging growth of employment has been reflected to an increasing degree in the rising numbers of unemployed slum dwellers in the urban areas. The order of magnitude of the problem is illustrated by the figures based on Turnham (1971) and given in Table 1.2. The assumptions underlying the table are simple; yet they make eminent sense, given our elementary notions about unemployment levels. The period 1950–1965 is taken as reference for projections to 1980. The supply of labor for the 30-year period is known with tolerable accuracy from population statistics. The demand for labor is crudely determined by trends in output and productivity. Since the latter is not known, one can only make assumptions about it. One can assume (optimistically) that the growth in output during the period 1950–1965 was just sufficient to keep the overall rate of unemployment constant. Still, as shown in the first column of the table, the unemployment rate would be expected to increase by an average of 7 percent between 1965 and 1980 just to account for the higher growth in the labor force, which is virtually inevitable given the age distribution of the population and other demographic

[3]The farm exodus has been fanned partly by the rising wage rates in the industrial sectors. For a means of reconciling the phenomenon of increasing urban unemployment with that of rising wage rates, the reader will have to await the discussion in Chapters 12 and 13.

Table 1.2 *Projected Unemployment Rates, 1965–1980, and Output Growth Rates Required for Reducing Unemployment Rates to 5 Percent in 1980 in Less Developed Countries, by Region (Percent)*

	Increment in Unemployment as Percent of Labor Force, 1965–1980	Range of Unemployment as Percent of Labor Force, 1980	Required Annual Output Growth Rate for Reducing Unemployment Rate to 5 percent in 1980
LDC Average	7	12–17	6.4
North Africa	19	24–29	7.7
Sub-Sahara Africa	3	8–13	6.0
West Asia	12	17–22	8.6
South Asia	7	12–17	5.8
East Asia	8	13–18	7.7
Middle America	7	12–17	9.2
South America	4	9–14	8.3

Source: Adapted from Turnham, D. (1971), *The Employment Problem in Less-Developed Countries: A Review of Evidence.* Paris: OECD Development Center, p. 116.

characteristics of LDCs. Some countries and regions will be expected to experience larger than average increases in the rate of unemployment, and others, smaller ones, the range being from 3 to 19 percent for the different regions of the world. If, on the other hand, unemployment is assumed to have increased from 5 percent in 1950 to 10 percent in 1965, the unemployment rate in 1980 would, on the average, be somewhere between 12 and 17 percent, as shown in the second column of Table 1.2. With the labor force growing by 40 percent in the LDCs in the 15-year period, the increase in the absolute number of unemployed would be even more alarming. Another way of looking at the magnitude of the unemployment problem is to calculate (on the basis of past trends) the growth in output required to hold (or reduce) the unemployment rate to 5 percent in 1980. These growth rates, shown in the last column of Table 1.2, are considerably higher than the rates achieved historically. We have noted that the population increase and the technology of production are the statistical parents that beget increasing rates of unemployment. This proposition is itself a potentially dysgenic marriage of Malthusian and Marxian economics.

With higher average incomes and more people without jobs, it follows that the distribution of personal income within LDCs has become more unequal. That this is the case has been substantiated by some recent, though tentative, studies on income distribution.[4] Therefore, the fact that development and higher rates of growth do not necessarily provide proportionate increases in employment or reduce income inequality can be regarded as the third lesson of the Development Decade of the 1960s. It is in the hope of overcoming or at least mitigating this effect that the "Second Development Decade," the decade of the 1970s, has been dubbed the "Employment and Income Distribution Decade."

Dark Spots and Other Costs

There are other costs, besides unemployment and inequality, that some critics would debit to the ledger of growth in LDCs. These costs vary with one's perception of development and perhaps inversely with the time horizon of the development process.

[4]See, for example, Adelman and Morris (1973), Chenery et al. (1974).

The principal—and with little exaggeration one could say the only—cost of development recognized by classical and neoclassical writers was the increment of abstinence from consumption in the interest of net saving. Abstinence and waiting by savers are rewarded with increased profits.

Marx, who supplied his own paradigm, had a special interest in discrediting the abstinence theory of development. Instead, he viewed capital as coming into the world "dripping from head to foot, from every pore, with blood and dirt." It is not the "waiting of the rich that should be rewarded, but rather the general deprivation of the poor" (Gurley 1971, p. 59). Thus, in contrast to the prevailing classical and neoclassical perceptions, in Marxian thought the costs of development loomed as important even in the long run.

To the orthodox Marxist, the costs of development are forced labor and the direct expropriation of property. Bronfenbrenner (1953, p. 98) remarks that "Economic development in every country has been hastened by whips on the backs of the slaves, peons and other debtors, vagrants, 'sturdy beggars,' convicts, war prisoners, and now 'class enemies.'" A variant of the forced labor cost is the exploitation of the working class that appears in the form of an ever widening gap between the productivity of the necessary productive workers and the wage share that accrues to them. This constitutes the ever increasing economic surplus, which may be applied either to development or to the production of waste.[5] When the surplus is not applied to development, expropriation of the resources that give rise to it may be necessary.

Expropriation can take different forms and refer to different kinds of property—most commonly to precious metals, often to the rights to land and mineral resources, and at times to other forms of wealth, tangible or intangible. It can take place directly, as with land reform movements, or it can be indirect, as in the case of the British enclosures movements and the uncompensated liberation of the slaves after the American Civil War. Ex-

[5]For such an interpretation of the economic surplus, which parallels the classical view of Smith's "surplus" or Ricardo's "net produce," see Baran and Hobsbawm (1961). Paul Baran (1957, foreword to 1962 printing, pp. xix to xxi) gives an illustration of the proposition and also of the possibility that a constant or even rising share of labor in national income can coexist with rising surplus.

propriation is attractive because it can be done quickly and is usually popular. What is more difficult, and therefore more costly to achieve, is to channel the expropriated surplus into productive forms of investment and to sustain capital formation and efficiency after the expropriation (Baran 1957, pp. xxvi–xxvii in 1962 printing).

Expropriation may also take more subtle forms, such as inflation. During inflation (net) monetary creditors lose and (net) monetary debtors gain. When the debtor is the issuing monetary authority and the creditors are the money holders, inflation represents in a certain sense the expropriation of property of money holders by the state. In the Schumpeterian vision, entrepreneurial innovation, the basic fuel for economic development, is financed through short-term borrowing from credit-creating banks. Inflation and "forced savings" follow, which redistribute income in favor of profit receivers (Schumpeter 1934).[6] A number of countries, including Japan and more recently several countries in Latin America, have financed a good part of their development programs at the expense of the creditors of monetary assets. But even this subtle form of expropriation has its costs, in that it is likely to stimulate expenditures on consumer durables and to impede the growth of financial intermediation, which is vital to efficiency in resource allocation and to resource mobilization.[7]

International lending from capital-rich to capital-poor countries would seem an ideal adjustment mechanism for spreading development. But this process, too, has its costs. Creditors may incur tremendous losses by lending to inefficient borrowers and by paying the costs of corruption, default, and confiscation. Debtors, on the other hand, may have to bear interest charges over and above the normal cost of borrowing to cover the risks of confiscation and default as well as to line the pockets of the monopolistic sellers of capital. Thus, the more radical political economists see in this developmental process sources of tension and conflict, particularly between foreign

[6]For a careful discussion of Schumpeter's model of economic development and of the role of inflation in financing innovation, see Meier and Baldwin (1957, Chapter 4).

[7]Moreover, inflation may lead to policies that tend to repress existing capital markets and financial intermediation. For a discussion of the factors that give rise to inflation and its consequences in LDCs, see Shaw (1973) and McKinnon (1973).

elements (and their local allies) and the majority of the indigenous population.

> A thorough-going development program that reaches deeply into all the stagnant backwaters of society is clearly in the interests of the poor in underdeveloped countries, but it is not necessarily the top priority of those who rule them, nor of the foreign corporations engaged in exploiting their resources. The over-riding goal of the ruling oligarchies is usually to maintain, and if possible to enchance, their privileged positions of wealth and power in the economic, political, and social life of the country. The principal requirement of the foreign corporations is for a stable and highly favorable environment for their investment and trading activities. (Gurley 1971, p. 56.)

Ecological considerations may constitute another cost of economic development. There are two components of the ecological argument. First is the despoliation of the environment, which is an external diseconomy in the sense that the actions of some impose a cost upon the community as a whole, which results mainly from effluence. Second is the conservation problem, the depletion of natural resources. Both effluence and depletion can be expressed as the product of population times output per capita times waste (pollution) per unit of output. The rate of growth of ecological deterioration is the sum of the rates of growth of the three components. It is in this sense that a recent twist to the ecological argument combines environment and population control (Ehrlich and Ehrlich 1970). It is true that population growth is more rapid in the LDCs than in the DCs. However, the growth rate of consumption per capita and the growth rate of waste per unit of output would seem to be far more important components than the rate of population increase in explaining the rate of environmental deterioration. If so, the blame for despoiling the world's environment must be laid squarely on the DCs rather than on the development efforts of the LDCs. There is no evidence that the three-quarters of the world's population that live in LDCs have plundered their environment to any great degree in order to improve their present lot (if so, they must have been uniquely inefficient in achieving results). Besides, it is not immediately evident that the quality of life, including environmental quality, in DCs or LDCs has deteriorated as compared, for example, to the eighteenth or nineteenth century.[8]

Clearly, some of these costs of development can be mitigated or even possibly eliminated by the adoption of appropriate policies and thus do not necessarily have to be regarded as inevitable consequences of development. Nevertheless, political as well as economic considerations often make it difficult to implement such policies, thereby making it appropriate to count these effects among the costs of development. Moreover, other costs of development are inevitable, even with optimal policies. Among these are the breakdown of traditional social and economic arrangements, the loss of pride in one's work (associated with the decline of handicrafts), the violation of strong mores and rituals, and often the decline of certain art forms and of the sense of personal independence.

What is the balance in the ledger of development when both benefits and costs are considered? Although the costs of development are certainly not negligible, when development is the only alternative that can ensure the survival of millions of the world's population it seems clear that, on balance, development is beneficial and indeed imperative. It is equally imperative that a more serious effort be made to reduce the costs of development by designing and implementing appropriate policies. The appropriate policies, however, cannot be identified until the nature of the relationships between and among the benefits of development, the costs of development, and their determinants can be more clearly specified. Rather than suggesting that development as a goal should be eliminated, we would argue that the economics of development as a subject should be refined to give more recognition to developmental costs.

The Record of the Economics of Development

The Doctrine
We turn now from the record of LDCs to the record of the field of development economics.

Three interrelated ideas, which are part and parcel of the body of theory known as neoclassical economics, have had profound influence in shaping the economics of develop-

ment.[9] They have provided the theoretical building blocks for the study of development economics and have outlined the kind of policies appropriate for achieving economic development. First, neoclassical economic development is a gradual and continuous process. This fact leads to the policy prescription of marginal adjustments. Second, the process is harmonious and cumulative. It is thus based on automatic equilibrating mechanisms. Third, there is an optimistic outlook concerning the possibilities for and benefits of continued economic growth. This emphasizes the spread effects and the trickling-down effects of economic development.

The view that development is a gradual, smooth, and continuous process would seem to have its origins in the evolutionary theories of Darwin and Spencer. It was introduced into economics mainly by Marshall, who observed ". . . the maxim that 'Nature does not willingly make a jump' . . . is especially applicable to economic developments" (Marshall 1920, p. 6). This view implies that change is nondisruptive and propelled by marginal adjustments. The price mechanism reflects these adjustments and thus becomes an important device in promoting economic development. It implies also that static, partial equilibrium techniques are sufficient for analyzing economic development.

It is the stroke of genius of neoclassical economics (and of classical economics before it) that it restores order out of conflict, harmony out of selfish drives. The operation of automatic, equilibrating mechanisms, the counterpart of the classical Invisible Hand, guarantees that development generally benefits all major income groups. In the ruling paradigm of a harmonious world, rich and poor, capitalist and laborer all work together for increased output to mutual advantage.

The optimism of the neoclassical view refers both to the future possibilities for continued development and to its spread among groups and across nations. Exchange is capable of leading to a Pareto-optimal position, and everybody benefits, at least in the sense that the gainers can compensate the losers. The neoclassical theory of international trade is an even more definite statement of the position that free exchange will spread the benefits of

---

[8]For a prodevelopment view on the quality of life, see Beckerman (1973).

[9]For a detailed sketch of the neoclassical paradigm of development, see Meier and Baldwin (1957, Chapter 3).

development across the world through specialization and the division of labor. Development spreads and trickles down and can continue uninterrupted, at least during its early stages.

The neoclassical analysis involves a delicately balanced system full of sensitive feedback mechanisms that serve either to amplify or to counter changes that occur. In the specific case of development, these changes are smooth and continuous, they take place in the context of eventual harmony of interests, and their effects spread across and trickle down so that development becomes a universal nostrum that benefits all groups.

Neoclassical economics is a house of many mansions, and any brief outline of a few basic ideas will resemble a caricature more than a sketch. The early founders of the theory, starting with Marshall, provided for numerous exceptions and generous modifications.[10] Yet the three salient ideas we described accurately portray the red thread that runs through development economics, the ruling paradigm of neoclassical economic development. Any description, for example, of neoclassical economics that omits the gradual adjustment features of the model that make the application of marginal calculus possible would be grotesque. Likewise, a general approach that provides for automatic and persistent departures from equilibrium would be inconsistent with neoclassical analysis. Equally inconsistent with neoclassical optimism are theories of secular stagnation or hypotheses predicting that the same class of people will consistently remain outside the scope of development and at the bottom of the income distribution ladder.

The neoclassical approach has served well to explain a good deal of economic development, as we will see in succeeding chapters. Nevertheless, it is not the only approach available. Marx, for example, provided his own interpretations of historical facts and saw development in a different light. Instead of a world of smooth processes, tendencies toward equilibrium, and harmonies of interest, he perceived conflicts, disequilibria, and recurring breaks in the process of development. The backwash effects attained more importance than the spread effects and the trickling-down mechanisms. When it comes to choosing

among competing paradigms, an eclectic approach may be essential for a complete understanding of the process of development.

The Dogma

We have argued that economic development as a goal is crucial and must be retained, even though the costs of economic development are significant and must also be recognized. The field of development economics, which has thus far been based largely on neoclassical analysis, has considerably underplayed the costs, as opposed to the benefits of development. As a result, it needs both revision and refinement to fit the realities of developing countries. This is no small requirement, and it should not be surprising that no such revision has been achieved. What is disappointing is that nothing close to it has ever been attempted. In our opinion, no such attempt will be forthcoming until the range of choice over the individual building blocks of any such system can be narrowed considerably.

We have noted that the economics of development has been an active, and activist, field. Rather than being characterized by speculations on how neoclassical analysis should be modified, it has been marked (quite appropriately) by a desire to provide policy solutions to the practical problems confronted by the LDCs that hamper their efforts to achieve rapid economic growth. This is generally a healthy approach. Indeed, in other fields of science (and in other fields of economics), the search for solutions to practical problems has stimulated intellectual activity and allowed the science to progress. Within economics, international trade and public finance provide two examples in which the pursuit of policy has stimulated the development of economic analysis.

Unfortunately, this has not been true of the economics of development. As early as the 1950s, numerous contradictions and paradoxes in the conventional classical-neoclassical paradigm as applied to economic development were observed. Much subsequent intellectual effort has been devoted to explaining such discrepancies away. As a result, altogether too little progress has been made in providing a scientific-analytic link between the problems identified and the solutions prescribed. In general, contributions to the field, with a number of notable exceptions that will be referred to

[10]See *Ibid.* for the amendments to the theory.

liberally in succeeding pages, have tended toward one of two poles—introspective generalization and immanent empiricism—both of which fall short of scientific analysis.[11]

Introspective generalization has been inspired by the paradigm of the evolution and growth of the DCs exclusively. Starting from the methodological precepts of neoclassical economics (which were developed in the DCs in the light of DC experience) introspection leads to spinning simple and abstract theories and applying them to all countries, including the LDCs. Introspective generalization constitutes the basis for speculative and ideological discussions of development that have led to little else than verbal battles, at worst, and to the construction of more empty theoretical boxes, at best.

The opposite approach is shared by immanent empiricists among philosophers and institutionalists among economists. This approach assigns an infinite weight to the deviations from the "special case" of the DCs. Instead of looking for a theory, the immanent empiricist looks at the data hard enough and long enough until some "general principles" become clear, less by formal logic than by insight (Bronfenbrenner 1966).

The resultant of the two forces, introspective generalization on the one hand and immanent empiricism on the other, has made the economics of development replete with dogmas but lacking in operational theories, at least until the late 1960s. Moreover, each dogma has tended to look at only one aspect of development, naively overlooking the interdependencies and the trade-offs between different facets. Some examples will illustrate the point.

The Blind Spots

Unemployment and inequality are now recognized as the two darkest spots in the record of development. Yet in the development literature, they have been largely unanticipated. Introspective generalization from the ruling neoclassical paradigm of economic development is partly responsible for these blind spots.

Neoclassical analysis views unemployment as a temporary phenomenon caused by mone-

tary factors, wars, or the introduction of new productive techniques (Meier and Baldwin 1957, p. 71). In the long run, equilibrium with unemployment is impossible, because the system has built-in mechanisms to restore full employment through allowing prices to adjust.[12] A spin-off from the neoclassical paradigm is the theory of dualistic development, which derives from the existence (temporarily) of unemployment (labor with zero marginal product) in agriculture, or at least a wage differential between agriculture and nonagriculture. According to this conception, however, there are automatic mechanisms that drive labor out of the low-wage agricultural sector and into the high-wage nonagricultural sector. This transfer increases both employment and output in the latter sector and the wage rate in the former, eventually eliminating the original wage differentials and restoring full employment.

Neoclassical analysis recognizes income inequality as arising from differential initial endowments but does not view it as an unmitigated evil. It is instead the bedrock of the incentive system on which automatic responses and gradual development are based, especially since greater income inequality may be associated with higher (marginal) savings ratios. Inequality is not a problem, not because it does not exist but because there is no reason to believe it is undesirable or likely to increase over time. Indeed, the harmony that neoclassical economists have perceived in the process of development and the optimism they have adopted toward its spread have led them to great lengths in emphasizing how development benefits all major income groups, especially labor (Meier and Baldwin 1957, p. 71). In any event, should inequality fail to decrease, Keynesian economics added the

---

[11]To give some analytical bite to these characterizations and help overcome their shortcomings, in Chapter 3 we give special attention to examples chosen from the literature of development economics.

[12]With the exception of Marx and his reserve army of the unemployed and of Ricardo's somewhat belated thoughts about technological unemployment, traditional economic doctrine has not been notably successful in anticipating the problem. Malthus provided that the birthrate would adjust downward or the death rate upward to remove unemployment and reestablish equilibrium in the labor market. Smithian optimism supposed that the propensity for thrift would stimulate a supply of savings and investment sufficient to absorb the unemployed. Keynes placed confidence in monetary and fiscal policies for reducing unemployment to a rather temporary phenomenon. In some neo-Keynesian treatments, such as Phelps et al. (1970), unemployment could be permanent, but would be associated with investments in search and information, thereby constituting a productive use of labor.

safety valve of redistribution through appropriate tax and transfer policies.

Introspective generalization from the neoclassical development paradigm is inconsistent with the development experience of the last two decades. Income inequality has not been decreasing between countries or within LDCs. Unemployment has become a persistent feature, especially in the urban sectors of LDCs. Poverty, unemployment, and inequality can constitute an explosive combination of forces in the Third World—which composes three-quarters of the world's population.

Although the economics of development has until recently given far too little attention to unemployment and inequality (which have, not surprisingly, appeared conspicuously among the dark spots in the development record of most LDCs), far too much attention has been given to a variety of fundamentalist dogmas, such as capital fundamentalism, sectoral fundamentalism, import substitution fundamentalism, and planning fundamentalism.

Capital Fundamentalism
The monistic preoccupation with capital is again largely the result of direct international transference of approaches developed for the DCs, with minor modifications to fit the "special case" of the LDCs. As such, it is an abortive crossing of introspective generalization with immanent empiricism.

The theoretical linchpin of capital fundamentalism is the Harrod-Domar model, developed for advanced countries that had already taken to heart the Keynesian lessons of how to overcome the problems of excess supply. This model made the rate of growth the product of the savings rate and of the output-capital ratio.[13] Although hardly neoclassical in its inception, the model fitted conveniently into the neoclassical kit of tools after modification for the realities of LDCs. Under the assumptions that there is no substitutability between capital and labor, and that labor is in surplus supply, capital becomes the overriding constraint. A further prop for capital fundamentalism was provided by the portion of the literature on

technological change that views capital as the vehicle in which technology is embodied.

Capital fundamentalism was implemented with a battery of policies for increasing savings and their purchasing power over capital goods (Nurkse 1953; U.N.: ECAFE 1960). Income redistribution from the workers to the capitalists was countenanced (Galenson and Leibenstein 1955) and so were various inducements, such as tax exemptions and the granting of monopolistic positions, that encourage private individuals and enterprises to save and invest (W. A. Lewis 1955). If, ultimately, the private sector did not save sufficiently, it could be taxed to force savings and to redistribute resources from the private to the public sector, which was assumed to have savings propensities approaching unity (Kaldor 1955). Failing that, foreign savings might substitute for the domestic inability to save. Prices should be distorted in such a way as to make investment goods as cheap as possible relative to consumption goods. Hence, tariff and exchange rate systems should be designed to assure that the price of foreign exchange is lower for capital goods than for consumer goods (imported or exported) (Chenery 1953). Credit and foreign exchange licensing were also used to supplement the role of the price mechanism in stimulating savings and investment. The planning of a wide variety of projects simultaneously—even if they must be on a small scale—was looked upon with favor as a means of overcoming any tendency toward insufficient demand for investment (Nurkse 1953). A major criterion for granting foreign assistance should be the productivity of that assistance in inducing domestic capital formation (Millikan and Rostow 1957).

As a consequence of the underpricing of capital, some labor, even at wage rates at or near the subsistence level, may be unemployed. Capital may be underpriced to such a degree that it, too, is underutilized.[14] Distorted prices that favor imported capital goods may kill off the domestic manufacture of capital goods and thereby limit the possibilities of creating a technology adapted to domestic needs and circumstances.

Capital fundamentalism was extended to cover human capital formation. Enormous subsidies were granted to education, especially

---

[13]In fairness to Domar and especially to Harrod, it should be pointed out that capital fundamentalism in the LDCs has been based upon an excessively mechanical interpretation of the relationship between these variables. Harrod's treatment in particular can hardly be described as mechanical.

[14]For estimates of the extent of this underutilization, see U.N.: ECLA (1966), UNIDO (1967), and Winston (1971).

higher education, with the result that in many countries, such as India and Sri Lanka, the function of higher education is to swell the ranks of the white-collar proletariat. The attendant underutilization of human capital is evidenced in the high rates of unemployment for university graduates and in the hoarding of skilled labor by the public sector.

A consequence of excessive capital-intensity of investments—of physical or human capital—is excessive specialization. Concomitant with excessive specialization is underutilization caused by low substitutability in the process of production. A physician specialist is unlikely to serve as a general practitioner, much less to pitch in during the harvest season. The institution of the "barefoot doctor" in China—the practitioner with only the minimum qualifications necessary to administer medicine—is a felicitous example of conserving investment in human capital. Lack of excessive specialization in human capital creates the circumstances for simultaneous part-time employment in different jobs and may lead to easing seasonal peaks in labor requirements and reducing seasonal unemployment through extending labor substitutability. There is no reason that physical capital could not also be designed for multiple uses—at the cost, of course, of some efficiency.

Industrial and Agricultural Fundamentalisms
There is a time-honored tendency among economists to associate development with industrialization. Long-established dogmas can make strange bedfellows. No less than three patriarchs of the literature on development, Paul Baran (1952, p. 77), Ragnar Nurkse (1953), and W. Arthur Lewis (1954), who occupy different political and analytical positions among development economists, agree that industrialization alone can raise agricultural wages, modernize agriculture, and provide employment for labor displaced by the machine. Those rare exhortations of LDCs to devote more attention to agriculture have tended toward the other extreme position, agricultural fundamentalism, and have generally been received with resentment and interpreted as evidence of the conspiracy to keep the poor nations tied to their farms, leaving industrial production to the DCs.

Industrial fundamentalism has pointed to the positive correlation between the shares of industry and per capita income. Insufficient consideration has been given to the direction of causation in the relationship. Industrial fundamentalism, of course is justified only if industrialization is the cause of higher income per capita, rather than vice versa. Agricultural fundamentalism, on the other hand, points to the fact that at low levels of income per capita the vast majority of the population is employed in agriculture and has its consumption and investment requirements satisfied by agriculture. It concludes that productivity changes in agriculture alone can make any significant difference and thus that increased agricultural productivity is a prerequisite to increased income and industrialization.

Industrial fundamentalism has resulted in the establishment of artificially implanted, inefficient "hothouse" industries, dependent on imported technology, capital, and management but lacking the raw materials (locally produced or imported in return for exports) or foreign exchange to keep them going. It has also resulted in a distribution of income tilted to the extreme in favor of industrialists and against farmers, workers, and consumers. Agricultural fundamentalism, on the other hand, has generally resulted in growth without development, as a result of the failure to establish linkages among sectors, and in a distribution of income skewed in favor of the landed aristocracy.

It is true that industry and agriculture compete for scarce resources, but the extent of complementarity has not been sufficiently appreciated; in the long run, industry is hurt if agriculture is starved. The interdependence between the sectors should be made more explicit in our analysis. Continued concern with the industry versus agriculture dichotomy is dysfunctional.

Import Substitution Fundamentalism
In many a country, import substitution has been the operative content of planning. Borrowing from the Keynesian model of deficiency in demand with infinite elasticity of supply, and still imbued with industrialization fundamentalism, many development economists came to the conclusion that development (and industrialization) could best be initiated by starting to produce those commodities for which demand already exists. This calls for import substitution that is implemented through the imposition of tariffs

and quotas (Prebisch 1959; Chenery 1960; Papandreou 1962).

This type of intervention in foreign trade may offset existing distortions, thereby increasing efficiency. Promoting self-sufficiency decreases dependence on the terms of trade and on uncertain foreign markets. What went long unnoticed, however, is that import substitution for final goods increases imports of intermediate goods and raw materials. As a result, overcapacity is built at the final stages of production and too little capacity at the intermediate stages, which after all are the ones endowed with the most significant linkage effects and the ones that lead to the development of locally adapted technology. In addition, tariff and quota protection act as a disincentive to exports, which earn the foreign exchange for the capital and intermediate goods imports. Without taking advantage of the export market, it is not possible to exploit economies of scale, which may well be substantial in industrial commodities. Only very gradually, especially in the recent works of Little, Scitovsky, and Scott (1970) and Balassa and associates (1971), have the shortcomings of this variety of fundamentalism become fully appreciated. Numerous cases have now been identified in which protection was combined with overvalued exchange rates, distorting the prices of imported inputs and the output prices of the stimulated industry to such a degree that the value added by a particular activity to the economy was negative.

Planning Fundamentalism
Fascinated by the probably quite unrepresentative performance of countries during wartime, which have seemed to belie economic laws by having both more guns and more butter under regimes of centralized decision making and controls, development economists and LDC governments have tended to succumb to the fundamentalist belief that planning is the magic door to development. Any planning is better than no planning at all; more planning is better than less planning. The only legitimate arena for rational debate is on the issue of which form of planning—centralized or decentralized—is better. Planning fundamentalism has been carried so far that the existence of a plan—at first just a macroeconomic plan but more recently detailed sectoral, physical, and financial plans—

is taken as a prerequisite for development. Planning fundamentalism has often been justified by the generally invalid contention that development can be achieved without any cost in scarce resources, simply by utilizing unused resources.

Insufficient attention has been paid to the fact that many planning models do not fit the past well, and thus, if for no other reason, the countries that adopt them for future guidance may be driving hell-bent in the wrong direction. Furthermore, in the fundamentalist tradition, the assumptions of the superiority of planning activities over market activities or the existence of free or surplus resources from which other scarce resources can be created have, until recently, been left unquestioned.

The Anatomy of Failure and the Scope of this Book

As a field of analytical economics and a method for the study of development, the economics of development has foundered on three points.

First, the subject has largely been composed of a vast number of recipes for "how to do it." This kind of economic engineering has had a stultifying effect on economic development as a scientific field of inquiry.

Second, there has been too much emphasis on certain fundamentalist dogmas, such as those discussed in the previous section. The fundamentalism of any one approach has deliberately overlooked, or at least acted to camouflage, the linkages between one problem and another. There have been exceptions, but usually these have been tautological utterances, such as "everything depends on everything else" or "this is one of the vicious circles of underdevelopment and poverty." Discussion of the merits of alternative fundamentalisms was solicitous and has served to divert attention from appreciation of the interdependencies among different aspects of development.

Third, there has been too much emphasis on development as a uniform, smooth, and equilibrating process of continuous marginal adjustments. Conversely, too little attention has been devoted to the study of structure and of discontinuous processes and disequilibria, such as those that appear as "costs" of development. Efforts to deal with disequilibrium and structural change have been limited either to describing institutions or to discovering correlations among variables. Seldom, if ever, have discussions of disequilibria and structural change delved into cause and effect relationships in an analytic way. Yet to a large extent, development is the study of disequilibrium and structural change, the causes and effects of which must be understood. As Boulding (1953) once remarked, the growth processes of different organisms have many common principles. What is true of biological processes—that successful growth is associated with changes not only in size but also in structure—tends to hold also with respect to other processes. After all, by doubling the linear dimensions of an object, one increases its surfaces by the square and its volumes by the cube. A thousand-fold enlargement of a fly would fly no more, and it could survive only if it were transmogrified into an elephant! Such principles can apply with equal validity to processes in economic development: as an economy grows, its structure changes. There is a qualitative difference between the state of stationary underdevelopment and the process of sustained growth. As a result, the more complex process cannot be explained solely on the basis of the less complex situation. This is an almost Hegelian proposition.

Our approach to the economics of development is designed to overcome these three specific shortcomings of existing textbooks and monographs. Indeed, our attempts to overcome each of these shortcomings in turn, and all of them simultaneously, constitute the main features of this book.

In the first place, we attempt to pull together the building blocks for a complete theory of development. We nurse no illusions about having formulated such a theory ourselves. A general theory of development inevitably consists of a set of hypotheses that have been verified by empirical observations, and we cannot pretend to have done this adequately for any one hypothesis, let alone every hypothesis that has been featured in the literature. We attempt to set the stage for such work by carefully selecting topics in terms of relative importance to that general theory and then demonstrating how economic theory and statistical procedures can be applied in each case to explain the most important features in the process of economic

development and to predict its course. The basic focus of the book is on empirical analysis; therefore, we expect that the reader who is already familiar with empirical techniques will be comfortable with our approach. However, for the reader who is unfamiliar with such techniques, our treatment is self-contained in that the tools are presented, explained, and then applied in a comprehensible manner. For this reason, we include a discussion of the methodology of positive economics (Chapter 2), which is further illustrated with respect to various themes in the development literature (Chapter 3). This also explains why we include the fundamentals of input-output and of linear programming analysis (Chapter 4) for use in studying economic structure and planning (Chapters 9, 15, 16, and 21), and the neoclassical tools of production analysis and the marginal rules for efficiency analysis (Chapters 4–7) for studying smooth and equilibrium growth throughout Parts II and III and in Chapters 17 (Part V) and 20 (Part VI). We attempt to indicate the advantages and disadvantages of each tool and to roughly map out the areas of application in which each would appear to have a comparative advantage. For example, we will conclude that the human capital model works fairly well in explaining who invests in education and why, but not in determining the specific type of education that should be chosen or in explaining certain types of migration.

Although it was not our primary intention to do so, the topics we cover virtually exhaust the subject of development as presented in conventional undergraduate textbooks. Our topic coverage includes discussion of some of the more traditional determinants of growth, such as production functions for agriculture and industry (Chapter 4), the analysis of static efficiency in resource allocation, factor utilization, consumer choice, market organization, and international trade (Chapters 5–7), the response of economic agents to price and quantity signals (Chapter 8), the aspects of technological change and their implications (Chapter 9), the determinants of physical and human capital formation (Chapters 10 and 11), the supply and demand for labor (Chapter 12), and the determinants of the level and structure of international trade (Chapter 17). Many of these topics and the analytical tools developed for dealing with them would be common also to the study of economic growth in DCs, although our applications are confined almost entirely to LDCs. More exclusively relevant to LDCs is our treatment of surplus labor (Chapter 12), migration (Chapter 13), the causes and effects of dualism and income inequality (Chapter 14), interdependencies between agriculture and industry and the role that each sector plays in economic development (Chapter 15), structural change and its causes and effects (Chapter 16), the backwash effects of trade and exchange (Chapters 17 and 18), economic integration (Chapter 19), project evaluation (Chapter 20), and microeconomic, sectoral, and policy planning (Chapter 21). However, we deliberately omit issues and topics about which our understanding is still extremely fragmentary (e.g., inflation and population growth) or those that may be largely determined by noneconomic factors (e.g., institutions, entrepreneurship, and population growth).[15] These omitted topics generally lie at the frontiers of the discipline. Eventually, they may become fully integrated into the operational subset of development economics. In order to bridge these gaps, Chapter 3 touches upon some of these topics and on the methodological difficulties they involve.

The second feature of the book is that we attempt to avoid empty discussions about the merits of one form of fundamentalism relative to another by concentrating on interdependencies between different aspects of development. Thus, instead of discussing the relative merits of agriculture versus industry, we look at both sectors in terms of the statics of interdependencies (Chapter 15), the dynamics of structural change (Chapter 16), and statics and dynamics combined, as in the planning models (Chapters 20 and 21). The

advantages of openness and export growth are treated (Chapter 17), but not without considering some of the drawbacks to openness and trade dependence, such as instability and deterioration in the terms of trade (Chapter 18) and structural distortions (Chapter 16). Likewise, both causes and effects are generally treated jointly. For example, not only do we treat the causes of income inequality (Chapters 9 and 14) but we also discuss its effects, as in capital formation (Chapter 10) and the means of offsetting these effects, as in evaluating projects from the point of view of income distribution (Chapter 20).

The third, and most important, feature of the book is that it combines two different paradigms of development and explores two radically differing perceptions of change: the dominant neoclassical one and the challenging paradigm of disequilibria, structural breaks, and backwash effects.

The ruling paradigm of the process of economic development rests on the classical-neoclassical views of a world with gradual, marginalist, nondisruptive, equilibrating, and largely painless change. Incentives are the bedrock of economic growth, which, once originated, becomes automatic and all pervasive. Development spreads among nations and trickles down among classes so that everybody benefits from the process. This view is analogous to the communicating vessels of elementary hydraulics: the pressure in the vessels with higher initial endowments leads to raising the water level in the other vessels. The mechanism that trips off change and restores equilibrium is the pressure created by nonidentical endowments and the pipeline that connects the vessels. Development is initiated by incentives based on inequality; it is promoted by the market mechanisms that connect the rich and the poor. Thus, according to this paradigm, development is largely a question of creating the proper incentives, of perfecting the market mechanisms, or of initiating changes that will lead to self-propelled takeoffs. The largest part of the development literature and a good deal of development experience fall within the classical-neoclassical framework. This framework and the areas of its application are covered in Parts II and III.

An alternative view of development substitutes conflict for the classical harmony of interests, disequilibrating and disruptive change for equilibrating and smooth processes,

---

[15]Another glaring but intentional omission from our coverage is the simulation of dynamic systems based on elaborate difference or differential equations —the "magnificent dynamics" (to adapt Baumol's characterization of the systems of Marx and Schumpeter) replete with the derivation of asymptotic properties of convergence, and so on, as exemplified in the works of Fei and Ranis (1964), Paauw and Fei (1973), Kelley, Williamson, and Cheetham (1972), and Zarembka (1972). We exclude this type of analysis for two reasons: first, the asymptotic convergence to equilibrium, if at all relevant for the problems of development, must refer to the very distant future—well beyond the horizon of most individuals or governments; second, it is difficult to carry out empirical analysis with equilibrating behavior that has not yet been realized.

jolt and backwash effects for spread effects and trickling-down mechanisms. Development is a process of disequilibrium. If left unchecked, it will enlarge rather than diminish the existing differences and inequalities. The analogy of the communicating vessels is now inappropriate but can be replaced by that of the siphon. In the siphon, as a result of vacuum and suction unequal initial endowments are magnified rather than balanced when the vessels are joined. The implication is that development can take place only within segmented and isolated compartments, not in the context of universalist tendencies. If suction cannot be stopped, the line that connects the two vessels must be ruptured. The existence of free communications and of unhampered markets not only fails to eliminate dualism; it even increases it. According to this view, universalist development is chimeric; dualistic development is the appropriate approach. Various aspects of developmental disequilibria are covered in Parts IV, V, and VI.

Chapter 2
An Excursion into Methodology

Methodology is necessary when one is in trouble; otherwise, one can do better without it. Thus, there is no reason for a chapter on methodology to be included in a book, for example, on public finance. Economic development, though, is still an underdeveloped field and at best an unstructured part of science. We consider it apposite, therefore, to start our discussion from some principles involved in formulating operational hypotheses and submitting them to empirical tests.

The Scientific Method

Facts and *habit of mind* are the two components of science. The scientific method consists of appealing to facts in a special systematic manner (K. Pearson 1937, p. 96; Reichenbach 1958, p. 8).

The use of facts in science involves *classification* and *generalization*. The mere collec-tion of observable phenomena serves at best to buttress a thesis with episodic argument; at worst, it constitutes purposeless anecdotology. Citing facts may be entertaining, but from the point of view of scientific discovery, unrelated facts are often better forgotten than remembered. The first precondition for the appeal to facts within the scientific method is classification, which as an ingredient of theory has no substantive content. It is a language, a set of tautologies, a mere filing cabinet (Friedman 1953, p. 7). Purely classificatory sciences have disappeared with old-time botany and zoology.

Generalization is characterized as connecting classified facts with chains of reasoning. It is formulating theories or hypotheses[1] by

[1]Distinctions between hypotheses and theories have been suggested in terms of the degree of their applicability and generality. See M. R. Cohen and Nagel (1938, p. 205) and Margenau (1935, p. 67).

building logical statements of the form "if A, then B." The "if" part of the statement is called the premise of the hypothesis; the "then" is the inference, the implication, or the prediction of the hypothesis.

The distinction between *positive* and *normative* statements can be formulated with reference to facts. Positive statements concern what is. Normative statements involve what ought to be. Disagreements over positive statements are then appropriately settled by appealing to facts. This is not true of normative statements, which are intertwined with moral, religious, and cultural values. Normative statements involve value judgments.

Although the scientific method that appeals to facts is not adequate to handle value judgments, the scientist should not stop short as soon as a normative statement comes up. "Private enterprise promotes rapid capital accumulation" is a positive statement, which can be confirmed or rejected by appealing to facts. "It is my opinion that LDCs ought to emulate the Chinese model of development" is a normative statement. At this stage, it cannot be judged by reference to facts. It is, however, in order for the practitioner of positive economics to ask "why?" Then the description of the consequences of the Chinese model of development and the international transference to other LDCs would constitute positive propositions that can be resolved by appealing to facts. The pursuit of a normative statement will turn up positive hypotheses, subject to investigation by the scientific method.

The scientific method is "an institutional mechanism for sifting warranted beliefs." According to the "uniformitarian" conception, science progresses by the dialectic application of the scientific method on a continuous process of stockpiling facts and techniques. Science becomes dominated by "paradigms," which are "universally recognized scientific achievements that for a time provide model problems and solutions to a community of practitioners" (Kuhn 1962, p. x). A paradigm enables scientists to take for granted the foundation of their knowledge and to concentrate on the solution of problems or "puzzles." A ruling paradigm in economics is the theory of economic equilibrium via the market mechanism. Once this is taken for granted, economists can concentrate on concrete problem-solving, such as the optimal allocation of resources or the mathematical properties of equilibrium.

Thomas S. Kuhn (1962), in an influential book, *The Structure of Scientific Revolutions*, has challenged the uniformitarian conception of scientific progress in favor of the "catastrophic" view. Instead of being a smooth process, progress in science has been punctuated by periodic discontinuities, breakdowns, and changes in direction. These are initiated by an increasing number of "anomalies" that are observed in the application of the ruling paradigm. These eventually become "critical"; a sense of crisis develops as the inadequacy of the ruling paradigm becomes increasingly apparent, and research is diverted from puzzle-solving to paradigm-testing (Coats 1969, p. 291). The challenge to the ruling paradigm arouses scientific passions. And if it is finally overthrown, its defeat is due to a "conversion experience," a "transfer of allegiance," rather than to "the logical structure of scientific knowledge." The criteria that will decide the battle of succession of the ruling paradigm are the possibilities inherent in the new paradigm, and not any demonstrable proof of its superiority.

The "Keynesian revolution" is an example of a change in the ruling paradigm through Kuhn's catastrophic view (Coats 1969). The major rethinking of development currently underway may represent a similar revolt against the ruling paradigm of neoclassical development economics.

Operational Hypotheses

The Facts

A statement is called operational if empirical conditions can be specified in which the statement could be "definitely"[2] rejected (Braithwaite 1953, p. 160). The empirical conditions that refer to the rejection of the statement are called the demarcation rule.

We can distinguish two important categories of operational statements, universal and existential. A *universal statement* is a general proposition ("all swans are white") that specifies empirical conditions under which the statement is definitely false. We test the truth content of the statement by comparing its empirical implications with the facts (the observed color of swans). Since it bears di-

---

[2]The word "definitely" is placed in quotation marks because the definition will be modified.

rectly on the terminology we use in evaluating a test, we should note a certain asymmetry in the empirical implications of such a statement. If the implication is observed to be true, it is still possible for the statement to hold in one instance and to be false in another. The statement cannot be proven true but can only be confirmed. Confirmation is always provisional. It can be reversed at any time by the observation of a contrary implication. On the other hand, if the implication is observed to be false in one instance, this is sufficient to prove the statement false, that is, to reject it or to refute it.

An *existential statement* is a partial proposition ("some swans are white"). Its empirical conditions are specified in such a way that the statement can be confirmed by an instance, but there is no definite number of contrary instances that will lead to rejection. Since the statement can be definitely accepted but not definitely rejected, it has failed the demarcation rule that we set for operational statements. Notice also that the asymmetry in the treatment of the implications of existential statements is the reverse of the asymmetry in the treatment of the implications of universal statements.

We have dealt to this point with *deterministic* operational statements. The demarcation rule must be modified when it is applied to the empirical content of a *probabilistic* or *stochastic* statement. "The probability of a child's being born a boy is 51 percent" is a stochastic statement. It is also a universal statement of the form, "The probability of every child's being born a boy is 51 percent." The demarcation rule that refers to deterministic operational statements has to be modified accordingly to encompass probabilistic statements (Braithwaite 1953, pp. 153–154). Instead of matching its implications directly to the observed facts, the confirmation or rejection of a probabilistic statement depends on whether or not a certain ratio of a set of n observations falls inside or outside a certain confidence interval, for example, two standard deviations from the mean. This modification of the demarcation rule bears upon the definitiveness of the test of a probability statement. Rejection or confirmation of a probability statement is not contingent only on the empirical implications of the statement. It also depends on the size of the sample we chose

from the parent population and on the confidence interval adopted by the investigator. Changing the sample size or the confidence interval can alter the results. Both confirmation and rejection of a probability statement can only be provisional. This becomes a salient characteristic of "inexact" (nondeterministic) science.

Although empirical statements are especially useful in science, one should not refuse to examine nonempirical statements. Nonoperational statements can still be useful in the sense that they might contain the germ of an important idea worth exploring further, or in the sense that they might be parts of the black box that helps us formulate empirical statements. The statement, "Every increase in income is associated with an increase in utility" is a nonoperational statement, because utility cannot ordinarily be defined or measured uniquely. Nevertheless, the concept of utility is still useful, since it leads to the formulation of empirical statements about income elasticities and downward sloping demand curves.

The Habit of Mind

We have defined a scientific hypothesis as a logical apparatus that refers to facts. Testing a hypothesis consists of putting it in competition with alternative hypotheses and critically confronting it with observation. This requires a criterion for deciding which hypotheses to match in competition as well as for judging their performance. In this section, we deal with the former question, which refers mainly to the scientific habit of mind. We will refer to the evaluation of the assumptions of a hypothesis, to its simplicity, elegance, fruitfulness, and consistency with other theory. In the following section, we will return to the question of confronting hypotheses with facts and judging their predictive ability.

One step in matching competing hypotheses is the comparison of their logical apparatus. The assumptions of a hypothesis are a part of that logical apparatus. There has been a long discussion, both in economics and in the methodology of science in general, about the importance of these assumptions.

The "traditional view" is as follows (Robbins 1935, pp. 78, 79): Once the validity of the deductive logic, which allows one to move successfully from the assumptions of the theory to its implications, has been established, one would be able to place confidence in the implications *if* the assumptions were realistic. Hence, the point at which we investigate the correspondence between the theory and the real world should be limited to the assumptions of the theory. According to the traditional view, progress in economics consists of gradually selecting theories with assumptions that are more appropriate (or more realistic) to the environment of the events we study.

Milton Friedman (1953) severely attacked the traditional view. Pointing out that the function of theory is not to reflect reality but to simplify by abstracting from reality, Friedman concludes that the realism of the assumptions is not what is relevant in testing the usefulness of a theory. The real test of theory is "does it work?" Citing the case of the law (theory) of gravity, the appropriate question is, "Does a rock dropped from the Leaning Tower of Pisa fall as if it were in a vacuum, that is, so that the wind resistance does not significantly affect the time it takes for the rock to reach the ground?" A vacuum is certainly not required to obtain good predictions from the law of gravity. But if a pound of feathers were dropped from the same tower under the same conditions, the law of gravity would not yield successful predictions, because the assumptions of the theory of gravity would not be realistic enough. Hence, how realistic the assumptions must be is relative to the situation. Friedman's extreme position is that the more descriptively false the assumptions of the theory are, the more important and powerful are the implications of the theory. In fact, theories that have tremendous power in terms of their policy implications are generally based on very strong and often unrealistic assumptions. But does this empirical generalization imply that the more unrealistic the assumptions, the better the theory?

Samuelson (1963) and Melitz (1965) have challenged Friedman on this point. Realistic implications from unrealistic assumptions might just indicate that the implications of the theory only "happened" to be right. Theories, they say, are useful only if both assumptions and implications are realistic.

The discussion has indeed been acrimonious and in part sterile because of differences in semantics. If one recognizes that the ingredients of the assumptions of the theory have different structures and fulfill very different roles, the disagreements can presumably be resolved. Machlup (1955) has distinguished between "fundamental" and "nonfundamental" assumptions and Melitz between "generative" and "auxiliary" assumptions. The justification for the first set of distinctions is that while fundamental assumptions, like the postulate of "economic man," cannot be tested and therefore should not be tested, nonfundamental assumptions, such as the applicability theorems of Papandreou (1958), which specify the time and space to which the hypothesis refers, can and should be tested. The second set of distinctions is based on the view that auxiliary assumptions (like *ceteris paribus*) are relevant to the validity and meaningfulness of the test, whereas the realism of the generative assumptions (like profit maximization) is relevant only to the truth of the theory.

In considering the logical apparatus of a hypothesis, the investigator generally wishes to consider a number of criteria in combination, some of which are complementary and some competitive. Aside from the realism of the assumptions, other criteria that merit consideration are the simplicity and elegance of the hypothesis, its fruitfulness, its consistency with other theory, and its specificity.

Simplicity refers to the initial knowledge needed to make a prediction within a given set of phenomena (Friedman 1953, p. 10). Simpler theories have appeal both because they are easy to explain to others (including policy makers) and because they require less information and computation and thus involve lower costs. Simple models, although they may not have the greatest ultimate value, are more easily testable, for they make strong statements about phenomena, which have been simplified to become easily managed.

Elegance may be closely related to the simplicity of a hypothesis. It may also be less an inherent attribute of economics than of the economist's palate.

Fruitfulness is the logical fertility of a hypothesis. A theory entailing many inferences is preferred, because it yields predictions within a wider area and suggests additional lines of research. Another advantage of fruitful hypotheses is that as more implications are derived from the hypothesis the possibility increases that an effective means of testing the hypothesis can be devised.[3]

Consistency with other theory is a criterion generated from notions about the universality of scientific explanation. In macroeconomics, for example, theorists prefer to work with hypotheses that are consistent with commonly accepted principles in microeconomics.

Because of the many levels on which the comparison of hypotheses is carried out, it is highly unlikely that a particular hypothesis will dominate in all respects. It is no wonder, therefore, that the comparison of hypotheses is often indecisive. It is not pigheadedness that makes for disagreement over hypotheses, even after they have been submitted to a good deal of empirical work. It is rather the subjective coloring that the investigator strokes in assigning weights to each criterion. It is conceivable nevertheless that on occasion the situation itself will dictate where the emphasis must go. For example, if one were interested only in the United States economy during a certain period of time, specificity would be more important than fruitfulness.

Since many criteria are highly subjective, primary attention will be given at present to the criterion of the ability to predict.

The Ability to Predict

A scientific hypothesis is a rational machinery for passing from premises to observational inferences. The purpose is to generalize from experience. In formulating a scientific hypothesis, one collects, classifies, and analyzes past events in such a way that one can describe observations that have not yet been made.

The link between premises and observational inferences may be made in two ways with vastly different consequences in economics (Conrad and Meyer 1964, pp. 7–8). The first is that of conjunction of properties in the sense of correlation. The second is that of sequential conjunction in the sense of regression analysis.

Consider the statements: (1) "The percent of population in urban areas increases with per capita income" and (2) "In periods of inflation, the debtors gain and the creditors lose." In both statements, observable facts have been classified and linked by a chain of reasoning. In statement 1, the chain of reasoning is reversible, for either urbanization or increase in income can be the premise, the other being the implication. (In fact, both may be implications of yet another premise, such as "change in the structure of productive activities.") The statement explains the phenomena of urbanization and increasing income, and predicts (in the loose sense of the word) the sign of the correlation coefficient that joins the two phenomena.

In statement 2, however, the chain of reasoning is irreversible; inflation causes the gains and losses rather than the reverse. Statement 2 is stronger and more operational than 1 because the causality runs only one way, from the premises (inflation) to the implications (gains and losses). When such irreversibility of conjunction exists, we can distinguish between exogenous and endogenous variables (Orcutt 1952, pp. 195–200). The technique of regression analysis then becomes relevant, and it yields not only correlation coefficients but also (partial) regression coefficients. Formal explanation and prediction in this case are possible in the sense that even if one had an as yet "unobserved"[4] case of inflation one could predict that debtors would gain and creditors would lose. Furthermore, if one has the quantitative information to compute the functional form, one can say something not only about the sign of the relationship (from the correlation coefficient) but also about its expected magnitude (from the regression coefficient). Finally, and in contrast to 1, in statement 2 deductive reasoning is possible—going from the premises to the implications of the hypotheses.[5]

---

[3]For an excellent example of the derivation of interesting secondary implications that facilitate rigorous testing, see Conrad and Meyer (1964).

[4]The expression "unobserved phenomena" should not be considered in historical context. We have an unobserved phenomenon as long as a fact or a statement is not contained in the hypothesis by construction. For example, if we derived the relationship between consumption and income from the years 1950 to 1970, the year 1973 is an unobserved phenomenon that we can predict. The universal statement, "Given the demand, if the supply curve shifts to the left the price goes up" can be anchored by the statement, "During the Peloponnesian War, the price of bread in Athens went up." We test this hypothesis by checking the unobserved statement in Thucydides.

[5]By structuring the line of reasoning from general to particular observations, we do not appear to include among scientific hypotheses inductive reasoning, that is, the procedure of obtaining a general conclusion from a set of observations. Suppose I observe the color of birds called ravens, and then I formulate

Scientific explanation and prediction are basically related to the process of learning from experience and not necessarily only to the accuracy of the results. The formulation of scientific hypotheses allows for the stepwise elimination of error. It constitutes a dialectic process on which learning is based.[6] The hunch of the wise man or the intuitive guess of the experienced practitioner may have better predictive results than abstract theories spun out from a few assumptions. The only problem is that from wise men and experienced practitioners we never "learn."

In judging the performance of the hypothesis, its ability to explain the facts is of central importance—indeed, according to Popper (1959, pp. 32–33, 40–42), it is the only relevant criterion. His injunction is: formulate an empirical scientific hypothesis in a way that it is given the chance to be proven wrong, and then try to refute it. A hypothesis is accepted or refuted according to how well it predicts relative to its rivals.

This is the ultraempiricist view.[7] It makes all *ceteris paribus* statements, which are so popular in economics, strictly nontestable. Consider the statement, "*ceteris paribus*, the imposition of a tax on automobiles will raise their price." This statement cannot be refuted in Popper's sense, because if a tax on automobiles were imposed and an increase in price not observed, one could always argue that "other things" did not remain constant. Nevertheless the statement is a hypothesis, for it has been derived by a chain of reasoning from certain constructs of economics, such as de-

mand, supply, and so on. It is readily comparable, for example, to the statement, "*ceteris paribus*, the imposition of a tax on automobiles will not raise their price." The comparison takes place by deriving the conclusions of each statement from some general principles and by checking the chains of reasoning they employ. On these grounds, the first statement would presumably be declared superior. Still, if we continually found that when taxes were imposed prices of automobiles did not go up, we would start having doubts of its validity, which would eventually induce us to reformulate the statement.

The Ability to Predict: An Example

We will illustrate the ability to predict by using variants of the hypothesis of the consumption function. The expression

$$C_t = f(Y_t)$$

relates consumption at time t, C_t, to income at time t, Y_t. It is an explanation in the sense that it segregates the factors associated with consumption in a relevant or meaningful way (e.g., income) from the factors considered irrelevant and omitted (e.g., size of household). It also assigns causality in the sense that the relationship between consumption and income is not reversible. The functional expression is an operational hypothesis.

The validity of this hypothesis should be judged in competition with rival hypotheses. Let us set up two alternative explanations: (1) the null hypothesis that consumption is not a function of income and (2) the naive hypothesis that consumption is a function of time. The three hypotheses will now be judged from the point of view of their adequacy in describing the facts and of their ability to predict the future. They have to be cast in an explicit form, which requires further specification of their initial assumptions. For the purpose of simplicity, assume linear relationships and consider the following forms.

Income hypothesis: $\qquad C_t = a + bY_t \qquad$ (1)

Naive hypothesis: $\qquad C_t = a' + b'T \qquad$ (2)

These are the "exact" or deterministic forms of the income hypothesis and the naive hypothesis. (The null hypothesis does not require a special form, because it consists of the rejection of the other hypotheses.) Testing

---

the universal statement: "If a bird is a raven, it is black." There are two views on whether this inductive statement represents a scientific hypothesis. First, this represents a correlation of species and color without any established scientific system in which the generalization appears as a consequence. Lacking causality, the blackness of all ravens may be accidental (Braithwaite 1953, p. 304). Second, there exists causality, although it may be dim or unverbalized. Without reason, one would not go about associating the color rather than the size of ravens to the species. As Darwin has remarked (quoted in Wisdom 1952, p. 50), "About thirty years ago there was much talk that geologists ought only to observe and not to theorize; and I well remember someone saying that at this rate a man might as well go into a gravel-pit and count the pebbles and describe their colors."

[6]Fred Hoyle's *The Black Cloud* (1957), an amusing and illustrative novel on the methodology of science, provides good examples of this point.

[7]For a proponent of this view in economics, see Hutchison (1938). For a discussion, see Klappholz and Agassi (1959, 1960) and Hutchison (1960).

the hypotheses consists of fitting the above equations and then using them for predicting as yet unobserved phenomena. Assume that we use data on consumption and income and the time variable for the period 1950–1970 to estimate the values of the "behavioral" parameters a, b, a', and b'. For prediction, we would require observations for a year that we did not include in the estimation procedures (e.g., 1973). We then see whether or not by supplying the values of the behavioral parameters we could predict the "unobserved" level of consumption from the observed level of the independent variable.

The fact that becomes immediately obvious by intuition is that it would be surprising if consumption stood in an exactly linear relationship to income or to time. Does this result mean that both the income and the naive hypotheses (in their deterministic forms) are refuted and the null hypothesis comes out triumphant? Presumably, this is the meaning of strict Popperian refutability. Yet it is hard to accept such a harsh judgment. One can always try to invent an alternative naive hypothesis that exactly describes the data: we should be able to find some polynomial with turning points at the right places. It is evident, however, that this comparison is unfair. The new naive hypothesis, although "it washes well," is decidedly inferior to the alternative hypothesis in terms of the criteria we established in the previous section—simplicity, fruitfulness, realism of the assumptions, elegance, and consistency with other theory. A good rule of thumb to adopt at this stage of judging the empirical results is that the naive hypothesis must have no fewer degrees of freedom than its serious rival (Archibald 1966).[8]

It is time to drop the exact or deterministic approach and recognize hypotheses as probabilistic statements. Their proper form then is the probabilistic or stochastic form, which consists basically of an additional "error" term (or terms) attached to the hypothesis in some way. The two main hypotheses can then be rewritten.

$$C_t = a + bY_t + e_t \qquad (1a)$$

$$C_t = a' + b'T + u_t \qquad (2a)$$

where e_t and u_t are the respective error terms.

[8]We draw upon Archibald heavily in the subsequent discussion of this section.

This seemingly small modification of the two hypotheses has great importance. Our new equations, besides recognizing the existence of systematic or nonrandom behavior in the universe, also admit the existence of the "unique," the random, or the unsystematic component.[9] The systematic factors explain central tendencies, that is, "representative," mean, median behavior, and so on. This can be expressed in the form of

$$\hat{C}_t = a + bY_t = C_t - e_t$$

where $\hat{C}_t$ is the "explained" part of consumption. It differs from the observed consumption, C_t, by the error term, e_t, or the "deviant" behavior. An obvious criterion of the "goodness" of the explanatory and predictive power of a hypothesis lies in the comparison of the two components, the systematic and the random elements.

Such a measure is the coefficient of determination, r^2, where

$$r^2 = 1 - \frac{\Sigma\, e^2}{\Sigma\, C^2}$$

Further discussion of the sources of error will help to illustrate two points: (1) The existence of an error term is an immutable feature of the universe or, what comes to the same thing, $r^2 < 1$. Strict refutability, therefore, in the sense of assigning to a hypothesis probabilities of 0 or 1, is impossible. (2) Selection among alternative hypotheses involves more than merely ranking them on the basis of their coefficients of determination. Actually choosing among competing hypotheses is more of an art (black magic, the cynic might say) than a science.

There are three sources of error: (1) errors in the model; (2) errors in measurement; and (3) "noise" in the universe.

Errors in the model are the easiest to detect and conceivably to handle. They are "specification errors," which arise from the fact that some important variables (variables with systematic influence on the dependent variable) are missing from the explanation. For example, consumption is not only a function of income at time t but also of the level

[9]This specification implies that the error term is randomly distributed. The existence of an error term that has systematic behavior (e.g., it is correlated with income, etc.) suggests that there exists a probably curable ailment in the model, such as an insufficient number of explanatory variables.

of income experienced in the past—the relative-income hypothesis. Statistically, the existence of this source of error may be revealed by low r^2, "badly behaved" residual terms, and unreliable estimates of coefficients.[10] Conceptually, this error can be treated easily: incorrect specification means that the hypothesis is wrong. Therefore, low tolerance of this kind of error is prescribed. The error can usually be cured by adding variables—another reason why one should be liberal in rejecting hypotheses with errors in the model.

Unlike errors in the model, errors in measurement result, not from flaws in the conceptual apparatus, but from imperfections in the tools. For example, in the consumption hypothesis, we might have liked to measure permanent income, or wealth. Instead, what we observe includes transitory elements. A priori we do not know much about the distribution of errors in measurement[11], although in a specific context we might know that they are "high," "low," or "moderate." We do not want to reject a correct hypothesis because of errors in measurement of variables.

Noise in the universe is the classical source of error. Suppose we have a variable subject to certain important, systematic influences. It is also subject to many individually independent and insignificant influences—the "free will" in the universe which means freedom to depart from the systematic part of the equation. The consumption function does not predict, nor does it intend to predict, the consumption expenditure of individual a or b, since that may vary because of taste, sickness, marriage, or other factors. For many individuals, however, the sum of a large number of such independent random variables (with finite means and variances) will be normally distributed. This is the central limit theorem, which makes individual behavior subject to statistical analysis.

Assume that we had eliminated the first

source of error, errors in the model, and that the remaining kinds of error were normally distributed. Since two separate normal distributions (with the same mean) produce a normal distribution, the combined effect of the second and third sources of error is a normally distributed residual. We know that in normal distributions 95 percent of the observations lie within two standard deviations and 99 percent within three standard deviations from the mean.

Under these conditions, the only question that remains in framing a rule for acceptance or rejection of the hypothesis is whether, for example, a 95 percent probability limit is "high" or "low." The answer is not unequivocal; it depends on which type of error one is trying to avoid: "Type I" error, the rejection of the correct hypothesis, or "Type II" error, the acceptance of the wrong hypothesis. Thus, if one were more concerned with avoiding Type II error than Type I error, 95 percent might be high error tolerance. But if one were more concerned with trying to avoid Type I error, 95 percent might be low error tolerance. How can one tell which type of error is more important? If the source of error is thought to be primarily errors in measurement and noise in the universe, it may be more important to avoid Type I error. This would also be the case when the competing hypothesis is the naive hypothesis.[12] On the other hand, if the errors are thought to arise primarily from the first source, which is errors in the model, it would be more important to avoid Type II errors. Although the choice between Type I and Type II errors appears uncertain, one should keep in mind that in economics, unlike in engineering or pharmacology, decisions are always reversible and hypotheses are accepted or rejected only provisionally, pending fresh evidence or more serious contestants. One might as a result choose to avoid Type I error when the naive hypothesis is being considered and Type II error when a hypothesis of good standing and long service is put to test. The choice between Type I and Type II errors can be formalized in terms of the criterion of minimizing total cost, where costs are of two kinds: the costs

---

[10]Another example of specification error is causation running from consumption to income and not from income to consumption: $Y = F(C)$ since $Y = C + I$. Such specification error biases the regression coefficient but not the correlation coefficient (or the r^2), since correlation says nothing about causality (Archibald 1966, p. 283).

[11]Under general circumstances, we have some information about errors in measurement. If a number of people perform the same operation of measurement, they will produce errors that are normally distributed around the mean. In economics, however, the same measurement operation is not performed by a number of people, nor is the measuring stick always the same.

[12]In fact, Bayesian statisticians generally believe that testing a hypothesis against the naive hypothesis is a meaningless exercise, since a priori information in support of the serious hypothesis is likely to more than offset any negative results which may be obtained in the test (Pratt 1965).

of accepting an hypothesis that is false and those of rejecting an hypothesis that is true.[13] In general, these costs will not be symmetric, and their relative magnitude will be determined by the situation.

Interpreting the outcome of tests and discriminating among alternative hypotheses is not simple. Still, this difficulty should not lead one to despair or to denounce empirical research in social science. Empirical research can supply predictions and provide answers to pressing problems of policy. Although the answers are not always unequivocal, they may well be better than the alternative—approaches based exclusively on impressionistic hunches and casual empiricism.

One should always try to remedy the causes of error in the tests. One way of doing so would be to obtain more and better data, of course at a cost. Even short of creating new data, much can often be done by utilizing other kinds of available data that are relevant to discriminating between alternative hypotheses. For example, if time series data are limited, is there a possibility that cross-section data might be useful? (Although much attention in the literature of methodology has been directed to the "best" means of testing, perhaps too little has been devoted to determining the feasibility of alternative methods of testing.) If prior information is available, it should be brought into the decision by putting it in terms similar to the "posterior" information. Information about the probable ranges of values of certain variables and parameters, for example, may facilitate choice among alternative hypotheses. Similarly, one can attempt to ascertain the influence that other factors, ignored for the sake of simplicity, would be likely to have. Would they offset or reinforce each other? If they would tend to offset each other, they can be safely excluded; if not, their exclusion would likely distort the results. A great deal can be gained by expanding the list of hypotheses to be considered, for it will facilitate discrimination between hypotheses supported only by spurious correlations and those reflecting true cause and effect relationships.

Finally, one should not forget that besides predictions—predictions now—the purpose of science is the stepwise elimination of error through the dialectic process of learning. We

also learn from mistakes and from incorrect hypotheses.

The Nature of Predictions of "Inexact" Science

Often a distinction is drawn between physical and social science, or exact and inexact science. The difference is intended to refer both to the methodology used by a science and to the confidence one can place in its predictions. Physical and exact sciences employ precise terms and exact derivations and produce reliable conclusions. They are deterministic. Social and inexact sciences use vague terms and intuitive insights and are confronted by virtual unpredictability. They are stochastic.

The preceding discussion has sufficiently illustrated that precision and determinism are the wrong criteria for distinguishing between exact and inexact science. In parts of aerodynamics and the physics of extreme temperatures, exact methods are still intermingled with intuitive insights. Furthermore, not only are probability statements an immutable part of sciences that otherwise use exact methods ("the probality that this bridge will collapse is . . ."), but also they do not present any special problem from the point of view of scientific prediction.

Still there *is* a difference between economics and aerodynamics, let alone between economics and solid state physics. It is connected with the multiplicity of often contradicting criteria used for discriminating among hypotheses in economics: the predictive validity and the degrees of freedom, simplicity of the hypothesis, elegance, fruitfulness, consistency with other theory, specificity, and realism of its assumptions. The first two criteria are not employed by inexact science in a way that is different from other science. They engage the probabilistic concept of relative frequency in the same way it is engaged in physics. The other criteria, however, involve "personal probability," which does not necessarily enter other science. It is this element of personal probability that makes the role of expertise important for prediction in economics.

[In inexact science] knowledge about past instances or about statistical samples—while indeed providing valuable information—is not the sole and sometimes not even the

---

[13]For an interesting example and clear explanation of this point, see Archibald (1966, pp. 288–289).

main form of evidence in support of rational assignments of probability values. In fact the evidential use of such *prima facie* evidence must be tempered by reference to background information. . . . (Helmer and Rescher 1959, pp. 37–38.)

This background information can often be intuitive in character and may refer to the knowledge of regularities in the behavior of people and in the character of their institutions as expressed in traditions and customs, in fashions and mores, in national attitudes and climates of opinion, and so on. An expert in economics is a person with such background knowledge who assigns weights to the different criteria employed in discriminating among hypotheses in a way that shows a record of comparative successes in the long run. Expertise in economics is almost synonymous with success.

Chapter 3

Some Refractory Hypotheses of Economic Development

In the previous chapter, we set strict standards for that interesting and valuable subset of statements known as operational scientific hypotheses. Two steps are involved in formulating and testing such hypotheses; first, a causal link must be established between the premises and the observational inferences of the logical statement; second, the truth content of the statement must be examined by reference to the facts. It should not be surprising that strictly operational hypotheses are scarce in most fields of science, including economic development, since their requirements are exigent. On the other hand, nonoperational and partially operational hypotheses abound. These should not be dismissed lightly for at least three reasons. First, even nonoperational hypotheses may contain the germs of an important idea that could conceivably be developed into a testable proposition. Second, even incomplete hypotheses can

contribute to the dialectic process of learning through which new hypotheses are born and old hypotheses die. Third, it is often the unfortunate blessing of nature that there is an inverse relationship between the importance and testability of hypotheses, the more important hypotheses being more difficult to test. As Braithwaite has pointed out, the difficulty of testing hypotheses may not necessarily be attributed to the lack of scientific rigor but rather to the way science progresses.

> . . . Science, as it advances, does not rest content with establishing simple generalizations from observable facts: it tries to explain these lowest-level generalizations by deducing them from more general hypotheses at a higher level. Such an organization of a science into a hierarchical deductive system requires the use of subtle deductive techniques, which are provided by pure mathe-

matics. As the hierarchy of hypotheses of increasing generality rises, the concepts with which the hypotheses are concerned cease to be properties of things which are directly observable, and instead become "theoretical" concepts—atoms, electrons, fields of force, genes, unconscious mental processes—which are connected to the observable facts by complicated logical relationships. (Braithwaite 1953, p. ix.)

This chapter is devoted to hypotheses that constitute higher level generalizations in the economics of development. Many such hypotheses emphasize noneconomic determinants of economic development. Since subsequent chapters are devoted largely to economic factors, this chapter presents a sampling of issues that would otherwise be entirely overlooked in our analysis. Another characteristic of some of the hypotheses presented in this chapter is that they are not fully operational on the basis of the criteria set out in Chapter 2. In such cases, we discuss (1) how these hypotheses have traditionally been stated; (2) what the difficulties that arise in testing them are; and (3) as far as possible how they can be reformulated to become operational. For this reason, this chapter can be considered an extension and an illustration of Chapter 2. These two characteristics—the comprehensiveness that extends to noneconomic factors and the nonoperational formulation—make the hypotheses of this chapter especially difficult to handle, that is, refractory.

As examples of incompletely operational hypotheses, we discuss two quite different approaches to stage theories (those of Rostow and of Adelman and Morris), attitudinal determination, status withdrawal, and a number of different "threshold" theories. Each illustrates a different type of shortcoming that renders empirical testing difficult or impossible.

In many fields of natural science, it has been found useful to distinguish the different stages through which organisms pass in their growth and evolution. For example, it is common and useful to distinguish a caterpillar from a cocoon from a moth. A successful stage theory must at least specify the various attributes of a caterpillar that are different from a cocoon and from a moth. However, it must do more than that: it must also specify unambiguously conditions under which the

organism moves from one stage to another. In the case of the caterpillar, the kinds of foods the caterpillar must eat, the temperature it requires, and the time it takes to spin the cocoon would be among the conditions to be specified. If and only if the stages can be distinguished and the conditions for changing from one stage to another can be specified is it possible to make predictions from the theory. Finally, by applying a demarcation rule to observations in which the conditions are fulfilled, the theory can be tested.

The complex process of economic development has also been approached from the point of view of stage theory. In fact, there has been a long line of stage theorists who have gone about identifying the various stages of economic development in different ways. Some have defined stages in terms of population density, the progression of stages being manifested in the shifts from areas of lesser density to those of greater density. Others have defined stages in terms of the sectoral composition of economic activity and the progression of stages from those in which the primary sectors (agriculture and mining) are dominant to those in which the manufacturing and/or service sectors are dominant.[1]

We shall discuss two of the more recent and popular stage theories: Rostow's historical stage theory and the Adelman and Morris social-political-economic brand of stage theory. Since each utilizes different analytic techniques and is incompletely operational for different reasons, they can profitably be discussed separately.

Rostow's Stage Theory

Rostow's stage theory[2] is designed not along the lines of a "rigid Newtonian derivation from a few axiomatic assumptions" but rather as a "kind of biological theory of process and pattern" (Rostow 1962). His theorizing is clearly motivated by what he considers the failure of economic theory. As a result, Rostow's theory is based on various observations taken from the histories of developed countries which, he feels, reveal a considerable degree of uniformity in the patterns and processes of development.

[1]For a presentation and analysis of stage theories of development, see Hoselitz (1960).
[2]The theory is most completely expressed in Rostow (1961, 1962).

Five stages are identified—"traditional society," "preconditions for takeoff," "takeoff into self-sustaining growth," "the drive to maturity," and "age of mass consumption"— through which every society would pass in achieving economic growth. Unfortunately, the distinctions drawn by Rostow between some of these stages, such as that between the traditional society stage and the preconditions for takeoff stage, are not sharp. For example, one characteristic of traditional society that is not a characteristic of the next stage is a "pre-Newtonian science and technology" and "pre-Newtonian attitudes to the physical world" (1961, p. 1). Since it is difficult to determine what kinds of science and attitudes are pre-Newtonian and which are not, it is possible to limit the analysis to three stages—pre-takeoff, takeoff, and post-takeoff —at virtually no cost in analytic power.

For each stage, Rostow specifies a number of distinguishing characteristics. The preconditions stage is characterized by a dramatic rise in agricultural productivity, political stability, heavy migration to the cities, substantial development of transportation and other forms of social overhead capital, and increasing capital goods imports financed by capital inflows as well as by raw material exports. The takeoff stage is characterized by a jump in the rate of productive investment from 5 percent or less to 10 percent or more of national income; the development of one or more substantial manufacturing sectors with a high growth rate; the existence or quick emergence of a political, social, and institutional framework ". . . which exploits the impulses to expansion in the modern sector and the potential external economy effects of the take-off and gives to growth an on-going character"; and a marked rise in the rate of growth of national income, aggregate and per capita (1962, p. 284). Furthermore, the time required for the takeoff period should be relatively short, no longer than 20 to 30 years. Finally, the post-takeoff stage is characterized by a shift of leading sectors, an eventual smoothing out of the growth rate, and less and less structural change.

Although some of these attributes of the different stages may not be operational, probably a sufficient number could be defined more precisely to permit at least a meaningful classification of particular countries. Unfortunately, as a result of qualifications he liberally introduces, Rostow's schema does not even provide a satisfactory classificatory scheme. Even the various characteristics that in the earlier versions of his theory were stated as necessary conditions are later compromised considerably. For example, in reference to the preconditions stage, Rostow subsequently distinguishes between the general case (Europe) and the special case of the "born-free" countries (the United States, Australia, Canada, etc.). He also hedges on the necessity of capital imports (1962, p. 285) and on the jump in the investment rate (1962, p. 292). In contrast to his earlier emphasis on uniformity in the growth process, these later qualifications lead him to conclude: "Perhaps the most important thing to be said about the behavior of these variables in historical cases of take-off is that they have assumed many different forms. There is no single pattern" (1962, p. 292). It is no wonder that much of the discussion of Rostow's stage theory has been limited to discussions as to whether or not his particular designations for particular countries at specific points in time are "correct."

The building of a classificatory system does not, by itself, constitute stage theory. What is also needed is an explanation of how and why a country moves from one stage to another at a particular time. In that respect also, Rostow's efforts are incomplete and unsuccessful, and his facts are often incorrect. For example, he says that the necessary condition of a rise in agricultural productivity could come from land reform and the breakup of feudalism, but alternatively, it could be induced by a favorable trend in the terms of trade. Moreover, in the final analysis, the rise in agricultural productivity may not be necessary if the area under cultivation can be expanded easily. Similarly, in explaining the transition to takeoff, Rostow suggests that industrialization and takeoff may be induced by a favorable shift in the terms of trade resulting from the rise in agricultural productivity in the preconditions stage. However, capital imports, urbanization, education, entrepreneurship, the opening up of foreign markets, and numerous other factors provide alternative explanations.

The result of this ambivalence is that one can never formulate a demarcation rule for deciding whether or not a specific case lies within or without the acceptable bounds of one's model. By backing away from the original determinancy of the model (presumably in an attempt to "save" the model), Rostow has rendered his theory nonoperational. Rostow attempts to defend his position by emphasizing the importance of stochastic elements, such as entrepreneurship and public policy, viewing his theory as a stochastic theory and as a "noncommunist manifesto," that is, a more realistic alternative to Marx's extremely deterministic (and powerful) theory of growth. As we suggested in Chapter 2, however, the fact that a statement is stochastic does not imply that a demarcation rule cannot be specified. Although the probabilistic element is relevant in determining the number of observations on the wrong side of the demarcation rule that one is willing to tolerate before rejecting the hypothesis, it does not obviate the need for a clearly stated demarcation rule. Lacking such a rule, Rostow's model, judged as a whole, is at best a classificatory scheme and at worst a series of entirely uninteresting existential statements of the form, for example, "there existed takeoffs that followed a rise in agricultural productivity." Since such existential statements can never be rejected, they do not lead to knowledge.

What could be done with his theory to make it more operational? We will suggest briefly how a central point of Rostow's theory could be reformulated. First, we would identify a country as being at the takeoff stage if, over a period of 20 to 30 years, that country is observed to: (1) achieve an increase in the annual rate of net investment from 5 percent or less of national income to 10 percent or more; (2) stabilize its population growth at 1.5 percent per annum or less; and (3) increase its allocation of investment to the capital goods industry. Second, we would state the theory as follows: if and only if a country satisfies all the characteristics of takeoff will it achieve an increase in the rate of growth of national income and national income per capita of at least 1 percent per annum sustained over a period of at least two decades. Finally, we could state a demarcation rule: if in more than 5 percent of the cases in which the conditions of takeoff are fulfilled, growth rates are not increased on a sustained basis by at least one percent per annum, the theory should be rejected.[3]

Kuznets (1963a) and Fishlow (1965b) have

summarized the statistical evidence available for a number of countries with respect to this version of Rostow's thesis. The findings are: (1) in a few of the cases in which sustained growth was subsequently obtained, the net investment rate had jumped by as much as 5 percent in the preceding 20 to 30 years and (2) in most of the cases in which the investment rate did rise by as much as 5 percent, the rise in the income growth rate was either less than 1 percent per annum or was temporarily higher but was not sustained. Clearly, the rise in the investment rate has proven to be neither a necessary nor a sufficient condition for sustained growth. This stricter version of Rostow's theory must therefore be rejected.

It is certainly possible to restate the theory in a weaker or more qualified manner to make it consistent with the evidence. As we have pointed out, however, weaker formulations run the risk of becoming nonoperational. Even if a more operational version of Rostow's stage theory had been confirmed with respect to the available economic histories of DCs, additional questions could be raised about the validity of such results for contemporary LDCs.

Social, Political, and Economic Stage Theory

Adelman and Morris and their associates share with Rostow and others the view that the process of economic development can best be analyzed in terms of stages. They use different techniques in distinguishing these stages, explaining growth within each stage, and identifying the factors that determine the transition from one stage to another. By dealing with political, social, and cultural factors as well as with economic ones, and by focusing on the experience of LDCs, Adelman and Morris have simultaneously extended the scope of analysis of the development process and molded a stage theory that has more assured relevance to contemporary countries. By prodigious effort, they manage to quantify all these factors, including the noneconomic ones, and they provide empirical results that underscore the importance of noneconomic factors in explaining growth within and between different stages of development. Without going into detail, we will briefly review some of their prolific writings, to give at least an intuitive understanding of some of their meth-

---

[3]For other but somewhat similar formulations of the Rostow model, see Bićanić (1962), Peterson (1965), Thweatt (1968), and especially Kuznets (1963a).

ods, summarize their results, and illustrate some methodological problems that confront their interesting but refractory hypotheses.

Adelman and Morris use a variety of statistical techniques, including factor analysis, discriminant analysis, canonical correlations, and analysis of hierarchical interactions.[4] These techniques represent different forms of multivariate analysis. The basic difference between univariate and multivariate analysis is that while in the former we study the characteristics of the distributions of a scalar variable, in the latter we study the characteristics of the distribution of a vector of variables that are jointly dependent. For example, in univariate analysis we study the total consumption as a function of family income and family size. In multivariate analysis, on the other hand, we study the demand of each one of n commodities as a function of the family income and the n prices of the commodities.[5] Both relationships can be fitted with m observations of family survey data.

The early applications of Adelman and Morris used factor analysis, upon which their subsequent studies also rely. We shall, therefore, present a brief and intuitive exposition of this form of multivariate analysis.[6]

Factor Analysis
Not unlike regression analysis, factor analysis is basically an analysis of variance technique. It decomposes the variance of a variable into several components based on its association with other variables. Unlike regression analysis, however, these other variables are not observable. Instead, they are hypothetical or latent variables, called factors, consisting of clusters of the original variables.

The factor analysis problem can be expressed in matrix form. Suppose we have data for m countries consisting of n indicators, such as GNP per capita, level of education, and so on. We can denote the decomposition of the variance of each indicator as

$$\mathbf{x} = \begin{pmatrix} x_1 \\ \vdots \\ x_n \end{pmatrix} = \mathbf{A} + \mathbf{Bf} + \mathbf{u}$$

where $\mathbf{x}$ is a column vector of n indicators, $\mathbf{A}$ is a vector of $1 \times n$, $\mathbf{B}$ is a matrix of $n \times q$, $\mathbf{f}$ is a vector of $q \times 1$, and $\mathbf{u}$ is a vector of $n \times 1$.

In matrix form for m countries, we write

$$\mathbf{X} = \mathbf{A} + \mathbf{BF} + \mathbf{U}$$

where $\mathbf{X}$ is a $m \times n$ matrix, with elements the observable indicators for each country. The elements of the vector $\mathbf{F}$ are the latent variables, the factors. $\mathbf{B}$ then consists of the coefficients of these factors, called factor loadings. The major aim of factor analysis is to determine the factor loadings, that is, the coefficients that relate the observed variables to the common factors. Factor loadings play the same role in factor analysis as regression coefficients in regression analysis. The squared factor loadings represent the relative contribution of each factor to the standardized variance of each indicator, x_i. If a given factor, f_i, appears only in a subset of the elements of $\mathbf{X}$, it is called a *group factor*. It is possible, however, that a factor f_i appears in all the elements of $\mathbf{X}$. Then it is called a *common factor*, and the *commonality* for each variable is represented by the sum of the squares of its factor loadings. The commonality indicates the extent to which the common factors account for the total unit variance of the variable x_i. It is akin to the coefficient of multiple determination in regression analysis, the R^2. Besides the common factors and the group factors, we may also have a *specific factor*, one that appears only in the element x_i. This appears in the residual u, which also includes errors in measurement and noise in the universe.

Factor analysis is primarily helpful to organize and simplify complex statistical data. While it may be possible in our example to fully describe each of the m countries in terms

---

[4]The analysis of hierarchial interactions that refers to the study of income distribution is presented in Chapter 14.

[5]As an example of this application of multivariate analysis, see the Stone (1954) linear logarithmic demand function:

$$q_k = \alpha_k \mu^{\beta_{k0}} \prod_j p_j^{-w_j \beta_{k0} + \beta_{kj}}$$

where

q_k = quantity of commodity k, $k = 1$ to n, consumed by a family
p_j = price of commodity j, $j = 1$ to n
$\mu = \Sigma\, p_j q_j$, that is, the income of the household
$w_j = \dfrac{p_j q_j}{\mu}$, that is, the weight of commodity j in the total budget.

In this system, the coefficient β_{k0} describes the income effect, $-w_j \beta_{k0}$ the indirect effect of price on income, and β_{kj} the substitution effect.

[6]For the technical presentation of the method, the reader is referred to Adelman and Morris (1967), Harmon (1960), Thurstone (1961), and Horst (1965).

of the whole array of the n indicators, it is more economical to do so by first arranging (or reducing) clusters of indicators in a small number of factors that can be interpreted intuitively, and then utilizing the smaller number of factors to describe or classify the countries. This is what factor analysis does, making for a somewhat different relationship between variables than in regression analysis. While in regression analysis the independent variables are by hypothesis uncorrelated, in factor analysis the variables, the factors, are interdependent. Thus, while regression analysis may make it possible to identify causality and dependence, factor analysis may be thought of as identifying only interdependence (Adelman and Morris 1971, p. 94). Another problem that arises in factor analysis but not in regression analysis is that the factor loading matrix, **B**, is not estimable as such. Instead, one can estimate only the product of **B** and its inverse, BB^{-1}. "Factor rotation" is a procedure for decomposing BB^{-1} into its two components and thus involves principal component analysis.[7]

Application of Factor Analysis to the Identification of Stages

As we have seen, the first step in stage theory is to classify, that is, to define the characteristics of a stage and to identify countries with respect to particular stages. With reference to a sample of 74 LDCs, Adelman and Morris heuristically obtain quantitative or semiquantitative data for each of 41 different social, political, and economic indicators of development. Some of these development indicators are traditional, such as per capita GNP, but some (especially the social and political ones) are distinctly nontraditional (e.g., "character of agricultural organization," "extent of leadership commitment to economic development," "degree of modernization of outlook," "extent of social mobility," and "character of basic social organization").

The complete list of 41 indicators appears

in Table 3.1 and distinguishes three groups: sociocultural, political, and economic.

Some of these indicators are, in turn, based upon two or more subindicators. For example, indicator 6, "extent of social mobility," is measured by: (1) "the ratio of the population five to nineteen years of age that is enrolled in primary and secondary schools"; (2) "the importance of the indigenous middle class"; and (3) "the presence or absence of prohibitive cultural or ethnic barriers to upward social mobility." As the authors admit, many of the other indicators are also based on a variety of qualitative characteristics that have been distinguished implicitly in the minds of the "experts" interviewed, not explicitly.

After defining the indicators and subindicators, Adelman and Morris resourcefully assign each of 74 LDCs a letter grade with respect to each indicator.[8] Finally, the letter-grade scales for these indicators, many of which are only qualitative, are converted to a numerical scale. The resulting "ordinal" scores are the basic data for their application of factor analysis and for their subsequent extensions of that analysis with other tools of multivariate analysis.

The first application of the technique is to interactions of the social and political indicators in the process of economic development (Adelman and Morris 1965, 1967). For this purpose, all the economic indicators given in Table 3.1 except one, per capita GNP, are omitted, and even this indicator is kept separate from the four factors into which the social and political indicators are clustered. The results appear in Table 3.2. Factor 1 (F_1 in the table) refers broadly to the extent of social differentiation and integration, that is, "processes of change in attitudes and institutions associated with the breakdown of traditional social organization." Factor 2 (F_2) is associated with political systems, indicating the transition from "centralized authoritarian political forms to specialized political mechanisms capable of representing the varied group interests of a society and of aggregating these interests through participant national political organs." Factor 3 (F_3) relates to leadership, "the strength of industrializing elites relative to traditional elites." Factor 4 (F_4) refers to social and political stability.

---

[7]Referring to the previous notation for the factor analysis problem, we can specify the distributions of **f** and **u**, respectively, as $f \sim N(0, I)$ and $u \sim N(0, \Sigma)$, where Σ is the variance-covariance matrix. Then, since we have introduced a vector of constants, **A**, we can specify $E(f) = 0$. Similarly, since the elements of **B** are completely unspecified, we can assume that the variances of the elements of **f** are all equal. Given the observations on x, we can only estimate $\phi = BB^{-1} + \Sigma$. If Σ were known, identifying the elements of **B** in this context would be equivalent to the problem of decomposing a positive semidefinite matrix (Dhrymes 1970, pp. 77–82).

[8]Where subindicators enter the definition of an indicator, the letter grade is assigned after an implicit weight is attached to each subindicator.

Table 3.1 *Indicators of Social, Political, and Economic Structure Utilized by Adelman and Morris*

Sociocultural Indicators	Political Indicators	Economic Indicators
1. Size of the Traditional Agricultural Sector	13. Degree of National Integration and Sense of National Unity	25. Per Capita GNP in 1961
2. Extent of Dualism		26. Rate of Growth of Real per Capita GNP
3. Extent of Urbanization	14. Extent of Centralization of Political Power	27. Abundance of Natural Resources
4. Character of Basic Social Organization	15. Strength of Democratic Institutions	28. Gross Investment Rate
5. Importance of the Indigenous Middle Class	16. Degree of Freedom of Political Opposition and Press	29. Level of Modernization of Industry
6. Extent of Social Mobility	17. Degree of Competitiveness of Political Parties	30. Change in Degree of Industrialization
7. Extent of Literacy	18. Predominant Basis of the Political Party System	31. Character of Agricultural Organization
8. Extent of Mass Communication	19. Strength of the Labor Movement	32. Level of Modernization of Techniques in Agriculture
9. Degree of Cultural and Ethnic Homogeneity	20. Political Strength of the Traditional Elite	33. Degree of Improvement in Agricultural Productivity
10. Degree of Social Tension	21. Political Strength of the Military	34. Adequacy of Physical Overhead Capital
11. Crude Fertility Rate	22. Degree of Administrative Efficiency	36. Effectiveness of the Tax System
12. Degree of Modernization of Outlook	23. Extent of Leadership Commitment to Economic Development	37. Improvement in the Tax System
	24. Extent of Political Stability	38. Effectiveness of Financial Institutions
		39. Improvement in Financial Institutions
		40. Rate of Improvement in Human Resources
		41. Structure of Foreign Trade

Source: Adelman, I. and C. T. Morris (1967), *Society, Politics, and Economic Development.* Baltimore: Johns Hopkins University Press, pp. 16–17.

The square of the rotated factor loadings represents the proportion of the variance in an indicator that is explained by a particular factor, after allowing for the contributions of the other factors. Thus, a factor 1 loading of 0.89 for the size of traditional agricultural sector implies that about 81 percent of the variance of this indicator is attributed to factor 1, that is, to social differentiation and integration. This is the usual interpretation of factor analysis. Adelman and Morris, however, go one step farther. The per capita GNP indicator was not included with any of the other indicators in any single factor, but was included in the factor analysis, and thus there are factor loadings for it with regard to each of the four factors. These factor loadings are used in a rather controversial way (from the technical point of view) to draw generaliza-

tions about the relationship between the per capita income and the four factors (Rayner 1970; Adelman and Morris 1970). The factor loadings for the per capita GNP are −0.73 for factor 1, 0.31 for factor 2, −0.26 for factor 3, and −0.03 for factor 4.[9] Since the squares of the factor loadings indicate the percent of the variance in the variable "explained by" or associated with each of the factors, Adelman and Morris claim that 53 percent of the intercountry variation in per capita GNP in 1961 is explained by factor 1, an additional 10 percent by factor 2, another 7 percent by factor 3, and about one-tenth of

[9]The reader might want to compare the rotated factor loadings of Adelman and Morris (1967), upon which the above discussion is based, with those of (1965). The difference in both weights and signs of the indicators illustrates the earlier point about the arbitrary nature of the factor matrix inversion.

1 percent by factor 4. The sum of the squared factor loadings, in the case of GNP per capita 70 percent, is the "commonality" of each indicator, and it represents the proportion of the total variance that is "explained" by the four factors taken together. The finding that 70 percent of the variance in GNP per capita is "attributed" to the sociopolitical indicators grouped in the four factors leads Adelman and Morris (1967, p. 150) to conclude that ". . . it is just as reasonable to look at underdevelopment as a social and political phenomenon as it is to analyze it in terms of intercountry differences in economic structure." A further interpretation of the rotated factor loadings is given. The loading of −0.73 of GNP per capita for factor 1 and the 0.89

for the size of the traditional agricultural sector included in factor 1 implies that GNP per capita is inversely related to the size of the traditional sector, and so on for the other rotated factor loadings.

The authors proceed with further applications of factor analysis to the same set of data for 74 LDCs. Since factor 1 is both the most important factor and constitutes a much broader index of development than other conventional measures, each country is then scored relative to factor 1 (Adelman and Morris 1965, 1967). These factor scores are used in turn to divide the sample of countries into three groups, identified as different *stages* of development—the "lowest," "intermediate," and "highest" stages. Separate factor analyses

Table 3.2 *Rotated Factor Matrix for Per Capita Gross National Product Together with 24 Social and Political Variables*

Political and Social Indicators	F_1	F_2	F_3	F_4	Commonality
	Rotated Factor Loadings				
Per Capital GNP in 1961	−0.73	0.31	−0.26	−0.03	0.699
Size of the Traditional Agricultural Sector	0.89	−0.21	0.17	−0.08	0.869
Extent of Dualism	−0.84	0.14	−0.30	0.04	0.824
Extent of Urbanization	−0.84	0.13	−0.12	0.02	0.741
Character of Basic Social Organization	−0.83	0.24	0.10	0.03	0.761
Importance of the Indigenous Middle Class	−0.82	0.14	−0.23	−0.08	0.755
Extent of Social Mobility	−0.86	0.21	−0.18	−0.18	0.848
Extent of Literacy	−0.86	0.32	0.03	−0.11	0.845
Extent of Mass Communication	−0.88	0.28	−0.06	−0.02	0.858
Degree of Cultural and Ethnic Homogeneity	−0.66	−0.30	0.34	−0.21	0.680
Degree of National Integration and Sense of National Unity	−0.87	−0.07	0.01	−0.18	0.792
Crude Fertility Rate	0.63	−0.14	0.05	0.18	0.448
Degree of Modernization of Outlook	−0.75	0.31	−0.39	−0.03	0.805
Strength of Democratic Institutions	−0.48	0.72	−0.26	−0.19	0.857
Degree of Freedom of Political Opposition and Press	−0.33	0.82	−0.02	−0.10	0.802
Degree of Competitiveness of Political Parties	−0.32	0.79	0.08	0.25	0.801
Predominant Basis of the Political Party System	−0.43	0.70	0.04	0.01	0.681
Strength of the Labor Movement	−0.38	0.63	−0.36	−0.05	0.678
Political Strength of the Military	−0.26	−0.58	0.36	0.41	0.706
Extent of Centralization of Political Power	−0.07	−0.65	0.08	−0.02	0.432
Political Strength of the Traditional Elite	0.08	−0.07	0.73	0.05	0.543
Extent of Leadership Commitment to Economic Development	−0.14	−0.02	−0.80	−0.21	0.699
Degree of Administrative Efficiency	−0.39	0.37	−0.59	−0.16	0.663
Degree of Social Tension	0.22	0.02	0.02	0.87	0.816
Extent of Political Stability	−0.07	0.05	−0.39	−0.82	0.821

Note: The figures in the boxes indicate the factor to which each variable is assigned. Percentage of overall variance explained by factors: 73.7. Percentage of variance explained by last factor included: 5.0.

Source: Adelman, I. and C. T. Morris (1967), *Society, Politics, and Economic Development*. Baltimore: Johns Hopkins University Press, p. 151.

are then computed for three different sets of countries, that is, regional subsamples for Africa, Asia, and Latin America, with the same set of indicators. Since the three different regions correspond at least roughly to different stages of development, the authors find that the characterization of the factors varies somewhat from stage to stage, social factors dominating intragroup differences in per capita GNP in the "lowest" group (Africa) and political factors playing the dominant role in explaining such differences at later stages. These results would seem to confirm the meaningfulness of the factor analytic classification system adopted by Adelman and Morris, and defend the logic of a stage theory approach.

In another application of factor analysis, Adelman and Morris (1967) investigate the interactions of social, political, and economic factors using all indicators in Table 3.1 (including the economic factors). This analysis is applied separately to each of the three different stages identified on the basis of the country scores with respect to factor 1. In these cases, the rate of growth (1950–1964) instead of the level of per capita income is the dependent variable. The results, which are interpreted as short-run effects, are in general akin to those of the previous applications. For the countries at the lowest end of the socioeconomic scale, the growth process requires both economic and social transformation. For the countries at an intermediate level of development, the statistical results are rather inconclusive, with some evidence that the crucial economic influences are those governing the process of industrialization. Finally, the political preconditions for development are important in the countries at the high end of the socioeconomic scale. The crucial correlates of economic performance in these countries are the effectiveness of economic institutions and the extent of national mobilization for development.

Further Applications of Multivariate Analysis

In subsequent studies using other multivariate techniques, Adelman, Morris, and their associates have gone on to produce other results which, they argue, support their thesis of the relative importance of social and political factors in development.

For instance, in Adelman and Morris (1968a), the technique of discriminant analysis has been utilized to identify the specific indicators that best "predict" the development performance potential of individual countries or, in the language of the technique, best discriminate among different development performance groups. Their results indicate that four indicators (39, 35, 12, and 23 in Table 3.1 by order of importance) account for more than 99 percent of the discriminable variance among the different development performance groups.

Subsequently, Adelman and Morris (1968b) attempted to explain each of the four indicators identified in their discriminant analysis in terms of the remaining indicators by utilizing the technique of stepwise regression. In this way, for each of the four indicators, they identified and obtained regression coefficients for a small number of the initial indicators that would explain the preponderance of the intercountry variation in that indicator. Going further, they tried to explain the intercountry variation in each important determinant of the indicators in the discriminant function, and then that of the determinants in terms of other indicators iteratively, until all indicators that entered the model and could be explained satisfactorily were explained. The variables that could not be explained were identified as exogenous variables, for which multipliers expressing their effect on all endogenous variables could be calculated. In this way, they arrived at a fairly large-scale quantitative social-political-economic model of development. The variables with the highest multipliers on development performance were variables 39, 12, and 2.

In still another study, Adelman, Geier, and Morris (1969) applied the technique of "canonical correlation" to estimate the relationship between one endogenously chosen set of variables, identified as "instruments," and another set, identified as "goals." By this technique, they obtain some interesting estimates of: (1) the degree of inconsistency among the various goals; (2) the relative importance of the instruments in achieving the respective goals; and (3) the relative sensitivity of different kinds of goal satisfaction to the manipulation of various "policy instruments."

Critique of Adelman and Morris

The scope and complexity of the work that Adelman, Morris, and their associates have carried out are indeed stupendous. The data collection task for their work is of staggering magnitude. Deriving such indicators as "character of basic social organization" or "importance of indigenous middle class" might appear to be a futile exercise, not unlike defining Rostow's "pre-Newtonian science and technology." Yet through a heroic effort, Adelman and Morris have managed to obtain at least quasi-quantitative estimates for these indicators for an impressive sample of countries. Moreover, their attempt to broaden the analysis and scope of the study of economic development by treating social and political variables operationally is imaginative. Given the scope of such research, it should come as no surprise that one can question the validity and accuracy of some of their measurements, disagree with some of their judgments, and criticize some of their interpretations and conclusions. Some such questions and criticisms may be minor. Some, however, may compromise the validity of the results to a considerable degree.

Let us discuss the data problems first. Some indicators are based, at least partially, on the same subindicators, and thus may have introduced some spurious correlation among the variables. This is especially true with respect to the twelve social indicators associated with factor 1 in the original factor analysis, the results of which were presented in Table 3.2. As a result, spurious correlation among the variables of factor 1 may contribute significantly to the high factor loadings reported for these variables in Adelman and Morris (1967), the large multipliers for these variables reported in Adelman and Morris (1968b), and the heavy emphasis on social variables in the broadly defined index of development in Adelman and Morris (1965, 1967).

Another set of problems arises as a result of the ordinal measurement of the indicators included in the analysis (Brookins 1970; Adelman and Morris 1970). Ordinal variables are inappropriate for deriving "elasticities" and "multipliers" that are subject to the usual interpretation. Moreover, ordinal variables have no average, and hence one should properly use majority rule as a means of making classifications, but with the accompanying problems of intransitivity of rankings that Arrow (1951) has demonstrated. Lastly, when at least one of the series is strictly ordinal,

the appropriate measure of correlation is the Spearman rank-correlation coefficient instead of the simple correlation coefficient Adelman and Morris use as the basis for their analysis.

Many of the assumptions made at various points in the analysis are arbitrary, and some are quite unjustified. Procedures such as stepwise regression and factor analysis inevitably involve certain arbitrary judgments, such as how to draw the line between one factor and another or what variables to start with in deciding which and how many variables to add. The results are often quite sensitive to such arbitrary choices. For example, in their attempt to define a more satisfactory and comprehensive index of development, Adelman and Morris (1965; 1967, Table IV–1) did not include any economic indicators (except GNP per capita), even though these indicators were included in the subsequent "short-run" analysis (Adelman and Morris 1967, Tables V–1, VI–1, VII–1). We have released the arbitrary assumption that economic variables do not matter in the long-run analysis and have rerun the first "long-run" factor analysis with the economic variables included. Our results indicate that most of the economic variables (e.g., indicators 28, 29, 32, 34, 36, 38, 40) also associate with factor 1. Similarly, we have found that the results change if one allows the GNP per capita indicator to be included in factor 1, which seems reasonable, since it is included in the factor analysis. The decision to include or exclude variables is defensible on grounds of a priori knowledge, but such information is inadmissible in multivariate analysis (as we will demonstrate). Thus, the authors seem to make their decisions about what indicators or subindicators to include or exclude simply on the basis of whether or not they work out well.[10] This, of course, makes the results tautological.

While Adelman and her associates cannot be criticized for the ultraempiricist spirit in their work, they should have been more consistent in recognizing its limitations and in avoiding confusion between hypothesis formulation and testing. By the authors' own admission, no explicit theoretical statements are made:

---

[10]Some examples of this are the exclusion of "openness of access to political leadership" (1967, p. 34), "achievement motivation," and "social attitudes toward economic activity" (1967, p. 16).

The philosophy underlying the procedure used for constructing the model is quite overtly empiricist. Since there are no firmly validated theories of the process of socio-economic and political change, we consciously avoided *a priori* specification of the functions we wished to fit. Instead, we let the data specify the model. (Adelman and Morris 1968*b*, p. 1184.)

This, in general, multivariate analysis can do well. It "hunts for correlations," and it exposes possible interactions among the variables. Correlations are instructive in the process of constructing hypotheses through inductive reasoning. Without any specific theoretical underpinning, however, the transition from correlation to causality is impossible.

In view of this limitation, factor analysis (as well as discriminant analysis and canonical correlation) can serve three distinct purposes (Rayner 1970): it can be a ranking device, a descriptive device, or a tool for further analysis, for example, in suggesting new hypotheses. In each of these respects, it can be particularly useful when large numbers of variables, which for the sake of efficiency can be reduced to a smaller number of factors, are involved.

At times, however, the Adelman and Morris studies go beyond these legitimate uses of their techniques by relapsing into the habit of interpreting the associations established as indicating causality or indicating that certain conditions must be satisfied in order to achieve development. For example:

> The analysis in this chapter makes it clear that at the lowest end of the socioeconomic scale the nature of the growth process *requires* both economic and social transformation. It is apparent that for this group of countries the extent to which the sway of tribal society has been reduced and the degree to which the modernization of social structure has proceeded are important *determinants* of the rate of improvement of purely economic performance. These social transformations are *required* for the enlargement of the sphere within which economic activity operates independently of traditional social organization. (Adelman and Morris 1967, p. 202, italics added.)

A more appropriate interpretation of the work of Adelman and Morris is that by classifying

complex data and reading the correlations in the data they have formulated specific hypotheses.

One such hypothesis would be that four factors (the extent of social differentiation and integration, the political transformation from authoritarian regimes to representative governments, the quality of leadership, and the extent of social and political stability) account for the variance observed in a number of sociocultural and political indicators from a large sample of LDCs. Another hypothesis would be that the relative importance of the factors varies from stage to stage, with social factors being more important in the early stages, political and economic factors in the later stages.

However, Adelman and Morris cannot validly use the same set of data and interpret their correlations as evidence that their hypotheses are correct. A new set of data, independent evidence, and methods with greater emphasis on determinacy and causality and less on correlation would be required for this purpose. The lesson of this example is clear: for testing such hypotheses, one is much better off formulating the theory on a priori considerations (as difficult as this might be) before one lets the data "speak."

From the Scylla of Uniformity to the Charybdis of Uniqueness: Motivational and Threshold Theories

In addition to noting their common as well as distinct shortcomings, which prevent them from being fully operational theories of development, our lengthy discussion of the Rostow and Adelman-Morris approaches has illustrated an important feature that permeates much of the literature: the search for sweeping similarities or uniformities in development patterns. As we have seen, these similarities, once discovered, tend to be elevated to the status of "preconditions" or "necessary requisites" for development, but usually at the risk of being wrong.

At the other extreme is the approach to development that places ultimate importance on the unique event, the random element, or the accidental factor. If uniformity is a Procrustean bed that presents the danger of emasculating the study of development, uniqueness pursued to the extreme may either negate the need for the study of development or at least make such study operationally impossible. In the following paragraphs, we discuss briefly the theories on historical accidents, development-oriented tastes and attitudes, and thresholds that illustrate this limitation to varying degrees.

Historical Comparisons

Gerschenkron (1962, pp. 31–51), among others, has taken issue with the universality of prerequisites for economic development, making use of historical comparisons. He rejects the idea that "major obstacles to development *must* be removed and certain things propitious to it *must* be created before industrialization can begin" (p. 31). What impresses Gerschenkron more than the uniformity of industrial development is the diversity in patterns of growth. He argues that latecomers to development are not likely to follow the sequence of their predecessors but instead can be expected to change the sequence around, to violate preconditions, and to skip certain stages entirely. After observing differences among the already developed countries in their growth processes, Gerschenkron formulated a series of specific hypotheses of the form: "the more X a country has, the more likely it is to do Y." By defining X and Y in measurable terms, many such hypotheses can be made operationally feasible. Specifically, Gerschenkron argues that the more relatively backward a country is, the more likely its subsequent development will be characterized by: (1) higher rate of growth in manufacturing; (2) greater stress on large scale in plant and firm size; (3) more emphasis on capital goods; (4) more downward pressure on consumption standards; (5) greater centralization in financial institutions and entrepreneurial guidance; and (6) a smaller role for agriculture in the development process. These hypotheses can be far more easily tested than the uniformity hypotheses, thereby constituting a happy compromise between hypotheses that emphasize uniformity and those that emphasize uniqueness.

Attitudinal Factors and Status Withdrawal

Uniqueness hypotheses are exemplified by the hypotheses that have attributed economic development to fortuitous combinations of attitudes, which commanded considerable attention for a while. Many such hypotheses are rendered nonoperational by the extreme difficulty of measuring the relevant attitudes. A few, such as McClelland's (1961) Need-for-Achievement Motivation (N-Ach),[11] have overcome this hurdle but nevertheless suffer from a basic defect that severely limits their usefulness in the scientific process of the stepwise elimination of error, in that they fail to explain how attitudes are determined. The lack of such an explanation implies that attitudes, and therefore development, must be attributed to a "unique" or random occurrence, to a nonsystematic factor.

Hagen (1962) has gone a step farther by advancing an attitudinal hypothesis in which attitudes are explained in terms of exogenous events (usually political or social) that deprive people of their accustomed status. Specifically, Hagen argued that, starting from childhood and continuing into adulthood, people search and strive for an identity and for status respect, especially from the members of their reference groups—groups whom they respect and whose esteem they value. A hierarchical, authoritarian, traditional economic system offers secure status to an individual with respect to his higher elite group. It is a system at a stable equilibrium.

The basic agent of change in the system is an historical accident that entails the withdrawal of the status that the highest elite had traditionally bestowed on the middle- or lower-level elite groups. This accident might be the accession to power of a new group by force, the derogation of valued systems, the nonacceptance of an immigrant group, and so on. The social tension that ensues leads the derogated group to deviate in its behavior from traditional patterns and to reject the traditional values of the derogating elite. This leads the derogated group to social withdrawal and in the course of a few generations to a less consistent control of children, with the result that the children of the deviant minority are freer to use their initiative and to become innovative than are other children. Thus, in a Schumpeterian finale, these entrepreneur-innovators constitute the engine of economic development, and deviance constitutes the fuel that will feed that engine in the future. This may or may

[11]For other examples of the literature on N-Ach, see LeVine (1966), Ostheimer (1967), McClelland and Winter (1969). For critics, see R. W. Brown (1965), Child and Storm (1956–1957), MacArthur (1953), and Schatz (1965).

not be so. The test of the hypothesis notwith-standing, the obvious question arises whether or not deviance is a necessary condition for developing entrepreneurship.

Threshold Hypotheses

The idea of the threshold of economic de-velopment appears in both the stage theories and in the hypotheses emphasizing the unique event. In the takeoff, the threshold hypotheses examine that optimum moment in the life of an economy when breaking away from back-wardness is relatively easier. In the unique-ness hypotheses, this moment is a result of a particular stimulus. Analytically, this stimulus may be conceived of in terms of Toynbee's re-lation between challenge and response. While small challenges may be dissipated, larger challenges generate, up to a point, effective responses.[12]

A number of hypotheses examine the re-lationship between the challenge and the re-sponse. Leibenstein (1957) advanced the "crit-ical minimum effort thesis," which emphasized the relationship between population size and agricultural development. Rosenstein-Rodan's (1961) "big push" hypothesis focused on ex-ternal economies. Nurkse (1953) emphasized balanced growth as a way of overcoming the supply and demand impediments to capital formation in poor countries. As we have al-ready noted, Gerschenkron (1962) tied the tension between the backwardness of pre-industrialization conditions on the one hand and the benefits expected from industrializa-tion on the other to the response which over-comes the obstacles to development and liberates the forces that make for industrial growth.

Each of these versions facilitates testing by specifying a particular development process yet suffers from the difficulty of specifying a priori what level of effort is sufficient to provoke growth, while not so excessive as to thwart it.

Hirschman (1967) provides a good ex-ample of the nature of the set of hypotheses that employ the challenge-response idea. He studied 11 well-diversified and matured proj-ects financed by the World Bank in different parts of the world to explain their respective success or failure. His approach was to dis-cern common themes running through the different experiences and to trace these themes to "the principal structural characteristics" of the projects.

Each project comes to the world with its own germs and antibodies: the unsuspected threats to its profitability and the unsuspected remedial action. The combination of these two constitutes the Toynbeean principle of chal-lenge and response, which Hirschman elabo-rates as "the principle of the Hiding Hand." In this application, he suggests that creativity is underestimated. People do not seek chal-lenge; instead, they plunge into new tasks because they erroneously think that the tasks are easily manageable. As a result, if the full cost of the projects and the myriad of problems that ensue in their implementation could have been foreseen, the projects would never have been undertaken. The job of the benevolent Hiding Hand is to disseminate misinformation so as to underestimate the difficulties associated with the project or to exaggerate the prospective benefits so that one is tricked into undertaking a task that other-wise one would not dare tackle.

Lest this sounds like the praise of folly, an invitation to financial disaster, and a chase of white elephants, let us point out that Hirschman qualifies his thesis by arguing that there is an optimum amount of challenge that will elicit successful response. "One has to be rather lucky to be lured by the Hiding Hand into ventures whose emergent problems and difficulties can be successfully tackled" (p. 28). Examples of too much challenge that thwarts response are the international promoters' gim-micks of "pseudoimitation" ("the project is a straightforward application of a well-known technique that is widely used in the United States") and "pseudocomprehensiveness" ("the previous techniques of handling the problem failed because they were 'piecemeal' ").

The difference between Hirschman and the more conventional challenge-response theory of action is that the challenge has to be camouflaged. Once this is done, one has to wait and see whether or not the unan-ticipated difficulty that subsequently arises is overcome. "If the difficulty is encountered and overcome, the benefits that accrue as a result are likely to be higher, the greater were the odds against a favorable outcome" (p. 36). The drawback to such an approach is that one can only identify a good project by wait-

---

[12]The "up to a point" qualification is usually in-troduced to account for the possibility that an ex-cessively strong challenge may be counterproductive.

ing to see whether or not it does unexpectedly well. Furthermore, Hirschman's pursuit of uniqueness goes so far as to negate not only the possibility of generalization but even, it seems, of simple classification. "It is now seen that the project analyst must be still more modest: he cannot even pretend to classify uniformly, for purposes of decision making, the various properties and probable lines of behavior of projects, as either advantages or drawbacks, benefits or costs, assets or liabilities" (p. 188).

Although nonoperational, Hirschman's treatment of the topic is perceptive. He does point out some interesting limitations of existing methods of cost-benefit analysis. Although that analysis is capable of dealing with projects in which indirect benefits and costs and the external effects are likely to swamp direct and internal effects, the technique is not capable of dealing with outputs of the project, which are at the same time inputs essential to the project's success and survival. Marginal analysis and linear programming methods are unable to deal with this situation (although integer programming may become applicable). Hirschman is persuasive in stating that the dynamic interrelationship and feedback between outputs and inputs of a project deserve as much notice as the static transformation of specific inputs to certain outputs. Thus, his thesis provides an excellent example of how even a nonoperational hypothesis can provide many useful insights.

Part II
Development Statics

The classical vision of development, dating back to Adam Smith, is one of smooth, gradual, and nondisruptive change. Harmonic interests gravitate toward equilibrium processes, and departures from equilibrium activate automatic adjustment mechanisms. The classical approach to development is covered in Part II, in terms of development statics, and in Part III, as development dynamics.

Two basic questions are at the heart of development statics. First, what are the possibilities of substitutability between labor, which is plentiful in LDCs, and capital, which is scarce? Second, how is it possible to obtain more output from the existing resources? Chapters 4 to 7 focus, therefore, on the production function and on the study of efficiency.

The principal tool for our exposition of development statics is the production function, introduced in Chapter 4. Through neoclassical marginal productivity comparisons for the factors of production, we can gauge the departure from equilibrium and thus the force with which adjustment mechanisms are expected to operate. In order to determine the possibilities of substitution among factors of production, one must first determine which specific production function is applicable. If the production function is of the Cobb-Douglas form, no problem arises in connection with factor substitution. If it is of the Leontief type, no possibilities of substitution exist. If the production function is of the constant elasticity of substitution type, the substitution possibilities are not restricted to the two previous cases, and the exact range depends on the specific value of the elasticity of substitution parameter. Finally, if the appropriate form is linear programming, the question becomes one of imposing constraints that reflect the limitational resource endowments. It is also important to distinguish between the degree of factor substitutability before the plant and equipment are installed (i.e., the choice of technology), and that attainable after installation (i.e., adaptation).

The importance of departures from equilibrium is addressed in Chapter 5 through the measurement of efficiency. The partial production function analysis of Chapter 4, drawn to its logical conclusion, negates the concept of the production function itself. We start, therefore, by releasing the strict assumptions introduced earlier. Instead of firms having the same production function, we allow for shifts in the constant term, thereby representing differences in technical efficiency. Firms may also differ in their ability to maximize profits. We account for this by introducing the concept of price efficiency. Finally, firms may not encounter the same prices for inputs and outputs. Since prices do not enter the production function as exogenous variables, at this level of analysis the production function as a tool breaks down.

Chapter 6 starts at this point. The test of economic rationality purports to determine both the extent to which firms maximize profits and the importance of factor and output prices in determining the observed levels of factor utilization. The conclusions of this discussion lead directly to the formulation of the profit function and to the simultaneous measurement of technical and price efficiency in a context in which production functions vary, prices vary, and firms may commit mistakes in maximization.

The measurement of efficiency in Chapter 6 leads to the question addressed in Chapter 7, namely, how important is the cost of inefficiency and resource misallocation in the economy as a whole? Unlike the microeconomic analysis presented thus far, this is a question of macroeconomics. It is first approached within the partial equilibrium framework by measuring the consumption cost of monopoly in terms of social welfare. If one calculates this cost with the traditional model and the conventional, though highly restrictive, assumptions, one finds that the cost of inefficiency is relatively small, amounting to only a fraction of 1 percent of GNP. This might seem to suggest that the static efficiency payoff for economic development is negligible. The calculations change drastically as soon as more realistic assumptions are introduced, even within the static framework. The discussion culminates in the introduction of general equilibrium and *dynamic considerations. When the consumption and production costs of tariff protection are measured in this context, they are found to amount to a sizable fraction of GNP. The discussion is concluded by further relaxation of the limiting assumptions by introducing inter-dependencies among various sources and types of inefficiency, including dynamic aspects.*

Part II focuses on partial equilibrium and static processes. The typical case is represented by the production function with a set of exogenous variables, the inputs, each of which is independent of the other. Equilibrium processes are defined in terms of the payoff in increased output that results from adjusting the level of one input, holding the other inputs constant. In equilibrium, however, this gain in output is zero. This is an extremely restrictive frame-work which is maintained only for purposes of didactic exposition. It leads naturally to the formulation of a dynamic general equilib-rium system, in which the levels of exogenous variables are simul-taneously determined.

In the linear programming model of Chapter 4, for example, the prices become endogenous variables determined simultaneously with the activity levels. In the discussion of efficiency in Chapter 5, the usefulness of the distinction between technical and price efficiency leads directly to considerations of the dynamics of economic evolu-tion, such as in the life-cycle hypothesis of international trade. Similarly, the general equilibrium treatment of static inefficiency gives rise to certain dynamic effects.

Throughout Part II, therefore, dynamic aspects crop up but are not central to the analysis. Their systematic treatment will await Part III.

Chapter 4
The Analysis of Production

Our discussion of the methodology of science singled out three crucial steps in the process of learning: classification, generalization, and prediction. The objective of econometric research is to make the science of economics operational by devising methods that can be used for classifying economic observations, generalizing, and deriving predictions about economic phenomena. The production function is a tool of economic theory that has been sharpened by econometric research to a point at which it is highly operational and quite sophisticated. Indeed, many empirical approaches to the economics of development rest heavily on the concept of the production function. The type of the engineering production function, for example, that underlies a specific set of data is at times sufficient to determine the range of substitutability among factors of production and to answer questions relating to productivity change, labor absorp-

tion, unemployment, excess capacity, or skill bottlenecks. The production function, combined with the conditions for economic maximization, sheds further light on these issues and opens up new areas for empirical research, such as productivity change, efficiency, bias in technological change, and aspects of income distribution.

In the first section of this chapter, we discuss the mathematical and economic properties of a specific form of the production function, the Cobb-Douglas (C-D) production function. This is followed by somewhat briefer discussions of the constant elasticity of substitution (CES), input-output (I-O), and linear programming (LP) production functions. Finally, we make reference to some other more general production functions and to some limitations of the production function concept. The chapter concludes with an appendix devoted to two examples of fitting the C-D and the CES production functions. Subsequent chapters deal with applications of the production function for the economics of development.

The Cobb-Douglas Production Function

Properties and Economic Interpretation

Intuitively, the production function describes the transformation of a set of inputs into output. More specifically, and for each combination of inputs and ouput, it represents the minimum quantity of inputs that yields a given quantity of output. For a group of homogeneous firms, we can note the production function as

$$Y = f(X_1, \ldots, X_i, \ldots, X_n) \tag{1}$$

where Y is the observed output of firms having different sets of inputs, $X_1, \ldots, X_i, \ldots, X_n$. The next step is to choose a specific algebraic form to describe this function. The choice among numerous alternative forms is usually made on the basis of such criteria as compliance with a priori notions about the engineering and the economic laws of production, computational manageability, and so on. The popularity of the Cobb-Douglas function can be attributed largely to its basic consistency with the established body of economic theory, especially to its computational simplicity.

We may note the C-D form as

$$Y = AX_1^{b_1} \cdots X_i^{b_i} \cdots X_n^{b_n} \tag{2}$$

where Y is the output, X_i are the inputs, A is a constant term, and b_i defines the transformation parameter for the level of input, X_i. All variables are measured in physical units. The computationally attractive characteristic of this form is that it becomes linear in the logarithms of the variables. Thus, we may write

$$\log Y = \log A + b_1 \log X_1 + \cdots + b_i \log X_i$$
$$+ \cdots + b_n \log X_n \tag{3}$$

We can now present the main economic properties of the C-D production function.

The marginal productivity of a factor is one of the most crucial concepts in the theory of production. It represents the change in output that results from a (small) change in any one input, when all the other inputs are held constant. As such, it is expressed by the partial derivative of output with respect to an input. Thus, differentiating equation 2 with respect to one input, X_i, we write

$$\frac{\partial Y}{\partial X_i} = b_i AX_1^{b_1} \cdots X_i^{b_i-1} \cdots X_n^{b_n} = b_i \frac{Y}{X_i} \tag{4}$$

Assuming that b_i is a positive constant and smaller than one, that is, $0 < b_i < 1$, the marginal product of factor i is positive. Furthermore, since Y/X_i obviously declines as X_i increases, the marginal product of any factor generally declines as the level of the input of that factor increases. However, by the same token, the marginal product of any factor, i, rises with an increase in any other factor, j, $j \neq i$. These properties make eminently good sense and are considered desirable properties for any production function. If, for example, the marginal productivity of a factor did not decrease as the quantity of that factor increased, an acre of land in Laguna could produce all the rice for the Philippines, even for the world, by the mere application of ever greater quantities of labor or fertilizer.

The marginal product is employed in the derivation of the elasticity of production with respect to an input, which is defined as the percentage change in output with respect to a percentage change in input. By substitution from equation 4, we write

$$\eta_{YX_i} = \frac{\partial Y/Y}{\partial X_i/X_i} = \left(b_i \frac{Y}{X_i}\right) \frac{X_i}{Y} = b_i \tag{5}$$

Therefore, we see that in the case of the C-D production function, the elasticity of production with respect to any (and all) input(s) is constant. Furthermore, it is directly estimable in terms of the exponents of the respective inputs as, for example, in equation 2. The assumption that $0 < b_i < 1$ implies that a 1 percent increase in any input (holding other inputs constant) will always increase output by less than 1 percent.

Another and closely related property of any production function is the extent of economies of scale. This can be determined by changing all inputs simultaneously by the same percentage and by recording the effect on output. In the C-D function, with both A and b_i (for all i) assumed to be constant, an increase in all inputs $(X_1, X_2, \ldots, X_n)$ by 1 percent increases output by the percent indicated by the sum of the input coefficients. If, for example, the sum of b_i is less than one, a 1 percent increase in all inputs leads to an increase in output of less than 1 percent. This is defined as decreasing returns to scale. Increasing and constant returns to scale are defined, by correspondence, as sum of b_i greater than and equal to one, respectively.

Equation 4 shows that in the C-D function the marginal products are proportional to the average products Y/X_i, the factor of proportionality being the associated exponent. We have also noted that the marginal product of any factor, i, declines with the level of input of i but increases with the level of input of factor j ($i \neq j$). These characteristics can also be seen from the second derivative of output with respect to any input, X_i, which is obtained by differentiating equation 4 with respect to X_i. This yields

$$\frac{\partial^2 Y}{\partial X_i^2} = b_i(b_i - 1)\frac{Y}{X_i^2} \qquad (6)$$

which is negative since $0 < b_i < 1$.

Instead of the relation between the output and one input (out of the n inputs), we now examine the relation between any two inputs. Empirically, interesting implications arise concerning isoquants, marginal rates of substitution, and expansion paths.

An isoquant curve, for example that given by Y_0Y_0 or Y_1Y_1 in Figure 4.1, expresses one input as a function of another, for the given

output. Any point on a particular isoquant represents a particular combination of the inputs X_1 and X_2 that would produce the same level of output. Setting $Y = Y_0$ and solving equation 2 for X_1 in terms of X_2, we write for an isoquant

$$X_1 = \left[\frac{Y_0}{X_2{}^{b_2}(AX_3{}^{b_3}\cdots X_i{}^{b_i}\cdots X_n{}^{b_n})}\right]^{1/b_1} \qquad (7)$$

All such isoquants are downward sloping and convex to the origin at all points, as one can see by taking the first and second derivatives of equation 7 with respect to X_2. By solving for different levels of output, we can derive a constant product map in inputs X_1 and X_2.

Taking differentials of equation 2 with respect to the two factors, X_1 and X_2, we can derive an expression for the quantity of one factor required to compensate for a certain change in the quantity of the other in order to keep output on the same isoquant.

$$\frac{\partial Y}{\partial X_1}dX_1 + \frac{\partial Y}{\partial X_2}dX_2 = dY = 0 \qquad (8)$$

The marginal rate of substitution, r, is defined from equation 8 as the ratio of the differential of the two inputs or, alternatively, as the ratio of the marginal products

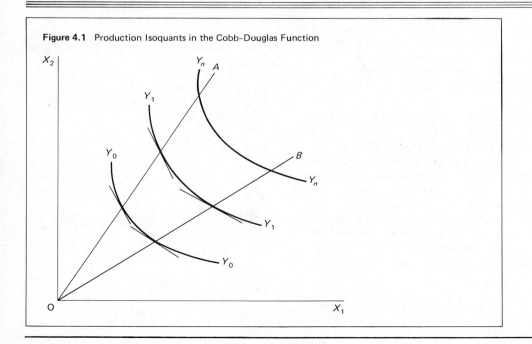

Figure 4.1 Production Isoquants in the Cobb-Douglas Function

$$r = -\frac{dX_1}{dX_2} = \frac{\frac{\partial Y}{\partial X_2}}{\frac{\partial Y}{\partial X_1}} \qquad (9)$$

For the C-D case from equation 4, the marginal rate of substitution of two factors is a linear function of the ratio in which the two factors are combined:

$$r = \frac{b_2\frac{Y}{X_2}}{b_1\frac{Y}{X_1}} = \frac{b_2}{b_1}\frac{X_1}{X_2} \qquad (10)$$

This equation can be interpreted as a relationship between the factor proportions X_1/X_2 and the marginal rate of technical substitution, r. As such, it is a relationship with important empirical implications. The marginal rate of substitution depends on the units in which the two factors are measured. It is useful to restate the relationship to make it independent of the units of measurement by expressing both X_1/X_2 and r in terms of their percentage changes. The ratio of the two percentage changes is defined as the elasticity of substitution σ:

$$\sigma = \frac{d\left(\frac{X_1}{X_2}\right)\Big/\left(\frac{X_1}{X_2}\right)}{\frac{dr}{r}} \qquad (11)$$

The obvious interpretation of the elasticity of substitution is that it expresses the degree to which the factor proportions adjust to a given change in the marginal rate of substitution.

Defining dr from equation 10 as

$$dr = d\left(\frac{X_1}{X_2}\right)\left(\frac{b_2}{b_1}\right) \qquad (12)$$

and substituting both equation 12 for dr and 10 for r in 11, one can see that in the C-D production function with constant returns to scale, $\sigma = 1$. This implies that a certain percentage change in the marginal productivity ratios of the two factors (or in their relative prices, as we will see immediately below) will induce an equiproportional change in their utilization ratio in the opposite direction

$$\sigma = \frac{d\left(\frac{X_1}{X_2}\right)\left(\frac{X_2}{X_1}\right)}{d\left(\frac{X_1}{X_2}\right)\left(\frac{b_2}{b_1}\right)}\left(\frac{b_2}{b_1}\right)\left(\frac{X_1}{X_2}\right) = 1 \qquad (13)$$

That σ should take exactly this value is obviously a fairly restrictive property of the C-D function.

Profit Maximization and Other Economic Properties

All the preceding properties of the C-D function are defined strictly in physical or technical terms. Nothing has yet been said or assumed with respect to prices or values of any of the inputs or output. All inputs and output are measured in physical units, the production function summarizing the physical transformation relationship between them.

Profits, Π, however, are defined in value terms as

$$\Pi = P_Y Y - P_1 X_1 - P_2 X_2 - \cdots - P_n X_n \qquad (14)$$

where P_Y is the price of output and P_1, P_2, ..., P_n are the prices of the various inputs.

Assuming that producers wish to maximize profits, Π^*, will be defined as:

$$\Pi^* = \max\ [\Pi - \lambda(Y - AX_1{}^{b_1}X_2{}^{b_2}\cdots X_n{}^{b_n})] \qquad (15)$$

Assume also that there is perfect competition in both commodity and factor markets, such that the prices of inputs and output are given to each firm. We can differentiate equation 15 with respect to λ, then with respect to Y, and then with respect to X_1, X_2, ..., X_n to derive the various (first order, i.e., necessary but not sufficient) conditions for profit maximization:

(a) $\dfrac{\partial \Pi^*}{\partial \lambda} = -Y + AX_1{}^{b_1}X_2{}^{b_2}\cdots X_n{}^{b_n} = 0$

(b) $\dfrac{\partial \Pi^*}{\partial Y} = P_Y - \lambda = 0$

or

$P_Y = \lambda$

(c) $\dfrac{\partial \Pi^*}{\partial X_1} = -P_1 + \lambda b_1 \dfrac{AX_1{}^{b_1}X_2{}^{b_2}\cdots X_n{}^{b_n}}{X_1} = 0$

or

$P_1 = P_Y b_1 \dfrac{Y}{X_1}$

(d) $\dfrac{\partial \Pi^*}{\partial X_2} = -P_2 + \lambda b_2 \dfrac{AX_1{}^{b_1}X_2{}^{b_2}\cdots X_n{}^{b_n}}{X_2} = 0$

or

$$P_2 = P_Y b_2 \frac{Y}{X_2}$$

$$\vdots$$

(p) $\dfrac{\partial \Pi^*}{\partial X_n} = -P_n + \lambda b_n \dfrac{AX_1{}^{b_1}X_2{}^{b_2}\cdots X_n{}^{b_n}}{X_n} = 0$

or

$$P_n = P_Y b_n \frac{Y}{X_n} \tag{16}$$

Condition b is the well-known product rule of perfect competition: "produce the quantity of output at which price equals marginal cost." Likewise, conditions c to p represent the well-known factor rule: "each factor should be used up to the point at which the value of its marginal product is equal to its price," that is,

$$\frac{\partial Y}{\partial X_i} = b_i \frac{Y}{X_i} = \frac{P_i}{P_Y} \tag{17}$$

Since this relationship should hold for each and every factor of production, in equilibrium the marginal rate of substitution, r, with respect to any two factors, X_1 and X_2, should also be equal to the ratio of their prices,

$$r = \frac{\dfrac{\partial Y}{\partial X_2}}{\dfrac{\partial Y}{\partial X_1}} = \frac{P_2}{P_1} \tag{18}$$

Equation 17 can be reexpressed as

$$b_i = \frac{P_i X_i}{P_Y Y} \tag{19}$$

Since b_i is assumed to be constant, the C-D function under perfect competition implies that the value share of each factor in total revenue is constant and equal to the elasticity of output with respect to that factor. This additional property of the C-D function holds only in the case of constant returns to scale, that is, when

$$\sum_{i=1}^{n} b_i = 1$$

Absence of constant returns to scale makes the equilibrium conditions more complicated. It turns out that the factor shares depend not only on the real factor prices and the inverse of the average product but also upon the demand elasticity for output and the supply elasticities for inputs.[1] Since demand elasticities for outputs and supply elasticities for inputs are not usually available, the assumption of perfect competition, for lack of a better alternative, is commonly used for detecting resource misallocation in production function analysis.

The implication of increasing returns to scale is that the sum of the shares of the factors overexhausts the product. Decreasing returns to scale, on the other hand, imply that a share of the product is left over for factors that were not included in the specification of the variables. Thus, when the sum of the elasticities add up to less than one, the remaining share of the product is sometimes attributed to management or entrepreneurship, because the latter certainly contributes to output, yet cannot be measured well enough to justify inclusion as a separate input in the production function.[2]

Another interesting property of any production function is the shape of the expansion path of output. This can be determined by holding the relative factor prices constant. From equation 18, the stability of relative prices implies that the marginal rate of substitution will remain constant and therefore, from equation 10, further implies that the factor proportions, X_1/X_2, will remain constant no matter what the level of output, Y, or the price of output, P_Y. The expansion path of output is thus a straight line from the origin. This is shown in Figure 4.1, where, any individual isoquant curve, such as $Y_0 Y_0$, $Y_1 Y_1, \ldots, Y_n Y_n$, represents all (technically) efficient combinations of X_1 and X_2 that yield the same quantity of output, $Y_0, Y_1, \ldots, Y_n$. The two expansion paths of output, OA and OB, are straight lines, because the marginal rates of substitution given by the slope of the output isoquants at points along each such ray are the same.

---

[1] The factor share under imperfect markets becomes:

$$\frac{P_i}{P_Y} \frac{X_i}{Y} = b \left(\frac{1 - \dfrac{1}{\eta}}{1 + \dfrac{1}{\varepsilon}} \right)$$

where η = elasticity of demand for output and ε = elasticity of the factor supply.

[2] A specific application is provided in Chapter 5, with the measurement of management bias.

The Advantages and Drawbacks of the Cobb-Douglas Function for Empirical Research

The C-D production function has become the workhorse of econometric research. Its simple functional form is computationally economical and yields statistically significant estimates of the coefficients without imposing excessive demands upon data accuracy. Its estimation provides important information that is generally consistent with some a priori notions of economic theory, such as the extent to which a factor's marginal productivity declines as the level of input increases, given the quantities of all other factors of production. Similarly, measurements of returns to scale and of relative factor shares have important economic policy implications. The C-D function is applied to Greek agriculture in the first part of the appendix to this chapter.

The assumption of perfect markets is not necessary for the C-D production function, although it is convenient if we are to say anything about resource misallocation or to interpret the input coefficients as factor shares. The concept of the marginal product, to the extent that it is tied to the marginal productivity condition, can become inexpedient in empirical research. Suppose we make the assumption of optimal allocation, thereby implying the marginal productivity condition. Does it make sense then, from the viewpoint of economic policy, to talk about the effect on output of a change in the quantity of one factor, *ceteris paribus*? Should the quantity of a factor change, the other factors would be expected to change in order to restore the marginal productivity condition. It would be more meaningful under these circumstances to estimate *mutatis mutandis* elasticities, that is, the effect upon output of a change in one factor, with all other factors taking on their optimal values. But this is impossible to do in the production function that considers the quantities of inputs as the exogenous variables. Perhaps it would be more realistic to treat the prices of the variable factors of production as the exogenous variables that are considered by the entrepreneur in setting endogenously in the production process both the quantity of output and the quantity of the variable factors. This involves the profit function, which will be discussed in Chapter 6.

Several properties of the C-D function seem quite realistic; for example, the proper-ties of positive but declining marginal products, variable returns to scale, the inverse relation between the marginal rate of substitution and factor proportions. There are also some properties that would intuitively seem unrealistic, however, such as the unitary elasticity of substitution among factors or the strictly linear expansion path. These shortcomings become more obvious when one considers more than two factors of production, because the properties of unitary elasticity of substitution and linear expansion paths must hold for each and every pair of factors.

Constant Elasticity of Substitution Production Function

Properties and Economic Interpretation

One of the crucial implications that derive from a production function is the degree of substitutability between any two inputs. As we indicated in the previous section, this is expressed by the value of the elasticity of substitution.

The extent to which capital and labor can be substituted for each other becomes an empirical question. For a long time, the theory of production had focused on two convenient values for the elasticity of substitution, $\sigma = 1$ and $\sigma = 0$. We have seen that the former is represented by the C-D production function with constant returns to scale. We will see below that the latter is the case of the Leontief-type input-output (I-O) production function. As an alternative case, the linear production function implies infinite elasticity of substitution.[3]

Several pieces of empirical evidence have turned out to be inconsistent with any of these assumptions.[4] For example, although one would have expected the marginal product of any factor to be the same in its alternative uses, Arrow, Chenery, Minhas, and Solow (1961) found capital-labor proportions to vary

---

[3]The linear production function is

$$Y = \alpha_1 X_1 + \alpha_2 X_2$$

From the definition of σ from equation 11,

$$\sigma = \frac{d\left(\frac{X_1}{X_2}\right) \bigg/ \frac{X_1}{X_2}}{d\left(\frac{\alpha_2}{\alpha_1}\right) \bigg/ \frac{\alpha_2}{\alpha_1}}$$

Since α_1 and α_2 are both constant, $d(\alpha_2/\alpha_1) = 0$, implying that $\sigma = \infty$.

[4]Arrow, Chenery, Minhas, and Solow (1961) detail such evidence.

among countries much more in some sectors than in others. This suggests that capital-labor proportions do not vary simply as a result of variations in marginal productivities. Furthermore, for various industries in an international cross-section sample, a linear (or log linear) relationship between value added per unit of labor and the wage rate was observed. However, the coefficient of the wage rate was significantly different from either zero or one—the values that would obtain if the true functions were of I-O or C-D form, respectively. This led Arrow, Chenery, Minhas and Solow to their pathbreaking formulation of the constant elasticity of substitution (CES) production function:

$$Y = \gamma[\delta K^{-\rho} + (1 - \delta)L^{-\rho}]^{-1/\rho} \qquad (20)$$

where γ is the efficiency parameter, δ is the distribution parameter ($0 \leq \delta < 1$), and ρ is the substitution parameter ($-1 < \rho < \infty$). Furthermore, it can be shown that ρ specifies the elasticity of substitution, since $\sigma = 1/1 + \rho$. Although this specification restricts σ to constancy, it permits a much wider choice among alternative values. Since $-1 < \rho < \infty$, the range for the elasticity of substitution becomes $\infty > \sigma > 0$. The three examples of production functions mentioned are special limiting cases of the CES, as one can see by substituting the appropriate values. If $\rho = -1$, $\sigma = \infty$, and the production function becomes the linear production function; if $\rho = \infty$, $\sigma = 0$, and the production function takes on the Leontief I-O form with fixed factor proportions; finally, if $\rho = 0$, then $\sigma = 1$, and we have the C-D production function.

The elasticity of substitution measures the sensitivity of the factor proportions to changes in the marginal rate of substitution. These changes in the marginal rate of substitution are the result of operating at different points on an isoquant, that is, at points where the marginal productivities of factors differ. Furthermore, as we pointed out for the C-D function in equation 18, under the assumptions of perfect competition and profit maximization the marginal rate of substitution should be equal to the ratio of the factor prices, that is,

$$r = -\frac{dK}{dL} = \frac{P_L}{P_K} \qquad (21)$$

where P_L and P_K are the prices of the factors of production, the wage rate, and the interest rate (or more appropriately the "user cost of capital"). Thus, we can rewrite the elasticity of substitution as

$$\sigma = \frac{\dfrac{d\left(\dfrac{K}{L}\right)}{\left(\dfrac{K}{L}\right)}}{\dfrac{d\left(\dfrac{P_L}{P_K}\right)}{\left(\dfrac{P_L}{P_K}\right)}} \qquad (22)$$

By allowing values of σ other than one, the CES production function admits the possibility that a certain change in the ratio of relative factor prices will induce a change in the relative factor utilization ratios that is not necessarily equiproportional in the opposite direction. We will see that this property has important empirical implications.

Other properties of the CES function are similar to those of the C-D function. For example, assuming constant returns to scale, by differentiating equation 20 with respect to K and then with respect to L, we obtain the following expressions for the marginal products of capital and labor:

$$\frac{\partial Y}{\partial K} = \delta \gamma^{-\rho} \left(\frac{Y}{K}\right)^{1+\rho} \qquad (23)$$

$$\frac{\partial Y}{\partial L} = (1 - \delta)\gamma^{-\rho} \left(\frac{Y}{L}\right)^{1+\rho} \qquad (24)$$

Since the parameters δ and γ and the variables Y, K, and L are all positive, the marginal product of any factor, i, is positive and decreasing with the level of factor i but increasing with the level of factor j, $j \neq i$. Furthermore, the function can be rewritten as

$$Y = \gamma[\delta K^{-\rho} + (1 - \delta)L^{-\rho}]^{-\nu/\rho} \qquad (25)$$

where the special parameter ν measures returns to scale.

The marginal rate of substitution, r, is given by dividing equation 23 by equation 24. Assuming competitive product and factor markets and profit maximization, r should be equal to the ratio of the factor prices, P_K/P_L, that is,

$$r = \frac{\dfrac{\partial Y}{\partial K}}{\dfrac{\partial Y}{\partial L}} = \frac{\partial L}{\partial K} = \frac{\delta}{1 - \delta}\left(\frac{L}{K}\right)^{1+\rho} = \frac{P_K}{P_L} \qquad (26)$$

The CES production function, equation 20, can be estimated either directly by using maximum likelihood techniques or indirectly by utilizing the relationship between the average productivity of labor and the wage rate, which yields the value of the elasticity of substitution as the coefficient for the wage rate. Since this is an important property of the CES function, it bears elaborating in detail.

Any linear homogeneous production function, that is, one with constant returns to scale, $Y = F(K, L)$, can be written as

$$y = f(x) \tag{27}$$

where $y = Y/L$ and $x = K/L$. Then the marginal products of capital and labor are, respectively, defined as

$$\frac{\partial Y}{\partial K} = \frac{\partial [Lf(x)]}{\partial K} = L \frac{1}{L} f'(x) = f'(x) \tag{28}$$

and

$$\frac{\partial Y}{\partial L} = \frac{\partial [Lf(x)]}{\partial L} = f(x) + Lf'(x) \frac{\partial x}{\partial L}$$
$$= f(x) - xf'(x) \tag{29}$$

The assumption of profit maximization under perfect competition implies the equality of factor prices to marginal productivities, that is,

$$P_K = f'(x) \tag{30}$$

and

$$P_L = f(x) - xf'(x) \tag{31}$$

For the CES production function, this relationship can be expressed as

$$P_L = \gamma [\delta x^{-\rho} + (1 - \delta)]^{-1/\rho} - \gamma x \left(-\frac{1}{\rho} \right)$$
$$[\delta x^{-\rho} + (1 - \delta)]^{-(1/\rho)-1}(-\rho)\delta x^{-\rho-1}$$
$$= \gamma [\delta x^{-\rho} + (1 - \delta)]^{-1/\rho}$$
$$\left[1 - \frac{\delta x^{-\rho}}{\delta x^{-\rho} + (1 - \delta)} \right]$$
$$= f \cdot \left[\frac{\delta x^{-\rho} + (1 - \delta) - \delta x^{-\rho}}{\delta x^{-\rho} + (1 - \delta)} \right] \tag{32}$$

Noting that

$$(f)^{-\rho} = \gamma^{-\rho} [\delta x^{-\rho} + (1 - \delta)] \tag{33}$$

we have as the denominator above

$$\delta x^{-\rho} + (1 - \delta) = \left(\frac{f}{\gamma} \right)^{-\rho} \tag{34}$$

Therefore,

$$P_L = f \frac{(1 - \delta)}{\left(\dfrac{f}{\gamma} \right)^{-\rho}} = f^{(1+\rho)} \gamma^{-\rho} (1 - \delta) \tag{35}$$

Transforming with logs, we have

$$\log P_L = (1 + \rho) \log f - \rho \log \gamma + \log(1 - \delta) \tag{36}$$

or

$$\log f = \frac{1}{1 + \rho} \log P_L$$
$$- \frac{1}{1 + \rho} \log[\gamma^{-\rho}(1 - \delta)] \tag{37}$$

that is,

$$\log f = \log y = \sigma \log P_L - \sigma \log c \tag{38}$$

where c is a constant given by

$$c = \gamma^{-\rho}(1 - \delta) \tag{39}$$

Consequently, the CES function implies a log linear relationship between average productivity of labor and the wage rate. In this relationship, the elasticity of output per unit of labor with respect to the wage rate is identical with elasticity of substitution, that is,

$$\frac{df}{dP_L} \frac{P_L}{f} = \sigma$$

The value of the elasticity of substitution has important empirical implications, not only with respect to the substitutability between factors of production but also with respect to income distribution. An elasticity of substitution equal to one implies that factor shares will remain constant even if capital substitutes for labor over time as a result of changes in the factor intensity of technology and/or of changes in relative factor prices. However, if $\sigma < 1$, the share of the factor whose price has risen (and therefore whose quantity has fallen) will increase. The opposite is true if $\sigma > 1$. This has important implications for the policy of economic development, especially if, as the available empirical evidence suggests, the elasticity of substitution in industry is generally less than one while in agriculture it is more than one. As the wage rate increases, we would expect the share of agricultural labor to decline. The result of technological change would then be to shift the distribution of labor income from agriculture to manufacturing.

It is easy to demonstrate this implication of the elasticity of substitution. Assuming perfect competition and profit maximization from equation 22, we obtain

$$\sigma = \frac{d\left(\dfrac{K}{L}\right)}{d\left(\dfrac{P_L}{P_K}\right)} \frac{P_L L}{P_K K} \qquad (40)$$

Observe that

$$\frac{d\left(\dfrac{K}{L}\right)}{d\left(\dfrac{P_L}{P_K}\right)} > 0$$

Furthermore, dividing both sides of equation 26 through by L/K

$$\frac{P_K K}{P_L L} = \left(\frac{\delta}{1-\delta}\right)\left(\frac{L}{K}\right)^{\rho} \qquad (41)$$

Now, if $\sigma > 1$ ($\rho < 0$) and the relative price ratio, P_K/P_L, falls by 1 percent, L/K will fall more than 1 percent, and therefore $P_K K/P_L L$ will increase, that is, the share of K will increase and the share of L will decrease. If $\sigma < 1$ and P_K/P_L falls by 1 percent, L/K will fall by less than 1 percent and, consequently, $P_K K/P_L L$ will rise. When $\sigma = 1$, relative shares do not change. Therefore, the share of the factor whose price has risen will increase when $\sigma < 1$ and decrease when

$\sigma > 1$. The rationale is clear. The parameter σ reflects the facility with which factors can be substituted for each other. If it is relatively easy to do so, the factor whose price has increased will be substituted for; but if substitution is not easy, the share of the factor whose price rose will increase.

In the second part of the appendix to this chapter, we provide an example of fitting the CES production function with data from Indian agriculture.

The Input-Output Production Function

Properties and Economic Interpretation

In neoclassical production functions of the C-D and CES varieties, we have seen that output isoquants are typically smooth and continuous as depicted by the curves Y_1, $Y_2, \ldots, Y_n$ of Figure 4.1. In contrast, the basic characteristic of the input-output (I-O) production function is that isoquants are right angles, as shown by Y_0 and Y_1 in Figure 4.2. Indeed, since points on the horizontal and vertical lines emanating from points A and B are clearly less efficient than points A and B themselves, each of these right angle isoquants ultimately collapses to an individual point isoquant, that is, to points A and B respectively.

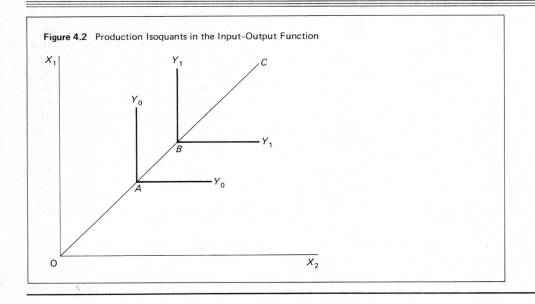

Figure 4.2   Production Isoquants in the Input-Output Function

In the I-O production function, we can express the relationship between output, Y, and any of the n inputs, X_i, as

$$X_i = a_i Y \tag{42}$$

where a_i is the proportionality coefficient, which may vary for different inputs. Thus, for the kth input, $(k \neq i)$, $X_k = a_k Y$ and a_k is not necessarily equal to a_i. Furthermore, a number of different processes, industries, or activities, Y_j, $j = 1, 2, \ldots, m$, can be distinguished, each with its own set of proportionality coefficients corresponding to the set of n inputs,

$$X_{ij} = a_{ij} Y_j \tag{43}$$

for all $i = 1, 2, \ldots, n$, and $j = 1, 2, \ldots, m$.

Thus, the proportionality or input-output coefficients, a_{ij}, will generally vary not only from input i to input k but also from activity $j = 1$ to activity $j = 2$, or activity $j = m$. Nevertheless, it is assumed that equation 43 holds between each and every input, i, and each and every activity, j. If X_i and Y_j are measured in different physical units, such as kilograms, meters, or cubic meters, the coefficients a_{ij} could be thought of as taking on any nonnegative value, $a_{ij} \geqq 0$. In most applications of I-O functions, however, the various inputs and outputs (or activities), X_{ij} and Y_j, are homogenized in value terms through the use of market prices. In such cases, the value of any input is constrained to be less than the value of output, that is, $0 \leqq a_{ij} < 1$. In fact, the sum of all such input coefficients for any activity, j, is constrained to be less than or equal to output, that is,

$$\sum_{i=1}^{m} a_{ij} \leqq 1$$

for all j.

The points A, B, C on different output isoquants in Figure 4.2 indicate the minimum combination of inputs X_1 and X_2 used in producing different amounts of commodity j, Y_1, Y_2, and so on. The angle that OC cuts with respect to the horizontal axis is obviously determined by a_{1j}/a_{2j}. The fact that OC passes through the origin and is a straight line indicates that I-O functions are homothetic. They also have constant returns to scale. Furthermore, the average and marginal productivities of any factor i, Y_j/X_{ij} or $1/a_{ij}$, are equal at the point isoquants on OC, but drop off to zero at points off OC. The marginal rates of substitution are thus in general indeterminate (0/0), and the elasticities of substitution indicating the possibilities of substituting one factor for another are clearly zero.

General Equilibrium Applications

While the properties of I-O functions are generally considered less realistic than those of the neoclassical functions, an important shortcoming of the latter is that they are not practical for showing empirical interrelationships among sectors or for obtaining general equilibrium solutions to systems with more than a few commodities (sectors). The neoclassical tools are thus primarily applicable to partial equilibrium analysis. As such, they do not provide answers to questions referring to the effect of a change in the final demand for industry j on the output of industry i. The I-O function is an especially useful tool for empirical analysis of general equilibrium systems.

There is nothing in the assumptions of I-O functions that limits attention to the factor as opposed to commodity or other inputs. Indeed, the input coefficient, a_{ij}, may refer to the input of a raw material of intermediate good i per unit of output of commodity j, just as well as it may refer to a factor input. Thus, in this respect, I-O functions are more general than the neoclassical function. I-O analysis emphasizes the relationships between the commodity and service inputs per unit of output. The conceptual distinction between inputs, $X_1, \ldots, X_n$, and outputs, $Y_1, \ldots, Y_m$, therefore disappears. Inputs are simply negative outputs. The interrelationships among sectors are introduced by considering the simultaneous determination of all of the m outputs, $Y_1, \ldots, Y_m$, and nm inputs, X_{ij}. For any region or country, the output of any commodity k must be equal to the demand for that commodity by all industries (including industry k) indicated by

$$\sum_{j=1}^{m} a_{kj} X_j$$

plus the net final demand for the commodity, B_k

$$X_k = a_{k1} X_1 + a_{k2} X_2 + \cdots + a_{kn} X_n + B_k$$

For the entire system of m commodities ($m = n$), this relationship can be represented in matrix form by

$$(I - A)X = B \qquad (44)$$

Given estimates of all the n^2 coefficients a_{ij} and a vector of final demands, $B = (b_1, b_2, \ldots, b_m)$, this system can then be solved to obtain the equilibrium output vector, $X = X_1, X_2, \ldots, X_n$, which would satisfy the net final demands with the given technology,

$$X = (I - A)^{-1} B \qquad (45)$$

Since a breakdown of net final demand—usually defined as private consumption (C) plus government consumption (G) plus investment (I) plus net exports ($X - M$)—into its m commodity components is fairly easy to obtain, the ability to use I-O analysis for general equilibrium solutions of output in any region or country depends upon the existence of an I-O Table with the whole matrix (A) of coefficients a_{ij}, such as that represented by Table 4.1. The matrix of I-O coefficients (A) can then be subtracted from the identity matrix, I, to yield the $I - A$ matrix, known as the Leontief matrix. The diagonal elements in this matrix (those in which $i = j$) have positive values given by $1 - a_{ij}$, while the off-diagonal elements have negative values given by $-a_{ij}$. Although the original I-O Table, A, need not be square (have an equal number of rows and columns), the $I - A$ Leontief matrix must be square ($m = n$), because only then can solutions be obtained by inverting the $I - A$ matrix and postmultiplying by the vector of final demands.

Although I-O was developed to deal mainly with the problems of structural change in mature economies, particularly in the United States, it may well be that its most important use lies with LDCs. According to some recent bibliographies (Taskier 1961; U.N.: Statistical Office 1967; U.N.: Department of Economic and Social Affairs 1972) I-O tables are now available for a large number of LDCs.[5]

Contrary to popular belief, the usefulness of I-O does not depend on the stability of the input-output coefficients over time or between countries but only on their predictability. Thus, only if technological changes in input requirements cannot be predicted with sufficient accuracy is I-O analysis likely to be unreliable for answering the kinds of questions posed above. Furthermore, by crafty aggregation and disaggregation, treatment of imports, and specification of the exogenous and endogenous variables, the assumptions can be made more realistic than they might otherwise seem.[6]

The predictive validity of the I-O model for a particular country can be determined in the following steps: (1) substitute the matrix of I-O coefficients, A, for that country and time period and the actual final demands, B, for the same country and period into equation 44; (2) solve for X as in equation 45; and (3) compare the "predicted" values of X obtained in this manner with those attainable from alternative naive or more sophisticated methods (e.g., multiple regression analysis).

Construction of an Interindustry Transactions Table

While the matrix of I-O coefficients, A, could in principle be obtained directly from engineering data, in practice almost all estimates of such coefficients are obtained from interindustry transactions tables, X, such as that for the Ecuadorian economy in 1963, shown in Table 4.2, constructed in Nugent (1967a).

The interindustry transactions, X_{ij}, appear in nine rows and nine columns. A characteristic of Table 4.2 is that each row-column cell has a place for two entries, one marked by N and the other by M. The former represents the domestic component of interindustry transactions; the latter is the import component. The $X_{1,1}$ cell, for example, in the northwest corner, contains the element N of 183, which

Table 4.1 *Input Coefficients Matrix:* **"A"** *Matrix*

Supplying Industry	Consuming Industry					
	1	2	$\cdots$	j	$\cdots$	n
1	a_{11}	a_{12}	$\cdot\ \cdot$	a_{1j}	$\cdot\ \cdot$	a_{1n}
2	a_{21}	a_{22}	$\cdot\ \cdot$	a_{2j}	$\cdot\ \cdot$	a_{2n}
$\cdot$	$\cdot$	$\cdot$		$\cdot$		$\cdot$
$\cdot$	$\cdot$	$\cdot$		$\cdot$		$\cdot$
i	a_{i1}	a_{i2}	$\cdot\ \cdot$	a_{ij}	$\cdot\ \cdot$	a_{in}
$\cdot$	$\cdot$	$\cdot$		$\cdot$		$\cdot$
$\cdot$	$\cdot$	$\cdot$		$\cdot$		$\cdot$
m	a_{m1}	a_{m2}	$\cdot\ \cdot$	a_{mj}	$\cdot\ \cdot$	a_{mn}

[5]Examples are Spain, Yugoslavia, Poland, Sudan, Algeria, Argentina, Colombia, Peru, Ecuador, British Guiana, Antigua, Cyprus, India, Mexico, Portugal, Greece, El Salvador, Israel, Iraq, Egypt, Taiwan, South Korea, and so on.

[6]See Chenery and Clark (1959, Chapters 2, 3, 5, 6).

Table 4.2 *Interindustry Transactions Table for Ecuador, 1963 (in Millions of Sucres at Current Consumer Prices)*

Sector of Origin		Agriculture 1	Livestock 2	Mining 3	Manufacturing 4	Construction 5	Electricity 6	Transport 7	Commerce 8	Other Services 9	Imports 10
		Sector of Destination									
1. Agriculture	*N*	183	160	1	809					8	
	M	1	2		114						
2. Livestock	*N*				138					2	
	M										
3. Mining	*N*				215	191		1			
	M				119						
4. Manufacturing	*N*	144	59	26	1,173	193	55	290	39	134	
	M	104	20	80	1,082	76	2	169	23	10	
5. Construction	*N*										
	M										
6. Electricity	*N*	2	3	13	110		2		30	20	
	M										
7. Transport	*N*	458	102	15	360	42		37			55
	M							3			200
8. Commerce	*N*	1,049	161	5	746			7	11		200
	M										
9. Other Services	*N*	63	15	9	304	26	15	45	167	110	
	M					8	15			10	
Total Inputs	*N*	1,899	500	69	3,855	452	72	380	247	274	255
	M	105	22	80	1,315	84	17	172	23	20	200
Value Added		4,618	1,184	352	2,523	590	216	648	1,804	3,720	
Wages, Salaries		1,099	483	172	1,038	427	66	200	1,000	2,715	
Interest, Profits		3,519	701	180	1,485	163	150	448	804	1,005	
Gross Production		6,622	1,706	501	7,693	1,126	305	1,200	2,074	4,014	3,215

Note: *N* = Domestic, *M* = Imports.
Source: Nugent, J. B. (1967*a*), "The Construction and Use of Input-Output Tables in Determining the Consistency of Ecuador's First Development Plan," *Planificación*, 4 (Spring), pp. 23–27.

indicates the purchase of agricultural products by Ecuadorian farmers from one another during 1963. The element in the same cell for *M* of 1 indicates the amount of agricultural raw materials imported for use by Ecuadorian farmers. Similarly, the $X_{4,5}$ element of 193 in the *N* row and 76 in the *M* row represent the amount of domestically produced and imported manufactured goods, respectively, purchased by the construction sector.

A tenth row, labeled "total inputs," separately sums the interindustry transactions of domestic and imported raw materials. The imported raw materials become intermediate inputs for a sector only after a service component is added for their transportation and distribution. This appears in column 10 as the output of the transport and commerce sector. The entry 55, for example, in $X_{7,10}$ under *N*, represents the domestic transport services that were provided for the distribution of imported raw materials, and the entry $X_{8,10}$ of 200 similarly represents the domestic markups for imports. The entry 200 for *M* in $X_{7,10}$ represents the foreign transport component of imported raw materials. Column 10 is also summed in the row of total inputs, thus making the table a square 10 $\times$ 10 interindustry transactions table.

The table also includes the value added (composed of wages and salaries in one row and interest and profits in another row), and finally the total value of gross production in each sector. The columns at the right side

				Government Consumption G		Subsidies Less Indirect Taxes B–T		
Inter-industry Demand	Private Consumption C	Fixed Investment I	Changes in Stocks ΔS		Exports E		Final Demand	Total Demand
1,161	3,250		49	130	2,140	−108	5,461	6,622
117	60		1	10			71	188
140	1,400		134	50	2	− 20	1,566	1,706
							0	0
407	30		13	15	36		94	501
119			12				12	131
2,113	3,901	722	156	524	492	−215	5,580	7,693
1,566	284	300					584	2,150
		1,126					1,126	1,126
							0	0
180	140			10		− 25	125	305
							0	0
1,069	200			28		− 97	131	1,200
203	170						170	373
2,179						−105	−105	2,074
							0	0
754	2,700			299	354	− 93	3,260	4,014
33	215			125			340	373
8,003	11,621	1,848	352	1,056	3,024	−663	17,238	25,241
2,038	729	300	13	135			1,177	3,215
15,655				1,031		−861		
7,200				1,031				
8,455						−861		
25,696	12,350	2,148	365	2,222	3,024	1,524	18,415	

of the table show the sectoral composition of the elements of final demand (private consumption, government consumption, fixed investment, changes in stocks, and exports) inclusive of net indirect taxes, net indirect taxes on final demand, final demand, and total demand. By utilizing the convention that inputs are negative outputs, from equation 43 we can write $X_{ij} = a_{ij}X_j$. The matrix of input-output coefficients, **A**, can thus be computed directly from the interindustry transactions, X_{ij}, of Table 4.2 by dividing the row elements of each column j by the gross production element in that column. For example, a_{11} is computed by dividing the domestically produced component of $X_{1,1}$, 183, by the total agricultural gross production, X_1, of 6,622. This gives

0.028. Similarly, a_{12} is $X_{1,2} = 160$ divided by $X_2 = 1,706$, or 0.094. Subtracting the resulting matrix, **A**, from the unit or identity matrix, **I**, gives us the elements of the corresponding Leontief matrix, **I** − **A**, shown in Table 4.3. This explains why the first element in that matrix is $1 - a_{11}$, or 0.972, while the second element, $-a_{12}$, is −0.094, and so on.

Once the Leontief matrix of Table 4.3 has been obtained, only two steps remain: to invert the matrix and to postmultiply it by the 10×1 vector of final demands, **B**. Since the latter step is perfectly straightforward, we shall confine our comments and presentation to the inversion process itself and to the interpretation of the inverted Leontief matrix.

Matrices can be inverted by a number of

Table 4.3 Leontief Matrix for Ecuador, 1963

Sector of Origin	Sector of Destination									
	Agriculture 1	Livestock 2	Mining 3	Manufacturing 4	Construction 5	Electricity 6	Transport 7	Commerce 8	Other Services 9	Imports 10
1. Agriculture	0.972	−0.094	−0.002	−0.105					−0.002	
2. Livestock		1.000		−0.018					−0.001	
3. Mining			1.000	−0.028	−0.170		−0.001			
4. Manufacturing	−0.022	−0.035	−0.052	0.848	−0.171	−0.180	−0.242	−0.019	−0.033	
5. Construction					1.000					
6. Electricity		−0.002	−0.026	−0.014		0.993		−0.014	−0.005	
7. Transport	−0.069	−0.060	−0.030	−0.047	−0.037		0.967	−0.006		
8. Commerce	−0.158	−0.094	−0.010	−0.097			−0.006	0.995		−0.018
9. Other Services	−0.010	−0.009	−0.018	−0.040	−0.023	−0.049	−0.038	−0.081	0.973	−0.049
10. Imports	−0.016	−0.013	−0.160	−0.171	−0.075	−0.056	−0.141	−0.011	−0.005	1.000

Source: Table 4.2.

different procedures. For matrices of substantial size, such as the 10×10 Leontief matrix of Table 4.3, and in cases in which extreme accuracy is not required, the easiest method is an approximation method. By this method, the inverse can be approximated by the formula

$$(\mathbf{I} - \mathbf{A})^{-1} \simeq \mathbf{I} + \mathbf{A} + \mathbf{A}^2 + \mathbf{A}^3 + \cdots + \mathbf{A}^n \tag{46}$$

As n becomes larger in number, the approximation is closer and closer to the true inverse. The calculations for obtaining the inverse can always be checked by computing: $(\mathbf{I} - \mathbf{A})^{-1}(\mathbf{I} - \mathbf{A}) = \mathbf{I}$.

The inverse of the 10×10 Leontief matrix of the Ecuadorian economy in 1963 is shown in Table 4.4. The approximation method for calculating the inverse (equation 46) provides an intuitive explanation of why the ijth element of the inverse matrix should be interpreted as the direct plus indirect (or total) increase in production of commodity j required to meet a unit increase in final demand of commodity i. The first matrix on the right side gives the direct requirements to meet a unit increase in final demand. The second matrix, $\mathbf{A}$, accounts for the first round of interindustry inputs that would be required in each sector to produce the additional output to meet the additional final demand. The third matrix, $\mathbf{A}^2$, would account for the additional inputs that would be required to satisfy the additional interindustry demand generated by the output required to meet the original increase in final demand. Similarly, matrices of higher power include further indirect effects of the original change in final demand. The indirect effects become smaller and smaller, until, eventually, they approach zero.

Thus, the northwest element of the inverted Leontief matrix given in Table 4.4 (1.034) indicates the total (direct plus indirect) increase in agricultural output that would be required to meet a unit increase in the final demand for agricultural products. The second element in the first row of the same matrix (0.104) represents the increase of agricultural output required to meet an increase in the final demand for livestock.

We shall demonstrate some useful applications of such inverse matrices in the context of intersectoral relations and linkages, as in Chapters 15 and 16, and in the planning context, as in Chapter 21.

The Linear Programming Production Function

Properties and Economic Interpretation

Some of the more restrictive assumptions of I-O functions can be relaxed in a linear programming (LP) approach. While in I-O the a_{ij} is unique and invariant with such factors as the level of output and relative prices, LP introduces the possibility of technical choices among alternative combinations of input vectors, each of which yields a given amount of output. Moreover, one can impose constraints on the amount of output with any set of I-O coefficients so as to associate different levels of output of a particular commodity with different sets of input coefficients. Increasing costs (decreasing returns to scale) can be introduced by ordinary linear programming methods; decreasing costs (increasing returns to scale), however, can be handled only by more complicated methods, such as integer programming.

Figure 4.3 illustrates how various production isoquants, $Y_0, Y_1, \ldots$, might look under such circumstances. Take the isoquant Y_0. Since four alternative techniques (labeled 1, 2, 3, 4) can be used to produce the commodity under investigation, let us assume that the amount Y_0 could be produced with technique 1 and the factor proportions given by point A. Alternatively, with technique 2, Y_0 could be produced with the inputs of X_1 and X_2, indicated by point B; with technique 3, point C indicates the minimum combination of X_1 and X_2 required; and with technique 4, point D represents the corresponding efficient combination of inputs. Since all the alternative techniques are possible, so are various combinations of techniques indicated by points on the line segments connecting the points A and B, B and C, C and D. The entire isoquant is thus $Y_0 ABCD Y_0$, the shape of which approaches the smooth convexity of neoclassical functions.

The other generalization that LP functions can provide is illustrated by the relationship between the two isoquants, that is, there may be decreasing returns to scale in some techniques, such as 3 and 4, but constant returns to scale in technique 2. Moreover, while technique 1 may be valid for output up to the level Y_0, at greater levels of output the ratio of I-O coefficients, a_1/a_2, reflected in the slope of OA may change. Thus, LP production func-

Table 4.4 Inverse of the Leontief Matrix for Ecuador, 1963

Sector of Origin	Sector of Destination									
	Agriculture 1	Livestock 2	Mining 3	Manufacturing 4	Construction 5	Electricity 6	Transport 7	Commerce 8	Other Services 9	Imports 10
1. Agriculture	1.034	0.104	0.011	0.134	0.026	0.025	0.034	0.003	0.008	0.001
2. Livestock	0.001	1.001	0.001	0.022	0.004	0.004	0.006	0.001	0.001	
3. Mining	0.002	0.002	1.002	0.034	0.176	0.006	0.009	0.001	0.001	
4. Manufacturing	0.054	0.069	0.080	1.218	0.235	0.223	0.307	0.030	0.043	0.007
5. Construction					1.000					
6. Electricity	0.004	0.005	0.028	0.021	0.009	1.001	0.006	0.016	0.006	0.001
7. Transport	0.077	0.073	0.039	0.075	0.060	0.015	1.056	0.002	0.003	0.020
8. Commerce	0.172	0.120	0.829	0.154	0.037	0.031	0.052	1.010	0.006	0.050
9. Other Services	0.030	0.026	0.027	0.068	0.042	0.064	0.058	0.086	1.031	0.005
10. Imports	0.039	0.039	0.181	0.229	0.153	0.098	0.204	0.018	0.014	1.005

Source: Table 4.3.

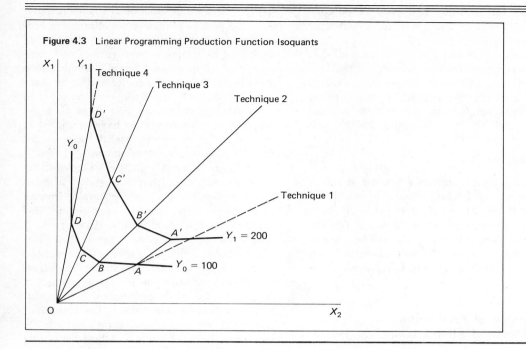

Figure 4.3 Linear Programming Production Function Isoquants

tions may be constrained in such a way as to be nonhomothetic. They also can be restricted in such a way as to make the whole range of technical choices, techniques 1-4, open and applicable before the plant and machinery are installed but to eliminate substitution once the plant and machinery are in place.

General Equilibrium Applications

Like I-O models, LP production functions for different sectors can be fitted together to constitute an interdependent system of equations for a cluster of sectors for a region or for a country. One formal difference between the two is that I-O models, as given by equation 44, are formulated as strict equalities; whereas in LP models, the same variables and relationships can be defined in terms of inequalities

$$(I - A)X \geqq B \tag{47}$$

where **B** is the vector of final demands.

Another important difference is that, because LP (in contrast to I-O) allows for alternative techniques, LP solutions are not always unique. In fact, if there is more than one feasible solution, the number of feasible solutions will be infinite. This implies the need for a criterion for choosing an optimal

solution from the infinite number of possible solutions. Typically, such a criterion might be to minimize costs, defined as the linear combination of unit cost, C, and output,

$$\min \mathbf{C'X} \tag{48}$$

The LP system is completed by excluding negative output,

$$\mathbf{X} \geqq 0 \quad \text{for all } X \tag{49}$$

Corresponding to any cost minimization problem of the type defined by relationships 47–49 is a maximization problem of the form:

$$\max \mathbf{B'P} \tag{50}$$

$$(\mathbf{I} - \mathbf{A})^{-1} \mathbf{P} \leqq \mathbf{C} \tag{51}$$

$$\mathbf{P} \geqq 0 \tag{52}$$

where **P** is a vector of shadow prices determined endogenously. P_i represents the social marginal productivity or social opportunity cost in terms of the objective function, **CX,** of an additional unit of the ith resource.

The existence of a set of endogenously determined shadow prices in general equilibrium models constitutes another major advantage of LP functions. While in I-O the general equilibrium solutions of output are computed in such a way as to be independent of prices (prices being presumed to be constant), prices and quantities are determined simultaneously in LP models.

According to the duality theorem of LP, if there exists an optimal solution to the first problem (inequalities 47–49 which constitute the so-called primal problem), there also exists an optimal solution to the second or dual problem defined by inequalities 50–52, such that

$$\min \mathbf{C'X} = \max \mathbf{B'P} \tag{53}$$

Thus, LP is an operational extension of classical general equilibrium theory in which all activity levels, $\mathbf{X}$, and shadow prices, $\mathbf{P}$ (both of which are constrained to nonnegativity) are determined simultaneously. As will be demonstrated in Chapter 21, such a model has obvious possibilities for use in economic planning.

Limitations of Production Functions and Alternatives

The preceding discussion of several forms of production functions has illustrated both their advantages and their limitations. Some of these limitations are shared by all the forms we discussed. The elasticity of substitution is constant (whether zero, one, infinite, or another value between the two extremes), although one can conceive of situations in which it should be varying for different factor proportions and different levels of output. Similarly, the elasticities of substitution could be varying for different pairs of factors. Furthermore, the functions we have presented treat only a single output at a time, whereas in fact most processes yield several products (some desired and some undesirable) from a given set of inputs. Joint production cannot be readily analyzed within our framework.

Some of these limitations can be handled with alternative forms. The variable elasticity of substitution function, for example, and the transcendental logarithmic production function both allow for different σ at different input-input and input-output ranges.[7] The latter function can also readily handle the problem of pairwise differing elasticities of substitution for a set of several factors of production as

well as for joint production. In general, however, the gain of realism from alternative production function forms comes at the cost of additional information requirements and computational difficulties. These complications often make the use of simpler and more manageable functions definitely advantageous. In subsequent chapters, we will show that the simple functional forms we have presented in detail can be extremely useful tools in the analysis of economic development.

A more general criticism of production function analysis is that it is static, whereas actual production decisions generally involve simultaneous determination of a whole time stream of outputs and inputs. As a result, it misses the important advantages of specialization and the fuller utilization of the various productive factors over time that have characterized the substitution of mass production techniques for craft techniques (Georgescu-Roegen 1970; Alchian 1959a). The conditions and rules of profit maximization that are applied to these functions in a dynamic setting should recognize the importance of adjustment costs in changing factor proportions over time (Nadiri and Rosen 1969).

Summary and Conclusions

Efficiency and factor substitution are two extremely important issues in the partial analysis of development statics. The extent of substitutability between capital and labor delineates the range of alternatives that capital-scarce, labor-abundant LDCs face in the organization of production. The study of productive efficiency determines whether output can be increased without increasing resources but merely by reallocating the existing ones. Preliminary to the study of these issues, Chapter 4 has been devoted to the analysis of production.

Knowledge of the engineering production function that characterizes an activity—whether of the C-D, CES, I-O, or LP form—is sufficient to answer a number of questions relating to factor substitution. But by introducing factor prices and the economic rules of maximization, an even broader range of issues can be approached through the production function. For example, from marginal productivity and factor prices, one can determine the optimum allocation of resources; from the

---

[7]For presentation of these functions, see Lu and Fletcher (1968), Sato and Hoffman (1968), and Christensen, Jorgenson, and Lau (1973).

elasticity of substitution, one can determine the direction and the extent to which the income distribution will change as a result of factor price changes. These possibilities were illustrated with the C-D and the CES production functions.

Still, the C-D and the CES functional forms have a number of restrictive features. Prices, for example, can enter only indirectly through the maximization conditions, or inputs are considered as independent from one another. Such features limit the usefulness of the production function for the study of interdependencies. To illustrate how interdependencies can be studied through general equilibrium analysis, we have introduced the I-O and LP production functions and their applications. In Chapter 6, the neoclassical production function will also be reformulated to become amenable to general equilibrium applications.

Concepts from the analysis of production developed in this chapter will be used in subsequent chapters to study specific issues in the economics of development. Neoclassical production analysis, for example, will be utilized in Chapters 5 and 6 for the study of efficiency, in Chapter 9 for the study of technological change, in Chapter 16 to construct a general equilibrium model of the agricultural sector, and in Chapter 19 to measure the effects of customs union participation. I-O analysis will be used in studying linkages and sectoral articulation in Chapters 15 and 16. The study of planning for economic development in Chapter 21 will be based on I-O and LP approaches.

Appendix

Examples of Production Analysis with the Cobb-Douglas and Constant Elasticity of Substitution Functions

This appendix will fix the concepts of the production function by presenting examples in which the C-D and CES functions are fitted with data from the agricultural sectors of Greece and India, respectively. Detailed discussion of the way estimates obtained can be utilized for the study of empirical hypotheses in the economics of development is deferred to other parts of the book (e.g., in Chapter 5, with regard to the marginal productivities obtained from fitting the C-D with the Greek data). Likewise, application of I-O and LP production functions is postponed until Chapters 15, 16, and 21.

The Cobb-Douglas Production Function

The data for this application were collected by one of the authors by interview questionnaire of 430 farm households randomly selected from a random sample of 110 villages in Epirus, the least developed area in Greece. The purpose of the main study based on these data was to yield some insights into the agricultural operations in Epirus, and more generally in Greece, especially with respect to questions of efficient use of inputs in farms of different size.[8]

The primary purpose of the estimation of the production function is to obtain estimates of the regression coefficients. A computer printout presents these estimates and also additional information necessary for the economic interpretation of the relationship. For illustration, we present in Table 4.5 the information most likely to be contained in a printout, and we discuss the data and some of the relevant statistics.

Output is defined in terms of gross value of agricultural production. The farm house-

[8]This research is reported in detail in Yotopoulos (1967a).

Table 4.5 *Sample of Printout Information, Cobb-Douglas Production Function for Greek Agriculture*

		Output Y	Labor X_1	Land X_2	Plant Equipment X_3	Live Capital X_4
I						
Partial Regression Coefficients (b_i)			0.4446	0.1245	0.0818	0.2300
Standard Errors (S_{b_i})			0.0593	0.0411	0.0163	0.0331
t-Ratios			7.4938	3.0287	5.0126	6.9460
Beta Coefficients			0.3743	0.1318	0.1644	0.2891
Table of Correlation Coefficients (zero order)	Y	1.0000	0.7336	0.6251	0.4434	0.6683
	X_1	0.7336	1.0000	0.7156	0.3964	0.6913
	X_2	0.6251	0.7156	1.0000	0.3779	0.5648
	X_3	0.4434	0.3964	0.3779	1.0000	0.2797
	X_4	0.6683	0.6913	0.5648	0.2797	1.0000
Partial Correlation Coefficients			0.3416	0.1454	0.2363	0.3193
Means (of logs)		3.9919	2.2461	1.0877	3.2335	3.8107
Standard Deviations (of logs)		0.4027	0.3390	0.4263	0.8093	0.5063
Geometric Means (antilog)		9815.0	176.2	12.24	1712.0	6468.0

II				
Number of Observations k	430	k-n-1 Degrees of Freedom		425
Intercept (logs)	1.7169	F-ratio		175.6826
Intercept (antilogs)	52.11			
Durbin-Watson Test (d)	1.3418			
Standard Error of Estimate	0.2484	Standard Error of Estimate Adjusted		0.2507
Coefficient of Multiple Determination R^2	0.6231	Adjusted Coefficient of Determination $\bar{R}^2$		0.6195

Source: Yotopoulos, P. A. (1967a), *Allocative Efficiency in Economic Development: A Cross Section Analysis of Epirus Farming.* Athens: Center of Planning and Economic Research, Table 10.1, p. 180.

holds in the study were engaged in mixed farming. As a result, the physical output, which would have been a more appropriate variable in a production function, had to be homogenized by the use of farm-gate prices to give the dependent variable.

The labor input is in physical terms and expresses homogeneous man-workdays (i.e., after conversion of work performed by women and children into man-workdays-equivalent) of agricultural activities on the farm for the period of the year. The land input refers to cultivated stremmata[9] converted into standard units by allowing for differences in quality, especially for irrigation. The capital inputs (plant and equipment) and live capital (trees and animals) are expressed in terms of drachmas for annual service flows.[10] As compared to stocks, service flows are more appropriate variables for the estimation of a production function.[11] The concept is equivalent to the price one would have to pay to rent, for example, the services of a tractor or of a milking cow for a year instead of owning the capital asset outright.

[9]One stremma is equal to 0.247 acres.

[10]One dollar was equivalent to 30 drachmas in 1963–1964 prices.

[11]For the biases that arise if a stock concept of capital is used instead, as well as the methodology of transforming capital stock information into capital flow concepts, see Yotopoulos (1967b) and Day (1967).

The regression coefficients are coefficients of technical transformation, since they describe the transformation of man-workdays of inputs into drachmas of output. In the specific case of the log linear relationship, the regression coefficients are output elasticities, as shown in equation 5. For example, an increase in labor by 1 percent, the other inputs being held constant, is expected to result in a 0.44 of 1 percent increase in output. Moreover, under constant returns to scale and with the assumptions of perfect competition and profit maximization (i.e., marginal product of each factor is equal to its opportunity cost), the regression coefficients represent the relative shares of the factors of production (equation 19). In Table 4.5, for example, the estimated share of land is 12 percent of total output.

Under perfect competition, the sum of regression coefficients measures returns to scale. In the example, we have decreasing returns to scale, since an increase in each resource input by 1 percent would lead to only a 0.881 of 1 percent increase in output. There may be a priori theoretical reasons to believe that constant returns to scale must prevail if all relevant inputs are included in the function. If so, the discrepancy between the a priori expectations and the regression results should be sought in specification errors in connection with the variables. A brief summary of the main results of the technical discussion on the specification errors sheds some light on why the regression coefficients add up to only 0.881.[12] The most common specification error is the omission of variables. If the omitted input variables are positively correlated with the included ones—which is what we might usually expect—the result will tend to overestimate one or more of the coefficients of the included variables. The converse is true in the case of a negative correlation between included and omitted variables.[13] The results of mistakes in the aggregation of nonhomogeneous components within a variable are less clear. Ignoring qualitative differences within a factor is equivalent to omitting several variables, plus including the imperfectly specified variable. The result of the former part is to tend to

bias the coefficients of the included variables upward—assuming that the omitted and included variables are positively correlated. The inclusion of the misspecified variable, however, may complement or counteract this bias. The results of aggregation over different inputs are still more unpredictable. They will, however, be minimized by treating resource categories that are perfect complements, as well as resource categories that are perfect substitutes, as a single input.

The leading candidate among specification errors is the omission of management or entrepreneurial ability. In accord with the preceding discussion, and assuming that over the range of the sample observations the management factor varies less than proportionately with the included factors of production, the omission of managerial input from the production function should have led to an underestimation of returns to scale.[14]

The goodness of the fit of the overall relation is judged by the multiple coefficient of determination, $\overline{R}^2 = 0.620$, and by the standard error of estimate, adjusted for degrees of freedom. In interpreting the latter, one should keep in mind that it is always stated in the same units as the dependent variable. Thus, in the example of Table 4.5, the standard error adjusted is the logarithm 0.251. That would mean that the estimates of log Y are likely to agree with the logarithm of the true values to within ± 0.251, two-thirds of the time—at the 95 percent level of significance.

Once the relationship itself has been judged generally satisfactory, one may proceed to examine its individual components. The question of the reliability of the estimates of the regression coefficients arises here. It is formulated as a test of significance by calculating confidence limits for the coefficients or, equivalently, by testing to see if the estimates are significantly different from a specific value, for example, one. The appropriate statistic is the ratio of the regression coefficient to its standard error, or the *t*-ratio. Conventionally,

---

[12]The interested reader is referred to the crucial paper by Griliches (1957); see also Goldberger (1968, Chapter 5) and Heady and Dillon (1961, pp. 212–217).

[13]For further discussion of this point, see Chapter 5 on management bias.

[14]Mundlak (1961); also Yotopoulos (1967a). The effect of management is a shift of the entire production possibility curve to the right, thus producing more output from a given amount of resources. This change is reflected in the increase in the marginal productivity of each input factor. At given input prices, the quantity demanded of each resource would increase, and it is likely that this increase would be more than proportional to the change in the management factor.

a probability value of 5 percent is chosen, so one wants the regression coefficients to be (in absolute terms) at least twice as large as their standard errors, or t-ratios exceeding 2.

A potential problem in estimating a multiple regression is "high" correlation between some (or all) of the independent variables with one another. Multicollinearity, which is a question of "more or less" rather than "yes or no," reduces the precision of the individual regression coefficients. An intuitive explanation of multicollinearity is the following. A multiple regression coefficient quantifies the effect that a certain change in the relevant independent variable has upon the dependent variable, if the other variables are held constant. If there is multicollinearity in the independent variables, however, it is not possible to hold other things equal when we vary one independent variable. Therefore, the interpretation of the regression coefficients becomes invalid. The extent of multicollinearity is ascertained by examining the table of auxiliary correlation coefficients. A correlation coefficient between a pair of independent variables greater than $|0.8|$ is usually taken as evidence of "high" multicollinearity. This does not appear to be a problem in our example.

If the assumption of the least squares estimation about zero covariance in the error terms is violated, autocorrelation in the errors arises. Autocorrelation may appear in time series analyses because of problems with the data, as in errors in measurement, or because of problems with the functional form, as when the wrong model is used or important variables are omitted. The test for autocorrelation in the errors is provided by the Durbin-Watson statistic, or d-test. Tables of d statistics provide the lower, d_l, and upper, d_u, bounds for a given probability level and sample size. A d-value below the tabled d_l indicates significant positive serial correlation, while a d-value above the tabled d_u indicates significant negative serial correlation (or, since the test is usually applied to discover positive serial correlation, insignificant positive serial correlation). A value between the two limits means that the test is inconclusive. The example of Table 4.5 is a cross-sectional study and therefore such a text is not relevant. Should it have been based on time series, the fact that the d-statistic of 1.34 lies between the tabulated values of d_l and d_u for the 5 percent level of significance and 425 degrees of freedom indi-

cates that the test for autocorrelation of the errors would have been inconclusive.

The results in Table 4.5 of fitting the C-D production function with the Greek data will be utilized in Chapter 5 in the discussion of efficiency.

The Constant Elasticity of Substitution Production Function

We illustrate estimation of the CES production function with data from a sample of Indian farms. The purpose was to determine the value of the elasticity of substitution between capital and labor in Indian agriculture, as reflected in the sample data. The answer to this question is crucial if economic hypotheses regarding Indian agriculture are to be cast in the proper functional form. By establishing, for example, that the elasticity of substitution is not significantly different from one, the C-D function becomes the appropriate tool for further analysis. This conclusion is used in Chapter 6, in which we formulate a test for relative efficiency and apply it to Indian data.

The comparison of the two fitted functions in Table 4.6 indicates the superiority of the C-D as the analytical form that describes the data from Indian agriculture. First, and most important, since the value of ρ is not significantly different from zero, the elasticity of substitution, $\sigma = 1/(1 + \rho)$ must not differ from one. As a result, the functional form of the C-D can be accepted as appropriately describing the data. Both the efficiency parameter γ and the coefficient of land are not significant. Even more disturbing is the negative value of the distribution parameter for capital (computed as $1 - \delta_1 - \delta_2$), which suggests that there might be serious problems in the definition and measurement of this variable. The insignificant coefficient of capital in the C-D function corroborates this interpretation. Labor is the only variable with a significant coefficient in the CES function. In the C-D function, on the other hand, the values of the coefficients of labor and land of 0.52 and 0.46, respectively, are not far off from the values estimated for other countries.

As a result of this comparison, Yotopoulos, Lau, and Somel (1970) utilized the C-D in their further analysis of Indian data. The extra sophistication of the CES seemed both unnecessary and unwarranted by the quality of the available data.

Table 4.6 *Constant Elasticity of Substitution Production Function and Comparison with the Cobb-Douglas, Sample of Indian Farms*

Parameter Estimated	CES	Parameter Estimated	C-D
γ	3.881	A	3.052
	(2.876)		(8.833)
δ_1	0.102	β_1	0.459
	(0.250)		(0.060)
δ_2	0.919	β_2	0.517
	(0.205)		(0.074)
ρ	0.349	β_3	0.033
	(0.599)		(0.036)
$\overline{R}^2$	0.981	$\overline{R}^2$	0.961

Notes: The estimating equations are:

$$\ln Y = \ln \gamma - \frac{1}{\rho} \ln \left[\delta_1 T^{-\rho} + \delta_2 L^{-\rho} + (1 - \delta_1 - \delta_2) K^{-\rho} \right]$$

$$\ln Y = A + \beta_1 \ln T + \beta_2 \ln L + \beta_3 \ln K$$

where

Y is output in rupees per farm
T is cultivable land in acres per farm
L is labor in rupees per farm
K is interest on fixed capital in rupees per farm.

Source: India, Government of: Ministry of Food and Agriculture (1957–1962), *Studies in the Economics of Farm Management*. Delhi.

Chapter 5

The Study of Efficiency: What Can We Learn from the Production Function?

An intuitive notion of efficiency refers to the achievement of maximum output from a given set of resources: the greater the output relative to the inputs, the higher the level of efficiency. This beguilingly simple notion suffices to establish the importance of the concept in the economist's quest to identify and explain the components of economic growth. Growth that follows from an increase in the amounts of available resources is both predictable and easy to understand. However, such growth lacks the mystique and appeal of growth that might occur without any increase in the measured inputs of production. Because increased efficiency represents a kind of "manna from heaven," it is not surprising that the study of efficiency has received much attention in recent years, culminating in some significant analytical innovations.

This chapter is composed of three sections. First, we deal with some conceptual considerations of economic efficiency. We identify the two component parts, technical and price efficiency, and we emphasize the implications of this distinction from the point of view of both microeconomic static analysis and dynamic characteristics of the structure of firms and product competition. Second, on the basis of the standard production function analysis of the previous chapter, we present techniques for measuring the technical component of efficiency. Third, we review the literature on "allocative efficiency," which purports to draw conclusions about the success with which a given set of resources have been combined. We show that conventional measures of allocative efficiency (via the production function) do not fully capture the component of price efficiency distinguished in our discussion and, besides, that the concept itself has its shortcomings.

The discussion builds up to Chapter 6,

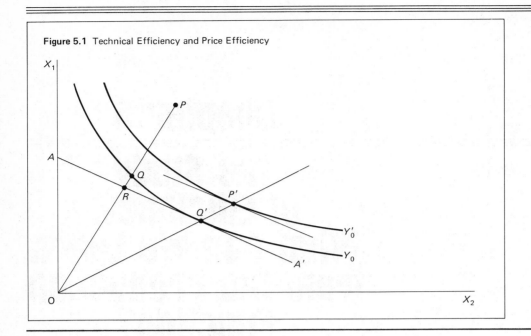

Figure 5.1 Technical Efficiency and Price Efficiency

which introduces the profit function for the unambiguous measurement of economic efficiency and its component parts, and also to subsequent chapters on technological change and sectoral interdependencies.

Conceptual Considerations on Efficiency

Two Components of Economic Efficiency: Technical Efficiency and Price Efficiency

Efficiency is an elusive concept which, to all appearances, is rather simple. Some classificatory housecleaning will help before discussing the operational aspects of the variants of efficiency.

Figure 5.1 shows the "unit isoquant" in inputs X_1 and X_2. The unit isoquant represents the combinations of X_1 and X_2 that yield one unit of output, Y_0. A firm that produces Y_0 at a point on the unit isoquant can also produce Y_0 by using combinations of inputs that lie above the unit isoquant—simply by throwing inputs away. To guarantee the uniqueness of the isoquant, we define it in the context of the production function, that is, as depicting the minimal combinations of inputs that can produce the unit output. Alternatively, the isoquant shows the maximum quantity of output that can be produced with any combination of inputs.

In Figure 5.1, we show the actual input utilization of two firms that produce one unit of output, one at Q and the other at P. Comparing the two firms, we observe that both use the same factor proportions, X_1/X_2. We also observe that the firm at Q produces the unit output with only OQ/OP as much of each factor as the firm at P. It is, therefore, natural to define the firm at Q as the *technically efficient* firm (relative to the one at P). We then measure the degree of technical efficiency of the firm at P as $(OQ/OP) \times 100$ on a percentage basis (Farrell 1957). An index of 70 percent for the firm at P implies that X_1 and X_2 can be reduced at a scale of 10 : 7, with the firm still producing one unit of output— provided that it "were like" the firm at Q.

Our description of technical efficiency up to this point is a purely engineering concept. It deliberately omits consideration of input prices. The price of X_1 relative to X_2 can be introduced quite simply. It is portrayed in our graph by line AA' or, for prices remaining unchanged, by any other line parallel to AA'.

By comparing the prices of inputs, as reflected by the slope of AA', to their marginal products, as reflected by the slope of the isoquant, we introduce the concept of price efficiency. The firm at Q' is *price efficient*, since the marginal product of input X_1 and the marginal product of input X_2 (or their ratio) equals, respectively, the price of input X_1 and the price of input X_2 (or their ratio).

The price line AA' is also an isocost line, which indicates the minimum cost for producing output Y_0 at given prices. The cost at Q' being the same as the cost at R, the price efficiency of firm Q can be expressed as OR/OQ. Furthermore, a simple relationship exists between price and technical efficiency at points P, Q, and R, since $OR/OP = (OQ/OP) \times (OR/OQ)$.

We can now combine the criteria of price efficiency and technical efficiency in order to define *economic efficiency*. The firm at Q is technical-efficient but price-inefficient and thus economic-inefficient. So is the firm at P', which is price-efficient but lies on the technical-inefficient isoquant Y_0'. Only the firm at Q' is economic-efficient. Price efficiency and technical efficiency are necessary, and also, when occurring jointly, they are sufficient conditions for economic efficiency.

Efficiency and the Production Function: A Case of Hunting the Heffalump

The production function, in a form as simple as output-input or input-input ratios, or in more sophisticated forms such as C-D or CES, is the tool that has conventionally been used for the study of efficiency. A number of examples will suggest the limitations of this kind of analysis.

The *Farm Management Studies* of the Indian Ministry of Food and Agriculture (1957–1962) have provided microeconomic data from cost-accounting records of about 3,000 holdings in the six main agricultural regions of India.[1] These data have been a valuable source for the analysis of Indian agriculture and have also provided an empirical testing ground for economic theory. A number of writers have approached the *Studies* with an eye on implications about the efficiency of Indian agriculture, especially on the comparative efficiency of small farms as distinguished from large (more than 10 acres).[2]

Some of the most celebrated findings of the studies suggest that there are significant differences in factor intensities, that is, input-input ratios, and in input-output ratios between different size classes of farms. More specifically, it has been observed that:

1. Output per acre is inversely related to farm size as measured by area.
2. Input per acre (in terms of a "cost" concept which includes, among other things, both hired and family labor) is inversely related to farm size.
3. Output per acre is directly related to non-labor input per acre.
4. Labor per acre is inversely related to farm size.
5. Output per unit of labor is directly related to farm size.

Different observers have drawn contradictory conclusions from these observations.[3] We will point out that contradiction is inevitable because such ratios are inappropriate indices for efficiency comparisons.

The intuitive definition of efficiency given at the start of this chapter was the achievement of maximum output from a given set of resources. Intuition is often misleading. On the basis of observation 1, small farms would seem more efficient in producing more output from their land. Observation 5 leads to the opposite conclusion, since large farms obtain higher output from their labor input. Observation 2 favors large farms that "conserve" inputs and have lower costs per unit of land —or do large farms underutilize their land resources by combining them with "too few" other inputs? The same problem arises with observation 4. Do large farms underutilize labor, or do they conserve labor inputs? Observation 3 favors large farms, which utilize land "intensively" by the application of large quantities of complementary factors of production.

Following 4, one can conclude that large farms substitute capital for labor to a greater extent than small farms. Would it be surprising if the ratio of output per unit of capital favored the small farms? An alternative interpretation of 2 and 3 combined is that costs per unit of land increase with farm size not only because of labor substitution but also because large farms pay a higher wage rate than do small farms, which employ their

[1]For details on the Farm Management Studies, see Lau and Yotopoulos (1971) and the studies cited there.
[2]See Paglin (1965), Bennett (1967), Sahota (1968b), Sen (1964), Yotopoulos, Lau, and Somel (1970), Lau and Yotopoulos (1971), Yotopoulos and Lau (1974),

[3]For a full discussion, see Yotopoulos, Lau, and Somel (1970).

family members whose opportunity costs are low. Should labor cost or labor days be the relevant unit for comparison?

The attempt to quantify economic efficiency through output-input and input-input ratios constitutes measurement without theory. It is not surprising that it leads to ambiguous interpretations. Economic theory specifies the conditions under which firms are expected to have identical ratios of inputs and outputs. Specifically, it is well known that all firms would have the same quantities of inputs and outputs (and as a result only one point on the production surface would be observable) if:

1. All firms had the same production function, that is, the same technical knowledge and identical fixed factors.
2. All firms faced the same prices in the product and factor markets.
3. All firms maximized profits perfectly and instantaneously.

Nevertheless, we observe firms that produce homogeneous outputs with different factor intensities and varying average factor productivities. It is, of course, sufficient to explain the world if we assume that firms behave randomly (that they are ignorant of their production, cost, and return functions and that no matter what prices are given, they

do not behave as if they maximized profits). But if this were the case, there would be no need to measure economic efficiency.

On the other hand, suppose we establish that firms behave according to a certain decision rule, which we can conveniently call profit maximization with respect to a set of exogenous variables, such as prices and fixed factors of production. Then the observed interfirm differences in factor intensities and productivities are in need of explanation. The two possible explanations are that: (1) firms have different input and output mixes because they face different prices and/or (2) firms have different input and output mixes because they have different endowments of fixed factors of production, that is, they have neutral differences in technical efficiency. This situation is illustrated in Figure 5.2 and Table 5.1.

Panels I through VI of Figure 5.2 present six different sets of unit-output isoquants for inputs X_1 and X_2, with the position of firms 1 and 2 indicated. All isoquants represent the possible alternative input combinations as determined by engineers. The panels are drawn so that, on the basis of the criterion of output per unit of X_1, firm 1 is more efficient than firm 2, and the converse is true for the criterion output per unit of X_2. The rankings for each panel are shown in Table 5.1.

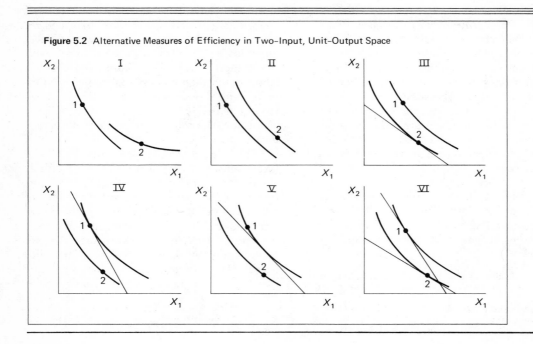

Figure 5.2 Alternative Measures of Efficiency in Two-Input, Unit-Output Space

Table 5.1 *Firm Rankings with Respect to Efficiency*

Efficiency Concept		Panel					
		I	II	III	IV	V	VI
Output/Input Ratio	X_1	1	1	1	1	1	1
	X_2	2	2	2	2	2	2
Technical Efficiency		?	1	2	2	2	2
Price Efficiency		?	?	2	1	—	1 and 2
Economic Efficiency		?	?	2	2?	2?	2

Efficiency comparisons of any kind are impossible in panel I, because the isoquants belong to production functions that differ not only by the constant terms but also by the value of the elasticities. In panel II, comparison of technical efficiency becomes possible, because the isoquants belong to production functions that differ only by the constant term. This term represents differences in endowments of fixed factors as well as the impact of nonmeasurable inputs, such as entrepreneurship. Technical efficiency is the shorthand notation for such differences. It favors firm 1, since it produces the unit output with smaller quantities of inputs than firm 2. In panel III, the economic information of relative prices is introduced. Firm 2 is technical-efficient, price-efficient, and economic-efficient, whereas firm 1 is inefficient with respect to both components of economic efficiency. In panel IV, although price efficiency changes in favor of firm 1, the ranking with respect to economic efficiency perhaps favors firm 2. In panel V, neither firm 1 nor firm 2 is price-efficient. Even though firm 1 might be slightly more price-efficient than firm 2, the latter's advantage in technical efficiency would seem to rank it above firm 1 in overall economic efficiency. The final panel introduces differences in prices. Firm 2 employs relatively cheap X_1 inputs, while firm 1 has cheap X_2 inputs. In this graph, both firms are price-efficient. The criterion of economic efficiency then favors firm 2, which has the advantage in technical efficiency over firm 1.

The point we have made in Figure 5.2 has relevance for interpreting the observations made from the Indian data. These observations are inconsistent with profit maximization within the same production function and the same price regime, since in that case both large and small farms would have identical ratios. If maximization is imperfect, the ratios observed are plausible but still do not yield conclusive determination of relative efficiency. Alternative explanations for these ratios are that small and large farms have differences in the production function, represented by differences in the constant term, and/or that they operate under different output or input price regimes.

The latter interpretation is especially plausible in peasant agriculture of the Green Revolution variety. The new seeds, fertilizers, and insecticides that have constituted the basis for increased yields in recent years have become selectively available mainly to large farms. This factor, if not counterbalanced by other technical efficiency advantages of small farms, would tend to produce higher output-input ratios for large farms, other things being equal. In addition, small farms are likely to operate with relatively cheap labor (since the opportunity cost of family members in a rural sector that has few alternative employment opportunities will be extremely low), relatively expensive capital (because of limited or no access to credit from official sources or institutions subject to interest rate ceilings), and, by definition, little land. Large farms, in contrast, have more land, access to credit on more favorable terms, and the ability to hire labor in the market at the going wage rate. These characteristics are sufficient to explain the observed variations in the input and output ratios. In the extreme case where labor is free for small farms and land is free for large ones, the maximization rule would lead the former to maximize output per unit of land and the latter to maximize output per unit of labor. These ratios are then purely definitional and convey no information about economic efficiency.

The search for economic efficiency through the medium of the production function inspires the pessimism of "hunting the Heffalump" of the children's fairy-lore—Pooh has never seen the animal; yet convinced of its existence, he is busily modifying traps in an attempt to capture it! We conclude that the production function is the wrong trap for capturing economic efficiency.

Technical efficiency, as distinct from economic efficiency, can be measured through the production function. And under certain strong assumptions, one can also say something about the price efficiency or inefficiency of different firms. These topics will be pursued in the balance of this chapter. The combination, however, of the technical and price efficiency components of economic efficiency can be measured only after the new tools presented in the next chapter have been incorporated into the analysis.

The Importance of the Study of the Components of Economic Efficiency

The preceding discussion of economic efficiency drew attention to two kinds of inefficiency: the inefficiency that lies in people, and the inefficiency that lies in people's stars! By the former, we mean price inefficiency, which has to do with managerial decision making about the allocation of the variable factors of production—factors that are within the control of the firm. Technical inefficiency, on the other hand, is related to the fixed resources of the firm. It is an engineering datum and as such, at least in the short run, it is exogenous and a given part of the environment.

The economist, the engineer, and the policy maker all have great stakes in the study of efficiency. The policy implications of economic efficiency permeate both the micro- and the macroeconomic levels, the static as well as the dynamic analyses. The relative importance of each component of economic efficiency varies from case to case, and the knowledge of which component offers the greatest scope for improvement can be important for achieving higher levels of income in LDCs, in both the short run and the long run. In some cases, the two components are quite independent of each other, whereas in others, they are interdependent.

The economic function of the firm is to bid resources away from alternative uses and to combine them in the production of a certain output basket. The manufacturer bids capital away from the construction industry to employ it in turning out steel; the farmer bids land away from tobacco to produce wheat; the worker shifts his labor from the consumption activity of leisure or from building a highway to the cultivation of his vegetable garden. As a result of such resource transfers, aggregate output may be increased or decreased. Under ideal circumstances (perfect markets, no externalities, etc.) the entrepreneur who masterminds this increase is rewarded by adding to his personal wealth, that is, by reaping profits. The one who transfers resources so as to decrease social output is usually accountable to society for making up this loss through the sacrifice of his personal wealth (Alchian 1959b). (Where markets are imperfect, externalities exist, and so on, more complicated methods must be used for determining whether society gains or loses from reallocation, and the penalties or rewards awarded by market forces may not be the appropriate ones. Such situations will be discussed in Chapter 20.)

One of the yardsticks economists use to gauge the relative success of firms in enhancing social welfare—and therefore in maximizing their profits—lies in the comparison of marginal costs and marginal revenues. As long as the last unit of a resource that a firm employs yields as much as it would have yielded in alternative employments (its opportunity cost), the firm is price-efficient. If the last unit of a resource yields less than what it could have produced elsewhere, the firm is wasteful and will be penalized by taking losses. If a resource yields at the margin more than its opportunity cost, the firm can expand its utilization of this resource and still add to its profit.

So much for price efficiency and how price inefficiency may arise. What accounts for variations in technical efficiency? One model is that of the classical "taut" economy, as incorporated, for example in the Schumpeterian model of dynamic competition. The genesis in the Schumpeterian world is a surge of innovations initiated by the engineer-entrepreneur: he has a technological invention, he takes his risks to make it an innovation in the marketplace, and he is rewarded with increased profits. Profits in the Schumpeterian cosmogony are begotten by technology. The profit-making firm is technically efficient, that is, it has lower cost curves than the technically inefficient firm. Technical efficiency giveth, and technical efficiency taketh away. The engineer-entrepreneur sets off a wave of imitators, the field becomes competitive, and profits decline. Should no new technological breakthrough be forthcoming, the firm will fall prey to the more vigorous newcomers. As Galbraith mockingly puts it, the economy is viewed ". . . as a biological process in which the old and the senile are continually being replaced by the young and the vigorous." This is one view, but not the only alternative.

At the confines of the classical world of the taut economy, there exists the neoclassical world, which allows for imperfect markets, mistakes in maximization, and entrepreneurial inertia. Variations in technical efficiency are attributable in this model to the "slack" in the economy that exists because of limited information. Instead of maximum profits, firms are on "a systematic temporal search for highest practicable profits" (Earley 1957, p. 334). This is the view that Baran and Sweezy (1966) and Papandreou (1972, pp. 47–49) adopt.

> The firm always finds itself in a given historical situation, with limited knowledge of changing conditions. In this context it can never do more than improve its profit position. In practice, the search for "maximum" profits can only be the search for the greatest *increase* in profits which is possible in a given situation, subject of course to the elementary proviso that the exploitation of today's profit opportunities must not ruin tomorrow's. (Baran and Sweezy 1966, p. 27.)

This description of the slack in the economy is related to technical inefficiency caused by limitations in a fixed factor, in this case, information.

There is more, however, in the concept of the slack economy than what Baran-Sweezy and Papandreou notice. In a slack economy, profits are a cushion providing the firm with latitude for deterioration. In a competitive economy, profits act as a beacon to other firms and set in motion the Schumpeterian forces that compete them away. In a monopoly economy, however, profits may also take the form of "a quiet life." This is a form of profit that cannot be easily competed away by market forces. Hirschman brings the point into focus:

> What if we have to worry, not only about the profit-maximizing exertions and exactions of the monopolist, but about his proneness to inefficiency, decay, and flabbiness? This may be, in the end, the more frequent danger: the monopolist sets a high price for his products not to amass super-profits, but because he is unable to keep his costs down. (Hirschman 1972, p. 57.)

If this view of the world is correct, it would seem that the Schumpeterian paradigm overlooks some important healing forces that may come into play when remediable lapses from technical efficiency occur. According to the new scenario, the manager-entrepreneur, being divested of his technological monopoly by the wave of imitators, comes to pay attention to the finer aspects of rationalization, resulting in increased price efficiency. This illustrates the point that the two components of efficiency may not be independent of each other.

The "product cycle" hypothesis is another variation of the dynamic competition model that involves both technical and price efficiency. This hypothesis explains world trade patterns on the basis of stages in a product's life. New products emanate from developed countries mainly because of the importance of technology in the early stages of a product's life. In later stages of the product's cycle, however, innovations spread, decreasing the technical efficiency advantage of the early innovator and increasing the importance of price competition. This has the effect of shifting the comparative advantage to countries that are more price-efficient, because they have more favorable factor price relations and/or a greater ability to rationalize the use of inputs.[4]

Technical Efficiency or Management Bias

We have seen that the combination of the assumptions of the same production function, the same prices, and perfect profit maximiza-

[4]For examples of the product life-cycle theory as applied to international trade, see Vernon (1966) and Wells (1972). See also Chapter 17.

tion for all firms invalidates the concept of the production function per se. All firms would produce the same quantity of output and use the same quantity of inputs.

The concept of technical efficiency was developed to introduce systematic deviations in the quantities of inputs that firms use and in the quantity of output they produce, while still retaining the idea of an "average" production function and keeping the assumptions of maximizing behavior by firms that face the same product and factor prices. Suppose we invented a factor called "entrepreneurship." It is a specialized and individual attribute of each firm, which cannot be bought on the market (Kaldor 1934). In the Cobb-Douglas production function it appears as a firm-specific multiplicative factor (Marschak and Andrews 1944). The other parameters of the production function remain the same among firms, and therefore, a certain percentage increase in any input will increase output for all firms by a constant proportion. The absolute change in output would nevertheless vary among firms, depending on the size of the entrepreneurial variable. A logical measure of efficiency is then the value of the individual firm's intercept in the production function. This approach was developed independently by Hoch (1955, 1962) and Mundlak (1961), and it employed the analysis of covariance of the production function.

The study of technical efficiency per se is an important aspect of the study of development, because it quantifies the productive contribution of factors that are not easily amenable to measurement, such as technology, management, and education. Furthermore, and from the point of view of econometric research, if one ignores differences in technical efficiency among firms, one biases the parameter values obtained in the estimation of the production function. As an illustration of this bias, consider the scatter diagram of Figure 5.3 with the (overall) log linear relationship, f'. Suppose the scatter of observations came from a population that was not standardized for one variable, management. Suppose, further, that good managers use more of all inputs of production and produce more output than bad managers. Then the relationship f' is obviously biased. The correct relationship would be f_2 for good managers and f_1 for bad managers. And the effect of good management, if we assume that it can be captured

by a neutral shift in the intercept, would be equal to the shift BC.[5]

We discussed earlier the applicability of the technique of analysis of variance to a wide range of problems in the economics of development. The question of management bias becomes a straightforward application of analysis of variance. Observations for individual firms are used for fitting a production function with the conventional inputs. Suppose now we partition the firm observations into a number of groups on the basis of a relevant criterion (such as the years of education of the managers, the size of input scale, or the years the firm has been in operation) and run separate regressions for each group. The basic proposition of the analysis of variance is that the total variation of output around the overall regression can be decomposed into the variation of individual firms around the group means (variation within groups) and the variation of the group means around the overall regression (variation among groups). If a test of significance (the F-test) reveals that the variation among groups is significant as compared to the variation within groups, the criterion used for the partition of the groups is deemed important for the explanation of the observed distribution of output.[6]

An uncomplicated approach quantifying differences in efficiency (reflecting differences in fixed factors, such as management) utilizes dummy variables in the production function (Mundlak 1961, 1964; Hoch 1955; Massell 1967a; Etherington 1973). Suppose we have at least two cross-sections, for example, a cross-section for a number of firms, and for each firm, we also have time series observations. Assume that the level of management (or technical efficiency) does not change considerably over time within the firm but that it

---

[5]This is part of the general category of problems of specification bias in econometric research. More precisely, in the case of misspecification due to omitted variables, it has been found (Theil 1957; Griliches 1957) that as long as the omitted variables are positively correlated with the included ones (which is the usual case) the result will have a tendency to overestimate one or more of the coefficients of the included variables. The converse is true in the case of a negative correlation between the included and omitted variables.

[6]The analysis of covariance is the general case of the one-way classification we have described so far. It means that there is more than one variable in the relation estimated. For details, see Goldberger (1964, p. 227 ff.) and Mood and Graybill (1963, Chapter 14).

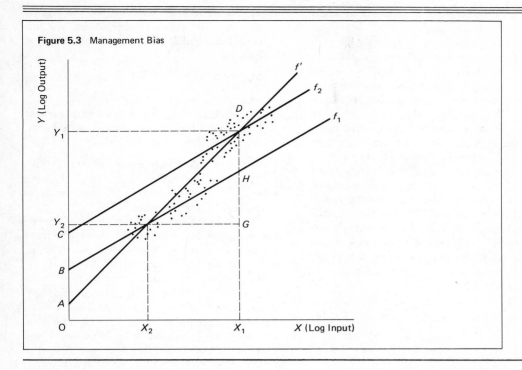

Figure 5.3 Management Bias

varies in the cross-section of the firms to the extent that some firms have good managers and some have bad ones. With the additional assumption that the production functions have the same coefficients but may differ by the constant term, we can measure technical efficiency by using dummy variables (values of one and zero for the two groups of firms we want to distinguish).

The production function is specified (with variables in logs) as

$$Y_{it} = B_0 + B_1 X_{1it} + \cdots + B_k X_{kit} + CM_i + \varepsilon_{it} \tag{1}$$

where

Y_{it} is output of the ith firm at time t

X_{kit} is input of the kth type by firm i at time t

M_i is management input of firm i

B_j and C are the elasticity coefficients of the variables to be estimated

ε_{it} is the error term.

The purpose of the research in management bias is to derive an estimate of M_i which is not directly observable and which, being omitted, has introduced bias in the estimates of equation 1. Furthermore, the esti-

mate of C in equation 1 provides empirical information on the elasticity of output with respect to management. Finally, we would also like to derive information on the elasticity of management with respect to the other factors of production.

Define the unobservable management input up to a multiplicative constant

$$A_i = CM_i \tag{2}$$

We can now write equation 1 as

$$Y_{it} = B_0 + B_1 X_{1it} + \cdots + B_k X_{kit} + A_i + \varepsilon_{it} \tag{3}$$

Assume that A_i is normalized as $\sum_i A_i = 0$. We can now obtain least squares estimates of B_0, B_j, and A_i, where B_0 is the constant term for the overall sample, B_j is the coefficient of each of the k inputs and by assumption is the same for the cross-section of firms and for the time series, and A_i is the dummy variable that refers to management and is also by assumption firm specific.[7]

[7]The sum of squares that is being minimized is
$$S = \sum_{it} (Y_{it} - B_0 - B_1 X_{1it} - \cdots - B_k X_{kit} - A_i)^2$$

With the assumption of the A_i normalized as $\sum_i A_i = 0$,

By fitting equation 3, instead of the usual function that omits management, we have estimated production coefficients that are free of specification bias. Furthermore, the estimate of A_i can be used in further analysis as the dependent variable for studies that explore the factors determining the quality of management. This is simply done by regressing such factors as education, age of the manager, years of operation of the firm, access to extension services for agriculture or accessibility of markets on the estimate of A_i. From equation 3, however, we do not directly obtain an estimate of the management component of each firm, M_i. This can be obtained from equation 2 by introducing outside information that specifies constant returns to scale in the production function, where all inputs are included. With this assumption, we can compute

$$C = 1 - \sum_{j}^{k} B_j \tag{4}$$

Therefore, from equation 2, it follows that

$$M_i = \frac{A_i}{C} \tag{5}$$

The next step is to examine how management is related to the other inputs of production, X_j. This is done by comparing the B_j coefficients of equation 1 with the coefficients of a function estimated in the usual manner, by omitting management. To obtain this function, we rewrite equation 1 with management inputs omitted

$$Y_{it} = b_0 + b_1 X_{1it} + \cdots + b_k X_{kit} + \varepsilon_{it} \tag{6}$$

In this case, Theil (1957) and Griliches (1957) have shown that in estimating b_j (the coefficient of the usual regression that omits M_i), the bias introduced is

$$E(b_j - B_j) = C d_j \tag{7}$$

In other words, the bias in the coefficients caused by the omission of management can be decomposed in two parts:

---

the following estimates can be derived.

$B_0 = Y_{..} - B_1 X_{1..} - \cdots - B_k X_{k..}$
$A_i = Y_{i.} - B_1 X_{1i.} - \cdots - B_k X_{ki.} - B_0$
$\mathbf{B} = (\mathbf{S}_{yx})(\mathbf{S}_{xx})^{-1}$

where a dot signifies averaging over the subscript that the dot replaces, and $\mathbf{S}_{yx}$ is the row vector of cross-products of Y_{it} and X_{1it}, and $\mathbf{S}_{xx}$ is the matrix of cross-products of X_{1it}, $l = 1 \cdots k$.

1. The (unobserved) coefficient of the regression of the omitted variable on the included ones, that is, d_j in the following regression 8

$$M_i = d_0 + d_1 X_{1i} + \cdots + d_k X_{ki} \tag{8}$$

and

2. The coefficient of the omitted management in the multiple regression that included it, that is, C in equation 1.

We can now obtain estimates of d_j in two ways: either by estimating b_j and utilizing equation 7 or by computing M_i from equation 5 and fitting it in equation 8.

The quantification of technical efficiency (or management component) requires the combination of two sets of observations on firms, and it employs the assumption that the functional form is the same for both sets, with the exception of the shift effect of management. Mundlak (1961, 1964) utilized a combination of cross-section and time series data. Massell (1967b), on the other hand, combined cross-section data at the firm level, with a crop-specific cross-section. Table 5.2 presents some of the results of Mundlak's analysis, which was based on 66 family farms in Israel for the years 1954–1958. The results indicate positive correlation between management and most of the inputs, signifying that good managers use more inputs to produce higher levels of output. The exception is X_4, and it indicates that good managers use fewer livestock and poultry barns to produce more output, other things being equal.

We return to Figure 5.3 to show the management bias as defined in equation 7 and for the case of one input, X. Since f' is the overall relation that does not account for the firm management effect, we have $b = (Y_1 - Y_2)/X_1 - X_2)$. With the management effect included, we have $B = (H - G)/(X_1 - X_2)$. Noticing that the slope of equation 8 for the case of one variable can be written $d = (M_1 - M_2)/(X_1 - X_2)$, we have

$$E(b - B) = Cd$$

$$\left(\frac{Y_1 - Y_2}{X_1 - X_2}\right) - \left(\frac{H - G}{X_1 - X_2}\right) = C\left(\frac{M_1 - M_2}{X_1 - X_2}\right)$$

or

$$\left(\frac{D - H}{X_1 - X_2}\right) = C\left(\frac{M_1 - M_2}{X_1 - X_2}\right)$$

As we suggested, the quantification of man-

Table 5.2 *Production Function Elasticities of Family Farms in Israel*

Item	X_1	X_2	X_3	X_4	X_5	Sum of Elasticities	Output Elasticity
1. Elasticity with Management Excluded (Equation 6)	0.130	0.692	0.004	0.103	0.037	0.967	
2. Elasticity with Management Included (Equation 3)	0.083	0.635	0.002	0.156	0.002	0.878	
3. Management Elasticity (Equation 7)	0.047	0.057	0.002	−0.053	0.035		0.122

Notes: The variables are defined as
Y is value of product
X_1 is number of labor days
X_2 is variable expense
X_3 is value of livestock
X_4 is value of livestock and poultry barns
X_5 is amount of land, homogenized for irrigation.
Source: Mundlak, Y. (1964), *An Economic Analysis of Established Family Farms in Israel 1953–1958.* Jerusalem: The Falk Project for Economic Research in Israel, p. 63.

agement can utilize either the left side of the above equation (as shown in Figure 5.3) or the right side, which requires estimating the regression of the other inputs on management with equation 8.

Allocative Efficiency as Seen Through the Production Function

The analysis of management bias just presented deals with only one component of economic efficiency, technical efficiency. The price component of economic efficiency has also been noticed in the literature through the discussion of allocative efficiency. Existing approaches to allocative efficiency, however, suffer from the large number of constraining assumptions used in measuring it as well as from technical econometric defects that greatly limit its usefulness.

The traditional test for allocative efficiency[8] is based on the assumption that firms use the same technology and that they face the same prices. It builds up to a comparison between the marginal product and the opportunity cost of the "average" firm by going through the following steps:

1. By fitting the production function, a stochastic isoquant for the "representative"

[8]For a discussion of allocative efficiency and empirical applications, see T. W. Schultz (1964), Hopper (1965), Yotopoulos (1967a, 1968) and Massell (1967a, b).

firm (i.e., the isoquant that minimizes the sum of squares of positive and negative deviations) is determined.

2. The physical marginal productivities for all factors of production are estimated from the production function at some value of the variables, for example, at their geometric means.

3. The physical marginal productivities are expressed in units of output per unit of each input. They are converted into marginal value productivities, dollars per unit of input, by multiplying by the price of output. These marginal value products represent the implicit price of each factor of production.

4. The implicit price of each factor is compared with the explicit, that is, market factor price. Allocative efficiency implies, for example, that the employment of labor should expand to the point that its marginal value product is equal to its opportunity cost. This comparison can easily be done by computing an index of marginal value product to opportunity cost, the expected value of which would be one.

Sometimes it is feasible to fit product-specific production functions, for example, different functions for wheat, barley, and so on. In this case, we can obtain product-specific marginal productivities. Allocative efficiency then implies that the marginal value product of each input is equalized in the production of each output. If, for example, the marginal value product of labor is higher in the production of wheat than it is in the production of barley, efficiency in the allocation of resources calls for shifting labor from barley to wheat until the implicit factor price is the same for each crop. This approach yields a more meaningful comparison of efficiency.

As an empirical application, we present the allocative efficiency test of Yotopoulos (1967a, 1968) for Greek agriculture.

The regressions in Table 5.3 describe the Cobb-Douglas production function, which underlies the agricultural operations of a random

Table 5.3 *Production Coefficients and Related Production Function Statistics for Sample of Greek Farms*

| Regression Number | Variable |||||||| Sum of Coefficients | R^2 | Farm Class |
	Output Y	Labor X_1	Land X_2	Plant X_3	Equipment X_4	Live Capital X_5	Education X_6			
COEFFICIENTS[a]										
R1	...	0.442	0.092	0.048	0.041	0.259	...	0.882	0.626	All
		(0.177)	(0.058)	(0.042)	(0.012)	(0.015)	(0.034)	...		
R2	...	0.441	0.093	0.046	0.044	0.247	0.138	1.009	0.794	All
		(0.177)	(0.057)	(0.042)	(0.012)	(0.015)	(0.035)	(0.067)		
R2.1	...	0.425	0.066*	0.056	0.063	0.223	0.143	0.976	0.714	Small
		(0.178)	(0.067)	(0.056)	(0.015)	(0.018)	(0.043)	(0.073)		
R2.2	...	0.550	−0.109*	0.024*	0.006*	0.261	0.086*	0.818	0.641	Large
		(0.171)	(0.122)	(−0.121)	(0.022)	(0.025)	(0.061)	(0.171)		
SAMPLE MEANS (GEOMETRIC)										
R1	9,817	176	12	366	335	4,558	...			
R2	9,817	176	12	366	335	4,558	2.24			
R2.1	6,884	128	7	258	214	3,027	2.14			
R2.2	20,320	338	35	744	838	10,543	2.41			
MARGINAL PRODUCTS[b]										
R1	...	24.64	75.26	1.29	1.20	.56	...			
R2	...	24.60	76.08	1.23	1.29	.53	604.80			
R2.1	...	22.86	...	1.49	2.03	.51	460.00			
R2.2	...	33.06	...	...	...	.50	...			

Notes: The production function used, as described in the text, is of the Cobb-Douglas logarithmic form. The primary data used, also described above, are annual figures per farm. Of the 430 farms surveyed, 289 were classed as small, 141 as large. One United States dollar was equal to 30 drachmas (drs.) in 1963–1964 prices. The variables are defined as:

Y is the gross value of agricultural production in drachmas.
X_1 is man-workdays.
X_2 is the number of stremmata cultivated. One stremma = 0.247 acres.
X_3 is the value of current services of plant plus operating expenses for plant, in drachmas.
X_4 is the value of current services of equipment plus operating expenses for equipment, in drachmas.
X_5 is the value of current services of live capital (i.e., animals and trees) plus operating expenses for live capital, in drachmas.
X_6 is the average number of years of education of farm household members age 15–69.

[a]Nonstarred coefficients *are* significantly different from zero at a probability level of $\leq$ 5 percent. Starred coefficients (*) *are not* statistically significant at a probability level of $\leq$ 5 percent. Numbers in parentheses are the calculated standard errors of the respective coefficients.

[b]Estimated at the mean values of input and output; not computed for the statistically nonsignificant coefficients. Expressed in the following dimensions: labor in drs. per man-workday; land in drs. per stremma; plant in drs. per dr.; equipment in drs. per dr.; live capital in drs. per dr.; education in drs. per year change in the average of household education.

Source: Yotopoulos, P. A. (1968), "On the Efficiency of Resource Utilization in Subsistence Agriculture," *F.R.I.S.* 8, No. 2, p. 129.

sample of 430 farm households drawn from a sample of 110 villages (also randomly selected) and three cities in Epirus, an underdeveloped area of Greece. The variables defined for this analysis were discussed in the appendix to Chapter 4. Here it is enough to remind the reader that output is defined as the gross value of agricultural production, labor is in homogenized man-workdays, and capital inputs are expressed in service flow terms, in drachmas.[9]

Education is expressed as an index, calculated as the sum of the years of education of all farm household members in the age bracket 15 to 69, divided by the number of farm household members in this age bracket. The reason for concentrating on the education of members in the 15–69 age bracket is that these members are more likely to participate directly in farm activities, and therefore, their education becomes relevant for estimating the agricultural production function.

The land input refers to cultivated acres converted into standard units by allowing for differences in quality, especially for irrigation. The land variable also serves to distinguish between small and large farms. The former are farms with cultivated areas less than the mean value for the whole sample (20 stremmata, or 5 acres). By splitting the sample into two farm-size groups, we can easily determine whether or not the same law of production underlies the entire range of independent variables; we "hold constant" the unobserved variables that are correlated with farm size (for example, entrepreneurship?); and most important, we can draw implications about relative efficiency as between the two groups of farms.

Four regressions are reported in Table 5.3. Regression R2 is fitted for the total sample of 430 farms, with the complete set of six independent variables. For purposes of comparing the effects of including education in the function, regression R1 is reported with only five independent variables. Regressions R2.1 and R2.2 pertain to the separate subsamples of small and large farms, respectively.

The marginal productivities in Table 5.3 are computed as the product of the input coefficient times the output-input ratio. This computation yields a marginal product of labor of 24.60 drachmas (standard deviation is 3.22

[9]One dollar was equal to 30 drachmas in 1963–1964 prices.

drachmas) or $0.81, per man-workday (R2). It is slightly lower for small farms (22.86 drachmas) and considerably higher for large farms (33.06 drachmas). This is as one might have expected: besides being more land intensive (by definition), large farms also use greater quantities of complementary inputs of production, as compared to small farms.

To evaluate allocative efficiency, we compare the marginal value product of labor to the market wage rate. The average wage for hired-in labor recorded in the questionnaire is 52.25 drachmas (standard deviation is 14.46), or $1.75. Since this is significantly different from the computed marginal productivity of labor,[10] it represents evidence of allocative inefficiency. This finding, however, may merely reflect that the wage rate is inappropriate for use as the opportunity cost of labor. The demand for wage labor in the agriculture of Epirus is only seasonal, concentrated mainly in the fall and spring seasons of peak agricultural activities. Agricultural labor "shortage" is prevalent during these seasons (Pepelasis and Yotopoulos 1962, especially Table 5; Yotopoulos 1964). On the other hand, because of the low degree of industrialization, in the off-peak seasons of winter and summer there are no alternative nonagricultural employment opportunities, and seasonal "surplus" labor is observed. During these seasons, the opportunity cost of family labor can be considered zero. By weighing the seasonal wage rate of 52.25 drachmas by 56 percent, which is the proportion of the total agricultural work in Greece that is performed in the two peak seasons (Pepelasis and Yotopoulos 1962, for the year 1960), we arrive at an approximation of the true year-round opportunity cost of labor of 29 drachmas, or $0.97. If this is true, the marginal productivity of labor in Table 5.3 is not significantly different from the year-round opportunity cost of labor.

Similar comparisons can be carried out for the other inputs as well, at least if the relevant opportunity costs are available. The rental of one stremma of land in the region lies, for example, between 80 and 100 drachmas. The efficiency index then for this factor of production is also close to one. On the other

[10]The relevant test is an F-test. It refers to the null hypothesis that the frequency distribution of the wage rates have the same means. For calculating the variance of the marginal productivity estimates, see Carter and Hartley (1958).

hand, the opportunity cost of one year's education per household member is unknown and allocative efficiency conclusions cannot be drawn about this input. Similarly, comparison of marginal products to opportunity costs is not possible for the capital inputs. Because of the definition of this variable, its marginal product is a profit margin, which expresses the return to a machine per year over the lifetime of the machine. This concept is not suited for comparison with market rates of interest or similar concepts of the opportunity cost of capital.[11]

The Problem of Simultaneous Equation Bias in Tests for Allocative Efficiency

The test for allocative efficiency involves not only the purely technological relationship between inputs and output but also an implicit assumption about profit-maximizing behavior. This assumption introduces other relationships between inputs and output, which hold simultaneously with the technological relationship of the production function (Walters 1963a; Marschak and Andrews 1944; J. Johnston 1963, p. 233; Nowshirvani 1967c). This source of simultaneous equation bias can easily be demonstrated by full specification of the model.

Assume the stochastic production function in two inputs and one output

$$Y_i = AK_i^\alpha L_i^\beta U_i \tag{9}$$

where Y is the output, K and L are capital and labor, U is a disturbance term randomly distributed between firms, and i is the firm subscript. Assume that firms buy their inputs and sell their output in perfectly competitive markets and at prices P_K, P_L, and P_Y for capital, labor, and output, respectively. Subject to the technical constraint of the production function, the market behavior of the firms leads to profit maximization. Denoting profit by Π and writing stars for maximum, we have

$$\Pi = P_Y Y_i - P_K K_i - P_L L_i \tag{10}$$

$$\Pi^* = P_Y Y_i - P_K K_i - P_L L_i - \lambda(Y_i - AK_i^\alpha L_i^\beta U_i) \tag{11}$$

The first order conditions for profit maximization are

$$\frac{\partial \Pi^*}{\partial \lambda} = -Y_i + AK_i^\alpha L_i^\beta U_i = 0$$

$$\frac{\partial \Pi^*}{\partial Y_i} = P_Y - \lambda = 0$$

$$\frac{\partial \Pi^*}{\partial K_i} = P_K + \frac{\lambda \alpha AK_i^\alpha L_i^\beta U_i}{K_i} = 0$$

$$\frac{\partial \Pi^*}{\partial L_i} = P_L + \frac{\lambda \beta AK_i^\alpha L_i^\beta U_i}{L_i} = 0$$

The first order conditions yield a set of three equations which hold simultaneously: the technological production function of equation 9 and the two factor price equations, which incorporate the condition that marginal value product equals the factor opportunity cost. Since $P_Y = \lambda$, the factor price equations can be written

$$P_K = P_Y \frac{\alpha}{K_i} AK_i^\alpha L_i^\beta U_i = P_Y \frac{\partial Y_i}{\partial K_i} \tag{12}$$

$$P_L = P_Y \frac{\beta}{L_i} AK_i^\alpha L_i^\beta U_i = P_Y \frac{\partial Y_i}{\partial L_i} \tag{13}$$

By rearranging equations 9, 12, and 13 and converting to logs, we have

$$\log Y_i = \log A + \alpha \log K_i + \beta \log L_i + \log U_i \tag{14}$$

$$\log K_i = \log \frac{\alpha P_Y}{P_K} + \log A + \alpha \log K_i$$
$$+ \beta \log L_i + \log U_i \tag{15}$$

$$\log L_i = \log \frac{\beta P_Y}{P_L} + \log A + \alpha \log K_i$$
$$+ \beta \log L_i + \log U_i \tag{16}$$

Thus, from equations 15 and 16, the level of use of factors K and L depends not only on the price of output and the respective prices of capital and labor but also on the error term in the production function. This violates the assumption of the least squares estimation of equation 9 that the independent variables are independent of the error term. Therefore, equation 9 cannot be consistently estimated by ordinary least squares. In the context of the discussion of allocative efficiency, this means that we can draw no conclusions from efficiency indexes that involve equations 12 and 13. If equations 12 and 13 hold, we cannot estimate the production function itself because of simultaneous equation bias.

A way to tackle the problem of simultaneous equation bias, with special reference to agricultural production functions, has been suggested by Hoch (1962).[12] Suppose farmers do not set the level of their inputs by maximizing profits within a production function such as equation 9 but within a variant of equation 9. More specifically, suppose that farmers do not maximize *actual* profit (which is uncertain, anyway, because of exogenous shocks, such as the weather, that may intervene); instead, they maximize *"anticipated"* profit with respect to inputs, and furthermore, these input levels are unaffected by "good" or "bad" weather. Formally, this amounts to assuming that U_i equals one and hence has no impact. Anticipated output is then defined as $Y_i^* = AK_i^\alpha L_i^\beta$ and differentiation with respect to capital yields

$$P_Y \frac{\partial Y_i^*}{\partial K_i} = P_Y \frac{\alpha}{K_i} AK_i^\alpha L_i^\beta = P_K \qquad (17)$$

and correspondingly for labor. Since U_i does not enter this decision equation, the model justifies single equation estimation of the technological production function of equation 17.

Maximizing "anticipated" profits is conceptually one way of employing a single equation estimation of the production function while avoiding the problems of simultaneous equation bias. In practice, however, this approach is not fully satisfactory. It relies on the assumption that the stochastic factor is exogeneous (e.g., the weather), and as such, it is independent of the level of inputs. But even in this case, it is likely that there is correlation between the independent variables and the error term. For example, during a drought farmers are likely to use more irrigation water, if available, or, lacking that, less labor and fertilizer.

Summary and Conclusions

In this chapter, we have employed the neoclassical tools of production analysis to study efficiency and the importance of departures from equilibrium. Should inefficiency exist, increases in output—and economic development—can be achieved by reallocating resources in the direction of optimality without necessarily increasing the quantity of productive factors. It is an alluring view of development, one that formed the foundation for the literature of "surplus labor," to be discussed in Chapter 11, and for the pollyannistic view that growth can be achieved by an "up-by-the-bootstraps" operation. This is the motivation for studying efficiency in a development statics framework.

Efficiency also has its dynamic aspects. In this chapter, we have alluded to some dynamic implications of efficiency, for example, those referring to the leadership of firms in the field of industrial organization and to the "product life-cycle" hypothesis in the field of international trade, which will be further discussed in Chapter 17. In Chapter 9, we will deal with other dynamic aspects of efficiency and changes in efficiency.

By distinguishing between variables that cannot in the short run be controlled by the entrepreneur, such as the fixed factors of production or the knowledge of technology, and those that can be controlled, such as the quantities of the variable factors of production hired, we have organized the discussion around the concepts of technical and price efficiency. The neoclassical production function is a perfectly adequate tool for the study of technical efficiency, and a procedure for its measurement through the analysis of variance has been illustrated. Our first approach to the measurement of price efficiency was through the comparison of marginal products and opportunity costs—which has come to be known in the literature as "allocative efficiency." At this point, both conceptual and empirical limitations of the production function became evident. To overcome the econometric defect of simultaneous equation bias, we have suggested that expected output might be specified with the error term excluded. More generally, however, the exogenous variables in the analysis of production are the prices rather than the quantities of the variable factors. A conceptual defect of the allocative efficiency approach refers to the "average" input price that is compared to the "average" point on the fitted isoquant in order to draw conclusions about the extent of resource misallocation. It is more realistic to allow for imperfect markets in which factor prices are firm-specific and also to allow for mistakes by firms in their attempt to maximize profits.

[12]For an alternative specification in which the inputs do not depend on the disturbance of the production function, see Zellner, Kmenta, and Drèze (1966).

In the following chapter, we present methods whereby these complicating factors can be handled. Specifically, by introducing the profit function, we can measure relative economic efficiency by identifying separately its technical and price efficiency components in a way that is free of the problems of the more traditional production function approach.

Chapter 6

Production Function and Profit Function: The Measurement of Relative Economic Efficiency

As we have seen in the preceding chapter, the study of relative efficiency can have important policy implications. For example, comparison of the efficiency of small traditional firms with that of large modern firms can be of great importance in shaping an appropriate antitrust policy, in designing credit institutions, or in deciding whether to undertake land reform and if so what kind of reform it should be. Indeed, if for no other reason, the importance of such issues and the magnitude of the social and political sensitivities they arouse require that the measurement of efficiency should be theoretically valid and subject to unambiguous interpretation.

The study of efficiency relates basically to the common observation that firms that produce homogeneous outputs have different factor intensities and varying average factor productivities. A test of efficiency must pro-vide a satisfactory explanation of this phenomenon.

One explanation could be that firms behave randomly. They are ignorant of their production, cost, and return functions, and no matter what prices are given, they do not behave as if they maximized profits. If this explanation were valid, however, the study of economic efficiency would constitute nothing more than an exercise in snipe hunting, which could profitably be abandoned.

On the other hand, suppose firms behave according to a certain decision rule, which we can conveniently call profit maximization, subject to a set of exogenous variables, such as prices and fixed factors of production. The observed interfirm differences in factor intensities and productivities could then be explained by one or more of the following: (1) different firms face different prices; (2) different firms have different endowments of fixed factors of production, that is, neutral differences in technical efficiency, and (3) different firms use different (nonideal) systematic behavioral rules.

A conclusive test of economic efficiency should, therefore, include two parts. First, given different regimes of prices of the variable factors of production and of quantities of fixed factors of production, it should determine if firms behave according to a decision rule, such as profit maximization. Second, if and only if a decision rule appears to be generally applicable, the question arises whether a group of firms is more economically efficient than another because it is more successful in responding to the set of prices it faces (price efficiency) and/or because it has higher quantities of fixed factors of production, including entrepreneurship (technical efficiency).

The first part is formulated and tested by the Wise-Yotopoulos (1969) test of economic rationality. The purpose of the rationality test is to compare the systematic with the random element of firm behavior and to determine if the hunt for efficiency is worth the prize. Anticipating our results, we find not only that the observed differences in firm behavior are overwhelmingly systematic but also that this systematic behavior is a function of the differences in the endowments of fixed factors, including entrepreneurship.

This finding suggests that the study of efficiency cannot take place in the narrow confines of the assumption of the same interfirm prices and technologies. This leads us to the second step, in which we formulate, à la Lau-Yotopoulos (1971), a test of relative efficiency in terms of the profit function. In contrast to the production function, the profit function specifically allows for differences in the prices of the variable factors of production and in the quantities of the fixed inputs. Moreover, we use the profit function in such a way as to allow interfirm differences in the ability to equate the value of the marginal products of the variable factors to their prices, that is, to maximize profits. As we shall demonstrate, the profit function is an appropriate tool for measuring economic efficiency and both of its components, technical efficiency and price efficiency.

Because of data availability, the relative importance of the agricultural sector, and the

widespread interest in land reform issues, our empirical study of efficiency refers specifically to Indian agriculture. In this context, we attempt to compare the relative efficiency of large and small farms with respect to economic efficiency as well as its components, price efficiency, and technical efficiency.

A Test for Economic Rationality

By rationality, we mean the ability of firms to successfully apply the profit-maximizing rule of behavior. By testing for rationality, we are, therefore, testing for price efficiency. Our test of rationality,[1] or price efficiency, is within a context of firms that face different price regimes and have different endowments of fixed factors. A by-product of the test of economic rationality is the estimation of supply elasticities for the variable factors of production.

The index of economic rationality, P, gives a measure of the extent to which firms are successful in setting their variable inputs at the *ex ante* correct, that is, the profit-maximizing levels. As we will indicate, an index of one suggests that firms perfectly maximize profits, given the constraint that some inputs must be considered as fixed.

Conditional Profit Maximization in the Cobb-Douglas Model

Consider the following deterministic model, which consists of the C-D production function, constant elasticity supply functions for the inputs, and a constant elasticity demand function for the output.

$$Q_i = A_i f(K_i, L_i) = A_i K_i^\alpha L_i^\beta \qquad (1)$$

$$K_i = k P_{Ki}^\eta \quad \text{or} \quad P_{Ki} = \left(\frac{K_i}{k}\right)^{1/\eta} \qquad (2)$$

$$L_i = l P_{Li}^\varepsilon \quad \text{or} \quad P_{Li} = \left(\frac{L_i}{l}\right)^{1/\varepsilon} \qquad (3)$$

$$Q_i = q P_{Qi}^{-\lambda} \quad \text{or} \quad P_{Qi} = \left(\frac{Q_i}{q}\right)^{-1/\lambda} \qquad (4)$$

where: Q_i, K_i, and L_i are respectively physical output, capital, and labor for firm i; P_{Ki}, P_{Li},

[1]This section is a condensed version of Wise and Yotopoulos (1969). © 1969 The University of Chicago. For a discussion of the test of economic rationality, see P. R. Johnson (1968, 1969) and Lianos (1969); and for rejoinders, see Yotopoulos and Wise (1969a,b,c). In the former of the Yotopoulos-Wise comments, the authors explicitly formulate the test of economic rationality to account for "traditional behavior."

and P_{Qi} are respectively the prices of capital, labor, and output for firm i; A_i is the technical efficiency parameter, which varies from firm to firm; α and β are the elasticity coefficients of production and are assumed constant across firms; and η and ε are the price elasticities of supply for capital and labor respectively, and λ is the demand elasticity for output, all three presumed constant across firms.

The total revenue from output for firm i is

$$V_i = P_{Qi}Q_i = \left(\frac{Q_i}{q}\right)^{-1/\lambda} Q_i = q^{1/\lambda}Q_i^{(1-1/\lambda)} \quad (5)$$

By making the market-clearing assumption, we substitute the production function, equation 1, into equation 5, obtaining the total revenue for firm i

$$V_i = q^{1/\lambda}[A_iK_i^\alpha L_i^\beta]^{(1-1/\lambda)}$$

and by setting $A_i' = q^{1/\lambda}A_i^{(1-1/\lambda)}$, we write

$$V_i = A_i'K_i^{\alpha(1-1/\lambda)}L_i^{\beta(1-1/\lambda)} \quad (6)$$

A_i' is the technical efficiency parameter that represents exogenously determined interfirm variations in the volume and quality of the fixed factors of production (e.g., land, entrepreneurship).

The total expense for capital and labor can be derived from equations 2 and 3 respectively as

$$C_k = P_{Ki}K_i = \left(\frac{K_i}{k}\right)^{1/\eta}K_i = \left(\frac{1}{k}\right)^{1/\eta}K_i^{(1+1/\eta)} \quad (7)$$

$$C_l = P_{Li}L_i = \left(\frac{L_i}{l}\right)^{1/\varepsilon}L_i = \left(\frac{1}{l}\right)^{1/\varepsilon}L_i^{(1+1/\varepsilon)} \quad (8)$$

By using equations 6, 7, and 8, we can obtain the total profit equation under the assumption of constant returns to scale

$$\Pi_i = V_i - P_{Ki}K_i - P_{Li}L_i \quad (9)$$

$$\Pi_i = A_i'K_i^{\alpha(1-1/\lambda)}L_i^{\beta(1-1/\lambda)}$$
$$- \left(\frac{1}{k}\right)^{1/\eta}K_i^{(1+1/\eta)} - \left(\frac{1}{l}\right)^{1/\varepsilon}L_i^{(1+1/\varepsilon)} \quad (10)$$

We have so far assumed that firms have knowledge of their production functions, cost functions, and returns functions. The economic rationality hypothesis implies that, given this knowledge and the level of the other factors, firms maximize profits with respect

to each factor of production, that is, $\partial\Pi_i/\partial K_i = 0$ and $\partial\Pi_i/\partial L_i = 0$. From equation 10—and by substituting from equation 6—the profit-maximization condition for capital inputs (whether or not labor inputs are at their correct levels) yields

$$\frac{\partial\Pi_i}{\partial K_i} = \alpha\left(1-\frac{1}{\lambda}\right)\frac{V_i}{K_i}$$
$$- \left(1+\frac{1}{\eta}\right)\left(\frac{1}{k}\right)^{1/\eta}K_i^{1/\eta} = 0$$

We can now write

$$\frac{V_i}{K_i} = \frac{\left(1+\dfrac{1}{\eta}\right)}{\alpha\left(1-\dfrac{1}{\lambda}\right)}\left(\frac{1}{k}\right)^{1/\eta}K_i^{1/\eta}$$

$$\log V_i = a + \left(1+\frac{1}{\eta}\right)\log K_i \quad (11)$$

where

$$a = \log\frac{\left(1+\dfrac{1}{\eta}\right)}{\alpha\left(1-\dfrac{1}{\lambda}\right)}\left(\frac{1}{k}\right)^{1/\eta}$$

By analogy, the maximization condition for labor inputs (whether or not capital inputs are at their correct levels) yields

$$\log V_i = b + \left(1+\frac{1}{\varepsilon}\right)\log L_i \quad (12)$$

where

$$b = \log\frac{\left(1+\dfrac{1}{\varepsilon}\right)}{\beta\left(1-\dfrac{1}{\lambda}\right)}\left(\frac{l}{1}\right)^{1/\varepsilon}$$

Since a and b are constant, equations 11 and 12 represent linear relationships between $\log V_i$ and $\log K_i$, and $\log V_i$ and $\log L_i$, respectively. The economic interpretation of these relationships is straightforward. Equation 11 describes the maximizing behavior of the firm that can control the quantity of capital it employs but must take the quantity of labor as constant, and vice versa for labor in equation 12. Each of these conditions, taken by itself, is a necessary but not a sufficient condition for complete profit maximization. The two taken together are both necessary and sufficient conditions and imply the third. The third partial condition for profit maximization refers to the firm that controls both capital and labor and has to achieve a specified level of output (whether or not the scale of output is correct). In other words, which are the factor proportions that a maximizing firm would employ to achieve a planned level of output? From equations 11 and 12, we write

$$\log K_i = \frac{(b-a)}{\left(1+\frac{1}{\eta}\right)} + \frac{\left(1+\frac{1}{\varepsilon}\right)}{\left(1+\frac{1}{\eta}\right)} \log L_i \qquad (13)$$

Since a and b are constant, equation 13 represents a linear relationship between $\log K_i$ and $\log L_i$ and is thus independent of V_i. This equation, if satisfied, implies that the two variable factors, capital and labor, have been combined in such a way that the cost of achieving a specified level of output, V_i, is minimized.

Equations 11, 12, and 13 represent, in a sufficiently simple form, the three partial conditions for profit maximization in a Cobb-Douglas model.

The Profit-Maximizing Variables as Functions of the Efficiency Parameter of the Individual Firm

Since equations 11 to 13 involve parametric constants that are the same for all firms, they would seem to lead to identical profit-maximizing input levels and output levels for all firms. However, the model does allow for systematic variation in the profit-maximizing inputs and output of the individual firm via the assumption that the technical efficiency term, A_i, is an exogenous variable that varies among firms. This becomes the source of the systematic variation in the profit-maximizing inputs and output between firms. We must, therefore, express the profit-maximizing variables of equations 11 to 13 as functions of the exogenous efficiency parameter of the individual firm.

By combining equations 11 and 12 with the production function, we form the system of simultaneous equations

$$\log A_i' + constant = \left[\left(1+\frac{1}{\eta}\right)\right.$$
$$\left. - \alpha\left(1-\frac{1}{\lambda}\right)\right] \log K_i - \beta\left(1-\frac{1}{\lambda}\right) \log L_i$$

$$\log A_i' + constant = - \alpha\left(1-\frac{1}{\lambda}\right) \log K_i$$
$$+ \left[\left(1+\frac{1}{\varepsilon}\right) - \beta\left(1-\frac{1}{\lambda}\right)\right] \log L_i \quad (14)$$

The solution of this system gives

$$\log K_i = \frac{g}{\left(1+\frac{1}{\eta}\right)} \log A_i' + constant \qquad (15)$$

$$\log L_i = \frac{g}{\left(1+\frac{1}{\varepsilon}\right)} \log A_i' + constant \qquad (16)$$

where

$$g = \frac{1}{1 - \frac{\alpha\left(1-\frac{1}{\lambda}\right)}{\left(1+\frac{1}{\eta}\right)} - \frac{\beta\left(1-\frac{1}{\lambda}\right)}{\left(1+\frac{1}{\varepsilon}\right)}}$$

Thus, we see that K_i and L_i are linear functions of A_i', the exogenous efficiency parameter of the individual firm. The same can also be shown for V_i. By substituting equations 15 and 16 into the production function, equation 6, we obtain

$$\log V_i = \log A_i' + \frac{\alpha\left(1-\frac{1}{\lambda}\right)}{\left(1+\frac{1}{\eta}\right)} g \log A_i'$$
$$+ \frac{\beta\left(1-\frac{1}{\lambda}\right)}{\left(1+\frac{1}{\varepsilon}\right)} g \log A_i' + constant$$

or

$$\log V_i = g \log A_i' + constant \qquad (17)$$

We have, therefore, established that the profit-maximizing inputs and output of the individual firm are subject to systematic variations that are caused by the differences in the exogenous efficiency parameter between firms. Specifically, we have expressed them as log linear functions of the exogenous efficiency parameter.

Stochastic Formulation of the Model: The Diagonal Regression Analysis

The equivalent systems of equations 11 to 13 and 15 to 17 are written in terms of profit-maximizing variables which are, of course, nonobservable variables and should be transformed into observable variables. Furthermore, if profit-maximizing behavior is to be tested, it should be formulated in a stochastic model that also allows for random variation. This is done with an errors-in-variables model.

Consider the following conceptual framework: what a firm does is determined by profit-maximization considerations plus an error term. In other words, the observed variables of capital, labor, and output each have two components: one, the systematic component, completely determined by *ex ante* profit maximization and expressed in the systems of equations 11 to 13 or 15 to 17; and another, the random component, which represents deviations from profit maximization. In other words, we define

$$\log K_i = X_{1i}{}^* = x_{1i} - u_{1i}$$
$$\log L_i = X_{2i}{}^* = x_{2i} - u_{2i}$$
$$\log V_i = Y_i{}^* = y_i - v_i \tag{18}$$
$$\log A_i{}' = Z_i$$

where $X_{1i}{}^*$, $X_{2i}{}^*$, and $Y_i{}^*$ are the systematic and unobserved components of log capital, log labor, and log output, respectively, x_{1i}, x_{2i}, and y_i are the observable actual amounts of inputs used and output produced (in the logs), while the error variables u_{1i}, u_{2i}, and v_i are the stochastic deviations from the profit-maximizing terms.

Assume that the errors in the inputs and output in the definitional equations 18 are due entirely to deviations from profit-maximizing behavior.[2] In this framework, a suitable index of economic rationality is the proportion of the variance (in the logs) of the (observed) quantities of a firm's inputs of labor and capital that is caused by the variation in the (unobserved) systematic profit-maximizing component of these inputs:

$$\frac{\text{var } X_{1i}{}^*}{\text{var } x_{1i}} = \frac{\text{var } X_{2i}{}^*}{\text{var } x_{2i}} = P \tag{19}$$

P is thus a measure of the extent to which the individual firm is successful in setting its inputs at the *ex ante* correct, that is, the profit-maximizing levels. We will show that this postulated relationship—that there is a uniform degree, P, to which each of the profit-maximizing input targets is actually achieved—enables us to identify and determine P from the simple correlation coefficient of equation

13 after it is transformed into an errors-in-variables equation. Similarly, the slope coefficients of the errors-in-variables regressions that correspond to equations 11 and 12 yield estimates of the elasticity of supply of capital and labor and are obtained by utilizing the ratio of the standard deviations of the observed variables (see below and also the appendix to this chapter).

With respect to the error terms in our variables, we assume

$$E(u_{1i}) = E(u_{2i}) = 0$$

that is, on the average, the values of the two inputs of production (in the logs) are the profit-maximizing values. This assumption, although usual, is not operationally necessary for the errors-in-variables model (Klein 1953, p. 285) and the more general alternative $E(u_{1i}) = $ constant and $E(u_{2i}) = $ constant is sufficient. In our case, however, the more general assumption would imply that the target is not profit maximization and thus would change the hypothesis. Therefore, zero expectation of the error terms of the inputs is the only assumption that is logically consistent with the model we use.

The assumption

$$\text{cov } (u_{1i}, Z_i) = \text{cov } (u_{2i}, Z_i) = 0$$

that is, uncorrelatedness of the errors in the inputs and the exogenous variable, is necessary for our estimates of both the slope parameters and P. Similarly, the assumption

$$\text{cov } (v_i, Z_i) = 0$$

is utilized in the estimation of the slope parameters.

The assumption

$$\text{cov } (u_{1i}, u_{2i}) = 0$$

that is, the errors in the capital and labor inputs are uncorrelated with one another, is used for the measure of P but is not required for the estimation of the slope parameters.[3]

---

[2]This is a strong assumption, for it ascribes to irrationality *all* deviations from *ex ante* profit maximization, including deviations that are due to measurement, errors in the model, and noise in the universe. To this extent, the index of economic rationality is an underestimate, that is, it describes the minimum degree to which the firm's behavior is consistent with *ex ante* profit-maximization considerations.

[3]The assumption cov $(u_{1i}, u_{2i}) = 0$ is crucial for estimating the index of economic rationality. Our estimate of P is an overestimate or an underestimate, depending on whether cov $(u_{1i}, u_{2i}) >$ or < 0. This crucial assumption, therefore, deserves further explanation. First, equation 19, on which this assumption is based, is usual and necessary in errors-in-variables models (Klein 1953, p. 290). In this sense, we *had* to make this assumption. Second, we also *wanted* to make the assumption. Since, in our model, capital and labor are under the control of the firm, there is no a priori reason to believe that a firm's ability to

The assumption

$$E(v_i) = 0$$

is not crucial for our statistical analysis. Instead, it is possible that $E(v_i) =$ constant, that is, there is a systematic bias in the efficiency parameter across firms.

By employing the definitions in equation 18, we rewrite the system of equations 11 through 13

$$y_i - v_i = a + \left(1 + \frac{1}{\eta}\right)(x_{1i} - u_{1i}) \qquad (11a)$$

$$y_i - v_i = b + \left(1 + \frac{1}{\varepsilon}\right)(x_{2i} - u_{2i}) \qquad (12a)$$

$$x_{1i} - u_{1i} = \frac{b - a}{\left(1 + \frac{1}{\eta}\right)} + \frac{\left(1 + \frac{1}{\varepsilon}\right)}{\left(1 + \frac{1}{\eta}\right)}(x_{2i} - u_{2i}) \qquad (13a)$$

Equations 11a–13a are cast in terms of observable variables and can be directly estimated.

Similarly, by employing the definitions in equation 18, we rewrite the system of equations 15–17

$$x_{1i} = \frac{g}{\left(1 + \frac{1}{\eta}\right)} Z_i + u_{1i} + \text{constant} = X_{1i}{}^* + u_{1i} \qquad (15a)$$

$$x_{2i} = \frac{g}{\left(1 + \frac{1}{\varepsilon}\right)} Z_i + u_{2i} + \text{constant} = X_{2i}{}^* + u_{2i} \qquad (16a)$$

$$y_i = g Z_i + v_i + \text{constant} = Y_i{}^* + v_i$$

From the specific property of the statistical model, equation 19, we have

$$\frac{\text{var } x_{1i}}{\text{var } x_{2i}} = \frac{\text{var } X_{1i}{}^*}{\text{var } X_{2i}{}^*}$$

and by substituting for the var $X_{1i}{}^*$ and $X_{2i}{}^*$ from equations 15a and 16a,

---

maximize with respect to labor is different from its ability to maximize with respect to capital. It is actually assuming, like the classical X^2 distribution, that the rifleman's N–S and E–W errors are independent. Third and last, although this assumption may be challenged on a priori grounds, its validity is empirically testable—and we tested for it. If we make the very strong statistical assumptions that var Y/var $y =$ var X_1/var $x_1 =$ var X_2/var x_2 and cov $(u_1, v) =$ cov $(u_2, v) =$ cov $(u_1, u_2) = 0$, the three separate product-moment coefficients of correlation among y, x_1, and x_2 all have the same value. This in fact is approximately satisfied by our results as revealed by the correlation matrix.

$$\text{var } X_{1i}{}^* = \frac{g^2}{\left(1 + \frac{1}{\eta}\right)^2} \text{ var } Z_i$$

$$\text{var } X_{2i}{}^* = \frac{g^2}{\left(1 + \frac{1}{\varepsilon}\right)^2} \text{ var } Z_i$$

we have

$$\frac{\text{var } x_{1i}}{\text{var } x_{2i}} = \frac{\left(1 + \frac{1}{\varepsilon}\right)^2}{\left(1 + \frac{1}{\eta}\right)^2}$$

or

$$\frac{\left(1 + \frac{1}{\varepsilon}\right)}{\left(1 + \frac{1}{\eta}\right)} = \left(\frac{\text{var } x_{1i}}{\text{var } x_{2i}}\right)^{1/2} \qquad (20)$$

Expression 20 is the diagonal regression coefficient relating x_{1i} and x_{2i}.

Furthermore, as shown in the appendix,

$$P = \rho_{x_{1i}, x_{2i}} \geqq 0$$

and it is the product-moment coefficient of correlation between x_{1i} and x_{2i}. We thus establish that the product-moment correlation coefficient gives an estimate of P, which is defined as the proportion of the variance of the log in both inputs due to variation in the systematic profit-maximizing component of the inputs.

Because of our use of the errors-in-variables model, the appropriate estimates of $1 + 1/\eta$, $1 + 1/\varepsilon$, and $(1 + 1/\varepsilon)/(1 + 1/\eta)$ —obtained from equations 11a, 12a, and 13a —are the diagonal regression estimates. Two alternative estimates of $1 + 1/\eta$ and $1 + 1/\varepsilon$ are: (1) the orthogonal regression on the assumption that var $u_{1i} =$ var $u_{2i} = 0$, which reduces to the ordinary least squares estimate of log output on log capital, and of log output on log labor, and yields $1 + 1/\eta$ and $1 + 1/\varepsilon$, respectively; and (2) on the alternative assumption that var $v_i = 0$, the instrumental variable estimate of log output on log capital and of log output on log labor, with output used as the instrumental variable, which also yield estimates of $1 + 1/\eta$ and $1 + 1/\varepsilon$, respectively. These two estimators, alternative to the diagonal regression estimate, provide the lower and upper bounds, respectively, for the values of $1 + 1/\eta$ and of $1 + 1/\varepsilon$. These alternative estimates are based on extreme assumptions, however, while the diagonal regression assumptions provide, at least a priori and within our model, the best first approximation of the slope coefficients.[4] As we will see, this is also confirmed by the results of our test.

An Empirical Application of the Test of Economic Rationality with Indian Data

We apply the test of economic rationality to data provided by the Farm Management Studies of the Indian Ministry of Food and Agriculture (1957–1962). The Studies report the data collected over a three-year period, 1955–1957, from cost-accounting records of 2,962 holdings in the six main agricultural regions of India.[5]

In this application we use the data on output, labor, and other costs that the Studies provide.[6] Output, V, is given in terms of revenue per farm in rupees. Labor, L, and other costs, K, are the variable factors of production. The former is expressed in terms of labor-days employed per farm. The latter includes all out-of-pocket costs, with the exception of wages paid to labor, rent of land, and interest imputed on own capital. In the specification of the two variable factors, therefore, land and fixed capital are subsumed in the intercept term and become part of the technical efficiency component.

We now turn to the interpretation of the results reported in Table 6.1. Suppose that firms operate under different price regimes and with differing endowments of fixed factors of production. How successful are firms in employing the maximizing rule of behavior once we control for these factors? We are therefore discussing the price-efficiency component of firms. This is given by P, the index of economic rationality. We note that the lowest value of P is 0.83 and does not vary

significantly between small and large farms. It means that at least 83 percent of the variance in the logs of both inputs is due to the variation in the systematic profit-maximizing component of these inputs. The balance of 17 percent is the maximum that can be attributed to "irrationality," because it reflects not only mistakes in maximization but also errors in the model and noise in the universe. The conclusion is that Indian farmers on farms of all sizes would seem to be remarkably price-efficient.

Another interesting aspect arises from the test of economic rationality. We have allowed for the fact that firms may operate within different price regimes. We can now check this assumption by referring to the estimated elasticity of supply of other costs and labor. The slope coefficients of log output on log other costs and log output on log labor, from the diagonal regression results presented in Table 6.1, differ from unity—the limiting value for perfect input markets. This difference, which is small enough to justify the assumption of relatively competitive markets,[7] suggests that interfirm differences in prices cannot be great and cannot account for much of the remaining interfirm variance in inputs used and outputs produced. This suggests that technical efficiency, the component that has been subsumed in the constant term in the present analysis, might assume a major role in explaining the differences in observed behavior among firms. The test of efficiency in the following section brings into play both components of economic efficiency and combines them for an overall comparison of economic efficiency.

A Test for Relative Efficiency

The minimum requirements for a useful concept of economic efficiency can now be restated:[8]

---

[4]The index P, being the product-moment coefficient of correlation between capital and labor, remains, of course, the same in all three alternative estimating procedures.

[5]For this analysis, we utilize data from the following states and years: West Bengal, Madras, Uttar Pradesh, Punjab, 1955–1956; Madhya Pradesh, 1956–1957. The latter is chosen because the 1955–1956 report of the Farm Management Studies for Madhya Pradesh does not contain information comparable with the others.

[6]Notice that the specification of variables here differs from that in the test of relative efficiency that follows. The reason is that, while for the rationality test we employ two variable factors, the profit function involves only one variable factor, labor, and two fixed, capital and land.

[7]The elasticity of supply of "other costs" and the elasticity of supply of labor are −16 and −1 respectively, both estimated for the whole sample. The "wrong" sign of the elasticity of supply should come as no surprise if one keeps in mind that these are "cross-section elasticities." It simply implies that the larger the firm, the lower the supply price of "other costs"—presumably for a number of reasons, including greater bargaining power and greater access to other input markets. This finding, together with the corroborating estimates of the elasticities of the two subsamples, indicates that as the size of the farm increases it is easier to expand output by substituting "other inputs" for labor.

[8]This section is a condensed version of Lau and Yotopoulos (1971).

Table 6.1 *Economic Rationality Coefficients and Related Statistics*

Relation Estimated	Quantity Estimated	Diagonal Regression Coefficients[a]		
		All Farms ($n = 34$)	Small Farms ($n = 16$)	Large Farms ($n = 18$)
1n Output, V on 1n Other Costs, K	$\left(1 + \dfrac{1}{\eta}\right)$	0.938 (0.026)	0.746 (0.044)	1.003 (0.039)
1n Output, V, on 1n Labor, L	$\left(1 + \dfrac{1}{\epsilon}\right)$	0.195 (0.017)	1.119 (0.001)	1.355 (0.040)
1n Other Costs, K on 1n Labor, L	$\dfrac{\left(1 + \dfrac{1}{\epsilon}\right)}{\left(1 + \dfrac{1}{\eta}\right)}$	1.274	1.502	1.351
ρ or P[b]		0.912	0.849	0.833
η		−16.1	−3.9	333.3
ϵ		−1.2	8.4	2.8

Notes: The estimating equations are 11 to 13 in the text, with the profit-maximizing variables transformed into observable ones in the errors-in-variables context of equations 11a to 13a in the text. The variables are defined as:

V is total output in rupees.

K is other costs, that is, total cash outlays, including depreciation of capital equipment, with the exclusion of outlays referring to labor and to land.

L is labor days.

η is the elasticity of supply of K.

ϵ is the elasticity of supply of L.

P is the index of economic rationality.

"1n" before a variable indicates natural logarithm of that variable.

[a]Estimated by using the property $\beta_{12} = \rho_{12}\,(\sigma_1/\sigma_2)$, where 1 and 2 are the dependent and the independent variable respectively, in the least squares regression. Since the diagonal regression coefficient is $\frac{\sigma_1}{\sigma_2}$ sign σ_{12}, it can be estimated by β_{12}/ρ_{12}. Standard errors (in parentheses) are first approximations of the standard errors obtained by assuming that var $(b/r) \simeq$ (var $b)/r^2$ for the diagonal regression. This implies that we are neglecting the terms involving cov (b, r) and var (r), which have opposite signs and which, therefore, tend to cancel out.

[b]The economic rationality index, P, is defined as the proportion of the variance of the log in both inputs, which is due to variation in the systematic profit-maximizing components of the inputs, that is, $P = (\text{var } X^*_1/\text{var } x_1) = (\text{var } X^*_2/\text{var } x_2)$. It is estimated by the product-moment coefficient of correlation between log other costs and log labor.

Source: India, Government of: Ministry of Food and Agriculture (1957–1962), *Studies in the Economics of Farm Management.* Delhi. Reports for the year 1955–1956: Madras, Punjab, Uttar Pradesh, West Bengal; Report for the year 1956–1957: Madhya Pradesh.

1. It should account for firms that produce different quantities of output from a given set of measured inputs of production. This is the component of differences in *technical efficiency.*
2. It should permit different firms to vary in their ability to maximize profits, that is, in equating the value of the marginal product of each variable factor of production to its price. This is the component of *price efficiency.*
3. It should account for the fact that firms may operate at different sets of market prices.

By using the profit function, we will encompass all these requirements into the single concept of economic efficiency.

Anticipating our argument, we shall find that the three elements can be combined in a profit function of the following form:

$$\Pi = A_* \prod_{j=1}^{m} q_j^{\alpha_j{}^*} \prod_{j=1}^{n} Z_j^{\beta_j{}^*} \tag{21}$$

where Π is profits, q_j is the real price of the jth variable factor of production (deflated by the price of output), Z_j is the quantity of the jth fixed factor of production, $\alpha_j{}^*$ and $\beta_j{}^*$ are the coefficients of prices of variable factors and quantities of fixed factors, respectively, and A_* is a constant. The justification for the use of the profit function can be explained in an intuitive way.

Profit is defined as

$$\Pi = V - \sum_{j=1}^{m} q_j X_j \tag{22}$$

where V is total value of output. Profit is the total value of output minus the total cost of the variable factors of production. It is equivalent to the "surplus" appropriated by the fixed factors of production.

We note the production function

$$V = pF(X_j, Z_j) \tag{23}$$

and the profit maximization condition

$$\frac{\partial F}{\partial X_j} = q_j \tag{24}$$

We can express the demand for variable input j of the maximizing firm as

$$X_j^* = f_j(q_j, Z_j) \tag{25}$$

where X_j^* denotes that this is the optimal quantity of factor j. Substituting equations 23 and 25 into equation 22, we can express profit as a function of the prices of the variable factors of production and the quantities of the fixed factors of production. It follows that two identical firms (to be defined later as firms of equal technical efficiency and equal price efficiency) that have successfully maximized profits would still have different values of profits as long as they faced different prices. This accounts for element 3 in the list of requirements.

Still we have not mentioned elements 1, technical efficiency, and 2, price efficiency. Consider two groups of firms with production functions identical up to a neutral displacement parameter. We can rewrite equation 23, with superscripts 1 and 2 identifying the firm group by number,

$$V^1 = pA^1F(X_j, Z_j); \quad V^2 = pA^2F(X_j, Z_j) \tag{26}$$

where A is the group-specific technical efficiency parameter. Firm group 1 would be considered more technical-efficient than firm group 2, that is, $A^1 > A^2$ if, given the same quantities of measurable inputs, it consistently produces a larger output. We have thus introduced element 1 from the above list of requirements.

We now introduce price efficiency. We have seen that a firm is price-efficient if it maximizes profits, that is, if it equates the value of the marginal product of each variable input to its price. Consider two complications in the definition of price efficiency. First, assume that the prices of inputs are different for each firm, so that price-efficient firms equate the value of the marginal product of each factor to its firm-specific opportunity cost. Second, assume that firms may not maximize profits. For such firms, the usual marginal conditions do not hold; it is assumed that they equate the value of the marginal product of each factor to a constant (which may be firm- and factor-specific) proportion, k, of the respective firm-specific factor prices. For firm groups 1 and 2, this can be expressed as

$$p \frac{\partial A^1 F(X_j, Z_j)}{\partial X_j} = k_j^1 q_j \quad p \frac{\partial A^2 F(X_j, Z_j)}{\partial X_j} = k_j^2 q_j \tag{27}$$

In this case, k_j^1 indexes the decision rule that describes the firm's "profit-maximizing" behavior with respect to variable factor j. It encompasses perfect profit maximization as a special case when $k_j = 1$ for all j. In a set of price-inefficient firms of equal technical efficiency and facing identical output and input prices, the firm with the higher profits within a certain range of prices is considered the relatively more price-efficient firm (within that range of prices).

We return now to the profit function of equation 21. The A_* constant encompasses the group-specific factors of technical efficiency, A^1 and A^2, and price efficiency, k_j^1 and k_j^2, in the comparison of the two groups of firms, 1 and 2.

First, we develop the concept of the profit function (Shephard 1953; McFadden 1970) in its general form, but without the components of technical and price efficiency. Next, we introduce the group-specific technical-efficiency parameter and the group- and input-specific price-efficiency parameter. The combination of the two defines the group-specific economic efficiency, relative to another group of firms. The concept becomes operational by casting it in the framework of the Cobb-Douglas production function. Finally, we apply it to Indian agricultural data again obtained from the Farm Management Studies of the Ministry of Food and Agriculture.

The Profit Function
Consider a firm with a production function with the usual neoclassical properties

$$V = F(X_1, \ldots, X_m; Z_1, \ldots, Z_n) \qquad (28)$$

where V is output, $\mathbf{X}$ represents variable inputs, and $\mathbf{Z}$ represents fixed inputs of production. Profit (defined as current revenues less current total variable costs) can be written

$$P' = pF(X_1, \ldots, X_m; Z_1, \ldots, Z_n)$$
$$- \sum_{j=1}^{m} q_j' X_j \qquad (29)$$

where P' is profit, p is the unit price of output, and q_j' is the unit price of the jth variable input. The fixed costs are ignored, since, as is well known, they do not affect the optimal combination of the variable inputs.

Assume that a firm maximizes profits given the levels of its technical efficiency and fixed inputs. The marginal productivity conditions for such a firm are

$$p \frac{\partial F(X; Z)}{\partial X_j} = q_j' \qquad j = 1, \ldots, m \qquad (30)$$

By using the price of output as the numeraire, we may define $q_j \equiv q_j'/p$ as the normalized price of the jth input. We can then rewrite equation 30 as

$$\frac{\partial F}{\partial X_j} = q_j \qquad j = 1, \ldots, m \qquad (31)$$

By similar deflation by the price of output and defining P as the *normalized restricted profit*[9], we can rewrite equation 29 as

$$P = \frac{P'}{p} = F(X_1, \ldots, X_m; Z_1, \ldots, Z_n)$$
$$- \sum_{j=1}^{m} q_j X_j \qquad (32)$$

Equation 31 may be solved for the optimal quantities of variable inputs, denoted X_j^*'s, as functions of the normalized prices of the variable inputs, and of the quantities of the fixed inputs,[10]

$$X_j^* = f_j(\mathbf{q}, \mathbf{Z}) \qquad j = 1, \ldots, m \qquad (33)$$

where $\mathbf{q}$ and $\mathbf{Z}$ are the vectors of normalized input prices and quantities of fixed inputs, respectively.

By substitution of equation 33 into equation 29, we obtain the *normalized restricted profit function*.[11]

$$\Pi' = p\left[F(X_1^*, \ldots, X_m^*; Z_1, \ldots, Z_n) \right.$$
$$\left. - \sum_{j=1}^{m} q_j X_j^* \right]$$
$$= G(p, q_1', \ldots, q_m'; Z_1, \ldots, Z_n) \qquad (34)$$

The profit function gives the *maximized* value of the profit for each set of values $(p; q_1', \ldots, q_m'; Z_1, \ldots, Z_n)$. Observe that the term within square brackets on the right-hand side of equation 34 is a function only of $\mathbf{q}$ and $\mathbf{Z}$. Hence, using p as a numeraire, as above, we can write the normalized restricted profit function as

$$\Pi = G^*(q_1, \ldots, qm; Z_1, \ldots, Z_n) \qquad (35)$$

We have thus expressed profit as a function of the prices of the variable factors of production and the quantities of the fixed factors of production. We were led to this transformation by utilizing the profit-maximization condition of equation 30, which defined the demand curve of each variable factor of the maximizing firm as a function of the prices of the variable factors and the quantities of the fixed factors, as in equation 33.

We may at this point introduce, without proof, a set of dual transformation relations that connect the profit function and the production function.[12] In terms of the profit function, the demand curve for a variable factor of production that was given in equation 33 is written

$$X_j^* = \frac{-\partial \Pi (\mathbf{q}, \mathbf{Z})}{\partial q_j} \qquad j = 1, \ldots, m \qquad (36)$$

This implies that profit is decreasing and convex in the prices of the variable inputs.

We can solve equation 34, which expresses profit in terms of the production function and the cost of the variable factors of production, for output. Then by substituting equation 36 into it, we can solve for the quantities of the variable factors of production, yielding the output supply function

---

[9]The terminology follows Jorgenson and Lau (1974). It is sometimes referred to as the unit-output-price (UOP) profit.

[10]To simplify notation, we will occasionally omit the subscripts. Thus, the unsubscripted variables $\mathbf{X}$, $\mathbf{Z}$, $\mathbf{q'}$, $\mathbf{q}$, $\mathbf{X^t}$, $\mathbf{Z^t}$, $\mathbf{q^t}$, and $\mathbf{k^t}$ are used to denote vectors. Superscripts, as above, denote groups of firms.

[11]One should be careful to distinguish between profit, as defined in equation 29, and the profit function, in equation 34.

[12]These relations are given and proven in McFadden (1970) and Lau (1969).

$$V^* = \Pi\,(\mathbf{q}, \mathbf{Z}) - \sum_{j=1}^{m} \frac{\partial \Pi(\mathbf{q}, \mathbf{Z})}{\partial q_j}\, q_j \qquad (37)$$

There are a number of advantages in working with the profit function of equation 35 instead of the production function of equation 30 (Lau and Yotopoulos 1971). We note here only one. The profit function, the supply function, and the derived demand functions we obtained are functions only of the normalized input prices and the quantities of fixed inputs, variables normally considered to be determined independently of the firm's behavior. Since these variables are exogenous, by estimating these functions we avoid the problem of simultaneous equations bias that arises in single-equation estimation of the production function, because the quantities of the variable factors that constitute the independent variables are not truly exogenous, as indicated by the conditions of profit maximization.

Relative Economic Efficiency

The discussion of the profit function in the preceding section is general. It does not consider possible differences in technical efficiency and price efficiency between groups of firms. Following the intuitive exposition above, in this section we introduce such differences and combine them in the concept of relative economic efficiency.

Our approach is straightforward. Given comparable endowments, identical technology, and normalized input prices, the normalized restricted profits of two firms should be identical if they have both maximized profits. To the extent that one firm is more price-efficient or more technical-efficient than the other, the normalized restricted profits will differ even for the same normalized input prices and endowments of fixed inputs.

Let us represent the situation as follows. For each of two groups of firms, the production function is given by

$$V^1 = A^1 F(\mathbf{X}^1, \mathbf{Z}^1);\; V^2 = A^2 F(\mathbf{X}^2, \mathbf{Z}^2) \qquad (38)$$

where superscripts identify groups of firms. The marginal conditions are given by

$$\frac{\partial A^1 F(\mathbf{X}^1, \mathbf{Z}^1)}{\partial \mathbf{X}^1} = k_j{}^1 q_j{}^1$$

$$\frac{\partial A^2 F(\mathbf{X}^2, \mathbf{Z}^2)}{\partial \mathbf{X}^2} = k_j{}^2 q_j{}^2$$

$$k_j{}^1 \geqq 0 \qquad k_j{}^2 \geqq 0 \qquad j = 1, \ldots, m \qquad (39)$$

At this point, it is useful to reiterate the basic differences in approach that equations 38 and 39 introduce, as compared to the presentation in the previous section. The previous formulation was general, as deduced from firm-specific variables, such as the level of profits for each firm, the prices a firm pays for each variable factor of production it employs, the quantity of the variable factors it hires. In this section, the formulation becomes group-specific. In the concept of relative efficiency, we compare two or more groups of firms on the basis of two rules of reference. First, we allow for neutral differences in the production functions in terms of the group-specific technical efficiency parameters, A^1 and A^2. They represent differences in environmental factors, managerial ability, and other nonmeasurable fixed factors of production. If two groups of firms are equally technical-efficient, then $A^1 = A^2$. Second, we allow the groups of firms to vary in terms of price efficiency, that is, in the degree to which they are successful in equating values of marginal products to the firm-specific factor prices, through the introduction of the group-specific and variable-input-specific k's.[13] If, and only if, two groups are equally price-efficient with respect to all variable inputs, then $k_j{}^1 = k_j{}^2$, $j = 1, \ldots, m$.[14] We have defined economic efficiency to encompass both technical and price efficiency. In terms of our notation, therefore, the null hypothesis of equal relative economic efficiency for group 1 and group 2 implies that $A^1 = A^2$ and $\mathbf{k}^1 = \mathbf{k}^2$. In this section, we develop a method that enables us to make this comparison.

Equations 38 and 39, which represent the technical- and price-efficiency components respectively, must be introduced in the general form of the profit function in equation 35. This is detailed in two steps. First, we write

---

[13]Of course, if a firm is perfectly successful in equalizing the normalized price of an input i to its opportunity cost, k_i assumes the value of one for that specific input.

[14]The price behavior specified by equation 39 can be rationalized in different ways for the case that $k \neq 1$. It may be that firms make decisions on the basis of expected prices, which deviate from actual prices; and/or firms may considerably overvalue or undervalue the opportunity cost of some of their resources. The hypothesis of disguised unemployment implies, for example, consistent undervaluation of the opportunity cost of labor. In terms of the discussion of economic rationality above, a decision rule, $k \neq 1$, implies that, although firms do not act randomly, they do not maximize profits either.

the profit function that corresponds to the production function in equation 38. Second, observe that the right-hand side of equation 39 may be interpreted as the "effective" prices facing the two groups of firms. Then we need to introduce these "effective" prices into the profit function. We may call the result the "*behavioral* normalized restricted profit function," since it represents profit maximization subject to the "effective" prices, in other words, imperfect profit maximization. We write the "behavioral" profit function for the two groups of firms[15]

$$\Pi_b{}^1 = A^1 G^* \left(\frac{k_1{}^1 q_1{}^1}{A^1}, \ldots, \frac{k_m{}^1 q_m{}^1}{A^1} ; Z_1{}^1, \ldots, Z_n{}^1 \right)$$

$$\Pi_b{}^2 = A^2 G^* \left(\frac{k_1{}^2 q_1{}^2}{A^2}, \ldots, \frac{k_m{}^2 q_m{}^2}{A^2} ; Z_1{}^2, \ldots, Z_n{}^2 \right)$$

(40)

Differentiating equation 40 with respect to the "effective" prices $k_j{}^i q_j{}^i$ (for $i = 1, 2$, the two groups of firms), we write the input demand function corresponding to equation 36

$$X_j{}^i = -A^i \frac{\partial G^* \left(\frac{k^i q^i}{A^i} ; Z^i \right)}{\partial k_j{}^i q_j{}^i}$$

$$= \frac{-A^i}{k_j{}^i} \frac{\partial G^* \left(\frac{k^i q^i}{A^i} ; Z^i \right)}{\partial q_j{}^i}$$

(41)

where

$i = 1, 2$ group of firms

$j = 1, \ldots, m$ variable inputs.

By correspondence from equation 37, the supply function is given by

$$V' = A^i G^* \left(\frac{k^i q^i}{A^i} ; Z^i \right)$$

$$- A^i \sum_{j=1}^{m} k_j{}^i q_j{}^i \frac{\partial G^* \left(\frac{k^i q^i}{A^i} ; Z^i \right)}{\partial k_j{}^i q_j{}^i}$$

$$= A^i G^* \left(\frac{k^i q^i}{A^i} ; Z^i \right)$$

$$- A^i \sum_{j=1}^{m} q_j{}^i \frac{\partial G^* \left(\frac{k^i q^i}{A^i} ; Z^i \right)}{\partial q_j{}^i}$$

(42)

where

$i = 1, 2$ group of forms

$j = 1, \ldots, m$ variable inputs.

[15]For details, see Lau and Yotopoulos (1971).

It should be emphasized at this point that $X_j{}^i$ and V^i, as given in equations 41 and 42, are the actual quantities of inputs demanded and output supplied by firm i given the firm-specific A^i and $\mathbf{k}^i$. When appropriate functional forms are specified for G^*, statistical tests can be devised to test the null hypothesis of equal economic efficiency, that is, $A^1 = A^2$ and $\mathbf{k}^1 = \mathbf{k}^2$.

The behavioral profit function focuses on the demand and supply functions and asks whether or not a firm behaves as if it equated marginal products to effective prices. An alternative approach to looking at the demand and supply functions is to examine the "*actual* normalized restricted profit function." It consists of looking at actual profits, that is, value of output minus the total cost of the variable factors. Solving equation 37 for Π and substituting from equations 41 and 42, we obtain the "actual" profit function

$$\Pi_a{}^i = V^i - \sum_{j=1}^{m} q_j{}^i X_j{}^i$$

$$= A^i G^* \left(\frac{k^i \mathbf{q}^i}{A^i} ; \mathbf{Z}^i \right)$$

$$+ A^i \sum_{j=1}^{m} \frac{(1 - k_j{}^i) q_j{}^i}{k_j{}^i} \cdot \frac{\partial G^* \left(\frac{k^i \mathbf{q}^i}{A^i} ; \mathbf{Z}^i \right)}{\partial q_j{}^i}$$

(43)

where $i = 1, 2$ group of firms.

Notice that equation 43 involves two types of variables. The group-specific variables are A^i and $\mathbf{k}^i$. The firm-specific variables are q_j and Z_j. Once we control for the observable variables q_j and Z_j, the actual profit function of the two groups is different only to the extent that $\mathbf{k}^1 \neq \mathbf{k}^2$ and/or $A^1 \neq A^2$. Therefore, one can also test the null hypothesis of equal relative economic efficiency by comparing the actual profit functions of the two groups when appropriate forms are specified for G^*. This is the approach that will be employed in our empirical analysis.

An additional test becomes relevant if we reject the joint hypothesis that $(A^1, \mathbf{k}^1) = (A^2, \mathbf{k}^2)$. In this case, an overall indication of the relative efficiency between the two firms within a specified range of normalized prices for variable inputs can be obtained by comparing the actual values of the normalized restricted profit functions within this range. If

$$\Pi_a{}^1 \geqq \Pi_a{}^2$$

for all normalized prices within a specified range, clearly the first firm is relatively more efficient within the range of prices than the second.

The Formulation of the Cobb-Douglas Case

In this section, we specify the appropriate mathematical form of the profit function and empirically formulate the test of relative economic efficiency. It simplifies matters if we again employ the C-D form for the production function.

A C-D production function in m variable inputs and with n fixed inputs is written

$$V = A\left(\prod_{j=1}^{m} X_j^{\alpha_j}\right)\left(\prod_{j=1}^{n} Z_j^{\beta_j}\right)$$

where the sum of the coefficients, α_j, is restricted to less than one, indicating decreasing returns to the variable factors,[16]

$$\mu = \sum_{j=1}^{m} \alpha_j < 1$$

The normalized restricted profit function is given by

$$\Pi^* = A^{(1-\mu)-1}(1-\mu)\left(\prod_{j=1}^{m} \left(\frac{q_j}{\alpha_j}\right)^{-\alpha_j(1-\mu)-1}\right)$$
$$\left(\prod_{j=1}^{n} Z_j^{\beta_j(1-\mu)-1}\right) \tag{44}$$

By direct substitution of the production function and of equation 44 into equation 37, the actual profit function is given by

$$\Pi_a^i = (A^i)^{(1-\mu)-1}\left(1 - \sum_{j=1}^{m} \frac{\alpha_j}{k_j^i}\right)$$
$$\left(\prod_{j=1}^{m} (k_j^i)^{-\alpha_j(1-\mu)-1}\right)$$
$$\left(\prod_{j=1}^{m} \alpha_j^{-\alpha_j(1-\mu)-1}\right)$$
$$\left(\prod_{j=1}^{m} (q_j^i)^{-\alpha_j(1-\mu)-1}\right)$$
$$\left(\prod_{j=1}^{n} (Z_j^i)^{\beta_j(1-\mu)-1}\right) \tag{45}$$

Observe that the terms in the first three brackets of equation 45 involve two types of variables: one is the coefficients of the production function, α and μ, which *ex hypothesi*

[16]The value of $\mu < 1$ is required, since constant or increasing returns in the variable inputs are inconsistent with profit maximization.

are constant for the overall group of observations; another type is group-specific variables, A and $\mathbf{k}$. On the other hand, the two last terms in brackets of equation 45 involve firm-specific variables, $\mathbf{q}$ and $\mathbf{Z}$. It should now become clear where the search for efficiency is leading us: since all the terms up through the third set of brackets consist solely of overall constants and the group-specific k's and A's, the variation observed in these terms in a fitted relationship can be assigned to variations in A and $\mathbf{k}$ between groups. An analysis of variance approach for these three terms becomes relevant.

Define the three first terms in equation 45 as

$$A_*^i \equiv (A^i)^{(1-\mu)-1}\left(1 - \sum_{j=1}^{m} \frac{\alpha_j}{k_j^i}\right)$$
$$\left(\prod_{j=1}^{m} (k_j^i)^{-\alpha_j(1-\mu)-1}\right)$$
$$\left(\prod_{j=1}^{m} \alpha_j^{-\alpha_j(1-\mu)-1}\right) \tag{46}$$

Then equation 45 is written

$$\Pi_a^i = (A_*^i)\left(\prod_{j=1}^{m} (q_j^i)^{-\alpha_j(1-\mu)-1}\right)$$
$$\left(\prod_{j=1}^{n} (Z_j^i)^{\beta_j(1-\mu)-1}\right) \tag{47}$$

By writing A_*^2 and A_*^1 for groups 2 and 1 respectively, and taking the ratio of the constant terms, we have

$$\frac{A_*^2}{A_*^1} = \left(\frac{A^2}{A^1}\right)^{(1-\mu)-1} \frac{\left(1 - \sum_{j=1}^{m} \frac{\alpha_j}{k_j^2}\right)}{\left(1 - \sum_{j=1}^{m} \frac{\alpha_j}{k_j^1}\right)}$$
$$\left(\prod_{j=1}^{m} \left(\frac{k_j^2}{k_j^1}\right)^{-\alpha_j(1-\mu)-1}\right) \tag{48}$$

Thus, one may write, from equation 45,

$$\Pi_a^1 = A_*^1\left(\prod_{j=1}^{m} (q_j^1)^{-\alpha_j(1-\mu)-1}\right)$$
$$\left(\prod_{j=1}^{n} (Z_j^1)^{\beta_j(1-\mu)-1}\right) \tag{49}$$

$$\Pi_a^2 = A_*^1\left(\frac{A_*^2}{A_*^1}\right)\left(\prod_{j=1}^{m} (q_j^2)^{-\alpha_j(1-\mu)-1}\right)$$
$$\left(\prod_{j=1}^{n} (Z_j^2)^{\beta_j(1-\mu)-1}\right) \tag{50}$$

Further defining

$$\alpha_j{}^* \equiv -\alpha_j(1-\mu)^{-1} \qquad (51)$$

and

$$\beta_j{}^* \equiv \beta_j(1-\mu)^{-1} \qquad (52)$$

and taking natural logarithms of equations 49 and 50, we have

$$\ln \Pi_a{}^1 = \ln A_*{}^1 + \sum_{j=1}^{m} \alpha_j{}^* \ln q_j{}^1$$
$$+ \sum_{j=1}^{n} \beta_j{}^* \ln Z_j{}^1 \qquad (53)$$

$$\ln \Pi_a{}^2 = \ln A_*{}^1 + \ln \frac{A_*{}^2}{A_*{}^1} + \sum_{j=1}^{m} \alpha_j \ln q_j{}^2$$
$$+ \sum_{j=1}^{n} \beta_j{}^* \ln Z_j{}^2 \qquad (54)$$

We note that if $A^1 = A^2$ and $\mathbf{k}^1 = \mathbf{k}^2$, then $A_*{}^1 = A_*{}^2$, and thus the two functions $\Pi_a{}^1$ and $\Pi_a{}^2$ (ln $\Pi_a{}^1$ and ln $\Pi_a{}^2$) should be identical. This implies that ln $(A_*{}^2/A_*{}^1) = 0$. We can therefore test the equal relative efficiency hypothesis by utilizing a firm dummy variable in the logarithmic normalized restricted profit function and examining whether its value is equal to zero.[17]

An Empirical Application of the Test of Relative Economic Efficiency with Indian Data

We have utilized the same data for India that we used in the previous section in our test of economic rationality. Output, V, is given in terms of revenue per farm in rupees, land, T, represents cultivable land per farm in acres, and capital, K, is defined in terms of interest charges paid or imputed on the quantity of fixed capital per farm.[18] Labor is given in

terms of labor days employed per farm as well as in terms of a labor cost per farm concept (cost of hired labor plus imputed cost of family labor). By dividing the latter labor concept through by the former, we define the money wage rate per day, q_L. Only three inputs are distinguished: labor, capital, and land. We treat labor as the variable input of production, and land and capital as fixed inputs. Finally, from the revenue, we subtract the total cost of variable inputs per farm (the wage bill) in order to define profit variable, Π.[19]

For the Cobb-Douglas case, the logarithmic profit function is given by equations 53 and 54

$$\ln \Pi_a{}^1 = \ln A_*{}^1 + \alpha_1{}^* \ln q_L + \beta_1{}^* \ln K$$
$$+ \beta_2{}^* \ln T \qquad (55)$$

$$\ln \Pi_a{}^2 = \ln A_*{}^1 + \ln \left(\frac{A_*{}^2}{A_*{}^1}\right) + \alpha_1{}^* \ln q_L$$
$$+ \beta_1{}^* \ln K + \beta_2{}^* \ln T \qquad (56)$$

where $\Pi_a{}^1$ and $\Pi_a{}^2$ are actual normalized restricted profit (total revenue less total variable cost, divided by the price of output), q_L is "normalized" wage rate, K is interest on fixed capital, and T is cultivable land. A maintained hypothesis is that the production function is identical on large and small farms up to a neutral efficiency parameter. This implies that the coefficients corresponding to ln q_L, ln K, and ln T are identical for large and small farms. In our stochastic specification, we assume that the error in the profits is caused by climatic variations, divergence of the expected output price from the realized output price, and imperfect knowledge of the technical efficiency parameter of the farm. The demand functions are exact, or in any case, if they are subject to error, the errors are uncorrelated with the profit function. Hence, one can estimate the profit function alone with the least squares estimator, which in this case turns out to be minimum variance, linear and unbiased.

---

[17]Notice that in our presentation so far it is impossible to identify separately the effect of technical efficiency, A, and price efficiency, $\mathbf{k}$. Only their combined effect, in terms of economic efficiency, is captured by our analysis. The two components of economic efficiency constitute two unknowns, and in order to separate them, we need two independent equations. This becomes feasible if we use equation 43 with equation 41. This method was developed and applied in Yotopoulos and Lau (1973).

[18]This definition of the capital concept is especially disturbing. Since the interest rate used in the imputation (3 percent) is uniform throughout the states and the years, the true quantity of fixed capital will be proportional to our measure. This implicitly assumes that the flow of capital services as a ratio of the stock of capital is constant across farms. Such

assumptions, as demonstrated by Yotopoulos (1967a, b), may lead to unreliable estimates of the coefficient of capital in a production function formulation. This may be the case with our estimated capital coefficient.

[19]Π and q_L, it may be recalled, enter the function in real terms. Unavailability of prices of output to be used as deflators posed a problem with the data. It was handled through state dummy variables, a detail that we will omit in this presentation. See Lau and Yotopoulos (1971, pp. 103–104) for specifics.

Table 6.2 *Cobb-Douglas Profit Function and Related Statistics*

Parameter Estimated	All Farms $(n = 34)$
α_0	4.582
	(0.548)
S	−0.567
	(−0.253)
D_1	1.614*
	(0.549)
D_2	−1.359*
	(−1.274)
D_3	−0.588*
	(−0.485)
D_4	0.296
	(0.715)
α_1*	−2.141**
	(−1.200)
β_1*	−0.588
	(−0.274)
β_2*	1.797
	(0.233)
σ_2	0.185
$\overline{R}^2$	0.896
F-Statistic	36.4

Notes: The estimating equation is

$$\ln \Pi = \alpha_0 + S + \sum_{i=1}^{4} D_i + \alpha_1{}^* \ln q_L + \beta_1{}^* \ln K + \beta_2{}^* \ln T$$

The variables are defined as:

Π is ln of profit, that is, total revenue less total variable costs.

S is dummy variable for farm size, with value of one for large farms (greater than 10 acres) and zero for small farms (less than 10 acres).

D_1 is regional dummy variable, with D_1, D_2, D_3, D_4 taking the value of one for West Bengal, Madras, Madhya Pradesh, and Uttar Pradesh, and zero elsewhere, respectively. The purpose of the dummy variable is to express the money variables in real terms.

q_L is ln of wage rate.

K is ln of interest on fixed capital.

T is ln of cultivable land in acres.

* Starred coefficients are not significantly different from zero at a probability level $\geq$ 95 percent.

** Double-starred coefficients are significantly different from zero at a probability level $\geq$ 95 percent, but they are significantly different from zero at a probability level $\geq$ 90 percent. All other coefficients are significantly different from zero at a probability level $\geq$ 95 percent.

Two-tail test applies to the dummy variables; one-tail test to all other variables.

The standard error of the estimated parameters are given in parentheses.

Source: Lau, L. J., and P. A. Yotopoulos (1971), "A Test for Relative Efficiency and Application to Indian Agriculture," *A.E.R.*, 61 (March), p. 105.

The results of the estimation are presented in Table 6.2. The F-value indicates that the hypothesis stating that all coefficients (except α_0) are equal to zero should be rejected. As expected, the coefficient of the wage rate is negative, while the coefficient of land is positive. The negative coefficient of capital can only be attributed to the misspecification of this variable caused by the implicit assumption of proportionality between capital service flow and capital stock (Yotopoulos 1967a, b).

As we have indicated in the previous section, the hypothesis of relative efficiency can be cast in terms of the constant by which the two profit functions, one for small and one for large farms, differ. The null hypothesis is that this constant factor is equal to one. Furthermore, if one takes natural logarithms before estimating the profit function, the constant term becomes the coefficient of a dummy variable that differentiates the two groups of farms, and the test becomes one of determining whether or not the coefficient of the dummy variable is significantly different from zero. Our results, therefore, reject the hypothesis of equal efficiency between the two groups. Furthermore, the sign of the dummy variable indicates that small farms are more profitable, that is, more efficient, at all observed prices of the variable input, given the distribution of the fixed factors of production.

Policy Implications from the Study of Relative Economic Efficiency

A crucial feature of the profit function analysis is that it assumes firms behave according to certain decision rules, which include the profit-maximization rules, given the price regime for output and variable inputs and given the quantities of their fixed factors of production. In our analysis, the existence of these systematic decision rules is a maintained hypothesis. As noted in the previous section, however, large and small Indian farms were alike in their remarkable ability to adhere to such roles, that is, they were equally price-efficient.

Since the conclusion of the test of relative economic efficiency is in favor of the small farms (less than 10 acres) and yet no significant differences were observed in price efficiency between groups, the overall advantage of the small farms must be attributed to their greater technical efficiency.

This conclusion can be validated if, instead of using equations 53 and 54, in which it is impossible to identify separately the components of technical and price efficiency, we estimate the simultaneous restricted equations 41 and 43. In this way, the two unknowns subsumed under A_*, technical efficiency, A, and price efficiency, $\mathbf{k}$, can be directly compared. This approach was followed in Yotopoulos and Lau (1973) and served to confirm our tentative conclusion that large farms are as price-efficient, but not as technical-efficient, as small farms.

This result, though tentative, merits further consideration. Equal relative price efficiency might suggest that, after all, small and large farm operators alike can habitually and easily perform marginal calculations (Machlup 1946). The result of technical efficiency can be analyzed if one first examines what is missing from the specification of the factors of production and is thus incorporated in the A term. The functional form is misspecified to the extent that it does not account for nonmeasurable factors of production and for quality differences in the inputs measured. Entrepreneurship and diligence, as well as the quality of the labor force, are largely ignored in the production function formulation. Could this be precisely where the superior technical efficiency performance of the small farms rests? Could the supervisory role of the owner-manager and the superior labor inputs of diligent and motivated family members be instrumental in explaining the higher levels of economic efficiency attained by small-scale agriculture?

Some evidence from subsequent Indian data is not inconsistent with affirmative answers to such queries. For example, Sidhu (1974) studied three samples of wheat-producing farms in Punjab, covering the years 1967–1968, 1968–1969, and 1970–1971: one sample covering 150 farms in Ferozepur, another covering 128 farms in three different agroclimatic regions, and a third consisting of 304 farms in the "tractor cultivation sample." He distinguished between small (less than 10 acres) and large farms and between tractor-mechanized and non-tractor-mechanized farms. He performed the Lau-Yotopoulos test of relative economic efficiency and also tested the null hypothesis, in which the price and technical efficiency components are not significantly different between groups. The results indicate that small and large farms, as well as tractor-mechanized and non-tractor-mechanized farms, display no significant differences in relative economic efficiency, nor in price efficiency or technical efficiency components. While at first sight these findings seem inconsistent with the Yotopoulos-Lau results, Sidhu suggested an explanation for the differences that would seem plausible. Between the time period to which our sample pertained, that is, the mid-1950s, and that of the Punjab sample utilized by Sidhu, that is 1967–1968 to 1970–1971, Punjab agriculture had been modernized, relying on new varieties of seeds, fertilizers, and other chemical inputs, and on irrigation. Since these modern inputs became available sooner and more fully to large farms than to small farms, large farms were able to catch up with small farms in terms of technical efficiency.

The lack of significant differences in technical efficiency in the current period as between tractor-mechanized and non-tractor-mechanized farms is even more disturbing, especially considering the tremendous subsidies that have been offered for tractor mechanization by many LDC governments. These policies have been achieved only at very high cost in terms of foreign exchange, substantial distortion of the relative prices of capital and labor (B. F. Johnston and Cownie 1969), reduced opportunities for employment, and greater income inequality. If, as suggested by the results cited above, no increase in total output can be credited against these costs as a result of tractor mechanization, the termination of such programs should be given serious consideration.

Summary and Conclusions

We concluded in Chapter 5 that the production function is the proper tool for measuring differences in efficiency that arise from differential endowments of the fixed factors of production which are not under the short-run control of the entrepreneur, that is, for measuring differences in technical efficiency. Should firms also face different prices for the variable factors of production, however, or should they fail to maximize profits perfectly, the production function is no longer a satisfactory tool for the study of efficiency. This chapter has attempted to fill the gap by forging new tools for the study of economic efficiency and by applying them to data from Indian agriculture.

Our test of economic rationality has addressed two questions: First, to what extent do differences in the price regimes that different firms face explain differences in observable behavior as expressed in different output-input and input-input ratios? A by-product of investigating this question is the estimation of input-supply elasticities for a sample of Indian farms. The large farms in the sample were found to face a perfectly elastic supply of "other costs" but a supply of labor that is much less elastic than that of the small farms, which generally have large numbers of family members whose opportunity cost is low. The elasticity of the supply of other costs to the small farms was found to be negative, suggesting that the smaller the farmer, the more he must pay for his purchased inputs. This finding has important implications for employment and mechanization policies for agriculture.

The second question addressed by the test of economic rationality is how closely do farmers in their behavior approximate the rules of profit maximization, and how important are the mistakes in maximization? The test has confirmed the rationality of traditional farmers—an issue that was much discussed a short time ago. However, mistakes in profit maximization may account for up to one-fifth of the observed interfirm differences in factor and output ratios. Therefore, even though farmers strive to maximize profits, mistakes in profit maximization should be explicitly incorporated in the model.

Our test of relative efficiency has been built on the knowledge gained from performing the test for economic rationality. It allowed for interfirm differences in technical efficiency, it allowed for mistakes in maximization (differences in price efficiency), and it allowed for imperfect markets by entering the prices of output and of the variable factors directly into the functional form as exogenous variables. Relative economic efficiency among firms was thus measured by combining the components of technical and price efficiency. The startling conclusion reached from applying this test to Indian data is that small farms are more efficient than large farms. Should this conclusion be buttressed by other studies, it might well turn out that the land reform issue, which is usually posed as a dilemma: "equity versus productivity," is not a dilemma after all. Reform may achieve both equity and productivity. Even more surprisingly, when the test was extended by decomposing economic efficiency into its technical and price efficiency components, it was found that while small and large farms alike are equally price-efficient, the former are superior from the point of view of technical efficiency (except when large farms are favored by the availability of new and superior technology). Within our framework, differences in technical efficiency are attributed to the use of differential quantities of fixed factors of production, including such nonmeasurable factors as diligence, motivation, or entrepreneurship. We thus suggest the probative hypothesis that the difference may lie in the superior quality or intensity of labor used by small owner-operated farms. Should this turn out to be correct, the appeal of small-size agriculture might ultimately rest not only on output but also on employment considerations. At the present state of knowledge, however, these hypotheses must be considered tentative and speculative. The tools for their further investigation, nevertheless, have been developed fully in this chapter.

The introduction of the profit function allows us to take a more sanguine view of the production function. Its analytical power is severely circumscribed by its inherent assumptions. Consider the interpretation of the elasticities of production. They measure the response of output to a change in the quantity of one factor, holding the quantities of all other factors of production constant. This constitutes a contradiction in terms. A given increase in the quantity of land will shift upward the marginal productivity curve of labor (as well as that of the other factors of production). As a result, the profit-maximizing firm will employ more labor than before, and the interpretation of the coefficient of land becomes ambiguous. Similarly, consider the demand curve of labor derived from the production function. By equating the marginal product of labor to the wage rate, we have one point on the labor demand curve. Other points are derived by changing the wage rate and determining the quantity of labor that restores the equality of marginal product to wage. This operation is appropriate when labor is under the control of the entrepreneur—which is inconsistent with the formulation of the production function that treats labor, together with the other factors, as exogenous variables. As we demonstrated in the preceding chapter, this becomes the source of the simulanteous-equation bias in the production function.

A more realistic interpretation of the process of production through the profit function circumvents these problems. The entrepreneur has exogenously determined the prices of output and of variable factors of production and the quantities of the fixed factors of production. He is maximizing profits within these restrictions by setting both output and quantities of variable factors at their optimum levels—corrected for mistakes in maximization in the way we suggested in our efficiency analysis.

This alternative formulation, which treats the price of output, the prices of variable inputs, and the quantities of fixed factors as exogenously determined variables and the quantities of output and of the variable factors as control variables in the process of profit maximization, is consistent with our a priori notions and our experience of the world at the microeconomic level. It is cor-

rect for the firm, or for the village. At the aggregate level, however, the prices and quantities of output and the variable factors of production are jointly determined as endogenous variables in a system that treats as exogenous variables the factors that determine the supply and demand curves of inputs and the supply and demand curve of output. In Chapter 15, we will demonstrate an application of such an extension of profit function analysis in the context of a general equilibrium model of the agricultural household. Thus, we will actually have extended production function analysis in two respects: first, as in the profit function applied in this chapter, by treating prices of output and of variable factors as exogenous variables that determine their respective quantities; and second, in Chapter 15, by constructing an operational macro-model in which both prices and quantities of output and variable factors are endogenously determined in an equilibrium analysis.

Appendix

The Diagonal Regression Model for Errors-in-Variables Relationships: The Index of Economic Rationality

Consider the following model, in which a and b are constant parameters and x, y, and z are random variables.

$$x = az + u \tag{1}$$

$$y = bz + v \tag{2}$$

Then az and bz are the systematic components of x and y respectively.

Let us assume that

$$E(u) = E(v)$$
$$= 0$$
$$\text{cov } (u, z) = \text{cov } (v, z)$$
$$= \text{cov } (u, v) \tag{3}$$
$$= 0$$

Further, let us make the simplifying assumption

$$\frac{\text{var } u}{\text{var } x} = \frac{\text{var } v}{\text{var } y} = 1 - P \tag{4}$$

P is thus the ratio of the systematic components of x and y to var x and var y respectively.

Then from equations 1, 2, 3,

$$\text{var } x = a^2 \text{ var } z + \text{var } u \tag{5}$$

$$\text{var } y = b^2 \text{ var } z + \text{var } v \tag{6}$$

$$\text{cov } (x, y) = ab \text{ var } z \tag{7}$$

From equations 5 and 6,

$$\frac{\text{var } x}{\text{var } y} = \frac{a^2 \text{ var } z + \text{var } u}{b^2 \text{ var } z + \text{var } v} \tag{8}$$

and from equation 4,

$$\frac{\text{var } x}{\text{var } y} = \frac{\text{var } u}{\text{var } v} \tag{9}$$

Thus, from equations 8 and 9,

$$\frac{\text{var } x}{\text{var } y} = \frac{a^2 \text{ var } z}{b^2 \text{ var } z} = \frac{a^2}{b^2} \tag{10}$$

But from equation 7,

$$\text{sgn } ab = \text{sgn cov } (x, y) \tag{11}$$

so that, from equations 9 and 10, if $b \neq 0$,

$$\frac{a}{b} = \left(\frac{\text{var } x}{\text{var } y}\right)^{1/2} \text{sgn cov } (x, y) \tag{12}$$

which is the diagonal regression estimator.

From equations 4, 5, and 6,

$$P = a^2 \frac{\text{var } z}{\text{var } x} = b^2 \frac{\text{var } z}{\text{var } y}$$

and from equations 7 and 11,

$$P = \frac{\text{cov } (x, y)}{(\text{var } x \text{ var } y)^{1/2}} \text{sgn cov } (x, y) = |\rho_{x, y}| \tag{13}$$

In the economic model we are considering,

$a > 0$ and $b > 0$, so that sgn cov $(x, y) = 1$. Thus,

$$\frac{a}{b} = \left(\frac{\text{var } x}{\text{var } y}\right)^{1/2} \tag{12a}$$

and

$$\rho_{x, y} > 0,$$

so that

$$P = \rho_{x, y} \tag{13a}$$

In our specific application for economic rationality, equations 1 and 2 correspond to the K and L equations. The index of economic rationality is therefore given by the simple correlation coefficient of the relationship of log other costs on log labor.

Chapter 7
The Macroeconomics of Efficiency

In the preceding chapters, we have presented some techniques for analyzing and measuring both technical and allocative efficiency. We started from the more traditional measures and progressively relaxed assumptions to achieve greater realism. While our examples demonstrated that the methods of analysis and measurement are operational, how important inefficiency is remains a moot question.

This chapter will demonstrate that the study of efficiency is indeed important. We shall examine several different sources of inefficiency that may have pervasive effects for LDC economies. For each source examined, we shall attempt to measure the overall effect of the inefficiency in social welfare terms and at the same time to test the sensitivity of the results to alternative methods of estimation. The approach we use relies heavily on the well-worn tool of consumer surplus analysis. For detailed examination of this method and

some of the conceptual problems inherent in it, the reader is referred elsewhere.[1]

Our specific applications of the macroeconomics of inefficiency are semihypothetical—as opposed to fully empirical. Still, as far as they help to identify priorities for empirical research, these quantitative exercises are useful.

In the first section of this chapter, we demonstrate the use of partial equilibrium methods for measuring the welfare cost of monopoly. In the second section, general equilibrium methods of measuring welfare cost are applied to the case of distortions from tariffs. In the final section, we discuss interdependencies among sources and types of inefficiency.

While existing estimates of the importance of the various sources of inefficiency have varied from source to source and from study to study, the general presumption has been

[1]For a well-balanced and up-to-date critical survey, see Currie, Murphy, and Schmitz (1971).

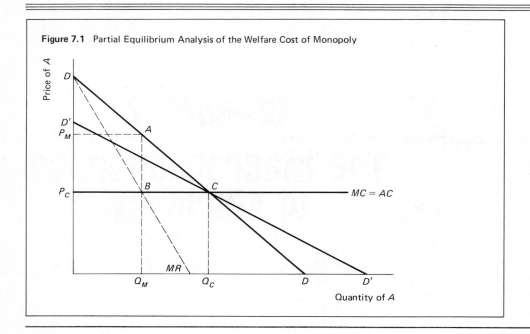

Figure 7.1 Partial Equilibrium Analysis of the Welfare Cost of Monopoly

that the overall effect of such distortions has been fairly small.[2] The result of our analysis is that such conclusions are at best premature and at worst misleading and incorrect. Indeed, various sources of price inefficiency would seem to constitute an important part of the economic landscape of LDCs. Any one of these types of price distortion may account for very substantial losses in social welfare, the effects of which may serve to compound inefficiencies of other sorts and maintain the economic and social equilibruim at low levels of income.

Partial Equilibrium Analysis of the Welfare Cost of Monopoly

Let us consider the output of an individual industry, A, in the absence of foreign trade. For simplicity, assume that marginal costs of producing A are constant and (at least within the relevant range of output), equal to average costs, and that the demand curve for A is a straight line.[3]

These assumptions are reflected in Figure

7.1, where the linear demand curve is DD and the horizontal long-run supply curve is $P_C BC$. The welfare cost of monopoly can be calculated in this familiar partial equilibrium context by subtracting the total economic surplus attainable in the (pure) monopoly case from that attainable under perfect competition.

If industry A is a pure monopoly, the equilibrium output and price will be Q_M and P_M respectively, whereas if industry A is competitive, equilibrium output and price will be Q_C and P_C. Consumers' surplus is $P_C DC$ in the competitive case but only $P_M DA$ in the monopoly case. The reduction in consumers' surplus resulting from monopolization of industry A is thus $P_M ACP_C$. Part of this, $P_M ABP_C$, is transferred to the producer in the form of monopoly profits. If it can be assumed that the redistribution of income from consumers to the monopolist does not affect the demand for A and also that there exists the possibility of potential compensation,[4] the income distribution effect of monopoly can be ignored. The other part of the loss in consumers' surplus, ABC, is the net "deadweight loss" attributable to monopoly. Quantitatively,

---

[2]See, for example, Harberger (1954, 1959) and and Leibenstein (1966).

[3]Some of these strong assumptions will be released in further modifications of the model.

[4]For this to be the case, it must be possible for the monopoly profits to be taxed away by appropriate lump-sum taxes and redistributed to consumers in the form of neutral income subsidies.

this loss is equal to $1/2(P_M - P_C)(Q_C - Q_M)$ or $1/2(\Delta P \, \Delta Q)$.

Harberger (1954) demonstrated how this model can be used to estimate the welfare cost of monopoly on an industry by industry basis. The procedure was as follows:

1. Obtain data on profits, Π, sales, Q, and capital stock, K, for each and every industry for a particular period of time. (This time period should be one in which accounting values approximate actual values and during which the structure of industry and demand remain relatively constant.)
2. Compute the average rate of return ($R = \Pi/K$) for each industry j, R_j and for the economy as a whole, $\overline{R}$. ($\overline{R}$ is defined as a normal or competitive rate of profit.)
3. Compute $R_j - \overline{R}$ for each and every industry j, $j = 1, 2, \ldots, n$. $R_j - \overline{R}$ is defined as the excess rate of profit attributable to monopoly power in the industry.
4. Multiply $(R_j - \overline{R})$ by K_j to obtain the amount of excess (monopoly) profits in industry j, $(R_j - \overline{R}) K_j$. (This corresponds to the area $P_M A B P_C$ or $Q_M \Delta P$ in Figure 7.1.)
5. Multiply $(R_j - \overline{R}) K_j$ by an assumed elasticity of demand, η_j. Since $\eta = \Delta Q/Q \cdot P/\Delta P$, $\eta(Q_M \Delta P)$ approximates $P_C \Delta Q$ which in terms of Figure 7.1 can be interpreted as the amount of resources misallocated, BCQ_CQ_M.[5]
6. If the quantity and price units are defined in such a way that $P_C = 1$, the amount of resources misallocated is also ΔQ or $Q_C - Q_M$.
7. Calculate $\Delta P = P_M - P_C$ by dividing the excess profits calculation from step 4, $Q_M \Delta P$, by the sales data, Q_M.[6]

8. Calculate the welfare cost of monopoly $(1/2 \, \Delta P \, \Delta Q)$, where ΔQ is taken from step 6 and ΔP is taken from step 7.

This procedure has been applied by Harberger (1954) to United States industry data for the 1920s, by Schwartzman (1959, 1961) to industry for the United States and Canada for the 1950s, and by Rees (1963) to labor union data for the United States. None of these studies has yielded an estimate of the welfare loss of monopoly that is as high as one-tenth of 1 percent of national income! However, since all such studies are based on similar methods, the consistency of their findings is hardly surprising. As a number of critics have pointed out,[7] the validity of the results of these studies depends on a number of questionable assumptions and on certain parameter values used in estimation. These, most probably, have led to underestimating the welfare cost of monopoly. If, for example, long-run marginal cost curves are upward sloping, or if the elasticity of demand is higher than the specific parameter value adopted in step 5 (which is usually assumed to be either 1 or 2), the estimate of welfare loss is biased downward. This bias can be substantial, as demonstrated by Kamerschen (1966), who merely adjusted profits to reflect items such as advertising expenditures, royalties, or salaries to executives. He found that his relatively minor modifications yielded estimates of the social cost of monopoly for the United States ranging from 1 percent to 8 percent of GNP, with 6 percent as the best guess. Moreover, important components of monopoly costs are totally overlooked by this approach— for example, the possible effects of monopoly on technical and price efficiency[8] or on the propensity to innovate[9]. So too the social cost

---

[5]Thus, if $\eta = 1$, the amount of resources misallocated, $P_C \triangle Q$ from step 5, is identical to the amount of excess profits, $Q_M \triangle P$ from step 4.

[6]As an alternative method of computing $\triangle P$ and one which is not dependent on the arbitrary assumption that the average rate of profit in the economy is the competitive rate, Bain (1951) and Schwartzman (1959, 1961) have suggested the following procedure:

(1) Obtain data on total sales, PQ, total variable costs, TVC, and the quantity of output, Q, for each of several industries, j, in each of several countries, i.

(2) In each case, divide sales, PQ, and total variable costs, TVC, by quantity, Q, to obtain price, P, and average variable cost, AVC, respectively.

(3) Compute $(P/AVC)_{ij}$ for each industry j, $j = 1 \ldots n$, and country, $i = 1, \ldots, m$, and relate these ratios to an independent index of monopoly power, M_{ij}, such as the concentration ratio (Gini coefficient).

For example, one could postulate the linear relationship:

$$\left(\frac{P}{\text{AVC}}\right)_{ij} = a + bM_{ij}$$

This method would have the effect of relaxing the assumption that any increase of price above marginal cost is due to monopoly power.

[7]See, for example, Mack (1954), Stigler (1956), Worcester (1969), Mishan (1968), Bell (1968), Alonzo (1969).

[8]See discussion in Chapter 5.

[9]It should be admitted that the effect on innovation could, in theory, be either positive or negative. According to Schumpeter (1934), monopoly may be conducive to innovation by allowing the innovating firm itself to capture the benefits (in the form of greater profits), which in competition would be passed

of creating the monopoly (through legal or criminal behavior, lobbying, and bribery of the officials involved in investment licensing and external trade regulations, etc.) remains entirely unaccounted for (Tullock 1967). Finally, as we will demonstrate immediately, single market, partial equilibrium analysis is not designed to capture the full extent of all the distortions in relative prices among all the sectors of the economy.

Estimates of the welfare cost of monopoly specifically for LDCs are not available.[10] We would, nevertheless, venture the guess that monopolistic influences may impose larger welfare losses in LDCs than in DCs.[11]

General Equilibrium Analysis of the Welfare Cost of Tariffs

The partial equilibrium framework assumes that the price and quantity effects of any efficiency-reducing distortion are confined to the sector in which the distortion occurs.

---

on to consumers in the form of lower prices. However, in LDCs, where original innovation (requiring costly investments in research and development) is less common than imitative innovations which may be motivated more consistently by competitive pressures, the negative effects of monopoly are likely to dominate over the positive effects.

[10]See, however, Harberger (1959) and Alonzo (1969).

[11]Several justifications may be proposed for such an hypothesis: (1) With smaller domestic markets, and yet operating on the portions of the cost curve that are more steeply downward-sloping, domestic firms are more likely to try harder to restrict the entry of other firms. (2) Historically, colonial powers found the granting of monopolistic and monopsonistic companies an inexpensive and politically acceptable way of achieving territorial ambitions (S. R. Pearson 1971). (3) Wealth tends to be more highly concentrated in LDCs than in DCs, and individuals and their governments who possess that wealth have every incentive to preserve their economically and politically monopolistic positions. (4) While monopoly is usually confined to the industrial sector in advanced countries (land markets being competitive), in LDCs land ownership is often highly concentrated (Bottomley 1966). As a result, monopoly and monopolistic practices often permeate the agricultural sector as well. (5) Trade restrictions in LDCs are heavily biased toward quantitative restrictions that (as will be demonstrated in the final section of this chapter) enable domestic producers to take greater advantage of monopoly power than they would be able to from tariffs. (6) While in the advanced countries, activist antitrust policy or at least the threat of it has tended to lessen the concentration of industry, antitrust policy is virtually nonexistent in the LDCs. (7) With some possible exception, there is little other countervailing power in LDCs (e.g., in the form of strong labor unions) that would favor a theory of second-best justification for monopoly.

While this assumption may be fairly realistic in considering a particular distortion in a small sector, such as the effect of monopoly power in the straw hat industry, it cannot be realistic in considering the overall efficiency effects of general types of distortions, such as monopoly, tariffs, or excise taxes, which affect large segments of the economy. In such a context, therefore, partial equilibrium estimates of distortion-induced inefficiency are unreliable. General equilibrium analysis is required.

The purpose of this section is to demonstrate how the tools for measuring inefficiency can be applied in the context of general equilibrium. Specifically, we consider the case of tariff distortions because of the significant extent to which these distortions permeate the economy, especially in LDCs. Our analysis is, however, general in the sense that it could be used to deal with any type of distortion.

The Two-Commodity Case

Suppose we have an open economy with two commodities: exportables, X, and importables, Y. There exist productive opportunities for exchanging X for Y via the transformation function (derived from underlying production functions of unknown form) and also as a result of the open economy specification, international market opportunities for exchanging them. This situation can be depicted in Figure 7.2, where the curve PP represents the transformation curve, and the slope of the parallel price lines w_0w_0, w_1w_1, and so on represents the relative price at which X and Y can be exchanged in international markets. The fact that the latter lines are straight reflects the small country assumption, namely that the extent to which a country participates in the international markets can have no effect on prices in those markets. Let us also assume a set of community indifference curves, given by U_0, U_1, U_2, and so on, each higher numbered indifference curve representing an unambiguously higher level of welfare.

If free trade prevails, X and Y will exchange both domestically and internationally at world prices, given by the slope of w_0w_0, w_1w_1, and so on. If producers and consumers are both technically and allocatively efficient, maximum welfare of U_3 will be achieved by producing X_1 of X and Y_1 of Y, as at point A,

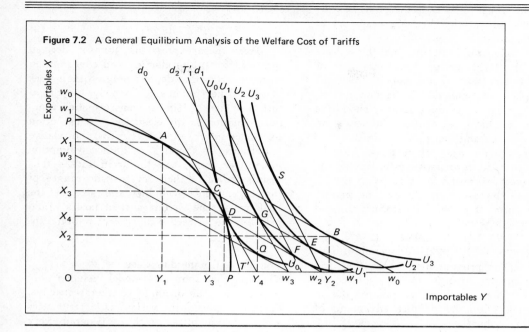

Figure 7.2 A General Equilibrium Analysis of the Welfare Cost of Tariffs

and by trading $X_1 - X_2$ of X in the world markets for $Y_2 - Y_1$ of Y so as to arrive at the optimal consumption point B on U_3. Consumers will thus be able to consume X_2 of X and Y_2 of Y. Welfare would be given by w_0 either in terms of X (on the X axis) or in terms of Y (on the Y axis).

The imposition of a tariff on importables will raise the price of Y relative to X for domestic producers and consumers. Suppose the new price ratio is given by the slope of the parallel lines, d_0, d_1, and so on. The optimal production point would now be at point C, where X_3 of X and Y_3 of Y would be produced. The country would still be in a position to trade in international markets, exchanging $X_3 - X_4$ of X for $Y_4 - Y_3$ of Y so as to arrive at the allocatively efficient consumption point, G. Point G is on the community indifference curve, labeled U_1.[12] Point F is the point on U_1 at which there is tangency with respect to world prices, $w_2 w_2$. Welfare can again be measured either in terms of X (on the X axis) or Y (on the Y axis); in this case, it is w_2.

The welfare cost of the tariff in absolute terms is the maximum welfare attainable under free trade, w_0, less that attainable under

[12]This analysis assumes that all tariff revenues collected by the government are returned to consumers in the form of neutral income subsidies.

tariffs, w_2. In relative terms, expressed as a percentage of national income in the free trade case, it is $(w_0 - w_2)/w_0$.

It is often desirable and convenient to break this aggregate welfare cost of the tariff down into its two components, production cost and consumption cost. If the distortion in relative prices caused by tariff could be confined to production, equilibrium in production would still be at C, but equilibrium in consumption would be at E on indifference curve U_2, which is obviously lower than U_3 but higher than U_1. The *production cost* of the tariff (in absolute terms) would therefore be measured by $w_0 - w_1$ on either axis. As has already been shown, however, when the price distortion of the tariff extends to consumption, equilibrium is at G, and the community is on the lower indifference curve U_1. The additional welfare cost attributable to the tariff's distorting effect on consumption, that is, the *consumption cost* of the tariff, is therefore measured by $w_1 - w_2$ in absolute terms.

The higher the tariff, the steeper the price line becomes until it attains the slope given by the line $T'T'$. Such a line is sufficiently steep to be tangent to both the transformation curve, PP, and the highest attainable indifference curve, U_0, at point D. This is clearly the point at which trade becomes unprofitable. Thus, point D is the point of self-sufficiency, or autarky. Welfare evaluated at international prices is measured by w_3, which is clearly below w_2, indicating that the welfare cost of the tariff increases with the size of the tariff. However, an increase in the tariff rate applied to commodity Y beyond the increase sufficient to produce autarky should be expected to have no further influence on domestic prices and hence on welfare.

This general equilibrium model can be used to provide quantitative estimates of the welfare cost of tariffs by estimating or, alternatively, by assuming the specific mathematical form that the transformation and utility functions take.

Lage (1967, 1970), Cabezon (1969), and Evans (1970, 1971, 1972), for example, have utilized linear programming production and utility functions to measure the welfare cost of tariffs. These methods, as pointed out in Chapter 4, offer the distinct advantage of facilitating disaggregation. However, LP functions that are based ultimately on production relationships of the I-O variety require both strong assumptions about the underlying relationships between inputs and outputs, and vast amounts of information for empirical estimation. Since the resulting welfare cost changes have tended to be very sensitive to various parameters (other than the tariff rates) in the model, which cannot be estimated with any degree of confidence, it has been difficult to gauge the reliability of the results.[13]

H. G. Johnson (1965b) enjoyed considerably greater success by assuming transformation and utility functions of more general form. Specifically, he assumed that the transformation function[14] between exportables X, and importables, Y, was of the following nature

$$X^2 + MXY + Y^2 = K^2 \qquad (1)$$

The utility function he assumed was of the

CES form,

$$U = [AX^{-\rho} + BY^{-\rho}]^{-1/\rho} \qquad (2)$$

From these expressions, Johnson derived formulas for the production and consumption costs of tariffs that depend only on the values of several key parameters, namely, the curvature coefficient, M, in the transformation function, equation 1, the elasticity of substitution (in consumption) $\sigma = 1/(1 + \rho)$, the relative importance of X and Y in total consumption under free trade, and the tariff rate, t. His results indicated that, for realistic ranges of the parameters (including the size of the tariff rates), the welfare cost of tariffs would probably not exceed 4 percent of national income.

The Three-Commodity Case

The fact that Johnson's model included only two goods is unfortunately rather restrictive, because it ignores the variations in tariff rates among commodities, which are generally very substantial.[15] In the subsequent presentation, we follow Nugent and Akbar (1970) in extending Johnson's model to three goods, exportables, X, and two classes of importables, Y and Z. To make our results comparable with those obtained by Johnson, we shall adopt the same forms for the transformation and utility functions and use the same ranges of values for the various parameters. The extension to three goods permits the comparison of welfare cost calculations obtained from cases in which a single homogeneous tariff rate applies with those in which different tariff rates apply to different commodities.

Let us define the quantity units in which each of the three goods in the model is measured in such a way that the prices of each would be equal to unity in the world market. The imposition of a tariff on either Y or Z can be treated as equivalent to a tax on consumption of the protected commodity combined with a subsidy to domestic producers of the same commodity. Negative protection, which can arise either through the imposition of an export tax or through a tax on industry's inputs at a higher rate than its output, can be treated in the opposite way, that is, as a subsidy to consumption of the commodity combined with a tax on its production. The proceeds of all taxes are assumed to be re-

---

[13]Note especially the qualifications admitted by Lage (1970).

[14]Although this function was not derived from any specific underlying production functions, it has the advantage of being mathematically convenient while at the same time characterizing the transformation function as it is generally portrayed in graphical analysis. Note, for example, that when $M = 0$ the formula reduces to a circle of radius OP in Figure 7.2. On the other hand, when $M = 2$, the formula is that of a straight line (as would be expected if the underlying production functions were of the I-O type).

[15]See Macario (1964), Balassa and Associates (1971), Little, Scitovsky, and Scott (1970).

turned to the community in the form of a general income subsidy, while the costs of subsidies are assumed to be financed by a general income tax.

Derivation of the Production Cost of Tariffs
Let us first compute the production cost of the tariff. In three dimensions, the transformation function given by equation 1 is

$$X^2 + Y^2 + Z^2 + MXY + LZY + NXZ = K^2 \tag{3}$$

where there are now three curvature coefficients, M, L, and N, instead of one, M, as in equation 1. Nevertheless, the values of these parameters play the same role that (as explained in footnote 14) the value of M played in equation 1, namely, to determine how sharply the transformation surface bends. The surface is that of a flat plane when $L = M = N = 2$, but it increases in curvature to that of a quarter of a circular sphere when $L = M = N = 0$.

One can easily derive from equation 3 the marginal rates of substitution of Y for X, of Z for X, and of Z for Y, which are as follows

$$\frac{\partial Y}{\partial X} = \frac{2X + MY + NZ}{2Y + MX + LZ} \tag{4a}$$

$$\frac{\partial Z}{\partial X} = \frac{2X + MY + NZ}{2Z + LY + NX} \tag{4b}$$

$$\frac{\partial Z}{\partial Y} = \frac{2Z + LY + NX}{2Y + MY + LZ} \tag{4c}$$

Our assumption about the units in which X, Y, and Z are measured permits the world prices of all commodities to be equal to unity. Assuming that complete autarky is not achieved, despite the possible imposition of tariffs of t_1 on Y and t_2 on Z, the domestic price ratios ($d_0, d_1, d_2, \ldots$ in Figure 7.2) would be[16]

[16]The assumption that all domestic prices are determined by world prices plus the tariff is simplistic and restrictive as far as general equilibrium is concerned. More generally, one might wish to admit some nontraded goods the price of which would be determined endogenously in the process of market-clearing. See, for example, J. E. Anderson (1970).

$$\frac{P_y}{P_x} = 1 + t_1 \tag{5a}$$

$$\frac{P_z}{P_x} = 1 + t_2 \tag{5b}$$

$$\frac{P_z}{P_y} = \frac{1 + t_2}{1 + t_1} \tag{5c}$$

Allocative efficiency in production requires that the marginal rates of transformation derived in equations 4a, 4b, and 4c should be equated to the domestic price ratios given by equations 5a, 5b, and 5c respectively. Setting equation 4a equal to equation 5a, equation 4b equal to 5b, and equation 4c equal to 5c, we arrive at the following equations in X, Y, and Z

$$(2 - M - Mt_1)X + (M - 2 - 2t_1)Y + (N - L - Lt_1)Z = 0 \tag{6a}$$

$$(2 - N - Nt_2)X + (M - L - Lt_2)Y + (N - 2 - 2t_2)Z = 0 \tag{6b}$$

$$(N + Nt_2 - M - Mt_1)X + (L + Lt_2 - 2 - 2t_1)Y + (2 + 2t_2 - L - Lt_1)Z = 0 \tag{6c}$$

Regarding the curvature coefficients (L, M, and N) and the tariff rates as given constants, these three relations comprise a system of linear equations in X, Y, and Z. We solve for both X and Y in terms of Z

$$X = \left[\frac{(2 + 2t_2 - L - Lt_1)(M - L - Lt_2) - (N - 2 - 2t_2)(L + Lt_2 - 2 - 2t_1)}{(2 - N - Nt_2)(L + Lt_2 - 2 - 2t_1) - (N + Nt_2 - M - Mt_1)(M - L - Lt_2)} \right] Z = EZ \tag{7a}$$

$$Y = \left[\frac{(N - 2 - 2t_2)(2 - M - Mt_1) - (N - L - Lt_1)(2 - N - Nt_2)}{(M - 2 - 2t_1)(2 - N - Nt_2) - (M - L - Lt_2)(2 - M - Mt_1)} \right] Z = DZ \tag{7b}$$

where E and D are the complicated expressions inside the brackets of equations 7a and 7b respectively.

Substituting equation 7a for X and equation 7b for Y in the transformation function 3 yields

$$(E^2 + D^2 + MDE + LD + NE + 1)Z^2 = K^2 \tag{8}$$

Solving for Z and taking the positive root only, we find

$$Z = \frac{K}{\sqrt{E^2 + D^2 + MDE + LD + NE + 1}} = \frac{K}{B} \tag{9}$$

where B is defined as the complicated expression in the denominator.

Substituting equation 9 into equations 7a and 7b, we obtain the following solutions for X and Y

$$X = \frac{EK}{B} \tag{10a}$$

$$Y = \frac{DK}{B} \tag{10b}$$

Gross national product at world prices, y, is clearly

$$y = X + Y + Z \tag{11}$$

Substituting equations 9, 10a, and 10b into equation 11, we obtain

$$y = \frac{K(1 + E + D)}{B} \tag{12}$$

By referring to the definitions of B, D, and E in the previous equations, it can be seen that equation 12 is an expression for aggregate welfare that is a quadratic function of the curvature coefficients L, M, and N and the tariff rates t_1 and t_2.

The maximum GNP attainable under tariff protection but evaluated in international prices, y_t, can thus be computed by substituting appropriate values of L, M, and N (between 0 and 2) and the actual (or assumed) values for the tariff rates t_1 on Y and t_2 on Z. Likewise, the maximum GNP attainable under free trade, y_f, can be calculated by setting $t_1 = t_2 = 0$.

The production cost of the tariffs expressed as a percentage of GNP under free trade, PC, is simply

$$PC = \frac{y_f - y_t}{y_f} = 1 - \frac{y_t}{y_f} \tag{13}$$

Derivation of the Consumption
Cost of Tariffs
Now let us turn to the consumption cost of protection. Following H. G. Johnson (1965b) in his choice of the CES utility function given by equation 2, but again extending it to include the second class of importables, Z, we have

$$U = (AX^{-\rho} + BY^{-\rho} + CZ^{-\rho})^{-1/\rho} \tag{14}$$

where A, B, and C (with $C = 1 - A - B$) are the distribution parameters, and ρ is the substitution parameter, which is related to the elasticity of substitution, σ, by $\sigma = 1/(1 + \rho)$. The assumptions that A, B, and C add up to unity and that ρ is constant imply that the income elasticities of demand for X, Y, and Z add up to unity and that the marginal utility of income does not vary with the level of income. Utility can thus be expressed in terms of aggregate income, y, as in equation 11.

The marginal utilities of each of the three goods may be derived as follows

$$\frac{\partial U}{\partial X} = A\left(\frac{U}{X}\right)^{1+\rho} \tag{15a}$$

$$\frac{\partial U}{\partial Y} = B\left(\frac{U}{Y}\right)^{1+\rho} \tag{15b}$$

$$\frac{\partial U}{\partial Z} = C\left(\frac{U}{Z}\right)^{1+\rho} \tag{15c}$$

Allocative efficiency in consumption requires that the ratio of any two of these marginal utilities should be equal to the ratio of their domestic prices, which were defined in equations 5a, 5b, and 5c. Taking the ratios of the various marginal utilities and setting each equal to the corresponding domestic price ratio from equations 5a, 5b, and 5c, we obtain

$$\frac{\frac{\partial U}{\partial Y}}{\frac{\partial U}{\partial X}} = \frac{B}{A}\left(\frac{X}{Y}\right)^{1+\rho} = \frac{P_y}{P_x} = 1 + t_1 \tag{16a}$$

$$\frac{\frac{\partial U}{\partial Z}}{\frac{\partial U}{\partial X}} = \frac{C}{A}\left(\frac{X}{Z}\right)^{1+\rho} = \frac{P_z}{P_x} = 1 + t_2 \tag{16b}$$

$$\frac{\frac{\partial U}{\partial Z}}{\frac{\partial U}{\partial Y}} = \frac{C}{B}\left(\frac{Y}{Z}\right)^{1+\rho} = \frac{P_z}{P_y} = \frac{1 + t_2}{1 + t_1} \tag{16c}$$

Equations 16 can be restated in terms of the ratios X/Y, X/Z, and Y/Z, or preferably for X or Y or Z in terms of each other,

$$\frac{X}{Y} = \left[\frac{A}{B}(1 + t_1)\right]^{1/(1+\rho)}$$

or

$$X = \left[\frac{A}{B}(1 + t_1)\right]^{1/(1+\rho)} Y$$

or

$$Y = \left[\frac{B}{A}\left(\frac{1}{1 + t_1}\right)\right]^{1/(1+\rho)} X \tag{17a}$$

$$\frac{X}{Z} = \left[\frac{A}{C}(1 + t_2)\right]^{1/(1+\rho)}$$

or

$$X = \left[\frac{A}{C}(1 + t_2)\right]^{1/(1+\rho)} Z$$

or

$$Z = \left[\frac{C}{A}\left(\frac{1}{1+t_2}\right)\right]^{1/(1+\rho)} X \qquad (17b)$$

$$\frac{Y}{Z} = \left[\frac{B}{C}\frac{(1+t_2)}{(1+t_1)}\right]^{1/(1+\rho)}$$

or

$$Y = \left[\frac{B(1+t_2)}{C(1+t_1)}\right]^{1/(1+\rho)} Z$$

or

$$Z = \left[\frac{C(1+t_1)}{B(1+t_2)}\right]^{1/(1+\rho)} Y \qquad (17c)$$

With the use of the accounting identity 11, the expressions for X, Y, and Z in terms of aggregate income, y, now become

$$X = \frac{\left[\frac{A}{B}(1+t_1)\right]^{1/(1+\rho)}}{\left[\frac{A}{B}(1+t_1)\right]^{1/(1+\rho)} + \left[\frac{C(1+t_1)}{B(1+t_2)}\right]^{1/(1+\rho)} + 1} \, y \qquad (18a)$$

$$Y = \frac{1}{\left[\frac{A}{B}(1+t_1)\right]^{1/(1+\rho)} + \left[\frac{C(1+t_1)}{B(1+t_2)}\right]^{1/(1+\rho)} + 1} \, y \qquad (18b)$$

$$Z = \frac{\left[\frac{C(1+t_1)}{B(1+t_2)}\right]^{1/(1+\rho)}}{\left[\frac{A}{B}(1+t_1)\right]^{1/(1+\rho)} + \left[\frac{C(1+t_1)}{B(1+t_2)}\right]^{1/(1+\rho)} + 1} \, y \qquad (18c)$$

After substituting equations 18 into equation 11 and dividing and multiplying the resulting expression by $B^{-1/\rho}$, we obtain the following expression for the maximum utility attainable at the given domestic price ratios but measured in world prices

$$U = \frac{\left[\left(\frac{A}{B}\right)^{1/(1+\rho)}(1+t_1)^{-\rho/(1+\rho)} + \left(\frac{C}{B}\right)^{1/(1+\rho)}\left(\frac{1+t_1}{1+t_2}\right)^{-\rho/(1+\rho)} + 1\right]^{-1/\rho} B^{-1/\rho}}{\left(\frac{A}{B}\right)^{1/(1+\rho)}(1+t_1)^{1/(1+\rho)} + \left(\frac{C}{B}\right)^{1/(1+\rho)}\left(\frac{1+t_1}{1+t_2}\right)^{1/(1+\rho)} + 1} \qquad (19)$$

By substituting appropriate values of the distribution parameters A, B, C, the substitution parameter ρ, and the tariff rates t_1 and t_2 into equation 19, we can compute the maximum utility attainable under tariffs, U_t, and again that attainable under free trade, U_f, that is, where $t_1 = t_2 = 0$.

As before, the welfare cost can be expressed as a percentage of the maximum welfare attainable under free trade. Thus, for the consumption cost of tariffs, CC, we write

$$CC = \frac{U_f - U_t}{U_f} = 1 - \frac{U_t}{U_f} \qquad (20)$$

Recalling that $\sigma = 1/1 + \rho$ and defining R_x as the ratio of X to Y under free trade and R_z as the ratio of Z to Y under free trade, from equations 16 we can rewrite equation 20 as

$$CC = 1 - \frac{\left[R_x(1 + t_1)^{\sigma-1} + R_z\left(\frac{1 + t_1}{1 + t_2}\right)^{\sigma-1} + 1 \right]^{\sigma/(\sigma-1)} (R_x + R_z + 1)^{1/(1-\sigma)}}{R_x(1 + t_1) + R_z\left(\frac{1 + t_1}{1 + t_2}\right) + 1} \qquad (21)$$

We further define $r_x = X/y$ and $r_z = Z/y$. From equation 11, R_x and R_z can be expressed in terms of r_x and r_z

$$R_x = \frac{X}{Y} = \frac{\dfrac{X}{y}}{\dfrac{Y}{y}} = \frac{\dfrac{X}{y}}{1 - \dfrac{X}{y} - \dfrac{Z}{y}} = \frac{r_x}{1 - r_x - r_z} \qquad (22)$$

$$R_z = \frac{Z}{Y} = \frac{\dfrac{Z}{y}}{\dfrac{Y}{y}} = \frac{\dfrac{Z}{y}}{1 - \dfrac{X}{y} - \dfrac{Z}{y}} = \frac{r_z}{1 - r_x - r_z} \qquad (23)$$

Equations 22 and 23 can be substituted into equation 21 to yield an expression for the

consumption cost that is stated in terms of the more familiar shares of each commodity in aggregate consumption under free trade (r_x, r_z, and $r_y = 1 - r_x - r_z$), and again in terms of the tariff rates t_1 on Y and t_2 on Z and the elasticity of substitution, σ. From such an expression, one can compute the consumption cost of tariffs for assumed plausible values of the parameters indicated.

However, when $\sigma = 1$, equation 21 is not amenable to computation, and the CES utility function defined by equation 14 must be abandoned in favor of the Cobb-Douglas utility function, which is, of course, the CES function in the special case in which $\sigma = 1$,

$$U = X^{r_z}Y^{1-r_x-r_z}Z^{r_z} \qquad (24)$$

Following the same steps to obtain an expression for the consumption cost of tariffs when equation 24 is used instead of equation 14, we obtain another expression in terms of the r_x, r_z, and t_1 and t_2,

$$CC = \frac{(1 + t_1)^{r_x}\left(\dfrac{1 + t_1}{1 + t_2}\right)^{r_z}}{1 + r_x t_1 - r_z + r_z\left(\dfrac{1 + t_1}{1 + t_2}\right)} \qquad (25)$$

Table 7.1 *Estimates of the Production Cost of Tariffs*

Value of Curvature Coefficients ($L = M = N$)	Value of the Average Tariff Rate[a]	Assumptions about the Relation of t_1 to t_2 Consistent with the Average Tariff Rate Shown at the Left				
		$t_1 = t_2$ (1)	$t_1 = t_2 - 0.20$ (2)	$t_1 = t_2 - 0.40$ (3)	$t_1 = t_2 - 0.60$ (4)	$t_1 = t_2 - 0.80$ (5)
0.5	0.20	0.0077	0.0111	0.0215	0.0392	0.0649
	0.40	0.0266	0.0282	0.0333	0.0422	0.0555
	0.60	0.0513	0.0520	0.0543	0.0601	0.0646
1.0	0.20	0.0153	0.0219	0.0416	0.0741	0.1186
	0.40	0.0512	0.0542	0.0635	0.0795	0.1027
	0.60	0.0915	0.0967	0.1006	0.1101	0.1181
1.5	0.20	0.0369	0.0521	0.0952	0.1596	0.2371
	0.40	0.1088	0.1212	0.1395	0.1550	0.1696
	0.60	0.1924	0.2106	0.2193	0.2385	0.2502

Notes: These estimates are based upon equations 12 and 13 in the text and are expressed as a proportion of GNP under free trade.
[a] Assuming that the sectors are equally weighted, the average tariff rate is $\frac{1}{2}(t_1 + t_2)$.
Source: Nugent, J. B., and M. A. Akbar (1970), "The Welfare Cost of Tariffs When the Tariff Structure Is Inhomogeneous," University of Southern California (mimeo).

Simulation Results

Having derived expressions for the production cost of tariffs, *PC*, that is, in equations 12 and 13, and for the consumption cost of tariffs, *CC*, that is, in equations 21–23 or in equation 25, we are now in a position to calculate the likely magnitude of these costs. This can be done by substituting into the relevant equations likely values for the various parameters appearing in these expressions.

Let us first consider the production cost. The magnitude of this cost has been shown to depend upon the curvature coefficient (*L*, *M*, and *N*) and the tariff rates (t_1 and t_2). As has been pointed out above, the realistic range for the curvature coefficients is between zero and something less than two. A relevant range for "average" tariff rates for LDCs is probably 20 percent to 100 percent, the lower part of the range being relevant to some of the smaller and more open LDCs, particularly those in Asia, and the higher part of this range relevant to larger LDCs, especially those in Latin America and Africa. The middle range is probably more typical of Central America and the Middle East. Nugent and Akbar (1970) followed H. G. Johnson (1965*b*) in substituting alternative values for each parameter throughout the expected range, obtaining a large set of alternative estimates of the production cost.

For present purposes, however, we may confine our attention to a limited number of alternative values within the most likely (or middle range of possible) values of the relevant parameters. We assume, therefore, values of 0.5, 1.0, and 1.5 for *L*, *M*, and *N* and average tariff rates of 20 percent, 40 percent, and 60 percent. The higher the curvature coefficient, the flatter the transformation surface, implying that the composition of output can be adjusted considerably (even to the point of complete specialization) without requiring much sacrifice in the marginal rate of transformation.

The results are given in Table 7.1. Column 1 gives the production cost of tariffs when tariff rates t_1 on *Y* and t_2 on *Z* are identical. Column 2 gives the production cost when the two tariff rates differ in absolute terms by 20 percent. Likewise, columns 3, 4, and 5 give the corresponding costs when the tariff rates differ by 40 percent, 60 percent, and 80 percent respectively. These results demonstrate that the production cost of tariffs increases with the size of the curvature coefficients, the

average tariff rate, and also the variance in the tariff rates around the average.

Before commenting further on these results, let us turn to the estimates of the consumption cost of tariffs. The formulas derived in equations 21–23 (or, alternatively, in equation 25 for the special case in which $\sigma = 1$) express the consumption cost in terms of the elasticity of substitution in consumption, σ, the relative shares of each commodity in total consumption, *r*, and in terms of tariff rates, t_1 and t_2. Again, we shall confine our attention to the most likely values of these parameters. We assume, therefore, that the elasticity of substitution takes on values of 0.5, 1.0, or 2.0 and that the product shares, r_x, r_y, and r_z, are approximately equal, that is, 0.4, 0.3, and 0.3 respectively. For tariff rates, we take the same values utilized in Table 7.1.

The resulting values of the consumption cost, *CC*, are given in Table 7.2. It can be seen that *CC* increases with σ, the average tariff rate, and the degree of dispersion among tariff rates.

The total welfare cost of any given tariff structure and values of *L*, *M*, *N*, and σ can be computed by adding the appropriate estimate of *PC* from Table 7.1 to the corresponding estimate of *CC* from Table 7.2. For example, when *L*, *M*, *N*, and σ are all equal to 1.0, and $t_1 = t_2 = 0.20$, the total cost of the tariff is the production cost of 0.0153 plus the consumption cost of 0.0040 or slightly less than 2 percent of GNP under free trade.[17] As we have already seen, however, it is not only the average degree of distortion in the protected sectors that reduces welfare but also the variation in the distortions among such sectors. Thus, if the degree of distortion increases to the point that $t_1 = -0.20$ and $t_2 = 0.60$, the total welfare cost of the tariff increases to more than 15 percent of GNP under free trade, that is, the *PC* of 0.1186 plus the *CC* of 0.0352.

The absolute size of the welfare loss is fairly sensitive to the choice of parameter values (about which it is difficult to be precise). Moreover, any conclusions are subject to the

[17]When t_1 and t_2 are equal, there is of course no need to distinguish between the two different importables, *Y* and *Z*, and thus, our three-commodity model should yield the same results reported by Johnson for his two-commodity model for the same selection of parameter values. Indeed, the interested reader can verify that this is the case by comparing the results for $t_1 = t_2$ in Tables 7.1 and 7.2 with those reported by H. G. Johnson (1965*b*, Tables 1A, 1B, 1C, and 2).

Table 7.2 *Estimates of the Consumption Cost of Tariffs*

Value of the Elasticity of Substitution σ	Value of the Average Tariff Rate[a]	Assumptions about the Relation of t_1 to t_2 Consistent with the Average Tariff Rate Shown at the Left				
		$t_1 = t_2$ (1)	$t_1 = t_2 - 0.20$ (2)	$t_1 = t_2 - 0.40$ (3)	$t_1 = t_2 - 0.60$ (4)	$t_1 = t_2 - 0.80$ (5)
0.5	0.20	0.0020	0.0026	0.0053	0.0101	0.0176
	0.40	0.0068	0.0069	0.0085	0.0111	0.0161
	0.60	0.0131	0.0136	0.0139	0.0160	0.0187
1.0	0.20	0.0040	0.0058	0.0113	0.0208	0.0352
	0.40	0.0137	0.0148	0.0182	0.0241	0.0327
	0.60	0.0267	0.0274	0.0296	0.0330	0.0387
2.0	0.20	0.0082	0.0075	0.0174	0.0319	0.0546
	0.40	0.0277	0.0271	0.0294	0.0336	0.0448
	0.60	0.0532	0.0537	0.0509	0.0515	0.0547

Notes: These estimates are based on equations 21–23 and 25 in the text and are expressed as a proportion of GNP under free trade.

[a] Assuming that the sectors are equally weighted, the average tariff rate is $\frac{1}{2}(t_1 + t_2)$.

Source: Nugent, J. B., and M. A. Akbar (1970), "The Welfare Cost of Tariffs When the Tariff Structure is Inhomogeneous," University of Southern California (mimeo).

realism of the assumptions of the underlying model, most notably the specific forms assumed for the transformation and utility functions. Nevertheless, the results are undoubtedly robust enough to warrant that some attention be given to their implications. First and foremost, the results suggest that, in focusing on the average distortion (in this case, the average tariff rate) and thereby ignoring the variations in the degree of distortion among the different sectors, existing studies may have considerably underestimated the welfare losses associated with various sources of price distortion. Indeed, our results indicate that tariff rates of the size and degree of variation among sectors that are typically observed in LDCs[18] could well imply welfare losses amounting to considerably more than 10 percent of GNP. The elimination of such inefficiencies might thus be expected to add 1 percent to the annual growth rate of GNP over a whole decade. An important policy implication is that LDCs would do well to rationalize their protective structures, for example, by giving all industrial sectors a common effective tariff rate or by adopting a dual exchange rate.[19]

Interdependencies Among Inefficiencies and Their Effects

Up to this point, we have dealt with one source of inefficiency at a time, neglecting any other sources of inefficiency or other effects emanating from the same source, which might have the effect of compounding or offsetting the welfare loss. Now we shall provide an example of how two sources of inefficiency—protection and monopoly—can become interdependent, compounding the welfare loss. The section will be concluded with an analysis of the case in which monopolization may bring about technical or "X-efficiency" gains, which tend to offset the efficiency losses.

Combination of Trade Restrictions and Monopoly: The Case of Quotas

An example of how the two sources of inefficiency, monopoly and tariffs, may interact with each other and compound resource mis-

[18]For references, see those of footnote 15 as well as various other individual studies of effective protection in LDCs, for example, Lawrence (1968), Humphrey (1969), Bergsman and Malah (1970), Korean Development Association (1967), Power (1966), Sun (1966), Nugent (1968).

[19]The validity of this implication would be reduced by the presence of other distortions, which might give rise to the second-best argument for tariffs. However, since trade restrictions are the most important source of price distortion in LDCs, this qualification is probably rather unimportant.

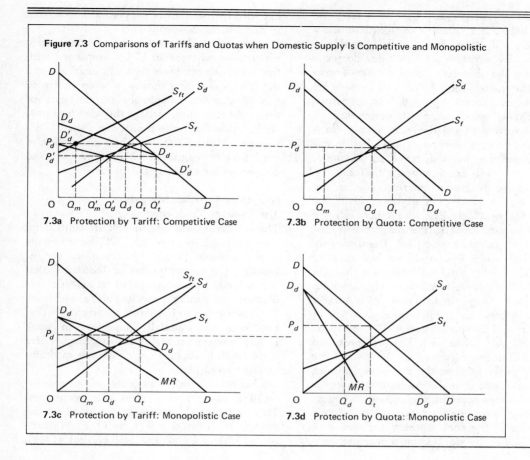

Figure 7.3 Comparisons of Tariffs and Quotas when Domestic Supply Is Competitive and Monopolistic

7.3a Protection by Tariff: Competitive Case

7.3b Protection by Quota: Competitive Case

7.3c Protection by Tariff: Monopolistic Case

7.3d Protection by Quota: Monopolistic Case

allocation is the use of import quotas for protection combined with monopoly in domestic production and/or in the holding of import quotas.[20]

When foreign and domestic supplies are competitive and competition prevails among quota holders, quotas and tariffs are equivalent in the sense that, if imports would be restricted to the same level by a tariff as by a quota, the distortion the tariff would impose on domestic prices would be equivalent to that imposed by the quota. This can be seen in Figures 7.3a and 7.3b for the case of the tariff and the quota respectively.

In both cases, D represents the demand curve, while S_f and S_d represent the foreign and domestic supply curves in the absence of tariffs. In Figure 7.3a, D_d' is the demand curve for domestic output in the absence of taxes; that curve is obtained by subtracting S_f

[20]Our presentation of this issue benefits from the analysis of Bhagwati (1965) and Kindleberger (1968).

from D. In the case of free trade, therefore, S_d and D_d' intersect to determine the domestic price P_d' and at that price Q_d' is produced while Q_m' is imported.

Either a tariff or a quota may be imposed to protect domestic supply. The imposition of a tariff in Figure 7.3a shifts the foreign supply curve (after taxes and in domestic currency terms) up to S_{ft}, which also has the effect of shifting the demand curve for domestic output from D_d' to D_d. The price now becomes P_d, at which Q_d is supplied domestically and Q_m is imported. Figure 7.3b shows what happens when a quota of Q_m, i.e., equivalent in its effect to the tariff shown in Figure 7.3a, is imposed. The domestic demand curve D_d in this case is simply the total demand curve D less the quota Q_m. The result is that all variables—Q_m, P_d, and Q_d—take on the same values in Figure 7.3b as in Figure 7.3a.

When domestic output is supplied by a monopolist, the "equivalence" between restriction by tariffs and that by quotas no longer holds. If a quota is designed to allow the same volume of imports that would be permitted by a certain tariff rate, the domestic price will be distorted to a greater degree under the quota system. This can be seen by reference to Figures 7.3c and 7.3d, in which equilibrium domestic output is determined by the intersection of the domestic supply curve and the marginal revenue curve that is derived from the demand curve for domestic output, D_d. One can easily see that the domestic price is higher in the case of the quota (Figure 7.3d) than in the case of the tariff (Figure 7.3c). The difference can, of course, be attributed to the difference in the way the D_d curves are derived. The difference would have been greater if we had invoked the usual small country assumption that the foreign supply curve is infinitely elastic within the relevant range. In this case, with a tariff the domestic supplier cannot take advantage of his potential monopoly power. Yet since he would be able to do so if he were protected by a quota, the existence of quotas can be said to convert a potential monopoly into an actual one. Indeed, if the domestic producer is awarded a monopoly in holdings of the quota (a situation not without precedent in colonial history or in the contemporary experience of several LDCs), he will become a pure monopo-

list with two sources of supply to choose from in maximizing his profits.

The relatively greater use of quantitative restrictions on trade in LDCs, combined with the small size of their domestic markets and the absence of any means or even desire to control domestic monopoly on the part of their governments, raises the distinct possibility that the trade policies of many LDCs impose welfare losses on their economies of even greater magnitude than those indicated by our earlier calculations for tariffs.

Monopoly-Creating Mergers: The Welfare Trade-offs

The apparent lack of interest in controlling monopoly on the part of LDC governments is not without possible justification. By increasing the concentration of industries that are subject to economies of scale, cost reductions can quite conceivably be obtained. The assumption of U-shaped cost curves makes this argument especially important in small LDCs, where in many industries market size is too small to support more than one medium- or large-sized plant.

Let us consider the case of monopoly-creating mergers that yield cost reductions. This case, which has been discussed in the context of antitrust policy by O. E. Williamson (1968) and DePrano and Nugent (1969),

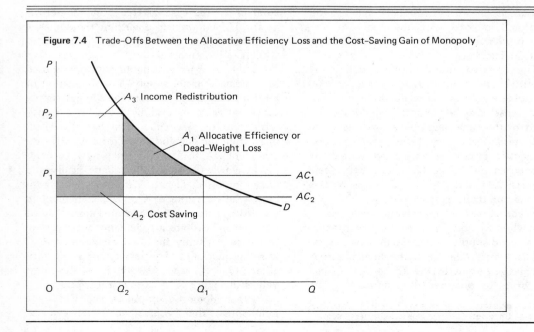

Figure 7.4   Trade–Offs Between the Allocative Efficiency Loss and the Cost-Saving Gain of Monopoly

is shown in Figure 7.4. Before the mergers, competition prevails, and average and marginal costs are constant at AC_1. Equilibrium output and price are Q_1 and P_1 respectively. As a result of a monopoly-creating series of mergers, costs are assumed to be reduced to AC_2 and equilibrium output and price are now Q_2 and P_2. The dead-weight loss from monopoly is given by the shaded area, A_1, but this is now offset by a welfare gain measured by the area of the shaded rectangle, A_2. The former may be approximated by $\frac{1}{2} \Delta P \Delta Q$ and the latter by $Q_2 \Delta AC$. If $Q_2 \Delta AC > \frac{1}{2} \Delta P \Delta Q$, there will even be a net welfare gain resulting from the monopolizing mergers.

The condition for a welfare gain from the monopoly-creating series of mergers is thus

$$Q_2 \Delta AC - \frac{1}{2} \Delta P \Delta Q > 0 \qquad (26)$$

Since the elasticity of demand, η, is equal to $(\Delta Q/Q)(P/\Delta P)$, we can substitute $Q\eta(\Delta P/P)$ for ΔQ. Then, dividing the revised version of equation 26 by Q and P_1 and remembering that $P_1 = AC_1$, we obtain

$$\frac{\Delta AC}{AC_1} - \frac{1}{2}\eta\left(\frac{\Delta P}{P_1}\right)^2 > 0 \qquad (27)$$

For a given elasticity of demand, expression 27 allows us to calculate the percentage price increases that could be offset by different percentage cost reductions. However, costs and prices are obviously not independent of each other. Indeed, the monopolist who is not constrained by the threat of antitrust activity or by potential entry will set price according to Joan Robinson's (1933) well-known rule: $P = (\eta/\eta - 1)MR$. In this case, it would mean that $P_2 = (\eta/\eta - 1)AC_2$, since from our diagram we know that $P_1 = AC_1$, $P_2/P_1 = (\eta/\eta - 1)(AC_2/AC_1)$. Converting this expression into one involving percentage changes in price and cost, to permit comparison with equation 27, we obtain

$$\frac{\Delta P}{P_1} = \frac{1 - \eta\left(\frac{\Delta AC}{AC_1}\right)}{\eta - 1} \qquad (28)$$

The percentage change in price in this relationship represents the change that would be expected on the basis of profit maximization for assumed values of η and $\Delta AC/AC$ from a monopoly-creating merger.

Thus, although they represent fundamentally different relationships, equations 27

and 28 involve the same three elements: (1) the elasticity of demand, η; (2) the percentage change in average cost associated with the merger; and (3) the percentage change in price. In both formulas, given any two of the three elements, the third can be calculated. We proceed by assuming several alternative cost reductions varying from 0.12 percent to 80 percent and elasticity of demand values of 1.1, 1.5, and 2.0, and we calculate the percentage change in prices from equation 27 and then from equation 28.

The assumed percentage cost reductions are given in column A of Table 7.3; the assumed elasticities of demand are given at the top of the table. In columns B of the same table, we give the price increases whose welfare effects could be offset by the cost reductions, as computed from equation 27. In columns C, computed from equation 28, we present the price increases that would result from monopolization accompanied by the assumed cost reductions.

Note, for example, that if $\eta = 2.0$ and $\Delta AC/AC = 5$ percent, from column B, based on equation 27, the percentage price increase, whose welfare effects would be offset by the cost reduction, would be 22.36 percent. However, according to column C, based on equation 28, the expected profit-maximizing price increase under these conditions would be 90 percent. This implies that, should the cost reduction associated with the monopoly-creating merger be only 5 percent and should profit-maximizing price behavior prevail, the monopoly-creating merger would lead to an unambiguous loss in social welfare. Even a 20 percent cost reduction would be insufficient to bring about a welfare gain, because the expected increase in price (60 percent in column C) would be greater than that which could be offset (44.27 percent in column B).

With lower elasticities of demand, even smaller cost reductions are necessary to offset the welfare effects of a given price increase. However, lower elasticities would lead to even higher price increases for any given cost reduction resulting from a merger. For example, when the elasticity is 1.1, column B would indicate that a cost reduction of 0.50 percent would be sufficient to eliminate the negative effects of a 12.72 percent price increase, but from column C, it is seen that a 0.50 percent cost reduction at that elasticity would be associated with an approximately tenfold increase

Table 7.3 *Relationships Between Cost Reductions and Price Increases*

Percentage Cost Reduction	Elasticity of Demand					
	2.0		1.5		1.1	
	Percentage Price Increase					
(A)	(B)	(C)	(B)	(C)	(B)	(C)
0.12	3.40	99.76	3.92	199.60	6.18	998.75
0.25	5.00	99.50	5.76	199.20	9.09	997.25
0.50	7.00	99.00	8.07	198.50	12.72	994.50
1.00	10.00	98.00	11.53	197.00	18.18	989.00
2.00	14.14	96.00	16.30	194.00	25.21	978.00
3.00	17.32	94.00	19.97	191.00	31.49	967.00
4.00	20.00	92.00	23.00	188.00	36.36	956.00
5.00	22.36	90.00	25.78	185.00	40.65	945.00
10.00	31.62	80.00	36.48	170.00	57.48	890.00
20.00	44.27	60.00	51.04	140.00	80.48	780.00
30.00	54.76	40.00	63.14	110.00	99.55	670.00
40.00	63.24	20.00	72.92	80.00	114.97	560.00
50.00	70.71	0.00	81.53	50.00	128.55	450.00
60.00	77.45	−20.00	89.30	20.00	140.80	340.00
70.00	83.66	−40.00	96.46	−10.00	152.09	230.00
80.00	89.44	−60.00	103.12	−40.00	162.60	120.00

Notes:
Column *A:* Cost reductions
Column *B:* Price increases whose welfare effects could be offset by the cost reductions
Column *C:* Price increases that would result from monopolization with the given cost reductions
  Source: DePrano, M. E., and J. B. Nugent (1969), "Economies as an Antitrust Defense: Comment," *A.E.R.,* 59 (December), Table 1, p. 949.

in price after the merger. Comparison of columns *B* and *C* shows that only very large cost reductions would be sufficient to offset the price rise that might be expected to accompany monopoly-creating mergers in the industry. When the demand elasticity is 2.0, the cost reduction must be over 20 percent; with an elasticity of 1.5, the cost reduction would have to be over 40 percent; and at an elasticity of 1.1, a cost reduction greater than 70 per cent is necessary!

Even if firms were constrained by antitrust authorities or the threat of entry by other firms from raising prices to the full extent indicated by the calculations given in columns *C* (possibilities which we have argued seem rather unlikely in most LDCs), the related cost reductions and price increases forthcoming from such mergers would still be unlikely to give net welfare gains. Moreover, our assumption that monopoly would be associated with lower costs may be incorrect. Firms that are not subject to competitive pressures may see little reason to invest in the

adoption of new techniques. Monopoly producers in typical LDCs are likely to have lower "X-efficiency" (Balassa and Associates 1971; Bergsman 1974). They may also be less likely to invest in the search for lower cost sources of raw materials or to resist the cost-increasing pressures of labor unions, preferring instead to pass cost increases on to their consumers in the form of higher prices (Bell 1968).

As has already been mentioned, it is conventional to ignore the income distributional effects (such as that represented by area A_3 in Figure 7.4), because they do not necessarily imply changes in welfare. Usually, it is argued that the redistribution of income from consumers to the monopoly producer could be compensated for by an appropriate combination of tax, expenditure, and transfer policies. In practice, however, it may be very difficult to bring about such compensatory policies. Even if they could be instituted, they might have undesirable consequences. Most importantly, the tax or transfer activities that would mitigate or compensate for the effects of mergers on income distribution would also have the effect of decreasing the intersectoral income differentials which could otherwise serve to improve the allocation of resources to the industry. This involves an unpleasant choice between equity and efficiency. This choice is avoided by policies that remove the artificial barriers to entry and open the industry to competition, eliminating monopoly power. Both greater equity and improved efficiency in resource allocation would be achieved by the elimination of monopoly. Thus, in practice, it may be unwise to ignore the income distribution effects of price distortions. Income distribution can be a fundamental part of the allocative process.

Other cases of possible interdependencies between one type of efficiency and another could be cited. Vanek (1971), for example, has explored the possible trade-offs between the allocative inefficiency of tariff distortions and the dynamic efficiency of increased investment and growth attainable through the investment of the tariff proceeds. In such cases, tariff and other distortions can be, on balance, beneficial. By and large, however, positive interdependencies among distortions, which compound the welfare losses attributable to any single distortion, seem at least as likely as the negative interdependencies investigated here.

Summary and Conclusions

In Chapters 5 and 6, we studied the microeconomics of efficiency. Chapter 7 has been devoted to the macroeconomic question of the aggregate cost of inefficiency. While the two previous chapters emphasized partial equilibrium analysis of efficiency, this chapter started from partial equilibrium considerations and proceeded to general equilibrium in the context of two- and three-commodity models. The analysis in the previous chapters started by assuming perfect markets, an assumption that was eventually relaxed to allow for firm-specific prices of inputs and output. This chapter has concentrated on cases of market imperfections by studying inefficiency in the case of monopolies, and price distortions owing to the imposition of tariffs and quotas. By simulation methods, we have estimated the costs of inefficiency under various alternative assumptions that are likely to hold in many LDCs.

The welfare cost of monopoly was studied within the usual partial equilibrium, consumer surplus framework. When this framework has been utilized, as in empirical studies of monopoly in DCs, the first-pass results have generally yielded estimates of negligible magnitude—as low as one-tenth of 1 percent of GNP. When, however, more realistic assumptions are introduced into the model, the cost for the DCs has been found to increase substantially to as high as 6 or 8 percent of GNP. Although specific studies for LDCs are not available, there are reasons to believe that the welfare costs of monopoly in LDCs are even higher.

The consumer surplus approach to the cost of inefficiency was extended in a general equilibrium framework utilizing two- and three-commodity models. Quantitative estimates of welfare costs of tariff distortions have been based on an international trade model with one exportable and two importable commodities. The crucial parameters used in our simulation experiments were measures for the curvature of the production possibility curve and of the utility function, the size of the price distortion, as measured by the average tariff rate, and the variation of individual tariff rates from the average. The results presented in Tables 7.1 and 7.2 were dramatic. First, it was observed that the production cost of tariffs tends to be more important than the consumption cost, rising, under extreme assumptions, to as high as 25 percent of GNP. Second, and under assumptions generally realistic for LDCs, the total welfare loss (including both the production and the consumption costs) due to tariff protection may well amount to 10 percent or more of GNP. This implies that the elimination of inefficiencies of this kind could well add 1 percent to the annual rate of growth of a number of LDCs over a period of 10 years. Barring complete elimination of tariffs, the rationalization of protection in LDCs, for example, by giving all industrial sectors a common effective tariff rate or by adopting a dual exchange rate, would substantially decrease the welfare cost of inefficiency. These results will be further utilized in Chapter 19, in the study of economic integration.

If the domestic production sector is competitive, the imposition of a quota is equivalent to the imposition of a tariff. Under monopolistic conditions, however, this equivalence does not hold, and the welfare cost of protection by quotas is higher than the cost of protection by tariffs. This case was studied in the last section of Chapter 7, in which we concentrated on interdependencies between different sources of inefficiency, such as protection and monopoly, or between different effects of monopoly-creating mergers, such as cost reductions and increases in monopoly power. Since quotas often substitute for tariffs and at the same time provide monopolistic positions for favored producers, the actual welfare costs of the market imperfections existing in most LDCs are probably very large.

Part III
Development Dynamics

In Part II, we discussed development statics as based on the neoclassical theory of economic maximization. The process of change originated from marginal adjustments and was achieved through smooth processes, which lead to equilibrium (also covered in Part III). The basic difference, however, between our treatment of statics and of dynamics is that in the latter case equilibrium is not achieved instantaneously but requires time. Once time is explicitly introduced into the system, variables, such as capital, labor, and technology, previously treated as independent (exogenous) variables in the production function, become endogenous. In the dynamics of development, therefore, we concentrate on the process of accumulation with respect to productive factors and technology.

Consider, for example, the case of efficiency that we studied within the development statics framework. The degree to which technical and price efficiency prevail in a given situation may make a considerable difference as far as welfare in the short run is concerned. However, differences in economic efficiency between DCs and LDCs are certainly insufficient for explaining more than a small portion of differences in per capita income among countries. This is, of course, because the process of development requires time, during which changes in technology, prices, resource endowments, and accumulation patterns are witnessed. People react to these changes. In the long run, the extent and nature of the reaction to changing circumstances is likely to be of far greater importance in explaining international differences in income or growth than the degree of efficiency attained at any single point in time. In this process, resource endowments change and accumulation occurs. Such are the concerns of development dynamics.

We begin our discussion of development dynamics, in Chapter 8, by studying how individuals respond to changes in relative prices. This is the dynamic counterpart to allocative efficiency. Some of the earlier literature in development economics has challenged the usefulness of economic analysis on the grounds that actual behavior in LDCs tends to be either unresponsive or even perversely responsive to changes in relative prices. In other words, it has been alleged that actual behavior is inconsistent with the predictions of economic theory. We shall show that the kinds of phenomena that have been cited as examples of "perverse" behavior are not necessarily inconsistent with economic theory—even that of the simplistic variety—when properly understood! We also demonstrate some analytic tools that have proved useful in measuring responsiveness. When these methods are applied, they generally indicate a considerable degree of responsiveness to incentives.

Next, in Chapter 9, we study technological change. The reader may recall from the development statics framework of Part II that technical efficiency is measured by the constant term in the production function. Furthermore, differences in technical efficiency among (groups of) firms were assumed to be of a certain kind, that is, neutral displacements of the isoquant reflecting only changes in the constant terms while the other parameters of the production function remained the same. In a dynamic framework, the constant term in the production function may change over time. Furthermore, in response to changes in exogenous variables, such as prices, other characteristics of the production function may also change. The study of technological change is concerned with these issues, and it is organized around four characteristics of technology: (1) the technical efficiency of production; (2) the scale of operation of production; (3) the factor intensity (or technological bias); and (4) the elasticity of substitution. Our analysis leads to the study of the causes and effects of technological change. The fact that several characteristics of technology vary from sector to sector provides the basis for technological dualism, discussed in Chapter 14. When these differences increase over time, they suggest that dualism is likely to be not just a temporary state but rather an immutable fact of development.

Of crucial importance in development dynamics are the rate and nature of factor accumulation. The dominant constraints on factor accumulation may be on either the supply or the demand side—of course always recognizing the fundamental interdependence between the two. Capital formation may take one of two forms, physical (such as roads, buildings, machinery, or transport equipment) or human (such as education, health, or on-the-job training). In each case, we present analytical tools that allow us to formulate operational hypotheses concerning the determinants of investments in physical and human capital. When one compares the properties and implications of alternative hypotheses and subjects them to empirical tests, the set of candidate hypotheses can be narrowed considerably.

Labor has also traditionally been treated in the economic literature within the context of factor mobilization—primarily from the viewpoint of existing surplus resources. A particular view of development consisted of considering unemployment and underemployment as a surplus of a valuable resource that could be transferred (cheaply) from its origin in the agricultural sector to fill the new jobs created in the nonagricultural sector. A popular strategy of development was based on this labor transfer. This transfer, it has been thought, sets in motion an equilibrating mechanism that culminates in the "break-out" point and the elimination of economic dualism.

With the recent rapid growth of urban unemployment throughout the Third World, attention has shifted radically to the issues of employment generation and labor force participation. Of particular importance in determining unemployment rates in the future are the various groups who presently exist in that nefarious land of hidden unemployment and underemployment that lies between open unemployment, on the one hand, and employment on the other. We develop a utility maximization model of surplus labor in the agricultural sector that combines the objective and subjective factors that jointly determine the behavior of these individuals. Our analysis suggests that this group is likely to be dominated by inframarginal individuals with above-average capability, training, and ambition rather than by the marginal or unemployable individuals who have traditionally been supposed to constitute the unemployed. This analysis sets the stage for the study of rural-urban migration, in Chapter 13. It also raises an important question for empirical investigation: "Who migrates?" If the migrants are more highly qualified inframarginal individuals in hidden unemployment, migration cannot be an equilibrating mechanism but rather one that reinforces existing dualism and disequilibrium. Since theory as well as empirical findings suggest that this is the case, the study of migration is postponed until Part IV, where developmental disequilibria are treated.

As the reader will see, even when the adjustments and processes with which we are concerned are no longer those of the instantaneous type considered in the development statics of Part II, but rather require time and thus are the concern of development dynamics, one would still characterize the analysis in terms of generally equilibrating mechanisms and smooth and complete adjustments. Nevertheless, several of the hypotheses, models, or phenomena dealt with in development dynamics admit to assumed differences between groups in some respects. For example, we may find that capitalists save larger proportions of income than workers (or alternatively that the rich save larger proportions of income than the poor, or that people with unstable incomes save more than those with stable incomes). We may also find that workers in industry are more productive (at least at the margin) than those in agriculture or that the rate of return to education varies among racial or ethnic groups or among different regions. Private rates of return may differ from social rates of return. If these phenomena are realistic and, more important, if they are persistent and recurring features of the economic milieu, the classical conception of development as a smooth process of continuous and complete adjustments and equilibrating mechanisms must have failed to describe fully the process of growth. Moreover, in studying the phenomena of hidden unemployment and migration, we find the suggestion that the classical mechanisms of adjusting to disequilibria, namely, exchange and factor mobility, may be selective in such a way as to increase rather than diminish the extent of disequilibrium. These considerations outline the limitations of development dynamics and suggest the need for the study of development disequilibria, the subject of the rest of this book (Parts IV, V, and VI).

Chapter 8
Response
to Incentives

We have examined in some depth the question of whether or not, and why, firms, industries, or economies vary in their technical efficiency, price efficiency, and overall economic efficiency at any point in time. However, we have thus far ignored what may be the more important and relevant question: if they should for one reason or another be inefficient, or if circumstances change, how rapidly and to what degree would they adjust? To what extent would they respond to economic and other incentives in order to maintain or improve their efficiency and mobilize their resources?

As we shall show, a failure of individuals, firms, and economies to respond to purely economic incentives may not necessarily imply that economics is useless in formulating policies for economic development. It does imply, however, that the theories that deal with development must be general ones, encompassing both economic and noneconomic motivations. After an introductory discussion on the response to incentives in a general sense, that is, including both economic and noneconomic incentives, we discuss two particular kinds of behavioral response: the supply of labor and the supply of agricultural output. In the first of these cases, incentives are defined broadly with both pecuniary and nonpecuniary elements. In the second case, they are defined more narrowly in economic terms alone. We conclude the chapter with a discussion of some shortcomings of existing approaches.

Pecuniary and Nonpecuniary Aspects of Utility Maximization

Response to incentives is closely connected with the discussion of rationality. Economic theory postulates the existence of a utility function and leads to predictions about behavior connected with the maximization of this function. Utility derives from a basket of pecuniary and nonpecuniary elements. The former are goods and services available in the marketplace. The latter are taste-satisfying elements, such as leisure, security, prestige, glory, and love for fellowman, which cannot generally be bought and sold. Maximization of utility implies the equimarginal principle—the equalization (at the margin) of the "return" per unit of "cost" for each element that enters the utility basket.[1] This leads to predictions about observable phenomena: when the return or the cost for any element of the utility basket changes, we should observe marginal readjustments in the quantities of the elements in the basket.

The pecuniary elements can be readily homogenized and aggregated through the use of prices to give income. In this form, they are relatively easy to handle. If the cost of champagne increases, there is a readjustment that involves less champagne and more of some other elements, say wine, in order to maximize the utility function—income in the case of pecuniary goods. If there is an increase in the return of labor, the readjustment involves more labor, so that the equality of return per unit of cost at the margin is restored.

The convenience of handling the pecuniary elements in the utility function often leads to neglecting the nonpecuniary elements—to assuming that the nonpecuniary elements have zero weight. This at times can be done with impunity. But the more this assumption departs from reality, that is, the greater the weight of nonpecuniary elements relative to pecuniary elements, the more likely we are to observe "strange" economic behavior, and the less satisfactory the concept of income becomes as a scalar proxy for the utility function.

Nonresponse to incentives is usually meant to indicate that a change in the return per unit of cost in the pecuniary part of the basket does not lead to any marginal readjustments in observable behavior, or, in the extreme case, it leads to "perverse" readjustments. Suppose that the return to employment of labor in mines increases. Suppose also that the quantity of labor supplied does not increase or that it decreases. This would be nonresponse to economic incentives; yet it would not necessarily imply that the utility function does not exist or that people are not maximizing their utility. It would only imply that the pecuniary part alone is not a good proxy for the entire utility function and would suggest that the refractory nonpecuniary part should be explicitly introduced into our model. Thus, even if it should be important to consider leisure, security, or the satisfactions derived, for example, from staying with the tribe, economics need not become useless—only more complicated; it can still lead to predictions.

The farmer who lives at the brink of starvation and yet refuses to experiment with high-yielding varieties of rice behaves rationally according to a risk-aversion hypothesis like that of Friedman and Savage (1948). In order to explain such behavior, it would be sufficient to assume that the marginal utility of income does not decrease monotonically as income rises, but rather it increases after a certain threshold level of income is reached, before decreasing again. Consider the farmer who thinks, for example, that if he experiments he either doubles his income if he succeeds or starves his family if he fails. No matter what probability value he attaches to the failure of the experiment, he still should rationally prefer the payoff of the present yields, which is virtually certain because his family may have survived for generations on the same land, with the same techniques and yields. This hypothesis can be tested. It predicts that, other things being equal, rich farmers would be more likely to experiment with new crops than poor farmers. If the hypothesis is confirmed, it can lead to interesting policy implications. For example, poor farmers would be more willing to experiment if the government guaranteed their present level of output in case the experiment failed. A number of "innovative insurance" schemes seem to have met with success, precisely as the hypothesis would have predicted.[2]

Another aspect of uncertainty minimization that carries an important weight in the objective function of producers in LDCs is food grain self-subsistence. The cultivator who

---

[1] If we write utility, U, as a function of returns, R, and costs, C, maximization of utility implies $dU = (\partial U/\partial R)dR + (\partial U/\partial C)dC = 0$.

[2] According to Taiwanese newspaper reports, Taiwan has a highly successful insurance program of this sort. For an example of a similar insurance proposal, see Marglin (1965).

produces food grain for self-consumption runs the risk of a poor crop. So does the cultivator who produces cash crops exclusively for the market. The latter, however, also runs a double risk on prices. The price of his cash crop may have fallen by harvest time, and the price of food grain for his consumption may have increased by the time he is ready to buy it. This probability of adverse movement in prices increases the risk to the cultivator who produces cash crops—and the higher the ratio of self-consumption to cash crops (the higher the ratio of a particular nonpecuniary element in the utility function, subsistence crop, to the one pecuniary element, cash crop), the greater this risk element. It is not surprising, therefore, to find small farmers concentrating in self-subsistence production and in the production of low-risk crops (Falcon 1964). This does not imply that such farmers are ignorant or insensitive to incentives. Rather, it is proper behavior that leads to maximizing an objective function, including nonpecuniary taste-satisfying elements, in addition to the usual pecuniary component. Formulated as a testable hypothesis, this can lead to a number of important predictions. For example, we would expect to find that the ratio of cash crop areas increases with the size of the farm.

Even "perverse" responses to economic incentives, for example, the backward sloping supply curve of labor, can be perfectly consistent with standard economic theory, as we demonstrate in the next section.

Labor Supply Response: The Backward Sloping Supply Curve Hypothesis

One extremely important kind of response to economic incentives is the response of labor to changes in wage rates. A perverse labor reaction, often postulated in the literature, is that the quantity of labor supplied decreases when the wage rate is increased.

Explanations for the backward sloping supply curve of labor have ranged from the fixity of wants—unitary elastic demand curve for real income—to the grudging accommodation of the phenomenon as an economic curiosity.[3] The didactic exposition in terms of indifference curves that follows proposes to

establish that there is nothing anomalous about backward bending supply curves of labor. Fixity of wants is sufficient to produce such a supply curve. It is, nevertheless, an overly restrictive and specious assumption. Instead, we will conclude that the backward bend is normal when the one who demands leisure is also the supplier of labor, which is *par excellence* the case of the worker. The increase in money income that results from an increase in the wage rate is analyzed into two effects, the *income effect* and the *effect on income*, which, in combination with the *substitution effect*, can produce backward sloping supply curves of labor. The analysis will conclude that the precise combination of the three effects necessary for the backward bend in the supply curve is less likely to occur in LDCs than in DCs.

Consider a set of indifference curves, U_0, $U_1, U_2, \ldots U_n$, as in Figure 8.1, between X, representing the rate of leisure per unit of time available to an individual (e.g., 168 hours per week or 365 days per year), and Y, representing real income, or the composite demand for all other goods (except leisure) that the individual consumes per unit of time. By the usual assumption of diminishing marginal utility and lack of interdependence of utilities, the indifference curves are well behaved.

We draw the opportunity lines of the individual at different wage rates, QM, QM', and so on, and designate the preferred income-leisure combinations, that is, the respective tangencies of the opportunity lines with the indifference curves, P, A, B, C, D, and so on. The curve, QPR, that joins all possible tangency points is the price-consumption curve. It indicates the way consumption of leisure (or supply of labor) varies when the price of leisure changes.

The price-consumption curve provides sufficient information to derive the supply curve of labor (or the demand curve for leisure). The slope of the opportunity line, QM, expresses the marginal rate of substitution between leisure and income (or the price of leisure in terms of income, OM/OQ). For steeper opportunity lines, the marginal rate of substitution (or the price of leisure in terms of income, OM'/OQ) increases. Given our indifference map, with an increasing marginal rate of substitution, the quantity of labor supplied increases (or the quantity of leisure de-

[3]For examples of the fixity-of-wants approach, see references in Berg (1961). Smith (1937, pp. 80–82) and Marshall (1952, pp. 438–439) recognized the phenomenon and approached it as a curiosity.

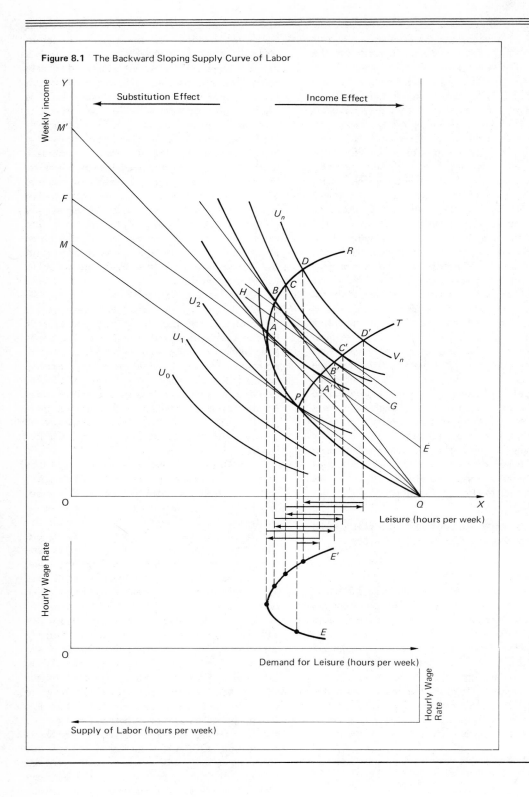

Figure 8.1 The Backward Sloping Supply Curve of Labor

manded decreases) for the range up to point A; but at higher marginal rates of substitution, the quantity of labor supplied decreases (or the quantity of leisure demanded increases) for the range beyond point A. In other words, the price-consumption curve, QPR, reveals information about an eventually upward sloping "demand curve" for leisure. This has been plotted against the wage rate as curve EE' on the lower diagram of Figure 8.1. Since leisure is by definition the time spent not working, it follows that curve QPR, as transformed in EE', can easily be expressed in terms af labor. If read (from right to left) against the scale for labor added at the bottom of Figure 8.1, the curve EE' shows an individual's supply curve of labor that initially slopes upward, then flattens out, and eventually slopes backward.

In order to explain the backward bend in the supply curve of labor, it would be useful to dissociate the income effects from the substitution effects resulting from changes in the slope of the opportunity line, QM, QM', and so on. This can be done by holding the marginal rate of substitution between leisure and income constant, but shifting the market opportunity curve upward from QM to EF, GH, and so on. This yields the series of new equilibrium points, P, A', B', C', D'. The income-consumption curve, PT, shows the way consumption varies when income increases and the marginal rate of substitution remains unchanged. It represents the income effect. The move away from the income-consumption curve as a result of changes in the marginal rate of substitution represents the substitution effect.

The explanation of the income and the substitution effect is now simple. When the price of leisure in terms of income (the marginal rate of substitution between leisure and income or the wage rate) increases, the individual who is the supplier of leisure becomes better off and moves along the income-consumption line, PT. Since we assume neither leisure nor income to be "inferior" commodities, the slope of the income-consumption line is upward and to the right. It indicates that the richer the individual is, the more of everything he buys—more of the composite commodity and more leisure as well. The same increase in the price of leisure, however, means that the individual who is also a demander of leisure is willing to substitute the composite commodity that has become relatively cheaper for leisure. This time the substitution effect is in operation, and the individual moves from the income-consumption to the price-consumption line—from point A' to A, B' to B, and so on—for different levels of income.

Can we determine in advance the result of the combination of the income and substitution effect? The substitution effect always pulls to the left—an increase in the price of X, per se, will always result in substitution of Y for X. The income effect agrees with the substitution effect when X is an "inferior" good—i.e., if it is largely consumed at low levels of income but is replaced, or partially replaced, by other goods (in this instance by Y) as income rises. In this case, the net result of the combined income and substitution effect is unequivocal. It yields a normal downward sloping demand curve for leisure or an upward sloping supply curve of labor.

But for leisure to be an "inferior" good is the exception rather than the rule. In the usual case in which we assume leisure to be a "noninferior" good, the two effects work counter to one another, and the net result depends upon their relative strength. Follow, for example, the change of the opportunity line from QM to QM' in Figure 8.1. At point P, the individual sells relatively little labor (or buys much leisure), so that an increase in the price of labor (from OM/OQ to OM'/OQ) does not make him much better off. On the other hand, the new opportunity line, QM', indicates a relatively large increase in the price of labor, given the fact that we started from a comparatively low initial position. As the arrows at the bottom of the graph show, the substitution effect is larger than the income effect, and the net result is that the individual increases the quantity of labor he sells (or decreases the quantity of leisure he buys).

The next movement is from point A to point B. Since at A the individual sells more labor, an increase in its price accounts for a relatively strong income effect. The relative increase in price being less this time, the substitution effect is weaker than the income effect, as shown again by the arrows. So the individual decreases the quantity of labor he sells (or increases the quantity of leisure he buys). When one moves to an even steeper opportunity line, the quantity of labor sold (or leisure bought) decreases, and so the income effect is relatively weaker in comparison to what it was before. Since the relative change in price is now smaller, however, the substitution effect is also weaker in relation to what it was before—so much so that the income effect still counterbalances it—and we continue moving on the backward sloping part of the supply curve of labor.

The operation of the income and substitution effect upon the demand curve for a commodity may be summarized as follows:

> The demand curve for a commodity must slope downwards, more being consumed when the price falls, in all cases when the commodity is not an inferior good. Even if it is an inferior good, so that the income effect is negative, the demand curve will still behave in an orthodox manner so long as the proportion of income spent upon the commodity is small, so that the income effect is small. Even if neither of these conditions is satisfied, so that the commodity is an inferior good which plays an important part in the budgets of its consumers, it still does not necessarily follow that a fall in price will diminish the amount demanded. For even a large negative income effect may be outweighed by a large substitution effect. (Hicks 1946, p. 35.)

In reference to the response to incentives, there are two differences between the demand for any other commodity and the demand for leisure. First, in the case of the demand for leisure, the income effect and the substitution effect work in *opposite* directions—save in the exceptional case when leisure is an "inferior" good. What is the rule in this case is the exception for the demand of any other commodity. There, the income and substitution effects work in the *same* direction—with the exception, again, of "inferior" goods. Second, in the case of the demand for any other commodity, the negative income effect will be small and most likely swamped by the substitution effect if the proportion of income spent upon the commodity is small. This is extremely unlikely to happen in the case of leisure, which is a general category that absorbs a good part of the individual's real budget.

Both these differences, however, seem to be contingent upon a more general asymmetry that exists between demand and supply curves. Usually, we assume the purchaser's income to be fixed in terms of money. In the case of the demand for leisure, however, the individual comes to the market not only as a buyer but also as a seller, and this directly affects his *money income*. If the price of leisure (the wage rate) increases, the substitution effect is well defined. It will work toward decreasing the quantity of leisure demanded (increasing the quantity of labor supplied). But with regard to income, the effect is double. A higher price of leisure (higher wage rate) means that the demander of leisure suffers a decrease in real income. As a result of this *income effect*, he is likely to purchase less leisure. On the other hand, by the same token the supplier of labor receives more money income. As a result of this *effect on income*, he is likely to buy more of everything, including more leisure. The demander of leisure and the supplier of labor is the the same individual.

Since sellers usually derive large parts of their incomes from the commodity they sell, the effect on income dominates any time the consumer comes to the market not only as a buyer (of leisure) but also as a seller (of labor). The supply of all factors of production is an example. The awkward upward sloping demand curve or the downward sloping supply curve we may derive in such cases is attributed to the fact that the condition of *ceteris paribus* has been violated by an increase in the income of the demander.

At this point of the analysis, we may return to the utility function of the previous section, with its pecuniary elements and the refractory nonpecuniary elements. Since an increase in the wage rate leads to an effect on income, the individual engages in marginal readjustments within his utility basket by increasing the quantity of some elements. Some of these elements, the goods and services, can be acquired through the market; others, such as leisure, security, family esteem, and salvation, can be obtained through nonmarket activity. Whether the effect on income will lead on balance to purchasing more pecuniary goods and services or purchasing more nonpecuniary elements by even decreasing the absolute quantity of market elements that are bought depends largely on the weight given to nonpecuniary relative to pecuniary elements. This may explain why originally the backward bending supply curve of labor was associated with "the more ignorant and phlegmatic of races"—the underdeveloped market economies. The initial low wage rate at which the income effect becomes dominant reflects a limited range of choice and a lack of familiarity with market goods. As tastes develop and knowledge spreads, there is a rise in the wage rate at which the income effect, which reduces work effort, dominates. The contemporary LDCs that are immutably exposed to strong international demonstration effects are unlikely to be facing the same problems they did when they were inhabited by Marshall's "ignorant and phlegmatic" denizens! Therefore, the wage rate at which the backward bend occurs must be considerably higher —at a level, perhaps, that only the DCs can afford.

Another factor that may affect the point at which the supply curve bends backward by influencing the shape of the indifference map in Figure 8.1 is expectations referring to the wage rate. In the preceding discussion, we implicitly assumed that the higher wage rate is expected to be permanent. If, however, a higher wage rate is viewed as only temporary, the reaction to it may reveal that the income effect swamps the substitution effect at wage rates that are relatively higher than what they would have been if the wage increase were considered permanent. Such behavior constitutes an attempt to take advantage of the opportunity offered by a higher wage rate while the opportunity lasts, thereby postponing the purchase of leisure. Friedman (1962, pp. 205–206) offers this as an explanation of the wartime experience in the United States, where the average number of hours worked per week was substantially higher than in the prewar period.

Supply Response in Agriculture

The preceding section encompassed both economic and noneconomic incentives. In this section, we limit the discussion to response to economic incentives. More specifically, the supply response to price changes is formulated as a testable hypothesis, and it is tested in the context of LDC agriculture.

Three alternative hypotheses of supply response on the part of LDC farmers to agricultural price changes can be postulated.

Hypothesis I: Farmers in LDCs respond to relative price changes normally, that is, they increase the quantity of crops supplied as a result of an increase in prices, and they decrease the quantity supplied when prices decrease.

Hypothesis II: Farmers respond to relative price changes "perversely," that is, the quantity they supply is inversely related to price.

Hypothesis III: Farmers' response to price incentives is insignificant.

The test for the three alternative hypotheses consists of measuring the elasticity of supply with respect to price. Hypotheses I, II, and III predict, respectively, that the price elasticity of supply of agricultural products in LDCs is positive, negative, and zero. It is important to investigate the elasticity of supply in LDC agriculture, both for its implications for agricultural policy and also as an adjunct to the discussion of the applicability of economic theory to LDCs. In view of the size of the agricultural sector in the LDCs, of its potential contribution to the cause of development through an investable surplus,[4] and of the recently rekindled concern about world food shortages and the threat of starvation, the implications for policy have vital importance.

The diversity of opinion about the effects of the surplus food disposal program of the United States (Public Law 480) upon agricultural production in recipient countries provides an example of the importance of the question of supply responsiveness.[5] If foreign surpluses and domestic produce are disposed of in the same markets, the foreign surpluses obviously compete directly with domestic production. Even if they are channeled into a separate market, they compete indirectly with domestic production as long as arbitrage is possible. The first period effect of surplus food disposal, given the domestic supply, is a decrease in price by an amount that depends on the elasticity of demand. Given the lower price for food, the second period effect upon domestic food production depends on the

---

[4] The surplus of agricultural production over the consumption of the farm population may be exported, thus procuring important foreign exchange resources for economic development. Alternatively, the agricultural surplus can be devoted to domestic consumption, and then it can lead to significant intersectoral transfers, whether in the form of lower relative food prices or of direct taxes upon agriculture. For an example of this process, see Owen (1966). We will return to this question in Chapter 15.

[5] For a quantitative analysis of the impact of PL 480 imports, see Mann (1967).

elasticity of supply of domestic producers with respect to price. If the elasticity of supply is normal, foreign surplus food disposals discourage increases in domestic supply—and the higher the value of the elasticity, the more the discouragement (T. W. Schultz 1960b, p. 1028; Beringer 1963, p. 319). On the other hand, if farmers do not respond to price incentives, surplus food is irrelevant from the point of view of domestic production (Dantwala 1963, p. 87).

Even more extreme is the view that holds supply curves for marketed surplus to be downward sloping. In this case, the depressing effect that foreign surplus disposal has upon domestic prices leads to increases in the marketed quantities. This rather surprising thesis merits further examination. Khatkhate (1962) bases this conclusion on a postulated unitary elasticity of demand for money income: when price falls, the farmer increases the marketed surplus to maintain the same level of money income. P. N. Mathur and Ezekiel (1961) reach the same conclusion by postulating that subsistence farmers have an inelastic demand for cash to pay debt obligations, rent, and a Ricardian-type bundle of nonagricultural subsistence goods. However, since this argument assumes that both the income elasticity of demand for commodities other than home-produced foodgrains and the substitution effect are zero, it is a dubious one.[6]

Foreign surpluses could also be used to provide buffer stocks to stabilize the prices of domestic production. If farmers have aversion to price fluctuations, such stabilization could lead to increased domestic production, even if the stabilized price is lower than the mean level of the fluctuating price (F. M. Fisher 1963, pp. 863–869). If farmers are insensitive to price, stabilization through buffer stocks can only affect and benefit consumers.

Economic policies that fragment the market raise another set of questions, the answer to which is contingent upon the study of supply responsiveness. In certain countries (e.g., India, Indonesia, Thailand), exports of some staple foods are prohibited, not just from the country as a whole but even from one state or province to another. This policy, of course, penalizes producers in potential surplus-producing areas and also consumers of potential importing states; it benefits consumers of potential surplus-producing states and producers in potential importing states. However, if the elasticity of supply in all states is greater than zero, in the long run the policy decreases the available marketable surplus and may lead to higher prices and food shortages, even in the potential surplus-producing states.

The investigation of supply responsiveness in the agricultural sector in LDCs also relates to our discussion of labor supply and its response to changing wage rates. This is because straightforward tests of supply responsiveness that measure the elasticity of supply are incomplete, in the sense that they can only confirm the hypothesis of response to (price) incentives but cannot reject it. Suppose that we find a negative elasticity of supply to price for a certain cash crop. Such a finding is consistent with maximizing behavior and normal income and substitution effects, with leisure treated as a noninferior good. The reason was pointed out in the discussion on the backward bending supply curve of labor in terms of the income effect and the effect on income. The latter may be especially strong in LDCs, where producers derive a great part of their income from the supply of one cash crop and where the range of choice of pecuniary goods offered through the market is greatly restricted. A finding of a negative supply response, therefore, does not demonstrate that the response to incentives is perverse. At best, it reveals something about "perverse" Engel's curves—an increase in income leading to more than proportionate increases in the consumption of nonpecuniary elements.

The deceptive simplicity of the two-dimensional leisure-agricultural-income model may also be responsible for seemingly perverse responses. The problem of allocation of time for the farm household does not include only the choice between earning income from a cash crop and consuming leisure, but also the time to be spent on nonagricultural activities, such as making pottery, repairing implements, constructing a house, or making clothes. Labor devoted to these "Z-goods" can be important in rural areas. A fall in the price of the cash crop, accompanied by an increase in the cash crop output supplied, may occur

---

[6]Nowshirvani (1967a) has assailed this view on dynamic stability grounds. A negative unitary price elasticity for marketed surplus would imply that the urban elasticity of demand for food is greater than one. Empirical evidence suggests that this value is implausible.

simultaneously with a decrease in the price of Z-goods. Under these circumstances, it is only natural for the farmer to allocate more time to production of the cash crop and less to the Z-goods, which can now be purchased at lower prices.[7]

Simple Models of Supply Response

The purpose of supply response studies is to examine how output is related to a number of important factors, such as prices, technology, and weather. Of special interest is the relationship between output and price. This can be investigated by holding the other variables that enter the output function constant, that is, by estimating the partial regression coefficient of the price variable in a multiple regression of output on all relevant factors.

Output is a result of acreage planted and yield. Writing Q for output, A for acreage, and Y for yields, we have

$$Q = A \cdot Y \tag{1}$$

If the acreage planted and yields obtained (through intensity of work, etc.) are functions of price, P, by totally differentiating equation 1 we write,

$$\frac{dQ}{dP} = Y \frac{\partial A}{\partial P} + A \frac{\partial Y}{\partial P}$$

Assume that other inputs are varying in proportion to acreage and the production function is homogeneous of the first degree (constant returns to scale). Dividing the above equation through by Q/P, we can express the response of output with respect to price in terms of the elasticities of output, η_{qp}, acreage, η_{ap}, and yields, η_{yp} as

$$\frac{\frac{dQ}{dP}}{\frac{Q}{P}} = \frac{\frac{Q}{A}\frac{\partial A}{\partial P}}{\frac{Q}{P}} + \frac{\frac{Q}{Y}\frac{\partial Y}{\partial P}}{\frac{Q}{P}} = \frac{\frac{\partial A}{\partial P}}{\frac{A}{P}} + \frac{\frac{\partial Y}{\partial P}}{\frac{Y}{P}}$$

or

$$\eta_{qp} = \eta_{ap} + \eta_{yp} \tag{2}$$

One can make a further simplifying assumption if, in the specific context, this would seem sufficiently realistic. Suppose that the elasticity of yields with respect to price is nonnegative. Then we consider only the term η_{ap} and by regressing acreage on price we

derive a lower bound estimate of the price elasticity of output.[8]

Why should one regress acreage and not output on price? The variable we want to explain is planned output. This is an unobserved variable, and thus a proxy must be utilized. Realized output may be used as a proxy for planned output. In agriculture, however, the weather and other environmental factors have an important influence, which cannot be readily (inexpensively) controlled in empirical studies. As a result, realized output may vary significantly and systematically from the farmer's planned output. It is, therefore, common to use actual acreage as such a proxy, because acreage is thought to be more directly under the farmer's control and, once planted, cannot be varied during the production period by factors outside the farmer's control.[9]

A further problem arises in specifying the price that enters the output response function. The relevant price that should be considered is the price of the crop in question deflated by the price(s) of alternative crop(s) and by the prices of the inputs of production. Assuming that the prices of the inputs are constant over either time or crops, we can simplify the specification of the price variable by expressing it as a ratio of the price of the crop in question to a weighted average of the prices of competing crops.

Since we are interested primarily in the intentions of the farmer as expressed by planned output (and proxied by actual acreage planted), the relevant price variable becomes the "expected" price. Expected prices are also nonobserved variables, and a hypothesis of the way price expectations are formed is required.

The above discussion can be summarized

[7]For an interesting exposition of such a model, see Hymer and Resnick (1969).

[8]For examples of cases where the price elasticity of yields can be safely assumed as negligible, see Falcon (1964) and Behrman (1968, p. 154). In other instances, this assumption may be unrealistic, and then the response of yields to price has to be investigated specifically. Nerlove (1958, p. 67) mentions the example of the United States, where increased yields successfully substituted for acreage controls, and as a result, total output increased. Barker (1966) has pointed out the possibility of a negative effect of price upon yields, which works indirectly through acreage: the increased price of output expands cultivation to lands of marginal fertility, which has the effect of decreasing average yields.

[9]In agricultural areas of exceptionally high population density and a single crop, such as in some parts of Asia, acreage may not be a decision variable but rather an exogenously determined constant.

in a single equation model of supply response. We rewrite equation 1 using stars for planned or expected values

$$Q^* = A^* \cdot Y^* \qquad (3)$$

If, for reasons given above, actual acreage A is taken to be an adequate measure of planned acreage A^*, and if $\partial Y^*/\partial P$ is zero, the supply response function for an individual crop, i, in time period, t, may be specified as

$$A_{it} = f(P_{it}^*, P_{it}^{*f}, F_{it}^*, Y_{it}^*, W_t^*, t \cdots) \qquad (4)$$

where P_{it}^* is the expected price of crop i relative to that of alternative crops; P_{it}^{*f} is the price of the inputs to crop i relative to the price of inputs for alternative crops; F_{it}^* is a factor for expected technology in crop i relative to that of alternative crops; Y_{it}^* is the expected yield in crop i relative to that of alternative crops; W_t^* is expected weather; and t is a time trend.

Assuming for simplicity that P_i^{*f}, F_i^*, Y_i^*, and the various factors expected to change with time are all constant, that $P_{it}^* = P_{it-1}$, and that the elasticities of planned acreage with respect to expected price, η_{ap}, and weather, η_{aw}, are constant, equation 4 can be restated as

$$A_{it} = CP_{it-1}^{\eta_{ap}} W_t^{*\eta_{aw}}$$
$$\log A_{it} = \log C + \eta_{ap} \log P_{it-1} + \eta_{aw} \log W_t^* \qquad (5)$$

This model has been used to test for the supply responsiveness of Javanese rice farmers by Mubyarto and Fletcher (1966, p. 21), with time series data for 1951–1962. Their results (with standard errors in parentheses) are as follows:

$$\log A_{it} = 0.474 + 0.565 \log P_{it-1}$$
$$(0.187)$$
$$+ 0.141 \log W_t \quad R^2 = 0.577$$
$$(0.157) \qquad (6)$$

where P_{t-1} is the lagged price of rice relative to alternative crops and W_t is the amount of rainfall during the rice-growing season. The estimate of the elasticity of planned output with respect to price, η_{ap}, is thus 0.565, which is significantly different from zero at the 0.05 level. Moreover, since this estimate assumes away the probably positive influence of price on yields, this might well be a lower bound estimate of the true elasticity.

Nerlovian Supply Response Models

In the previous section, we treated expectations rather cavalierly: expected output was proxied by planted acreage and expected prices by the prices of the previous year. Furthermore, no attempt was made to introduce expectations with respect to acreage. The beginnings of a more satisfactory treatment of expectations in supply response relationships may be attributed to Nerlove (1958). Before we proceed to the presentation of a Nerlovian supply response model, however, the concept of adaptive expectations with respect to prices should be introduced.[10]

The adaptive expectations model was developed by Cagan (1956) along Hicksian (1946) lines. Expectations in this model are revised in proportion to the error associated with the previous levels of expectations (Cagan 1956, p. 37). We illustrate with an example from Hicks by considering expectations about prices. We define a person's elasticity of expectations, η_e, as the ratio of the percentage change in expected future prices to percentage change in present prices,

$$\eta_e = \frac{\dfrac{P_{t+1} - P_t}{P_t}}{\dfrac{P_t - P_{t-1}}{P_{t-1}}}$$

An elasticity of expectations equal to one then means that a person expects future prices to change by the same percentage as current prices. An elasticity of expectations equal to zero implies that the change in current prices is expected to have no effect on future prices. Finally, a negative elasticity of expectations would imply that people expect prices to revert from their current levels back toward their old levels. In general, then, the price that people expect for period t is the price that they expected for the period $t - 1$ plus a factor that depends on the elasticity of expectations and the actual price of period $t - 1$.

Cagan gave the following specific formulation of the adaptive expectations model. Writing starred (*) for expected and nonstarred for observed prices, P, we have

$$P_t^* = P_{t-1}^* + \beta[P_{t-1} - P_{t-1}^*], \quad 0 < \beta \leq 1 \qquad (7)$$

---

[10]For a survey of the literature on distributed lags, see Griliches (1967).

This can be written

$$P_t{}^* = (1 - \beta)P_{t-1}{}^* + \beta P_{t-1}$$
$$= \beta P_{t-1} + (1 - \beta)[(1 - \beta)P_{t-2}{}^* + \beta P_{t-2}]$$
$$= \beta P_{t-1} + (1 - \beta)\beta P_{t-2}$$
$$\quad + (1 - \beta)^2[(1 - \beta)P_{t-3}{}^* + \beta P_{t-3}]$$
$$= \beta P_{t-1} + (1 - \beta)\beta P_{t-2}$$
$$\quad + (1 - \beta)^2 \beta P_{t-3} + \cdots$$

$$P_t{}^* = \sum_{i=0}^{T} \beta(1 - \beta)^i P_{t-1-i} \qquad (8)$$

Equation 8 implies that expected prices assume a geometrically declining lag form as a function of all past prices. For example, if the expected prices for the year 1974 are expressed as a function of the observed prices of the three previous years ($i = 0$ to 2), the β term in the power of one refers to 1973, the squared term to 1972, and the cubed term to 1971 ($t - 1 - i = 1971$).

The definition of expectations in equation 7 can be utilized in a general model that makes X, output (or acreage), a function of expected prices,

$$X_t = a + bP_t{}^* + u_t \qquad (9)$$

From equations 8 and 9, we write

$$X_t = a + b \sum_{i=0}^{T} \beta(1 - \beta)^i P_{t-1-i} + u_t \qquad (10)$$

Operationally, the estimation of this equation requires iteration on β to maximize R^2. It has been shown that the resulting estimates from such a search procedure are maximum likelihood estimates.[11]

Nerlove (1958, p. 58 ff.) incorporated Cagan's adaptive expectations model into a partial adjustment model, which provides the skeleton of an acceptable rationale as well as a feasible estimation procedure that has appli-

cability to a wide range of problems. The adaptive expectations model, as applied to acreage response, consists of two hypotheses. First, price expectations (in the simplest case, actual current prices) determine the equilibrium output (or acreage), $X_t{}^*$. Second, in each period of production, output is adjusted (only partially) in proportion to the difference between last period's actual output and the long-run equilibrium output. In symbols

$$X_t{}^* = a + bP_t + u_t \qquad (11)$$

$$X_t - X_{t-1} = \gamma(X_t{}^* - X_{t-1}) \qquad (12)$$

Substituting equation 11 into equation 15, we obtain

$$X_t = a\gamma + b\gamma P_t + (1 - \gamma)X_{t-1} + \gamma u_t \qquad (13)$$

The reduced form equation 13 is simpler than equation 10, in that it can be easily estimated by least squares. It is similar to the Koyck-type reduced form (equation 1n in footnote 11), except that the error structure, and therefore the autocorrelation problems, differ.

From equation 13, we can estimate both the short-run and long-run elasticities of acreage with respect to price. The short-run elasticity ($\gamma = 1$) is the response of acreage to price in one time period, and for the mean of prices and acreage, it is given by[12]

$$\eta_{sr} = b\gamma \frac{\overline{P_t}}{\overline{X_t}} \qquad (14)$$

The long-run elasticity is defined as the elasticity over the time period necessary for complete adaptation, that is, $(1 - \gamma)^t = 0$. We have[13]

---

[11]Under the condition of a geometric lag distribution, Koyck (1954) has produced an equation that is easier to estimate. The price for this simplification is that if the original disturbances, u_t, were serially independent, they are no longer so in the transformed equation. Lagging equation 10 once, we have

$$X_{t-1} = a + b \Sigma \beta(1 - \beta)^i P_{t-2-i} + u_{t-1}$$

Multiplying by $1 - \beta$ and subtracting from equation 10,

$$X_t - (1 - \beta)X_{t-1} = b\beta \Sigma (1 - \beta)^i P_{t-1-i}$$
$$\quad - b(1 - \beta)\beta \Sigma (1 - \beta)^i P_{t-2-i} + u_t - (1 - \beta)u_{t-1}$$

or, since the interim periods cancel out,

$$X_t = b\beta P_{t-1} + (1 - \beta)X_{t-1} + u_t - (1 - \beta)u_{t-1} \qquad (1n)$$

This model is much easier to estimate.

[12]Since equation 13 is a first order difference equation, from it we can generate any X_t as

$$X_t = A_t X_0 + C \frac{1 - A^t}{1 - A}$$

where

$$C = a\gamma + b\gamma P_t \quad \text{and} \quad A = 1 - \gamma.$$

By substitution for A and C, we have

$$X_t = (1 - \gamma)^t X_0 + (a\gamma + b\gamma P_t) \frac{1 - (1 - \gamma)^t}{\gamma}$$

$$\frac{dX_t}{dP_t} = (b\gamma) \frac{1 - (1 - \gamma)^t}{\gamma} = b - b(1 - \gamma)^t$$

We then define the elasticity in general as

$$\eta = [b - b(1 - \gamma)^t] \frac{\overline{P_t}}{\overline{X_t}} \qquad (2n)$$

From 2n, we define the short-run and the long-run elasticity.

[13]This is again derived from equation 2n, in footnote 12.

$$\eta_{lr} = b\frac{\overline{P_t}}{\overline{X_t}} \qquad (15)$$

For $\gamma = 1$, that is, when present prices are expected to hold in the future, the long-run and short-run elasticities are equal. For $0 < \gamma < 1$, the two values differ. When $\gamma = 0.50$, five periods must be included in order to incorporate in the model past prices with weights totaling at least 0.95; when $\gamma = 0.30$, nine past prices must be included; and when $\gamma = 0.10$, 28 past prices must be included for complete adaptation.

Nerlovian supply response models are thus obviously much more general than the naive supply response models presented in the previous section, which were based on an equation of the form

$$X_t = a + bP_{t-1}$$

or

$$\log X_t = \log a + b \log P_{t-1}$$

Such models are adequate if $\gamma = 1$. But for γ less than one, not only is the naive model misspecified in that it omits lagged prices, P_{t-2}, P_{t-3}, and so on, but also the coefficient or elasticity of supply response, b, is underestimated.[14]

One can build "pure" partial adjustment supply response models by utilizing and appropriately modifying equations 11 and 12. Alternatively, one can construct more elaborate partial adjustment models that incorporate adaptive expectations along the lines of equation 7. An example of the former is provided by Krishna (1963); the latter, by Behrman (1968).[15] Generally, such methods yield considerably larger estimates of supply response than had been obtained from the more naive models.

[14]Nerlove (1956, p. 505) provides some comparative examples of United States farm output elasticities estimated with $\gamma = 1$ and unrestricted. They are, respectively, cotton 0.20 and 0.67 (actual $\gamma = 0.51$); wheat 0.47 and 0.93 (actual $\gamma = 0.52$); corn 0.09 and 0.18 (actual $\gamma = 0.54$). The effect of the misspecification appears by examining the improvement in the fit of the equation. For $\gamma = 1$ and γ unrestricted and for cotton, wheat, and corn, respectively, R^2 rises from 0.59 to 0.74; 0.64 to 0.77; and 0.22 to 0.35.

[15]For a complete list of references and results on estimating supply elasticities, either with partial adjustment models or with models that incorporate adaptive expectations, see Behrman (1968, pp. 15–19) and Krishna (1967, pp. 506–507).

Supply Response of Marketed Surplus

Thus far, output, acreage, and yields have been assumed to be determined primarily by price. We now consider a simple model that introduces income. In this way, we will become more aware of the significance of the nonpecuniary elements that enter the utility function, discussed at the beginning of this chapter.

A feature of subsistence agricultural economies is that the market supply is the residual of total output produced after household consumption needs have been satisfied. We write

$$M = Q - C \qquad (16)$$

where M is marketed surplus, Q is total quantity produced, and C is home consumption. In this model, M and Q are functions of P, the price of the crop relative to alternative crops. C is a function of P but also of I, the income of the household. Assume there is an increase in the price of the crop the farmer produces relative to alternative crops. The price effect of this change is for C to decrease to the extent that the farmer can substitute in his consumption function the alternative crops, which have now become cheaper. The income effect makes the farmer poorer, since an item he consumes has increased in price. The effect on income, however, makes the farmer richer, because the same marketed quantity as before, M, brings in higher real income. As a result of this effect on income, the producer consumes more of everything—even more of the crop he produces. These three effects of an increase in the price of the crop upon household consumption should be considered together with the positive effect of the price increase upon the quantity supplied in deciding whether the marketed surplus will increase, decrease, or remain the same.

By taking the first partial derivative of equation 16 with respect to price, we have

$$\frac{\partial M}{\partial P} = \frac{\partial Q}{\partial P} - \frac{\partial C}{\partial P} - \frac{\partial C}{\partial I}\frac{\partial I}{\partial P} \qquad (17)$$

Whereas $\partial M/\partial P$, $\partial C/\partial P$, and $\partial C/\partial I$ are conceivably quantities that can be observed either from supply response functions or from consumption functions, $\partial I/\partial P$ is unobservable. However, since the peasant is assumed to be both a producer and a consumer of the crop, the change in his income caused by a one-unit change in the price of the crop is approximately equal to the difference between the number of units he produces (his income gain derived from the price rise) and the number of units he consumes (his income loss associated with the price rise),[16]

$$\frac{\partial I}{\partial P} \simeq Q - C = M \tag{18}$$

By the substitution of equation 18 into equation 17, we have

$$\frac{\partial M}{\partial P} = \frac{\partial Q}{\partial P} - \frac{\partial C}{\partial P} - M \frac{\partial C}{\partial I} \tag{19}$$

By rearranging terms and multiplying by P/M so that we express the lefthand side as an elasticity, we write

$$\frac{P}{M}\frac{\partial M}{\partial P} = \frac{Q}{M}\frac{P}{Q}\frac{\partial Q}{\partial P}$$
$$- \left(\frac{Q}{M} - 1\right)\left(\frac{P}{C}\frac{\partial C}{\partial P} + \frac{M}{Q}\frac{PQ}{I}\frac{I}{C}\frac{\partial C}{\partial I}\right) \tag{20}$$

Define:

η_m = price elasticity of the marketed surplus,
η_q = price elasiticity of output,
η_c = price elasticity of home consumption of the crop in question,
η_e = income elasticity of home consumption of the crop in question, and
$k = PQ/I$, the total value of production relative to the net income of the producer.

We can now write

$$\eta_m = \eta_q \frac{Q}{M} - \left(\frac{Q}{M} - 1\right)\left(\eta_c + \eta_e k \frac{M}{Q}\right) \tag{21}$$

Since η_c is negative, and since η_e, k and M/Q are all smaller than one and thus their product, $\eta_e k(M/Q)$, is rather small, the term in the right-hand parentheses would either be positive but small or negative. Therefore, the elasticity of the marketed surplus, η_m, should be expected to be greater than the price elasticity of output, η_q. Also, the more diversified the portfolio of different crops, the higher η_m would become; the more specialized producers become (the closer the ratio Q/M approaches unity), the lower will be the value η_m.

An example of approximating the price elasticity of the marketed surplus by the first

term of equation 21 is given in Mangahas, Recto and Ruttan (1966). With an elasticity of planned output with respect to price (approximated by the elasticity of acreage with respect to price) for rice in a certain region of the Philippines of 0.11 and a ratio of marketed to produced rice of 37 percent, the elasticity of the marketed surplus is 0.30 (0.11 × 100/37). This may be an underestimate to the extent that the product term that includes η_c (an elasticity that is expected to be negative) exceeds $\eta_e k(M/Q)$ in the second term of equation 21.

An alternative approximation of η_m can be obtained if there exist cross-section data from which to estimate the elasticity of the marketed surplus with respect to output. We write

$$\eta_m = \frac{\frac{\Delta Q}{Q}}{\frac{\Delta P}{P}}\frac{\frac{\Delta M}{M}}{\frac{\Delta Q}{Q}} = \eta_q \frac{\frac{\Delta M}{M}}{\frac{\Delta Q}{Q}} \tag{22}$$

Krishna (1965) found the output elasticity of market supply, $(\Delta M/M)/(\Delta Q/Q)$, of wheat in many villages of India to lie between 1.04 and 1.6. With a price elasticity of output, η_q, of around 0.1 or 0.2, the price elasticity of marketed supply was estimated between 0.104 and 0.32.

Two problems arise in connection with Krishna's approach to the elasticity of the marketable surplus. First, the transition from equation 20 to equation 22 implies that the only income relevant in determining the demand for home consumption of crop i is the cash income derived from the marketed surplus of that crop. But it is the total net income of the household that is relevant. Second, consumption is not a function of the price of crop i relative to alternative crops in household production, but of the price of crop i relative to alternatives in household consumption. Behrman (1966, 1968) derives the elasticity of the marketable surplus by incorporating these two effects: the effect on income (the change in the net income of the household) and the income effect (the change in the initial value of consumption.)[17]

Other Considerations in Supply Response
While the use of distributed lags has made it possible to generate expectational hypotheses

---

[16]This is an approximation, because the first partial derivatives of Q and C with respect to P are excluded, despite the fact that both Q and C are functions of P.

[17]For the same argument, see Nowshirvani (1967b).

that are both more general and more highly operational than the earlier naive expectational hypotheses, we can hardly avoid acknowledging some glaring weaknesses. Most such hypotheses are still quite mechanical. For example, in the various supply response formulations we have considered—Cagan's in equation 7, Nerlove's in equations 11 and 12, and Koyck's in equation 1n of footnote 11—the crucial reaction coefficients are assumed to remain constant in the face of changing circumstances without any learning process over time. These models therefore ignore the question of how expectations are formed.

Another shortcoming in existing supply response models is that they generally fail to include constraints on the flexibility of various complementary factors. Thus, institutional and other constraints may be responsible for lack of response to incentives. For example, the Peronist restrictions of the late 1940s on the hiring and firing of agricultural workers have undoubtedly had some effect on making it more costly for agricultural enterprises in Argentina to adjust to changing market opportunities. Similarly, the responsiveness to emerging industrial opportunities may have been deterred by the need to obtain investment licenses, by fiscal disincentives, or by the formation of labor unions. Also, the monopsonistic powers in rural labor markets of large landowners, often buttressed by monopolies of political and economic power, may have limited farmers' willingness to respond to favorable opportunities. The lack of response in such cases may merely reflect the failure of our models to recognize the institutional constraints that impose costs on adjustments to changing circumstances.

Supply response models generally assume that price changes are the only signals that should elicit behavioral responses. But this may be far from the truth. In many instances, quantities (e.g., queues, unfilled orders, inventories, or vacancies) may be relatively more important signaling devices than prices.[18] Particularly where large and risky investments are required to initiate a certain economic activity, a (temporary) price change may be much less powerful in influencing positive investment and production decisions than orders to buy fixed quantities. Moreover, the pervasiveness of controls and quotas throughout a world composed of diverse economic and political systems suggests that the information generated by quantitative signals may constitute a necessary condition for successful market operation.

Summary and Conclusions

Maximization, the process that constituted the basis for the study of development statics in Part II, was considered within a rather restrictive framework. It was confined to maximization in terms of pecuniary factors (profit maximization), and it was considered to be achieved instantaneously without adjustment costs. Chapter 8 provides the link between development statics and development dynamics and broadens both the content and the time horizon of maximization.

The purpose of Chapter 8 has not been to present the host of evidence (whether of the impressionistic or the "hard" variety) that has been accumulated on the question of whether or not people in LDCs act "rationally."[19] Instead, this chapter has been designed to further pursue the theme developed in Chapters 5 and 6, namely, that rational response to incentives takes place within certain constraints and may refer to an objective function that includes components other than profits (narrowly defined). There is no inconsistency with economic theory, for example, if farmers adjust their behavior to decrease the risk of crop failure—even if the price of the cash crop has increased and the acreage devoted to it has decreased. Such an event merely suggests that the economic model used for the study of farmers' behavior must explicitly take account of risk. Neither does the observation that the quantity of labor supplied decreases in the face of an increase in the wage rate indicate that behavior is "perverse" or that economic theory is inapplicable. It merely suggests that the labor supply response cannot be studied within a partial equilibrium production-analysis framework but must also incorporate the

[18]Sanchez (1972) has provided evidence that raw sugar production throughout the world is much more responsive to unfilled orders (in this case announced quotas) than to price changes and, furthermore, that price changes lag behind quantity adjustments in that industry. For an example of an empirical attempt to combine output and input responses to changing prices and quantities, see Nadiri and Rosen (1973).

[19]For examples of this literature, see Jones (1960) and Doyle (1974).

consumption equilibrium that determines the choice between income (which increased because of the wage increase) and leisure. A dynamic and general equilibrium framework becomes necessary, as Chapter 15 will further illustrate.

We have also paid due attention to responsiveness of agricultural output to changes in prices and other variables. Since adjusting the level of output involves time, behavior must be described in terms of time derivatives. Moreover, as a minimum, the model must express output as a function of its price. This cannot be done within the framework of the production function which, as suggested in Part II, does not treat the price of output as an independent variable. We presented, therefore, both simple and Nerlovian supply re-

sponse models with which to treat this problem. As was already mentioned in Chapter 6 (and will be further discussed in Chapter 15), the profit function that treats the price of output as an independent variable provides an alternate method for estimating the elasticity of supply.

Our presentation of the supply response of the marketed surplus has further illustrated the point that maximization must be considered within a general equilibrium framework that involves both production and consumption decisions. The model we presented included consumption decisions in a simple yet fairly satisfactory manner in the form of the elasticities of home consumption with respect to price and income. A more sophisticated model will be outlined in Chapter 15.

Chapter 9
Technological Change

In Chapters 4 through 6, we studied within a partial equilibrium, comparative statics framework several characteristics of technology, such as technical efficiency, economies of scale, factor intensity, and the elasticity of substitution. In Chapter 9, we examine these characteristics as they interact with each other and as they change over time in response to changes of exogenous variables, for example, prices. This constitutes the study of technological change, which has important implications for the economics of development in terms of its impact on resource allocation, factor proportions, income distribution, and size-of-plant decisions. Does the optimum scale of operations increase in the process of development? Does the elasticity of substitution among factors, more specifically between labor and capital, decrease? Can agricultural labor be expected to command a decreasing share of GNP because of the nature of technological change?

A great deal of the confusion surrounding the discussion of technological change is no doubt due to the ambiguity that shrouds the term in its conventional usage. Technological change is frequently employed in a qualitative sense to describe gradations from "more" to "less." While such cardinally unquantifiable usage of the term is sufficient for many purposes, it presents problems when one is attempting to measure changes in the existing technology and either to determine or to explain the effects of these changes.

Especially since World War II, prodigious efforts have been expended to make the concept of technological change unambiguous and operational. Since there exist competent reviews of this literature (Mansfield 1968; Nadiri 1970; Kennedy and Thirlwall 1972), this chapter will not attempt to provide another. Our more selective exposition is organized around the previous discussion (which, for convenience, is partly restated here) of the characteristics of production functions and technical efficiency, and we emphasize operational methods for measuring changes in technology. Once technological changes can be measured successfully, the testing of theories explaining their causes or effects can proceed.

Technology is a stock concept indicating the body of knowledge that can be applied in productive processes. Consequently, technological change implies changes in this stock. Since technology can be summarized by an appropriately defined production function, technological changes are reflected in changes in production functions. This is a purely technical concept that must be modified to account for economic viability.

The concept of economic viability is introduced through the Schumpeterian distinction between latent technology (or invention) and economically feasible technology (or innovation). While an invention increases the stockpile of known technology, to be adopted by the innovator-entrepreneur, the invention must also be technically and economically feasible. Early innovators will eventually be followed by other imitators in the same field or industry. This constitutes the third and most vital step in the process of technological change, the "diffusion" stage.

In this chapter, we will concentrate primarily on the effects of technology that has already been diffused, that is, technology that has made an impact on the current processes of production.

The Production Function and the Ingredients of Technological Change

In the analysis of technological change, we distinguish between four basic elements: (1) the technical efficiency of production; (2) the scale of operation of production; (3) the bias of technological change; and (4) the elasticity of substitution. The combination of these four ingredients gives a composite picture of the changes in technology that are reflected in actual production processes.

Technical Efficiency and the Scale of Operations
We have already discussed both technical efficiency and economies of scale at considerable length. An increase in the technical efficiency of production refers to a reduction in the quantities of all factors used in producing the unit output. Alternatively, it can be seen as a reduction in the unit cost of all factors of production attributable to the application of better techniques. The reduction of cost, or of physical input, is of a specific kind: it is equal for all factors. This is reflected by a homothetic shift in the isoquant or by the shift in the constant term of the production function.

The second characteristic of technology is the scale of operation of the production process. While technical efficiency is defined in terms of the maximum quantity of output with inputs held constant, returns to scale (economies or diseconomies) refer to the change in output that results from an equiproportional change in all inputs. Increasing, decreasing, or constant returns to scale, it will be recalled, are defined depending on whether total output increases more, less, or equally in proportion to increases in all inputs.

Factor Intensity and Bias
The bias in technological change, the change in factor intensity, is the third characteristic of a technology. Factor intensity, of course, may change as a result of changes in factor prices. In order to distinguish sharply changes in factor proportions that have a purely technological origin from those induced by relative factor price changes, we shall assume that the relative prices of capital and labor remain constant. This feature can be determined empirically in terms of the marginal rate of substitution of two factors. It may be recalled that the marginal rate of substitution, r, of any two factors, such as capital for labor, r_{KL}, is defined as the ratio of their marginal products

$$r_{KL} = \frac{\frac{\partial Q}{\partial L}}{\frac{\partial Q}{\partial K}} \tag{1}$$

In Chapter 4, we showed that for the Cobb-Douglas production function

$$Q = AK^\alpha L^\beta \tag{2}$$

where Q is output, K is capital, L is labor, and α and β are the elasticities of production, the marginal rate of substitution of capital for labor (from Chapter 4, equation 10) is

$$r_{KL} = \frac{\beta K}{\alpha L} \tag{3}$$

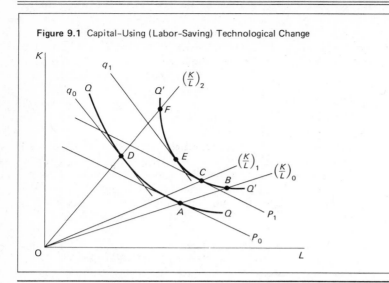

Figure 9.1 Capital–Using (Labor-Saving) Technological Change

Since in a competitive equilibrium r will be equated to the factor price ratio, our assumption of constant factor prices implies that r is also constant. Consider two output isoquants (given in terms of K and L), such as the isoquants Q and Q' in Figure 9.1. The marginal rate of substitution is, of course, the slope of the isoquants at a particular point. This is obviously changing continuously as one moves along the isoquant. Assume that the prices of K and L are such that the two factors exchange at the rate indicated by the parallel lines p_0, p_1. We have drawn p_0 tangent to Q at point A, and p_1 tangent to Q' at point C. Since the capital-labor ratio at C, $(K/L)_1$, is higher than that at A, $(K/L)_0$, technology Q' is more capital intensive than technology Q. Frequently, Q' will be more capital intensive than Q at all factor price ratios. In this case, however, notice that at factor prices given by q_0, q_1, Q at D is more capital intensive than Q' at E.

Returning to our assumption that factor prices are given by the original price lines, p_0, p_1, we have seen that technology Q' at C is more capital using (labor saving) than technology Q at A. Meanwhile, the marginal rate of substitution of capital for labor, that is, the ratio of their marginal products, as defined in equations 1 and 3, is the same for the two isoquants at points C and A. Therefore, the coefficient of capital α must be higher in isoquant Q' than it is in Q, and

correspondingly the coefficient of labor β must be lower. This also appears from equation 3. For a given r, K/L varies inversely with β/α. However, since in the C-D function β and α are both constant by hypothesis, the technology with the lower β/α will have the higher K/L and is thus the more capital-intensive technology for all factor-price ratios. In other words, the technology with the lower marginal rate of substitution between capital and labor is the more capital-using technology.

The Elasticity of Substitution

The fourth characteristic of a technology is the ease with which one input can be substituted for another. We have shown in Chapter 4 that this characteristic is measured by the elasticity of substitution, σ.

$$\sigma = \frac{d\left(\frac{K}{L}\right)\Big/\left(\frac{K}{L}\right)}{d\left(\frac{f_L}{f_K}\right)\Big/\left(\frac{f_L}{f_K}\right)} = \frac{d\left(\frac{K}{L}\right)\Big/\left(\frac{K}{L}\right)}{\frac{dr}{r}}$$

$$= \frac{d\log\left(\frac{K}{L}\right)}{d\log r} \qquad (4)$$

where f_K and f_L are the marginal products of capital and labor respectively. This shows the intimate relationship between two characteristics of technological change, r and σ.

In perfect competition, we have seen that r is equated to the ratio of the wage of labor,

P_L, to the price of capital, P_K. Therefore, equation 4 can be rewritten as

$$\sigma = \frac{d\left(\frac{K}{L}\right)\bigg/\left(\frac{K}{L}\right)}{\frac{dr}{r}} = \frac{d\left(\frac{K}{L}\right)\bigg/\left(\frac{K}{L}\right)}{d\left(\frac{P_L}{P_K}\right)\bigg/\left(\frac{P_L}{P_K}\right)}$$

$$= \frac{d\log\left(\frac{K}{L}\right)}{d\log\left(\frac{P_L}{P_K}\right)} \qquad (4a)$$

which can be restated as

$$d\log\frac{K}{L} = \sigma \, d\log\left(\frac{P_L}{P_K}\right) = \sigma \, d(\log r) \qquad (4b)$$

From equation 4b, we observe that changes in the relative ratio of capital to labor depend on the product of two terms, the elasticity of substitution, σ, and the changes in the marginal rate of substitution, dr/r. If either $\sigma = 0$ or $dr/r = 0$, that is, where we have a Leontief-type isoquant, no possibilities exist for substituting capital for labor or vice versa. The factor proportions are fixed. Conversely, if $\sigma = \infty$ (i.e., if K and L are perfect substitutes), an arbitrarily small change in relative factor prices would lead to an infinitely large change in factor proportions. The cases of $\sigma = 0$ and $\sigma = \infty$ are, however, the extreme cases. More commonly, $0 < \sigma < \infty$, and thus an increase in the price of labor relative to capital, (P_L/P_K), of 10 percent will cause an increase in the ratio of K to L by less than, exactly, or more than 10 percent, depending on whether $\sigma < 1$, $\sigma = 1$, or $\sigma > 1$.

Neutral and Nonneutral Technological Change

Two of the four ingredients of technological change, technical efficiency and returns to scale, are independent of the ratio of the marginal productivities of the factors. The marginal rate of substitution and the elasticity of substitution are not independent of the marginal productivities by definition. The effect that technological change has on the ratio of the marginal products, or the marginal rate of substitution, has led to the definition of neutrality and nonneutrality. If technology changes and the ratio of marginal products remains constant, technological change is said to be "neutral." On the other hand, if changes in technology result in changes in the ratio

of marginal products, technological change is "nonneutral."

Neutrality may be defined in three alternative ways, corresponding to the three possible ways of measuring the marginal product of two inputs in a two-factor, one-product production function. Technology is Hicks-neutral if, with the capital-labor ratio constant, the ratio of marginal products is also constant. Harrod-neutral and Solow-neutral technological change, on the other hand, refer respectively to cases in which the ratio of marginal products remains constant when measured with respect to identical capital-output or labor-output ratios. The bias in technological change may therefore be measured in terms of the rate at which the ratio of marginal products changes when one or another of these factor-factor or factor-output ratios is held constant. We may define, for example, Hicks-bias as

$$B_{\text{Hicks}} = \frac{\partial r_{KL}}{\partial t} \qquad \text{for given } \frac{K}{L}$$

$$= \frac{\partial \frac{(f_L L)}{(f_K K)}}{\partial t} \Bigg|_{\frac{K}{L} \text{ constant}}$$

$$\begin{aligned}
&> 0 \quad \text{labor-using (capital-saving)} \\
&= 0 \quad \text{neutral} \\
&< 0 \quad \text{capital-using (labor-saving)} \qquad (5)
\end{aligned}$$

Similarly, we may define Harrod-bias as $B_{\text{Harrod}} = \partial r/\partial t$ for given K/Q, and Solow-bias as $B_{\text{Solow}} = \partial r/\partial t$ for given L/Q. These three cases do not exhaust the possibilities for defining the bias or its absence—the neutrality—of technological change, but they are the most common definitions.[1] We shall return to the cases of Harrod and Solow bias later in this chapter. In the meantime, our emphasis shall be on the Hicksian case.

We will illustrate the concept of technological bias in the C-D and CES production functions. In the former, as given in equation 2, and under the assumption of constant returns to scale and competitive equilibrium, the marginal rate of substitution of capital for labor is defined as

---

[1] For alternative definitions of neutrality and bias in production functions with two factors and a single output, see Beckman and Sato (1969). Moreover, the possibilities multiply further if additional products or factors are considered.

$$r_{KL} = \frac{\frac{\partial Q}{\partial L}}{\frac{\partial Q}{\partial K}} = \frac{\beta K}{\alpha L} = \frac{P_L}{P_K} \quad (6)$$

from which follows

$$\frac{\beta}{\alpha} = \frac{P_L L}{P_K K} \quad (7)$$

We can now see that the definition of the bias in technological change given by expression 5, which refers to the change in the marginal rate of substitution, also implies a change in factor shares. Neutral technological change, therefore, can be defined either in terms of constant shares or in terms of constant marginal rates of substitution. But it is clear from equation 7 that shares may remain constant if P_L/P_K and L/K change inversely. As a result, the bias of technological change can be measured in terms of changes in the ratio of shares, β/α, along a constant capital-labor ratio. This is illustrated in Figure 9.1. Points A and C have the same marginal rate of substitution, r_{KL}. From equation 7, and since $(K/L)_1$ at C is higher than $(K/L)_0$ at A, it follows that β/α has decreased in the move from A to C. Since the values of β and α are constant in any one isoquant, the move from A to B also implies a decrease in β/α, or, by definition 5, a capital-using technological change.[2]

We can now relax the simplifying assumption of the C-D that $\sigma = 1$. Consider the more general CES function

$$Q = \gamma[\delta K^{-\rho} + (1 - \delta)L^{-\rho}]^{-1/\rho} \quad (8)$$

where $\sigma = 1/(1 + \rho)$. Since any of the parameters of the CES (including σ) may be subject to change over time, this function allows us to observe more interesting relationships between the bias of technological change and the elasticity of substitution.

[2]Hicks presents a simple explanation of why we observe constancy of β/α in fitting Cobb-Douglas production functions. Suppose there has been a secular trend for capital to increase faster than labor, that is, K/L increases. This tends to increase the ratio of the price of labor to capital, P_L/P_K. The two trends may result in constant shares of the factors. M. Brown and Popkin (1962), in an historical analysis of the United States nonagricultural sector, observe that the relative shares remain constant within technological epochs, but they change between epochs. For the period 1890–1958, they distinguish three epochs: 1890–1918 and 1919–1937 with labor-saving technological bias (β/α decreases) and 1938–1958 with capital-saving technological bias (β/α increases).

From equation 8, the marginal products in the CES function are given by

$$\frac{\partial Q}{\partial K} = \delta\gamma^{-\rho}\left(\frac{Q}{K}\right)^{1+\rho}$$

and

$$\frac{\partial Q}{\partial L} = (1 - \delta)\gamma^{-\rho}\left(\frac{Q}{L}\right)^{1+\rho}$$

The technological bias is then defined

$$B = \frac{(1 - \delta)}{\delta}\left(\frac{K}{L}\right)^{1/\sigma} \quad (9)$$

For a given capital-labor ratio, technological change will be nonneutral if the variations in $(1 - \delta)/\delta$, the factor intensity parameter, or in σ, the elasticity of substitution, are nonoffsetting. We can separately consider the effects that changes in δ or in σ would have in terms of changes in the technological bias.

From equation 9, we write

$$\frac{\partial B}{\partial \delta} = \frac{-B}{\delta(1 - \delta)} \quad (10)$$

and

$$\frac{\partial B}{\partial \sigma} = \frac{-B}{\sigma^2}\log\frac{K}{L} \quad (11)$$

Suppose, for example, that the coefficient, δ, of capital increases over time. From equation 9, this implies a decline in B. This in turn means that from the definitions of bias given by equation 5, technological change would be capital-using (labor-saving), in the Hicksian sense at all (constant) values of K/L.

On the other hand, a change in σ may also be a source of biased technological change. Suppose, for example, that σ falls over time—a possibility that is not unlikely, as we will suggest. This will either lower or raise B, depending on whether K/L is less than or greater than one. Returning to the two isoquants Q and Q' in Figure 9.1, the fact that Q' was found to be more capital intensive than Q at $(K/L)_0$ but less capital intensive than Q at $(K/L)_2$ can apparently be attributed to the fact that σ of Q' is greater than σ of Q. Starting from a position in which $K/L = 1$ (by so defining the units of K and L that this is true at a particular point in time), if labor grows more rapidly than capital, K/L will decline to a value less than one. The fall in σ would have the effect of lowering r, making technological change capital-using (or labor-saving). Conversely, if capital grows more rapidly than labor from the initial K/L of unity, the increase in σ will have the effect of lowering r, thereby making technological change capital-using (or labor-saving). Since LDCs are generally afflicted with more rapid growth in population and labor force and smaller saving and investment ratios than DCs, the universal decline in σ associated with modernization of technology would likely be more capital-using (labor-saving) than in DCs. Such changes could provide one explanation for the increasing rates of unemployment observed in most LDCs in recent years, which will be discussed in Chapter 12.

In summary, we have singled out four characteristics of the production function (some of which are closely interrelated) that are salient for the investigation of technological change: (1) the degree of technical efficiency of a technology; (2) the extent of economies of scale; (3) the degree of bias in technological change; and (4) the possibilities of substitution between inputs. The change of one or several of these characteristics over time constitutes a technological change.

Measurement of Technological Change

Whether or not an observed increase in output is the result of technological change becomes an empirical question. And if it is, for at least two reasons we may wish to know which specific characteristics of technology have changed and by how much. First, different kinds of technological change have very different implications for resource allocation, factor proportions, income distribution, and size-of-plant decisions. Second, each different type of technological change may have its own determinants, knowledge of which may be useful for predicting or controlling changes in technology and indirectly the growth of income and employment.

One approach to measuring technological change is to estimate all the parameters of the production function for different periods of time, or "epochs." As we have seen in Chapter 4, the estimation of the production function is based on a number of assumptions, for example, that the functional form is known and estimable and that the quantities of inputs are exogenous variables that have been measured without error. Also, if techno-

logical change is embodied in the inputs (e.g., new machinery and/or present-day workers are more efficient than old machinery or past workers), this change must be properly specified and accounted for in the aggregation of each input. If, and only if, these assumptions are warranted can technological change be measured by estimating the parameters of a complete production function in two different "epochs" and comparing them.[3] In practice, however, some of these assumptions become especially crucial, and the results of estimating the production function are rather sensitive to changes in specification and measurement. Aggregation problems that are solved arbitrarily often restrict the usefulness of the aggregate production function (Fisher 1969). Consequently, alternative specifications with distinctly different implications often become equally consistent with the same set of data (Nelson 1973).

For these reasons, serious attention has been given to shortcut methods, which permit estimation of one or more of the technological parameters of the production function and of their changes without direct estimation of the complete function itself.

We shall discuss briefly some possible approaches to estimating changes in each of the four key parameters of technology already introduced. We start with the measurement of economies of scale, where the methods employed have strayed farthest from production function estimation, and we finish with the measurement of bias, in which the production function is most intimately involved.

Measurement of Economies of Scale

The economies of scale parameter can be measured by direct estimation of the production function. By fitting, for example, a Cobb-Douglas production function, in which the elasticities of output with respect to the several factors are not constrained to add up to unity, we determine increasing, constant, or diminishing returns to scale depending on whether the sum of the elasticities is greater than, equal to, or less than one. However, to the extent that changes in the quantities of the inputs occur simultaneously and/or inputs, such as management and resources, are omitted, estimates of economies of scale

[3]For a review of the problems in such an approach along with an empirical application, see M. Brown (1966).

obtained directly from the production function are likely to be biased—usually in a downward direction.

Cost functions are an alternative method for measuring economies of scale. Particularly in regulated industries, such as electricity and natural gas, where the quantity and price of output are exogenously determined, cost functions can be estimated on the basis of costs experienced in plants of different scale.[4]

An alternative approach utilizes the relationship between size of plant and profit rates or the relationship between size of plant and industrial market share.[5] If larger firms have higher profit rates than small firms or if they are observed to increase their market shares over time, economies of scale may be inferred. However, such an inference may not be valid, because the higher profit rates or larger market shares of large firms may arise from their greater degree of monopoly power.

Another method for determining economies of scale utilizes international cross-section comparisons of (per capita) value added in different industries. A positive relationship between per capita value added in any particular industry and a measure of market size (such as population size or GNP) would be interpreted as indicative of economies of scale. It should be obvious that these measures of size may be positively correlated with many other factors, and hence, it is dangerous indeed to interpret such results as indicative of economies of scale in any strict sense.[6]

Because of the shortcomings of all these approaches, for practical estimates of economies of scale economists commonly rely on engineering estimates of long-run total cost from different scales of plant. Scale is usually measured in terms of output per time period.[7]

Writing C_i and C_j for the long-run total cost for two different scales of plant, i and j, and Q_i and Q_j for respective outputs, the engineering economies of scale are expressed as

$$\frac{C_i}{C_j} = \left(\frac{Q_i}{Q_j}\right)^\alpha \quad \text{or} \quad d \log C = \alpha \, d \log Q$$

where α is the elasticity of costs with respect to scale. A value of α less than one is indicative of economies of scale, whereas a value of α greater than one reflects decreasing returns to scale. Based on their knowledge of certain physical relationships, for example, that the material requirements of a cylindrical mill increase less than in proportion to the volume of materials that the mill processes, engineers have proposed that α will be generally in the vicinity of 0.6, thereby displaying substantial economies of scale (Moore 1959; Chilton 1950).

Table 9.1 presents a compendium of such estimates of α for a number of manufacturing activities derived from different sources. The reader is warned that estimates obtained from the different sources may not be comparable, since somewhat different estimation procedures and definitions of cost and capacity output may have been employed. However, the results indicate a fair amount of consistency in the estimates for the same industry. They reveal the general existence of economies of scale in modern types of manufacturing activities, but also considerable variation in the magnitude of such economies from sector to sector, the "0.6 rule" being appropriate for some sectors but not for others. For example, economies of scale seem relatively large in industrial gases and food processing and relatively small in some metallurgical industries.

Over time, do economies of scale grow larger or smaller? Evidence on this issue is understandably more difficult to come by. Nevertheless, increasing plant size in most industrial sectors provides at least crude evidence to suggest that economies of scale have been growing larger, in several industries at least (Pryor 1972; Sanchez 1972).[8]

[4]For applications of this method in such industries, see Nerlove (1965) and Dhrymes and Kurz (1964).

[5]For applications of this method, see Stigler (1958) and Silberston (1972).

[6]For applications of this approach, see Chenery (1960), United Nations (1963), Chenery and Taylor (1968). For demurrals, see Keesing (1965).

[7]Two difficulties arise in connection with this approach. First, the engineering concept of scale differs from that of the economist, since changes in output may not correspond to equiproportional changes in all inputs. Second, capital costs, which are an important component of total costs, are generally estimated from quotations from equipment suppliers of individual units of different capacities. Since economies in selling costs are built into these quotations, the

resulting estimates of scale economies will be biased upward.

[8]Note, however, that various other factors, such as changes in the size and location of the population, in transport and distribution costs, and in tax policies, can also influence plant size. Hence, changes in plant size may not necessarily reflect changes in economies of scale (Scherer 1973).

The Elasticity of Substitution

How large is the elasticity of substitution in different sectors? This question can be answered by estimating the CES production function in different sectors either by linear approximation or nonlinear estimation. In Chapter 4, we employed the latter method with reference to a sample of Indian farms. The results showed that the elasticity of substitution in Indian agriculture is not significantly different from one. This finding of a relatively high σ in agriculture has been corroborated by other studies for other countries. In contrast, when Arrow, Chenery, Minhas, and Solow (1961) and others have applied the same method to industry, they have consistently found estimates of σ that are less than one, in some cases even approaching zero. It is generally agreed, therefore, that the elasticity of substitution is considerably larger in agriculture than in industry. This suggests that with existing technologies the agricultural sector offers at the margin better opportunities for substituting labor for capital than does the industrial sector, a finding with obvious policy implications with respect to employment and unemployment (the subject of Chapter 12).

What is likely to happen to the elasticity of substitution as modern processes replace traditional ones with the passage of time and in various sectors? In Chapter 6, we noted some evidence suggesting that the adoption of modern technology of the "Green Revolution" variety has lowered the elasticity of substitution in agriculture.

How about the industrial sector? Some evidence is provided by comparing the estimates of σ for a sample of "modern" Peruvian and U.S. firms in manufacturing industries obtained by Clague (1969) with those obtained by Witte (1970, 1971) for a sample of "traditional" Peruvian manufacturing firms.[9] The latter estimates of σ were generally closer to 1.0, while Clague's were considerably lower, normally around 0.2. This tends to confirm the hypothesis that σ secularly declines as modern technology replaces traditional tech-

nology.[10] These findings suggest another form in which technological dualism is evident.

Changes in Technical Efficiency or Factor Productivity

Substantial and often lumpy investments are required to take advantage of economies of scale, while changes in the elasticity of substitution are more difficult to measure and generally bring mixed blessings. The parameter, therefore, whose change offers the most alluring benefits from both the conceptual and the measurement point of view is that of technical efficiency (or total factor productivity).

Abstracting from changes in economies of scale and the ease of substitution, it has been suggested that increases in factor productivity could be measured by simply subtracting the increases in real output attributable to increased real inputs from the actual increase in real output. If the indexes of the different inputs could be weighted in some reasonable way (for example, by their relative contribution to output in a base period), it would seem that even a rough index of the growth in real inputs and output would be sufficient for estimating the changes in output attributable to increasing factor inputs. By subtracting this component from the actual increase in output, one could estimate the increase in total factor productivity. Direct estimation of a complete production function would be either unnecessary or even inappropriate. This is the logic behind the so-called productivity index approach to measurement of changes in technical efficiency.

Two such indexes of total factor productivity will be presented and illustrated in this section: the arithmetic index and the geometric index. Although at first sight they seem to provide practical shortcuts to measurement of changes in technical efficiency, closer inspection reveals that any such index is inevitably based on a particular production function. Indeed, the validity of any such in-

---

[9]Clague has utilized the simple method of estimating σ from equation 4. Witte, on the other hand, used the alternative method described in Chapter 4, and fitted

$$\log \frac{Q}{L} = \sigma \log P_L - \sigma \log [\gamma^\rho(1 - \delta)].$$

[10]While Clague's study allows technical efficiency to vary between Peru and the United States, Witte assumes that all firms have the same technical efficiency. Since P_L is usually estimated by taking total wages and salaries, W, and dividing by the number of employees, L, that is, $P_L = W/L$, there is a positive spurious correlation between $\log Q/L$ and $\log P_L$ which biases the Witte estimates upward. Such differences act to highlight the importance of assumptions with respect to the underlying production function in empirical investigations of this sort.

Table 9.1 *Engineering Estimates of Economies of Scale*

Industry or Process	Chilton (1)	Haldi and Whitcomb (2)	Manne (3)	Moore (4)	OECD (5)	Silber-ston (6)	UN (7)
Acetaldehyde							0.60
Acetylene		0.68–0.82					0.67
Acetylene Carbide		0.94					0.60
Aircraft						0.68	
Alumina		0.68	0.90	0.88–0.93			
Aluminum Ingots	0.90	0.72–0.87	0.77–0.90	0.92–1.00			
Aluminum Rolling				0.88			0.96
Aluminum Extensions				1.00			
Ammonia	0.81	0.53–0.98	0.63–0.88				0.73–0.88
Ammonium Nitrate		0.74					0.71
Automobiles						0.82	
Ball Bearings							0.65
Beer					0.48	0.37	
Benzol							0.91
Bread						0.62	
Bricks					0.50	0.62	
Butadene	1.02						0.59
Calcium Carbide				0.80			0.50–0.60
Calcium Oxide							0.58
Canning of Fruits and Vegetables							0.54
Carbon Black				0.20–0.60			0.58–0.60
Cement		0.70	0.54–0.68	0.77	0.61	0.77	0.64–0.77
Chlorine Gas		0.38					
Chlorine Soda (Caustic)		0.75	0.77				0.76–0.80
Coke		0.60					
Computers						0.82	
Cylinder Blocks						0.80	
Desalination		0.49–1.00					
Detergents						0.74	
Diesel Engines						0.86	
Dyes						0.47	
Engineering Castings						0.86	
Ethanol		0.60					
Ethylene						0.62	0.54
Fertilizers		0.72					
Fish Canning					1.00		
Footwear						0.93	
Generators (Turbine)						0.86	
Glass Containers							0.75
Hydrogen		0.73–0.74					
Isopropanol		0.60					0.50
Jute Manufactures					0.91		
Machine Tools						0.86	
Magnesium	0.62						
Methanol		0.55					0.78
Motors (Electric)						0.74	
Newspapers						0.51	
Nitric Acid		0.67					
Oxygen Gas	0.47–0.59	0.36–0.80		0.63			
Petroleum Refining (Aviation Fuel)	0.88	0.97–1.17					
(Catalytic Cracking)	0.71–0.81	0.80					
(Gasoline)	0.51	0.71–0.83				0.66	

Table 9.1 *(Continued)*

Industry or Process	Chilton (1)	Haldi and Whitcomb (2)	Manne (3)	Moore (4)	OECD (5)	Silberston (6)	UN (7)
(General)	0.75	0.89–0.97					
(Tapping, Thermal Cracking)	0.60	0.52–0.69					
(Thermal Cracking)	0.48–0.62	0.60					
Polyethelene		0.67					0.87
Polymer						0.70	
Polyvinyl Chloride		0.92					0.55
Pulp and Paper		0.74–0.98			0.82		
Refrigerators						0.84	
Rubber	0.82	0.78–1.33		1.10			
Shipbuilding		0.44–0.96					
Soap					0.45		
Soda Ash (Solvay Process)				0.70			
Sodium Hydroxide	0.48						
Steel						0.80	
Steel Rolling						0.82	0.90
Styrene	0.53	0.65–0.75		0.90			0.76
Sugar					0.38		0.40
Sugar Refining							0.50
Sulphur		0.70–0.86					
Sulphuric Acid	0.68–0.91	0.66–0.90		0.80		0.75	0.65–0.80
Tar							0.82
Titanium Dioxide							0.61
TNT		1.01					
Urea			0.73				0.67
Vegetable Oil		0.70			0.46		0.40

Notes: Values of α computed from $C_i/C_j = (Q_i/Q_j)^{\alpha}$ where C is cost and Q is output for plant sizes i, j.

Almost all estimates are based upon an extremely limited number of observations, usually two, three, or at the most six or seven.

The reported variations from a single source for the same industry result from comparisons of different processes or different countries.

Variations in estimates between sources for the same industry may be due to consideration of different ranges in scale, with lower elasticities reflecting larger economies of scale at lower ranges of scale. However, they can also be due to different methods of estimation.

Most of the estimates derive from engineers' estimates and data from actual plants for the United States in the period 1948–1950. Only the Haldi and Whitcomb; Manne; and the Vietorisz estimates for the United Nations, pertain in some instances to a somewhat later period (the late 1950s or early 1960s). The Manne data refer to India and certain other countries.

Sources:

Chilton, C. H. (1950), "Six-Tenths Factor Applies to Complete Plant Cost," *Chemical Engineering*, 57 (April), pp. 112–114.

Haldi, J., and D. Whitcomb (1967), "Economies of Scale in Industrial Plants," *J. P. E.*, 75 (August), Part 1, pp. 373–385.

Manne, A. S., ed. (1967), *Investments for Capacity Expansion: Size, Location and Time Phasing.* Cambridge: M. I. T. Press.

Moore, F. T. (1959), "Economies of Scale: Some Statistical Evidence," *Q. J. E.*, 73 (May), pp. 232–245.

OECD (1968), *Industrial Profiles, Manual of Industrial Project Analysis in Developing Countries.* Paris. Annex to Vol. 1.

Silberston, A. (1972), "Economies of Scale in Theory and Practice," *E. J.*, 82 (March Supplement), pp. 369–391.

U.N. (1963), "Pre-investment Data for the Cement Industry," *Studies in the Economics of Industry*, No. 1 (ST/ECA/75). New York, pp. 1–29.

U.N. (1966), "Pre-investment Data for the Aluminum Industry," *Studies in the Economics of Industry*, No. 2 (ST/CED/9). New York.

U.N.: FAO (1966), *State of Food and Agriculture, 1966* (CL 47/2). Rome.

U.N.: Department of Economic and Social Affairs (1959), "Problems of Size of Plant in Industry in Underdeveloped Countries," *Industrialization and Productivity*, Bulletin No. 2 (ID/Ser. A) (March), pp. 7–25.

U.N.: Department of Economic and Social Affairs (1964), "Plant Size and Economies of Scale," *Industrialization and Productivity*, Bulletin No. 8 (ID/Ser. A) (December), pp. 53–61.

U.N.: Department of Economic and Social Affairs (1966), "Programming Data for the Chemical Industry," Thomas Vietorisz in *Industrialization and Productivity*, Bulletin No. 10 (ID/Ser. A) (February), p. 55.

dex depends rather critically on the proper specification of the relationship between input and output, that is, on the form of the production function, on the proper measurement of input and output, and on the weighting scheme used for their aggregation.

The Arithmetic Index of Productivity

The arithmetic index of productivity was introduced by Abramovitz (1956) and J. W. Kendrick (1961). It expresses all variables of an underlying production function as index numbers with a common base period and appropriate weights. The productivity index, C, is defined as

$$C = \frac{\dfrac{Q}{Q_0}}{\dfrac{P_{K0}K_0}{Q_0}\left(\dfrac{K}{K_0}\right) + \dfrac{P_{L0}L_0}{Q_0}\left(\dfrac{L}{L_0}\right)} = \frac{Q}{P_{K0}K + P_{L0}L} \quad (12)$$

where Q/Q_0, K/K_0, and L/L_0 are indexes of output, capital, and labor respectively, and P_{K0} and P_{L0} are the base-year prices of capital and labor. The weights for capital and labor are their base-year respective shares in output.

By rearranging terms, it can be seen that this index is based upon a production function in which output is a linear combination of the inputs,

$$Q = C(P_{K0}K + P_{L0}L) \quad (13)$$

This function presents some uncomfortable theoretical problems.[11] For example, differentiation of equation 13 shows that the marginal products of inputs change only through changes in the productivity constant, C, and furthermore, their ratio (the marginal rate of substitution) remains the same regardless of how fast capital is growing in relation to labor. This is evident also *ex hypothesi*, since the arithmetic weights for capital and labor are their base-period (constant) prices, and since theory suggests that under perfect competition marginal productivities are equal to the respective input prices. An index of productivity that does not associate changes in marginal products with changes in input ratios (factor proportions) is a rather limiting index, because it would be difficult to think of a better reason for changes in marginal pro-

[11]See for example, Domar (1962) and also Lave (1966, pp. 6–10).

ductivities than changes in factor proportions.[12]

The Geometric Index of Productivity

In a pioneering article, Solow (1957) presented an alternative productivity index, the geometric index, which represented a substantial refinement over the previous arithmetic index in that the prices of the inputs, and therefore their marginal products, were allowed to vary. These advantages were based upon the fact that the index was formally derived from the more general production function

$$Q = A(t)f(K, L) \quad (14)$$

Since A varies with time and independently of K and L, technological change is by assumption both disembodied and Hicks-neutral. More specifically, although not necessarily, we can assume that the function is of Cobb-Douglas form with exponential shifts in the constant term. We may thus rewrite equation 14 as

$$Q = Ae^{rt}K^{\alpha}L^{\beta} \quad (14a)$$

Differentiating equation 14 totally with respect to time, we obtain

$$\frac{\partial Q}{\partial t} = \frac{\partial A}{\partial t}f + A\left(\frac{\partial f}{\partial K}\frac{\partial K}{\partial t} + \frac{\partial f}{\partial L}\frac{\partial L}{\partial t}\right) \quad (15)$$

Redefining $\partial Q/\partial t = \dot{Q}$, and so on, and dividing equation 15 by Q, we have

$$\frac{\dot{Q}}{Q} = \frac{\dot{A}}{A} + A\frac{\partial f}{\partial K}\frac{\dot{K}}{Q} + A\frac{\partial f}{\partial L}\frac{\dot{L}}{Q} \quad (16)$$

If competitive conditions prevail, $\partial Q/\partial L = P_L/P$ and $\partial Q/\partial K = P_K/P$. Since $(\partial Q/\partial K)(K/Q)$ is the share of capital, α, and $(\partial Q/\partial L)(L/Q)$ is the share of labor, β, by substituting α and β into equation 16 we obtain

$$\frac{\dot{Q}}{Q} = \frac{\dot{A}}{A} + \alpha\frac{\dot{K}}{K} + \beta\frac{\dot{L}}{L} \quad (17)$$

and therefore,

$$\frac{\dot{A}}{A} = \frac{\dot{Q}}{Q} - \alpha\frac{\dot{K}}{K} - \beta\frac{\dot{L}}{L} \quad (18)$$

[12]Kendrick attempts to sidestep this shortcoming by changing the arithmetic weights often. In this case, however, the interpretation of the index becomes very ambiguous (Domar 1962). Furthermore, in the limiting case of continuous change in weights, for example, by using moving weights, surprisingly enough it turns out that the productivity index is approximately constant through time (M. Brown 1966, pp. 98ff).

Table 9.2   *Calculations of the Solow Measure of Technological Change: U. S. Economy, 1909–1949*

Year	$\dfrac{Q}{L}$ (1)	$\dfrac{\dot{q}}{q}$ (2)	A (3)	Corrected $\dfrac{Q}{L}$ (4)	Contribution to Growth in Productivity (5)	Explanation (6)
1909	$0.623		1.0			
		$0.652				
1949	1.275		1.809	$0.705	$0.082	Due to capital intensity
					0.570	Due to increased labor productivity
					0.652	TOTAL

Source: Solow, R. M. (1957), "Technical Change and the Aggregate Production Function," *R. E. Stat.*, 39 (August), pp. 312–320.

In discrete approximations of the time derivatives, we can rewrite equation 18 as

$$\frac{\Delta A}{A} = \frac{\Delta Q}{Q} - \alpha\frac{\Delta K}{K} - \beta\frac{\Delta L}{L} \tag{18a}$$

Equations 18 and 18a can be estimated for any time period for which we have data for output, capital, labor, and the capital and labor shares. The term $\Delta A/A$, which is not observable, is derived as a residual and is the expression for technological change.

Utilizing the assumption of constant returns to scale, that is, $\alpha + \beta = 1$ or $\beta = 1 - \alpha$, dividing equation 18 by L, and defining $q = Q/L$ and $k = K/L$, we obtain

$$\frac{\dot{q}}{q} = \frac{\dot{A}}{A} + \alpha\frac{\dot{k}}{k} \tag{19}$$

Then the estimation of $\dot{A}/A$ is made from time series data on output per man-hour, capital per man-hour, and the (constant) share of capital. Equation 19 can serve to answer the question of how much of the increase in output per man-hour is due to increased productivity, $\dot{A}/A$, and how much to an increase in capital per man-hour. Solow's results, which appear in Table 9.2, provide an empirical illustration of the method. Solow finds that in the period 1909–1949 real GNP per man-hour in the United States increased from $0.623 to $1.275 ($\dot{q}/q = \$0.652$). In the same period, technological change shifted the intercept, A, of the production function from a value arbitrarily set at 1.0 in 1909 to 1.809 in 1949. Dividing the 1949 GNP per man-hour ($1.275) by the

1949 shift in the production function (1.809), one obtains the "corrected" GNP per man-hour of $0.705, which is shown in column 4 of the table. This represents the value of Q/L in 1949 that would have been expected had there been no technological change. The difference between the Q/L for 1949 (technological change excluded) of $0.705 and Q/L for 1909 of $0.623 is $0.082. This is the amount of the total increase in Q/L attributable to the increase in K/L. The total increase in Q/L ($0.652) less that portion attributable to the increased capital intensity ($0.082), or $0.570, is the proportion attributable to increased productivity.

The finding that in the United States during the period 1909–1949 technological change accounted for about 90 percent of the increase in labor productivity, Q/L, and only the remainder can be attributed to capital deepening (increase in K/L) seems surprising at first. Since this result has been confirmed by parallel studies based on the same method,[13] one might conclude that the assumption of neutral and totally disembodied technological change is responsible for the odd finding that one can obtain considerable growth in output without investing and, vice versa, that the payoff to increasing the rate of investment is rather small.

In order to analyze the biases that enter the Solow measure of technological change, we return to equation 18, which we write in more complete form

[13]One of the earliest is Massell (1960) for the manufacturing sector.

$$\frac{\dot{A}}{A} = \frac{\dot{Q}}{Q} - \left(\frac{Kf_K}{Q}\frac{\dot{K}}{K} + \frac{Lf_L}{Q}\frac{\dot{L}}{L} \right) \qquad (20)$$

where dots, as before, indicate time derivatives, and f_L and f_K are, respectively, the partial derivatives of output with respect to labor and capital.

From equation 20, we can distinguish three possible sources of bias in the magnitude of the residual $\dot{A}/A$ and its stability (Nadiri 1970; Kennedy and Thirlwall 1972). The first is misspecification of the form of the production function. Suppose the production is of the Cobb-Douglas form, with constant returns to scale, $Q = AK^\alpha L^\beta$. The constancy of α and β implies that the factor shares are invariant with respect to $\dot{K}/K$ and $\dot{L}/L$. Equation 20 therefore reduces to equation 18. On the other hand, if the production function is CES, with input shares constant (as suggested by Nelson 1965), equation 20 should be rewritten as

$$\frac{A}{\dot{A}} \simeq \frac{\dot{Q}}{Q} - \left(\alpha\frac{\dot{K}}{K} + \beta\frac{\dot{L}}{L} \right)$$
$$- \frac{1}{2}\alpha\beta(\sigma - 1)\sigma\left(\frac{\dot{K}}{K} - \frac{\dot{L}}{L} \right)^2 \qquad (21)$$

This measure of technical change then differs from equation 18 by the last term of 21. If $\sigma = 1$, this term is zero, and we are again in the C-D case. If $\sigma < 1$, the term in question is positive, and any estimate of $\dot{A}/A$ that ignores it is an underestimate. In other words, the increase in output due to capital-labor substitution has been overestimated. The converse, of course, is the case of $\sigma > 1$. The intuitive reason for this bias is simple. The smaller the elasticity of substitution, the more difficult it becomes to increase output by increasing one factor; the greater the elasticity of substitution, the easier it becomes; and if both capital and labor expand at the same rate, the case of Hicks-neutral technological change, growth in output is independent of the elasticity of substitution.

The second possible source of bias in the residual is errors of measurement in K and L. If K and L are misspecified by a multiplicative factor, g_3 and g_2 respectively, which refers to quality improvement over time, we can show that

$$\frac{\dot{A}}{A} = \alpha\left(\frac{\dot{g}_3}{g_3} \right) + \beta\left(\frac{\dot{g}_2}{g_2} \right) \qquad (22)$$

In this case, the residual becomes the weighted average of the quality changes embodied in the misspecified inputs.

Finally, the third source of bias is omission of other pertinent variables from the production function. Suppose the function, properly defined, includes education, E, with a share γ. If so, under constant returns to scale, equation 18 should be rewritten as

$$\frac{\dot{A}}{A} = \frac{\dot{Q}}{Q} - \alpha\frac{\dot{K}}{K} - \beta\frac{\dot{L}}{L} - \gamma\frac{\dot{E}}{E} \qquad (23)$$

Since total factor shares exhaust the product, it is evident that the residual $\dot{A}/A$ in equation 18 overestimates the true increase in productivity by including with it the contribution of education to total productivity.

In the Solow formulation of technological change, one can directly test for the assumption of neutrality, that is, for the assumption that technological progress leaves the marginal rate of substitution (the ratio of the marginal product of the factors) unaltered at given capital-labor ratios.[14] One can also embody part or all of technical progress in the inputs in the form, for example, of improvement in education of the labor force, decrease in the average age of capital, improvement in the efficiency of capital with newer vintages, and so on. The most general approach to embodied technological change is to use independent evidence to improve each input series separately by allowing for changes in its quality. The result is to increase the contribution of inputs to the rate of growth and to decrease accordingly the residual component attributed to neutral technological change. We will return to some of these attempts below.

The Johansen Measure of Neutral Technological Change

Of the statistical parents of the Solow measure of technological change (the output series, the capital series, the labor series, and the weights of capital and labor), the capital series is usually the weakest. There exists a difference of opinion on whether the input of capital in a production function should be measured by service flows or by capital stocks (Haavelmo 1960; Yotopoulos 1967b). Further-

---

[14]Solow tested for neutrality by regressing $\triangle A/A$ on K/L. He interprets the absence of a relationship between them as indicating that technological progress was neutral "on the average." However, this is not a conclusive test. See Brown (1966, p. 104) and references therein.

more, in either case, figures for capital inputs are generally scanty and unreliable. This led Johansen (1961) to develop an ingenious method that obviates the necessity of using capital data in measuring neutral technological change.

The Johansen method is appropriate for cross-section analysis of interindustry productivity between two time periods. Assume a Cobb-Douglas production function for industry i at time t as

$$Q_{it} = A_{it} K_{it}^{\alpha_i} L_{it}^{\beta_i} \qquad (24)$$

With the assumption of constant returns to scale, that is, $\alpha_i + \beta_i = 1$, and constancy of α_i and β_i over time, we can write for labor productivity, q_{it},

$$q_{it} = \frac{Q_{it}}{L_{it}} = A_{it} K_{it}^{\alpha_i} L_{it}^{(1-\alpha_i-1)} = A_{it}\left(\frac{K_{it}}{L_{it}}\right)^{\alpha_i} \qquad (25)$$

For purposes of computing an index of productivity change between periods $t = 1$ and $t = 2$, we can write the ratio

$$\frac{q_{i2}}{q_{i1}} = \frac{A_{i2}}{A_{i1}}\left(\frac{K_{i2}}{L_{i2}}\right)^{\alpha_i}\left(\frac{L_{i1}}{K_{i1}}\right)^{\alpha_i} = \frac{A_{i2}}{A_{i1}}\left[\frac{\left(\dfrac{K_{i2}}{K_{i1}}\right)}{\left(\dfrac{L_{i2}}{L_{i1}}\right)}\right]^{\alpha_i} \qquad (26)$$

Equation 26 states that the increase in labor productivity depends upon the neutral shift in the production function and the increase in capital per worker. This is familiar from the Solow index of productivity.

A set of crucial assumptions at this point allows elimination of capital from equation 26. Assume that producers minimize costs for a given level of output, given the wage rate, P_{Li}, and the price of capital, P_{Ki}. The familiar first order conditions of constrained minimization,

$$\frac{P_{Lit} L_{it}}{Q_{it}} = (1 - \alpha_i), \text{ and } \quad \frac{P_{Kit} K_{it}}{Q_{it}} = \alpha_i$$

yield

$$\frac{P_{Lit} L_{it}}{(1 - \alpha_i)} = \frac{P_{Kit} K_{it}}{\alpha_i}$$

For the interperiod index, we write

$$\frac{P_{Li2} L_{i2}}{P_{Li1} L_{i1}} = \frac{P_{Ki2} K_{i2}}{P_{Ki1} K_{i1}}$$

By rearranging and defining the ratio of the wage increase to the price-of-capital increase as the "relative increase in wages," W_i, we have

$$\frac{\dfrac{K_{i2}}{L_{i2}}}{\dfrac{K_{i1}}{L_{i1}}} = \frac{\dfrac{P_{Li2}}{P_{Li1}}}{\dfrac{P_{Ki2}}{P_{Ki1}}} = W_i \qquad (27)$$

We can now substitute W_i in equation 26. However, equation 26 is still not estimable so long as the term in parentheses has an i subscript. At this point, the second crucial assumption is made. Assume that the relative increase in wages is the same for all industries, that is,

$$W_1 = W_2 = \cdots = W_I = W \qquad (28)$$

This amounts to assuming that there exists a pattern of wages, $P_{L1} : P_{L2} : \ldots : P_{LI}$, and a pattern of capital costs, $P_{K1} : P_{K2} : \ldots : P_{KI}$, that either remain constant or move in parallel as the prices of labor and capital rise.

By substituting equation 28 into equation 26, we obtain

$$\frac{q_{i2}}{q_{i1}} = \frac{A_{i2}}{A_{i1}} W^{\alpha_i} \qquad (29)$$

By defining $\varepsilon_i = \log\left(\dfrac{A_{i2}}{A_{i1}}\right)$,

we rewrite equation 29 as

$$\frac{q_{i2}}{q_{i1}} = W^{\alpha_i} \varepsilon_i$$

For purposes of estimation, we add a constant to the above equation, and after taking logs, we have

$$\log\left(\frac{q_{i2}}{q_{i1}}\right) = \log C + (\log W)\alpha_i + \log \varepsilon_i \qquad (30)$$

If we assume that α_i and ε_i are uncorrelated, we can fit equation 30 from cross-section data of labor productivity for two periods and cross-section data of the (constant through time) share of capital. The coefficient of α_i (antilog) is interpreted as the contribution of the "relative increase in wages," or from equation 27, as the contribution of changes in the capital-labor ratio to changes in labor productivity per unit share of capital, α_i. It represents the effect of capital deepening upon the productivity index. The constant term (antilog) is interpreted as the unweighted average of technological progress within the group of industries. The residual, ε_i, indicates whether the technological progress component for a specific industry, i, lies above or below the average technological progress for the group of industries under consideration.[15]

There are two alternative formulations of the Johansen measure that have been fitted by Lave (1966, Chapter 3). By substitution from equation 27 to equation 26, we have

$$\frac{q_{i2}}{q_{i1}} = \frac{A_{i2}}{A_{i1}} \left(\frac{P_{Li2}}{P_{Li1}}\right)^\alpha \left(\frac{P_{Ki2}}{P_{Ki1}}\right)^\alpha$$

The second term in parentheses is dropped from this equation by assuming that P_{Ki} is constant through time. Then one can obtain data on the relative change of wages from other sources and, in the absence of data on α_i, can fit to solve for α. Finally, if one has independent evidence on $\left(\frac{K_{i2}}{L_{i2}}\right) \Big/ \left(\frac{K_{i1}}{L_{i1}}\right)$ one can again fit for α by substituting these data for the first term in parentheses in the above equation.

The Johansen method is remarkably simple and parsimonious as far as data utilization is concerned. Furthermore, Lave (1966) has shown that by considering small time intervals and by expanding equation 26, the Johansen measure converts to the Solow measure. Both measures, then, give remarkably close estimates of the component of technological progress.

For illustrative purposes, we use the Johansen method to analyze neutral technological change in the Hawaiian economy, 1952–1964 (Yotopoulos and Miklius 1970). The data consist of value added per employee and capital share in value added for ten sectors of the Hawaiian economy, the sectors being classified according to the two-digit international standard industrial classification (ISIC). The results of estimating equation 30 are as follows

$$\log\left(\frac{q_{i2}}{q_{i1}}\right) = 0.3392 + 0.3871\ \alpha_i$$
$$\phantom{\log\left(\frac{q_{i2}}{q_{i1}}\right) = 0.3392 + } (0.2751)$$
$$r^2 = 0.1983$$

[15]This interpretation of the residual is somehow loose, since by assumption, the residuals are randomly distributed. Another problem arises with the assumption that α_i and e_i are uncorrelated. If increases in labor productivity are correlated with increases in output, increases in output are correlated with ϵ_i and thus with α_i, then the above assumption does not hold. Johansen has tried to handle this problem by splitting the sample in three subgroups on the basis of labor productivity and by fitting different intercepts for each group by the use of dummy variables.

where 0.3871 is log W, that is, the coefficient of α_i, and represents the results of capital deepening; 0.3392 is the intercept, showing the extent of the "average" shift in the production function; and the number in parentheses is the standard error of the regression coefficient.

We can employ these results to attribute the increase in labor productivity to its two component parts: growth in capital per worker and shifts in the production function. For the "average" industry, that is, the sector that has a share of capital, $\alpha = 0.3487$, which is the mean sample value, the term log $(W)\bar{\alpha}$ equals 0.1350. As a result, the growth in capital per worker accounts for a growth in labor productivity of 36 percent (antilog 0.1350 − 1). Shifts in the production function account for a 118 percent (antilog 0.3392 − 1) increase in labor productivity. The total growth of output per worker for 1952–1964 was 198 percent (antilog 0.4742 − 1), leaving 44 percent for the interaction between the factors.

Alternative estimates of the components of increasing labor productivity can be obtained by distinguishing between different broad categories of industries, such as service- and commodity-producing. When this was done, it had the effect of raising the r^2 and also of assigning greater weight to the effects of the shift in the production function (as compared to the increase in capital per worker) in the service-producing sectors than in the commodity-producing sectors. This difference may be attributed to greater difficulty in substituting capital for labor in the former than in the latter. Thus, these results provide additional evidence of interindustry differences in technology and in changes thereof over time and in the process of development.

Embodied Technological Change and the Measurement of Bias

Until now we have been able to treat changes in individual characteristics, or parameters, of technology as if they were quite independent of each other. In the case of measuring bias or the change in factor intensity, this is no longer possible because of the intimate relationship between the marginal rate of substitution and the elasticity of substitution.

We have seen that equation 21 provides a fairly net estimate of the residual change in output, that is, change not associated with increases in the quantities of inputs as traditionally measured. The approach of embodied technological change is to treat the residual as the consequence of "mismeasurement" of traditional inputs, that is, failure to account for qualitative changes. Qualitative changes in inputs are considered to have "input-augmenting" effects. To the extent that augmentation is not equal for all inputs, the ratios of the marginal productivities of different inputs will change over time, suggesting that technological change is nonneutral. Thus, three concepts are interwoven at this level of analysis: the concept of "embodiment," which allows for qualitative changes in measured inputs; the concept of technological bias, which allows for changing ratios in the marginal productivities of measured inputs and thus in the ratio of their utilization; and the elasticity of substitution, which may differ from one, and which is captured through the relevant coefficient in the CES production function.

To accommodate the concept of embodiment, we return to the definition of neutral and nonneutral technological change. Embodiment refers to the specific way the technological change function is introduced in the production function. The Hicks-neutral technological change we examined earlier is incorporated in the constant term of the production function

$$Q = A(t)f(K, L) \tag{31}$$

In this case, since the marginal productivities of the two factors are not disturbed, technological change is disembodied and considered as "manna from heaven." In the conceptual complement of this case, technological change is embodied or introduced in the variable inputs themselves. This is accomplished by redefining the units in which the inputs are measured, for example, in efficiency units rather than in conventional units. Neutrality is then defined relative to the new units of measurement, in the sense that, thanks to the redefinition of the units exclusively, the marginal rates of substitution remain unchanged. We can thus define two cases of neutral but embodied technological change.

Harrod-neutral technological change occurs when technological change is embodied in the labor input; thus,

$$Q = f[K, \beta(t)L] \tag{32}$$

This form of technological change is also called labor-augmenting, and its neutrality is defined in efficiency units of labor, that is,

$$\bar{L} = \beta(t)L$$
$$Q = f(K, \bar{L})$$

Solow-neutral technological change occurs when technological change is embodied in the capital input and is represented as

$$Q = f[\alpha(t)K, L] \tag{33}$$

Neutrality is defined in efficiency units of capital, that is,

$$\bar{K} = \alpha(t)K$$
$$Q = f(\bar{K}, L)$$

Obviously, the basic characteristics of these three concepts of technological change—disembodied, labor-embodied, and capital-embodied—can be synthesized. For example, Nelson (1964) synthesizes them as follows

$$Q = A(t)f[\alpha(t)K, \beta(t)L] \tag{34}$$

In both the Harrod and the Solow formulations, neutrality is defined by changing the measurement of inputs in terms, for example, of efficiency units. The implication is that technological advance "augments" new inputs so that they become more efficient than old inputs. This is the basic idea of the embodiment of technological change. From equations 32 and 33, the production function can be rewritten as

$$Q = f[\alpha(t)K, \beta(t)L] \tag{35}$$

where $\alpha(t)$ and $\beta(t)$ are the coefficients of factor augmentation. It can be shown that the coefficients of factor augmentation define the kind of technological change. Harrod-neutral (labor-augmenting) technological change implies that $\beta(t)$ is constant. Solow-neutral (capital-augmenting) technological change requires that $\alpha(t)$ remain constant. Finally, Hicks-neutral technological change requires that the ratio $\alpha(t)/\beta(t)$ is constant. Likewise, the Hicksian bias in technological change B can be defined (Solow 1967) as

$$B = \left[\frac{d\alpha(t)}{\alpha(t)} - \frac{d\beta(t)}{\beta(t)}\right]\left[1 - \frac{1}{\sigma}\right] \tag{36}$$

Equation 36 suggests that this bias is zero when either α/β is constant or $\sigma = 1$. This explains why technological change in the

Cobb-Douglas production function is always Hicks-neutral ($B = 0$).

How can embodied technological change be quantified? The ensuing discussion suggests that from the conventional measures of inputs and outputs, it is possible to infer the rate of labor augmentation and the rate of capital augmentation and, thus, the bias in technological change.

Consider the production function with the usual neoclassical properties, but in this case, without disembodied technological change

$$Q = f(K, L; t) \qquad (37)$$

Furthermore, let us assume that f is homogeneous of degree one in the factors of production, and the marginal productivity conditions hold both with respect to f_L for the wage rate, P_L, and with respect to f_K for the price of capital, P_K. This allows us to define the shares of the factors of production, S_K and S_L

$$\frac{f_K K}{f} = S_K = 1 - S_L; \qquad \frac{f_L L}{f} = S_L \qquad (38)$$

The rate of technological progress, R, can be defined strictly in terms of the productive factors

$$R = \frac{\dfrac{\partial f}{\partial t}}{f} = \frac{\dfrac{\partial f_K}{\partial t} K + \dfrac{\partial f_L}{\partial t} L}{f} \qquad (39)$$

By multiplying the first and second terms of the right-hand side of equation 39 by f_K/f_K and f_L/f_L respectively, we have

$$R = (1 - S_L)\frac{\dfrac{\partial f_K}{\partial t}}{f_K} + S_L\frac{\dfrac{\partial f_L}{\partial t}}{f_L} \qquad (40)$$

The bias in technical progress is defined as

$$B = \frac{\partial\left(\dfrac{f_K}{f_L}\right) \Big/ \left(\dfrac{f_K}{f_L}\right)}{\partial t}$$

$$= \frac{\partial f_K}{\partial t}\frac{1}{f_K} - \frac{\partial f_L}{\partial t}\frac{1}{f_L} \qquad (41)$$

We wish to express the rate of change in factor shares in terms of the rate of progress, the bias in technological progress, the elasticity of substitution, and the capital-labor ratio, k. David and van de Klundert (1965) and Ferguson (1969, pp. 224–227, 241–243) have shown that the rate of growth of the marginal product of labor can be expressed as

$$\frac{\dot{f_L}}{f_L} = R - (1 - S_L)B + \frac{(1 - S_L)}{\sigma}\left(\frac{\dot{k}}{k}\right) \qquad (42)$$

The rate of growth of the marginal product of capital can be expressed in corresponding terms. The rate of growth of output can be written

$$\frac{\dot{f}}{f} = R + (1 - S_L)\frac{\dot{k}}{k} + \frac{\dot{L}}{L} \qquad (43)$$

Differentiating equation 37 totally with respect to time and remembering that $S = S_K + S_L = (1 - S_L) + S_L$ and $S_L = f_L L/f$, we divide both sides by S and obtain

$$\frac{\dot{S_L}}{S_L} = \frac{\dot{f_L}}{f_L} + \frac{\dot{L}}{L} - \frac{\dot{f}}{f} \qquad (44)$$

By substituting equations 42 and 43 into equation 44, we obtain

$$\frac{\dot{S_L}}{S_L} = -(1 - S_L)\left[B + \left(\frac{\sigma - 1}{\sigma}\right)\left(\frac{\dot{k}}{k}\right)\right] \qquad (45)$$

Equation 45 suggests that the rate of change in the relative share of labor depends on the bias in technological progress, B, the elasticity of substitution, σ, and the rate of factor substitution, $\dfrac{\dot{k}}{k}$.

If technological progress is neutral ($B = 0$), the elasticity of substitution and the direction of change in the relative input supplies are the only factors governing the rate of change in the share of labor. If the capital-labor ratio is increasing over time, the share of labor will increase or decrease depending on whether σ is less or greater than one.

Technological progress, however, may not be neutral. The effect of nonneutral technological change on factor shares can be investigated by introducing the ratio of the marginal products of capital to labor from the definition of B (e.g., from equation 41) into equation 45.

The production function 37, from which equation 45 was derived, did not, however, consider factor-embodied technological change. To determine the relationship corresponding to equation 45 for the case of factor-embodied technological change, we start with the CES production function with constant returns to scale and factor-augmenting technological change

$$Q = \{[\alpha(t)K]^{-\rho} + [\beta(t)L]^{-\rho}\}^{-1/\rho} \qquad (46)$$

where α and β are the productivity-augmenting quality changes in capital and labor respectively, which are functions of time. A simple specification of α and β is the exponential

$$\alpha(t) = \alpha_0 e^{\lambda_K t}$$

$$\beta(t) = \beta_0 e^{\lambda_L t}$$

Bias in the case of factor-augmenting technological change was defined in equation 36. In terms of the present specification, it would be

$$B = \left(\frac{\sigma - 1}{\sigma}\right)\left(\frac{\dot{\alpha}}{\alpha} - \frac{\dot{\beta}}{\beta}\right) \tag{47}$$

By substitution into equation 45, we can express the rate of change in the share of labor as

$$\frac{\dot{S}_L}{S_L} = -(1 - S_L)\left[\left(\frac{\sigma - 1}{\sigma}\right)\left(\frac{\dot{k}}{k} + \frac{\dot{\alpha}}{\alpha} - \frac{\dot{\beta}}{\beta}\right)\right] \tag{48}$$

Compared to equation 45, equation 48 expresses the change in the share of labor after adjusting the changes in capital-labor ratio for qualitative improvements in the factors of production. If, for example, $\sigma > 1$, the share of labor will increase as long as the change in capital-labor ratio, adjusted for changes in capital productivity, exceeds the change in labor productivity.

In order to fit equation 48, we need estimates of σ as well as of $(\dot{\alpha}/\alpha - \dot{\beta}/\beta)$, an unobserved variable.

By using the exponential specification of the quality changes in capital and labor, we can write the ratio of the marginal products of the true factors

$$\frac{f_L}{f_K} = \left[\frac{\beta_0}{\alpha_0}e^{(\lambda_L - \lambda_K)t}\right]^{-\rho}\left[\frac{K}{L}\right]^{1+\rho} \tag{49}$$

By substituting the respective prices for the marginal products and by rearranging terms, we obtain

$$\frac{K}{L} = \left[\frac{P_L}{P_K}\right]^{\sigma}\left[\frac{\beta_0}{\alpha_0}e^{(\lambda_L - \lambda_K)t}\right]^{1-\sigma} \tag{50}$$

or

$$\log\frac{K}{L} = \left[(1 - \sigma)\log\left(\frac{\beta_0}{\alpha_0}\right)\right]$$
$$+ \sigma\log\frac{P_L}{P_K} + (\lambda_L - \lambda_K)(1 - \sigma)t \tag{51}$$

Equation 51 can be fitted to give estimates of σ and $(\lambda_L - \lambda_K)$.

An alternative way to estimate σ and λ_L, without using information on capital, utilizes the marginal product of labor

$$f_L = \left(\frac{Q}{L}\right)^{1+\rho}(\beta_0 e^{\lambda_L t})^{-\rho} \tag{52}$$

By dividing through by $P_L = \partial Q/\partial L$ and rearranging, we obtain

$$S_L = P_L{}^{1-\sigma}(\beta_0 e^{\lambda_L t})^{\sigma-1} \tag{53}$$

or

$$\log S_L = (\sigma - 1)\log\beta_0 + (1 - \sigma)\log P_L$$
$$+ \lambda_L(\sigma - 1)t \tag{54}$$

Two comments are appropriate in reference to estimating equations 51 and 54. First, by disregarding the term $(\lambda_L - \lambda_K)$, either equation can yield the conventional estimates of the elasticity of substitution under the assumption of Hicks-neutral technological change (J. W. Kendrick and Sato 1963). If this neutrality assumption is not warranted, the estimates of σ are biased: in the case that $(\lambda_L - \lambda_K) > 0$, that is, the bias is labor augmenting, the elasticity parameter is overestimated, while the converse is true if the bias is capital augmenting. In an empirical application of the equations to aggregate data of the United States between 1899 and 1960, David and van de Klundert (1965) found that the bias had been labor augmenting and that the elasticity of substitution was less than one. Second, Lianos (1971), by estimating equations 51 and 54 for U.S. agriculture, 1949–1968, found an elasticity of substitution $\sigma = 1.524$ and a value of $\lambda_L - \lambda_K$ significantly less than zero. Given the definition of bias that we employ—equations 5, 41, and 47—the process in agriculture would seem to have been labor saving. Starting from a certain capital-labor ratio, the increase in the marginal product of capital in agriculture has led producers to substitute capital for labor, thus increasing the capital-labor ratio. From equation 48, we see that the change in the share of labor depends on the original labor share, the change in the capital-labor ratio, the $\lambda_K - \lambda_L$ component, and the elasticity of substitution. Thus, the fact that the latter was greater than one, combined with the increase in capital-labor ratio, has led to a decline in the relative share of labor in agriculture.

Srivastava and Heady (1973) fitted equation 51 under the assumption of Hicks-neutral technological change, $\lambda_L - \lambda_K = 0$, to agricultural cross-section data in two regions of India for the years 1956–1957 and 1967–1969 and obtained quite different results. The object was to obtain estimates of the elasticity of substitution and of the constant term (interpreted as σ times the ratio of the distribution parameters of capital and labor) to explain the decline in the relative share of labor in Indian agriculture. They found that the elasticity of substitution, which in all cases was significantly less than one, increased slightly between the two time periods. The distribution parameter for labor increased, as did the ratio of wages to price of capital. In spite of these favorable factors, the relative share of labor decreased. The authors attribute this paradoxical result to capital-labor substitution that occurred with the technological changes of the Green Revolution variety. Such substitution is not reflected in the recorded wage rates, since the latter are peak-season rates that are much higher than the year-round opportunity cost of agricultural labor. A more likely interpretation of these results derives from their omission of the measure of bias $(\lambda_L - \lambda_K)$. If $\lambda_L - \lambda_K$ in equation 51 were really negative, as one might suspect, the value of the elasticity of substitution would have been underestimated. If so, this capital-augmenting or labor-saving technological change would have induced producers to substitute capital for labor, which, given the higher value of the elasticity of substitution, would have led to the observed decline in the share of labor.

Summary and Conclusions

In this chapter, we have introduced dynamic considerations, namely technological changes, into the analysis of production presented in Part II. Our approach has centered on the four basic characteristics of the production function: technical efficiency, economies of scale, technological bias, and the elasticity of substitution. Our purpose has been to specify how these characteristics change in the process of economic development, how they respond to changes in exogenous variables (such as prices), and how they interrelate.

Economies of scale can be measured by the complete specification and estimation of production functions at different points in time, or alternatively, through a number of shortcut procedures. If they are carefully done, engineering estimates may constitute a satisfactory shortcut. Our compendium of existing engineering estimates of economies of scale in different industries indicates that many industries may be subject to economies of scale but also that the magnitude of the scale economies tends to vary considerably from industry to industry. The increases in actual plant size that have occurred in most industries may indicate that scale economies increase over time.

The study of the changes in the elasticity of substitution has led to two basic conclusions. First, we have found that the elasticity of substitution is generally less than one in industry and probably considerably lower than the elasticity of substitution in agriculture. Second, as more modern technology is adopted, the elasticity of substitution declines. Both findings suggest that as a country develops its ability to substitute labor for capital decreases. If other things would remain equal, this factor alone could be expected to make unemployment a more serious problem as development occurs.

Secular changes in technical efficiency have traditionally been measured in terms of disembodied shifts in the constant term of a production function that is restricted in its other parameters. The startling conclusion emerging from such studies has been that an overwhelming proportion of the increase in output (as high as 90 percent in some instances) can be attributed to increases in labor productivity; only the small remainder is due to capital deepening. Such findings imply that the payoff to increases in the rate of investment is relatively small—which does not seem plausible. This shortcoming has led to the formulation of "embodiment" hypotheses, which admit qualitative changes in the factors of production in the process of development. In the process of formulating embodiment hypotheses, it has been possible to define the bias in technological progress in terms of changes in factor intensity. It is of crucial importance to determine if a certain production process is capital saving or labor saving. Furthermore, changes in factor intensity, combined with changes in the elasticity of substitution between factors, determine changes in factor shares as development occurs and the quantity of output increases.

The evidence on these issues is scanty. It would appear that in the United States, at least, technological progress in agriculture has been characterized by an increase in the capital-labor ratio, which, combined with an elasticity of substitution greater than one, has led to a decline in the relative share of labor in agriculture.

Our study of the technological parameters of production and of their dynamic properties points to some seeds of trouble that will eventually mature, leading to the conclusion that development may not be as smooth and equilibrating a process as development statics and neoclassical dynamics has generally described it. For example, the existence of economies of scale suggests that neoclassical marginal productivity considerations may be insufficient for explaining the functional distribution of income. Variations in the economies of scale parameter among industries or technologies and over time suggest that some industries may be dominated by large firms and others by small firms. Moreover, if there are different technologies in the same industry, no one of which is dominant in all respects, these differences may explain how large and small firms may coexist. So, too, if the elasticity of substitution decreases either over time or as technology becomes more modern, we would expect that LDCs will have difficulty in absorbing their relatively abundant endowments of unskilled labor.

The consequences of these seeds of trouble will be explained more fully in the context of our treatment of development disequilibria in Parts IV, V, and VI. Even at this point, however, we should point out that certain rather unorthodox policy prescriptions may be required if these seeds of trouble are sufficiently serious. For example, if the only in-dustrial technologies available to LDCs are extremely capital intensive with low elasticities of substitution, it may be beneficial to subsidize the development of alternative technologies better suited to local conditions. If economies of scale are large but market size is small, perhaps deliberate attempts should be made to take advantage of international trade. Alternatively, LDCs may be justified in distorting their productive structures in favor of agriculture and other sectors that have higher elasticities of substitution and more labor-intensive technologies. If, in some sectors, productivity-increasing learning occurs to a greater extent and more rapidly than in other sectors, perhaps it is desirable to deliberately favor the expansion of the former sectors at the expense of the latter.

There are still other problems less amenable to explanation on the basis of the traditional paradigm of neoclassical production and growth theory. Productivity changes that have been shown to account for a large portion of the overall growth in output must be intimately related to the process of invention, innovation, and diffusion. Yet the Schumpeterian process of invention, innovation, and diffusion defies explanation within the neoclassical framework. So does the observed heterogeneity in the world with regard to choice of techniques, scale of operations, factor proportions, even prices observed across firms, let alone among industries and countries. A full explanation of technological change and growth must certainly involve more than what the comparative statics or neoclassical dynamics can offer.[16]

---

[16]For an interesting yet far from complete alternative "evolutionary theory" of technological change and growth, see Nelson and Winter (1974).

Chapter 10

Savings
and Capital
Formation

Capital accumulation has long been considered the central issue on the economics of development. The view is certainly an oversimplification that comes from the notion that capital is the relatively scarce factor and the most serious bottleneck in the LDCs. Although not the single most important issue, the position of capital is certainly unique in the process of development. Aside from being one of the traditional factors of production, the effect of capital is also interactive and cumulative: capital accumulation leads to increases in income, which increase savings and lead to additional capital formation. Finally, capital accumulation involves decision making over time in a fundamental way; through time discounting, which links income and wealth, capital formation can in a sense be considered almost synonymous with development, in that through efficient capital formation the availability of present as well as future income streams can be increased.

This chapter is organized into three sections. In the first, we present the simple economics of capital formation. In the next section, we analyze the supply of savings and present alternative hypotheses of saving behavior. In the final section, we focus on the demand side of investment. In Chapter 20, which is a companion to this one, we discuss project appraisal and investment criteria. While the emphasis in Chapter 20 is appropriately on how capital is to be allocated rather than on its accumulation, we also discuss there cases in which inadequate accumulation can affect the optimal pattern of allocation and vice versa.

The Simple Economics of Capital

The Link Between Income and Wealth

Labor is a convenient factor of production, because, excluding slavery, there is only one way it can be acquired: by renting its services for a particular time period. In comparison, capital is more complicated. It can be used in production by renting the services of a capital asset; alternatively, the asset itself can be bought outright and used as a joint input in more than one production period. There are, as a result, two prices of capital at any time, the service price and the asset price. There are two links between these two prices, the time element (purchase for one period or for the asset's lifetime) and the risk element. By and large, we will abstract from risk considerations and concentrate on time discounting as the link between service flows and asset stocks.

The same conceptual relationship between service flows and asset stocks also applies to income and wealth. Wealth is simply the present discounted value of future income streams. For a constant discount rate, r, the relationship between wealth, W, and income, Y, is

$$W = \frac{Y_1}{(1+r)^1} + \frac{Y^2}{(1+r)^2} + \cdots + \frac{Y_n}{(1+r)^n} \quad (1)$$

Naturally, numerous different streams of income with the same present discounted value or wealth can be found. In order to facilitate the distinction between certain activities that may raise income in one or more periods at the expense of income in other periods (leaving wealth unchanged)[1] from those that increase wealth, one income stream that is given particular attention is the annuity stream. An annuity income, which we will define as a "permanent income," Y_p, is a sequence of equal incomes at equal intervals, $Y_p = Y_1 = Y_2 = \cdots Y_i \cdots = Y_n$. Substituting this expression for Y_p into equation 1, the expression for wealth simplifies to

$$W = \sum_{i=1}^{n} \frac{Y_p}{(1+r)^i} = \int_{i=1}^{n} Y_p e^{-ri} di \quad (2)$$

for a finite series of n periods.[2] For an infinite horizon, equation 2 is further simplified as

$$W = \frac{Y_p}{r} \quad (2a)$$

and we can subsequently define

$$r = \frac{Y_p}{W} \quad (2b)$$

In equation 2b, r has the usual interpretation of a ratio, that is, it expresses the price of wealth in terms of permanent income streams. It is a pure number, since it involves division of dollars of Y_p by dollars of W. Conversely, we can invert equation 2b and have

$$\frac{1}{r} = \frac{W}{Y_p} \quad (2c)$$

where $1/r$ can be interpreted as the price of permanent income streams in terms of wealth per unit of time.

It will be convenient to define permanent income as \$1 streams. We can then analyze the demand and supply of permanent income streams as in Figure 10.1a and the demand and supply of wealth as in Figure 10.1b.[3] Consider Figure 10.1a. Curve D_{yp} is a demand curve for permanent income streams. It represents the behavior of the purchasers of capital assets who buy them as sources of permanent income streams to acquire future income. Curve S_{yp} is the supply of permanent income streams, that is, of investment goods. The suppliers are the firms that produce for sale the sources of permanent income streams. The intersection of demand and supply gives the price of permanent income streams, for example, the \$20 that one is willing to pay to acquire a \$1 annuity to perpetuity if the rate of discount is 5 percent. Consider price P_1, which is below the equilibrium price of permanent income streams, P_0. At P_1, there is excess demand for permanent income streams, $D_{yp} > S_{yp}$, which implies a willingness to give up present consumption to acquire sources of permanent income streams or capital. The converse is the situation at prices above the equilibrium price.

The case of economic growth can be represented in terms of increasing the supply of permanent income streams. Start from the static case represented in Figure 10.1a, where no sources of permanent income streams are capable of being reproduced, that is, the supply curve is perfectly inelastic. An increase in the quantity of permanent income streams in that case involves an exogenous shift of S_{yp}' to the right. This results in excess supply, which drives the price down to a new equi-

---

[1] The predatory exploitation of the land, as an example, increases present income but also depletes the soil and thus decreases future income streams.

[2] For small values of r, the expression e^r is equal to $1 + r$, since $e^0 = 1$, $e^{0.01} = 1.01$, $e^{0.02} = 1.02, \ldots$, $e^{0.10} = 1.11$.

[3] This terminology and analysis is based upon Friedman (1962, Chapter 13).

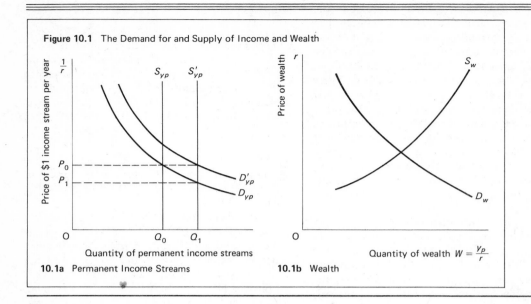

Figure 10.1 The Demand for and Supply of Income and Wealth

10.1a Permanent Income Streams

10.1b Wealth

librium at P_1. At this price of permanent income streams, individuals are willing to give up consumption to acquire more sources of income. This means that society generates its own savings, as shown by the shift of D_{yp}' to the right. Equilibrium is restored at P_0 with a larger quantity of permanent income streams, Q_1. The interpretation is similar if the supply of permanent income streams is upward sloping, instead of perfectly inelastic. In that case, a shift either in S_{yp} or in D_{yp} to the right is sufficient to generate a greater quantity of permanent income streams, that is, greater levels of future income growth. The search for the means of raising incomes in LDCs then consists of identifying factors that bring about shifts in the demand (supply) and supply (demand) for permanent income streams (wealth).

Figure 10.1b is in terms of stocks, capital assets, or wealth, in contrast to Figure 10.1a, which is in terms of flows. Wealth, as in equation 2a, is nothing else but the capitalized value of permanent income streams. A given stock of capital yields a given amount of permanent income streams. A complication, however, arises in Figure 10.1b. Changes in r affect the capitalized value of permanent income streams, that is, they change the capital value, or wealth. This is the disadvantage of working with capital stock figures. If, on the other hand, we measure a stock of capital by the quantity of the permanent income streams it yields, the measure is not affected by r.

Equation 2c indicates that the price of permanent income streams is equivalent to the capital-output ratio, or perhaps the incremental capital-output ratio (ICOR). Why, then, are the typical values for the price of permanent income streams between $10 and $20 ($r$ between 0.05 to 0.10), while the typical values for ICORs are between 3.0 and 8.0? The reason is that the definition of the price of permanent income streams is closer to the internal rate of return, that is, how much a machine will yield per year to perpetuity. The capital-output ratio, on the other hand, is expressed in terms of the lifetime of the machine. At the limiting case of capital assets of infinite longevity, the capital-output ratio approaches the price of a permanent income stream. This also explains why wide variations in capital-output ratios are observed in countries at different stages of development. Early in development, when more capital goes for infrastructure investment of long time horizons, the capital-output ratio is high. It declines as development proceeds, and the capital composition shifts from infrastructure to short-lived productive assets, such as machinery and transport equipment. For this reason, the capital-output ratio is a risky tool to use for decisions on allocating investment. We will return to this point in Chapter 20.

Sometimes capital is broadly defined to be synonymous with wealth. It is easy to see that such a definition makes capital accumulation the *sine qua non* of economic development. However, the differences in (1) the markets for the different forms of wealth, (2) the responsiveness of each different form to changing conditions, and (3) the ways each relates to the permanent income streams are usually sufficiently great to make it profitable to distinguish the various forms of wealth—at least among physical capital, human capital, land, money, and other financial assets.[4]

Supply and Demand Relationships for Capital and Savings

We have already introduced savings, although indirectly, in terms of the excess demand for sources of permanent income streams at price P_1 in Figure 10.1a. We will further examine the interrelationships between capital and savings in terms of Figure 10.2. S_{yp} and D_{yp} represent the supply and demand curves of permanent income streams (denominated in terms of one dollar streams) with the intersection of P_0 and Q_0 indicating a state of

[4] For example, the market for land and money tends to be better organized and more perfect than the market for physical capital, which in turn tends to be more perfect than that for human capital. The optimal portfolio or composition of wealth among its alternative forms will depend upon such factors as demographic patterns, the rate of inflation, and the rate of interest.

stationary equilibrium. In stationary equilibrium, net saving and investment are, of course, zero.

We can now portray the case of the growing economy. Suppose that the demand for permanent income streams was D_{yp}', representing, for example, a 10 percent savings ratio devoted to buying new sources of capital. If the sources of capital available are only Q_0, the stationary state equilibrium quantity, the increased demand will drive the price up to P_1. At a price of Y_p above the equilibrium price, it would be profitable to supply additional physical capital sources of income streams by sacrificing current consumption. This would lead to a shift in the supply curve. Suppose, on the other hand, that the supply curve of permanent income streams shifts first to S_{yp}', say a 10 percent investment ratio. The excess supply now drives the price of permanent income streams down to P_2, and as a result, suppliers convert the additional sources of capital to current consumption. Between P_1 and P_2 there is a price, P_3 in the graph, at which the intersection of D_{yp}' and S_{yp}' indicates the creation and purchase of new sources of permanent income streams at a level of savings and investment equal to 10 percent of permanent income. At this point, the stock of sources of permanent income

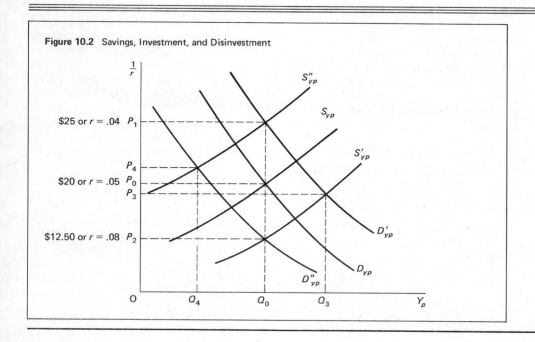

Figure 10.2 Savings, Investment, and Disinvestment

streams is growing, as indicated by quantity Q_3.

The case of dissavings and disinvestment is analogous. A shift of the demand curve to the left, that is, a negative savings ratio indicated by D_{yp}'', given the quantity of permanent income streams, Q_0, leads to a decrease in their price. As a result, sources of capital are devoted to present consumption, implying a negative net investment ratio. A decrease in supply without a corresponding decrease in demand drives the price up. The long-run equilibrium that combines the two shifts, with dissavings being equal to disinvestment, is shown at price P_4 and quantity Q_4.

The analysis, given thus far in graphical terms, can also be presented algebraically in the following system of equations:

$$I = f(K, r) \qquad \text{Demand for investment} \qquad (3)$$

$$S = g(K, r) \qquad \text{Supply of savings} \qquad (4)$$

$$S = I \qquad \text{Equilibrium condition} \qquad (5)$$

$$Y_p = rk \qquad \text{Stock-flow conversion} \qquad (6)$$

where S, I, and Y_p are the flows of savings, investment, and permanent income respectively, r is the interest rate, and K is the stock of physical capital (what we have been calling wealth).

Equation 3 can be viewed alternatively as the demand for capital in terms of the interest rate for a given investment rate or (from the stock-flow conversion) in terms of the supply of permanent income streams. However, the explicit form in which it is given in equation 3 is usually interpreted as demand-for-investment equation in terms of the interest rate for given values of K or Y_p. Similarly, equation 4 expresses the supply of savings in terms of the interest rate and either K or Y_p.

Equations 3–6 thus comprise a system of four equations in five unknowns for which an infinite number of solutions exist. In the special case of stationary long-run equilibrium, we have $S = I = 0$, and thus, equations 3 and 4 become a simpler system of two equations in K and r, from which K and r can be determined. From the solutions of K and r, equation 6 provides the solution to Y_p. Alternatively, in the more general case of short-run equilibrium in terms of constant Y_p but nonzero values of S and I, the constancy of Y_p reduces the number of unknowns (variables) to four, and the system of four equations yields the short-run (temporary) solutions for K, r, S, and I.[5]

It is conceivable, of course, that the only equilibrating interest rate would be a negative one. However, in a monetary economy in which, as an alternative to physical capital, individuals and institutions might store wealth in the form of money; at a zero interest rate, wealth holders would be likely to hold their entire wealth in this form, thus putting a floor of zero on the nominal interest rate. Numerous other specifications of supply and demand for savings are possible and will be discussed in subsequent sections. Nevertheless, the simple four-equation model given above provides a framework for combining the supply and demand aspects of capital formation.

The Supply of Savings

In discussing the relationship between savings and investment in the previous section, we have emphasized the supply of savings as the determinant of investment. As Keynes (1936) and Nurkse (1953) have pointed out, situations can also arise in which the causality goes from investment demand to savings. The intermediate position is, of course, that savings and investment are merely interdependent.[6]

Although comparable time series data on savings and investment are fairly scarce for LDCs, in column 1 of Table 10.1 we present estimates of the average shares of gross capital formation (investment) in GDP for a sample of 18 DCs and 30 LDCs for the decade of the 1960s. Note that both the weighted and unweighted averages of investment ratios were higher in the DCs than in the LDCs. With population growing faster in LDCs than in DCs, this implies that the gap in capital endowments of the average citizen between DCs and LDCs has been growing wider

[5]One well-known example of a temporary equilibrium system is that of Keynes' (1936) "General Theory." This is a system of seven equations in seven unknowns, including income, employment, savings, investment, and the demand for money, in which an exogenous money supply is a major determinant. It is a theory of temporary equilibrium in which the time dimension is long enough for the effects of investment on income to be realized, but short enough so that the effect of investment on capital stock and productive capacity is not realized. See, for example, Ackley (1961, Chapters 14 and 15) for an exposition of this model.

[6]An excellent review article on which this section draws is Mikesell and Zinser (1973).

despite some overly zealous efforts of LDCs to stimulate capital formation.

The averages conceal considerable variation from country to country, especially in the LDCs, where investment-GDP ratios vary from a low of 0.10 for Madagascar to a high of 0.28 for oil-rich Libya. Note also from column 2 that the countries that have maintained high investment ratios throughout the decade were generally among the best performers in terms of growth rates of GDP.

The intercountry variations are even more noticeable when it comes to the various sources of financing, shown in the remaining columns, and there are some very striking differences between DCs and LDCs as a whole. While foreign savings are small or even negative in DCs, they can comprise a substantial portion of gross capital formation in LDCs, especially in the poorer ones. The oil-rich LDCs, such as Iran and Libya, apparently have difficulty absorbing all their funds, and thus foreign savings are negative. Of the sources of domestic net savings, the household sector is usually most important in the DCs, but in LDCs, this is frequently not the case. For example, household savings are insignificant in Colombia and Korea and negative in Chile and Panama. Government savings, on the other hand, are quite sizable in some LDCs.

The measurement of savings is unfortunately subject to substantial error, since savings are frequently obtained as a residual.[7] This is particularly true of household savings, which are a kind of residual of residuals, in the sense that they are measured as the residual between disposable income and household consumption, which in turn is often measured as the residual item in aggregate expenditure. The validity of the savings data depends not only on the validity of the methods used in constructing the national accounts but also on both the rather arbitrary choice of the rate at which capital depreciation is allowed and the foreign exchange rate (Hooley 1967). When the price of foreign exchange is set too low, as it frequently is in LDCs, the estimate of the contribution of foreign savings is biased downward and that of domestic savings is biased upward (S. R. Lewis 1969).

[7]A description of the methods for estimating gross domestic product consumption and savings in LDCs is provided in OECD (1970).

If one is willing to sacrifice length in the time series—which is desirable for diminishing the influence of extraordinary year-to-year variations in the levels of inventories, government and business savings, and investment— one can gain greater country coverage. In so doing, the general patterns of change in capital formation proportions and in the sources of finance become clearer. For example, Table 16.1 will show that the investment share tends to rise from 12.7 percent in countries whose per capita income is $50 to 25.2 percent in countries with per capita income of $2,000. The ratio of foreign savings to GDP falls from 4.9 percent in countries with per capita income of $50 to 1.8 percent in countries with per capita income of $2,000. The rise in the gross national savings ratio is even more dramatic, from 7.8 percent to 23.4 percent.

Government Taxes and Savings

We begin our discussion of the supply of savings with government savings which, as shown in Table 10.1, have provided a substantial portion of total domestic savings in some LDCs. Government savings can be generated by decreasing expenditures while holding revenues constant or by increasing taxes while holding expenditures constant. In either case, savings are defined as total government revenues less current expenditures, and they appear in the government capital account. This introduces an ambiguity to the concept, since the distinction between current and capital expenditures is in most cases opaque and can be further confused by political expediency and book juggling. Certain kinds of expenditure on education are regarded as current, although properly they should be considered as investment in the human agent. On the other hand, expenditures for purchasing a fleet of government limousines, or for building presidential palaces are commonly included in government investment, while more appropriately they could be classified as consumption.

The raising of revenues through taxation has been viewed as the main source of government savings. Foreign donors have in fact placed exclusive emphasis on this mechanism by labeling virtually any method for increasing revenues as evidence of "self-help," which has apparently been used as one of several criteria in allocating assistance among countries. The empirical question that arises is to what exent an increase in government revenue increases domestic savings? What is the relationship between the increase in taxes and the level of savings in a country, and what is the marginal propensity of governments to save as compared to that of private individuals?

The effect of government taxes on savings ratios has been investigated by Landau (1971) by fitting time series data for Latin American countries to the equations

$$\frac{S}{Y} = a + b\left(\frac{T}{Y}\right) \tag{7}$$

or

$$\frac{S_g}{Y} = a + b\left(\frac{T}{Y}\right) \tag{8}$$

where S is savings, S_g is government savings, T is taxes, and Y is gross national product. Despite the problems of serial correlation that seem to lead to poor results, the test appears to support the "Please effect" (Please 1967, 1970) that the marginal propensity of government to consume out of increased revenues is sufficiently high that in several cases increased taxation might reduce domestic savings. Using similar methods, other researchers have ob-

Table 10.1 *Capital Formation Shares, Rates of Growth, and Sources of Finance, 1960–1969*

Country	Average Ratio of Gross Investment to GDP	Average Rate of Growth of GDP	Proportion of Gross Capital Formation Financed by:					
			Foreign Saving	Depreciation	Domestic Net Saving	Corporate Saving	Government Saving	Household Saving
DEVELOPED COUNTRIES								
Australia	0.26	5.4	$\cdots$	0.36	0.64	0.13	0.22	0.29
Austria	0.26	4.3	$\cdots$	0.38	0.62	0.15	0.21	0.26
Belgium	0.21	4.5	−0.01	0.44	0.57	0.09	0.04	0.44
Canada	0.23	5.7	$\cdots$	0.55	0.45	0.19	0.10	0.16
Denmark	0.21	4.5	−0.01	0.40	0.61	—	0.24	—
France	0.23	5.6	$\cdots$	0.40	0.60	0.14	0.17	0.29
Germany	0.25	4.4	−0.01	0.37	0.64	0.17	0.22	0.25
Ireland	0.19	3.9	$\cdots$	0.40	0.60	0.17	0.04	0.39
Italy	0.21	5.2	$\cdots$	0.35	0.65	0.07	0.08	0.50
Japan	0.32	10.6	$\cdots$	0.33	0.67	0.14	0.19	0.34
Netherlands	0.25	5.2	$\cdots$	0.33	0.67	0.15	0.15	0.37
New Zealand	0.22	—	0.08	0.26	0.66	—	—	—
Norway	0.28	5.0	$\cdots$	0.46	0.54	—	0.25	—
South Africa	0.22	6.1	$\cdots$	0.38	0.62	0.16	0.16	0.30
Sweden	0.24	4.6	$\cdots$	0.39	0.61	0.10	0.32	0.19
Switzerland	0.26	4.0	$\cdots$	0.36	0.64	0.16	0.18	0.30
United Kingdom	0.18	2.9	$\cdots$	0.43	0.57	0.23	0.13	0.21
United States	0.17	4.9	$\cdots$	0.54	0.46	0.14	0.05	0.27
Average (unweighted)	0.23							
Average (weighted by GDP)	0.20							
LESS DEVELOPED COUNTRIES								
Brazil	0.17	4.6	0.04	0.32	0.64	—	—	—
Chile	0.16	4.6	—	0.73	0.27	0.18	0.29	−0.20
Colombia	0.18	4.9	—	0.49	0.51	0.31	0.16	0.04
Costa Rica	0.21	5.0	0.02	0.37	0.61	—	0.04	—
Dominican Republic	0.12	2.9	0.42	0.35	0.23	—	—	—
Ecuador	0.12	—	—	0.36	0.64	—	0.20	—
El Salvador	0.13	—	—	0.43	0.57	—	—	—

Table 10.1 *(Continued)*

Country	Average Ratio of Gross Investment to GDP	Average Rate of Growth of GDP	Proportion of Gross Capital Formation Financed by:					
			Foreign Saving	Depreciation	Domestic Net Saving	Corporate Saving	Government Saving	Household Saving
Greece	0.24	7.3	0.02	0.27	0.71	—	0.10	—
Honduras	0.14	5.5	0.07	0.35	0.58	0.19	0.05	0.34
India	0.15	—	0.01	0.35	0.64	—	0.16	—
Iran	0.17	9.2	−0.12	0.35	0.77	—	—	—
Jamaica	0.21	4.6	0.20	0.31	0.49	0.25	0.09	0.15
Jordan	0.16	—	0.10	0.18	0.72	—	—	—
Korea	0.17	9.7	0.03	0.39	0.58	0.16	0.39	0.03
Libya	0.28	23.8	−0.25	0.20	1.05	—	0.75	—
Madagascar	0.10	—	0.17	0.32	0.51	—	—	—
Malaysia	0.14	—	−0.03	0.39	0.64	0.02	0.41	0.21
Mexico	0.16	7.2	0.07	0.23	0.70	—	—	—
Morocco	0.12	—	0.02	0.18	0.80	—	—	—
Panama	0.17	7.8	—	0.53	0.47	0.46	0.23	−0.22
Paraguay	0.14	4.4	0.33	0.39	0.28	—	—	—
Philippines	0.17	4.9	—	0.40	0.60	0.14	0.06	0.40
Portugal	0.18	6.1	—	0.30	0.70	0.02	0.16	0.52
Spain	0.21	7.4	0.01	0.29	0.70	0.21	0.20	0.29
Sudan	0.17	4.7	0.18	0.45	0.37	—	—	—
Taiwan	0.19	10.3	0.07	0.29	0.64	0.08	0.12	0.44
Tunisia	0.21	4.1	0.40	0.19	0.41	—	—	—
Uruguay	0.13	0.3	—	0.28	0.72	—	—	—
Venezuela	0.18	5.9	—	0.42	0.58	—	—	—
Zambia	0.21	6.5	—	0.25	0.75	—	—	—
Average (unweighted)	0.17							
Average (weighted by GDP)	0.17							

Notes:
··· indicates zero or negligible.
— indicates information is lacking or incomplete.
Source: U.N. (1973, 1974), *Yearbook of National Account Statistics*, Vol. 1, International Tables 1971, 1972. New York, Tables 1A, 2A, 4A, 8, and 9.

tained results which cast some doubt on the Please effect (Krishnamurty 1968; J. G. Williamson 1968; Singh 1972). Singh, for example, confirms the low marginal propensity to save on the part of governments and finds a high degree of substitutability between government and private savings. (An incremental dollar of government savings implies the reduction of private savings by 57 cents.) However, he also observes the paradoxical result (earlier noticed by Houthakker 1965) of a positive relationship between the tax rate and the private savings rate.

Besides increasing the tax burden, an alternative that governments often rely on for increasing revenues and presumably also savings is deficit financing. Its effects are generally ambiguous. Deficit financing is accomplished either through public borrowing or through printing money. In either case, an increase in prices is likely to result, the effects of which we will discuss presently.[8]

[8]Although certain attempts have been made to work out precise formulas for "safe" deficit financing (Ezekiel 1967) and in fact foreign donor institutions may follow certain rules of thumb, the topic is still shrouded with ignorance. In general, not much is known about the effect of inflation on income distribution, real balances, savings, and capital formation. There is some evidence to suggest that inflation may be a more costly form of taxation than alternative methods (M. J. Bailey 1956; Marty 1967).

Theories of Savings

The Level of Income Hypothesis

The logical starting point for theories concerning the relation of saving to income is the Keynesian hypothesis that the average propensity to save, S/Y, increases with the level of income. This hypothesis, which derives from Keynes' "first psychological law" (Keynes 1936, Chapter 10), is expressed by the savings function

$$S = a_0 + a_1 Y \qquad (9)$$

where $a_0 < 0$ and the marginal propensity to save (MPS) is $0 < a_1 < 1$. Under this specification of equation 9, the average propensity to save (APS) rises with the level of income. If $a_0 \geq 0$, the average propensity to save is less than or equal to the marginal propensity to save.

Another specification of the level of income hypothesis that derives from Keynes' "second psychological law" is that the marginal propensity to save is an increasing function of the level of income

$$\ln S = b_0 + b_1 Y \qquad (10)$$

where $b_0 > 0$ and $b_1 > 0$. Yet another specification relies on the constant income elasticity of savings

$$\ln S = c_0 + c_1 \ln Y \qquad (11)$$

where c_1 is the elasticity coefficient. All these specifications of the hypothesis are consistent with the familiar "vicious circles" argument that savings in LDCs are low because income is low. The specifications of equations 10 and 11 are stronger than specification 9, because they imply that people in LDCs will be able to save a smaller proportion of a certain increment in income than individuals in DCs.

A number of tests of the level of income hypothesis are available for LDCs. In Table 10.2, we report the results of Mikesell and Zinser (1973) for time series of a sample of Latin American countries. The basic finding of this and other similar studies is that, contrary to the Keynesian hypothesis, the MPS is not uniformly greater than the corresponding APS. This observation is also consistent with observations from DCs that the APS tends to remain constant over long periods of time despite significant increases in income.

Table 10.2 *Savings Functions for Latin America*

Country	Period	a_0	t_0	a_1	t_1	$\bar{R}^2$	$\overline{APS}$
Argentina	1950–1968	−100.82*	5.075	0.294*	13.987	0.915	0.182
Bolivia	1953–1968	537.02	2.083	0.097	1.510	0.096	0.059
Brazil	1950–1967	4.15	0.599	0.140*	14.468	0.925	0.147
Chile	1960–1968	1.64	1.826	0.047	0.886	−0.028	0.146
Colombia	1950–1968	0.73	1.750	0.151*	8.359	0.793	0.187
Costa Rica	1953–1968	−165.14	1.683	0.107*	6.177	0.726	0.139
Dominican Republic	1953–1968	193.71*	5.038	−0.114**	2.442	0.262	0.132
Ecuador	1953–1967	1.22*	4.405	0.035	1.778	0.134	0.126
El Salvador	1958–1968	42.72	1.149	0.087*	4.282	0.634	0.112
Guatemala	1953–1968	−68.15*	3.618	0.163*	9.989	0.884	0.100
Honduras	1953–1968	−27.67**	2.307	0.148*	7.688	0.806	0.101
Mexico	1950–1967	−4.54**	2.935	0.159*	16.487	0.941	0.135
Nicaragua	1953–1968	−98.17	0.963	0.164*	4.912	0.623	0.128
Panama	1960–1968	−59.95**	3.024	0.238*	6.962	0.856	0.129
Paraguay	1962–1970	−4.76	1.620	0.190*	3.860	0.630	0.120
Peru	1950–1968	4.67*	3.412	0.122*	6.095	0.668	0.198
Uruguay	1955–1968	0.82	0.253	0.076	0.396	−0.069	0.125
Venezuela	1950–1968	1.41*	4.452	0.186*	13.624	0.911	0.256
Average				0.132			0.139
Median				0.150			0.130

Notes: Estimated from the relation $S = a_0 + a_1 Y$. Starred coefficients (*) are significant at the 1 percent level; (**) indicates significance at the 5 percent level.

Source: Mikesell, R. F., and J. E. Zinser (1973), "The Nature of the Savings Function in Developing Countries: A Survey of the Theoretical and Empirical Literature," *J. E. L.*, 11 (March), p. 5.

Besides the time series tests of the level of income hypothesis, international cross-sections have also been used to study the relationship between savings and national product, or savings per capita and GNP per capita, for countries at different levels of development (Kuznets 1960; Landau 1969; Singh 1972). The guarded result that emerges is that high per capita income countries have higher savings ratios than poorer countries.

To explain the apparent contradiction between higher savings ratios for richer individuals, groups, and countries than for poor ones and savings ratios that are constant in the long run, three alternative hypotheses have been developed: the relative-income hypothesis, the permanent-income hypothesis, and the life-cycle hypothesis.

The Relative-Income Hypothesis

Most analyses of savings assume that the consumption (or savings) components of individuals or of time series observations are independent. An important exception is the relative-income hypothesis, or the "demonstration effect" (Brady and Friedman 1947; Duesenberry 1949; Modigliani 1947), in which the consumption of one person, group, or time period is made a function of the consumption of other persons, groups, or time periods.

Nurkse (1953) extended this hypothesis to the international context by arguing that the availability of information concerning (higher) consumption standards in DCs to people in LDCs induces an imitative behavior, which raises the (average and perhaps marginal) propensity to consume (and lowers the propensity to save) relative to that which would be expected on the basis of income alone. As a number of critics have pointed out, however, one might want to know why the demonstration effect would affect only consumption patterns and not investment patterns. If investment is also subject to imitative behavior, it would tend to offset the consumption demonstration effect and thus nullify any negative effect on the *ex post* propensity to save.

The relative-income hypothesis can be expressed as

$$C_i = a + b_1 Y_i + b_2 C_j \qquad (12)$$

where C_j is consumption in country j, which is supposed to induce imitative consumption behavior in country i, C_i. An estimate of $b_2 > 0$ would confirm the international demonstration effect. Alternatively, the relative-income hypothesis could be expressed as (Suits 1963)

$$\frac{C}{Y} = a + b\left(\frac{Y}{Y_i}\right) \qquad b < 0 \qquad (13)$$

where Y_i is the income of the other country or group, and for time series data, Y_i is the previous peak income observed. A negative coefficient b in this expression would be consistent with the hypothesis that the proportion of income consumed will increase as the distance from the standard of comparison increases. The time series counterpart to this formulation is that, as income in the current year, Y, falls relative to the highest previous income, Y_i, the propensity to consume rises. This implies that people resist declines in their consumption standard. The relative-income hypothesis is thus one of several hypotheses asserting that consumers may not adjust their consumption spending (and therefore savings) immediately and completely to the current level of income.

The Permanent-Income Hypothesis

Friedman's (1957) permanent-income hypothesis is the starting point for a number of alternative specifications of savings behavior and, as we will see in Chapter 18, it is sufficiently robust to be applied in other contexts, such as the study of export instability. The cornerstone of the hypothesis is the concept of permanent income we introduced in Figures 10.1 and 10.2. It is defined in terms of a long-run expectation over a planning period. The difference between permanent income and measured income is transitory income. It is hypothesized that the marginal and average propensities to consume from transitory income are smaller (zero in the original extreme version of the hypothesis) than those from permanent income. In general, therefore, the higher the transitory component of income, the higher the savings ratio. In its simplest form, the hypothesis can be expressed as

$$S_t = a_0 + a_1 Y_{pt} + a_2 Y_{tt} \qquad (14)$$

where Y_{pt} is permanent income and Y_{tt} is transitory income in year t. Since Y_{pt} and Y_{tt} are not observable for fitting the above equation, a more detailed specification of the hypothesis is necessary.

Consider the following specification:

$$C_p = k(r, w, u)Y_p \tag{15}$$

$$Y = Y_p + Y_t \tag{16}$$

$$C = C_p + C_t \tag{17}$$

$$\rho(Y_p, Y_t) = 0; \qquad \rho(C_p, C_t) = 0;$$

$$\rho(Y_t, C_t) = 0 \tag{18}$$

where C and Y are actual measures of consumption and income, and the subscripts p and t refer to the permanent and transitory components of these variables. The constant k depends on r, w, and u, which represent respectively the interest rate, the ratio of non-human wealth to permanent income, and the various taste factors that enter the individual's consumption behavior. Friedman assumes, as in equation 18, that there is no correlation (represented by ρ) between: (1) permanent and transitory income; (2) permanent and transitory consumption; and (3) transitory consumption and transitory income. Permanent consumption is a constant proportion (k) of permanent income, and thus, the ratio of present consumption to permanent income is independent of the income level. Furthermore, Friedman argues that over time, at least in the United States, the effects of r, w, and u have tended to cancel each other out and hence for simplicity may be ignored.

Compare the results of specifications 15–18 to the usual specification, in which permanent and transitory components are not distinguished:

$$C = a + bY \tag{19}$$

It can be shown that b is related to k in the following way[9]:

$$b = k\frac{\Sigma(Y_p - \overline{Y}_p)^2}{\Sigma(Y - \overline{Y})^2} = kP_y \tag{20}$$

where P_y is the ratio of the variance of the permanent component of income to the total variance of income. From equation 20, it appears that the estimate of b, the marginal propensity to consume out of measured income, is biased downward to the extent that $P_y < 1$. Consequently, the estimate of a in equation 19 must be biased upward. Friedman's hypothesis is that $a = 0$, which is consistent with the evidence cited above suggesting that, in the United States at least, the average propensity to consume is constant in the long run.

To obtain an estimate of k, we have to derive a measure of permanent income. An approximation of permanent income for time series applications is a weighted average of present and past measured income. The weights and the number of years considered can be determined by the formula given by Friedman (1957, p. 144)

$$Y_p(T) = \beta \int_{-\infty}^{T} e^{(\beta - \alpha)(t-T)} Y(t)\, dt \tag{21}$$

where β is the adjustment coefficient between measured and permanent income, α is the average annual growth rate of income, T is the present time period, and t is the index of time period. Since the observations are in discrete terms, we express

$$Y_p{}^t(T) = \beta[Y_t + e^{(\beta - \alpha)}Y_{t-1} + e^{2(\beta - \alpha)}Y_{t-2}$$
$$+ \cdots + e^{T(\beta - \alpha)}Y_{t-T}] \tag{22}$$

The weights decline through time, implying that consumption plans are influenced more by present than by past income.

Friedman, in his application to United States data, found the relevant consumer horizon to be three years. Similarly, J. G. Wil-

[9]The proof is as follows: The marginal propensity to consume, b, in equation 19 is estimated by the ratio of the covariance of C and Y around their average values, $\overline{C}$, $\overline{Y}$, to the variance in Y around its mean.

$$b = \frac{\Sigma(C - \overline{C})(Y - \overline{Y})}{\Sigma(Y - \overline{Y})^2} \tag{1n}$$

substituting equations 16 and 17 into the numerator of equation 1n, we obtain

$$b = \frac{\Sigma(C_p + C_t - \overline{C}_p - \overline{C}_t)(Y_p + Y_t - \overline{Y}_p - \overline{Y}_t)}{\Sigma(Y - \overline{Y})^2}$$

$$= \frac{\Sigma(C_p - \overline{C}_p)(Y_p - \overline{Y}_p) + \Sigma(C_p - \overline{C}_p)(Y_t - \overline{Y}_t) + \Sigma(C_t - \overline{C}_t)(Y_p - \overline{Y}_p) + \Sigma(C_t - \overline{C}_t)(Y_t - \overline{Y}_t)}{\Sigma(Y - \overline{Y})^2} \tag{2n}$$

Substituting equation 15 for C_p in the first two terms of equation 2n and its converse for Y_p in the third term yields

$$b = \frac{k\Sigma(Y_p - \overline{Y}_p)^2 + k\Sigma(Y_p - \overline{Y}_p)(Y_t - \overline{Y}_t) + \frac{1}{k}\Sigma(C_t - \overline{C}_t)(C_p - \overline{C}_p) + \Sigma(C_t - \overline{C}_t)(Y_t - \overline{Y}_t)}{\Sigma(Y - \overline{Y})^2} \tag{3n}$$

From the assumptions about the independence of Y_p and Y_t, C_p and C_t, and C_t and Y_t, the last three terms are zero, thus allowing us to simplify equation 3n to equation 20.

liamson (1968), in his study of the saving function in a number of Asian countries, used a three-year moving average of income to represent permanent income. Three-year averages have also been used by other researchers, such as Gupta (1970) in his study of per capita household Indian saving and Friend and Taubman (1966) in their pooled time series study of personal savings in 22 DCs and LDCs. Singh (1972) used a two-year horizon.

An equivalent but simpler procedure is the distributed lag method. The reduced form of the consumption function model, which can be estimated, is as follows

$$C_t = \lambda C_{t-1} + k(1 - \lambda)Y_t + v_t \qquad (23)$$

where $0 \le \lambda \le 1$ and v_t is a composite error term. C_{t-1} and v_t are correlated, and hence, ordinary least squares will give biased and inconsistent estimates. Empirical applications of this model have used maximum likelihood estimation and the Bayesian approach to estimation (Zellner and Geisel 1970).

Our presentation of the permanent-income hypothesis to this point has been built upon time series data. Cross-section data can also be utilized to estimate k of equation 20. In the simplest specification of the hypothesis, and following Friedman, permanent income from budget studies can be approximated by group means in the household survey. It is hypothesized that the income of individuals of a particular group will contain transitory components, but that the average measured income for the group is equal to its average permanent income. In this approach, the number of observations available to estimate the parameters of the consumption function is limited by the number of groups one can identify. The most frequently used grouping criterion is occupation, but other criteria also appear, such as race or location (Mayer 1966).

Holbrook and Stafford (1971) extend the permanent-income hypothesis within a multivariate framework to analyze three-year panel data of a sample of United States families. They distinguish five sources of family income (husband's, wife's and other household member's, transfer, mixed capital-labor, and other capital income) and find that the marginal propensity to consume from each source of income differs significantly from case to case.

The permanent-income hypothesis has been applied in LDCs both in its strict form

(with the assumption that the marginal propensity to consume out of transitory income is zero) and also by allowing some consumption to take place out of transitory income. In general, the marginal propensities to save out of permanent and transitory income diverge quite markedly. For example, J. G. Williamson (1968) in his study of eight Asian countries estimated MPS_p to be from 0.20 to 0.29, as compared to a range of 0.37 to 1.12 for MPS_t. Friend and Taubman (1966) estimated the marginal propensities for 22 countries as 0.06 for MPS_p and 0.41 for MPS_t.

The permanent-income hypothesis is a good example of a higher level hypothesis that enables the formulation and testing of a number of subsidiary hypotheses. Among these are the following:

1. Measured income might be expected to be less than permanent income in the early and late years of a working lifetime, and higher in the middle. Thus, one would expect lower propensities to save out of measured income in one's early and mature years than in the "prime of life" years.[10]

2. Since measured incomes of consumer units with relatively constant incomes are probably closer during any period of time to their permanent incomes, than those with nonconstant incomes, the APS should be lower for constant-income families and should vary more with the level of income than the *APS* of nonconstant-income families.[11]

3. The more narrowly defined the job and industrial classification of the worker, the more likely it is that differences in measured income are attributable to differences in transitory income rather than permanent income, and thus the higher the expected APS.[12]

4. In a few cases, such as in the United States after the National Service Life Insurance dividend of 1950 and in Israel after restitution payments were granted by Germany, it has been possible to test the permanent-

---

[10]See Friedman (1957, p. 91).

[11]Using consumer survey data for the United States, Friend and Kravis (1957) found evidence inconsistent with the hypothesis.

[12]Using United States cross-section data, Friedman (1957) and Houthakker (1958) have presented conflicting evidence on this implication. Somewhat similarly, Mayer (1966) utilized international data to reject the permanent-income hypothesis in its strict form.

income hypothesis directly by studying the effect of changes in transitory income on consumption. As pointed out above, the strict version of the model assumes that the marginal propensity to consume transitory income is zero.[13]

5. Countries with unstable export prices and export revenues might be expected to have higher savings rates than countries with stable exports and income. If export and income instability are more characteristic of LDCs than of DCs, one would expect to find higher savings ratios in LDCs than in DCs.[14]

6. If foreign assistance and the immediate increases in income and expenditures which it permits were considered permanent by LDCs, the propensity to consume would rise, thereby lowering the domestic savings ratio.[15] By the same token, the fact that United States foreign aid must be funded annually by congressional appropriation bills, thereby impeding long-term commitments, may contribute to having foreign assistance considered as part of transitory income, thereby increasing the *APS*.

Functional Sources of Income and Savings
A direct implication of the permanent-income hypothesis is that the propensity to consume could vary depending on the source of income. In Friedman's model, the propensity to consume depends on interest rates, the ratio

of human to total wealth, tastes, and uncertainty, which enter the transitory component of income. In terms of uncertainty, if measured income originates from sources that have different permanent and transitory income components, the propensity to consume would be expected to vary. Similarly, the propensity to consume would vary were we to compare groups of income recipients that differ in interest rates, ratios of human to total wealth, and tastes. In the process of aggregation, these differences appear as differences in the propensity to consume in different functional income groups.

The distinction among alternative income sources that has received the most attention from the point of view of the analysis of savings is the distinction between wage (and salary) income and property income. Houthakker (1961) found that savings out of labor income tend to be zero in most countries. J. G. Williamson (1968), in his study of several Asian countries, finds the marginal propensity to save out of nonwage income significantly higher than that out of wage income. These results are consistent with the findings of Holbrook and Stafford (1971). Within the context of the permanent-income hypothesis, a ready explanation of these findings suggests itself. Suppose that the economy of LDCs is characterized by "fragmented investment opportunities," that is, capital market imperfections (McKinnon 1973). Investment in physical capital is characterized by a certain "lumpiness" and has generally high, and differing, rates of returns. Investments in financial assets, such as bank deposits, have low, government-controlled interest rates, which may even be negative after one allows for inflation. Investment in human capital has rates of return somewhere between the bank deposit rate and the rate of return in physical capital. In this fragmented capital market with different rates of interest, one may expect entrepreneurs (or capitalists) to have higher savings ratios because of the high rate of return to investment opportunities in physical capital, as compared to laborers whose opportunities are limited to those with low rates of return (either as bank deposits or as investment in human wealth). This is the theoretical point that underlies McKinnon's (1973) advocacy of liberalizing capital markets and increasing bank deposit interest rates as a means of capital accumulation in the process of economic development.

[13]Bodkin (1959) used the United States case to argue there is no significant difference between the marginal propensity to consume transitory income and permanent income, while Kreinin (1961) used the Israeli case to argue that there is a significant difference, although the marginal propensity to consume transitory income is not zero as in the strict version of the hypothesis. Bodkin (1963) presented several possible explanations as to why Kreinen's results might still be consistent with his own.

[14]MacBean (1966) provides some evidence to support the first part of this hypothesis, but additional evidence to deny the latter part. However, this study is marred by the use of unsatisfactory measures of instability and other problems. Knudsen (1972) uses a more sophisticated expectations index of instability and confirms the permanent-income hypothesis. This subject will be discussed in detail in Chapter 18.

[15]Friedman (1957, pp. 233–236) makes this point but allows for a possible offsetting influence in the form of higher interest rates resulting from a higher growth rate and greater inducements to invest. Oner (1968), Wolf (1964), Rahman (1968) and Chenery and Eckstein (1970) have used international cross-section analysis to show that foreign savings may substitute for domestic savings with, but possibly even without, a reaction lag. However, these results have been strongly challenged by Dalloul (1969).

The Life-Cycle Hypothesis

The life-cycle hypothesis, associated with the writings of Modigliani, Ando, and Brumberg[16], postulates utility maximization over a lifetime, subject to a wealth constraint. It is assumed that individuals attempt to spread their consumption evenly over their lifetimes. They accumulate enough savings over their earning years to maintain their consumption standard during retirement and to have zero assets at the end of the life horizon. The distinct empirical implications of the hypothesis are two. First, in a society with stationary population, if we control for income there will be no aggregate net personal savings, since the dissavings of the retired would exactly offset the savings of the employed. Second, controlling for population, in a society with stationary per capita income there will be no aggregate net personal savings. If per capita income is growing, however, the amount of savings necessary to maintain an individual's consumption level in retirement is also increasing. Two crucial variables, therefore, that enter the analysis are the rate of population increase and the rate of increase in per capita income.

The two basic assumptions of the life-cycle hypothesis refer to the utility function that is maximized and to the horizon for maximization. The utility function is a homogeneous function of the present and future stream of consumption flows (C_t, C_{t+1}, C_{t+2}, . . . , C_T) for the T years of the individual's lifetime. More specifically, individuals formulate their consumption plans for their lifetimes so that they consume all their wealth (ignoring bequeathals) at a constant rate of γ per year. This is the implication of the homogeneity assumption. For any individual of age K, therefore, with $T - K$ years remaining in his lifetime, the constant rate of consumption is $\gamma^K = (1/T - K)$, which is independent of the level of his wealth, W. In one's youth, $T - K$ is large and thus γ^K is small. However, the proportion of wealth consumed increases gradually until, in the final year of life (where $K = T - 1$, that is, $\gamma^K = 1$), the proportion of remaining wealth that is consumed is one, leaving a net worth of zero at death. The consumption function of the life-cycle hypothesis can therefore be written

[16]The seminal references are Modigliani and Brumberg (1955), Ando and Modigliani (1963, 1964). See also Modigliani and Ando (1957) and Modigliani (1966, 1967).

$$C_t^K = \gamma_t^K W_t^K \quad \text{where} \quad \gamma^K = \frac{1}{T - K} \qquad (24)$$

Two forms of wealth are distinguished: nonhuman wealth, A, and human wealth, Y. The human wealth of an individual at age K is the discounted sum of labor incomes for the individual's lifetime,

$$\sum_{i=1}^{N} \frac{Y_i}{(1 + r)^i}$$

where $N = T - K$. We can distinguish labor income, and therefore human wealth, in two parts, current labor income, Y_t^K, and the average annual flow of future labor income, Y_E, multiplied by the number of years remaining in the individual's lifetime, $N - K$. Assuming for simplicity that the interest rate is zero, for the nonhuman and human wealth of an individual of age K, we can write

$$W_t^K = A_t^K Y_t^K + (N - K)Y_E \qquad (25)$$

Substituting equation 25 into equation 24, we obtain

$$C_t^K = \gamma_t^K [A_t^K + Y_t^K + (N - K)Y_E]$$
$$= \frac{1}{T - K} A_t^K + \frac{1}{T - K} Y_t^K + \frac{N - K}{T - K} Y_E \qquad (26)$$

Equation 26 can easily be aggregated for all individuals in the same age group. The hypothesis can then be tested by comparing estimates of γ^K from data for individuals or groups in different age classes.

The life-cycle hypothesis is cast in terms of an individual household member, with each member's consumption flow equalized through life. Savings, however, are measured per family, and savings ratios are expressed as a proportion of income. Family incomes are observed to follow roughly parabolic paths over the earning span, rising sharply to a peak in the 35–54 age range and declining thereafter. Family size is also correlated with household age, reaching a peak at ages 35–44 and declining thereafter as children establish their own households. As a result of these two forces, income per household member reaches a low at ages 35–44 and rises thereafter. After considering the age-of-household correlates of income and family size, equalization of consumption per household member would predict that average savings as a proportion of family income are high in the age groups

45–64 and low in the age groups 25–44 and at retirement.

Two applications of the life-cycle hypothesis to data from LDCs are Landsberger (1970) for Israel and Kelley and J. G. Williamson (1968) for Indonesia. Landsberger estimates a linear consumption function for two groups of families, those whose head is no older than 34 years and families whose head is 35–44.[17] The independent variables are family current income, age of head of family, and two wealth variables, restitution receipts and other lump sums. The restitution receipts (paid to Israeli families by the West German government) are regarded as windfall increases in wealth; hence, their coefficient is regarded as an estimate of the marginal propensity to consume out of windfall wealth. The test is performed for two time periods, 1963–1964 and 1957–1958, and the results suggest, though weakly, that the marginal propensity to consume out of windfall income was higher for families belonging to the older age group.

Kelley and Williamson (1968) have data on income, savings, and family size, classified by the age of the head of household into five groups for a sample of Indonesian families in the Jogjakarta region. They perform two tests. First, they interpret the hypothesis as implying constant per capita consumption over the life-cycle, defined as the average consumption in the sample of households. By multiplying the per capita consumption figures by the average family size of each age group, they predict consumption, savings, and the average propensity to save. This is compared with the observed values of these variables. The results of this test were disappointing, presumably because education varied within household age depending on location. The second test examined savings behavior within age groups by regressing savings per capita on family income per capita. As the household grows older, labor income declines in proportion to nonhuman wealth, because wealth is set aside to finance consumption at retirement age. Data for nonhuman wealth are not available for this test. Therefore, the model would predict that the marginal propensity to save out of

income increases as the household grows older. With the exception of the group age 40–49, this pattern was confirmed. The marginal propensity to save rises from 0.05 for age group 20–29 to 0.60 for age group 60–69 for all households, and from 0.13 to 0.76 for rural households alone.

The life-cycle hypothesis can also be utilized to derive aggregate saving functions. Assume that the proportionality parameter, γ, of every age class, K, the age distribution of the population, and the distribution of wealth among age groups all remain constant over time. One can then aggregate equation 26 over the different age groups to arrive at

$$C_t = a_1 A_t + a_2 Y_t + a_3 Y_{E_t} \qquad (27)$$

Using current income or current income adjusted for the proportion of the total labor force to the employed labor force (or alternatively a distributed lag of present and past incomes) as the measure for Y_E, equation 27 can be estimated from aggregate time series data on C, Y, and A. The coefficient a_1 could be interpreted to be the propensity to consume out of nonhuman wealth, while a_2 would be the short-run propensity to consume out of income, and the sum of a_2 and a_3 would be the long-run propensity to consume out of income, which in turn is a multiple of the marginal propensity to consume out of human wealth. Ando and Modigliani (1963) report results from time series data for the United States, which show that the marginal propensity to consume out of nonhuman wealth, a_1, is significantly positive and not significantly different from the propensity to consume out of human wealth $(a_2 + a_3)/(N - K)$. Furthermore, they demonstrate that this wealth approach improves upon both the ordinary level of income hypothesis and the distribution of income hypothesis.

Dividing both sides of equation 27 by current labor income, we obtain

$$\frac{C_t}{Y_t} = a_1 \frac{A_t}{Y_t} + a_2 + a_? \frac{Y_{E_t}}{Y_t} \qquad (28)$$

Assuming (1) that the interest rate or the rate of return on nonhuman capital assets, r, is no longer necessarily zero but rather is constant over time, and (2) that income and, nonhuman wealth, Y and A, grow at the same rate, in the long run, Y_E/Y is unity and A/Y is constant, thereby reducing equation 28 to

---

[17]Only families whose head-of-household age is less than 45 were considered in order to standardize for the family size effect, since family size was found to be increasing up to that age but decreasing thereafter.

$$\frac{C_t}{Y_t} = a_1 \frac{A_t}{Y_t} + a_4 \quad \text{where} \quad a_4 = a_2 + a_3 \quad (29)$$

and thereby explaining the long-run constancy of the average propensity to consume. On the other hand, during cyclical recessions, where income grows more slowly than either non-human wealth or expected income, the ratios A_t/Y_t and Y_E/Y rise, causing the propensity to consume to rise. During cyclical booms, where current income is rising more rapidly than either wealth or expected income, these same ratios fall, causing a decline in the propensity to consume. In this way, it is seen that the life-cycle is consistent with both the observed long-run constancy of the average propensity to consume and the frequently noted inverse relation between the average propensity to consume and the level of income in the short run.

Substituting into the left-hand side of equation 29 the accounting identities

$$S_t = Y_t - C_t$$

and

$$S_t = \Delta A = A_{t+1} - A_t$$

we obtain

$$\frac{Y_t - \Delta A}{Y_t} = \frac{Y_t - A_{t+1} + A_t}{Y_t} = a_1 \frac{A_t}{Y_t} + a_4$$

$$(30)$$

Designating the long-run rate of growth in income and wealth by g, end-of-year wealth is related to beginning-of-year wealth by

$$A_{t+1} = (1 + g)A_t \quad (31)$$

Substituting for A_t from equation 31 into equation 30 and solving for A_{t+1}/Y_t, we have

$$\frac{A_{t+1}}{Y_t} = \frac{(1 - a_4)(1 + g)}{a_1 + g} \quad (32)$$

Finally, substituting the long-run solution for A_t/Y_t of equation 29, we find

$$\frac{C_t}{Y_t} = a_1 \frac{(1 - a_4)(1 + g)}{(a_1 + g)} + a_4$$

$$= \frac{a_1 + (a_1 - a_1 a_4 + a_4)g}{a_1 + g} \quad (33)$$

Note that in the steady-state equilibrium where $g = 0$, the long-run propensity to consume is unity, and thus, the propensity to save is zero. Recalling from the definition of a_4 above ($a_4 = a_2 + a_3$) that a_4 must be posi-

tive but less than 1, C/Y will decline, and hence, S/Y will rise as the rate of growth in income and nonhuman wealth increases. Assuming, for example, that $a_1 = 0.10$ and $a_4 = 0.80$, the propensity to save would be 0.03 at a growth rate of 2 percent, 0.06 at a growth rate of 5 percent, 0.09 at a growth rate of 10 percent, and 0.12 at a growth rate of 20 percent. Thus, the S/Y rises with the rate of growth of income and wealth, but at a decreasing rate. Likewise, assuming alternative values of a_1 and a_4 of 0.07 and 0.7 respectively, the propensity to save would rise from zero at $g = 0$ to 0.005 when $g = 0.01$, 0.04 when $g = 0.02$, 0.075 when $g = 0.05$, and 0.106 when $g = 0.10$. This implication of the life-cycle hypothesis is amenable to testing on the basis of a cross-section of time series data on income and saving or investment and is an implication that is distinguishable from any of the other hypotheses thus far considered. Modigliani (1966) reports favorable results obtained from an international cross-section of time series data from approximately 1954 to 1960 for some 36 DCs and LDCs. While admitting that the test could be biased by the favorable effect of the savings (and hence investment) ratio on the rate of growth, Modigliani finds that his results hold even when this simultaneous equation bias is mitigated or eliminated by the use of two-stage least squares as opposed to ordinary least squares.

Demographic factors may also have an important influence on aggregate savings. Thus, Leff (1969) estimates an aggregate savings function in terms of income per capita, the rate of increase in per capita income, the dependency ratio, and the two components of the dependency ratio (the percentage of population age 14 or less and the percentage of population age 65 or older). His results, based on an international cross-section of 47 LDCs, 20 DCs, and 7 communist countries, indicate a negative relation between savings and dependency ratios, with coefficients higher for LDCs than for DCs. He concludes that high birthrates are among the important factors in accounting for the great disparities in aggregate savings rates between DCs and LDCs.

Investment Demand

In this section, we shift our analysis to the demand side of capital-formation. The focus here, however, is on the factors explaining levels of investment demand through time in a macro as well as micro setting. Criteria for the optimal allocation of investment are covered in Chapter 20.

Econometric studies of investment demand have undergone several modifications since the simple accelerator model of J. M. Clark (1917). In this model, investment represents the simple difference between the initial actual level of capital stock and the desired level of capital. In other words, actual capital is equal to desired capital, and the latter in turn is proportional to output. More recently, there have been major modifications, particularly in the assumed time structure of the investment process and the specification of the desired level of capital stock. Research in the field, while confined mostly to DCs, has been relatively active. It is summarized in a number of competent survey articles.[18]

Recently, studies of investment demand have taken a neoclassical turn, following Jorgenson and his associates.[19] In the following paragraphs, we present briefly the main points of this neoclassical investment-demand theory, because it provides a more complete theoretical structure in that it considers both technological and price factors, and because it has performed relatively better in a statistical sense.

Investment decisions are made by firms and, therefore, should be related to the decision rule that firms use to obtain their objective, given technology and product and factor prices. The firm's objective in selecting its production plan is to maximize market value, the discounted sum of cash flow less direct taxes. Cash flow is the difference between net revenue and the implicit rental value of capital services. This implies that for a given production function, the firm maximizes profit at each point of time.

Profit is defined as

$$\Pi_t = p_t O_t - s_t L_t - c_t K_t \tag{34}$$

where

Π = profit
p = price of output
Q = quantity of output

s = wage rate
L = quantity of labor
c = the "shadow," or accounting, price of capital services before taxes
K = capital stock.

The shadow price of capital reflects a number of factors, which together determine the effective rental price of capital that, an entrepreneur considers in maximization of profits. These factors are the cost of capital, the price of investment goods, the rate of change of the price of investment goods, and the tax structure.[20] The formula used by Jorgenson and Siebert (1968a) to estimate c is[21]

$$c_t = \frac{q_t}{1 - u_t}\left[(1 - u_t w_t)\,\delta + r_t - \frac{q_t - q_{t-1}}{q_t}\right] \tag{35}$$

where

q_t = price of investment goods
u_t = rate of taxation
r_t = cost of capital
w_t = proportion of depreciation at replacement cost deductible from income for tax purposes
δ = rate of replacement
$\dfrac{q_t - q_{t-1}}{q_t}$ = rate of capital gains.

To determine the profit-maximizing conditions, specify a Cobb-Douglas production function with constant returns to scale of the following form[22]

$$Q = AK^\alpha L^{1-\alpha} \tag{36}$$

Maximizing profits requires that the marginal product of each factor be set equal to the ratio of factor cost to product price.

---

[18]See Meyer and Kuh (1957), Eisner and Strotz (1963), and Jorgenson (1971).

[19]For example, in Jorgenson and Siebert (1968a) and Jorgenson and Stephenson (1967).

[20]The rate of change of the price of investment goods represents capital gains. Jorgenson estimates two measures of the price of capital services. One assumes capital gains are taken into account in decision making, and the other assumes capital gains are transitory and thus are excluded. See Jorgenson and Siebert (1968a).

[21]Notice the similarity between the formulas used by Jorgenson and his associates to estimate the accounting price of capital service and those suggested by Yotopoulos (1967a, Chapter 7) for estimating the service flow of capital.

[22]The most important issue raised so far against Jorgenson's formulation is the validity of this C-D constant returns specification of the underlying production function of the firm. Eisner and Nadiri (1968) cite several studies which indicate that the elasticity of substitution is less than unity. But Jorgenson, Hunter and Nadiri (1970) conclude from the review of evidence that the assumption of unitary elasticity of substitution and constant returns to scale is reasonable.

$$\frac{\partial Q}{\partial L} = \frac{s}{p} \tag{37}$$

$$\frac{\partial Q}{\partial K} = \frac{c}{p} \tag{38}$$

From the second marginal productivity condition, we can determine the desired amount of capital, K^*. Since by definition $\partial Q/\partial K = \alpha(Q/K)$, then

$$K^* = \alpha \frac{pQ}{c} \tag{39}$$

where α is the elasticity of output with respect to capital services. The desired level of capital therefore depends on both technological and market conditions, as represented by the elasticity of output with respect to capital services and the price of the product relative to that of the capital services, respectively.

With this specification of the desired level of capital, we can derive a neoclassical theory of investment behavior cast within the framework of the flexible accelerator model. We have thus far discussed the factors determining the desired capital stock. This capital stock is generally achieved over several time periods, and investment represents the realization of these additions to the capital stock at each time period. Assume that capital is adjusted toward its desired level by a constant proportion of the difference between desired capital and actual capital, K. Net investment, which is the measure of the flow of capital in one time period, is therefore specified as a distributed lag function of the following formulation

$$I_n = K_t - K_{t-1} = (1 - \lambda)(K_t^* - K_{t-1}) \tag{40}$$

A complete theory of investment behavior must also involve an explanation of replacement investment, which constitutes a major portion of investment expenditure at the aggregate level (Kuznets 1961a). Thus, gross investment depends on the behavior of both net investment and replacement investment.

$$I_g = (1 - \lambda)(K_t^* - K_{t-1}) + \delta(K_{t-1}) \tag{41}$$

Replacement investment (the last term in equation 41) in this formulation is defined as proportional to capital stock. This definition is widely adopted in empirical estimation of investment demand and assumes that the mortality distribution of investment goods is geometric.

Jorgenson in his survey article (1971) characterizes equation 41, which utilizes the flexible accelerator mechanism as the basic model of most econometric studies of investment demand. Alternative investment-demand models, however, differ in the specification of the desired level of capital, the lag structure in the investment process, and replacement investment. In the neoclassical investment theory that Jorgenson and others have proposed, the desired level of capital is determined from conditions of profit maximization, subject to a production function as shown in equation 39.[23] They also have used a rational lag distribution, in contrast to the geometric distributed lag function first proposed by Chenery (1952), although the latter is a special case.[24]

In the test of performance of various investment models using a common set of data, Jorgenson and Siebert (1968a,b) for individual manufacturing firms and Jorgenson, Hunter, and Nadiri (1970) for two-digit manufacturing industry groups have shown that the neoclassical theory based on optimal theory of capital accumulation provides the best explanation of investment behavior so far proposed. This judgment of performance of the various models is based on goodness of fit and absence of autocorrelation in errors. Among the alternative models, the ranking that emerged was: (1) neoclassical; (2) expected profits; (3) accelerator; and (4) liquidity.

Empirical investigations of the nature of investment demand have focused mainly on the DCs, particularly the United States manufacturing sector. The neoclassical formulation may adequately express the behavior of investor decision making in such countries where the price of capital services generally reflects the real scarcity of financial resources in the economy. In LDCs, however, where capital and capital-goods markets are relatively imperfect and the financial infrastructure is woefully inadequate, changes in finance

[23]Other specifications of desired capital have been classified by Jorgenson and Siebert (1968a) as: (1) Accelerator: $K_t^* = \alpha Q_t$, where Q is the output and α is the desired capital-output ratio; (2) Liquidity: $K_t^* = \alpha L_t$, where L is a measure of liquidity and α is the desired ratio of capital to the flow of internal funds available for investment; and (3) Expected profits: $K_t^* = \alpha V_t$, where V is the market value of the firm and α is the desired ratio of capital to market value of the firm.

[24]A detailed discussion of the choice of appropriate distributed lag functions is given in Jorgenson and Stephenson (1967).

costs or in costs of capital goods, which play a major role in the neoclassical investment demand model, may not capture the full significance of the financial constraints. A rise in the interest rate, which would normally be expected to reduce the desired capital stock and investment to remedy the shortage of loanable funds, is often not allowed under institutional conditions in LDCs, where interest rates and prices of capital goods are usually controlled. In these situations, capital rationing through credit or some form of investment licensing is undertaken. Supply of internal financing under these circumstances may become an important consideration in a firm's investment decisions.

One attempt to explain aggregate investment behavior in an LDC was undertaken by DePrano and Nugent (1966) for the postwar period in Ecuador. A major part of investment in the nonagricultural sector of Ecuador appears to be externally financed, and interest rates and prices of capital goods are to a large extent determined by government policy. Given these conditions and the data available, DePrano and Nugent have estimated a gross investment equation of the following form for the Ecuadorian economy for the postwar period

$$I_t = a_0 + a_1 Y_{t-2} + a_2 K_{t-1} + a_3 M_{t-1} + a_4 R_t$$
$$(42)$$

where M represents high-powered money, and R is the stock of credit. Note that in this formulation, the planning and implementation stages are combined in a single equation. A more appropriate alternative would be to separate the two steps by estimating a sequence of two equations—first a planned investment equation and then an investment realization equation. But the paucity of data for Ecuador caused the study to be limited to the single-equation approach.

Except for the stock of credit, all variables on the right-hand side of equation 42 are predetermined, since they are lagged. The income variable is lagged by two time periods in this model. The stock of credit may also be considered predetermined if it is a policy instrument. In the case of Ecuador, however, R has been treated as an endogenous variable that depends on M, the stock of high-powered money. To avoid the problem of inconsistent estimation that arises, two-stage least squares has been utilized instead of ordinary least

squares. Based on the time series data from 1950–1965, the following results were obtained (standard errors in parentheses)

$$I_t = -71.466 + 0.243\, Y_{t-2} + 0.113\, K_{t-1}$$
$$(0.066) \qquad (0.105)$$
$$+ 0.235\, M_{t-1} + 1.006\, R$$
$$(0.110) \qquad (0.373)$$
$$R^2 = 0.602 \qquad DW = 2.33 \qquad (43)$$

It appears that past income, the stock of capital in the previous period, and the supply of high-powered money have had a significant influence on the level of investment in the Eucadorian economy.

Summary and Conclusions

Chapter 10 has been devoted to capital accumulation—a subject that has long been considered the linchpin of economic development. Although the role of capital formation in economic development may have been exaggerated in capital fundamentalism, a careful study of capital in the economics of development is rewarding. The process of capital accumulation–increase in income–increase in savings–capital accumulation is one of the few *virtuous* circles suggested in the development literature. Furthermore, to the extent that economic development involves Alice's crucial choice of "no jam today versus more jam tomorrow," time discounting, the link between income and wealth deserves serious attention.

Our presentation has started with the neoclassical approach to capital accumulation in terms of the relationship between the demand and supply of permanent income streams. The characteristic of this exposition is that savings is considered as a direct determinant of investment, as opposed to the Keynesian formulation of underemployment equilibrium that makes savings a function of income and income a function of investment. The former formulation emphasizes the supply side of capital, especially important in LDCs, which commonly face capital shortages. The Keynesian formulation emphasizes the demand side. Besides being directly applicable to situations of deficiency of demand, a general feature of DCs, the Keynesian formulation also has a bearing on the complementarities that may arise between specific kinds of investment demand. In this sense, it becomes crucial in the study of balanced growth, as will be suggested in Chapter 16.

Since the empirical hypotheses relating to both the supply of savings and the demand for investment do not lend themselves to a detailed summary, we content ourselves with a brief reprise of some of our findings.

The government sector remains a potentially important source for increased savings, although usually its effectiveness is much compromised by the "Please effect," in that the marginal propensity of the government to consume out of increased revenues is generally quite high. On the other hand, however, there apparently exists a positive relationship between the tax rate and the savings rate in the private sector. Thus, it appears that the government can play a crucial role in capital accumulation, especially if taxation is judiciously applied. Tax increases should be trained on individuals or types of income that have high marginal propensities to consume.

Aside from its ability to generate public savings without reducing private sector savings, the government can also play an important role in influencing savings behavior in the private sector. Moreover, to influence the private sector in an effective and expeditious manner, the determinants of savings and investment decisions must be properly understood. There are numerous different theories of savings, which investigate the propensities to save and consume under different circumstances and for different sources of income. While it is well established that, at least as far as measured savings are concerned, DCs have higher savings ratios than LDCs, there is no universal agreement on the reason for these differences.

One explanation is the absolute income hypothesis, in which the average (and even perhaps the marginal) propensity to consume rises with income, constituting an inevitable vicious circle of poverty and insufficient savings for poor countries. However, the evidence provided by historical accounts of individual countries suggests that the average propensity to save does not rise as income goes up. Alternative theories point to the sources of income, the subjective way it is viewed by the income recipient, the time in the person's life-cycle in which the income is received, and so on, as the basis for the explanation for the different behavioral patterns in DCs and LDCs.

There seems to be considerable merit in several of these factors. For example, the distinction between the permanent and transitory components of income seems to be appropriate in devising tax and other policies for LDCs. The marginal propensity to save out of transitory income is decidedly higher than that out of permanent income. This distinction seems to carry over validly to foreign assistance policies and to stabilization of export earnings policies. We return to this last subject in Chapter 18. There is also considerable empirical support for the proposition that the marginal propensity to save out of wage income is lower than that of nonwage (e.g., property or profits) income. Savings ratios also tend to be higher among families in the age groups 45–64 than those in other age groups. Savings rates are also higher in countries whose incomes are growing rapidly than in those with stagnant incomes. Savings also appear to be affected by demographic factors, such as the rate of growth of population and the dependency ratio.

We have concluded the chapter with a brief treatment of the demand side of capital formation, starting from the neoclassical theory of investment demand. Because of the lag between the time in which investment decisions are made and investment expenditures are carried out, investment expenditures seem to be most strongly influenced by lagged variables, including monetary factors, which influence the ability to implement positive investment decisions.

In the last several chapters, we have had ample opportunity to witness the importance of the classical concept of accumulation for the dynamics of development. Accumulation requires behavioral reactions to changing circumstances. Once accumulation is accomplished, it changes the endowments from which current and future outputs and income are generated. This raises the possibilities for further accumulation, and the process goes on. The concept of accumulation is general and need not be limited to technology and physical (tangible) capital, which have been the concerns of Chapters 9 and 10.

Indeed, the concept of accumulation is also applicable to the cluster of factors, including nutrition, education, on-the-job training, and migration, which has received considerable attention in recent years.[1] The common

thread among these factors is that they all affect the quality of labor and require present sacrifices to derive certain future advantages. In other words, each represents an investment, not of the usual type, such as physical capital (plant, equipment, and buildings) or financial capital (money, bonds, and equity shares), but rather in "human capital."

Our presentation begins with the specification of a general model capable of analyzing how human capital decisions are made in a variety of settings. This is followed by a discussion of alternative sources of discrepancies between the private and social benefits of human capital investments. Next, we demonstrate the use of the general model in calculating the private rate of return to different levels of education and then estimate the response of educational investments to variations in the rate of return. We also demonstrate how such estimates of educational response can be used to estimate the costs of public programs to

---

[1]Among the most important contributions to the subject have been T. W. Schultz (1960a, 1961, 1962), Becker (1962, 1964), and Stigler (1962).

achieve specific educational targets and/or to equate the private and social benefits of investments in education. Finally, we consider certain limitations and deficiencies in the human capital model and some alternative approaches.

A General Model of Human Capital Investments

Let us consider an individual whose life expectancy is n years. In his gth year, this individual has a human capital stock i of level $i = K$ (from which he earns an income of Y_{Kj} in any year, j, from $j = g$ to $j = n$). He considers making an investment in his future earning capacity (such as going to school an extra year, moving his place of residence, or receiving medical care). Such an investment would have the effect of raising the individual's human capital stock from level $i = K$ to level $i = K'$ ($i = K, K', \ldots$), thereby enabling him to earn a different stream of incomes $Y_{K'j}$ in each year, j, through the $n - g$ years remaining in his lifetime ($j = g$ to n). The costs incurred in year j are composed of the direct cost of the human capital investment, in this case $C_{K'j}$, as well as an opportunity cost owing to the loss in income during the period in which the investment is made.

Writing for $i = K, K', \ldots$, the investment will be economically advantageous if, and only if,

$$\sum_{j=g}^{n} \frac{Y_{K'j} - C_{K'j}}{(1+r)^{n-g}} - \sum_{j=g}^{n} \frac{Y_{Kj}}{(1+r)^{n-g}} > 0 \qquad (1)$$

where r is an appropriately chosen discount rate assumed to be the same in all future years. Under conditions of allocative efficiency, r would be equal to the marginal rate of return on the best alternative investment. If there should be no investment alternative (the decision is strictly "invest or don't invest"), r is the individual's subjective discount rate representing the individual's evaluation of present relative to future income (consumption). In any case, intertemporal efficiency requires that the individual's marginal rate of substitution of future for present income (consumption) be equal to the marginal rate of transformation between present and future income (consumption) attainable from the available market and/or productive opportunities.

The Y_{ij}'s (in this case Y_{Kj} and $Y_{K'j}$) should be weighted by the probability of the person's being alive in any year j, p_{ij} (for $j = g, \ldots, n$), and by the probability of being employed (if alive) in year j, q_{ij} (i.e, q_{Kj} and $q_{K'j}$), so as to represent expected incomes. The resulting streams of expected incomes should reflect the rates of growth of income attributable both to appreciation of the human capital stock (from learning-by-doing and experience) and also to depreciation with increased age and obsolescence, both of which may vary with the level or type of human capital investment.

Alternatively, when inequality 1 is restated as an equation, it becomes

$$\sum_{j=g}^{n} \frac{Y_{K'j} - C_{K'j}}{(1+r)^{n-g}} - \sum_{j=g}^{n} \frac{Y_{Kj}}{(1+r)^{n-g}} = 0 \qquad (2)$$

This is the rate of return over cost criterion, in which one solves for r rather than taking it as given as in inequality 1. The decision rule associated with equation 2 is: invest if, and only if, r exceeds the marginal rate of return on alternative investment opportunities.

If time is treated as continuous rather than as divided into discrete periods, equation 2 would be reformulated as

$$\int_{j=g}^{n} (Y_{K'j} - C_{K'j})(t)e^{-rt}dt - \int_{j=g}^{n} Y_{Kj}(t)e^{-rt}dt = 0 \qquad (3)$$

Incomes and expenditures are usually defined in terms of annual flows, and the data utilized in empirical applications are generally taken from population censuses and surveys. These are available only at different points in time and pertain to discrete periods of time —usually a calendar year. Therefore, we shall confine our attention throughout this chapter to the discrete time versions, that is, to inequality 1 or equation 2.

From the human capital model, one would predict that human capital investments would be more profitable for, and therefore more likely to be undertaken by: (1) younger people with longer working lifetimes, $n - g$, over which to recoup their investments; (2) people in societies with lower mortality rates (higher p_j's), which also have the effect of raising the expected value of $n - g$; (3) individuals or groups that are most likely to enter and remain in the labor force (males in most societies); and (4) individuals or groups for whom the direct and opportunity costs of the investments are relatively low and are confined to a relatively short period of time.

We see that the human capital model represented by inequality 1 or equation 2 is sufficiently general to be applied to any of the above types of investment in human capital. For example, the investment might take the form of on-the-job training (OJT). Given data on incomes, Y_{ij}, of people with different levels i of OJT and ages j, and different direct costs of OJT, C_{ij}, the rate of return over cost, r, to OJT could be computed. Utilizing data of this sort for different age, sex, race, and educational groups, Mincer (1962) used equation 2 to compute r for OJT in different groups in the United States. His findings confirm at least two of the general implications of the model —that younger people are more likely to invest in OJT than older people, and that females (who generally expect to work a much smaller portion of their lifetimes than do males) will invest less in OJT than males.

Moreover, by showing that the rate of return to OJT was as high as that to formal education, and that the accumulated investments in OJT have been almost as great as for formal education, for United States males at least, Mincer has made a convincing case that human capital investments in the form of OJT are important and deserve greater attention.[2]

Investments in health can also be analyzed in terms of the human capital model. The benefits of health investments may take the form of greater vitality and productivity while at work, fewer days absent from work, or longer working lifetimes reflected in higher probabilities of survival, p_{ij}. Mushkin (1962) has called attention to the fact that this form of human capital investment has been of increasing relative importance, at least in the case of the United States, where it presently accounts for more than 6 percent of GNP.

The human capital model can also be applied to investments in migration, as will be discussed in the following chapter, and to job search as demonstrated by Stigler (1962). The most common application of the model, however, is to investments in education. Applications of this sort are, therefore, discussed in some detail.

[2]Simmons (1972) has also provided some evidence of this, showing that OJT contributes significantly to the earnings of shoe industry workers in Tunisia. However, Simmons did not specifically use the human capital model or any of its implications.

Discrepancies Between the Private and Social Returns to Human Capital Formation

Thus far, we have considered human capital investment decisions primarily from the point of view of the individual. The present value of the differences in income (less cost) streams attributable to the investment in inequality 1, measures the net pecuniary benefits/costs of the investment that accrue to the individual. (Any such investment may generate significant nonpecuniary benefits as well—prestige, increased sensitivity to experiences, or the ability to live life more meaningfully—but these benefits are likely to remain relatively difficult to measure and thus may have to be left out of the analysis.) However, the same conceptual apparatus can be applied at the group or societal level. When inequality 1 is applied at the societal level, one can determine the pecuniary social benefits derived from the investments. The social benefits of human capital investments may not necessarily coincide with the private benefits; when they do not, efficient private investment decisions will not be socially optimal.

There are three important sources of discrepancies between the private and social benefits of human capital investments: (1) consumers' surplus; (2) externalities; and (3) market imperfections (e.g., taxes, subsidies, or monopoly).

In considering the effect of consumers' surplus on the distinction between private and social benefits of investment in the human agent, assume there is a competitive market in human capital, with no taxes or subsidies. Consider the supply and demand curves for human capital investment in Figure 11.1. Suppose people increase their investment in the human agent, shifting the supply curve from S to S'. The increase in income to investors is $CEB'C' - A'EBA$, which is less than the increased income to society, $CBB'C' = CEB'C' + EBB'$. Part of that difference is captured by the employers, $A'EBA$, and part by society, EBB'. Capitalizing the private return $CEB'C' - A'EBA$ will thus lead to an underinvestment in human capital.

The external effects of human capital investments can take various forms, depending on the type of human capital; sometimes they can be extremely important. Consider, for example, the case of a person who purchases innoculations that give him immunity to a communicable disease he otherwise would have

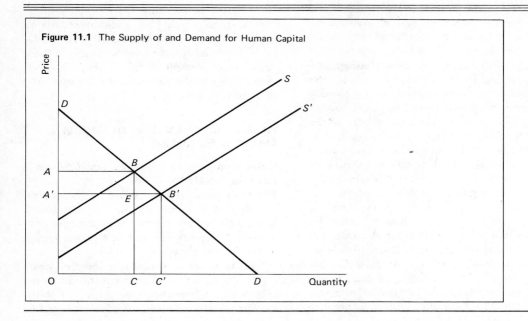

Figure 11.1 The Supply of and Demand for Human Capital

contracted. His investment in the innoculation benefits not only himself but also other individuals with whom he would have come into contact and to whom he would have transmitted the disease.[3]

Numerous examples of external benefits can also be cited in the field of education. School facilities can often be used to generate recreational benefits for individuals and groups other than those attending school. Moreover, education provides benefits not only to those receiving the education (investing in education) but also to the mothers of the children who, because of the child-care services provided by the schools, are able to take remunerative jobs. Empirical studies have demonstrated that education tends to stimulate some forms of socially productive behavior (such as contributions to voluntary and community services) and to diminish some forms of socially counterproductive behavior (such as criminal activities).[4] Although so-

ciety benefits from these effects, the individual generally receives no reward.

Almost all forms of investment in human capital, but particularly investments in education, tend to raise the productivity of complementary inputs, such as the labor services of one's co-workers. Moreover, education generates other kinds of externalities, which may have an even broader impact and become widely diffused through the society. For example, by making the public more literate, communications and the flow of information are facilitated, both of which make the market economy more efficient. At the same time, greater literacy makes for widespread use of checks as a means of payment and of written contracts for defining present and future transactions, thereby reducing the costs of transactions. Finally, since healthier and more educated parents tend to teach more to their children in the normal process of child-rearing than less healthy and less educated parents, investments in human capital often provide important intergenerational effects (Bowles 1972).[5]

[3]Weisbrod (1961) has used the human capital model to calculate the social benefits of eliminating three specific diseases in the United States.
[4]Weisbrod (1962, 1964) provides bibliographical references to effects of this sort. The effects of education on reduced crime rates imply social gains by reducing each of the following: (1) the direct losses to persons and property involved in the crimes, riots, and so on; (2) the costs of coping with them (the costs of maintaining prisons, police forces, etc.); and (3) the opportunity costs of the time criminals and

rioters would spend in jails instead of in productive activities.
[5]For further discussion of various kinds of externalities and the extent to which they lead to legitimate divergence between private and social rates of return, the reader is referred to Chapter 20.

Discrepancies between the private and social benefits of human capital investments may also be caused by specific kinds of market imperfections and price distortions. For example, when the direct costs of education, health, or job search are subsidized by the government, the private rate of return to such investments may well exceed the social rate of return.[6] On the other hand, when part of the higher incomes received by individuals who have invested in human capital is taxed away by the government, the private benefits of such investments may understate the social benefits. Since human capital generally provides inferior collateral for loans than a house, a bond, or a machine, it may be harder to borrow money for maintenance and investments in human capital than for physical or financial capital investments. Capital market imperfections of this type may, therefore, raise the private costs of education above what they should be and thereby lower the private rate of return relative to the social rate of return.

Monopoly or monopsony positions on the supply or demand sides of the labor market may also be responsible for discrepancies between the private and social rates of return to investments in human capital. For example, the private rate of return to nurse-training or teacher-training in societies where the government is a monopsonistic buyer of such services is likely to be depressed relative to the social rate of return to such human capital investments.

Where local communities, states, or countries subsidize human capital investments (such as health and education) because of the external benefits derived or in order to compensate for price distortions and market imperfections, migration introduces the possibility that the external benefits will be redistributed from the community providing the subsidies to the communities receiving the migrants. If communities foresee the out-migration of human capital, they will tend to "underinvest" in human capital, and therefore, there will be no external economies.

Finally, if equity in income distribution receives some weight in the social welfare function, and also if education constitutes an effi-

cient means of reducing the inequality of incomes, there might be underinvestment in education in the sense that additional education of people in poor families might increase social welfare even if there were no divergence between the private and the social rates of return.

Application of the Human Capital Model to Education

Rates of Return to Education and Dropout Rates in the United States

We shall demonstrate the use of the general human capital model by utilizing equation 2 to estimate the private rate of return over cost, r, to education for different race-region groups in the United States.

By referring to equation 2 and the subsequent discussion, the reader can easily see that the calculation of r requires: (1) information on incomes of individuals or groups with different levels of education i and age j, Y_{ij}; (2) estimates of the costs of education at each different level i and age j, C_{ij}; and (3) the probabilities of being alive and of being employed at educational level i and age j, p_{ij} and q_{ij} respectively. If the data from which Y_{ij} are taken include members of the labor force that are unemployed, q_{ij} weights become redundant and therefore unnecessary.

Given time series or cross-section data on Y_{ij}, C_{ij}, and p_{ij} for individuals or groups with education of level i (for example, individuals or groups with education of level K' as compared to those with level K), the rate of return for any incremental year of education, $r_{K'-K}$, can be calculated. By doing so for each pair of alternative educational possibilities consecutively (for one year of education compared to no years, two years compared to one year, etc.), one could easily trace the pattern of the rates of return for each additional year from the first year of elementary education to the last year of graduate school. In fact, if data permitted, this type of analysis could be extended to determine: (1) the relative rate of return to various types of educational programs, such as to classical curricula, including Greek and Latin, to modern liberal arts curricula with heavy doses of science, including social science; and even (2) the relative profitability of education in alternative institutions (i.e., the profitability of a BA from Harvard, relative to that of a BA from Princeton, Wis-

---

[6]Blaug (1967) and Bailey and Schotta (1972) have argued that governmental subsidies may account for virtually the entire difference between private and social rates of return in the field of higher education.

consin, or Podunk). However, income data classified by age, sex, and other important characteristics do not often come in sufficient detail for investigations of this sort.[7]

In the following paragraphs, we describe briefly how DePrano and Nugent (1968) obtained empirical estimates of the rate of return over cost from equation 2 for different race-region groups in the United States. Their estimates were based on data for males in 1949 and 1959 classified by age, race (white and nonwhite), region (North and South), and the following levels of educational attainment: 8 years, 9–11 years, 12 years, 13–15 years, and 16 years or more, from the 1950 and 1960 population censuses. For the younger age groups (ages 14–21), which are, of course, the most relevant for educational decisions, the income data are available only in terms of two-year intervals: 14–15, 16–17, and so on. In order to match alternative educational levels and age-income groups consistently, the following assumptions were made: the average male with 9–11 years of education would have 10 years of education and the average male with 13–15 years of education would have 14 years (a complete secondary education plus two years of college). Thus, the educational alternatives available to the individual were defined in terms of two-year increments. The individual could choose: (1) to have 8 years of education and begin earning income immediately thereafter; (2) to have 10 years of education but delay earning income by 2 years; (3) to obtain 12 years of education but delay earning income by 4 years; (4) to obtain 14 years of education but delay earning income by 6 years; or (5) to have 16 years of education but delay earning income by 8 years.

Since the tables from which the income data were taken also include unemployed persons without income, it was not necessary to obtain separate estimates of q_{ij}. Assuming that the p_{ij} coefficients are unaffected by the level of education, calculation of p_{ij} reduces to $p_j = (1 - m_j)$, which were calculated from age, sex, and race-specific mortality rates, m_j, taken from standard tables. The income growth rates, g_{ij}, which reflect the combined effects of learning-by-doing, depreciation of human capital, and secular changes in market conditions specific to each level of education,

i, and age, j, were calculated from the income data for each age, sex, region, and level-of-education cohort in the two censuses.[8] For example, the growth rate of income for a 30-year-old white male in the North of a particular education level, i, was computed by comparing the expected income of such a person in 1949 from the 1950 census with that of a 40-year-old white male in the North in 1959 from the 1960 census (the latter adjusted for changes in the cost of living).

It is in general especially difficult to obtain reliable mean income estimates or growth rates for those who are out of school but still of school age. The census data for these groups seemed so inconsistent as to suggest the presence of substantial reporting errors and other distorting influences, such as military conscription and enlistment. One approach is to use moving averages of adjacent data to estimate these figures (Hanoch 1965). However, if the data used for making such adjustments are inaccurate, so are the weighted averages. To avoid using unreliable data, DePrano and Nugent utilized the more reliable income data for middle-aged persons by extrapolating their incomes and the growth rates of their incomes backward to the younger age groups.[9]

Estimates of the direct costs of education are also fragmentary at best. However, since in the United States, the direct costs of education are commonly financed by earnings of part-time employment or by transfer payments from parents, we have assumed the direct costs of education, C_{ij}, to be zero.[10]

The resulting computations of the rate of return over cost, r, for each region and level of education considered are given in columns 1 and 2 of Table 11.1, for whites and non-

---

[7]See, however, Hunt (1963).

[8]The adjustment, suggested by Miller (1965), is important when the individual takes into consideration not only information about what people with different educational levels earn at a particular point in time but also what happens to their income (presumably the net of learning-by-doing and depreciation) over time. To implement it requires census data for at least two census years. In this case, we have used the 1950 and 1960 Censuses of Population for the United States.

[9]In order to test the sensitivity of the results to the approach used in estimating incomes of males in the younger age groups and also to other adjustments for time-in-place, family size, location, and so on, we present below results utilizing Hanoch's computations as well as those obtained by these extrapolations.

[10]This simplifying assumption probably introduces less error than would be introduced through the use of unreliable estimates of the direct costs of education.

Table 11.1 *Actual Rates of Return, Whites and Nonwhites, at Various Educational Levels, and Rates of Return and Cost Requirements to Equalize White and Nonwhite Dropout Rates*

Region	Levels of Education Compared	Rates of Return Over Cost (r)		Dropout Rates (D)		Required r to Equalize Dropout Rates (5)	Cost per Student (6)	Required Number of Students to Equalize Dropout Rate (7)	Total Cost (millions) (8)
		White (1)	Nonwhite (2)	White (3)	Nonwhite (4)				
North	10/8	0.45	0.26	0.1695	0.2849	0.37	$ 223	528,130	$117.8
North	12/10	0.23	0.38	0.2595	0.4228	0.54	360	336,711	121.2
North	14/12	0.25	0.31	0.5317	0.6131	0.39	447	139,527	62.4
North	16+/14	0.18	0.16	0.4377	0.5813	0.30	1,991	57,077	113.6
South	10/8	0.40	0.16	0.2615	0.5304	0.43	658	439,944	289.5
South	12/10	0.29	0.14	0.2677	0.4856	0.45	631	204,859	129.3
South	14/12	0.23	0.19	0.5044	0.6200	0.30	760	71,317	54.2
South	16+/14	0.25	0.14	0.4658	0.5560	0.23	1,520	29,208	44.4
Total									$932.4

Notes: Levels of education are compared as higher relative to lower.

Columns 5, 7: Rates of return and number of students required in order to lower nonwhite dropout rates in the same level as those for whites.

Column 6: Cost per student for the equalization described in columns 5 and 7.

Source: DePrano, M. E., and J. B. Nugent (1968), "Individual Educational Subsidies as a Remedy for the School Dropout Problem: A Procedure for Estimating Costs." Mimeo.

whites respectively. Note that the r's for whites are generally higher than those for nonwhites, especially in the South, indicating that (with certain exceptions in the North) education is more privately profitable for whites than for nonwhites.[11] The rates of return are generally very high, indeed unrealistically high. This is undoubtedly explained by our intentional neglect of the direct costs of education.

Rates of Return to Education: An International Comparison

How do estimates of r for the United States compare with those obtained for other countries? How do the private rates of return compare with the social rates of return? To provide tentative answers to these questions, a compendium of available estimates of private and social rates of return to secondary and higher education is presented in Table 11.2. The social rates of return to secondary and university education are presented in columns 1 and 2 respectively.[12] The private rate of return to university education is presented in column 3. Finally, estimates of the (private) cross-rates of return to university education are presented in column 4. These rates are taken from Psacharopoulos (1971) and represent the rate of return to the joint decision of receiving university education and then emigrating to a more developed country—in this case the United States. Since these estimates are taken from a large number of different sources, the comparability among countries is undoubtedly quite limited. Moreover, few (if any) of them appear to have received the desired adjustments for differing probabilities of survival, p_j, and income rates of growth, g_{ij}.

Nevertheless, the following patterns apparent in these estimates are probably quite representative:

1. The rates of return are highest in the least developed countries, especially those in which historically education has not received much emphasis.
2. The rates of return are higher for secondary education than for higher education (indicative of diminishing marginal productivity of investment in education).
3. In the more developed countries, in which enrollment rates at all levels of education have been high for some time, the rates of return to education have been reduced to the point at which they are roughly equal to (or even perhaps slightly below) the expected rate of return on financial capital. (Exceptions to the latter generalization are countries, such as New Zealand and Canada, in which all types of labor skills have been in short supply.)
4. The social rate of return is generally slightly below the private rate of return, reflecting the fact that reductions in the costs of education because of governmental subsidies generally more than compensate for the additional income taxes collected from the higher income streams to which the education gives rise.[13]
5. The cross-rates of return to the simultaneous decision to invest in education and then to migrate to a country where the educated members of the labor force receive even greater remuneration are higher than the direct rates of return to education.[14]

The Response of Educational Investments to Differences in the Rate of Return

Of greater importance than knowing the magnitude of the rates of return to education in different countries is knowing something about the degree to which educational investments respond to differences in the rate of return. The fact that the rates of return to education tend to fall rapidly with the level of development and the per capita stock of education implies that decisions on investment in education are quite responsive to variations in

[11]This finding is supported by other studies as well. See, for example, Fogel (1966), Hanoch (1965), Hirsch and Segelhorst (1965), Miller (1965), Weiss (1970), Zeman (1955). However, T. Johnson (1970) and to a certain extent Becker (1964) have presented conflicting findings.

[12]The social and private rates of return differ only insofar as: (1) income taxes are included in the income streams for calculating the social rate of return but are excluded from those used in calculating the private rates of return; and (2) the direct costs of education are limited to the nongovernment share of these costs in the case of the private rate of return but include all costs in the case of the social rate of return.

[13]This generalization might not necessarily hold if the various kinds of external economies from educational investments that were discussed above could be incorporated into the social rate of return calculations.

[14]Psacharopoulos (1971) has shown that variations in these cross-rates of return among countries explain more than 68 percent of the variation in the relative rates of brain-drain to the United States from the countries included in Table 11.2.

Table 11.2 *Estimates of Private and Social Rates of Return to Secondary and Higher Education in Different Countries in the 1960s*

Country	Reference Year	Social Rate of Return — Secondary Level (1)	Social Rate of Return — University Level (2)	Private Rate of Return — University Level (3)	Cross-Rate of Return (Private) — University Level (4)	Per Capita GDP in U.S. Dollars in 1965 (5)	Enrollment Index for 1969 1960 = 100 — Secondary Level (6)	Enrollment Index for 1969 1960 = 100 — University Level (7)	Enrollment Ratio Secondary Level 1960 (8)	Enrollment Ratio Secondary Level 1969 (9)	Enrollment Ratio University Level 1960 (10)	Enrollment Ratio University Level 1969 (11)
Belgium	1967		9	(12)	18	1585	110	113	76	84	9.1	10.3
Brazil	1962	17	14	38	(50)	207	227	275	11	25	1.6	4.4
Canada	1961	14	15	20	18	2161	108	188	49	53	13.5	25.5
Chile	1959	12	9	(12)	48	486	136	225	25	34	4.0	9.0
Colombia	1965	24	8	(11)	44	275	175	277	12	21	1.8	5.0
Denmark	1964		8	10	(16)	2078	134	182	56	75	9.7	17.7
Germany	1964		5	(8)	14	1667	124	207	55	68	5.8	12.0
Ghana	1967	11	16	(19)	50+	256	250	350	2	5	0.2	0.7
Greece	1964	3	8	(11)	(44)	591	154	272	39	60	4.0	10.9
India	1960	13	13	14	50+	95	200	212	10	20	1.7	3.6
Israel	1958	7	7	(10)	34	1243	117	194	48	56	10.2	19.8
Japan	1961	7	6	10	(38)	838	111	183	79	88	8.6	15.8
Kenya	1968	20	9	27	50+	99	300	1075	3	9	0.1	0.7
Malaysia	1967	12	11	(14)	(49)	260	219	411	16	35	0.5	1.9
Mexico	1963	17	23	29	45	441	244	177	9	22	2.6	4.6
Netherlands	1965	6	6	10	(25)	1400	106	143	67	71	13.2	18.9
New Zealand	1966	20	13	15	(17)	1878	113	177	60	68	14.2	25.1
Nigeria	1967		17	(20)	50+	74	133	1000	3	4	0.1	0.6
Norway	1966	7	5	5	18	1717	135	350	52	70	4.4	15.4
Philippines	1966	21	11	12	50+	240	173	174	26	45	11.6	20.2
Puerto Rico	1960	22	16	23	(40)	661	123	167	79	95	15.0	25.1
South Korea	1967	9	5	(8)	(50+)	107	141	153	27	38	4.7	7.2
Sweden	1967	10	9	10	(15)	2406	130	228	77	100	8.0	18.2
Uganda	1965	50	12	(15)	(50+)	83	280	147	5	144	0.2	0.2
United Kingdom	1966	5	8	12	36	1590	104	158	68	71	6.2	9.8
United States	1959	14	8	(11)	(11)	3233	117	149	86	101	32.2	48.1
Venezuela	1957	17	23	(26)	(35)	904	165	220	23	38	4.0	8.8

Sources:
Columns 1 and 2: Carnoy, M. (1972). "The Political Economy of Education," in T. J. LaBelle (ed.), *Education and Development: Latin America and the Caribbean*. Los Angeles: University of California, Latin American Studies Series, Vol. 18. Table I, p. 188.
Columns 3 and 4: Psacharopoulos, G. (1971). "On Some Positive Aspects of the Economics of the Brain Drain." *Minerva*, 9 (April), pp. 231–242, Table 1, columns 3 and 5. Figures in parentheses in column 3 are derived by adding 3 percent to the social rate of return of column 2. Figures in parentheses in column 4 are estimated from per capita income level relative to that of the United States, which varies inversely with the cross-rate of return.
Column 5: U.N. (1969), *Yearbook of National Account Statistics, 1969*. New York: U.N., Vol. 2, Table 1B.
Columns 6 and 7: Computed from figures for enrollment ratios presented in columns 8–9 and 10–11 respectively. Column 6 = column 9 ÷ column 8; column 7 = column 11 ÷ column 10.
Columns 8 to 11: UNESCO (1971), *Statistical Yearbook, 1971*. Geneva, Tables 2.7, 2.25. These ratios represent percentages of corresponding school age populations enrolled at the secondary and university educational levels.

the rates of return. High rates of return are typical only of countries in which the number of educated people is small relative to the total population. This is reflected in the fact that countries with high rates of return in columns 1–3 of Table 11.2 are typically those with very low enrollment ratios in the base year (1960), as shown in columns 8 and 10. Yet these same countries tend to increase their enrollment rates very rapidly, as shown by the enrollment indexes in columns 6 and 7 of the same table. According to the historical findings of Carnoy and Marenbach (1975), the fall in the rate of return is felt first in primary education, then in secondary education, and finally in higher education, until eventually investments in education generally claim no more than a normal rate of return (such as the marginal rate of return on alternative investment opportunities, say 6 to 10 percent per annum).

Despite the limited comparability afforded by these estimates of rates of return, we utilize them to explain the variations in the rate of change of enrollment ratios between 1960 and 1969 at the secondary and university levels for the same sample of countries. The latter rates of change are given in columns 6 and 7 respectively, of Table 11.2. Naturally, since the countries of the sample may vary in many respects other than the rate of return to education (the rates of return to alternative investments, the degree of capital market imperfections, and the nonpecuniary benefits of education) one would hardly expect the relationship to be very close. Indeed, it is not. Yet by regressing the relative change in enrollment ratios 1960–1969 of educational level i, ΔER_i, on the rate of return to education of level i, r_i, and on the initial enrollment ratio, ER_{i1960}[15] (and in the case of university level education also on the cross-rate of return, r_c), the following results are obtained (with t-ratios indicated in parentheses):

Secondary Education

$$\Delta ER_s = 117.82 + 3.31\, r_s \qquad r^2 = 0.25$$
$$ (2.90)$$

$$\Delta ER_s = 203.78 + 1.52\, r_s - 1.57\, ER_{s1960}$$
$$ (2.29) \quad (-6.129)$$

$$\overline{R}^2 = 0.73$$

[15]This variable is included to reflect the fact that countries with higher initial enrollment ratios will find it more difficult to increase these ratios than countries with smaller ratios.

University Education

$$\Delta ER_u = 117.77 + 6.28\, r_u + 4.34\, r_c$$
$$ (1.05) \quad (1.50)$$

$$\overline{R}^2 = 0.12$$

$$\Delta ER_u = 185.25 + 6.11\, r_u + 1.69\, r_c$$
$$ (1.02) \quad (0.47)$$

$$- 9.66\, ER_{u1960} \qquad \overline{R}^2 = 0.18.$$
$$(-1.25)$$

These results indicate a fair amount of overall responsiveness of educational decisions to variations in the rate of return among countries, especially in secondary education. Although educational policy makers may be interested in knowing what the aggregate rate of return to education is, and how the average person responds to it, they may also be interested in variations in the rate of return to education among different social groups, particularly insofar as these differences tend to perpetuate intergroup differences in educational attainment and therefore also intergroup differences in incomes.

By referring to the estimates of the rates of return in the United States, presented in columns 1 and 2 of Table 11.1, we can see that there may indeed be substantive differences in the private rates of return to education among different social groups. Returning to this example with respect to the United States, let us consider the following: (1) that the educational attainment of nonwhites tends to lag well behind that of whites in all regions; (2) that (as shown in columns 1 and 2 of Table 11.1) the private rates of return are generally higher for whites than for nonwhites; (3) that if all the external benefits of education were included, the social rates of return to education might well exceed the private rates of return; and (4) that a decrease in the disparity of incomes between whites and nonwhites might be considered socially desirable. Considering these four points, and assuming that equalization of the degree of educational attainment among whites and nonwhites would be a relatively efficient method of achieving the desired income redistributions,[16] it is not surprising that policy

[16]Whether or not this is the case has been disputed by a number of authors. On the negative side are Chiswick (1968), Tullock and Staaf (1973), Thurow and Lucas (1972). Some reasons for their doubts will be discussed in Chapter 13. On the positive side are Al-Samarrie and Miller (1967) and Aigner and Heins (1967).

makers in the United States have from time to time considered (and in some cases even implemented) programs that would subsidize higher levels of education for nonwhites. Many proposals of this sort have foundered, not only on the understandable difficulty of quantifying the benefits but also on the failure to quantify the costs.

In the following paragraph, we follow De-Prano and Nugent (1968) in demonstrating how estimates of the responsiveness to variations in the rate of return might be used to estimate the costs of one type of governmental program to achieve equality in educational levels between whites and nonwhites in the United States. The program considered is a GI Bill-type system of direct educational subsidies for nonwhites.

We measure the response of educational investments to variations in the rate of return in terms of the dropout rate. We define the dropout rate, D, for any race-region group and level of education for United States males in the 1950s in percentage terms as $1 - (a/b)$, where a represents the number of males of age 25–34 in 1960 (or 15–24 in 1950) who were reported in the 1960 census of population to have attained education of level "$i + 1$ or above," and b represents the corresponding number who were reported to have attained a level of education of level "i or above." The resulting estimates of the dropout rates, D, of whites for each level of education and region are given in column 3 of Table 11.1. The corresponding estimates for nonwhites are given in column 4 of the same table.[17] In each case, it can be seen that the dropout rate for nonwhites is higher than for whites. Also, the dropout rates tend to be higher at higher levels of education. Naturally, these findings are roughly consistent with our earlier findings of lower rates of return to education for nonwhites than for whites and also of lower rates of return to higher levels of education than for lower ones.

The marginal response of the dropout rate to variation in the rate of return is estimated by regressing the different values for D in columns 3 and 4 of Table 11.1 on the corresponding values of r in columns 1 and 2.

[17]By including some who may have dropped out of school prior to 1950, these estimates of dropout rates may be biased upward, but there is little reason to suspect any particular pattern to the bias varying in direction and intensity from group to group.

The following result was obtained (with t-ratios in parentheses)

$$D = 0.698 - 1.014\,r \qquad r^2 = 0.37$$
$$(-3.03)$$

Although these results might be modified by including other variables, the fact that the rate of return by itself explains more than 37 percent of the intergroup variance in dropout rates and that the regression coefficient is highly significant provides additional support for the hypothesis that investment in education is responsive to variations in the private rate of return.

By visual examination, it was found that the residuals in the dropout regression were not randomly distributed. Specifically, the residuals tended to be positive for nonwhites and negative for whites. At the same time, visual examination made it clear that, had we treated the two racial groups separately, the slope of the regression line would not have been significantly different from that obtained from the overall sample.[18] Therefore, the regression coefficient, −1.014, indicates the extent to which a unit increase in the rate of return would lower the dropout rate for any race-region group and educational level. One can easily compute the amount by which the rate of return over cost, r, would have to rise in order to lower the dropout rate of nonwhites to that of whites for each region and level of education. Since the differences in dropout rates are different in each such case, the required increases in r also differ. These values are shown in column 5 of Table 11.1. Assuming a discount rate of 10 percent per annum, the required increases in r are converted into increases in present values per student-year of nonwhite income streams that would be required for nonwhites to achieve

[18]In other words, the fact that nonwhite dropout rates are "off" the regression line in one direction and dropout rates for whites are off in the other direction is due to different positions of the response function not to different degrees of sensitivity to variations in the rate of return. In such a situation, one would normally want to try to include some socioeconomic variables associated with race which might help identify more precisely the nature of the racial difference or, failing that, to repeat the regression with a dummy variable for race. However, because of: (1) data limitations; (2) the fact that the use we shall make of the regression estimates is limited to the regression coefficient; and above all (3) our desire to keep the analysis and our exposition as simple as possible, for present purposes we shall utilize the above results without further amendment.

parity with whites in terms of dropout rates. These increases in present values are given in column 6 of Table 11.1; they represent our best estimate of the average annual payment per student that would induce the number of nonwhites given in column 7 to continue their education for an additional year. Finally, by multiplying the annual cost per student in column 6 by the required number of students given in column 7, we arrive in column 8 at our estimate of the total subsidies required: $932.4 million.[19]

One billion dollars per year would thus constitute a rough estimate of the cost of raising the educational attainment levels of nonwhites to those of whites. If the social benefits of the additional education induced by such a program plus the social value of the resulting improvements in distributional equity were expected to exceed this amount by and substantial margin, one might be reasonably confident in recommending such a program.[20]

The Human Capital Model: Criticisms and Reservations

A number of shortcomings arise in connection with the specification of the classical model of investment in the human agent.

Rate-of-return calculations are inevitably based on past income data. Consequently, utilization of the model for predictive or prescriptive purposes will be valid only to the extent that past rates of return reflect future rates of return, which may well not be the case. Indeed, present or past rates of return are likely to be particularly misleading if a rational subsidy policy is followed, with subsidies extended to levels and types of education with the highest rates of return, and if the impact of these changes on the stocks of human capital is substantial. In any case, a single rate-of-return calculation provides only one observation on the marginal efficiency of investment curve, whose whole contour would have to be traced out to arrive at valid conclusions for present and future policy.

A second defect in the model, or at least in its empirical application, stems from the exclusion of other factors that affect the decisions to invest in human capital. For example, in the case of education, the model fails to consider several factors that may affect the level of education and/or income: parents' income and education, ability and intelligence, motivation, and various educational factors (class size, the quality and quantity of materials, the grading system, the quality and experience of the teacher, the degree of student homogeneity with respect to social class, ability, and age, or the willingness to work long hours).[21] Even if one wanted to include them, valid and precise measures of these variables are exceedingly hard to obtain. The latter difficulty is particularly serious in the case of ability, where the shortcomings of any one measure, such as class standing, IQ level, or selective service induction mental test score, are well known. Since most of these variables tend to be positively correlated with both income and educational levels, and thus also with the rate of return to education, their exclusion leads to an upward bias in the estimates of the rate of return. It also compromises the usefulness of the rate of return in explaining human capital investment decisions.

---

[19]To achieve such reductions in dropout rates at every educational level simultaneously, might well require somewhat greater expenditures at the higher educational levels, and the resulting increase in the human capital stock would undoubtedly lower the rate of return to education and raise the cost of education, both of which would have to be compensated for if reductions in the educational attainment of whites were to be avoided. Nevertheless, the crudeness of the data and the limitations in number of observations notwithstanding, it is probably unlikely that these estimates understate the total cost of such a program to any large degree.

[20]However, even if all of these assumptions were fulfilled and if our calculations were correct, differences in profitability seem to explain less than 40 percent of the variation in dropout rate at various educational levels among various race-region groups. Therefore, it is still quite possible that additional research would uncover some other social or educational characteristic which, when manipulated, would achieve the same impact on dropout rates at a lesser cost than the GI Bill-type of educational subsidy program considered here.

[21]For evidence regarding the influence of parental income or education, see Masters (1969), Blau and Duncan (1967), Becker (1964), and Bowles (1972). The influence of the bias toward hard work in exaggerating the returns to education is stressed by Lindsay (1971). Balogh (1967) and Carnoy (1972) feel that political and social elites rig the rates of return to education in such a way as to mislead the masses into thinking that education really matters. Differences in the quality of education or different educational vintages are stressed by Sen (1966a). Hansen, Weisbrod, and Scanlon (1970) and Weisbrod and Karpoff (1968), on the one side; Ashenfelter and Mooney (1968), on the other, have disputed the importance of the bias in the returns to education introduced by the omission of intelligence and ability.

Although the concept of the cross-rate of return to joint or complementary investment decisions may help somewhat, even so modified the human capital model scarcely begins to consider the varying degrees to which different kinds or levels of human capital investment complement or substitute for one another. Failure to include these interdependencies can lead to either positive or negative biases, the magnitude or even the net direction of which may be difficult to determine a priori.

By these criticisms, we do not mean to imply that the human capital model is invalid or useless. Quite the contrary, even a superficial glance at the literature on the subject should be sufficient to convince the reader that the model is extremely fruitful. The various biases that may intervene in its application and which we described can often be handled simply by introducing additional variables. Should this not be enough, a further and more substantial modification is to add equations so as to arrive at a complete model, which traces the determination of every endogenous variable included back to a set of exogenous variables, allowing one to derive the (reduced form) solution to human capital decisions. Such an approach has been attempted on a modest scale in studies by Tolley and Olson (1971) and Bowles (1972), the latter spanning the discipline of sociology as well as economics. If the overall constraint on investments in human capital seems to be one of competing demands for time more than of wealth, the human capital model could perhaps be reformulated in terms of the allocation of time along the lines suggested by Becker (1965) and DeVany (1970). Not surprisingly, the seriousness of the limitations of the human capital model, and therefore of the importance of modifying it, depends to a large extent on the use to which the model is put. This underlines once again the importance of empirical investigations.

Summary and Conclusions

Our treatment of human capital is basically an extension of Chapter 10, on savings and capital formation. The framework that has been presented for the measurement of the rate of return to investment in the human agent was derived from Chapter 10—and it will recur in Chapter 20 in the discussion of neoclassical investment criteria. Similarly, a number of the empirical implications of the theory of investment in the human agent were already familiar as implications of the theories of savings presented earlier.

We have applied the model in estimating the rates of return to different years of educational investment for whites and nonwhites separately in the United States, North and South. Not unexpectedly, the rates of return to education were higher for whites, especially in the South—with a few exceptions in the North, where they were lower. We have also presented a compendium of rates of return to secondary and university education, private and social, for different countries, revealing that the rate of return to education at these levels is generally higher in LDCs than in DCs and higher for secondary than for university education.

The international cross-section of the rates of return to education was used as an explanatory variable of the observed enrollment ratios, 1960–1969, for the same countries. Similarly, the dropout rates observed for whites and nonwhites were regressed on the respective rates of return for the two groups in the United States. Both applications suggest that the relative magnitudes of the estimated rates of return to education can be used to predict the direction of educational investment, even though the absolute values may be grossly biased. And this may well be the case.

At the core of the literature on investment in the human agent is a basic assumption, in accord with neoclassical theory, that wage rates and therefore labor incomes are determined endogenously by the marginal productivity of the worker. The latter is in turn determined by exogenous characteristics, such as education, experience, or personality traits, which in shorthand notation are called investment in the human agent. As a result, wage differentials reflect differential endowments in terms of the human agent—which, not unlike technological change, may well be another name for our ignorance. Suppose, however, as we will suggest in Chapter 13, that wage rates are instead exogenous variables. Each job has a wage rate associated with it, and in imperfect "job competition" markets, individuals are picked out of a queue for a job (on the basis of a set of background characteristics, including education) and are assigned the wage rate of that job. If this model is applicable, the returns to investment in the human agent as conventionally measured are, of course, biased upward. They impute to education and to other personal characteristics what in effect is the return to monopoly—whether it arises from education working as a "filter," from family connections, or from racial origin.

Furthermore, the combination of market imperfections (which seem especially important as far as human capital is concerned), and the fact that rates of return to education may vary among individuals or groups inversely with their levels of income or wealth, might well provide yet another explanation for the phenomena of dualism and increasing inequality in the personal distribution of income, which are the subject of Chapter 14.

In any case, and for whatever reason, it seems possible that substantial discrepancies between the private and social rates of return to education may occur. If they do, nonoptimal investments in human capital will occur. If the wrong rates of return to human capital apply, wage rates, too, will presumably be incorrect, and consequently, several kinds of disequilibria may exist. Our discussion of human capital has added a number of items to our growing list of paradoxes, anomalies, and problems arising from the treatment of development as an equilibrium process.

Since investments in human capital, especially those in education and health, require long gestation periods before they begin to bear fruit, policies in respect to human capital investments must be planned carefully on the basis of appropriate criteria. The issue of educational planning will arise again in discussing national planning models in Chapter 21.

Chapter 12

Employment, Unemployment, and Labor Surplus

Employment is at once the most exhaustively covered and the least successfully studied subject in the economics of development. Long-held views on the role of labor in economic development have recently changed drastically. The main preoccupation of the literature of the 1950s, the classical theory of labor surplus, was with meeting the need for additional manpower in the nonagricultural sector of a developing economy. In this task, agriculture was thought to play the role of custodian of a national fund. The sector was viewed as having for some time employed the resources available to it at the wrong factor intensities. More specifically, it employed labor to the point that its marginal product was zero. With a minimum rearrangement of resources, therefore, agricultural labor could be transferred to the modern sector without any significant loss in agricultural output. The mobilization of surplus labor

resources by the nonagricultural sector would set in motion an almost painless "up-by-the-bootstraps" process of development.

The neoclassical literature on labor surplus that developed in the 1960s abandoned the assumptions of zero marginal product and of unlimited supplies of labor. It focused instead on the divergence in wage rates, and marginal products, between agriculture and nonagriculture, which were viewed as evidence of a dualistic disequilibrium. Yet it again relied on transfers of labor out of agriculture for initiating development and again emphasized the need to restore global optimality of resource utilization in the two sectors, thus eliminating dualism.

More recently, however, economists have been gradually coming to the painful conclusion that most of the discussion of the last two decades has been irrelevant, because it addressed the wrong problem. The real issue is not how to fill the need for additional workers in the modern sector but rather how and where productive opportunities for employing the surplus and unemployed labor can be found.

There are two factors responsible for this dramatic change. First, there is the continuing population explosion, which has brought about a spectacular increase in the labor force. Moreover, it is estimated that the number of persons wanting work in LDCs as a whole between 1970 and 1980 will increase by another 25 percent, as opposed to only 10 percent in the DCs. Second, there is the dismal failure of the industrial sector to absorb additional workers. In contrast to the promises of the advocates of industrial fundamentalism, the industrial sector has absorbed remarkably little labor in most LDCs despite, in many cases, rapid growth of industrial output. The explanation for this failure may lie partly in the policy biases that tend to lower the price of capital relative to labor: policies that refer to financial dualism (Chapter 14), to the undervaluation of foreign exchange (Chapter 17), and to the imposition of interest-rate ceilings and other price distortions (Chapter 7). The explanation may also lie partly in the choice of the wrong technology (Chapter 9) or the wrong industries, that is, those with capital-intensive technologies, fostered by import substitution fundamentalism. To get some idea of the magnitude of the problem, assume that, on the average, the nonagricultural sector employs 20 percent of the labor force in LDCs. To absorb the expected overall increase in the labor force of 3 percent per annum, it would need to create additional employment opportunities at the rate of 15 percent per annum. This is clearly impossible in any foreseeable circumstance (Turnham 1971, pp. 9–10).[1]

In view of the expected magnitude of the problem in the near future, the shift in emphasis from filling the modern sector's demand for labor to providing jobs for the masses of the unemployed has come none too soon. Unfortunately, measured unemployment may be no more than the tip of the iceberg. Some important categories of workers who stand at the twilight of the labor market, the "idle," the "poor," and the "willing," are likely to enter the labor market in increasing numbers, further swelling the rolls of the involuntarily unemployed. We will treat these groups under the headings of underemployment and hidden unemployment. This treatment, however, raises some conceptual problems of measurement, which can be overcome only by combining objective factors, namely, the job opportunities as reflected in the production function, with subjective considerations, such as the perceived need for work and the reservation price of labor. Fortunately, one strain of the surplus labor literature, the model which analyzes surplus labor within the context of utility maximization, combines these elements advantageously, thus providing a useful means of understanding the nature of the problem.

The measurement of the several variants of unemployment deserves special attention. The well-known survey techniques may be capable of accurately measuring unemployment in the modern, nonagricultural sector. Agricultural unemployment and underemployment require different approaches to measurement. We conclude this chapter by presenting and applying two such approaches to the measurement of surplus labor in agriculture —the labor utilization and labor productivity approaches.

The Magnitude of the Problem and Some Conceptual Considerations

Growth in the Labor Force

The rate of population growth and the labor-force participation rate of different population cohorts jointly determine the rate of growth in the labor force. Making only minimal allowance for changes in the labor-force participation rate over time, a rough idea of changes in the size of the labor force can be gathered from readily available population statistics. Some comprehensive estimates for LDCs, taken from a careful study by Turnham (1971), are presented in Table 12.1.

The table dramatically illustrates the problem confronting the LDCs. On the average, their labor force grows at more than twice the rate of the DCs, implying a total increase of about 25 percent for the decade 1970–1980. Starting from 1950, the rate of growth

---

[1]Assuming an annual increase in labor productivity of 3 percent, the nonagricultural sector would need to increase output by the same amount if only to maintain the current level of employment.

Table 12.1 *Rates of Growth of the Labor Force by Region, 1950–1980 (Percent)*

	1950–1965		1965–1980		1970–1980	
	Total	Annual	Total	Annual	Total	Annual
DCs	17.6	1.1	15.8	1.0	10.0	1.0
LDCs	28.1	1.7	39.0	2.2	25.2	2.3
Regions[a]						
Other East Asia	30.7	1.8	56.5	3.0	35.3	3.1
Middle South Asia[b]	23.2	1.4	33.1	1.9	21.6	2.0
Southeast Asia[c]	32.3	1.9	43.0	2.4	28.0	2.5
Southwest Asia[d]	31.8	1.9	50.4	2.8	31.3	2.8
West Africa	38.9	2.2	40.2	2.3	25.8	2.3
East Africa	21.1	1.3	30.8	1.8	19.8	1.8
Central Africa	16.0	1.0	19.4	1.2	12.9	1.2
North Africa	17.5	1.1	45.7	2.5	29.0	2.6
Tropical South America	48.3	2.7	55.6	3.0	34.7	3.0
Central America	52.0	2.8	62.7	3.3	39.1	3.4
Temperate South America	25.7	1.5	25.0	1.5	16.0	1.5
Caribbean	31.1	1.8	40.6	2.3	25.8	2.3

Notes:
[a]Excludes Sino-Soviet countries.
[b]Includes Ceylon, India, Iran, and Pakistan.
[c]Includes Burma, Cambodia, Indonesia, Malaysia, the Philippines, and Thailand.
[d]Middle East countries.
Source: Turnham, D. (1971), *The Employment Problem in Less-Developed Countires: A Review of Evidence.* Paris: OECD, Development Center, p. 31.

in the labor force of most LDCs has been consistently increasing and may be expected to increase further in the near future. In some areas, such as parts of East Asia (excluding China), Central America, and tropical South America, the annual rates of growth of the labor force are 3 percent or higher, amounting to between 30 and 40 percent for the decade of the 1970s.

To comprehend the impact such rates of growth in those seeking employment may have for LDCs, we must carefully examine some conceptual and definitional issues.

Conceptual Problems in Measurement
Labor Force, Participation Rates, and Involuntary Unemployment
The labor force is, by definition, the sum of the employed and the unemployed. Because both components of the labor force involve ambiguities, labor force, employment, and unemployment statistics can often be misleading.

Most statistical studies have defined a person as employed if he works a specified minimum number of hours during the week in which the employment census is taken. The amount of work sufficient to characterize one as employed therefore becomes a source of ambiguity in labor statistics. Persons are defined as unemployed (in the involuntary sense) if they do not have a job but are actively seeking one. The determination of whether or not an individual is actively seeking a job necessarily involves ambiguity and subjective considerations.

The labor-force participation rate is the ratio of persons at work, or seeking work, in a given population group. Given the size and age structure of a population, therefore, the participation rate determines the size of the labor force. Participation rates may vary substantially from country to country and from sector to sector, generally ranging between 0.25 and 0.50. Table 12.2 presents estimates of average participation rates for DCs and LDCs, separately for males and females. The rates for males are consistently larger in all age groups for LDCs than for DCs, but the same is not true for females. This discrepancy merits further comment, to demonstrate the ambiguity of labor statistics.

Variations in the labor-force participation rate are explained by a variety of factors, subjective as well as objective, noneconomic

Table 12.2 *Age- and Sex-Specific Participation Rates, Estimates for 1965 (Percent)*

Age Group	Males		Females	
	LDCs	DCs	LDCs	DCs
0–14	6.5	1.3	4.0	0.8
15–24	78.1	70.2	36.9	47.8
25–54	96.3	96.1	40.1	40.3
55–64	86.8	82.6	29.2	30.1
65+	57.5	30.0	14.5	9.2
Total (weighted)	53.2	58.3	22.9	26.8

Note: LDCs exclude Sino-Soviet countries, OECD countries, and Southern Africa, Australia, and New Zealand. DCs exclude Sino-Soviet countries.
Source: Turnham, D. (1971), *The Employment Problem in Less–Developed Countries: A Review of Evidence.* Paris: OECD, Development Center, p. 24.

as well as economic. One important objective factor is the age structure of the population. The population of LDCs is heavily skewed toward young age groups (with 42 percent of the population less than 15 years old as compared to 25 percent in Europe and 31 percent in North America). This decreases the current participation rates for LDCs relative both to what they would otherwise have been and to what they will be when the young age group reaches maturity. This explains why the labor-force participation rate for both males and females is lower in LDCs than in DCs, even though within age groups the converse tends to be true. Childbearing tends to keep women at home for a part of their adult lives. Since fertility rates are higher in LDCs than in DCs, female labor-force participation rates tend to be lower in the former than in the latter. In the long run, however, fertility rates will decline, which will raise female labor-force participation rates in LDCs. Noneconomic factors, such as social customs and conventions, also tend to account for lower labor-force participation rates among females in LDCs. This factor, too, will decline over time, raising female labor-force participation in LDCs. At lower levels of income—especially in the agricultural sector—the unit of production is the family, and employment within the household is more common for females. As the level of income rises and more employment opportunities arise in structured labor markets, some groups of women, such as the young and educated, will participate in the labor force to a greater extent. Moreover, as services that were formerly provided within the household, mostly by females, are sub-

stituted for by market activities, the utility of cash income increases, again raising labor-force participation rates of females in LDCs. Most of these factors suggest that LDC labor-force participation rates within age groups are likely to increase in the future, especially among females.

Of course, what will happen to employment and unemployment in the future will depend on how persons are divided between the categories of the employed and the unemployed. Because labor markets are less structured and more informal in LDCs than in DCs, the distinction between the employed and the unemployed is especially difficult to make. Straddling the fence that divides the clearly employed from the clearly unemployed are three important groups: (1) the "willing," people who are not actively seeking employment but would be willing to work under the right circumstances; (2) the "idle," people who worked, for example, less than 36 hours in a week; and (3) the "poor," people who are fully employed in a job that does not provide minimum subsistence (Krishna 1973). We will define hidden unemployment in terms of the "willing." Underemployment will include the "idle" and the "poor."

Hidden Unemployment
Hidden unemployment is composed of "discouraged workers" or persons outside the labor force, as commonly measured, who would be willing to enter it if they believed market opportunities were favorable.

Discouraged workers do not actively seek employment, because they attach a reservation price to their services above that which is feasible under the existing job conditions. The important element is a gap between their expected wage and the wage rate that prevails in the market. How long it takes discouraged workers to enter the labor force depends on the speed of adjustment of their expectations and on the objective improvement of available employment opportunities. Should labor-market conditions improve, discouraged workers may be able to move directly into jobs, without registering a corresponding decrease in measured unemployment. Similarly, the people in hidden unemployment are likely to seek to improve their opportunities for obtaining a job by migrating to another labor market. Indeed, in Chapter 13, we shall note some evidence suggesting that migrants come mostly from this fringe category rather than from the involuntarily unemployed. If employment opportunities do not improve, discouraged workers eventually revise their expectations and therefore must enter the labor force in the pool of the unemployed.

How important this group is and how significant are the flows between the categories of hidden unemployment, on the one hand, and of employment and unemployment, on the other, are not generally known.[2]

One would expect hidden unemployment to exist mostly among dependents who have other means of support. It is more prevalent in groups that face additional barriers to employment, such as mothers with young children to care for who otherwise would have accepted a suitable part-time job. Most important, discouraged workers are to be found among the young and those who are overeducated for the jobs an economy makes available. Turnham (1971, p. 42) reports the results of a sample survey for urban areas in India showing that 55 percent of the males in the age group 16–17 and 26 percent of those in the group aged 18–21 declared themselves as "students"—despite the fact that one hour's work in the reference week would have been sufficient to include them as employed members of the labor force. Similarly, the survey showed that 60 percent of females in the age group 16–17 and 75 percent of those 18–21 classified themselves as "home-

workers." By comparison, a study in Germany found that only 17 percent of males and females in the age group 16–17 and only 8 percent of those in the age group 18–21 were classified as (full-time) students. It is reasonable to expect that at least part of the discrepancy between the two surveys reflects the existence of discouraged workers in India. (If only 10 percent of the age group 18–21 in India would have accepted a suitable job if it had been available, the actual rate of unemployment in that group would have been 20 percent, as compared to the registered rate of 10 percent!)

Three conclusions emerge from this conceptual examination of hidden unemployment. First, to the extent that the available labor force statistics do not include hidden unemployment, the magnitude and importance of the unemployment problem may have been substantially underestimated. Second, an improvement in the objective labor market conditions will not be reflected in a decrease in unemployment as long as the new jobs go to people who were previously in the hidden unemployment group. Only the size of the labor force will increase. Third, since the hidden unemployed may consist of individuals with superior education and other background characteristics, it seems likely that it may be these discouraged workers and not the openly unemployed who migrate. If so, the role of migration as an equilibrating force that would tend to drain the pool of the unemployed and equalize wage rates may have been greatly exaggerated. We will return to this issue in Chapter 13.

Underemployment

This distinction between part-time and full-time employment is especially important in traditional and seasonal occupations. The large agricultural sector in LDCs fits both characteristics. The typical situation among family workers is work sharing and leisure rationing rather than open unemployment. The self-employed worker is unlikely to look for another job when he has little to do in his own firm. Adjustments for the peaks and troughs of seasonal activities are likely to occur through lengthening or shortening the hours of work.

The pronounced seasonality of agriculture imposes a pattern of labor utilization that alternates between substantial underemploy-

---

[2]Butler and Demopoulos (1974) present some evidence suggesting that the flows to and from hidden unemployment are more significant than those between unemployment and employment.

ment during trough periods and shortage of labor at peak times, such as at planting or harvest. This rules out permanent withdrawal of agricultural workers without loss in output (Pepelasis and Yotopoulos 1962; Yotopoulos 1964). Should permanent employment opportunities exist in other sectors, the social cost of maintaining underemployed labor in agriculture to handle peak demands is high. The alternative of mechanizing the peak-season activities is equally wasteful. The choice lies between keeping agricultural labor underemployed for long off-peak seasons or leaving specialized capital idle to handle the peak season work requirements. A better solution might be to decrease the work-force specialization so that workers from other occupations can help ease seasonal shortages of agricultural labor. This is the purpose of harvest brigades in Cuba, the innovation of the "barefoot doctor" in China, and the busing of urban workers to the farms in Tanzania. Perhaps, by decreasing labor specialization and compartmentalization, the peak labor demands in other sectors can be met at minimal social cost. The benefits of labor specialization in production, long taken for granted, may deserve more careful study in LDCs.

Invisible underemployment is another type of part-time employment. People are technically at work but virtually idle: the shopkeeper, the street-corner vendor, or the cab driver has to be on the job whether or not there is work to be done. So does the farmer during periods of inclement weather. "Invisible employment," the converse phenomenon, is also widespread in LDCs. The ubiquitous coffee shop is not necessarily the temple of leisure it might seem to be but rather is the office of the lawyer, the place where the middleman transacts his business, or the place where the elders adjudicate disputes. The existence of invisible underemployment and invisible employment goes a long way to reconcile casual observations of widespread idleness in LDCs with the findings of careful surveys that hours worked, even in rural areas, are long.[3]

The "additional worker," the individual who takes up paid work to supplement family income, presents another aspect of underemployment. The hypothesis, largely untested, suggests that as job prospects and family income improve, the additional worker will withdraw from the labor force and participation rates will decline.

The Evidence on Unemployment

Hard evidence on the size of unemployment in LDCs is both difficult to find and, when available, subject to understatement because of the considerations just discussed. Table 12.3 presents evidence for some LDCs compiled by Turnham (1971) and based on sample survey statistics. The reference points of the surveys are those recommended by the International Labor Office (1959): unemployment was defined in terms of those without full-time employment who actively sought work in the week previous to the survey. Despite this rather restrictive definition, it can be seen that unemployment rates in LDCs are high. Even LDCs with the lowest unemployment rates, such as Korea, the Philippines, and Chile, have rates higher than any DC has experienced in recent years (with the exception of Canada and Ireland). Considering that the labor-force participation rates of LDCs may increase and that population is still growing rapidly, the labor-force growth projections of Table 12.1 are probably conservative. Given past experience with employment generation, it seems likely that unemployment rates will grow rapidly, at least in many LDCs. Even if, by Herculean efforts in population control and employment generation, unemployment rates should be held constant, the projected growth rates of the labor force would imply rapid growth in the absolute number of unemployed persons.

Table 12.4 presents some estimates of unemployment rates for LDCs that permit comparisons between urban and rural sectors. Note that the unemployment rates are consistently lower in rural areas than urban areas. This finding is consistent with our previous suggestion that underemployment rather than unemployment is the crucial problem in agriculture. It may well be true that employment is always available in the traditional sector in the small owner-operated farm. It is the lack of the right kind of employment to attract the better educated and ambitious rural persons that creates conditions of hidden unemployment and eventually increases the rural exodus.

[3]For some evidence, see Turnham (1971, pp. 58, 61–63).

Table 12.3 *Unemployment as a Percentage of the Labor Force: Time Series for Selected Less Developed Countries*

	1957	1958	1959	1960	1961	1962	1963	1964	1965	1966	1967	1968
Africa:												
Egypt	5.1	3.4	4.9	4.8	3.2	1.8		1.5*				3.2*
Asia:												
Korea[a]			3.8	4.8	2.3	8.4	8.1	7.7	7.4	7.1	6.2	5.1
Philippines	7.9	8.2	6.8	6.3	7.5	8.0	6.3	6.4*	7.1	7.1	8.0	7.8*
Taiwan							5.3*	4.4	3.4	3.1	2.3	1.7
America:												
Argentine (Greater Buenos Aires)									5.3	5.6	6.4	5.0
Chile (Greater Santiago)	6.4	9.5	7.4	7.4*	6.7	5.3	5.1	5.3	5.4	5.4	6.1	6.0
Colombia (Bogotá)							8.7	7.2	8.8	11.5	12.7	11.6
Panama							5.8*	7.4*	7.6	5.1	6.2	9.1
Puerto Rico[b]	13.0	13.9	13.8	12.1	12.6	12.6	11.8	11.1	12.0	12.3	12.2	11.6*
Trinidad and Tobago									14.0	14.0	15.0	14.0

Notes: The data used are from sample surveys. Starred figures were collected at monthly dates different from the others included in the series.
[a]New series from 1962.
[b]Revised series after 1960.
Source: Turnham, D. (1971), *The Employment Problem in Less–Developed Countries: A Review of Evidence.* Paris: OECD, Development Center, p. 46.

Table 12.4 *A Comparison of Urban and Rural Rates of Unemployment, Selected Less Developed Countries*

	Year	Urban Rate	Rural Rate
Africa:			
Cameroons[a]	1964	4.6	3.4
Morocco	1960	20.5	5.4
Tanzania	1965	7.0	3.9
Asia:			
Ceylon	1959/60	14.3	10.0
	1968	14.8	10.4
China (Taiwan)	1968	3.5	1.4
India[b]	1961/62	3.2	3.9
Iran	1956	4.5	1.8
	1966	5.5	11.3
Korea	1965	12.7	3.1
Philippines	1967	13.1	6.9
Syria	1967	7.3	4.6
West Malaysia	1967	11.6	7.4
America:			
Chile	1968	6.1	2.0
Honduras	1961	13.9	3.4
Jamaica	1960	19.0[c]	12.4[d]
Panama	1960	15.5	3.6
	1967	9.3	2.8
Uruguay	1963	10.9	2.3
Venezuela	1961	17.5	4.3
	1968	6.5	3.1

Notes:
[a]Males only.
[b]The unemployed "available" but "not seeking" work are included in rural areas but not in urban areas. Deducting this group might reduce the rural percentage rate by about one-third. The urban figure relates to the age group 15–60.
[c]Kingston.
[d]All Jamaica less Kingston.
Source: Turnham, D. (1971), *The Employment Problem in Less-Developed Countries: A Review of Evidence.* Paris: OECD, Development Center, p. 57.

Surplus Labor in Agriculture

The discussion so far has related to employment and unemployment in general. Agricultural employment has attracted a good deal of special attention in the literature, at the level of both theory and measurement. The formulation of the surplus-labor hypothesis led to the prescription of a strategy for development based on the transfer of surplus labor from the traditional to the modern sector at a constant (and low) real wage.

The experience of LDCs during the last three decades suggests that surplus labor, as a development strategy, has foundered on two problems. First, there is no surplus labor that can be transferred from agriculture at no loss of output, except under rather special circumstances. Second, development has not been handicapped by the lack of additional workers for the modern sector. If anything, the problem that now looms paramount is how to find employment for increasing numbers of unemployed.

Despite the demise of the problem that the surplus-labor theory was designed to attack, some of the insights it has yielded are still useful. For example, we have seen that participation rates, employment, involuntary unemployment, hidden unemployment, and underemployment depend both on objective considerations, relating to the production function and to employment opportunities, and on subjective factors, such as the reservation price of labor and the willingness to work. These factors can be combined in a utility-maximization model developed from the surplus labor literature. Also, the techniques developed for measuring surplus labor in agriculture serve as useful complements to the survey methods commonly used in measuring unemployment in the nonagricultural sector. Finally, a number of interesting implications of the surplus-labor hypothesis can be tested.

From Zero Marginal Productivity of Labor to Neoclassical Dualism

The existence in LDCs of agricultural labor with zero marginal productivity was advocated as doctrine in the early post–World War II literature.[4] Zero marginal product can be interpreted in two ways: (1) that labor is working without contributing anything to output or (2) that some workers are marginal in the sense that removing them from the farms would stimulate the remaining workers to compensate for the loss in output by working harder. The implication of zero marginal productivity under either interpretation is that removal of labor is costless to the agricultural sector.

The most realistic, and historically the most venerable, version of surplus labor covers the range between the broad limits of zero marginal product of labor and of sectoral dualism. In W. A. Lewis' (1954) early version of the theory, as elaborated by Fei and Ranis (1964), unlimited supplies of labor exist as long as agriculture conforms to the classical model, in which the supply of labor is perfectly elastic at current wage rates. The current wage rate in the agricultural sector reflects the requirements for subsistence consumption. Under the income-sharing characteristics of the extended family system, this wage is closer to the average product of labor and higher than the "small" (or zero in the extreme case) marginal product of labor. Industry can therefore obtain unlimited labor from agriculture by paying a wage rate that is constant and slightly higher than the agricultural subsistence requirements. As capitalists reinvest their earnings, the demand for industrial labor shifts to the right, with wages remaining constant as long as the unlimited

supplies of agricultural labor last. After this point is reached, the labor supply curves slope upward, and wages start rising. The salient features of the classical labor-surplus model are zero marginal productivity of labor (as the limiting case), constant wage rates, and a dualistic wage structure between industry and agriculture.

An important theoretical contribution that emphasizes dualism while refuting the other features of the classical model is due to Jorgenson (1961). This model, which has become known as the neoclassical model, denies both that the agricultural wage differs from the marginal product of agricultural labor and also that the latter is zero. As a result, a withdrawal of workers from the farms will decrease agricultural output and raise the marginal productivity of the remaining workers. Laborers are paid according to their marginal products in both the agricultural and industrial sectors, resulting in an upward-sloping supply curve of labor to industry.

We will study the conditions for and implications of the existence of agricultural labor that has low (or zero) marginal product in the context of utility maximization at the household level. This model is sufficiently general to include the classical and neoclassical models as special cases.

Surplus Labor in a Utility-Maximization Model

Both the production and consumption behavior of the farm household must be studied simultaneously if one is to predict whether or not withdrawing agricultural workers will lead to a decrease in output. There exist a number of such general equilibrium models (Nakajima 1969; Jorgenson and Lau 1969; Yotopoulos and Lau 1974). For the study of surplus labor, a model that concentrates on the marginal valuations of labor (the marginal productivity of labor) and income is sufficient.

Sen (1966b) provided a cogent defense of surplus labor by distinguishing between the marginal productivity of a laborer in agriculture and the marginal product of a man-hour. The latter being zero is not a necessary condition for surplus labor to exist. More specifically, define household labor, L, as the product of the number of working members of the household, α, times the quantity of work, l, contributed by each individual. For output to decrease, the quantity of household labor, L, should decrease after workers, α,

---

[4]For examples, see Mandelbaum (1945), Nurkse (1953), Rosenstein-Rodan (1957).

are withdrawn. But this may not necessarily happen if l, the amount of work contributed by each remaining worker, increases at the same time. The analysis, as a result, focuses specifically on agricultural underemployment which, as we suggested earlier, may play an important role in swelling the rolls of the openly unemployed. The empirical question becomes: will l increase as a result of a decrease in α? If so, agricultural underemployment exists, and the provision of new jobs for the workers withdrawn from agriculture is not likely to decrease the magnitude of measured unemployment. To answer this question, both subjective (marginal utility of leisure) and objective (marginal productivity of work) considerations must be combined.

An individual will decrease the quantity of work he supplies, l, when the real cost of work rises. The real cost of work is the marginal disutility of work divided by the marginal utility of income. Consider a decrease in the number of workers in the household, α, by farm exodus. In order to maintain the quantity of household labor, L, unchanged, the quanity of work of each remaining worker, l, has to increase; as a result, the marginal disutility of work to each individual increases. In the meantime, the reduction in α leads to a rise in income for each remaining household member; as a result, the marginal utility of income decreases. Consequently, the real cost of labor rises, with both L and output decreasing. Nonreduction in output (surplus labor) is therefore possible if, and only if, both the marginal disutility of work curve and the marginal utility of income curve are flat in the relevant region. We can formalize this argument following Sen (1966b).

Define family labor supply, L, and family output, Q, respectively as

$$L = \alpha l \tag{1}$$

$$Q = \beta q \tag{2}$$

Here α is the number of workers in the household, β is the total number of members in the household ($\beta \geq \alpha$), l is the amount of work contributed by each individual worker, and q is the consumption per household member. The family output, Q, at a given point of time, is a function of L given the stock of capital and land, and the function is assumed to be smooth and normal, that is, with diminishing marginal productivity of labor

$$Q = Q(L) \tag{3}$$

with

$$Q'(L) > 0 \qquad Q''(L) < 0$$

Assume that the peasant family maximizes a welfare function, w, that is a linear combination of the individual utility of consumption, U_i, and the individual disutility of work, V_i, for all members of the household

$$w = \sum_{i=1}^{\beta} U_i(q_i) - \sum_{i=1}^{\alpha} V_i(l_i)$$
$$= \beta U - \alpha V \tag{4}$$

The utility and disutility curves (identical for each household member) have the normal properties:

$$U = U(q) \tag{5}$$

with

$$U'(q) > 0 \quad \text{and} \quad U''(q) \leq 0$$

that is, the marginal utility of consumption is positive, and

$$V = V(l) \tag{6}$$

with

$$V'(l) \geq 0 \quad \text{and} \quad V''(l) \geq 0$$

that is, the marginal disutility of work is nonnegative.

Family welfare is maximized when[5]

$$Q'(L) = \frac{V'(l)}{U'(q)} \equiv x \tag{7}$$

where x is the "real cost of labor," determined by the individual marginal rate of substitution between income and labor. The maximization rule suggests that labor is applied up to the point where its marginal product is equal to the real cost of labor.

The argument at this point will be simplified if we introduce two other auxiliary relationships. Not only is the marginal product of labor, $Q'(L)$, a function of L, but labor it-

---

[5]Rewrite equation 4 as $w = \beta U(Q/\beta) - \alpha V(L/\alpha)$, where $Q/\beta = q$ and $L/\alpha = l$. Differentiating with respect to L and setting equal to zero, we have

$$\frac{\partial w}{\partial L} = \beta U'(q) \frac{1}{\beta} Q'(L) - \alpha V'(l) \frac{1}{\alpha} = 0$$

Hence, a necessary condition for maximization is

$$U'(q)Q'(L) = V'(l)$$

which reduces to equation 7.

self is a function of $Q'(L)$.[6] Furthermore, since from equation 7 $Q'(L)$ is the real cost of labor, this relationship has a negative sign, that is, if $Q'(L)$ increases, L decreases. We write

$$L = \phi[Q'(L)] = \phi(x) \qquad (8)$$

with

$$\frac{dL}{d\phi} < 0$$

Since from equation 3 output is a positive function of labor, output is also a negative function of real labor cost

$$Q = \psi[Q'(L)] = \psi(x) \qquad (9)$$

with

$$\frac{dQ}{d\psi} < 0$$

Equation 3, together with the positive marginal productivity of labor condition, indicates that if family labor decreases, output also decreases and surplus labor is ruled out. Therefore, we have to approach the possibility of the existence of surplus labor with L constant: as α decreases, l increases to compensate for any decrease in α. By increasing l, the individual marginal disutility of work, $V'(l)$, is increased. The reduction in α leads to a rise in per capita income for the total, β, family members, and the marginal utility of income, $U'(q)$, decreases. As a result, the real cost of labor, x, increases, which, from equation 9, leads to a reduction in output. Nondecrease in output and hence surplus labor are possible only if both $V'(l)$ and $U'(q)$ are flat in the relevant region. Only under these circumstances will an increase in the individual's work leave the marginal disutility of work unchanged, and a rise in the individual's income leave the marginal utility of income unchanged. In this case, then, the real cost of labor is insensitive to the withdrawal of workers from the household and the possibility of surplus labor arises. This situation is depicted in Figure 12.1. If l, the actual quantity of work contributed by the individual worker of the household, is in the range l_1^* to l_2^*, the constancy of the real cost of labor is satisfied because the slopes of both $V(l)$ and $U(q)$ are constant. The withdrawal of workers will be compensated by the increase in individual work. Outside this range, however, for example, to the right of l_2^*, the increase in individual work will not be sufficient to compensate for the withdrawal of workers, because although the marginal disutility of labor is constant up to l_3^*, the marginal utility of income is not; nor will it be sufficient when l is to the left of l_1^* because neither curve is flat in that range.

Of the two conditions for the existence of surplus labor, constant marginal disutility of labor and constant marginal utility of income, the former is less objectionable than the latter. How can the flatness of the utility of income curve be rationalized? At a level of living close to the minimum subsistence, when a "decent" livelihood has not yet been achieved, nondiminution of the desire to earn more income as income rises may not be implausible. Even if the "decent" living standard has been achieved or, whether or not it has been achieved, we are still operating on the part of the marginal utility of income curve that is diminishing, one could devise a system of taxes that would wipe away the rise in income per head that resulted from the departure of some workers from the household. Then there would be no net increase in per capita income, and the invariance of the marginal utility with respect to the variation in income would not arise.[7] Given the possibility of designing and administering such a tax system, surplus labor would exist, of course, if the marginal disutility of work were also constant within the same range.

Under certain assumptions, we can generalize the model of the equilibrium of the peasant household to apply to the agricultural economy as a whole. Suppose we have a large number of identical families in the agricultural economy. Furthermore, assume constant returns to scale, assume that nonlabor resources can be reallocated among the households, and assume that the ratio $k = \beta/\alpha$ of the total members to workers in each household remains constant. The question is to determine the quantitative response of peasant output to a withdrawal of workers. In terms of elasticities, we want to determine the elasticity of output with respect to working members of the economy.

For the elasticity of output with respect

---

[6]The inverse function exists by virtue of the assumption $Q''(L) < 0$ throughout.

[7]This is the argument of Nurkse (1953, p. 43) in connection with the necessity of enforced savings for mobilizing surplus labor.

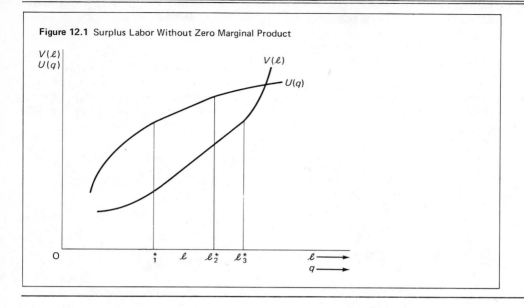

Figure 12.1 Surplus Labor Without Zero Marginal Product

to workers, we write

$$\frac{dQ}{d\alpha}\frac{\alpha}{Q} = \frac{dQ}{dL}\frac{dL}{d\alpha}\frac{\alpha}{Q} \tag{10}$$

Solving first for $dL/d\alpha$ we have[8]

$$\frac{dL}{d\alpha} = \frac{\left(\dfrac{V''(l)}{V'(l)}\cdot L\cdot k - \dfrac{U''(q)}{U'(q)}Q\right)}{\left(\beta\dfrac{V''(l)}{V'(l)} - \alpha\beta\dfrac{Q''(L)}{Q'(L)} - \alpha Q'(L)\dfrac{U''(q)}{U'(q)}\right)} \tag{11}$$

Then by substitution of equation 11 for $dL/d\alpha$

[8]The calculations, outlined in Sen (1966b, p. 433), are as follows:

$$\beta = k\cdot\alpha \text{ by assumption} \tag{1n}$$

$$\frac{dx}{d\alpha} = \left(\frac{\dfrac{dV'(l)}{d\alpha}U'(q) - \dfrac{dU'(q)}{d\alpha}V'(l)}{[U'(q)]^2}\right) \quad \text{from equation 7} \tag{2n}$$

$$\frac{dV'(l)}{d\alpha} = V''(l)\left(\frac{\left(\dfrac{dL}{d\alpha}\cdot\alpha - L\right)}{\alpha^2}\right) \tag{3n}$$

from equations 6 and 1

$$\frac{dU'(q)}{d\alpha} = U''(q)\left(\frac{Q'(L)\left(\dfrac{dL}{d\alpha}\right)\beta - Q\cdot k}{\beta^2}\right) \tag{4n}$$

from equations 5, 2, and 1n

$$\frac{dx}{d\alpha} = \frac{dL}{d\alpha}\frac{1}{\phi'(x)} = \frac{dL}{d\alpha}Q''(L) \tag{5n}$$

from equations 7 and 8.

Therefore, from equations 2n to 5n, we have equation 11.

in equation 10, we have

$$\frac{dQ}{d\alpha}\frac{\alpha}{Q}$$

$$= \frac{Q'(L)L}{Q}\left(\frac{\dfrac{V''(l)l}{V'(l)} - \dfrac{U''(q)q}{U'(q)}}{\dfrac{V''(l)l}{V'(l)} - \left(\dfrac{U''(q)q}{U'(q)}\dfrac{Q'(L)L}{Q}\right) - \dfrac{Q''(L)L}{Q'L}}\right)$$

or

$$E = G\left(\frac{n+m}{n+(mG)+g}\right) \tag{12}$$

where we define as follows:

$E = \dfrac{dQ}{d\alpha}\dfrac{\alpha}{Q}$ for the elasticity of output with respect to the number of workers

$G = \dfrac{Q'(L)L}{Q}$ for $dL = 1$ unit; the elasticity of output with respect to labor

$n = \dfrac{V''(l)l}{V'(l)}$ for $dl = 1$ unit; the elasticity of the marginal disutility of work with respect to hours of work

$m = -\dfrac{U''(q)q}{U'(q)}$ for $dq = 1$ unit; the absolute value of the elasticity of the marginal utility of income with respect to income

$g = -\dfrac{Q''(L)L}{Q'(L)}$ for $dL = 1$ unit; the absolute value of the elasticity of the marginal product of labor with respect to labor.

With equation 12, we can investigate the different conditions under which surplus labor may appear. Surplus labor implies that $E = 0$, that is, output remains unchanged with the withdrawal of workers. The following cases arise:

1. The extreme case occurs when $n = m = 0$. This coincides with the case in which the utility and the disutility curves are both flat within a certain region, as presented in Figure 12-1.
2. The case of $G = 0$ is the extreme classical case where the marginal product of labor and therefore the elasticity of output with respect to labor are zero. This case does not strictly follow.[9] Heuristically, however, one may conceive of making G smaller and smaller, which leads to infinitesimally small E.

The elasticity of output with respect to workers, E, can readily be determined empirically by fitting a production function. What relationship does this elasticity bear to the elasticity of output with respect to labor, G? By reference to equation 12, the relationship between E and G can be analyzed in terms of the following cases:

1. If the hours of work, l, are institutionally fixed, this leads to $E = G$. This, however, is not a realistic assumption for the peasant economy.
2. If n is very large, we have G approaching E. Heuristically, this corresponds to the case in which the marginal disutility schedule becomes vertical. It implies constancy of hours worked and thus coincides with the previous case.
3. A special case of $E = G$ arises when $m = g/(1 - G)$. We can visualize this case as follows:

> When some people are withdrawn from the peasant economy, with an unchanged number of hours of work per person, the marginal physical return from work will increase. On the other hand, since the people left behind will now enjoy a higher income, the utility value of a unit of output will now be lower. The condi-

tion quoted corresponds to the special case when the two forces just cancel out each other. (Sen 1966b, p. 435.)

4. The above are special cases. In general, we would not expect the elasticity of output with respect to workers to be identical with the elasticity of output with respect to labor. In fact one can verify from equation 12 that the condition reduces to

$$E \left\{ \lesseqqgtr \right\} G \quad \text{according as} \quad m \left\{ \lesseqqgtr \right\} \frac{g}{1 - G}$$

For the case of a Cobb-Douglas production function, we have $g = (1 - G)$, so that the condition reduces to

$$E \left\{ \lesseqqgtr \right\} G \quad \text{according as} \quad m \left\{ \lesseqqgtr \right\} 1 \text{[10]}$$

Extensions of the Model

We have presented a utility-maximization model of surplus labor based on rather conventional assumptions about the marginal productivity of labor and the marginal utility of leisure. This general model can be modified by introducing specific assumptions that enhance its realism. Stiglitz (1969) adds some realistic assumptions and strengthens Sen's results.

Sen does not allow for seasonal labor utilizations. In most agricultural activities (with dairy farming and specialized crops being the likely exceptions), the relationship between peak season and off-peak season labor utilization is one of complementarity rather than of perfect substitutability. It is useful to assume

---

[9]Marginal productivity of labor being zero requires, by equation 7, that the marginal disutility of labor be zero, too. This, however, has been ruled out in equations 11 and 12, which involve division by $V'(l)$.

[10]For the C-D production function with constant returns to scale, we write

$$Q(L) = AL^a$$

$$Q'(L) = a \frac{Q}{L}$$

Substituting into g, we have

$$g = -\frac{\frac{dQ'}{dL} L}{a \frac{Q}{L}}$$

$$= -\frac{\frac{d}{dL}\left(a \frac{Q}{L}\right) L^2}{aQ}$$

$$= -\frac{\left(\frac{Q'}{L} - \frac{Q}{L^2}\right) L^2}{Q}$$

$$= 1 - \frac{dQ}{dL} \frac{L}{a}$$

that the marginal productivity of labor supplied at harvest and planting times exceeds by a considerable amount the marginal productivity of labor at other times of the year. As a result, output is not simply a function of total labor supply, L (where $L = \alpha l$). Stiglitz rather assumes that the production function has two labor arguments, with workers being fully utilized in peak seasons (l being at the possible maximum), while at other times of the year the hours worked per week are determined to maximize utility. With this modification, Sen's results become even stronger. Labor can never be in surplus and total output must fall as workers migrate to the urban sector, regardless of the marginal utility of consumption and the marginal disutility of work—which are the crucial factors in Sen's argument. The empirical corollary of Stiglitz' analysis is that the supply price of labor to the urban sector is always upward sloping. Furthermore, assume that urban workers' marginal propensity to consume is close to one. An increase in wage rates in the urban sector that proposes to attract additional workers would result in decreasing the savings available for financing economic development.

Zarembka (1972, Chapter 1) has further elaborated Sen's model by specifying a CES production function in land and hours of work per family member and a CES utility function in hours of work and output per family member. The crucial parameters then become the elasticity of indifferent substitution in the utility function and the elasticity of factor substitution in the production function. If the former is greater than the latter, work hours per worker increase as a family member leaves the farm, and the potential for labor surplus exists. Sen's result is a special case of this. Another special case is the classical position of zero marginal productivity of a laborer, which is implied by an elasticity of indifferent substitution approaching infinity (Berry and Soligo 1968) or by an elasticity of factor substitution equal to zero. If the elasticity of indifferent substitution is equal to the elasticity of factor substitution, work hours are constant with respect to changes in the number of family members and output decreases with the withdrawal of labor. In such a case, it is not necessary to distinguish between labor, L, and the number of workers, α. Jorgenson's (1961) neoclassical model fits in this category. Finally, if the elasticity of indifferent substitution is

smaller than that of factor substitution, work hours per worker decrease as a family member leaves the farm.

Empirical Implications of the Analysis

Zero marginal productivity of labor has formed the foundation for a strategy of "painless" or "up by the bootstraps" process of development (Nurkse 1953). It is a misguided policy prescription, because as we have seen, zero marginal productivity of labor is neither a necessary nor a sufficient condition for withdrawing workers from agriculture without loss of output.

A special version of the zero marginal productivity of labor hypothesis has its origin in the "Agrarian Doctrine" and is related to the logic of feudal agriculture (Georgescu-Roegen 1960; Nicholls 1960; Dandekar 1962; Myint 1964; Desai and Mazumdar 1970). According to this version, in poor, overpopulated peasant agriculture, the real cost of labor is zero, $x = 0$, while the wage rate in the capitalist agricultural sector is positive, $P_L > 0$. The peasant sector, therefore, serves as a reserve of labor to be drawn upon, with no loss of output, in the process of development. It also, by applying more labor (per unit of land) than the capitalist sector, produces larger quantities of output. The preceding analysis implies that this argument, which is certainly of dubious empirical validity, is overly restrictive. The existence of constant (rather than zero) real cost of labor is sufficient to guarantee a labor pool. The existence of a "wage gap," $P_L > x$, is sufficient to produce higher labor utilization and greater output per unit of land in the peasant sector.[11]

A problem raised by the disguised unemployment literature is that of reconciling the zero marginal product of labor with the negative marginal utility of work. This problem becomes irrelevent once it is realized that all that is required for surplus labor to exist is constancy of the real cost of labor, that is, of the ratio of the marginal disutility of work to the marginal utility of income.

The origin of the wage gap between agriculture and manufacturing has been exten-

---

[11] Assume a production function with constant returns to labor and land. Thus, interpret Q and L in equation 7 as output and labor per unit of land respectively. From equation 8, we have $\phi(x) < \phi(P_L)$, therefore higher labor per unit of land in peasant farms. From equation 9, we have $\psi(x) < \psi(P_L)$, therefore higher output per unit of land.

sively discussed in the literature. Here it is sufficient to suggest an explanation based on the shape of the marginal disutility curve of labor in Figure 12.1. Wage employment takes the form of full-time work per day. Agricultural work, on the other hand, is subject to more flexible rules about hours of work per day. Interpret l as hours of work per day, and consider the case that full-time work in manufacturing lies to the right of l_3*, the point where the marginal disutility curve of labor starts rising, while the lower level of hours of work per person in the peasant equilibrium is to the left of l_3*. This is sufficient to cause a wage gap between agriculture and nonagriculture.

Flatness in the relevant range of the marginal rate of indifferent substitution between leisure and income is sufficient to account for surplus labor. In certain cases, even this condition can be released. This was suggested by Zarembka's (1972) generalization. Also, in an economy where part of the peasant output is marketed, the transfer of labor force from agriculture to manufacturing will lead to a change in the terms of trade in favor of agriculture. This will stimulate production by the remaining members of the peasant economy, and output can be maintained, post transfer, even though the flatness of the marginal disutility of labor and the marginal utility of income has not been satisfied.[12] Note, however, in such a case that the implications of the surplus labor doctrine for labor transfer do not necessarily hold, since the rise in agriculture's terms of trade will raise urban wages and directly and indirectly eat into the industrial sector's investable surplus.

The Measurement of Surplus Labor

Empirical work on surplus labor focuses on the question of whether or not workers can be withdrawn from the farms—without substantially compromising the *ceteris paribus* condition by additions of other factors of production or by radical reorganization of agriculture and change of techniques—while the level of output is maintained. There are two basic trends in the literature, the labor-utilization approach and the labor-productivity approach. The former method draws conclusions about surplus labor by comparing the

labor used for agricultural operations to the total labor available to the farm households. The latter directly utilizes a neoclassical production function.

There already exists a considerable literature on the measurement of surplus labor through both the labor-utilization and the labor-productivity approaches.[13] In the labor-utilization method, we can distinguish a number of variants, depending on the definition of labor requirements. Labor required to cultivate an acre of land with a specific crop or to produce one unit of output is one variant. The two empirical studies that will be presented below on the labor utilization method are of this type.[14] Another variant concentrates on the optimal density of population deemed adequate for a given type of cultivation. This density is compared to the actual density of population (Mujumdar 1961). A third variant utilizes the difference between the number of acres required under a given type of cultivation to provide a person with "a standard income." This is compared to the number of available acres and to the agricultural population.

The productivity approach focuses on the marginal product of labor. This can be directly estimated from a neoclassical type of production function, and it can be compared with some a priori and exogenous standards, such as the wage rate, the imputed cost of labor where the wage rate is not easily accessible or is unrepresentative, or a value like zero or "close to zero."

The Labor-Utilization Approach to Surplus Labor: Macroeconomic Analysis

As an example of the labor-utilization approach, we present the Pepelasis and Yotopoulos (1962) measurement of disguised unemployment for Greece. The authors start with a set of technical coefficients that express the man-day equivalents of labor required to cultivate one unit of land.[15] The coefficients, which are product-specific, are given by sample farm management surveys that studied the time spent in performing each agricultural

[12]For the specific conditions that lead to this result, see Sen (1966*b*, pp. 427–428, 438–439).

[13]For surveys of this literature, see Kao, Anschell, and Eicher (1964), Martina (1966), W. C. Robinson (1969), Wellisz (1968), and Islam (1964).

[14]Other examples of this variant are Rosenstein-Rodan (1957), A. Mathur (1964), Cho (1963, 1966).

[15]The technical coefficients are in terms of man-days per acre for crop production and man-days per animal or per unit of output for husbandry, and forestry and fishing, respectively.

operation. They represent a Leontief-type vector of coefficients which, when multiplied by the vector of land cultivated, give a product-specific vector of labor requirements:

$$r'X = R$$

where r_i is the product-specific labor coefficient, X_i is the area cultivated, and R_i is the labor requirements by product category. The column vector of the product is summed to give the total labor requirements of the agricultural sector in man-days, $\sum_{i=1}^{n} R_i$.[16]

The labor available for farm employment was calculated from the total size of the active agricultural population (15–69 years of age) as measured by census data. The active agricultural population, which was distributed by sex and by age brackets, was adjusted to account for institutional population, females in domestic employment, persons unable to work, and other groups. This adjustment gives the labor potential in agriculture expressed in labor days. Labor potential days were converted into homogeneous man-days by applying appropriate conversion coefficients for women, children, and the aged (65–69 years old). We may denote this total as $\sum_{i=1}^{m} D_i$, where D_i is labor available in man-days for m age groups.

The difference between labor available and labor required, $\sum_{i=1}^{m} D_i - \sum_{i=1}^{n} R_i = S_A$, is the *average annual surplus labor*. It is, however, a measurement deprived of any practical significance for certain kinds of policy questions. The existence of average annual surplus labor, for example, does not warrant the conclusion that part of the labor force can be withdrawn from the farms without any decrease in agricultural output. The inadequacy of the concept in this respect lies in the fact that it overlooks the seasonal nature of agricultural operations by averaging the seasonal employment peaks and troughs. Seasonality is a salient feature of agricultural production which is highly susceptible to the crop-cycle.

In order to recognize the crop-cycle pattern, surplus labor is reckoned in seasonal terms. For this purpose, the r_i vector of labor coefficients is converted into an $n \times 4$ matrix, where the n product coefficients are distributed for the four seasons of the year. The assumption is made that the total labor requirements are distributed proportionally to the seasonal sum of the labor coefficients. Similarly, the total labor available is distributed seasonally to account for the distribution within the year of the days that are not suitable for agricultural work (inclement weather, holidays, etc.). The difference between seasonal labor available and labor requirements is the *seasonal surplus labor*, S_S, which contributes to the productive operations for only part of the year and can thus be withdrawn only intermittently.

As a last step, a measurement of surplus labor is derived, which is better adapted to the study of the problem of permanently withdrawing labor from the fields. *Chronic surplus labor* is defined as the difference between the peak season actual employment (labor required) and the full employment level. Such chronically unemployed labor contributes nothing to the productive activities and therefore is directly removable from the farms.

Pepelasis and Yotopoulos found that in the period 1953–1960 the small initial level of chronic surplus labor rapidly declined, and starting in 1955, there existed permanent shortages of labor for at least two seasons of the crop year (fall and spring). Seasonal surplus existed for the other two seasons, ranging up to 25 percent for winter.

The major criticism of the Pepelasis-Yotopoulos study lies in the static nature of the labor-employment coefficients. They are derived from current practice. It would be surprising if the current practice did not reflect a technological and social bias to employ all labor available, at least during the peak seasons. A question that arises within the dynamic framework is whether or not agriculture would reorganize itself, that is, move to a higher production frontier, as labor is withdrawn. The coefficients that emerge if this process is taken to its limit are those that should be used in computing the surplus labor, chronic or seasonal.

The Labor-Utilization Approach to Surplus Labor: Microeconomic Analysis

A microeconomic study by Yotopoulos (1967a, Chapter 6), which utilizes farm survey data to

---

[16]An alternative approach to derive the product-specific labor coefficients would be from a detailed agricultural I-O Table by combining information about final plus intermediate demand and labor employment by agricultural subsector. This will be discussed in Chapter 15.

estimate agricultural production functions and to evaluate allocative efficiency in traditional agriculture, goes some way to meet this criticism of the Pepelasis-Yotopoulos study. With the aggregate method described above, the method employed treads some common ground. For each farm household in the sample, the total family labor supply (or labor potential), the family nonfarm labor supply, and the family farm labor supply (or labor available) are computed in a deterministic way by using assumptions similar to the Pepelasis-Yotopoulos study and also information directly derived from the questionnaire, such as days of sickness per household member, or employment outside the farm (which, being unusual in farm households, could be easily remembered). The question becomes how to estimate labor input in the farm by using indirect information on labor available. The difference between labor available and labor input gives an estimate of labor surplus.

The family labor available, A, for agricultural work is derived as the differences between the family labor potential, P, and the nonfarm family labor employment, N, as above, and it is expressed in equivalent man-days:

$$A = P - N \qquad (13)$$

Clearly, this does not necessarily measure the labor input in the family farm. For one thing, this total labor magnitude may also include overt idle labor that was never applied on the farm, since for some season or some phases of the production cycle, the marginal productivity of labor may have been zero or "low." On the other hand, hired-in labor, H_n, may also be employed on the farm. Thus, we write

$$F = A + H_n - U \qquad (14)$$

where F is the labor input in the family farm, A is the labor available for farm self-employment, H_n is the amount of hired-in labor directly available from the questionnaire, and U is the underemployment (overemployment if $U < 0$) component of the household. All are expressed in equivalent man-days. The problem is to estimate F for each sample farm, given A and H_n, with no direct information on U.

An assumption and a postulate are essential for this method of derivation of farm-labor input from data on family labor available and hired-in labor. It is assumed that there is a functional relationship between the labor input and the size of the agricultural operation in the sample of farms. This relationship is

$$F = f(D) \qquad (15)$$

where D is the size of the agricultural operation. It is also postulated that there exists a proper subset of the sample of farms where the underemployment component is equal to zero. By using the notation of equations 14 and 15, the relationship in the underemployment-free subset of farms is expressed as

$$\begin{aligned} F &= A + H_n \\ &= f(D) \end{aligned} \qquad (16)$$

From equation 16, Yotopoulos estimates the parameters used in order to compute the farm-labor input for the remaining farms in the sample, the complement of the underemployment-free subset in the universe. Thus, for this latter subset of farms, possible information on F provided by $A + H_n$ is completely ignored, and the labor input, F, is taken at the level implied from the relationship observed in the underemployment-free subset of the universe.

Some specific problems merit further discussion. How is the size of the agricultural operation, D, defined? What are the decision rules on selection of the underemployment-free subset? What is the statistical relationship between F and D? Is it possible to apply the same relationship to the subset of the remaining farms in the universe?

The Size of the Agricultural Operation

The independent variable, D, in equation 15 that expresses the size of the agricultural operation may be interpreted as a proxy for labor demand. It is derived for all farms in the universe by multiplying the size-of-agricultural-activity row vector by the column vector of the Leontief-type labor-intensity coefficients. This is a process of weighting the crop-specific land input by a cultivation-specific labor-intensity factor. The size of agricultural activity in acres of land is provided in the questionnaire. The labor-intensity coefficients were utilized in the same way as in the previous study.

The Underemployment-Free Subset of Farms
The decision rule of selection of the under-employment-free subset of farms involves a comparison of the family labor potential, P, and the size of agricultural operation, D, as defined above. The family labor potential includes the family labor employed in nonfarm activities, N, as well as the residual available for farm work, A, but it is net of hired-in labor, as shown in equation 13. The family labor potential may be interpreted as a proxy for the family total supply of labor. The implicit assumption made by taking P rather than A as a proxy for the labor supply is that N is an endogenous variable; it depends on the size of agricultural operation, D. In other words, the main profession of farmers being agriculture, it is assumed that farm work comes "off the top" of the labor potential, and that a household that has high farm-labor requirements (relative to its labor availabilities) will not accept outside, nonfarm employment.

For each farm in the sample, Yotopoulos constructs the ratio D/P of the farm-labor demand proxy and the family total labor supply proxy (both in equivalent man-days). The farms are ranked in a descending order of magnitude of the index D/P. We would then expect that the higher the value of the index, the more likely the farm is to belong in the zero-underemployment subset. Thus, the subset at stake is selected starting from the top of the D/P list. The empirical problem that arises is: at which point on the list should the line between the two subsets be drawn? Inspection of the D/P ratio for the farms in the universe reveals that it occupies a continuum with only 5 percent of the observations (24 farms) above the value of 0.50. Distinguishing the two subsets on the basis of the cardinal value of the index does not seem feasible. Instead, the ordinal ranking of the farms that the index produces is used. After inspection of the scatter diagram of the F on D relationship for the higher ranking farms, the subset at stake is arbitrarily defined as the one composed of the farms included in the top quintile of the distribution. The choice was based on the closeness of the fit of the regression of F on D.

The ranking criterion may assign two farms with the same values of $A + H_n$ and D to different subsets. This is as one would have expected because of the operation of the P factor. The farm that is assigned to the underemployment-free subset actually has a lower P value than the other; consequently, the latter has more members employed in nonfarm activities ($N = P - A$). On the other hand, the farm with the lower P has relatively fewer members working in nonfarm activities and therefore has greater "need" of farm labor.

Labor Input and the Measurement of Underemployment
By utilizing the value of D/P as a criterion a subsample of farms is selected for which it is postulated that the observed value of labor available on the farm plus hired-in labor is equal to labor input, F, with zero underemployment or overemployment component. For this subsample, the labor input variable is regressed on the observed labor-demand proxy by fitting the regression $F = A + H_n$. The estimate is (with standard errors in parentheses)

$$F = \begin{array}{c} 7.6 + 1.226\,D \\ (50.36)\ (0.133) \end{array} \qquad (17)$$

with $n = 84$ and coefficient of determination $r^2 = 0.629$.

Ex hypothesi, it is specified that the population regression relationship holds for all sample farms. The fitted equation 17, therefore, may be used to estimate the labor input for any farm whose size is known and that belongs to the same farm population from which the sample was drawn. The difference between labor available, computed for each farm, and labor input, estimated by the regression, gives the average annual surplus labor per farm. The analysis concluded that there existed annual shortages of labor for the larger farms (over 10 acres). On the other hand, the small farms (less than 10 acres) presented an annual surplus labor ratio of 0.6. The surplus labor ratio for the intermediate farms ranged between 0.4 and 0.2.

The microeconomic labor-utilization approach we described can be used for arriving at the appropriate labor input for running agricultural production functions. Given the institutional organization of agriculture around farm-household complexes, the distinction between agricultural population, agricultural workers, agricultural labor force, employed members of the agricultural labor force, and so on often becomes blurred. One can avoid misspecifying the crucial labor input by first estimating the subsidiary employment relationship from an underemployment-free subset of farms.[17]

Productivity Approach and the Marginal Productivity Theory of Wages

By fitting a production function, one can obtain estimates of the marginal product of labor. Such estimates can be used to test the hypothesis of disguised unemployment, whether it is formulated as marginal productivity close to zero or lower than an arbitrary (or observed) wage rate.

According to the marginal productivity theory, the marginal product of labor is equal to the wage rate. In a C-D model, for example, we have

$$\overline{P}_L = \beta \frac{Y}{L} \qquad (18)$$

where $\overline{P}_L$ is an "average" wage rate, Y is output, L is quantity of labor, and β is the labor coefficient in the production function. Given an estimate of β, we can solve for L in terms of β, Y, and $\overline{P}_L$. This would give us the quantity of labor that equates the marginal product to the wage rate. By comparing this estimate with the quantity of labor actually used, we can measure the extent of surplus labor.

B. Hansen (1966) tests with data from Egyptian agriculture the marginal productivity hypothesis and the alternative "conventional subsistence" or "institutional" wage specification hypothesis. He uses equation 18 to express the marginal productivity hypothesis, with Y defined as value of output. Adding a time subscript, t, to all variables and assuming β constant over time, we obtain the ratio of the marginal product at time t to that at time 0 as

[17]A simple, although relatively crude, approach for correcting for this misspecification has been suggested by Uppal (1969). Assume that agriculture is described by a well-behaved Cobb-Douglas production function, the coefficients of which present certain similarities across countries. Using this as a priori information, proceed to subtract a constant from each labor observation in the sample, and by trial and error, find the value of the constant that gives the best fit in the production relationship. (In the process, the observations that have labor input less than the arbitrarily selected constant are, of course, dropped from the sample.) The constant value, times the number of observations in the regression (plus the labor variable of the observations that were dropped as above) gives an estimate of the units by which labor had been misspecified. It can be treated as an estimate of surplus labor.

$$\frac{P_{Lt}}{P_{L0}} = \frac{\dfrac{Y_t}{L_t}}{\dfrac{Y_0}{L_0}} \qquad (19)$$

From equation 19, it follows that two indexes, one of wages, P_{Lt}, and the other of the average product of labor, $(Y/L)_t$, both having the same basis

$$P_{L0} = b\left(\frac{Y}{L}\right)_0 = 100 \qquad (20)$$

will always be equal. We write

$$P_{Lt} = \left(\frac{Y}{L}\right)_t$$

We can then formulate the statistical hypothesis of the marginal productivity theory of wages as

$$P_{Lt} = a + b\left(\frac{Y}{L}\right)_t + U_t \qquad (21)$$

The hypothesis is confirmed if the estimated values of a and b are zero and one respectively.

A definitive formulation of the "conventional subsistence" hypothesis is more controversial. A usual interpretation is that real wages (money wages over a cost-of-living index) are constant over time. We write

$$\frac{P_L}{P} = k \qquad (22)$$

where P is a cost-of-living index, and k is a constant. Forming indexes with $P_0 = 100$, we rewrite

$$P_{Lt} = P_t \qquad (23)$$

The statistical hypothesis becomes

$$P_{Lt} = a' + b'P_t + U'_t \qquad (24)$$

It is confirmed if a' and b' are zero and one respectively.

Hansen tests the two hypotheses with 17 observations of time series data from the period 1914 to 1959–1961. Besides the wage, the value of output, the labor employment, and the cost-of-living indexes, he also utilizes as an alternative to the last index a cost-of-maize subsistence index, $(P_M)_t$. The results are

$$H_1 : P_{Lt} = 31.31 + 0.88\left(\frac{Y}{L}\right)_t \qquad r = 0.973$$
$$\qquad\quad (15.21)\ \ (0.05)$$

$$H_{2a} : P_{Lt} = -5.09 + 1.33\,(P_M)_t \qquad r = 0.907$$
$$\qquad\quad (32.74)\ \ (0.16)$$

$$H_{2b} : P_{Lt} = -21.5 + 1.41 \, (P_C)_t \qquad r = 0.941$$
$$(26.88)(0.13)$$

On the basis of these results, the superiority of neither hypothesis is overwhelming. Further tests, however, gave an advantage to the marginal productivity hypothesis.[18]

A corollary of the unlimited supply of labor hypothesis is that there should not exist significant seasonal variations in wages. Hansen tests this hypothesis directly. He finds a national seasonal wage variation of 17 percent from peak to trough of labor demand in agriculture, with some provinces showing a variation of up to 300 percent. This is again consistent with the marginal productivity hypothesis and contrary to the "conventional subsistence" hypothesis.

Summary and Conclusions

The literature on labor in LDCs has come full circle. It was initiated after World War II, with the common-sense view that surplus labor represents a socially valuable and economically unexploited resource. Workers who have zero marginal product in agriculture, it was thought, should be able to contribute something in the process of development—even if they could only carry dirt or dig ditches with their bare hands! Development could then be achieved in a rather painless fashion. This classical approach was fully discredited by the early 1960s, when it became apparent that labor with marginal productivity approaching zero is unreal, and the expectation that workers could be moved out of agriculture at no loss of output, with other inputs remaining constant, was chimeric.

The neoclassical view of labor in a dualistic economy became fashionable in the 1960s. According to this view, the discrepancy in labor productivity between agriculture and industry was the automatic mechanism that would trigger resource transfers, which would continue until the dualism would eventually self-destruct, and self-sustained growth would occur. The dynamic models built were elegant,

replete with equilibrium conditions and convergence properties.

By 1970, the birds had come home to roost. Despite significant transfers of labor to the urban-industrial sector, dualism has continued and perhaps even increased. In the process, open unemployment has also increased. The demise of surplus labor has occurred as a result of the realization that unemployment is an important, perhaps even the most serious, problem in development—rather than a solution to the problems of insufficient capital formation and dualism. The magnitude of present estimates and future projections of unemployment in LDCs is a significant, though unhappy, finding. As a result, employment considerations must be given serious thought in evaluating projects and development plans, the subjects of Chapters 20 and 21.

This chapter has emphasized that it is both objective facts relating to the marginal product of labor and subjective considerations arising within a utility-maximization framework that determine the magnitude and importance of the problem of hidden unemployment, which will eventually show up as open unemployment. Our analysis points to four important conclusions. First, it is necessary to be precise about the different kinds of unemployment that exist, open, hidden, or disguised, for each gives rise to vastly different policy implications. Proper conception and measurement of each is therefore important. Second, the full implications of unemployment and the importance of divergence in wage rates and marginal productivities among different jobs and between the agricultural and the nonagricultural sector cannot be studied in a partial equilibrium context. This provides the motivation for our general equilibrium approach in Chapters 15 and 21. Third, the existence of underemployed resources (of labor, capital, or land) and the state of economic dualism cannot be properly understood in terms of the equilibrating processes of the classical or neoclassical type. Fourth, differential rates of unemployment and differential wage rates imply movements of people between sectors, that is, migration. Who migrates? If it is mainly the marginal workers and those who are openly unemployed (as would be predicted by the human capital model), there might be no reason for a separate chapter on migration. Or if there were need for special emphasis, a migration

---

[18]The results become more clear-cut in favor of the marginal productivity hypothesis when he takes first differences in order to eliminate the trend. Similarly, the fit for H_1 is better than for H_2 when the two hypotheses are formulated in terms of shares:

$$H_1 : \frac{P_{Lt}}{\left(\dfrac{Y}{L}\right)_t} = 1; \quad H_2 : \frac{P_{Lt}}{P_t} = 1$$

chapter would be appropriately placed in Part III, Development Dynamics. However, if it should be the better qualified "discouraged workers" who migrate, migration is not an equilibrating mechanism of the neoclassical human capital type but rather a process that perpetuates dualism and therefore disequi-librium. Since in this chapter we have found reason to believe that it is the inframarginal, better qualified members of the hidden un-employed who migrate, our chapter on migra-tion (which follows) is included among other subjects of disequilibrium in Part IV.

Part IV

Development Disequilibrium: Sectoral Articulation and Structure

We adhere to the view that development is a process of successive disequilibria. Yet economics does not possess a formal theory of disequilibrium. What we have, instead, are bits and pieces of a theory, individual building blocks on which an integrated development theory may eventually be founded. Parts IV, V, and VI, therefore, can be viewed as timid excursions into the economics of disequilibrium.

Several aspects of development characterize the process as one of disequilibrium. Development is not always a uniform and smooth process of marginal adjustments. More often it appears to be punctuated by some watershed effects. The selection of a growth path at any one time forecloses alternative choices that might have become available at a later stage of development. Change does not necessarily trigger autonomous control mechanisms. Rather than being gradual and nondisruptive, it often involves jolts and shocks. Trickling-down mechanisms and spread effects do not always work, and the backwash effects often dominate. Instead of gradualism, a certain amount of leap-frogging may be necessary if development is to be attained and sustained. Development involves changes not only in magnitude of the different variables but also in the structure of relationships among them. This introduces a qualitative difference between the requisites for understanding both stationary underdevelopment and the more complex process of sustained growth. The more complex process cannot always be explained solely on the basis of the less complex situation. All these are aspects of development disequilibrium with which we will deal in the remainder of the book.

Migration is the first topic to be studied within the framework of development disequilibrium. While according to the essentially neoclassical human capital model one would expect the differential rates of return that initially induce people to move from job to job and place to place to eventually be eliminated as a result of migration itself, experience has shown the converse. Substantial migration flows, for example, from the rural to urban areas, have persisted and sometimes accelerated despite growing unemployment in urban areas. Moreover, these flows have been incapable of decreasing, let alone of eliminating, rural-urban income differentials. Perhaps the roots of an adequate interpretation and explanation of this paradoxical behavior were anticipated in Chapter 12, where we suggested that the migrants, by and large, do not come from the set of the open unemployed but from the hidden unemployed—especially the "discouraged workers," who commonly have above-average qualifications and aspirations. In keeping with that suggestion, we shall introduce two models, the sequential job-search-under-uncertainty model and the job-competition model, that allow for the possibility that wage differentials increase and the distribution of income becomes more unequal despite significant migration rates and increasing levels of urban unemployment. It is in this sense that migration is a phenomenon of development disequilibrium.

Chapter 14 is devoted to dualism and income distribution. While the existence of dualism has posed certain problems for neoclassical statics analysis, as pointed out in Parts II and III, according to the elegant applications of neoclassical dynamics to development, the monster has been living (and prospering) on borrowed time! According to the scripts of neoclassical dynamics, the ending is always happy: dualism disappears and the "break-out" point of development occurs simultaneously. Yet in fact, as development has been taking place, dualism has often become more widespread.

Following from the neoclassical belief in a world of harmonies of interest and autonomous control mechanisms, it has generally been assumed that high growth rates of GNP would eventually be bound to filter down to the masses in terms of higher incomes and standards of living. And as an insurance that this would happen, Keynesian economics suggested that part of the increase in goods and services could always be taxed away to combat poverty. For these reasons, income distribution has been largely ignored in the economics of development, at least until very recently. Yet, despite respectable rates of growth, incomes within LDCs may have become more unequally distributed over time. It is in this sense that dualism and inequality of income distribution properly belong to the study of development disequilibrium.

Chapter 15 is devoted to the interactions between agriculture and nonagriculture. How the relations between the two sectors change in the process of development is part of the study of development structure. How the growth is transmitted from one sector to the other becomes an important part of the leap-frogging strategies. We shall demonstrate how changes in parameter values—such as changes in population, terms of trade, import policies, or the endowments of the fixed factors of production—which are ruled out in partial equilibrium economics and even in neoclassical dynamics, can be incorporated in a general equilibrium model linking the agricultural sector with the urban-industrial sector.

The way the structure of an economy changes in the process of development is studied in Chapter 16. Following up Chapter 15, on the interactions between agriculture and nonagriculture, we focus specifically on structural indicators that refer to sectoral patterns of change in the process of development. A long string of studies investigating the sectoral composition of output in the process of development has led to defining "normal" patterns of growth and identifying the factors that cause deviations from the normal pattern. Before one formulates policy prescriptions relating to sectoral patterns of growth, the effects of deviations from normal patterns must be investigated. We formulate hypotheses pertaining to these effects, which culminate in some strategies of leap-frogging to higher growth rates, such as those of balanced and unbalanced growth and of linkages.

Our analysis in Part IV will certainly fall short of supplying a formal theory of disequilibrium. In some respects, our analysis is still static; in other respects, it is largely equilibrium analysis, in the sense that we do not always explicitly account for the mechanisms by which resources in excess demand are rationed or resources in excess supply are disposed. Nevertheless, we explicitly recognize these disequilibria, and we incorporate them in our formulation of specific hypotheses.

Chapter 13
Migration

In preceding chapters, we have sporadically noted instances in which development resembles more a systematic process of successive disequilibria—with queues, surpluses, intersectoral disparities, and so on—than the workings of equilibrating mechanisms. Few, if any, of these disequilibria are more striking or more pervasive than the differences in wage rates between the traditional (rural) and modern (urban) sectors.

Chapter 11 presented the human capital model. Given the higher wages and incomes of urban areas relative to rural areas, the human capital model would predict labor flows, or migration, from rural to urban areas in LDCs. Chapter 12 presented a utility-maximizing version of the labor surplus model capable of specifying conditions under which agricultural labor surplus could exist and could be transferred to the urban sector at negligible cost—as in the classical model of Lewis and the neoclassical model of Ranis-Fei. We

showed there that the consequences of the labor transfer depend largely on who the migrants are and what their marginal products in agriculture had been. These are basically questions of the microeconomics of migration.

In this chapter, we will combine elements of the micro- and the macroeconomics of migration in order to address some broader questions: How significant and how persistent is rural-urban migration? What are its causes? What are the mechanisms that migration activates? What are its effects? Our presentation will develop as follows:

First, we present the "facts" of migration, which demonstrate that rural-urban movements have been taking place on a rather massive scale. Furthermore, migration has been accelerating without reducing wage differentials between the sectors. We also make reference to some studies on who the migrants are.

Next, we develop a series of alternative

models that purport to explain this migration. In each case, we give serious consideration to the implications of the model and identify those facts of migration the model can and cannot explain.

We begin with the human capital model developed in Chapter 11. This model is adequate for explaining both the direction of migration and, to a certain extent, who it is that migrates. The logical conclusion is that the wage differentials that triggered migration will gradually decrease and eventually disappear, with migration petering out. This is at variance with the observed facts.

The probability-of-employment model that we present next admits of the possibility that significant rates of migration may persist despite growing urban unemployment, but this possibility is introduced in the model almost by hindsight. It is attributed to basic imperfections in the labor market or to "urban solutions" to the unemployment problem, which maintain or even increase the wage differentials.

At this point, we return to the question of who the migrants are. Are they the marginal agricultural workers who leave the farms because they have small opportunity cost, and who thus increase the marginal product (and per capita income) in agriculture and decrease that in nonagriculture, setting off a process that restores equilibrium? Or are they, instead, people previously employed with high opportunity cost who by departing contribute to a further decrease in agricultural income and an increase in the urban per capita product? If the latter is the case, migration might be a disequilibrating factor. This aspect is studied within a model of sequential job search under uncertainty from the supply side of migration. It is approached with a job-competition model from the demand side of labor. These alternative interpretations of the labor market tend to emphasize more the backwash rather than the trickling-down effects of migration. They suggest the conclusion that dualism and income inequality, which are the subject of Chapter 14, may be far more immutable characteristics of countries in the development process than had generally been assumed.

The chapter is concluded with a short appendix, calling attention to some of the pitfalls in empirical application of even the simplest models of migration.

The Facts of Migration

Data on migration are usually obtained by comparing estimates of population by region (and better by age, sex, and other characteristics) for different time periods. Such differences combine the influence of different birthrates, death rates, and migration patterns. Birthrates are usually higher in rural areas than in urban areas. Therefore, even after accounting for the fact that death rates are lower in urban areas than in rural areas, in the absence of migration one would expect to find rural populations growing faster than urban populations and urban populations growing at a rate well below the physiological maximum rate, which is generally considered to be between 3.5 and 5.0 percent per annum (U.N.: Department of Economic and Social Affairs, 1969).

Table 13.1 presents some estimates of total, rural, and urban rates of population growth for various regions of the less developed world between 1950 and 1960. The evidence suggests that population growth in urban areas generally exceeds the physiological maximum and is from one-and-one-half to almost six times as great as that in the rural areas. When one compares the population of cities over 100,000 with that of towns or of rural areas, the divergence in the rates of growth is even more impressive. More recent data reported by Todaro (1971) suggest even more dramatic rates of growth in urban population for Africa, with estimates ranging from 4 to 12 percent per year for smaller cities and large towns and up to 14 percent per year for cities over 100,000. Such high rates of urban population growth could obviously not be achieved except by virtue of a massive exodus from rural areas. Indeed, this has been the case.

To put these estimates in perspective, in Table 13.2 we present estimates of the growth rates of urban, rural, and total population in different regions and time periods, beginning with the 1920s. This table reveals that rural-urban migration must be considerably larger in LDCs than in DCs, even though population growth is also considerably higher in the former than in the latter. The table also reveals that the massive rural-urban migration that has been taking place at least since 1920, has been accelerating rather than abating.

Comparative data on wage rates in the

Table 13.1 *Per Annum Population Growth Rates, 1950–1960, for World Regions, Less Developed Countries*

Region	Growth Rates					Ratio		City Population as Percent of Total Population[c] (8)
	Total (1)	Rural (2)	Urban (3)	Town[a] (4)	City[b] (5)	Urban/ Rural (Columns 3 ÷ 2) (6)	City/ Town (Columns 5 ÷ 4) (7)	
Northern Africa	2.4	1.7	4.3	3.9	4.6	2.5	1.2	21.0
Western Africa	3.4	2.9	6.9	5.8	9.4	2.4	1.6	7.4
Eastern Africa	2.5	2.2	5.5	3.6	10.0	2.5	2.8	4.9
Middle and Southern Africa[d]	1.8	1.3	7.7	5.7	12.0	5.9	2.1	6.0
Middle America	3.1	1.8	4.8	4.4	5.5	2.7	1.2	20.0
Caribbean	2.2	1.7	3.1	2.3	4.2	1.8	1.8	20.7
Tropical South America	3.1	1.6	5.4	3.9	6.9	3.4	1.8	32.1
East Asia	1.8	1.1	6.0	6.1	5.9	5.4	1.0	16.1
Southeast Asia	2.5	2.1	4.6	3.2	5.7	2.2	1.8	12.1
Southwest Asia	2.7	1.9	4.7	3.2	6.5	2.5	2.0	21.8
South Central Asia	1.9	1.8	2.7	1.8	3.5	1.5	1.9	9.8
Oceania	2.7	2.6	4.8	4.8	0.0	1.8	0.0	0.0

Notes:
[a]Less than 100,000.
[b]More than 100,000.
[c]Estimated for 1970.
[d]Excludes Union of South Africa.
Source: Browning, H. L. (1971), "Migrant Selectivity and the Growth of Large Cities in Developing Societies," in National Academy of Sciences, *Rapid Population Growth*, Vol. 2 (Research Papers). Baltimore: Johns Hopkins Press, p. 276.

various sectors are subject to grave measurement problems. The limited comparability of wage rates earned in different sectors under different conditions makes it unwise to present a specific set of estimates for fear that the numbers might be taken too literally. How-

Table 13.2 *Estimates of Average Annual Growth Rates of Total, Urban, and Rural Population In Various Areas, 1920–1960 (Percent)*

Item	Area	Period			
		1920–1930	1930–1940	1940–1950	1950–1960
Total Population	World	1.1	1.1	0.9	1.7
	Developed Regions	1.2	0.8	0.4	1.3
	Less Developed Regions	1.0	1.2	1.2	2.0
Urban Population[a]	World	2.4	2.5	2.1	3.6
	Developed Regions	2.3	2.1	1.2	2.7
	Less Developed Regions	2.9	3.4	4.1	5.1
Rural Population[b]	World	0.8	0.7	0.6	1.2
	Developed Regions	0.7	0.1	0.0	0.2
	Less Developed Regions	0.9	1.0	0.9	1.5

Notes:
[a]Living in cities or towns of more than 20,000.
[b]Living in communities of less than 20,000.
Source: U.N.: Department of Economic and Social Affairs (1969), *Growth of the World's Urban and Rural Population, 1920–2000.* New York, ST/SOA/Series A/44, Table 11, p. 27.

ever, the general conclusion from the available evidence is that urban-rural wage differentials are large (Singh 1970), especially in terms of sectoral per capita incomes, rather constant over time in relative terms, and slightly increasing over time in absolute terms (Ohkawa and Rosovsky 1968; Griffin 1969; Turner and Jackson 1970; Horowitz 1974). What is perhaps even more remarkable is that the stability or even widening of the wage gap is taking place at the same time that measured (open) unemployment rates are rising dramatically (as Table 12.3 showed).[1]

The final important "fact" of rural-urban migration is the selectivity among individuals in the decision to migrate. Rather than being the marginal and less employable members of the rural labor force, the migrants (as was predicted from our utility-maximization labor surplus model in Chapter 12) turn out to be younger, better educated, and more highly skilled than nonmigrants in the rural sector and often above average even with respect to the urban sector.[2]

Economic Models of Migration

A Simple Human Capital Model of Migration
In Chapter 11, we expressed investment in the human agent in terms of the capitalized lifetime earnings of an individual, net of costs. The decision rule for capital accumulation consists of comparing the capitalized alternative earnings streams of two activities, migration and nonmigration in the present case, given the parameter values for the rate of interest and for the duration of each activity. We can thus reformulate the general human capital model for the case of migration for

the discrete time period case as

$$\sum_{t=0}^{n} \frac{W(t)}{(1+r)^t} - C(0) - \sum_{t=0}^{n} \frac{R(t)}{(1+r)^t} > 0 \quad (1)$$

where W is the expected annual wage rate in the urban sector, R is the annual income from rural employment, C is the cost of migration, n is the number of years the individual expects to work in the rural or urban sector, and r is the relevant rate of interest. The costs of migration, not unlike the costs of education, examined previously, include two components: the direct costs, such as the cost of transportation and of the move in general, and the indirect opportunity costs, such as the income forgone during the period of the move, job search, and relocation.

For the continuous time case, the model is written

$$V_U(0) = \int_{t=0}^{n} W(t)e^{-rt}\,dt - C(0) \quad (2)$$

$$V_R(0) = \int_{t=0}^{n} R(t)e^{-rt}\,dt \quad (3)$$

where V_U and V_R are discounted present values, and the other symbols are defined as above. The urban wage rate and the rural income are now functions of time. We can write the urban-rural differential

$$\alpha = V_U(0) - V_R(0) \quad (4)$$

The α now becomes a function of the expected alternative income streams, W and R, the costs of migration, C, the period of work expected, n, and the rate of interest that becomes applicable in each case, r.

The interpretation of this simple model is that migration is determined by α, the capitalized value of the differential of the net urban-rural earnings streams. It is a rather parsimonious approach to migration, which nevertheless adequately explains a wide range of observations.

Empirical Implications of the Simple Model
This simple migration model is rich in empirical implications that have been borne out by a number of studies, such as Sjaastad (1962) and Bowles (1970) for the United States, Sahota (1968a) for Brazil, Herrick (1965) for Chile, and T. P. Schultz (1971) for Colombia. The model is indeed successful in explaining the "facts" of migration in a number of respects.

[1]There are several possible explanations for the higher wage in the urban sectors. To some extent, the higher wage may compensate for a higher cost of living, but this certainly does not account for all of the difference. It may partly result from the understandable attempt of urban employers to retain greater numbers of their employees, thereby averting the losses of the learning-by-doing benefits in the urban sector that high turnover rates would entail (Stiglitz 1974). To some extent, the higher wages may reflect greater skill requirements, but again, substantial differentials are apparent for any given skill group. At least part of the higher wage in the urban sector may result from monopoly power, economies of scale, agglomeration economies, labor union organization, and minimum wage legislation, all of which generally apply to a greater degree in the urban sector.
[2]See Myrdal (1957), R. B. Hughes (1961), Herrick (1965), Taeuber and Taeuber (1965), Lansing and Mueller (1967), Wertheimer (1970), Long (1962).

First, it explains the direction and the stages of migration. On account of urban-rural wage differentials, it correctly predicts that migration takes place from low-income rural regions to higher-income urban regions. Because of direct costs of migration, which undoubtedly vary with distance and the psychic costs of adjusting to unfamiliar environments, the human capital model successfully predicts that migration is likely to be accomplished by a series of intermediate moves—from farm to village, from village to town, from town to city. This stage approach to migration was formulated into one of the "laws of migration" by Ravenstein (1889) and has been substantiated in the LDC context by Herrick (1965) and others.

Second, the human capital model does a fairly good job in explaining who migrates, that is, the microeconomics of migration. For example, it correctly predicts that:

1. Younger people migrate. The pure effect of age is represented by n in equation 1, which is greater for the young, since they can expect a longer life horizon over which they can capitalize their earnings differentials. This pure age effect is strengthened by other age correlative influences (David 1973, p. 56): young people are poorer, which makes the R in the place of origin smaller; they have less place attachment and less seniority rights invested in a job, which makes the C (monetary and psychic) lower; they are also less risk averse, which can be reflected in assigning lower discount rates, r, to their future earnings streams.

2. Migrants are disproportionately single, because C is lower when there are no other family members or personal possessions to be moved.

3. Migrants to large cities have higher educational attainment than the populations from which they originate. This can be explained by the fact that the "cross-rate" of return to a joint decision to invest in education and migration is higher than the ordinary rate of return to either investment alone. (Evidence in support of this was presented in Table 11.2.) Interestingly enough, this implication of the human capital model and this fact of migration flies in the face of the view of the labor surplus theories of neoclassical dynamics that it is the amorphous mass of the unemployed or underemployed who leave the farms to become the marginal workers in the cities. However, this implication of the human capital model would seem to suggest that, since the marginal product of the educated migrants is above the average, both in the place of origin and at the destination, migration will lead to decreasing the average income in the rural areas and increasing it in the urban sector. But this would seem to be inconsistent with the neoclassical partial equilibrium character of the human capital model.

4. A substantial majority of migrants to large cities in developing areas have relatives or friends already living there (Browning 1971, p. 298). This correct description may be derived from the human capital model, because migrants with friends and relatives in the cities are able to lower C in both pecuniary and psychic terms.

While the simple human capital model of migration has enjoyed overwhelming success in explaining these observations in the real world, it fails to explain why migration could persist in spite of rising unemployment rates in urban areas.

The Probability-of-Employment Model

Todaro (1969) has suggested a simple modification of the migration model by making the urban-rural differential, α, both a determinant of the labor supply to the urban sector and a function of the pool of urban unemployment. This model has both realism and important empirical implications.[3]

The emphasis in this model is on the indirect costs of migration, especially the urban wage forgone while the worker is seeking an urban job. This becomes especially important in situations of overcrowding of urban occupations and severe unemployment. The process of labor transfer is not a one-step phenomenon, in which the worker migrates from a low-productivity rural job to a higher-wage urban job. Instead, another stage intervenes between the beginning and the end of the process. In this stage, the unskilled rural worker who migrates to the city spends his time eking out a parasitic existence in the no-man's land between marginal employment and

[3]For further exposition of the same model, see also Harris and Todaro (1970) and Zarembka (1972, Chapter 3).

open unemployment—he becomes yet another boot-black in the streets of Bombay, a *betjek* driver in Djakarta, or a self-appointed parking attendant and car dustman in Manila. There is little difference between open unemployment and this type of disguised unemployment. This period should certainly be considered for appropriately discounting the measured urban-rural differential.

Suppose the urban-rural differential, net of migration costs, is 100. If the probability of finding urban employment is only one-half, the real differential reduces to 50. This adjusted differential, α, can be written

$$\alpha = \pi W - R \tag{5}$$

where W and R are the urban and the rural wage rate respectively, both net of out-of-pocket migration costs, and π is the probability of obtaining a job in the urban sector in any one period.

The chance that a worker will find a job is related to the size of the existing pool of the unemployed and the rate of employment creation. We define

$$\pi = \frac{\gamma N}{S - N} \tag{6}$$

where N is urban employment, S is the size of the total urban labor force, and γ is the net rate of new urban job creation. By substitution, we redefine the rural-urban differential

$$\alpha = \frac{W \gamma N}{S - N} - R \tag{7}$$

An economic theory of migration, as already suggested, makes the supply of migrant labor to the urban sector, S, a function of the rural-urban differential

$$S = f_s(\alpha); \quad \frac{\partial S}{\partial \alpha} > 0 \tag{8}$$

On the demand side, the rate of urban job creation can be expressed as a function of the wage rate and a parameter, k, where k is the difference between the rate of industrial output growth and the rate of industrial labor productivity growth. In symbols

$$\gamma = f_d(W; k); \quad \frac{\partial \gamma}{\partial W} < 0; \quad \frac{\partial \gamma}{\partial k} > 0 \tag{9}$$

We can now determine the increase in the urban labor supply resulting from an increase in the labor demand conditions as represented

by k, that is, the increase in industrial output net of labor productivity changes (ignoring the role of W for the moment):

$$\frac{\partial S}{\partial k} = \frac{\partial S}{\partial \alpha} \frac{\partial \alpha}{\partial \gamma} \frac{\partial \gamma}{\partial k} \tag{10}$$

Differentiating equation 7 and substituting into equation 10, we have

$$\frac{\partial S}{\partial k} = \frac{\partial S}{\partial \alpha} W \frac{N}{S - N} \frac{\partial \gamma}{\partial k} \tag{11}$$

Urban unemployment increases if the increase in urban labor supply exceeds the increase in the jobs created, that is, if

$$\frac{\partial S}{\partial k} > \frac{\partial (\gamma N)}{\partial k} \quad \text{or} \quad \frac{\partial S}{\partial k} > \frac{N \partial \gamma}{\partial k} \tag{12}$$

By substituting from equation 11 into equation 12, we obtain

$$\frac{\partial S}{\partial \alpha} W > S - N \tag{13}$$

Multiplying by α/S, we can express the conditions of increasing urban unemployment in terms of the elasticity of labor supply with respect to the urban-rural differential

$$\frac{\frac{\partial S}{S}}{\frac{\partial \alpha}{\alpha}} > \frac{\alpha}{W} \frac{(S - N)}{S} \tag{14}$$

Finally, from equation 5 we can express the wage differential, α, explicitly in terms of the probability of finding a job, and we write

$$\frac{\frac{\partial S}{S}}{\frac{\partial \alpha}{\alpha}} > (\pi W - R) \frac{1}{W} \frac{(S - N)}{S} \tag{15}$$

The elasticity $(\partial S/S)/(\partial \alpha/\alpha)$ can be viewed as the "migration response function," that is, the elasticity of rural labor supply to the urban sector with respect to the urban-rural wage differential, properly discounted by the probability of finding a job. Inequality 15 relates the migration response function to the size of the urban-rural differential and a proportionality factor that involves the urban wage rate and the urban unemployment rate expressed relative to the urban labor force. As long as the "migration response function" exceeds the urban-rural differential, weighted as above, urban unemployment will continue to rise.

Since the "migration response function" is positive *ex hypothesi*, the probability of finding a job becomes crucial, for it determines not only the size but also the sign of the discounted urban-rural differential. Consider, for example, the case that $\pi = 0.50$, $W = 100$, and $R = 60$. The probability-weighted differential becomes -10. We know immediately that the rate of migration, $\partial S/S$, will decrease. Whether or not this will provide sufficient disincentive to eliminate unemployment from the urban sector will depend on the rate at which jobs are being created, γ in equation 6, as well as on the existing size of the pool of the unemployed, $S - N$. Equivalent to a decrease in π is a decrease in the money urban-rural differentials, either through wage restraint in the urban sector or through rapid growth of the demand for labor in the agricultural sector, and thus an increase in R. The combination of these two forces, besides decreasing $\partial S/S$, is also likely to lead to a more rapid exhaustion of the pool of urban unemployed, $S - N$, through the wage effect on the rate of urban job creation in equation 9.

Applications of the Probability-of-Employment Model

This model is obviously capable of explaining how wage differentials can persist despite high and perhaps rising unemployment. For instance, one can explain with it how purely "urban solutions" to the urban unemployment problems have tended to increase the pool of the urban unemployed, whereas "rural solutions" might help (Todaro 1971).

Two sets of policies, fairly familiar in developing countries, tend to increase the pool of urban unemployed. Policies that operate on urban labor demand and increase the urban employment are likely, *ceteris paribus*, to increase the rate of rural-urban migration by increasing the probability of finding a job. The pool of urban unemployed is certain to increase if the increase in the rate of migration exceeds the increase in the rate of urban employment creation.[4] Policies that tend to

increase urban wages at rates faster than the rural wages operate on the supply side and also tend to increase the pool of the urban unemployed.

An indirect increase in the real urban wage rate over the rural wage rate results from the operation of welfare policies in the urban sector. Governments, under the pressure of labor unions and political organization, have often engaged in subsidizing urban low-cost housing projects and in offering unemployment compensation and other welfare benefits to the workers of the urban sector. Such measures increase urban real incomes and exacerbate the rural-urban income gap. They tend, therefore, to increase migration and urban unemployment. An alternative policy is to devote these funds to bring "the city lights to the villages" by providing amenities, such as electricity, decent housing, water supply systems, and movie theaters. Such measures can be combined with increasing rural incomes directly through resettlement, extension services, training schemes, and rural-based industries. By decreasing the urban-rural differential, such policies will decrease migration, decrease urban unemployment, and decrease income inequalities.

Wage subsidies decrease the price of labor to the employer, that is, they distort the factor-price relationships opposite to the way in which the (usual) policies that decrease the price of capital do. As long as there is a negative elasticity in the demand for labor,[5] wage subsidies increase the rate of urban job creation (equation 9). This increases the probability of getting a job, and depending on the additional employment created, urban unemployment may increase (equation 15). Todaro (1971) suggests that wage subsidies may have to be coupled with a general policy of wage restraint to decrease the urban-rural differential. In a similar vein, Bhagwati and Srinivasan (1974) argue that wage subsidies in the urban sector should be accompanied by production subsidies in the rural sector.

As a means of restricting migration, Todaro (1971) and Gugler (1969) have suggested the use of government-run urban labor

---

[4]An example of such a policy is the Tripartite Agreement of the government of Kenya in 1964 (Todaro 1971, pp. 398–400). Under the agreement, the two parties demanding labor, the government and the employers, agreed to increase their employment by a rate of 15 percent and 10 percent respectively for the years 1964 and 1965. The suppliers of labor, the unions, for their part agreed to hold the line on all wage demands. There is some evidence that the agree-

ment failed—and incontrovertible evidence that it failed to decrease the pool of the urban unemployed. This is because of the increase in the probability of finding a job in terms of the migration model.

[5]Harris and Todaro (1969, p. 36) found a wage elasticity of demand for labor of -0.76 for Kenya.

exchanges. All employment openings are channeled through the labor exchanges and allocated among the potential migrants, who are registered by lot. The probability of finding a job thus becomes one for those selected and zero for all others. By eliminating uncertainty, this procedure increases the expected urban-rural differential and thus increases the value of the migration response function. Since, however, the potential migrants would not leave the farms without having been allocated a job, the result would be to inflate the labor exchange rolls rather than the ranks of urban unemployed.[6]

The shadow price of rural labor to the urban sector is conventionally expressed as the agricultural marginal product of the rural worker who migrates to the city to secure the additional urban job. As will be pointed out in Chapter 20, some modification may also be made for any additional consumption that derives from employment in the urban sector. Depending on the value of the migration response parameter, this shadow price (even so modified for consumption) might be an underestimate. If more than one worker migrates for each additional urban job created, the opportunity cost should also account for the marginal product of all those new migrants.

These policy implications are interesting and potentially of great importance. The probability-of-employment model may thus be extremely valuable in pointing to more appropriate policies with respect to the unemployment problems reviewed in Chapter 12. Nevertheless, the model has a major failing with respect to explaining one of the important "facts" of migration: the persistence and even increasing size of the urban-rural wage differential.

Migration and Dualism: Alternative Interpretations

As noted in Chapter 12, a number of "dual economy models" build on the initial disequilibrium between agriculture and nonagriculture and describe how equilibrium is being restored, primarily through labor transfers.[7]

A particular view of how the labor market works underlies this analysis. It is based on assuming that it is the marginal workers who are transferred, that is, who migrate.

Agriculture is assumed to employ large numbers of low-wage workers and nonagriculture small numbers of higher-wage workers. The marginal workers transfer out of agriculture, thus increasing wages and per capita incomes in the low-wage sector. At the same time, they increase the supply of labor to the high-wage sector, decreasing wages and per capita incomes there. Through the operation of the leveling force of migration, the dualistic features of the economy atrophy and agriculture becomes appended to nonagriculture in terms of rates of growth and development potential. This marks the end of the dual economy.

This particular view of the labor market is not congruent with a world where wage differentials are maintained, or even increase, in the face of substantial rates of migration and unemployment. Some recent research attempts to increase the realism of the labor market models. We will use these models as a point of departure to suggest that dualism might well be an immutable phenomenon in the world.

The probability-of-employment model, described in the previous section, implied an extremely simple theory of search. The migrant, as it were, pays a fixed fee, the cost of migration, to join the pool of the urban unemployed. From there, he continuously samples the job market, in which there is a certain distribution of wage offers from different potential employers that vary only slightly. The worker pays the variable costs of migration, forgone income, as long as he is unsuccessful in drawing a job.

Sequential Job Search under Uncertainty
Stigler (1962) described a more realistic search procedure. There are alternative labor markets that the migrant searches, and he collects a number of job offers which are, quite realistically, not uniform. When his sample reaches an optimum fixed size, he compares his varying offers and retrieves the best. Depending on the sectoral market in which the worker

---

[6]Inflation of the labor exchange rolls and thus decrease of the probability of an entrant to be selected can be circumvented by a rule such that no name will be allowed to remain in the pool for over a year.

[7]For examples of models of dualistic development, see W. A. Lewis (1954), Ranis and Fei (1961), Fei and Ranis (1964), Jorgenson (1961, 1967, 1969), Paauw and Fei (1973), Kelley, Williamson, and Cheetham (1972). For a review of the surplus labor literature, see Kao, Anschel and Eicher (1964).

obtains his job, he may by his employment increase or decrease the urban wage rate. Alchian (1970) and Phelps et al. (1970) have extended Stigler's analysis by making explicit the assumption that it is more efficient to search when unemployed, and by bringing in the notion of subjective expectations. The individual rationally chooses unemployment, which allows him to search more efficiently for a higher paying job as long as his subjectively determined expected wage is greater than the highest wage offer he has sampled. The longer he searches without finding a wage offer that equals his expected wage, the more likely he is to adjust his expected wage downward. This interpretation is actually consistent with our description in Chapter 12 of hidden unemployment and the discouraged worker. People move from hidden unemployment to open unemployment and finally to employment by revising their job expectations.

David (1973) presented an imaginative and elegant migration model that utilizes this view of job search and unemployment, with some further innovations. David's model is known as the model of sequential job search under uncertainty. The model is replete with policy implications that arise from consistent interpretations of observable phenomena. Of particular interest here is the use of this model in explaining a certain kind of migrant selectivity that may well cancel the trickling-down effects predicted by the conventional approach to the subject.

David describes a market in which it is not necessarily the unemployed who migrate. It may equally well be the workers who already hold a job and quit in search of another —a proposition for which there is considerable empirical support. Migration then involves three stages: (1) unemployment and the move; (2) random job search at destination; and (3) acceptance of a job of permanent tenure. In taking these steps, the migrant has to make two decisions associated with the costs of migration. First, he must select the market in which he will search. Each job market, say each city, has its own probability distribution of jobs (i.e., wage rates), and the relative variance of this distribution tends to be greater in the larger labor markets. The costs of migration at this stage are fixed— the cost of quitting one's job and moving to a labor market—and resemble a fixed entry fee for the search.

As in the conventional human capital model, part of the cost of migration is composed of the direct and opportunity costs of the move. Since, as in the Alchian and Phelps models, job search is more efficient while the worker is unemployed, part of the variable cost of migration is also the wages forgone while searching for a job. Unlike the Stigler fixed-sample-size search model, job offers are depreciating and obsolescing. The worker cannot accumulate a number of offers and then retrieve the best among them. Instead, he has the option: "Take it or leave it. You can start this afternoon!" Another part of the variable cost of migration, then, is the forgone wage of an offer that was turned down in favor of the expectation that a better offer would be received. The second decision the migrant has to make, then, is about a specified number of offers he will examine sequentially while maintaining the option to end the search any time he comes upon an offer which leads him to believe that the marginal expected gain from continuing the search is less than the marginal search costs (including turning down the present offer).

The migrant's statistical problem, as formulated by David, is that of choosing both the frequency distribution of the population he is going to sample and the optimum sample size. The aspect on which we wish to concentrate now, however, is straightforward. One can predict that labor will generally be drawn into job markets where the higher relative dispersion of offers prevails—perhaps the large city, or the self-employed occupations. This may or may not induce a change in the distribution of the job offers in that market. More importantly, job vacancy rates can even become negative, without strong pressure to make the offer distribution more compact or to skew it in a fashion that discourages migration. There is no a priori reason why one should associate the process of migration with equilibration and narrowing of the wage structure.

Job Competition

An alternative approach, which also emphasizes the backwash rather than the trickling-down effects of migration, is the job-competition model of Thurow (1969) and Thurow and Lucas (1972). It starts by challenging the wage-competition model of the neoclassical paradigm. Wage competition is viewed as the powerful mechanism of bringing into equilibrium the short-run supplies and demands of different kinds of labor and of inducing long-run adjustments, such as equalizing within-group wage differentials and setting the appropriate (in terms of productivity) wage differentials among groups. While one may debate the appropriate length of the run and the appropriate size of between-group differentials, the evidence presented in Chapter 12 suggests that the equilibrating process between agriculture and nonagriculture has not worked. And the casual evidence involved in this chapter suggests that wage differentials between the two sectors have been maintained or even increased in the face of both massive rural-urban migration and a growing pool of the unemployed in the urban sector. The automatic mechanism of wage competition needs rethinking if analysis is to become congruent with the observed world.

While in the wage-competition model individuals compete against each other on the basis of wages, in Thurow's job-competition model individuals compete for jobs according to their background characteristics. The unorthodox element in the theory is the concept of the job and the mode of competition.

It is not the marginal productivity of the worker that determines the wage rate the job carries. Instead, it is the marginal productivity of the job that will determine the wage rate to which a worker will be fitted. Wages are paid on the basis of the characteristics of a job. One characteristic of a job, for example, is the amount of capital it employs. Nonmarginal increases in the quantity of capital will increase the productivity of a job. As a result, workers who are hired for a capital-intensive job will be brought up to a higher wage rate, to match the productivity of that job, than workers who are hired for a noncapital-intensive job.

How are workers hired to fill a certain job? And why does competition in the labor market not bring wages of high-paying jobs into equality with wages of low-paying jobs? Workers come into the labor market with a set of background characteristics that determine each individual's relative position in the labor queue. Workers are distributed across job opportunities on the basis of their relative position in the labor queue. Position in the labor queue determines each worker's

probability of finding a job, conditional on the job opportunities for which he competes. The employers, in other words, start filling job vacancies from the top of the queue, with the best jobs going to the workers with the best set of background characteristics.

In the job-competition model, workers do not come to the labor market endowed with labor skills that allow them to enter directly in the production process. Most cognitive skills—knowledge of where to report for work, how to use the tools, how the specific work establishment functions—are acquired through formal or informal on-the-job training. Employers use the background characteristics—previous experience, education, sex, age, intelligence tests—as proxies to judge the trainability of the worker. By hiring workers with the best set of background characteristics, the employer minimizes his training costs. And the lower the training costs, the more skill characteristics, general or specific to the job, the employer will be able to generate with the given worker. Since the marginal product of capital depends on the quantity and quality of labor with which it is employed, employers will want to generate more job skills than workers will want to buy (by paying, for example, for on-the-job training in terms of accepting lower wages). As a result, employers will undertake on-the-job training even if they have to pay for most of it. And they will also try to minimize the cost of such training.

The pertinent lesson from the job-competition model is that by increasing the supply of job skills through educational investments or, as in the case of the two-sector dualism, through investments in migration from the farms, one cannot expect to decrease wage differentials and equalize the income distribution. The labor market is not primarily a place for determining the wage rate endogenously, by matching demands and supplies of different kinds of skills. Instead, the labor market matches trainable individuals with jobs that have training opportunities, the amount of on-the-job training required to bring a worker up to the marginal productivity of the job being endogenously determined. The job-competition model thus emphasizes the demand side of the market. The demand for job skills creates the supply of job skills, in the sense that the demand for labor determines which skills will be taught. "More potential plumbers will not lower the wages for plumbers since the market is structured in such a manner that individuals cannot learn plumbing skills unless there is a job opening available. Such a job will not exist unless it can generate enough marginal product to pay the current wage." (Thurow and Lucas 1972 p. 26).

Empirical Implications: Does Trickling-Down Work Through Migration?

We have discussed some views of the job market that emphasize the backwash effects of migration rather than the trickling-down effects. Both conceptual models we described, the sequential job search under uncertainty and the job-competition model, allow for the possibility that wage differentials and income inequality increase despite significant migration flows and increasing levels of urban unemployment. The models are somewhat complementary, the former explaining migrant behavior and selectivity and the latter the demand side of the market. Therefore, we use these models jointly to post-cast some of the tendencies that permeated the dual economy in the developing countries in the postwar years. For simplicity, consider two sectors, agriculture and nonagriculture. Agriculture employs unskilled workers. Nonagriculture has a capital-intensive subsector that employs skilled workers and an urban-traditional subsector that employs semiskilled workers.

The development literature and the development policies of the 1950s and 1960s emphasized rapid capital accumulation as the key to economic progress. This was reflected in distorted factor prices that undervalued capital through an arsenal of conscious policy measures: overvalued exchange rates, accelerated capital depreciation allowances, negative effective rates of protection for imported capital goods, tax rebates, and tying foreign aid to the importation of the donor country's capital goods. As a result, the capital intensity of the modern subsector increased,[8] and be-

cause of the complementarity between capital and labor, the marginal productivity of jobs in the capital-intensive subsector also increased. This led to more on-the-job training for the skilled workers of this subsector, bringing them up to the marginal productivity of the job. And it led to higher wage rates in the modern subsector—wage rates countenanced by governments that felt pressure from labor unions and civil servants. The wage differential between this subsector and the other sectors increased. With increasing size of the urban sector, the variation in wage rates—marginal products of different jobs—also increased. As a result, income inequality increased. The rate of rural-urban migration increased, lengthening the queue of employment seekers in the modern subsector and lowering the probability of getting a job. With the variation in wage offers increasing, potential migrants opt for migration and search at least until their expectations of likely wage offers are adjusted downward as a result of failure to get a high-paying job.

Can education of the labor force reverse these trends, decrease wage differentials, and decrease income inequality? Suppose education transforms unskilled workers in agriculture into skilled workers. If the number of skilled jobs does not increase, these new skilled workers would compete with the existing semiskilled workers and replace them in what used to be the best job opportunities for semiskilled workers. Semiskilled workers would therefore filter down to the unskilled occupations (i.e., they would return to the farms), replacing previously unskilled workers from what used to be the best job opportunities. As a result of this filtering-down process, the average wages of skilled, semiskilled, and unskilled workers would decrease, even though the wage differentials between them might increase. The income distribution would change at the two end points. Depending on this change, the entire distribution of income might become better or worse. Consider the case in which education changes semiskilled laborers into skilled laborers. The remaining semiskilled laborers find that they have to compete against more skilled laborers for the best semiskilled jobs. But they also have fewer semiskilled laborers against whom to compete. The average wage of skilled laborers decreases, while the average wage of semi-

---

[8]This factor-price distortion led to capital-intensive technology not only in the modern subsector but also in agriculture, as evidenced by premature tractor mechanization in a number of countries (B. F. Johnston and Cownie 1969). For simplicity, however, we will maintain our assumption that capital-intensive technology applied only to the relevant urban subsector.

skilled laborers increases. Wage differentials between the two groups decrease, but the income distribution among workers does not change.[9]

The way to increase employment in the job-competition model is therefore to increase the demand for skills, rather than the supply of skills. And in a model where skills are acquired through on-the-job training, the demand for skills can be directly increased by decreasing the cost of training to the employer, for example, by wage subsidies (Lefeber 1968). Wage subsidies can also be used to affect the income distribution. Workers with lower training costs who are higher in the employment queue are likely to have higher levels of wealth. The workers who are low in the queueing process have lower background characteristics and thus lower levels of human capital. Wage subsidies can be used to reverse the queueing process by subsidizing the training costs of employers who select high-cost workers who are more likely to be poor.

An empirically important implication of the job-competition model is that the orthodox literature on investment in the human agent mismeasures the returns to education because of a fundamental specification error. Marginal productivity differentials (wage differentials), capitalized, yield the capital stock invested in the human agent (and thus also the rate of return to that stock) only under the assumption that wages reflect the preexisting differences in workers' marginal productivities. This assumption is contrary to the job-competition model, in which wages are determined by a worker's rung in the job ladder and not by marginal productivity. The return to education depends on the pay of the jobs for which education fits one. The wage, in other words, is the independent variable in the economic model, and it is exogenously determined by considerations of status and prestige, in accordance with the value judgments of society.[10] If this is truly the case, "neither marginal or average income gaps between high school and college laborers serve to estimate the gains

from more education either to the individual or to society" (Thurow and Lucas 1972, p. 32). In contrast, the sequential job search under uncertainty model would suggest that government investment in labor market information could narrow differentials in wage rates and thereby lower search unemployment and possibly migration.

The more general question that arises in connection with viewing migration as an equilibrating force is, who are the migrants? The traditional wage-competition model, for example, as utilized in the analysis of surplus labor, implies that the migrants would be the marginal and unemployed workers who migrate in search of employment. As we have pointed out, this tends not to be the case. The swollen literature on the "brain drain" further suggests evidence that migration is a highly selective process that favors the inframarginal individuals.[11] Hirschman (1970, Chapter 4) has drawn the parallel with connoisseur goods and quality deterioration. When general conditions in a neighborhood deteriorate, for example, the residents who will move out first are those who valued most highly such qualities as cleanliness, safety, schools, and "neighborhood character." These residents have many alternatives, and they will seek the lost qualities in other high-priced neighborhoods. It may precisely be that the inframarginal workers—the professionals with high opportunity cost—are the first to leave the traditional sector of a dual economy. Their move, as we have mentioned, tends to increase rather than decrease the income differentials in the two sectors. Hirschman has drawn the analogy one step farther. Remedial mechanisms in a number of situations, such as quality deterioration, require less "exit" and more "voice"—the articulation of customer disaffection by politically powerful, quality-minded consumers. Should that be correct, the migration of precisely those individuals who can exercise "voice" may increase the cleavage between development in the advanced and in the traditional sectors. The more upward the social mobility, and the freer the migration, the more marked the economic and social dualism may become.

In view of the aforementioned sensitivity of policy choice to the particular version of a

[9]This is precisely what happened in the United States, where the distribution of skills, as measured by grade school, high school, and college training, changed dramatically in the postwar years in favor of college (from 20 to 28 percent between 1949 and 1969) and high school (from 38 to 51 percent for the same period) (Thurow and Lucas 1972, p. 34).

[10]For a discussion of the noneconomic factors that determine the wage rate, see Pen (1971).

[11]For a convenient review of that literature, see Myers (1972) and A. Scott (1970).

disequilibrium theory of migration employed, empirical testing of these alternative theories should be undertaken. In any case, rejection of the traditional neoclassical model narrows the choice considerably. Until more definitive results can be obtained, the seemingly greater realism of the job-competition model would seem to suggest that serious consideration should be given by policy makers to policies of investment in rural "turf" as opposed to investments in people that the theory of the "invisible foot" would suggest (Harrison 1974).

Summary and Conclusions

The theme in the chapters of Part III was the individual's responsiveness to price and quantity stimuli. The supply of output with respect to price is upward sloping; the differential between agricultural and industrial wage rates will draw workers off the farms; capital investment, in physical or human capital, will flow according to differential rates of return and increase with income and wealth. The same theme has been pursued in Chapter 13, but with a basic difference. While neoclassical dynamic processes are supposed to lead to equilibrium and to the eventual elimination of the existing differentials, migration flows (even massive ones) have been incapable of decreasing, let alone of eliminating, the existing differentials. Migration is a process that can better be studied as a state of disequilibrium.

The evidence from the major developing regions of the world suggests that a massive exodus of rural population into urban areas has been occurring at least since 1920, and that this exodus has accelerated in recent years. The direction of migration and most of the observed characteristics of the migrants are consistent with the simple neoclassical model of migration as investment in the human agent. However, some disconcerting evi-

dence has remained, which seems quite incongruous with the precepts of the model. First, if migrants move in response to wage differentials, what explains the large and even increasing flows of migration in the face of increasing urban unemployment? Todaro's model introduced a variable for the probability that the migrant obtains employment, thus allowing for the possibility that unemployment may be increasing despite significant migration flows. As a result, the neoclassical trickling-down mechanism is suspended when it comes to decreasing unemployment through migration.

Second, the neoclassical model errs in predicting the decrease and eventual elimination of wage differentials through migration. In the real world, rural-urban income differentials have been increasing. This has been a surprise for economists, although it had long been noticed by sociologists, who described the "positive selectivity" of migration. By and large, it is not the marginal workers who migrate but rather the ones whose marginal products are well above the average, certainly in the place from which they migrate, perhaps also in the place to which they migrate.

David's model of sequential job search under uncertainty allowed for the possibility that income differentials may persist and even increase, substantial migration flows notwithstanding. This model emphasizes the supply of labor in explaining migration. Thurow's unorthodox view of the labor market as a process of job competition, rather than wage competition, puts emphasis on the demand side. In any case, only by viewing migration as a disequilibrium process can economic analysis be made consistent with the facts. The neat trickling-down and spread effects of development, based on harmonies of interest and marginal adjustments, have become impossible to defend and justify.

Appendix

Common Pitfalls
in Empirical Investigations
of Migration

Since in this chapter we have departed from our general pattern of presenting detailed empirical tests, we owe the reader some warnings about common problems that arise in empirical studies of migration.

First, because of data availability and convenience, one is often forced to use net data on migration flows rather than gross flow data. At a minimum, this introduces measurement error, and if reverse migration is affected by factors other than those which affect the dominant migration, it also introduces specification error that is likely to exert an upward bias on estimates of the returns to migration (Hamilton 1965; Vanderkamp 1971, 1972; Eldridge 1965).

Second, the economic and other characteristics used to explain migration are likely to be imperfectly measured (e.g., by one-period wage differentials instead of by differences in present values of alternative income streams) and highly correlated, making it hard to obtain reliable estimates of the effects of each such influence (measurement error and multicollinearity).

Third, decisions to migrate are often made jointly with certain other decisions, such as to invest in health or education or to marry. If so, specification error and estimation biases will be introduced unless these other elements in the decision process are spelled out. The same is true if there are different steps in the migration path—first migration to a town, followed by migration to a city, and so on.

Fourth, there can be simultaneous equation biases of various sorts. Higher incomes, for example, stimulate migration, but migration, especially when the composition of the migrants is biased in favor of persons with higher skills and educational attainment, also increases income differentials (Muth 1971).

Fifth, there may be an aggregation problem, in the sense that more meaningful results could be obtained if one were to distinguish between different types of migration —short term, long term, autonomous (forced) as opposed to induced (chosen)—all of which may have different determinants.

Chapter 14
Income Distribution, Poverty, and Dualism

Economic development has traditionally focused on the gap between the rich and the poor *countries* and on ways the process of growth, especially in poor countries, could be accelerated. Only very recently has the gap between the rich and the poor *people* in DCs or LDCs been noticed. This belated concern with income distribution has presumably been promoted by the realization that, even though development occurs and per capita incomes grow, the numbers of poor people are also increasing.

The legacy of the neoclassical paradigm of development is probably as much responsible as any other single factor for the blindness of development economics with respect to income distribution. Three components can be distinguished in the traditional dogma on income distribution. First, income inequality is necessary for growth and efficiency. In the neoclassical paradigm, specialization and ex-

change are predicated on the existence of differing initial endowments. Differences in incomes merely reflect the underlying differences in physical and human assets. Moreover, income inequality is likely to increase the savings rate and thereby raise investment and the rate of growth. Second, in the presence of exchange and growth, income inequality is bound to decrease. Indeed, in the harmonious world of automatic and equilibrating adjustment mechanisms of the neoclassical paradigm, development trickles down and spreads. Therefore, should we be able to take care of the rate of growth in GNP, poverty would also be taken care of. Third, should unwanted income differences still exist after the operation of the trickling-down mechanisms, Keynesian economics offered another line of defense: the reliance on taxes and subsidies for redistributing income and reducing or even eliminating poverty. Such a scheme was especially attractive when it referred to redistribution of the increment of GNP, of the national dividend of growth, as it were, and therefore did not impair future growth possibilities.

The advocates of the traditional approach have, however, overlooked three critical points. First, the differences in personal incomes seem much too vast to be explained by differences in factor endowments alone. Second, the magnitude of the transfers necessary in order to reduce absolute poverty, or at least to decrease relative income inequality, has been seriously underestimated. This is a question of simple arithmetic. Consider a typical LDC, with 70 percent of the population and 50 percent of GNP in the agricultural sector and the rest in industry. Make the atypical assumptions that the economy grows by 10 percent in each sector and that the country has zero population growth. The gap between the rich and the poor may still be increasing, for the 10 percent growth in the nonagricultural half of GNP is shared by 30 percent of the population, while that of the other half is divided among the remaining 70 percent. The example, of course, is rather extreme. It assumes that agriculture and nonagriculture grow at the same rate and, more important, that incomes are equally distributed within each sector. Third, the traditional approach has failed to recognize that the institutions responsible for growth are not neutral to income distribution. Indeed, it is almost inevitable that the largest portion of the increment in GNP will go to the wealthiest few. Moreover, it is difficult to devise and virtually impossible to implement tax reforms that would redistribute the national dividend to any significant extent.[1]

That income distribution has long been a neglected subject in economics is also evidenced by the relative scarcity of analytical and empirical work on the subject. Despite conceptual shortcomings and paucity of data, the available estimates of income inequality almost invariably suggest that incomes are significantly more unequally distributed in LDCs than in DCs. Moreover, the relatively high level of income inequality in LDCs persists and in many cases increases, at least in the early stages of development (Kuznets 1955b; Adelman and Morris 1973; Ahluwalia 1974).

This evidence suggests that dualism of the "haves" and have-nots" exists and persists over time. In our opinion, this is explained by the persistence of the market imperfections that originally gave rise to dualism. These imperfections usually result from the efforts of individual groups to establish rent-maximizing positions. Motivations to enhance one's absolute as well as relative position are, obviously, neither temporary nor transitory phenomena. Moreover, once these positions are established, they tend to be reinforced by devoting the rents at least partly to attempts to further reduce effective competition. Public officials and civil servants can also benefit from market imperfections, forming a powerful political coalition for the preservation of distortions and for the unequal distribution of the rents that arise from them (Krueger 1974). In this way, dualisms and the unequal distribution of income are intimately interconnected and both are perpetuated.

This view of dualism is contrary to the neoclassical theory of dualistic development, which considers dualism a temporary aberration, bound to disappear as development takes hold. Our approach to the subject has much in common with that of the sociologists and anthropologists who have considered dualism as a permanent phenomenon to be reconciled with, as well as with that of the radical economists who have seen "separatism" or "ghetto economic development" as the most promising means of achieving growth with redistribution.[2]

Our treatment of income distribution and dualism proceeds as follows. We begin with the measurement of income inequality. We then use alternative measures of inequality to test theories concerning the determinants of income inequality. Finally, we explore alternative theories of dualism and their im-

---

[1]An example is provided by a scheme studied by the World Bank. It is based on redistribution of incremental investment, which is realized by transferring 2 percent of GNP from capital accumulation in the upper and middle income group to capital accumulation supporting incomes of the lowest group (the lowest 40 percent of the population). In the numerical simulation with parameters typical for an LDC, the income of that group will rise over a period of 10 years from 11.4 percent to 14.6 percent of GNP—or under more optimistic assumptions, from 12 percent to 16.2 percent (Ahluwalia and Chenery 1974, p. 228). This type of "incremental Marxism," even if it were feasible, seems to bring little benefit to the poor.

[2]For references to this literature, see Harrison (1974).

plications for development strategy and income distribution.

The Size and Measurement of Income Inequality

Two problems have handicapped the measurement of income inequality: the lack of data and ambiguities in measurement. The former problem can be attributed to the fact that priority in data collection has been given to production and input data, which may be adequate for describing the functional income distribution but which are useless for studying the personal distribution of income. Studies of family income and expenditure, which are necessary for the latter purpose, are much scarcer.

Comparative data on personal income distribution for international cross-sections have only recently become available. Table 14.1 classifies a number of countries by income levels and inequality. In interpreting the table, one must be mindful of the pitfalls that exist in international comparisons of GNP[3] and of the caveats about the comparative merits and significant inconsistencies among alternative measures of inequality—which we will proceed to discuss. Nevertheless, some broad trends are evident from the table, and they are aptly summarized by Ahluwalia (1974, pp. 6–16).

All socialist countries fall in the group with lowest inequality, Gini coefficient less than 0.40. This could have been expected, although the consistency of the observation is impressive. The DCs on the whole have more equality in income distribution than the LDCs. This may be the result of public transfer mechanisms, such as progressive taxation, social security, and certain public expenditures, that are more prevalent and have more redistributive orientation in DCs than LDCs. A striking feature of the table is that the LDCs vary considerably in the degree of income inequality, suggesting that income inequality is neither immutable nor solely determined by the level of per capita income. For example, the share of the lowest 40 percent of the population in the poorest of the LDCs (per capita income less than U.S.\$300

in 1964 prices) ranges from 6.5 percent to over 20 percent of GNP.[4]

The Gini Coefficient

An intuitive measure of inequality is the share of a certain percentile or decile of the population (e.g., the lowest, the highest) in total income. This is especially useful if the purpose of the study of inequality is well defined with respect to a certain group of the population, for example, to improve the lot of the bottom 20 percent. For a view of inequality with respect to all income groups, the cumulative distribution of income is usually plotted as the Lorenz curve and is described by the Gini coefficient of concentration.

In Figure 14.1, the degree of inequality is represented by the size of the shaded area, I, representing the difference between the actual distribution of income described by the curve between O and O' and the line segment OO', relative to the area, T, defined by the right angle triangle OBO'. This ratio is the Gini coefficient. If incomes are distributed equally, that is, all points lie on the diagonal line segment, the area of I is zero, and so is the index of inequality. On the other hand, if one person has all the income, the income distribution curve coincides with the right triangle, OBO', and the index of inequality is one. By approximating the areas of the figure with straight lines, one can easily derive the Gini coefficient of inequality.

By calling U the complement of I in the right triangle T, we write

$$G = \frac{I}{T} = \frac{T-U}{T} = 1 - \frac{U}{T}$$

For the population group denoted as ab in the figure, we write (by remembering the formulas for the area of a rectangle and a triangle)

$$U_{ab} = (bd)(ab) + \frac{1}{2}(ce)(ab)$$

$$= (bd)(ab) + \frac{1}{2}(ac - bd)(ab)$$

$$= \frac{1}{2}(ab)(bd + ac)$$

In order to calculate an overall coefficient of inequality, one would have to sum the area

---

[3]See, for example, Kuznets (1966, Chapter 7), Hagen (1968, Chapter 1).

[4]We will return to this point below, when we discuss Adelman and Morris' (1973) attempt to explain the patterns of income distribution with the set of their sociopolitical indicators.

Table 14.1 Classification of Countries by Income Levels and Inequality

High Inequality (Income Share of Lowest 40% less than 12%)					Moderate Inequality (Income Share of Lowest 40% between 12% and 17%)					Low Inequality (Income Share of Lowest 40%, 17% and above)				
Country (year)	Per Capita GNP US$	Lowest 40%	Middle 40%	Top 20%	Country (year)	Per Capita GNP US$	Lowest 40%	Middle 40%	Top 20%	Country (year)	Per Capita GNP US$	Lowest 40%	Middle 40%	Top 20%
PER CAPITA INCOME UP TO U.S. $300														
Kenya (1969)	136	10.0	22.0	68.0	El Salvador (1969)	295	11.2	36.4	52.4	Chad (1958)	78	18.0	39.0	43.0
Sierra Leone (1968)	159	9.6	22.4	68.0	Turkey (1968)	282	9.3	29.9	60.8	Sri Lanka (1969)	95	17.0	37.0	46.0
Philippines (1971)	239	11.6	34.6	53.8	Burma (1958)	82	16.5	38.7	44.8	Niger (1960)	97	18.0	40.0	42.0
Iraq (1956)	200	6.8	25.2	68.0	Dahomey (1959)	87	15.5	34.5	50.0	Pakistan (1964)	100	17.5	37.5	30.0
Senegal (1960)	245	10.0	26.0	64.0	Tanzania (1967)	89	13.0	26.0	61.0	Uganda (1970)	126	17.1	35.8	47.1
Ivory Coast (1970)	247	10.8	32.1	57.1	India (1964)	99	16.0	32.0	52.0	Thailand (1970)	180	17.0	37.5	45.5
Rhodesia (1968)	252	8.2	22.8	69.0	Madagascar (1960)	120	13.5	25.5	61.0	Korea (1970)	235	18.0	37.0	45.0
Tunisia (1970)	255	11.4	53.6	55.0	Zambia (1959)	230	14.5	28.5	57.0	Taiwan (1964)	241	20.4	39.5	40.1
Honduras (1968)	265	6.5	28.5	65.0										
Ecuador (1970)	277	6.5	20.0	73.5										
PER CAPITA INCOME U.S. $300–$750														
Malaysia (1970)	330	11.6	32.4	56.0	Dominican Republic (1969)	323	12.2	30.3	57.5	Surinam (1962)	394	21.7	35.7	42.6
Colombia (1970)	358	9.0	30.0	61.0	Iran (1968)	332	12.5	33.0	54.5	Greece (1957)	500	21.0	29.5	49.5
Brazil (1970)	390	10.0	28.4	61.5	Guyana (1956)	550	14.0	40.3	45.7	Yugoslavia (1968)	529	18.5	40.0	41.5
Peru (1971)	480	6.5	33.5	60.0	Lebanon (1960)	508	13.0	26.0	61.0	Bulgaria (1962)	530	26.8	40.0	33.2
Gabon (1968)	497	8.8	23.7	67.5	Uruguay (1968)	618	16.5	35.5	48.0	Spain (1965)	750	17.6	36.7	45.7
Jamaica (1958)	510	8.2	30.3	61.5	Chile (1968)	744	13.0	30.2	56.8					
Costa Rica (1971)	521	11.5	30.0	58.5										
Mexico (1969)	645	10.5	25.5	64.0										
South Africa (1965)	669	6.2	35.8	58.0										
Panama (1969)	692	9.4	31.2	59.4										

PER CAPITA INCOME ABOVE U.S. $750

High Inequality
(Income Share of Lowest 40% less than 12%)

Country (year)	Per Capita GNP US$	Lowest 40%	Middle 40%	Top 20%
Venezuela (1970)	1004	7.9	27.1	65.0
Finland (1962)	1599	11.1	39.6	49.3
France (1962)	1913	9.5	36.8	53.7

Moderate Inequality
(Income Share of Lowest 40% between 12% and 17%)

Country (year)	Per Capita GNP US$	Lowest 40%	Middle 40%	Top 20%
Argentina (1970)	1079	16.5	36.1	47.4
Puerto Rico (1968)	1100	13.7	35.7	50.6
Netherlands (1967)	1990	13.6	37.9	48.5
Norway (1968)	2010	16.6	42.9	40.5
Germany, Fed. Rep. (1964)	2144	15.4	31.7	52.9
Denmark (1968)	2563	13.6	38.8	47.6
New Zealand (1969)	2859	15.5	42.5	42.0
Sweden (1963)	2949	14.0	42.0	44.0

Low Inequality
(Income Share of Lowest 40%, 17% and above)

Country (year)	Per Capita GNP US$	Lowest 40%	Middle 40%	Top 20%
Poland (1964)	850	23.4	40.6	36.0
Japan (1963)	950	20.7	39.3	40.0
United Kingdom (1968)	2015	18.8	42.2	39.0
Hungary (1969)	1140	24.0	42.5	33.5
Czechoslovakia (1964)	1150	27.6	41.4	31.0
Australia (1968)	2509	20.0	41.2	38.8
Canada (1965)	2920	20.0	39.8	40.2
United States (1970)	4850	19.7	41.5	38.8

Notes: The income shares of each percentile group were read off a free-hand Lorenz curve fitted to observed points in the cumulative distribution. The distributions are for pre-tax income. Per capita GNP figures refer to GNP at factor cost for the year indicated in constant 1971 U.S. dollars.

Source: Ahluwalia, M. S. (1974), "Income Inequality: Some Dimensions of the Problem," in H. B. Chenery et al., *Redistribution with Growth.* Oxford: Oxford University Press, pp. 8–9. (Reprinted by permission of Oxford University Press, Oxford.)

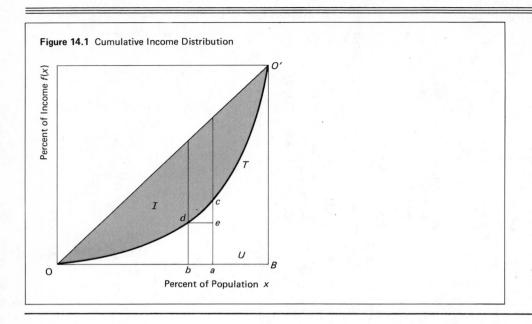

Figure 14.1 Cumulative Income Distribution

under the curve, U, for all the population groups. Furthermore, since T can be written as 1/2 (i.e., 1/2 $\times$ 1 $\times$ 1), we can write

$$G = 1 - \Sigma(ab)(bd + ac)$$

More generally, we can write

$$G = \frac{\int_0^{100} [x - f(x)]dx}{\frac{1}{2}(100)^2} \qquad (1)$$

where x is cumulative percent population and $f(x)$ is cumulative percent income.

Data can readily be converted to fit the needs of computing the coefficient G in equation 1. For example, on the basis of our diagrammatic presentation, one can obtain ab from the noncumulatively tabulated percent of units of population, while bd and ac represent the cumulatively tabulated shares of income. The straight-line approximation to the index of inequality, as calculated above, is quite satisfactory if the number of population groups is, for example, eight or more (Gastwirth 1972).

Other Measures of Inequality

Measurement of income distribution involves measurement of dispersion. The standard deviation is thus another natural choice as a measure of inequality. In order to account for nonidentical mean incomes in different distributions, the standard deviation is divided by the mean to give the coefficient of variation. Use of the coefficient of variation as a measure of dispersion is based on the assumption that income is normally distributed. Only in this case is the standard deviation an unbiased estimate of skewness. This brings us to the logarithmic measures of income inequality.

The Lorenz curve is actually based on a logarithmic concept. It is a descendant of Pareto's law,[5] the relationship that Pareto discovered between any randomly selected income, y, and the total number of people who earn at least this income, Ny. The relationship is described by

$$N_y = Ay^{-\alpha} \qquad (2)$$

with A and α being constants. The latter is an elasticity coefficient, which denotes that the number of income recipients earning incomes of at least y, N_y, decreases by a fixed percentage, α, as income increases by 1 percent. The measure α then is another measure of equality. The higher α, the more rapidly incomes level off as income increases. Plotted in logs, the relationship appears as in Figure

[5]For a fascinating history of the development of the measures of income inequality, see Pen (1971, Chapter 6).

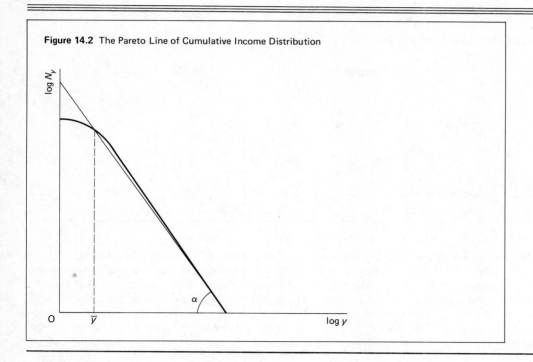

Figure 14.2 The Pareto Line of Cumulative Income Distribution

14.2. The heavy line represents the actual cumulative distribution of income recipients above a certain income, y. The straight line connecting the two axes shows the log-proportional relationship that Pareto postulated. The dotted line represents the position on the logarithmic scale of the average income, $\bar{y}$, and the constant slope of the postulated curve, α, is the elasticity coefficient. The figure suggests that Pareto's law better describes the relationship that exists at high income levels, for example, to the right of the mean, $\bar{y}$, than it does the relationship that exists at low income levels, to the left of $\bar{y}$.[6]

The next step from Pareto's law is to describe the income distribution in terms of a normal curve. The coefficient of variation discussed above assumes that incomes are normally distributed. This is unlikely, since there is a floor for income on which one can survive, while there is no ceiling for high incomes one can accumulate. We would expect, therefore, incomes to have a low bound and the distribution to be skewed to the right, as in Figure 14.3. Suppose we compact the right side of Figure 14.3 by plotting the logarithm of income instead of income. This implies that incomes, for example, of 10, 100, 1,000, and so on become 1, 2, 3, respectively. As a result of this transformation, it is no longer the absolute differences among incomes that matter but rather the relative percentage differences. The greater income inequality within the top incomes is compacted so that the transform of income of the form $u = a \log y + e$ is normally distributed. A distribution is lognormally distributed if the distribution of the logs of the variables is normal. In actuality, the lognormal income distribution is written as $u' = a \log (y - y_0) + e$, where y_0 represents a kind of Ricardian subsistence minimum.[7]

The measure of inequality suggested by the lognormal distribution is the standard deviation of the logs of income. As a measure of dispersion, the standard deviation of the logs incorporates both skewness and variance. It is independent of the mean and thus of the level of income and can be used for comparing two distributions. A high standard devia-

[6] The Lorenz curve is a direct outgrowth of Pareto's law. Instead of relating the cumulative number of recipients to an income, y, the curve relates it to their cumulative income, Y. We thus have $N_y = BY^\beta$, where β is the Gini coefficient of concentration.

[7] For the lognormal distribution, see Aitchison and Brown (1957).

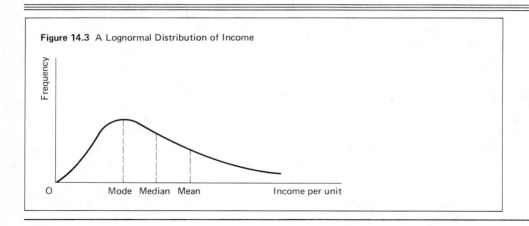

Figure 14.3 A Lognormal Distribution of Income

tion implies a high mean relative to the low mode, and thus both high variance and a high level of skewness. Because of the properties of logs, the standard deviation of the logs focuses on the distribution of income over the wide range of low and middle income, discounting inequality in the higher income levels.

Theil (1967) has defined still another index of income inequality, which is particularly useful for handling grouped as well as raw data and for providing explanations for the degree of income inequality. This "information theory" index is

$$\sum_i y_i \log \frac{y_i}{x_i} \qquad (3)$$

where y_i is the income share of group i, and x_i is the population share of the same group. When per capita income in all classes is the same, y_i/x_i is unity for each group, and thus log y_i/x_i is zero, giving the index a value of zero. When all income is attained by one individual or group, the index assumes a value of log N, where N is the number of individuals or groups. This measure of inequality is (like the Gini coefficient) free of assumptions with respect to the form of the income distribution. Moreover, because of its aggregation properties, this measure is particularly useful in that it permits decomposition of the total income inequality into its components. We will present below an application of Theil's index for the study of income distribution in Brazil.[8]

[8]It is worth noting that the index of the standard deviation of the logs has decomposition properties similar to the Theil index.

Comparison of Inequality Measures

We have discussed an array of measures of dispersion that can be used to measure income inequality. Empirical studies have shown, and A. B. Atkinson (1970) has proven theoretically, that an unambiguous ranking of income distributions is possible only when the Lorenz curves do not cross. Income distribution studies by Ranadive (1965) and Champernowne (1974) illustrate this ambiguity. For example, Ranadive ranked twelve distributions by five different commonly used measures of inequality and got five different rankings. The results appear in Table 14.2.

Consider the Lorenz distributions for India and West Germany, which cross as in Figure 14.4. The Gini concentration ratio ranks both distributions equally ($G = 0.410$). The standard deviation of the logs favors India (0.305 as compared to 0.369), but the coefficient of variation reverses this ranking by favoring West Germany (0.773 to 0.901). Indeed, the Gini coefficient and the coefficient of variation suggest that income is more unequally distributed in LDCs, with four out of the five LDCs coming at the bottom of the rankings. On the other hand, by focusing on the relative income distribution over a wide range of incomes, the standard deviation of the logs is less sensitive to large absolute income differentials. Use of the standard deviation of the logs for comparisons of income distributions shows a greater equality of income for the LDCs than for the DCs (Kuznets 1963b, p. 17), because as compared to DCs, inequality in LDCs is characterized by greater shares accruing to the upper income groups (captured by the Gini coefficient), while the in-

Table 14.2 Comparison of Alternative Measures of Inequality

Country	Gini Concentration Ratio	Standard Deviation of Logs of Income	Coefficient of Variation	Shares of		Equally Distributed Equivalent Measure		
				Lowest Quintile	Highest Quintile	ε = 1.0	ε = 1.5	ε = 2.0
1. India, 1950	0.410 (7)	0.305 (3)	0.901 (11)	7.8 (1)	55.4 (11)	0.297 (7)	0.359 (5)	0.399 (3)
2. Ceylon, 1952–1953	0.427 (8)	0.341 (6)	0.876 (10)	5.1 (5)	53.9 (10)	0.311 (10)	0.395 (6)	0.457 (6)
3. Mexico, 1957	0.498 (10)	0.395 (12)	1.058 (12)	4.4 (7)	61.4 (12)	0.401 (12)	0.492 (12)	0.550 (12)
4. Barbados, 1951–1952	0.436 (9)	0.383 (10)	0.842 (9)	3.6 (10)	51.6 (9)	0.315 (11)	0.433 (10)	0.524 (10)
5. Puerto Rico, 1953	0.394 (4)	0.317 (4)	0.783 (8)	5.6 (3)	49.8 (8)	0.256 (4)	0.341 (4)	0.408 (4)
6. Italy, 1948	0.378 (3)	0.301 (1)	0.748 (3)	6.1 (2)	48.4 (6)	0.241 (2)	0.319 (2)	0.379 (1)
7. Great Britain, 1951–1952	0.356 (1)	0.304 (2)	0.673 (1)	5.4 (4)	44.5 (1)	0.224 (1)	0.311 (1)	0.384 (2)
8. West Germany, 1950	0.410 (7)	0.369 (8)	0.773 (6)	4.0 (9)	48.0 (5)	0.299 (8)	0.411 (8)	0.498 (8)
9. Netherlands, 1950	0.406 (6)	0.355 (7)	0.781 (7)	4.2 (8)	49.0 (7)	0.290 (5)	0.395 (7)	0.478 (7)
10. Denmark, 1952	0.401 (5)	0.381 (9)	0.751 (4)	3.4 (11)	47.0 (4)	0.292 (6)	0.418 (9)	0.521 (9)
11. Sweden, 1948	0.406 (6)	0.393 (11)	0.752 (5)	3.2 (12)	46.6 (3)	0.303 (9)	0.435 (11)	0.540 (11)
12. United States, 1950	0.372 (2)	0.325 (5)	0.705 (2)	4.8 (6)	45.7 (2)	0.242 (3)	0.339 (3)	0.421 (5)

Note: Numbers in parentheses indicate rankings with respect to the inequality index at the left.

Sources:
Ranadive, K. R. (1965), "The Equality of Incomes in India," *Bulletin of the Oxford University Institute of Economics and Statistics,* 27 (May), Table 1, p. 122.
Atkinson, A. B. (1970), "On the Measurement of Inequality," *Journal of Economic Theory,* 2 (September), Table 1, p. 259.
Kuznet, S. (1963b), "Quantitative Aspects of the Economic Growth of Nations: Part 8, Distribution of Income by Size," E. D. C. C., 11, (January), Table 3, p. 13.

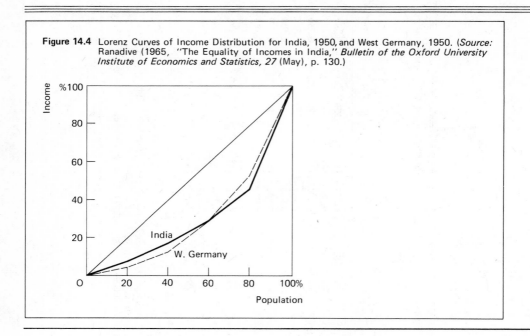

Figure 14.4 Lorenz Curves of Income Distribution for India, 1950, and West Germany, 1950. (*Source:* Ranadive (1965, "The Equality of Incomes in India," *Bulletin of the Oxford University Institute of Economics and Statistics, 27* (May), p. 130.)

comes below the top groups (emphasized by the standard deviation of the logs) are less unequally distributed in LDCs. Yet as a measure of dualism, the standard deviation of the logs is ambiguous. A low value could reflect an equal distribution of income or a high level of dualism.

In conclusion, we may say that the measurement of income inequality is riddled with ambiguities. No single measure is adequate to summarize all the important factors in a distribution. The use of multiple measures is, therefore, recommended, the choice among them depending on the aspect of inequality in which one is most interested. If, for example, relative inequality (inequality in the low ranges of income) is important, one would choose the standard deviation of the logs. If absolute inequality (inequality over the entire range), is the issue, the Gini coefficient is more appropriate. Finally, if relative inequality in the high or medium ranges is more important, Theil's information measure should be used.

A Welfare Measure of Income Inequality

The ambiguity of the different measures of income inequality is inevitable as long as the underlying social welfare function is not explicit. This is the starting point for the new measure of inequality proposed by A. B. Atkinson (1970). Consider a social welfare function that is an additively separable and symmetric function of individual incomes, y:

$$W = \int_0^{\tilde{y}} U(y)f(y)\,dy \qquad (4)$$

By making the conventional assumptions about the utility function, $U(y)$, Atkinson reduces the analysis of income distribution to the principles established in the theory of decision making under uncertainty (Arrow 1965; Arrow and Kurz 1970). He proceeds to define the concept of the equally distributed equivalent level of income, y_{EDE}, that is, the level of income per capita, which if equally distributed would give the same level of social welfare as the present distribution. Thus, equation 4 is written

$$U(y_{EDE}) \int_0^{\tilde{y}} f(y)\,dy = \int_0^{\tilde{y}} U(y)f(y)\,dy \qquad (5)$$

and the index is defined

$$I = 1 - \frac{y_{EDE}}{\mu} \qquad (6)$$

where μ is the mean income. The index takes the values from zero (complete equality) to one (complete inequality). The attractive feature of the index is that it lends itself to a simple interpretation. For example, an index of $I = 0.3$ means that, if incomes were equally distributed, only 70 percent of the present national income would yield the same level of social welfare—according to the particular social welfare function chosen.

If we specify that the distribution of income in one country, A, is simply a scaled-up version of the distribution in country B, that is, $f_A(y) = f_B(\theta y)$, the utility function that appears in equation 6 can be defined independently of the mean level of income, μ. Under such conditions, Arrow (1965) has demonstrated that the utility function has the form

$$U(y) = \begin{cases} A + B\dfrac{y^{1-\varepsilon}}{1-\varepsilon} & \text{if } \varepsilon \neq 1 \\ \ln y & \text{if } \varepsilon = 1 \end{cases} \tag{7}$$

where ε is a measure of the degree of inequality aversion, as will be explained immediately below. This implies that as the general level of income rises, that is, under proportional shifts in the distribution, the definition of inequality remains the same (there is constant relative inequality aversion). On the other hand, it is reasonable to assume that the utility function is not independent of the mean. As the general level of income rises, we are more concerned about inequality, that is, there is increasing relative inequality aversion.

Atkinson writes the index of inequality for the utility function of equation 7 as

$$I = 1 - \left[\sum_{i}^{n} \left(\frac{y_i}{\mu}\right)^{1-\varepsilon} f(y_i) \right]^{1/(1-\varepsilon)} \tag{8}$$

where $i = 1, \ldots, n$ for n discrete income categories. The case now becomes one of choosing ε, which is a measure of the degree of inequality aversion. As ε rises, we attach more weight to income transfers at the lower end of the distribution and less weight to transfers at the top.

Although social welfare functions are not known empirically, the Atkinson study is of interest for showing the sensitivity of the rankings of different measures of income distribution to ε. This is shown in the three last columns of Table 14.2. When $\varepsilon = 1$, the degree of relative inequality aversion is low, and the distributions are ranked similarly to the Gini coefficient. As the degree of relative inequality aversion increases, for example, when $\varepsilon = 2$, more weight in the index is given

to inequality in the low and middle income range, and rankings are similar to those based upon the standard deviation of the logs. Furthermore, the interpretation of the entries in the last three columns of Table 14.2 follows directly from the definition of the index of the equally distributed equivalent income. For example, for $\varepsilon = 1.5$, for the United States, $I = 0.34$. This means that if incomes were equally distributed, the present level of social welfare could be achieved in the United States with only two-thirds of the present national income. Similar interpretations hold for the other entries.

The Determinants of Income Distribution

If measurement of the degree of inequality in income distribution is deficient, the theory of income distribution is almost nonexistent.[9] The neoclassical equilibrium theory of income distribution concentrates on functional incomes rather than personal incomes. It relies on pure production relationships and factor supply conditions that generate competitive market equilibrium solutions, with the reward of the factors being determined by marginal productivity. At the other extreme is the classical or Marxist wage theory, with fixed real wages and a capitalist class that appropriates all surplus value.

Neither extreme position is consonant with reality. Had the Marxian thesis been correct, the observed income distribution would have been bimodal, one for the capitalists and one for the workers, with the latter being more or less flat at the subsistence wage rate. The neoclassical theory, on the other hand, is uninformative as far as personal income distribution is concerned and most likely wrong. It is inadequate for explaining how income is distributed in realistic circumstances such as when market imperfections or economies of scale are present, and even under unrealistic assumptions it cannot explain how personal, as opposed to functional, incomes are distributed. The differences in incomes seem much too vast to be explained by differences in factor endowments. Moreover, one would like to know how differences in inital endow-

[9]For reviews of the theories of income distribution, see Bronfenbrenner (1971), Pen (1971), Ferguson and Nell (1972), J. Robinson (1960), Marchal and Ducros (1968), Weintraub (1958).

ments are created in the first place—a question much overlooked in economic dynamics. As we have noticed in Chapter 11, on the measurement of human capital, such explanation cannot rely on the tautological definition of factor endowments as the capitalized streams of factor incomes. Finally, if market equilibrating forces had been operating, wage and income differentials should have been decreasing over time, especially in the face of increasing international trade and international capital movements. Yet as we have noticed in Chapter 13, this does not seem to have been the case.

Because of a dearth of theory, the emphasis has thus far been placed on describing (rather than explaining) the income distribution. Some measures of income inequality are more useful than others for assessing the determinants of income distribution.

Table 14.1 showed that there is greater inequality of incomes in LDCs than in DCs. This is a well-established finding of the literature on the subject.[10] Moreover, most of the inequality of incomes in LDCs is due to the larger share of income held by the 5 percent of the population at the top of the scale (Kuznets 1963b). These cross-section findings are also generally consistent with those from time series data for long periods, which have shown that inequality in income distribution has declined in the long run in the DCs.[11] On the other hand, over shorter periods of time or at certain stages of development, inequality of incomes may be increased, indicating an overall nonlinear relationship between growth and income inequality.[12]

In the short run, incomes and their distribution are determined by the distribution of wealth—although imperfectly, as we have already remarked. If different forms of wealth are more highly concentrated over the population than others (i.e., land and financial capital may be more unequally distributed than human capital), the degree of income inequality may be affected by the relative importance of different kinds of wealth[13] (Of

course, this raises the further question of how the present distribution of wealth came to be.) In the short run, the distribution of incomes generated from the given distribution of wealth will also be affected by differences in the rates of return to different forms of wealth. Here is where market imperfections, especially capital market imperfections, may come into play.

In the somewhat longer run, income distribution will be affected not only by the initial factor endowments, market imperfections, and other sources of dualism but also by the degree of geographic, sectoral, and social immobility within the society. Mobility may be limited by rigid barriers to entry by those holding monopoly positions—in the economic, political, or social sphere—by discrimination on the basis of caste, race, color, sex, or religion, by governmental restrictions, by the lack of willingness to undertake risk or of remuneration for undertaking it, by imperfections in capital markets,[14] and by information costs. A special case of mobility is intergenerational mobility, which effectively breaks the link between income and inherited wealth. The more intergenerational mobility exists, the less a son's income is determined by his father's, and the less likely it is that the poorest man this year will also be the poorest man next year. Inheritance taxes and public education increase intergenerational mobility to the extent that the wealth of a previous generation does not also determine the wealth, human and nonhuman, of the succeeding generation.[15]

In the presence of domestic and international trade and of labor and capital movements, one might suppose that inequalities in the distribution of wages, income, and other factors would be lowered considerably rela-

---

[10]See also Kuznets (1955b, 1963b), Kravis (1960, 1973).

[11]See Kuznets (1963b, 1966), Lampman (1962), Soltow (1965, 1968), Paukert (1973), T. P. Schultz (1968).

[12]See Kuznets (1963b), Oshima (1962), J. G. Williamson (1965), Weisskoff (1970), Adelman and Morris (1973), and especially Pryor (1973).

[13]Usually it is argued that labor income is distributed more equally than incomes from property or from capital (Kravis 1960, 1973); therefore, societies

with a large share of income going to labor are expected to have a lesser degree of income inequality. The degree of inequality in total income will also be affected by the correlation between labor and property income across the population (Pryor 1973).

[14]Imperfections in capital markets, especially in regard to human capital, which would thereby deprive poor but able and intelligent children of the opportunity to attend school, are one of the major arguments behind programs to subsidize investments in human capital. Note that this is an efficiency and not an equity argument.

[15]Some of these policies to reduce the inequality in the distribution of income may also reduce the motivations for risk taking, saving, and investment (H. G. Johnson 1973). For an interesting study, which simulates the effects of different rules with respect to inheritance and marriage on the distribution of income, see Pryor (1973).

tive to those in closed economies. This is not entirely consistent with observation. Hence, the origin of alternative explanations for the persisting differences in the production possibility sets of different sectors and countries, which will be discussed under the topic of dualism.

On the question of sectoral location, it has been observed that the poor are disproportionately located in rural areas and engaged in agriculture and related occupations, whereas the rich are located in urban areas. Within the agricultural sector itself, income is more equally distributed than within the nonagricultural sector, although the degree of inequality is still considerable. In a typical LDC, 80 percent of the rural population receives 50 percent of the rural income, with the rest of the income going to the upper 20 percent of the rural population (Ahluwalia 1974). It is not surprising, therefore, to find strategies to reduce income inequality based on reducing factor market imperfections and increasing the mobility of productive factors between sectors. Nevertheless, as we have seen in the previous chapter, even when capital and labor become mobile and flow from one sector to another, the result may not be equilibrating. Factor movements can also be disequilibrating, tending to accentuate existing dualisms and market imperfections. In such situations, a more appropriate method of reducing inequality may be to combat poverty directly, for example, by direct subsidies to the rural poor or by bringing productive jobs to them.

Such observations can be explained within a neoclassical framework in terms of sectoral differences in production possibility sets. But such an approach obviously raises the new question of how these differences are determined, that is, what explains dualism?

Once production possibilities and factor prices are determined, reductions in income inequality can be accomplished only by redistributive measures aiming at the pursuit of social justice. To the extent that recognition of the problem of income distribution is heightened, political leaders in many countries may strive toward social justice and redistribution. And this tendency is strengthened when the leaders are drawn from groups that have little affinity with private commercial enterprise— the military, the civil service, or the intellectual elites (Keesing 1974). Nevertheless, in no country has any redistributive mechanism brought about much in the way of *ex post* redistribution.[16] Massive redistributions seem politically infeasible.

Some Tests

We have highlighted some of the factors that seem to play important roles in explaining the distribution of income and the degree to which it changes over time: the institution of the family, the system of taxation, the level of education, the structure of the economy, and social and political forces. In the following paragraphs, we briefly describe some procedures by which the effects of each of these factors can be measured.

When the necessary data are available, it may be possible to compute Gini coefficients (and/or other measures of inequality) for the same country and time period, first at the family (household) level and then again at the individual level, affording the opportunity for a comparison between the index of inequality at the household level with that at the individual level. If the inequality index at the individual level exceeds that at the family level, it indicates that the institution of the family lessens inequality.

Comparisons of this sort have been carried out for Brazil in 1960 by Fishlow (1972) and for Mexico in 1963 by Weisskoff (1970), with conflicting results. As Fishlow has emphasized, however, any service that the institution of the family performs in decreasing the degree of inequality of incomes in the short-run (static) sense is likely to be offset by the intergenerational inequality it propagates. This is true because: (1) poor families tend to have more children (3.1 on the average in Brazil) than other families (1.7 on the average); (2) poor children are less likely to attend school than other children; (3) the educational level of one's parents has a positive effect on the productivity of schooling; and (4) savings rates are inversely related to family size.

The same method can be used to determine the effects of taxes and transfer payments on the size distribution of income. In this case, one would compare a suitable index of inequality based on incomes before taxes and transfers with the same index based on incomes after taxes and transfers. In this way, Kuznets (1963*b*) and Rosenberg (1970) have

---

[16]See, for example, Rosenberg's (1970) study of the the Philippines.

shown that taxes and transfers have modestly reduced the degree of inequality in the distribution of income in the United States and in the Philippines.

The effect of the average level of education on the degree of inequality of incomes can be estimated by regression techniques. For example, the Gini coefficients for different regions in a single country could be regressed against the region-specific median levels of education for people of working age. Using state data for the United States from the Census of Population, Aigner and Heins (1967) and Al-Samarrie and Miller (1967) showed that the higher the level of education, the lower the degree of income inequality. However, since income and educational levels both depend to a large extent on the rate of return to human capital, it may be preferable to regress the degree of income inequality on the rate of return to education as well as on the level of education. When this is done, as in Chiswick (1968) for the United States or in Fishlow (1972) for Brazil, the average level of education is shown either to have no effect on income inequality or even to increase it.[17]

Given data on incomes by the sector and location of employment, one may investigate whether or not these factors have had any effect on income distribution (Kuznets 1963b; Weisskoff 1970). Fishlow (1972) examined the effects of sector, location, education, and age on income distribution in Brazil for 1960. In order to distinguish the effect of any one of these factors from that of any other factor, Fishlow employed to great advantage Theil's "information theory" index of income inequality, given in equation 3. The advantage of the information theory index of inequality is that it allows one to express total income inequality as the sum of the between-group inequalities and within-group inequalities for any number of groupings specified.

For example, if data on income, y, and population, x, are available by state, q, and then can be aggregated into regions, p, the inequality index, I_{pq}, can be expressed as the sum of the interregional inequality index and the intraregional inequality, that is, as

---

$$I_{pq} = \sum_p Y_p \log \frac{Y_p}{X_p} + \sum_p Y_p \left[\frac{y_q}{Y_p} \log \frac{\frac{y_q}{Y_p}}{\frac{x_q}{X_p}} \right] \quad (9)$$

where the upper-case letters (Y_p, X_p) refer to the shares of a particular region, p, in total income and population respectively, whereas the lower case letters (y_q, x_q) refer to the shares of a particular state, q, in total income or population.

When the sets into which the individuals are aggregated are not of the primary-secondary variety, as in the preceding example, where they are aggregated first into states and then into regions, and the characteristics by which the sets are defined do not occur independently, the formulation is somewhat more complicated, because there are interaction terms. For example, if the income and population data are classified by sector of employment, j, and also by educational attainment level, k, the inequality index, I_{jk}, would be defined as

$$I_{jk} = \sum_j Y_j \log \frac{Y_j}{X_j} + \sum_k Y_k \log \frac{Y_k}{X_k}$$
$$+ \left[\sum_j \sum_k y_{jk} \log \frac{y_{jk}}{x_{jk}} - \sum_j Y_j \log \frac{Y_j}{X_j} \right.$$
$$\left. - \sum_k Y_k \log \frac{Y_k}{X_k} \right] \quad (10)$$

where the first term represents the income inequality index between sectors, the second term the inequality index between different educational attainment level classes, and the remaining terms, in parentheses, the interaction terms.

Inequality indexes, such as those in equations 9 and 10, can be defined with respect to any number of classifications. Fishlow (1972) defined such an inequality index with respect to income classes, i, sector, j, educational attainment level, k, age, m, and region, n, I_{ijkmn}. The number of terms in the formulation expands rapidly, and the nomenclature becomes rather complex with so many factors, but the spirit of the approach can be understood by expanding equation 10 to include a third characteristic, for example, the income group, i, in addition to the sector, j, and educational attainment level, k. The inequality index in this case can be expressed as

$$I_{ijk} = \sum_i Y_i \log \frac{Y_i}{X_i}$$

$$+ \sum_i Y_i \left[\sum_j \frac{Y_{ij}}{Y_i} \log \frac{\dfrac{Y_{ij}}{Y_i}}{\dfrac{X_{ij}}{X_i}} \right]$$

$$+ \sum_i \sum_j \frac{Y_{ij}}{Y_i} \left[\sum_k \frac{y_{ijk}}{Y_{ij}} \log \frac{\dfrac{y_{ijk}}{Y_{ij}}}{\dfrac{x_{ijk}}{X_{ij}}} \right] \quad (11)$$

where the first term represents the inequality between different income classes, the second term the inequality between different sectors within income classes, and the third term the inequality between different educational attainment groups within sector and income cells.

Equations 10 and 11 can be used jointly to assign different portions of the total inequality index from equation 11 to the different factors. Thus, the difference between equation 11 and 10, i.e., equation 11 less equation 10, can be identified as the portion of the total inequality of income that is due to variation in income within sector and educational attainment cells as well as to other characteristics omitted from the model. The total inequality less that computed for the within-sector and educational attainment cell portion (that given by I_{jk} in equation 10) can then be partitioned into the portion due to intersectoral inequality (from the first term of equation 10), the portion due to the inequality between educational attainment classes (from the second term of equation 10), and finally, the portion due to interaction between sector and educational attainment (from the terms in parentheses in equation 10).

Fishlow defines the five-dimensional index of income inequality, I_{ijkmn}, by considering age, m, and geographical region, n, in addition to the characteristics i, j, and k, and then a four-dimensional income inequality index, I_{jkmn}, along the lines given by the two-dimensional index of equation 10. By using both the five-dimensional index, I_{ijkmn}, and the four-dimensional index, I_{jkmn}, in the same way as equations 11 and 10 for the two- and three-dimensional examples, Fishlow is able to partition the total income inequality index into: (1) the within-sector, education level, age, and region cell component; (2) the individual components for inequality among sectors, education levels, age groups, and regions re-

spectively; and (3) to various interaction components.

Fishlow uses a stratified sample of 11,000 families drawn from the population census with data for income and population in Brazil for the year 1960. The data are classified into five sectors (agriculture and mining, industry and construction, services and commerce, transport and communications, and financial services and public administration), six educational attainment classes (no education, incomplete primary education, complete primary education, lower secondary education, upper secondary education, and university education), seven age groups (10–14, 15–19, 20–29, 30–39, 40–49, 50–59, and 60+), and three regions (Northeast, East and South). Fishlow computes I_{ijkmn} and then I_{jkmn}. This allows him to partition the total income inequality into the above-mentioned components.

Two different sets of results—one as it is (unadjusted) and the other adjusted for nonmonetary income and consumption, and so on—are presented in Table 14.3. The values for the total inequality index, I_{ijkmn}, are presented in the first row of Table 14.3 and are relatively high, especially the unadjusted one. The values for the within-sector, education level, age, and region cells, $I_{ijkmn} - I_{jkmn}$, are given in the second row. I_{jkmn} is given in the third row, and its subsequent partition into the portions attributable to variation among sectors, educational attainment classes, age groups, and regions is shown in rows 4–7. Fishlow also obtained a number of interaction terms which, because most of them were very small in size, are not shown. The greatest interaction was between the sector and education levels.[18] This is reflected in the fact that, when each of the other variables is held constant to eliminate interaction, the portions of income inequality attributable to variations in sector and educational attainment level are reduced significantly, whereas those attributable to age and region differences are affected only slightly.

Adelman and Morris (1973) have imaginatively and resourcefully attempted to probe further into social, political, and economic factors that determine income distribu-

[18]As Fishlow (1972, p. 395) notes, "limited education and employment in the agricultural sector together produce smaller incomes than would be expected from educational or sectoral classifications alone."

Table 14.3 *Decomposition of the Inequality Coefficient, Brazil, 1960*

	Unadjusted[b]	Adjusted[a,b]
1. Total Index (I_{ijkmn})	0.72	0.57
2. Within Sector, Education Level, Age, and Region Cells Portion of Index $(I_{ijkmn} - I_{jkmn})$	0.29	0.25
3. Between Sector and Education Level, Age, and Region Cells Portion of Index (I_{jkmn})	0.43	0.32
4. Portion of Index Attributable to Sector Variation	0.19 (0.05)	0.12 (0.03)
5. Portion of Index Attributable to Education Level Variation	0.25 (0.11)	0.20 (0.11)
6. Portion of Index Attributable to Age Level Variation	0.13 (0.09)	0.09 (0.09)
7. Portion of Index Attributable to Region Level Variation	0.05 (0.03)	0.04 (0.03)

Notes:
[a]The figures given in the columns designated "adjusted" pertain to the case where adjustments for nonmonetary income and consumption are made.
[b]The figures in parentheses represent the recomputations of the parameter next to it in the case where all other variables are held constant, so as to eliminate all interaction effects.
Source: Fishlow, A. (1972), "Brazilian Size Distribution of Income," *A. E. R.*, 62 (May), Table 3, p. 396.

tion. Specifically, they explain international differences in income inequality in a sample of 43 LDCs in terms of 35 social, political, and economic indicators, mostly familiar from Chapter 3.[19] The dependent variable is one of three alternative measures of inequality: (1) the income share of the lowest 60 percent of the population; (2) that of the middle quintile of the population; and (3) that of the wealthiest 5 percent of the population. This is related to the independent variables, the indicators, through the technique of "hierarchical interactions."

The analytical question is to select from the 35 social, political, and economic indicators the ones that best explain the variance observed in the sample of 43 countries with respect to each specific measure of inequality. Therefore, the technique of hierarchical interactions can be described with little loss of precision as an application of the analysis of variance. Recalling (from Chapter 3) that each country has a "score" with respect to each indicator, the procedure is as follows: with respect to any one index of income inequality,

Y_i, and any one indicator, j, that takes a number of distinct scores $(1, \ldots, n)$, that is, $X_{j1}, \ldots, X_{jn}$, the countries of the sample may be partitioned into two groups, with countries with values X_{j1} in one group and those with values $X_{j2}, \ldots, X_{jn}$ in the other. Next, the partition changes, with countries that have values of X_{j1}, X_{j2} in one group and $X_{j3}, \ldots, X_{jn}$ in the other. For each partition, the means of the index of inequality of the two groups and the variance of the group means from the grand means are calculated. The process is repeated for all mutually exclusive partitions of that indicator and then similarly for all the other indicators. The partition process aims at minimizing the sum of squares within groups or, alternatively, maximizing the sum of squares between groups. The indicator chosen for the first branching with respect to the inequality index is the one with the highest ratio of between-sums-of-squares to total-sums-of-squares (which is roughly analogous to r^2) for all the binary partitions in the sample. This ratio describes the total variance of the specific index of inequality explained by the chosen variable. As long as the result of one partition has produced groups of countries sufficiently large to be partitioned again, the process is repeated with another variable. In this manner, a hierarchy of partitions and variables is produced, resembling an asymmetrical tree branching.

Not unlike the other techniques of multivariate analysis employed by Adelman and Morris, the technique of hierarchical inter-

[19]The indicators include numbers 1, 2, 3, 5, 6, 7, 9, 19, 20, 21, 23, 25, 26, 27, 29, 30, 32, 33, 34, 36, 37, 38, 39, 40, in Table 3.1. To these are added: the size of population, the rate of population growth, an index of institutional structure in agriculture, an index of intersectoral patterns of development, the composition of exports, the level of socioeconomic development, the country size, the orientation of the development strategy, the extent of political participation, the type of colonial experience, the number of years a country has been self-governing, the extent of direct government economic activity.

actions merely produces classifications by identifying the common characteristics of the countries in each group. As in their previous work, Adelman and Morris do this by "subjective factor analysis." Once the meaningfulness of the classification is vindicated on a priori grounds, the authors draw conclusions about the relative importance of each indicator in explaining intercountry differences in income inequality. This is accomplished by counting the number of times each indicator appears as significant in the branching process. The six most important indicators turn out to be the rate of improvement in human resources, the extent of direct government economic activity, the socioeconomic dualism, the potential for economic development, the per capita GNP, and the strength of the labor movement. Not surprisingly, then, the authors conclude that the determinants of income inequality include social and political as well as economic variables.

Typology of Dualism

In the neoclassical paradigm of development, nonhomogeneity in the world and differences in initial endowments allow people to exercise their comparative advantage within the context of exchange and trade. However, as a result of trade, exchange, and factor mobility, economic development will trickle down and be diffused among countries, regions, groups, and individuals. Except for differences in initial endowments, there is little room for wage and income differentials and for the other signs of dualism. To the extent that dualism exists, it is a temporary aberration attributed to market imperfections; and in the process of development, dualism is bound to diminish, ultimately to self-destruct.

Sociologists and anthropologists, on the other hand, have been much less sanguine on the proposition that dualism contains the seeds of self-destruction. They tend instead to view the phenomenon as more stable and permanent than do economists. The implication of this view is that development economics must come to terms with dualism, and economic development can take place only within a dualistic society.

In the previous chapter, we reviewed evidence on one form of dualism, the wage differential between industry and agriculture. Likewise, in the preceding section of this chapter, we reviewed evidence on income inequality. We have seen that, concomitant with rapid development, both dualism and income inequality tend to persist or even increase. We have also suggested that the phenomena are intimately interrelated. In view of the stubbornness, persistence, and pervasiveness of dualism, we conclude this chapter by reviewing some types of dualism described in economic and other literature.

Sociocultural and Institutional Dualism

As we have emphasized earlier, the purpose of analysis is to reduce behavior, including its contrasts and riddles, to the lowest common denominator, consistent with other observed cases. There will always be an "unexplained" residual—both as evidence of the nonsystematic component of the universe and as challenge to the builders of new hypotheses. However, this unexplained residual can often be conveniently relegated to the dust bin of "fundamental differences in human species."

Indonesia, perhaps to a greater extent than other countries, is a country of contrasts and riddles that beg explanation. Impressed by the apparent failure of the liberal policies of the Dutch administration of the Dutch East Indies (Indonesia) and by the frustrations of his own personal experience as a civil servant there in 1910, Boeke (1953) chose to attribute the Indonesian riddles to fundamental differences in people and their attitudes.[20] Indonesia is described in terms of dualism, which in turn is defined in terms of sociocultural differences between the precapitalist traditional society, on the one hand, and the capitalistic modern sector, on the other. For Boeke, the traditional sector is that of the indigenous people, who have limited wants determined by social rather than economic factors; the modern sector is imported and capitalistic, and is based on unlimited needs. As a result of these different utility functions and attitudes prevailing in the different sectors, the behavioral pattern in each sector varies considerably. The behavioral patterns of the traditional sector, therefore, cannot and should not be analyzed in terms of the tools of Western economics, no matter how applicable those tools may be in explaining behavioral patterns in advanced Western

---

[20]For a generalized approach to sociocultural dualism outside the Indonesian context, see Sadie (1960) and Myint (1954).

countries and even in the modern sectors of LDCs.

Both the accuracy of Boeke's empirical observations and his analytical explanations are subject to challenge.[21] For example, Myrdal (1968) challenged Boeke's observations and the factors responsible for dualism, and substituted a list of attitudes and institutions that he feels are responsible for dualism. Analytically, economists are inclined to try to explain the universe in terms of observable and preferably quantifiable objective factors instead of attitudinal variables and motivations, which, as illustrated in Chapter 3, often reduce to interesting but untestable hypotheses.

From his analysis of dualism, Boeke (1953, p. 289) derived the following policy implications: first, as a general rule, one policy for the whole country is not possible; and second, what is beneficial for one section of society may be harmful for another.

Ecological Dualism

Geertz (1963) has provided a different characterization and explanation for dualism. Dualism is characterized by differences in ecological systems, each such system being self-contained and stable. Any ecological system prescribes certain social and economic patterns that conform with it, ensuring internal equilibrium. Interrelationships between the different ecological systems are likely to be nearly nonexistent, ruling out the possibility that the different systems will change, converge, or coalesce. Most ecological systems ". . . after having reached what would seem to be a definite form, nonetheless fail either to stabilize or to transform themselves into a new pattern, but rather continue to develop by becoming internally more complicated" (Geertz 1963, p. 81). This is defined as "involution," a process whereby an ecological system grows unto itself.[22]

The internal equilibrium of the ecological, social, and economic forces within any such system is sufficiently strong to resist any exogenous forces that may attempt to transform it or integrate it with other systems. Geertz defines the nature of ecological dualism with respect to the same example, Indonesia. Inner

Indonesia (Java) represents a labor-intensive ecological system typified by the intensive cultivation of rice, sugar, and other crops which require tropical or semitropical climatic conditions and much water. Outer Indonesia is typified by land- and capital-intensive, labor-extensive products, such as mining products, rubber, and oil palm. Geertz demonstrates the stability of this ecological dualism by showing that Indonesia's precolonial dualism was accentuated rather than diminished as a result of colonial intervention, whereas dualism in Japan—which escaped colonial intervention—was diminished. The integration of the different sectors in Japan is attributable in part to the development of an indigenous middle class. The entrepreneurial function in Indonesia was invariably performed by foreigners, who found it more natural to integrate the modern sectors of Outer Indonesia with foreign countries (mainly the Netherlands) rather than with Java.[23]

Thus, rather than being integrated into a system, the heterogeneous elements of plural societies lack the underlying common bonds— traditions, cultural aspirations, or indigenous entrepreneurs—that might impose an overriding control by social will. Plural societies are divided into groups of isolated individuals and separate sectors, which grow unto themselves and reach constantly higher levels of complication and intricacy without increasing the contact and interrelationships with one another (Furnivall 1948, pp. 303–306, 308– 312).

Economic Dualisms: Technological, Foreign Enclave, and Financial

While ecological dualism emphasizes differences in environments, each with its own stable equilibrium, and sociocultural and institutional dualism emphasizes idiosyncratic differences in people, technological dualism attributes differences between sectors to differences in knowledge of technical processes and their implementation, that is, to differences in production functions and factor endowments.

Production functions can differ in many respects. They can differ in the kinds of

---

[21]For a careful critique of Boeke, from the point of view of empirical relevance and of analytic validity, see the celebrated article of Higgins (1956).

[22]Geertz borrows the concept of involution from the anthropologist Goldenweiser (1936).

[23]For additional examples of how economic or political imperialism may accentuate and perpetuate dualism and kill off incipient tendencies toward development of home-grown entrepreneurship and industrialization, see Resnick (1970).

inputs that enter the function. For example, according to the two-gap models to be reviewed in Chapter 21, imports would appear as a factor of production in the modern sector. Jorgenson (1961) distinguishes between the modern and traditional sectors by including capital and labor as the productive factors in the modern sector, whereas land and labor are the productive factors in the traditional sector. Also, the sectors can differ in terms of one or more parameters of the production function, such as the economies of scale parameter, the efficiency parameter, or the elasticity of substitution parameter. For example, Eckaus (1955) argues that, in contrast to the traditional sector in which the elasticity of substitution approaches infinity, in the modern sector the elasticity of substitution approaches zero, that is, the modern sector is characterized by fixed coefficients.

Differences in the production function are sufficient to establish the case of technological dualism. Once this is done at the theoretical level, it becomes an empirical question as to whether or not such differences really exist in the world. Is production in the modern sector characterized by fixed coefficients? Does not the modern sector of LDCs eventually adapt to abundant labor supplies? If not, why not? Answers to these questions were sought in Chapter 9. Frequently, they take the form of measuring the bias in technological change in different sectors.[24] For example, utilizing time series data for agriculture and nonagriculture for Japan for the period 1905–1933, Watanabe (1965) found technological change to be capital using in manufacturing and indeterminate (sometimes capital saving and sometimes labor saving) in agriculture. The explanation of the capital-saving bias to technological change in the manufacturing sector (despite the alleged existence of "elastic supplies of labor at the going wage rate") lies in the importation of advanced technology. This technology, being primarily designed for countries where the price of labor with respect to capital is higher than in Japan, is of necessity more capital intensive.

A variant of technological dualism proposes to describe the situation that arises when a capitalistic wedge is introduced into the archaic indigenous economic structure. The wedge is a high-productivity, usually extractive industry (such as mines, oil wells, or plantations), which is capital intensive and supported largely by imported technology. This modern sector produces mainly for export. It coexists with a low-productivity, labor-intensive sector that mainly produces foods and textiles for the domestic market (Singer 1950; Furtado 1967; Myint 1964).

To provide an explanation for the stability of enclave dualism, one must answer two questions: (1) why do the development effects not spread from the modern sector to the rest of the economy to initiate a process of growth?; and (2) how does the modern sector remain capital intensive in a situation of abundant labor supplies?

The answers to both questions draw upon the model of technological dualism. The modern sector employs only a small fraction of the labor available. On the one hand, since wage rates are higher in the modern sector than in the traditional sector, the wage differential may prevent modern sector enterprises from attaining greater profitability than traditional enterprises, despite "superior" technology and other advantages, thereby preserving the static dualism (Nelson 1968). On the other hand, the wages paid to labor in the modern sector may not be determined by the marginal productivity of labor but by the living conditions prevailing in the region (Furtado 1967, p. 130). Since, in either case, wages constitute only a small portion of the value of the modern sector's output (the other and larger part accruing to the foreign economy of which the enclave sector is an economic, if not a geographic, appendage), the enclave modern sector has little impact on the local economy. Furthermore, the secondary and cumulative effects of investment are removed from the host country and placed in the investing country (Singer 1950, p. 477). This is basically an explanation for the lack of effective demand through low income levels in the traditional (local) sector.

Myint (1964, Chapter 5) and Bottomley (1964) go a step further in emphasizing the significance of the capital market as a basis for enclave dualism. The enclave sector can remain a capital-intensive sector, because it has easy access to long-term capital at low rates of interest in world capital markets.[25]

[24]For definition and measurement of bias, see Chapter 9.

[25]One reason for the easy access of the enclave sector to the world capital markets is the stability of the colonial-type currency, which precludes inflationary developments and stimulation of the effective demand from within.

The domestic sector, on the other hand, can borrow only from "noninstitutional" lenders, such as the village money lender, the landlord, the shopkeeper, and only at high interest rates—rates that partly reflect the greater premium for risk, partly the monopoly rent of the lender, and partly overall capital scarcity, especially during seasons of peak demand. Similarly, McKinnon (1973) emphasizes financial dualism in the domestic capital markets as a source of development disequilibrium. These types of financial dualisms imply differences in the relative prices of factors of production for the two sectors.

Dualisms and Income Distribution

Technological, foreign enclave, and financial dualisms are the economic analogues to institutional, sociocultural, and ecological dualisms. Both the economic and sociological varieties of dualism represent attempts to explain the existence of persistent differentials in wage rates and incomes between sectors in the face of widespread exchange and trade. Despite this similarity, however, economists draw entirely different implications from the existence of dualism than do sociologists and anthropologists.

For sociologists and anthropologists, dualism is inevitable and chronic. For economists, in the short run, a considerable amount of stretching of technology will take place, and thus, the cleavage between the two sectors will be bridged (Fei and Ranis 1972). In the long run, the sectors will adjust to relative factor endowments, factor prices, and so on, in a variety of ways, and dualism will eventually disappear (Fei and Ranis 1964; Kelley, Williamson, and Cheetham 1972; Zarembka 1972).

Not surprisingly, the policy implications are also very different. While the sociologists and anthropologists have advocated separatist and indigenous policies of growth for each sector of the dualistic society, economists, because of their confidence in the combined strength of the multiple forces that drive toward market equilibrium and therefore toward the elimination of dualism, have advocated trade, exchange, and the removal of market imperfections. Agriculture, for example, may be directly aided by "investment in place," which would tend to increase the marginal productivity of labor there. This may be a sufficient but not a necessary condition,

since an alternative is always available, "investment in people." Migration, for example, to the nonagricultural sector represents an investment in the human agent that also improves economic welfare and trips off the same equilibrating mechanisms. The success of these mechanisms depends on the resilience and the intersectoral mobility of outputs and factors of production which, in the view of the economists, and in the absence of monopoly restrictions, is certainly considerable.

The sociological view has recently been advocated among economists contributing to the literature on "ghetto economic development" (Harrison 1974; Vietorisz and Harrison 1973). The low-income sector, or the ghetto, is not a temporary staging area occupied by low-income potential migrants, to be abandoned as they adjust to social and technological institutions. Instead of the neo-Smithian theorem of the "invisible foot" (Tiebout 1956), the prevalent idea may well be investment in "ghetto turf." "People want to improve their community, not abdicate from it" (Samuelson 1958, p. 337). Should that be the case, economic policies ought to be designed for development within the dualistic sectors of society.

The implications of the two alternative views diverge significantly. If the equilibrating mechanisms of traditional economics work, improvement in one sector (agriculture) may be pursued indirectly through investment in the other sector (nonagriculture). This is essentially the surplus labor policy of development, which automatically trips off the mechanism that will close the gap between the sectors. On the other hand, if the mechanisms that lead to equilibrium are weak, or if development is a disequilibrium process, integrationist policies, such as the labor surplus strategy based on development of the industrial sector, will accentuate dualism and therefore be self-defeating. A more appropriate policy in the same context would be to invest in agriculture and to plug up the leakages to the nonagricultural sector in the form of the production squeeze or the expenditure squeeze, which are reviewed in the following chapter.

While we tend to view dualism in traditional economic terms, that is, in terms of factor endowments, production functions, and differential wage rates, the evidence concerning the prevalence and remarkable persistence of these symptoms of market imperfections leads us inescapably to the sociologists' conclusion that dualism and income inequality are facts of life in the LDCs, which are not likely to disappear quickly or easily. The negative feedback mechanisms of the development process apparently offset the equilibrating mechanisms, and as a result, dualisms and market imperfections persist, and the inequality of the personal income distribution is exacerbated.

Summary and Conclusions

Dualism has been at once the *deus ex machina* and the *bête noire* of neoclassical development economics. This distinguished appellation for "market imperfections" has given a certain degree of legitimacy to the observation, which is antithetical to neoclassical approaches, that the spread effects of economic development often seem to be abrogated. Development dynamics, on the other hand, has built elaborate models to describe how dualism gradually decreases and eventually disappears under the impact of automatic and equilibrating processes. Despite the elegance of the argument, the literature has left us singularly unprepared for the fact that dualism tends to persist or even to become more pronounced in the process of development.

As we suggested in Chapter 1, income distribution has been an ominous dark spot in the record of development. It has also been a failure of neoclassical development economics. The strategy for combating poverty, according to traditional theory, was an indirect one based on two implicit assumptions. First, in the classical world of harmonies of interest and gradual equilibrating processes, it was assumed that higher growth rates in GNP would eventually filter down to the masses. Should we take care of GNP, poverty would also be taken care of. Second, and as the next line of defense, Keynesian economics suggested that poverty can be attacked through fiscal policies for the redistribution of income. Neoclassical economics has left us unprepared for the startling realization that the trickling-down mechanism has not worked. This is a subject in the domain of development disequilibrium. The perception of harmonies of interest was impervious to the fact that the institutions that create growth are not neutral as to its distribution. The interdependencies among growth, institutions,

and distribution have formed the core of the political economy of development—a subject that is largely beyond the scope of this book.[26]

Our discussion of income distribution opened with problems of measurement. Since the measurement of inequality involves a number of ambiguities, we have presented the operational tools for constructing alternative indexes of inequality in income distribution, some of which are more appropriate in some situations and for some purposes than others. The personal income distribution within countries was also analyzed on the basis of the scant evidence available. The conclusion is that socialist countries have the highest degree of equality in income distribution, and DCs in general have incomes more equally distributed than LDCs.

After describing the inequality of income distribution, we turned to its explanation. Dearth of data is coupled with dearth of theory to make this endeavor rather tenuous at present. Various likely determinants of income inequality were noted, such as family, taxation, education, the relative importance of different forms of wealth, mobility, and social and political factors. The available evidence suggests that an increase in the average level of education lowers income inequality in the DCs, while in the LDCs, if it has any effect, it may increase income inequality. The institution of the family seems to reduce income inequality at any one point in time but, on the other hand, contributes to intergenerational inequality. Fishlow's estimates indicate that sectoral, regional, and age differences are also important in explaining the high degree of income inequality characteristic of Brazil and most other LDCs. Finally, we noted the results of Adelman and Morris, which place considerable emphasis on dualism as an explanatory variable in the analysis of income inequality.

Our brief survey of various theories of dualism has revealed striking differences between sociologists and economists in the extent to which they expect dualism to persist and in the strategies they advocate for achieving development with greater equality of in-

[26]Although unsystematically, we have made occasional references throughout the book to questions of political economy involving various aspects of development. A convenient reference for readings on the subject is Wilber (1973). For some political-economic considerations on the topic of income distribution, see Haq (1973).

comes. The evidence supports the view that dualism and income inequality are remarkably persistent, if not immutable, facts of life in development. The persistence of these phenomena can be explained by the fact that the rent-seeking behavior of those responsible for the market imperfections (which, in turn, give rise to dualisms and income inequality) is largely self-reinforcing. Those who gain from market imperfections are able to derive sufficient rents (and bribe enough officials and voters) to ensure their continuation.

Chapter 15

Interactions Between Agriculture and Nonagriculture

The discussion of migration and income distribution in the preceding chapters has pointed to the importance of agricultural development as a means of reducing urban unemployment and income inequality. Moreover, understanding the interactions between agriculture and the other sectors of the economy has been crucial for shaping appropriate development policies. These issues will be further discussed in the present chapter.

The interactions between agriculture and nonagriculture change significantly over time in the process of economic development. In the early stages, agriculture is of critical importance as the employer of one-half to three-quarters of the labor force and as the source of more than half of the GNP. As development takes hold, however, the relative importance of agriculture declines sharply, while that of industry increases. The secular decline in the relative importance of agriculture and

the secular increase in the relative importance of industry can be explained by a number of factors, which will be examined in greater detail in Chapter 16. First, and most important, is the role of changes in the composition of demand. As described by Engel's law, the income elasticity of demand for food is generally less than one, and it declines as income grows,[1] whereas the income elasticity of demand for industrial products is considerably

[1]For statistical estimates of the income elasticity of demand, see U.N.: FAO (1957). One might notice that Engel's law is at least partly the result of statistical illusions. The primary sector is largely identified with the production of food and raw materials, the demand for which is finite. The nonagricultural sectors, on the other hand, are so defined that they become the legatees of the principle of the insatiability of demand. They constitute an open-ended category that also includes the "want for new wants." As a result, one would expect the income elasticity of demand for the primary sector to be less than one, and that for non-agriculture to be greater than one.

larger than one. Second, are the input and output substitutions that take place in the process of development. Specifically, certain farm outputs are substituted by manufacturing output, while others undergo increasing degrees of processing in the nonagricultural sectors. Industrial inputs, on the other hand, substitute for farm inputs to an increasing degree as income rises; for example, chemical fertilizers substitute for manure, and tractors substitute for labor and farm animals. Finally, while the size of the market in a country grows as a result of population increases, rising per capita income, and monetization, changes in factor costs tip the balance in favor of manufacturing (Chenery 1960; Kuznets 1966; Chenery and Taylor 1968).

Attempts to systematize the discussion of the changing role of agriculture in the development process have led to the formulation of a number of "growth stage models" and of "dual economy models," which we have already discussed in other chapters.[2] This literature, voluminous and diverse as it is, treats the contributions of agriculture—of surplus labor or investable capital—as if they were strictly one-way transfers, failing to appreciate the full extent of the complementarities between agriculture and nonagriculture. In order to comprehend better the interactions between the two sectors, one has to capture both the intersectoral transfer of surplus and the sectoral market contributions. The latter refer to the linkages that connect agriculture and nonagriculture by providing market outlets for each other's products and factors (Ruttan 1968, pp. 19–20).

In this chapter, we analyze the roles of agriculture and industry in economic development through the interactions of the two sectors. First, we discuss the investable agricultural surplus that may be transferred and utilized in the development of the nonagricultural sector. This transfer can take place through the outflow of capital from agriculture, the outflow of labor, agricultural taxation, or the terms of trade (Nicholls 1963; Owen 1966). Next, we focus on the interdependence between agriculture and nonagriculture. This approach emphasizes the production function relationships and the market flows that link the agricultural and nonagricultural sectors.

More specifically, the development of agriculture may increase that sector's demand for the intermediate inputs, such as fertilizers, insecticides, and machinery, provided by nonagriculture; it may also increase the supply of agricultural raw materials to the nonagricultural sector. These two aspects will be studied through the backward and forward interindustry linkage effects. The development of agriculture also provides employment for agricultural workers and, as their incomes rise, an increased demand for consumer goods produced in the nonagricultural sector. The availability of such goods often acts as an incentive to greater work effort, savings, and productivity in the agricultural sector (Hymer and Resnick 1969; Freedman 1970).[3]

These factors will be studied through the employment and income-generation linkage effects. We call this process of increasing interdependence of the sectors "sectoral articulation."[4] Finally, we build a simple formal model that analyzes the general equilibrium of the agricultural sector in terms of prices and quantities supplied and demanded of agricultural output and labor. In this framework, we will be able to study the effect of a number of exogenous variables upon agriculture, such as the terms of trade, population, imports of agricultural commodities from abroad, taxation, land, and capital policies.

Sectoral Capital Flows

According to the Marxian thesis, the burden of providing surplus funds and surplus resources for the purposes of industrial capital formation in the early stages of economic development falls upon agriculture (e.g., W. A. Lewis 1954; Nurkse 1953). This raises two problems: (1) how to create a surplus in the agricultural sector and (2) how to extract this surplus for the financing of capital formation necessary for industrial growth. This view of the role of agriculture has been so broadly accepted that it has come to constitute orthodoxy. Only recently has it been challenged

---

[2]For a discussion of these models in the context of agricultural development, see Hayami and Ruttan (1971, Chapters 2 and 3).

[3]Other roles of the agricultural sector include exports, which utilize the relatively or absolutely surplus resources of land or labor to earn foreign exchange, which in turn permits importation of capital goods and technology (Caves 1965*a*). Since external structure is the subject of Part V, discussion of these effects will be postponed.

[4]The term sectoral articulation is owed to S. Robinson (1972).

(Ishikawa 1967; Ruttan 1968; Georgescu-Roegen 1969; Hayami and Ruttan 1971) on the grounds that modern, chemical-biological agriculture requires heavy investments in irrigation and water control. It therefore becomes necessary to stem or even reverse the resource outflow from agriculture if agricultural production is to keep up with the explosive population growth in many parts of the world.

In this section, we briefly sketch the conceptual framework for the thesis that there should be capital outflow from the agricultural sector. Next, we present the empirical basis for measuring the contribution of agriculture.

The Double Developmental Squeeze of Agriculture

The logic of extracting the agricultural surplus can be described in terms of the "double developmental squeeze" of agriculture.[5] This has two aspects, the production squeeze and the expenditure squeeze.

The production squeeze can assume different forms. In the Marxist-Leninist approach, output can be extracted directly through compulsory deliveries at low prices to the nonagricultural sector. Alternatively, it can be extracted through a combination of high farm prices and high farm taxes. The latter was the approach used in Meiji Japan, in the period 1881–1920. High farm prices stimulated the adoption of improved agricultural technology. Simultaneously, high farm taxes (in the form of a land tax), while transferring part of the agricultural surplus to the nonagricultural sector, also forced the peasants both to use their land intensively and to participate in manual work in the nonfarm sector in order to pay these taxes (Ohkawa and Rosovsky 1960).

The production squeeze can also assume an indirect form and operate through the market mechanism (the "Mill-Marshallian" model, as exemplified by economic development in the United States). Within a market-oriented and relatively perfectly competitive setup, the commercial family-farmer ". . . represents an individual Ricardian capitalist *par excellence,* forever reaching forward for new technologies in order to keep from losing position on that

reverse escalator of declining per unit average real costs, which is a characteristic of any industry that is making a positive contribution to general economic progress" (Owen 1966, p, 51). Competition giveth (by fostering technological progress) and competition taketh away (by taxing excess profits). Thus, the family farming system, through an intersectoral profit transfer brought about by technological progress, delivers to the nonfarm sector progressively increasing supplies of food at progressively lower prices.

The deterioration of the terms of trade is one reason for the relative decline of the agricultural sector. The pressure of a competitive system and a rapidly advancing technology is the other. Farmers who do not adopt and exploit new methods or technologies will either have to drift to the city to join the ranks of the urban unemployed and the slum dwellers, or become "the people who were left behind" and descend into the lost world of noncommercial subsistence farming. This constitutes the basis of what Owen calls "the expenditure squeeze."

The drift to the city is not costless for the farm sector. Indeed, the costs of rearing and educating the part of the nonfarm labor supply that originates in the farm sector represent a "capital" transfer from agriculture to nonagriculture. This can amount to a substantial outflow of capital. Second, in serving as the residual employer, the agricultural sector maintains at its own expense redundant quantities of labor until they can be absorbed at alternative employments in the nonfarm sector. This is especially true in countries where the extended family system is a prevalent institutional arrangement. There, the agricultural sector operates as an informal unemployment insurance and social welfare system.

There are then three aspects to the double developmental squeeze on agriculture. First, the sector is squeezed for the direct outflow of capital, represented by the net balance of purchases and sales of the agricultural sector. Second, it is squeezed by the deteriorating domestic terms of trade. Third, it is squeezed by the transfer of human capital through migration. The first and second aspects have been measured in Taiwan by Lee (1971) and by Lin (1973), both of whom employ the sectoral social accounting framework developed by Fei-Ranis (1964) and Ishikawa (1967).

---

[5]The double developmental squeeze has been developed in detail by Owen (1966).

Table 15-1 *Accounting Equations for Sectoral Capital Flows*

Inflows	Outflows

SECTORAL EQUATIONS

Nonagricultural Production Sector

$$X_{nn} + X_{an} + L_{an} + L_{nn} + K_{an} + K_{nn} + X_{mn} = C_{nn} + C_{na} + C_{ng} + X_{na} + X_{nn} + I_{nn} + I_{na} + E_n \quad (1)$$

Nonagricultural Household Sector

$$C_{nn} + C_{an} + S_{nn} + G_n + C_{mn} = L_{nn} + K_{nn} + K_{na} \quad (2)$$

Agricultural Production Sector

$$X_{aa} + X_{na} + L_{aa} + K_{aa} + K_{na} + X_{ma} = C_{aa} + C_{an} + X_{an} + X_{aa} + I_{aa} + E_a \quad (3)$$

Agricultural Household Sector

$$C_{aa} + C_{na} + S_{aa} + G_a + C_{ma} = L_{aa} + L_{an} + K_{aa} + K_{an} \quad (4)$$

Government

$$C_{ng} + S_g = G_a + G_n \quad (5)$$

Foreign Trade

$$F = X_{mn} + X_{ma} + C_{mn} + C_{ma} - E_n - E_a \quad (6)$$

CLEARING EQUATIONS FOR THE SYSTEM

$$S_{nn} + S_{aa} + S_g = I_{nn} + I_{na} + I_{aa} + E_n + E_a \\ - (X_{mn} + X_{ma} + C_{mn} + C_{ma}) \quad (7)$$

$$I_{nn} = S_{nn} + (S_{aa} - I_{aa}) - I_{na} + S_g + F \quad (7a)$$

CLEARING EQUATIONS FOR AGRICULTURE

$$(X_{an} + C_{an}) - (X_{na} + C_{na} + E_a) - (X_{ma} + C_{ma}) \\ + (K_{an} - K_{na}) + L_{an} + (I_{aa} - S_{aa}) - G_a = B \quad (8)$$

$$(X_{an} + C_{an} + E_a) - (X_{na} + C_{na} + I_a) \\ + (K_{an} - K_{na} + L_{an}) + G_a = B \quad (9)$$

Notes: The first of the double subscripts indicates the sector of origin and the second the sector of destination. The single subscript indicates the sector in which the designated activity takes place. The symbols are defined:

a = agriculture	C = consumption
n = nonagriculture	I = investment
m = imports	S = savings
g = government	E = exports
X = intermediate goods	G = taxes or subsidies
L = labor primary factor	B and F = balancing items
K = capital primary factor	

Sources:
Fei, J. C. H., and G. Ranis (1964), *Development of the Labor Surplus Economy: Theory and Policy*. Homewood, Ill.: Irwin, Chapter 2;
Lee, T. H. (1971), *Intersectoral Capital Flows in the Economic Development of Taiwan, 1895–1960*. Ithaca, N.Y.: Cornell University Press, Chapter 2;
Lin, W. L. (1973), "Economic Interactions in Taiwan: A Study of Sectoral Flows and Linkages," Ph.D. dissertation, Stanford University, Chapter 3.

Measurement

In measuring the sectoral capital flows, we distinguish two producing sectors, agriculture, a, and nonagriculture, n. In agriculture, we include landless farmers but not rentier landlords who, together with the service industry, are included in nonagriculture. Each sector incorporates both production and household activities.

The transactions among the sectors are described in terms of inflows and outflows as in Table 15.1. From equation 1, the nonagricultural production sector obtains intermediate goods, X, from both production sectors and also from imports, m, and labor, L, and capital goods, K, from the households of both sectors. It sells intermediate goods, X, to both sectors and to investment, I; consumption goods, C, to both household sectors and to government, g; and also exports, E, to foreign consumers. From equation 2, the nonagricultural household sector purchases consumption goods, C, from both sectors and from imports, pays taxes or receives subsidies, G, and creates savings, S. Its outflows are labor, which by assumption goes only to the nonagricultural production sector, and the services of accumulated capital that the households supply to both sectors. The interpretations for the agricultural production and household sectors (equations 3 and 4) are similar, except that nonagricultural labor cannot be employed in the agricultural production sector (as a result of the assumption that there is a net flow of labor out of agriculture) and also that the agricultural production sector provides neither consumer goods to the government nor capital goods to nonagriculture.

Equations 5 and 6, for government and foreign trade respectively, close the system. On the outflow side of the government sector are subsidies to the two sectors; on the inflow side are consumption and the balancing item, savings. Outflows from the foreign trade sector are the imports of intermediate goods and consumption goods to both agriculture and nonagriculture, net of the exports from both sectors to the rest of the world. The balance of these items, denoted as F, appears on the inflow side of the foreign trade equation.

By adding equations 1 through 5 and canceling out similar terms, we arrive at the clearing equation given by equation 7 in Table 15.1. From equation 6, equation 7 can be rewritten as 7a, to define capital formation in nonagriculture. Capital formation in nonagriculture is equal to the savings in nonagriculture, plus government savings, plus the net balance of payments term, plus the net sum of three terms that define the net transfers from agriculture to nonagriculture. These net transfers consist of the net difference between savings less investment in the agricultural sector and the net inflow of capital from the nonagricultural sector.

The transfer from agriculture to nonagriculture can be analyzed further by looking exclusively into the agricultural sector. By adding equations 3 and 4, and canceling out

similar terms, we have the clearing equation for agriculture given in equation 8. This can be simplified for purposes of empirical research, as in equation 9.[6] The capital flow from agriculture, B, can thus be represented in terms of three components: the difference between the total sales of agricultural products and total purchases of nonagricultural products, as defined in the two first parentheses, plus a term for transfer of primary factors of production and a term for government transfers.

The capital flow from agriculture may, but need not, occur in a direct fashion, as described in equation 9. As we have earlier remarked, the same flow in the Mill-Marshall model would operate through the change in the terms of trade against agriculture. Equation 9 must be cast in real terms by deflating by prices for the purposes of time series analysis.

We define the real capital flow from agriculture by considering four price indexes: agricultural prices, P_a, nonagricultural prices, P_n, factor prices, P_f, and the overall price index, P.

$$B' = \frac{X_{an} + C_{an} + E_a}{P_a} - \frac{X_{na} + C_{na} + I_a}{P_n}$$
$$+ \frac{K_{an} - K_{na} + L_{an}}{P_f} + \frac{G_a}{P} \qquad (10)$$

We can rewrite equation 10 in a form that separates the real capital flow transfer from the terms of trade effect,

$$B' = \frac{B}{P_a} + \frac{X_{na} + C_{na} + I_a}{P_n} \left(\frac{P_n}{P_a} - 1 \right)$$
$$- \frac{K_{an} - K_{na} + L_{an}}{P_f} \left(\frac{P_f}{P_a} - 1 \right)$$
$$- \frac{G_a}{P} \left(\frac{P}{P_a} - 1 \right) \qquad (11)$$

The first term represents the *visible real capital flow*, which consists of the difference between total sales of agricultural products and total purchases of nonagricultural products for agriculture, deflated by the agricultural price index. The remaining terms constitute the *invisible real capital flow* and account for pairwise changes in the terms of trade between agriculture, on the one hand, and nonagriculture, factor markets, and overall output,

[6]We have now redefined $I_{na} - S_{aa}$, the excess agricultural savings, so as to consist of capital goods that agriculture buys from nonagriculture, as well as imported intermediate and consumption goods for the use of agriculture, that is, $I_a = (S_{aa} - I_{aa} - I_{na} - X_{ma} - C_{ma})$.

Table 15.2 *Average Annual Intersectoral Capital Flows, Taiwan, 1952–1970*
(Billion New Taiwan Dollars, NT $, at 1964 Constant Prices)

	1952	1952–1955	1956–1960	1961–1965	1966–1970	1970
1. Total Agricultural Production	20.0	22.2	26.4	32.6	43.0	46.8
2. Sales of Agricultural Products $(X_{an} + C_{an} + E_a)$	10.8	12.5	15.4	20.3	26.8	29.9
3. Total Real Capital Outflow from Agriculture (B')	4.4	4.9	3.1	3.2	2.5	4.2
a. Visible real capital outflow from agriculture (B/P_a)	2.6	3.5	1.6	3.0	2.9	5.0
b. Invisible real capital outflow from agriculture (terms of trade)	1.8	1.4	1.5	0.2	−0.4	−0.8
4. Ratio of Real Capital Outflow to Total Agricultural Production (percent)	22	22	12	10	6	9
5. Net Real Capital Outflow per Farmer (NT $)	1073	1116	618	586	421	693
6. Net Real Capital Outflow per Capita Received by Nonagricultural Population (NT $)	1141	1194	603	518	318	479
7. Per Capita Real Income (NT $)	4017	4192	4741	6074	8042	8706

Source: Lin, W. L. (1973), "Economic Interactions in Taiwan: A Study of Sectoral Flows and Linkages," Ph.D. dissertation, Stanford University, Chapter 3.

on the other. The measurement of the total contribution of agriculture to capital formation in other sectors must, therefore, include the invisible as well as the visible real capital flows.

Implications from the Experience of Taiwan

Lee (1971) and Lin (1973) have painstakingly analyzed the Taiwanese sectoral capital flows for the periods 1895–1960 and 1952–1970 respectively, using a simplified version of the model presented in equations 9 and 11. Lin's results, appearing in Table 15.2, indicate that the transfer of investable surplus from agriculture to nonagriculture has been important and presumably instrumental in the process of Taiwanese economic development. The average annual transfer out of agriculture ranged from a high of 22 percent of total agricultural production in the early postwar years of Taiwan's development to a low of 6 percent in the late 1960s. Considering the large share of self-consumption in agriculture, the trans-

fer was even greater in relation to the sale of agricultural products. Furthermore, until very recently, the transfer represented a large proportion of per capita income.

The "production squeeze" of Taiwanese agriculture is measured in Table 15.2. It is composed of the visible outflow of capital, representing the balance of purchases and sales of the agricultural sector, and the invisible transfer obtained through the terms of trade. The latter was especially important in the early years of Taiwanese development. It was based largely on the rice-fertilizer barter price—a system that transferred to nonagriculture the profit from technological change in rice production. The high-yielding varieties of rice introduced in the 1950s and early 1960s required large quantities of chemical fertilizers. These were made available by the nonagricultural sector through direct barter for rice, at prices extremely unfavorable for agriculture, given the world prices of rice and fertilizer. Thus, as shown in Table 15.2, the production squeeze on agriculture and the intersectoral transfer of capital were maintained and relied upon for nonagricultural development.

The total contribution of agriculture to Taiwan's economic development should also include some items not included in Table 15.2: the intersectoral payments for the services of capital and intersectoral transfers of labor arising from the "expenditure squeeze." Migration from agriculture to nonagriculture has apparently been quite significant. Moreover, as we have pointed out in Chapters 12 and 13, since those who migrate are not marginal unemployed workers but rather those with high opportunity cost, farm out-migration in Taiwan has involved a substantial social cost for the agricultural sector. Similarly, to the extent that agriculture became the residual employer for marginal labor originating in the nonagricultural sector, a further sectoral capital transfer is involved. Thus, sectoral labor transfers arising from the expenditure squeeze undoubtedly have added significantly to the measured capital flows arising from the production squeeze, so that, together, the two squeezes have provided a substantial portion of the fuel for Taiwan's rather remarkable economic development.

Sectoral Articulation

The analysis to this point has been partial, capturing only intersectoral flows of output and factors from origin to destination. The interaction among sectors, however, also involves some underlying production function relationships. These can be described and accounted for by employing the input-output framework.

Table 15.3 gives a schematic representation of the relationships in a two-sector I-O model involving agriculture, A, and nonagriculture, N. The table is composed of four quadrants, distinguished by heavy lines. Quadrant I represents the final use, quadrant II the intermediate input use, quadrant III the primary factor use, and quadrant IV is reserved for the aggregates of the national accounting framework.

The capital flows approach of equations 1–6 and of the clearing equations 7 and 9 of Table 15.1 refers to flows across rows of Table 15.3. The production function relationships are described by the coefficients of the

intermediate use quadrant appearing in the first two columns of Table 15.3. A complete examination of the interrelationships between agriculture and nonagriculture should capture both the row and the column flows.

We can now formulate sectoral articulation, that is, the interdependence among sectors, in terms of the following three linkage effects: (1) the interindustry linkage effect, which refers to the effect of a one-unit increase in the autonomous portion of final demand on the level of production in each sector; (2) the employment linkage effect which, as one part of the more general concept of the primary factor linkage effect, measures the total use of labor in any one sector as a result of a one-unit change in the autonomous portion of final demand; (3) the income-generation linkage effect, defined as the effect on income of the exogenous change in final demand (Chenery and Clark 1959, pp. 63–64).

An autonomous increase in one unit of final demand increases the level of production within each sector through the interindustry linkage effect, and the level of employment through the employment linkage effect. The increases in output and employment arising from these linkages are also reflected in increased labor incomes, which through the income-generation linkage lead to increased demands for consumer goods, inducing more output and employment.

The interindustry, employment, and income-generation linkage effects describe the sectoral interdependence per unit of final demand. These effects must be weighted by each sector's component of final demand to give proper perspective to an individual sector's contribution to the process of sectoral articulation. Through this process, we derive measures of the linkage production potential, the linkage employment potential, and the linkage income-generation potential.

For an empirical study of sectoral interdependence, we again utilize data from Taiwan. The I-O analysis employs a 76×76 I-O Table for Taiwan in the year 1966. This table is consolidated to the 12×12 level of the sectors defined in Table 15.4.

Interindustry, Employment, and Income-Generation Linkage Effects

The interindustry linkage has three components: the backward linkage effect, the forward linkage effect, and the total linkage effect. The

Table 15.3 *Input-Output Format for the Sectoral Capital Flows and Sectoral Articulation Approaches*

From/To	Intermediate Use			Final Use					Total Use = Total Production
	A	N	Total Intermediate Use	Final Demand, k	Total Demand	Government	Investment	Exports	
A	X_{aa}	X_{an} (X_{mn})	$W_i = \sum_j X_{ij}$	$FD_{ik} = C_{aa} + C_{an}$ (C_{ma}) $+$ $C_{na} + C_{nn}$ (C_{mn})	$TD_i = \sum_j X_{ij} + \sum_j FD_{ik}$	G_a	I_a	E_a	$TP_i = TD_i - \text{Imports}$
N	X_{na} (X_{ma})	X_{nn}				G_n	I_n	E_n	
Total Produced Inputs	$U_j = \sum_i X_{ij}$	$\sum_i \sum_j X_{ij}$							
Primary Factor Inputs, m (Value Added)	L_{aa}	L_{nn} L_{an}							
	K_{aa} K_{na}	K_{nn} K_{an}							
Total Production	$TP_j = \sum_i X_{ij} + \sum_m V_{mj}$			FD	TD	G	I	E	

Table 15.4 *Total Interindustry Linkage Indexes and Their Rankings, Taiwan, 1966*

Groups	Industry	Total Interindustry Linkage, PL_j	Employment Linkage, EL_j	Income-Generation Linkage, YL_j
Agriculture	1. Agricultural Production for Food	1.898 (7)	0.852 (3)	1.637 (3)
	2. Agricultural Production for Raw Material	1.497 (10)	0.908 (1)	1.804 (1)
Industry	3. Working Capital for Agriculture	2.455 (3)	0.725 (10)	1.140 (8)
	4. Food Processing	2.158 (6)	0.673 (12)	1.089 (11)
	5. Mining	1.580 (11)	0.863 (2)	1.673 (2)
	6. Textiles and Rubber	2.623 (2)	0.819 (6)	1.100 (10)
	7. Nonmetal Products	2.172 (5)	0.764 (9)	1.110 (9)
	8. Metal Products	2.793 (1)	0.825 (5)	1.067 (12)
Services	9. Utilities	1.883 (8)	0.713 (11)	1.355 (6)
	10. Construction	2.417 (4)	0.839 (4)	1.416 (5)
	11. Transportation and Communications	1.858 (9)	0.787 (7)	1.329 (7)
	12. Other Services	1.286 (12)	0.768 (8)	1.517 (4)

Source: Lin, W. L. (1973), "Economic Interactions in Taiwan: A Study of Sectoral Flows and Linkages," Ph.D. dissertation, Stanford University, pp. 107, 121.

two former describe the direct effects (backward to the sectors providing inputs for the sector and forward to the sectors utilizing the output of the sector) that result from a one-unit increase in final demand in one sector. More specifically, backward linkage, L_{Bj}, and forward linkage, L_{Fi}, may be defined as

$$L_{Bj} = \frac{\sum_i X_{ij}}{TP_j} = \sum_i a_{ij}$$

and

$$L_{Fi} = \frac{\sum_j X_{ij}}{Z_i}$$

where X_{ij} represents the number of units of commodity i used in production of commodity j, and Z_i is total demand for commodity i, obtained by summing the demand for commodity i of industry, W_i, and of final demanders, FD_i.

The direct linkages, backward and forward, still capture only part of the interactions between industries. They measure only the first round of effects of the interrelationships—the contribution that intermediate inputs from other activities i make in the total value of production of industry j for the backward linkage, and the contribution which

the output of industry i makes to other industries j, rather than to final demand, for the forward linkage. In fact, however, there are also important indirect (second, third, . . . , round) effects. An increase in sector j's output will require not only an increase in the outputs of the sectors producing inputs to sector j but also increased outputs of the sectors contributing inputs to these sectors. We define the total interindustry linkage effects as those which combine both the direct and indirect repercussions of an increase in final demand.

The total linkage effect of a one-unit increase in the final demand (measured in value terms) for the product of any given industry on the total output of this and every other industry can be obtained from the inverted Leontief matrix $(\mathbf{I} - \mathbf{A})^{-1}$. Specifically, total interindustry linkage for the jth sector, PL_j, is defined as[7]

$$PL_j = \sum_i a_{ij}{}^* \quad \text{where} \quad a_{ij}{}^* = (1 - a_{ij})^{-1}$$

The $\mathbf{A}_{ij}$ matrix (where $a_{ij} = X_{ij}/TP_j$) is obtained from the 12×12 I-O Table for Taiwan in 1966. The total interindustry linkage effects and their rankings in descending order appear in the first column of Table 15.4.

[7]For further details, see Chapter 16.

The interindustry linkage effect of agriculture is relatively low compared to the other sectors.

To compute the employment linkage effect, we express each sector's utilization of the primary factors of production, specifically labor, relative to that sector's total production. We thus write, with reference to Table 15.3, $l_j = L_j/TP_j$, where l_j is the labor coefficient, that is, the labor input (in value terms) per unit of output of sector j. We recall that the elements of a column j of the inverse matrix express the output required in each sector i per unit of final demand for commodity j. By multiplying the labor coefficient by the elements of the inverse and by summing the row elements in each column, we obtain the employment linkage effect

$$EL_j = \sum_i l_i a_{ij}* \quad \text{where} \quad a_{ij}* = (1 - a_{ij})^{-1}$$

The interpretation of the employment linkage effect is similar to that of the total interindustry linkage effect: it expresses the total effect of any element in final demand, Y_j, on the factor of production, labor. The employment linkage effects for Taiwan, 1966, and their rankings in descending order appear in the second column of Table 15.4. We observe that this ranking of sectors differs greatly from that obtained with respect to total interindustry linkage, PL_j. In particular, agriculture is preeminent from the point of view of employment creation per unit of final demand, whereas from the point of view of interindustry linkage it is relatively unimportant.

In the analysis of interindustry and employment linkages, the level of income has been totally ignored, on the assumption that income is independent of the structure of production and, indeed, exogenous to the system. This assumption is certainly rigid. To the extent that employment is determined in part by interindustry structure, wage payments determine endogenously household income. Given the household's marginal propensities to consume different commodities, the structure of final demand is also affected. This induced household demand further stimulates a sector's demand for intermediate products and for labor, again with indirect effects on household income. This process describes the income-generation linkage effect.[8]

[8]In the definition of the income-generation linkage effect, we assume that incomes from capital and rent are relatively unimportant for the household.

Technically, the computation of the income-generation linkage effect rests on the augmentation of the interindustry input coefficients matrix by one row and one column vector.[9] The row vector is the labor-factor income supplied by households, the L row in Table 15.3. Under the assumption that households' marginal propensity to consume the output of any individual sector is proportional to their average propensity to consume, the elements of the extra column vector are ascertained by dividing every entry in the domestically supplied components of the final demand column by total household income. We have thus constructed from the original $n \times n$ I-O matrix a new matrix, D_{ij}, which is an $(n + 1) \times (n + 1)$ matrix. The last column of this matrix denotes the household sector's marginal (equal to the average) propensity to consume the output of each industry i. Therefore, household demand has been converted to the induced component of demand, even though government, investment, and export demands remain autonomous.

In order to capture both the direct and indirect income-generation effects, one inverts the $(I - D)$ matrix to get $(I - D)^{-1}$. The $(n + 1)$th row of the $(I - D)^{-1}$ is the income multiplier for each industry and defines the income-generation linkage effect, YL_j. The income-generation linkage effects for Taiwan, 1966, and their rankings (in decreasing order) are given in the last column of Table 15.4. It appears that one unit (in value terms) of expenditure in industry 2, agricultural production for raw materials, has the highest income-multiplier effect. This is presumably because of the combination of high interindustry demands for this sector, a high share of wages and salaries in value added, and a high marginal propensity to consume the output of this sector by households as a whole. Other industries with high income-generation linkages are mining and agricultural production for food, with the metal product industry ranking last.

The rankings of the three linkage effects that appear in Table 15.4 are consistent with a priori notions. First, sectors that generally

[9]Since the income linkage effect refers to the generation of household income from household expenditure and its further effects upon interindustry demand and household income, only the domestic interindustry input coefficients, D_{ij}, should be considered after deducting the input coefficients of interindustry demand.

rank high in interindustry linkage rank low in employment linkage, since labor is one component of the value added that complements intermediate demand to form the total value of output. Nevertheless, to the extent that the other primary factors, such as land and capital, are excluded from the value of L, the correlation should not be expected to be perfect. In fact, the Spearman rank-correlation coefficient between employment linkage and total interindustry linkage for the Taiwan table is only -0.20. Second, since employment generates income, the positive Spearman rank correlation of 0.61 between the rank of employment linkage and that of income-generation linkage is as expected. Because of the negative relation between interindustry linkage and employment linkage, on the one hand, and the positive relation between employment and income-generation linkages, on the other, the Spearman rank correlation coefficient of -0.76 between employment and income generation is also as expected.

Linkage Potential

The linkage effects are expressed per unit of final demand. The next step is to compute linkage potential by reflecting the level of demand that emanates from each sector, agriculture and nonagriculture. This operation can obviously change the linkage ranking of industries, especially in LDCs where agriculture accounts for 40 to 60 percent of GNP.

Had a breakdown of the final demand column of the I-O Table into its agriculture and nonagriculture components been available, this operation would have been simple and less arbitrary. Unfortunately, the finest available breakdown of final demand for any sector is according to the portion satisfied from the sector's own output and the part that comes from the other sectors. In Table 15.5, therefore, the final demand of the agricultural household sector is broken down only into C_{aa} and C_{na} and that of the nonagricultural household sector only into C_{nn} and C_{an}. This classification does not conform to the 12 $\times$ 12 classification of the Taiwan I-O Table in Table 15.4. To illustrate the method's application, therefore, we have arbitrarily chosen as the linkage effect coefficient for both C_{aa} and C_{an} the respective coefficient of industry 1, agricultural production for food. Similarly, the coefficient chosen for both C_{na} and C_{nn} is that for industry 4, food processing. One must

admit that this imputation is incomplete, since the outputs of the other industries are also partly used for final demand purposes. The validity of this expedient solution to the problem of data limitations rests on the implicit assumption that the marginal propensity to consume output of the other sectors does not differ greatly between agricultural and nonagricultural households—a tenuous assumption, indeed.

Besides final demand, another element reflected in the market contribution of the sectoral articulation approach is the interaction through the markets for intermediate products. In this regard, one should consider the demands of the agricultural sector for intermediate capital goods, for manufactured inputs, and for raw materials. In the 12 $\times$ 12 classification, these are given by industry 3, working capital for agriculture. Analogously, the intermediate demand of the nonagricultural sector for agricultural output is given by industry 4, food processing.

The three linkage potentials, production, employment, and income generation, for Taiwan are presented in Table 15.5. In each case, they are roughly equal for the two sectors, a result of the final demands for the two sectors being almost the same and of the simplifying assumptions we have made by totally disregarding the linkage effects of sectors 5 to 12. The interpretation of the items of Table 15.5 follows our description of the relevant concepts in the preceding paragraphs. The demand of agricultural households, which (as shown in the sectoral demand column) amounts to approximately NT\$21.7 billion, leads to production of both intermediate and final goods of almost NT\$44.1 billion, as shown in the production linkage potential column. The portion of this production that refers to wages and salaries amounts to about NT\$16.5 billion, as shown in the employment linkage potential column. Given the marginal propensity to consume of the agricultural household, the NT\$16.5 billion of employment potential leads to NT\$29.4 billion of income-generation potential.

Naturally, the policy implications from computing linkage effects and linkage potentials would vary, depending on the circumstances of the country to which the analysis is applied. If employment creation is important, agriculture should command special interest in development planning. (Moreover, the

Table 15.5 *Sectoral Final and Intermediate Demand and Production, Employment, and Income-Generation Linkage Potential, Taiwan, 1966*

	Sectoral Demand (NT $ million)	Production Linkage		Employment Linkage		Income-Generation Linkage	
		Index	Potential (NT $ million)	Index	Potential (NT $ million)	Index	Potential (NT $ million)
Agricultural Final Demand	*21,752*		*44,244*		*16,497*		*29,374*
C_{aa}	10,375	1.898	19,692	0.852	8,840	1.637	16,984
C_{na}	11,377	2.158	24,552	0.673	7,657	1.089	12,390
Nonagricultural Final Demand	*21,344*		*43,516*		*16,114*		*28,598*
C_{nn}	11,573	2.158	24,971	0.673	7,789	1.089	12,603
C_{an}	9,771	1.898	18,545	0.852	8,325	1.637	15,995
Agricultural Intermediate Demand from Nonagriculture							
X_{na}	6,271	2.455	15,395	0.725	4,546	1.140	7,149
Nonagricultural Intermediate Demand from Agriculture							
X_{an}	9,777	1.497	14,636	0.908	8,879	1.804	17,638
Gross National Product	125,496						

Source: Computed from Table 15.4 and Lin, W. L. (1973), "Economic Interactions in Taiwan: A Study of Sectoral Flows and Linkages," Ph.D. dissertation, Stanford University.

contribution of agriculture to employment is likely to be greater than one would conclude from Table 15.5, because wage rates are lower in agriculture than in nonagriculture.) A high income-generation potential is consistent with policies that promote income distribution. On the other hand, high income-generation linkage depends on high marginal propensities to consume, which may result in low rates of growth. Finally, since linkage potential does not account for possible supply constraints, and since supply shortages may be more chronic than deficiencies of demand in LDCs, high income-generation potential may lead to excess demand and inflationary increases in prices instead of increases in real output.

A General Equilibrium Model for the Agricultural Sector

The agricultural sector has been approached in this as well as previous chapters (for example, Chapters 4–6) primarily through partial analysis and microeconomic equilibrium. In partial equilibrium formulations, the prices of output, the prices of the variable inputs, and the quantities of the fixed factors of production have been treated as exogenous variables, while the quantities of output and the quantities of the variable factors of production have been treated as control variables determined in a microeconomic equilibrium system through the process of profit maximization. This may be realistic at the level of the firm or the village, for example, where the prices of output and of the variable factors and the quantities of the fixed inputs are determined largely as exogenous variables. At the aggregate level, however, the prices as well as quantities of output and of the variable factors of production are jointly determined as endogenous variables.

In this section, we introduce a theoretically consistent and empirically implementable method for the construction of general equilibrium models of the agricultural sector in LDCs.[10] A number of models will be developed, based on alternative assumptions about environmental and institutional characteristics of the agricultural sector. These models can be used for comparative analyses of the effects of changes in variables exogenous to the agricultural sector, such as support or ceiling prices, the terms of trade, the rate of agricultural taxation, or policies with respect to agricultural land and capital.

The method by which general equilibrium models are constructed can be divided into four parts. First, the microeconomic relations are formulated on the basis of the assumptions of utility and profit maximization and then estimated from microeconomic data. Second, the estimated microeconomic behavioral relations are aggregated across firms and households into the macroeconomic behavioral relations, to constitute the supply and demand functions for the agricultural sector. Third, alternative linkage equations between the agricultural sector and the rest of the economy are specified on the basis of alternative assumptions about the environmental and institutional characteristics of the agricultural sector. These linkage equations, once specified, may be estimated from time series macroeconomic data. Fourth, the macroeconomic behavioral relations and the macroeconomic linkage equations are combined to provide a general equilibrium solution of the agricultural sector.

To illustrate the method, we use data from Farm Management Studies of India's Ministry of Food and Agriculture to estimate the parameters of a rudimentary model of an agricultural household consisting of functions for output supply, labor demand, and labor supply. These functions are then aggregated across households to give the macroeconomic supply and demand functions. From aggregate time series data, we estimate a linkage equation between the agricultural sector and the rest of the national economy.[11] These results are used as components in several alternative equilibrium models of the agricultural sector, which reflect different specifications of the environmental and institutional characteristics.

The Microeconomic Model

The centerpiece of our approach consists of a model of a representative agricultural household, which both produces and consumes. It is assumed that the household maximizes utility, which is a function of leisure and other consumption commodities, subject to a resource constraint. In addition, it is assumed that family labor and hired labor are perfect substitutes and that the household participates in the labor market. Under this perfect labor-market assumption, Jorgenson and Lau (1969) have shown that the optimal production decisions of the household may be taken independently of the consumption decisions. In particular, this implies that at any given market wage rate the quantity of labor utilized on the household farm is independent of the quantity of labor the household is willing to supply. Hence, one is justified in analyzing first the production decisions and then the consumption decisions.

The Production Decisions

The production side of the agricultural household, as cast in a microequilibrium framework, has been presented in Chapter 6. The household may be visualized as a firm that maximizes profits (in the sense of revenues less variable costs) from agriculture in a single period, subject to a given technology, a given set of endowments with respect to the fixed factors of production—land and capital—and a given set of prices for output and the variable factors of production (mainly labor). By solving the maximization problem, we obtain the behavioral equations of output supply and factor demand at the level of the household firm.

The analysis in Chapter 6 starts with a neoclassical production function

$$V = F(X_1, \cdots, X_m; Z_1, \cdots, Z_n)$$

where V is output, X_i represents the variable inputs, and Z_i represents the fixed inputs of production. For this production function, there exists a *restricted profit function*

$$\Pi = G(p_A, q_1', \cdots, q_m', Z_1, \cdots, Z_n) \qquad (12)$$

where p_A is the price of output, and q_i' is the price of the ith variable input, which gives the maximized value of the profit for each set of values (p_A, q', Z).[12] The restricted profit

[10]The main part of this section has previously appeared in Yotopoulos and Lau (1974).

[11]The discussion on data and sources appears in Lau and Yotopoulos (1971, 1972).

[12]See Lau (1970) for a proof of these and the following results.

function is homogeneous of degree one in output and variable input prices, and thus the *normalized restricted profit function* is given by

$$\Pi^* = \frac{\Pi}{p_A} = G^*(q_1, \ldots, q_m; Z_1, \ldots, Z_n) \quad (13)$$

where $q_i = q_i'/p_A$. Under the assumption of free disposal, it can be shown that the normalized profit function is decreasing and convex in the normalized prices of variable inputs and increasing in the quantities of fixed inputs. It follows also that the normalized profit function is increasing in the price of the output.

A set of dual transformation relations connects the production function and the normalized restricted profit function.[13] The most important pair of relationships, from the point of view of our application here, is what is sometimes referred to as Shephard's (1953) Lemma, namely,

$$\chi_i^* = \frac{-\partial \Pi^* (q, Z)}{\partial q_i} \quad i = 1, \ldots, m \quad (14)$$

and

$$V^* = \Pi^* (q, Z) - \sum_{i=1}^{m} \frac{\partial \Pi^* (q, Z)}{\partial q_i} q_i \quad (15)$$

where V^* is the supply function. Equations 14 and 15 form the basis for our microeconomic formulation of the factor demand and output supply functions of the agricultural sector.

Once a specific functional form is chosen for the normalized restricted profit function, the output supply and factor demand functions can be derived directly and estimated jointly with microeconomic data. Note that specification of the normalized restricted profit function implies the specification of the output supply function and the factor demand functions. Moreover, since

$$\Pi^* (q, Z) = V^* (q, Z) - \sum_{i=1}^{m} q_i \chi_i^*(q, Z)$$

by the profit identity, only $(m + 1)$ of the $(m + 2)$ functions—the normalized restricted profit function given by equation 13, the output supply function given by equation 15, and the m factor demand functions given by equation 14—need to be estimated, because the remaining function can always be derived from the identity.

For our specific case of one variable input, labor, L, and two fixed inputs, fixed capital, K, and land, T, the normalized restricted profit function is given by

$$\Pi^* = G^*(q_L, K, T) \quad (16)$$

where q_L is the money wage rate divided by the money price of output, or the normalized price of labor. The derived demand function for labor is given by

$$L^* = \frac{-\partial \Pi^* (q_L, K, T)}{\partial q_L} \quad (17)$$

and the output supply function is given by

$$V^* = \Pi^* - \frac{\partial \Pi^* (q_L, K, T)}{\partial q_L} q_L \quad (18)$$

Equations 17 and 18 comprise the production sector of the microeconomic model.

In our illustrative application, the production function for each agricultural household is specified to be Cobb-Douglas in form. This implies that the normalized restricted profit function is

$$\Pi^* = A^*\left(\frac{q_L'}{p_A}\right)^{\alpha_1^*} K^{\beta_1^*} T^{\beta_2^*}$$

or

$$\ln \Pi^* = \ln A^* + \alpha_1^* \ln q_L' - \alpha_1'^* \ln p_A \\ + \beta_1^* \ln K + \beta_2^* \ln T \quad (19)$$

where q_L' is the money wage rate and p_A the money price of agricultural output. Labor demand, as given in equation 17, is[14]

$$\frac{q_L'}{p_A} L_D = -\alpha_1^* \Pi^*$$

or

$$\ln L_D = \ln (-\alpha_1^*) + \ln \Pi^* - \ln q_L' + \ln p_A \quad (20)$$

The output supply function is then given by

$$V_S = \Pi^* + \frac{q_L'}{p_A} L_D$$
$$= \Pi^* - \alpha_1^* \Pi^*$$
$$= (1 - \alpha_1^*) \Pi^* \quad (21)$$

Thus, the output supply and labor demand

---

[13]These relations are given and proved in McFadden (1970) and Lau (1970).

[14]Multiplying both sides of equation 17 by $-q_L/\Pi^*$ we have $-q_L L^*/\Pi^* = \partial \ln \Pi^*/\partial \ln q_L$, which for the C–D profit function is given in equation 20.

functions are given by

$$\ln V_S = \ln (1 - \alpha_1{}^*) + \ln A^* + \alpha_1{}^* \ln q_L'$$
$$- \alpha_1{}^* \ln P_A + \beta_1{}^* \ln K + \beta_2{}^* \ln T \quad (22)$$

$$\ln L_D = \ln (-\alpha_1{}^*) + \ln A^* + (\alpha_1{}^* - 1) \ln q_L'$$
$$- (\alpha_1{}^* - 1) \ln p_A + \beta_1{}^* \ln K$$
$$+ \beta_2{}^* \ln T \quad (23)$$

Equations 19, 22, and 23 are the estimating equations for the production decisions of the household. Two of the equations, that for labor demand and either the equation for normalized restricted profit or that for output supply, are independent and will be estimated jointly.[15]

Since, in equations 19 and 23, the variables on the left-hand side are the jointly dependent variables and those on the right-hand side include only the predetermined variables, consistent estimates can be obtained by applying ordinary least squares to each equation separately. In general, however, these estimates will be inefficient, because the fact that $\alpha_1{}^*$ appears in both equations 19 and 23 has been ignored. A natural and more efficient approach will be to estimate equations 19 and 23 jointly, imposing the condition that the two $\alpha_1{}^*$'s are equal. Assume that equations 19 and 23 have an additive error term with zero expectation and finite variance. For equation 19, this implies that farms maximize profits subject to unknown exogenous disturbances. The additive error in equation 23 may arise from differential abilities to maximize profits or divergence between expected and realized prices. Given this specification of the errors, Zellner's (1962) method, by which known constraints on the coefficients

in the equations are imposed, provides an asymptotically efficient method of estimation.

Equations 19 and 23 are first estimated jointly, imposing the condition that $\alpha_1{}^*$ is identical from both equations. These results as well as those of single equation ordinary least squares and of unconstrained Zellner's method are presented in Table 15.9 in the Appendix. One may note the marked improvement in the coefficients that results from joint estimation of both functions.

The Consumption Decisions

The consumption decisions of the household can be developed formally within a utility maximization model.[16] In this approach, by specifying an indirect utility function one can estimate the labor supply and the consumption demand functions of the household. In this section, however, we will simplify the consumption side of the household to make it consistent with our data limitations. We specify directly the labor supply function as a function of the wage rate, the price of agricultural output, money profits from agricultural production, fixed obligations,[17] the number of working family members, and the total number of family members in the household. Thus, the labor supply function can be written as

$$L_S = f\left(q_L', p_A, \frac{\Pi}{N_f}, \frac{O}{N_f}, N_w, N_f \right) \quad (24)$$

where O is fixed obligations less asset income, N_w is the number of workers in the household, and N_f is the total number of household family members, workers plus dependents, and the other symbols are as defined previously.

By distinguishing two kinds of household income, nonlabor agricultural income, Π, and fixed obligations, O, we allow that the effects on consumption of leisure of the two types of income may be different. On the other hand, it is not necessary to distinguish whether the labor hired out is for agricultural or nonagricultural activities so long as the net rate of compensation is the same. Once a specific functional form is chosen, the labor supply

---

[15]A remark about the stochastic specification of the model is appropriate. Given our assumptions of profit maximization with production functions concave in the variable inputs and the short-run fixity of the quantities of capital and land, the price-taking farm-firm's decision variables are the quantities of output and labor input. Consequently, output and labor input are the jointly dependent variables, and the prices of output and variable inputs and the quantities of fixed inputs are the predetermined variables in the model. Because of the profit identity, namely, that profit is equal to current revenue less current variable costs, an alternative set of jointly dependent variables consists of profits and total labor costs. From the specification of equations 19, 22, and 23, it can be seen that, given the predetermined variables, there is a one-to-one and onto correspondence between profits and total labor costs and the quantities of output and labor input.

[16]For further elaboration of this approach, see Yotopoulos and Lau (1974).

[17]The purpose of the variable fixed obligations is to capture the net nonfarm, nonlabor income of the household. It thus includes nonfarm asset income minus taxes and other fixed obligations of the household.

function can be directly estimated from micro-economic data.[18]

For the household labor supply function, we specify the following constant elasticity form

$$\ln L_S = \ln \gamma_0^* + \gamma_1^* \ln q_L' + \gamma_2^* \ln \frac{\Pi}{N_f}$$
$$+ \gamma_3^* \ln \frac{O}{N_f} - (\gamma_1^* + \gamma_2^* + \gamma_3^*) \ln p_A$$
$$+ \gamma_4^* \ln N_w + \gamma_5^* \ln N_f \quad (25)$$

where the condition of zero degree homogeneity in prices and income has been imposed.[19] This is the actual form used in the estimation. By substituting

$$\ln \Pi = \ln p_A + \ln \Pi^*$$
$$= \ln p_A + \ln V_S - \ln(1 - \alpha_1^*)$$

into equation 25 and using equation 21, we have

$$\ln L_S = \ln \gamma_0^* - \gamma_2^* \ln(1 - \alpha_1^*) + \gamma_1^* \ln q_L'$$
$$+ \gamma_2^* \ln V_S + \gamma_3^* \ln O$$
$$- (\gamma_1^* + \gamma_3^*) \ln p_A + \gamma_4^* \ln N_w$$
$$+ (\gamma_5^* - \gamma_2^* - \gamma_3^*) \ln N_f \quad (26)$$

Equation 26 is a reduced form equation for microeconomic labor supply, expressed only in terms of variables exogenous to the agricultural household.

Equilibrium of the Household

Thus, the agricultural household equilibrium values of output supply, labor demand, and labor supply are completely determined, given values of the money wage rate, the money price of output, the quantities of capital and land, fixed obligations, and the number of working and total family members. Of course, the labor demanded is not necessarily equal to the labor supplied, because of the existence of hired-in and hired-out labor. Nevertheless, as far as the household is concerned, there is no incentive to change any of the decision variables—output, labor demand, labor supply—unless the exogenous conditions change. But given changes in the variables exogenous to the household, it is possible to compute directly the changes in the equilibrium values of output, labor demanded, and labor supplied.

Rewriting the output supply, the labor demand, and the labor supply functions for the household in matrix form, putting the three endogenous variables on the left-hand side, we have

$$
\begin{bmatrix}
1 & 0 & 0 \\
0 & 1 & 0 \\
-\gamma_2^* & 0 & 1
\end{bmatrix}
\begin{bmatrix}
\ln V_S \\
\ln L_D \\
\ln L_S
\end{bmatrix}
=
\begin{bmatrix}
\ln(1-\alpha_1^*)+\ln A^* & \alpha_1^* & -\alpha_1^* & \beta_1^* & \beta_2^* & 0 & 0 & 0 \\
\ln(-\alpha_1^*)+\ln A^* & \alpha_1^*-1 & -(\alpha_1^*-1) & \beta_1^* & \beta_2^* & 0 & 0 & 0 \\
\ln \gamma_0^* - \gamma_2^* \ln(1-\alpha_1^*) & \gamma_1^* & -(\gamma_2^*+\gamma_3^*) & 0 & 0 & \gamma_3^* & \gamma_4^* & (\gamma_5^*-\gamma_2^*-\gamma_3^*)
\end{bmatrix}
\begin{bmatrix}
1 \\
\ln q_L' \\
\ln p_A \\
\ln K \\
\ln T \\
\ln O \\
\ln N_w \\
\ln N_f
\end{bmatrix}
$$

This can be solved to yield the reduced form output supply, labor demand, and labor supply functions, given by

$$
\begin{bmatrix}
\ln V_S \\
\ln L_D \\
\ln L_S
\end{bmatrix}
=
\begin{bmatrix}
\ln(1-\alpha_1^*)\ln A^* & \alpha_1^* & -\alpha_1^* & \beta_1^* & \beta_2^* & 0 & 0 & 0 \\
\ln(-\alpha_1^*+\ln A^*) & \alpha_1^*-1 & -(\alpha_1^*-1) & \beta_1^* & \beta_2^* & 0 & 0 & 0 \\
\ln \gamma_0^* + \gamma_2^* \ln A^* & (\gamma_1^*+\gamma_2^*\alpha_1^*) & -(\gamma_1^*+\gamma_3^*)-\gamma_2^*\alpha_1^* & \gamma_2^*\beta_1^* & \gamma_2^*\beta_2^* & \gamma_3^* & \gamma_4^* & (\gamma_5^*-\gamma_2^*-\gamma_3^*)
\end{bmatrix}
\begin{bmatrix}
1 \\
\ln q_L' \\
\ln p_A \\
\ln K \\
\ln T \\
\ln O \\
\ln N_w \\
\ln N_f
\end{bmatrix}
$$

---

[18]Note that while the production decisions of the household may be made independently of the consumption decisions, the consumption decisions depend on the outcome of the production decisions, specifically on the level of profits from the agricultural operation. In other words, the model of the agricultural household is a block recursive one, in which the household can be visualized as first making the production decisions according to the profit-maximization principle and then, subject to the level of planned profits, determining the optimal choice of leisure, work, and consumption. Given this recursive structure of the model, the appropriate estimation procedure consists of first estimating the parameters of the production block and then using the fitted value of the profits in the estimation of the labor supply functions.

[19]Observe that labor supply should be invariant with respect to a proportional change in the wage rate, price of agricultural output, money profits, and fixed obligations. Hence, it must be homogeneous of degree zero in q_L', p_A, Π and O. This implies that the sum of the elasticities of labor supply with respect to the money wage rate, money price of output, profits, and fixed obligations must be zero, that is,

$$\frac{q_L'}{f}\frac{\partial f}{\partial q_L'} + \frac{p_A}{f}\frac{\partial f}{\partial p_A} + \frac{\Pi}{f}\frac{\partial f}{\partial \Pi} + \frac{O}{f}\frac{\partial f}{\partial O} = 0$$

Table 15.6 *Coefficients of the Reduced-Form Output Supply, Labor Demand, and Labor Supply Functions: Microeconomic Analysis*

Endogenous Variables	Inter-cept	$\ln q_L'$	$\ln p_A$	$\ln K$	$\ln T$	$\ln O$	$\ln N_w$	$\ln N_f$
				Exogenous Variables				
$\ln V_s$	5.188	−1.166	1.166	−0.224	1.224	0	0	0
$\ln L_D$	4.569	−2.166	2.166	−0.224	1.224	0	0	0
$\ln L_s$	2.107	1.583	−2.078	0.224	−1.224	0.494	1.575	1.177

Note: For variable definitions, see Appendix.
Source: Yotopoulos, P. A., and L. J. Lau (1974), "On Modeling the Agricultural Sector in Developing Economies: An Integrated Approach of Micro and Macroeconomics," *J. D. E.*, 1 (June), p. 113.

Given our specification of the model, the coefficients of the matrix provide estimates of all the reduced form elasticities. For example, the elasticity of output supply with respect to the money wage rate is given by α_1^*. The elasticity of labor demand with respect to the money wage rate is given by $\alpha_1^* - 1$. The elasticity of labor supply with respect to the wage rate is given by $\gamma_1^* + \gamma_2^* \alpha_1^*$. Note that changes in the levels of fixed obligations (less asset income) and in family size and composition do not affect either output supply or labor demand, i.e., the elasticities are zero. This feature is a direct implication of our assumption of a perfect labor market.

Using estimates from Indian agriculture, details of which are presented in the Appendix, the coefficients of the reduced form output supply, labor demand, and labor supply functions have been computed and are presented in Table 15.6. The exogenous variables are the wage rate, the price of output, capital, land, fixed obligations, and the numbers of working and total family members. For the household, the elasticity of labor supply with respect to output price is negative. This is because an increase in the price of output leads to an increase in profits, the household's nonlabor agricultural income, which shifts labor supply to the left. A similar interpretation applies to the negative coefficient of labor supply with respect to land. The coefficients of output and labor demand, with respect to the price of output and the quantity of land, are positive, while that with respect to the wage rate is negative. Increases in the numbers of working family members or total household members, as well as increases in fixed obligations (e.g., taxes), lead to increases

in labor supplied.[20] With the exception of the reduced form coefficients of capital, our results are plausible and consistent with economic theory. The wrong signs of the capital coefficients are a direct consequence of the fact that the estimate of the capital coefficient in the normalized profit function has the wrong (negative) sign, which can probably be attributed to errors in the measurement of the capital input.[21]

Aggregation of Microeconomic Relationships
Given the estimated microeconomic relationships, one can derive the macroeconomic relationships by summing over all the households in the economy. We approximate these macroeconomic relationships by multiplying the estimated microeconomic behavioral functions by the total number of households in the agricultural sector, say *n*. This approximation will be exact if we assume that all households are identical in terms of their utility functions, production functions, initial endowments of fixed inputs, family size and composition, and fixed obligations. Although this seems an overly strong assumption, it is not unusual in macroeconomic analysis. Ideally, the macroeconomic relationships should be derived by integrating the microeconomic relationships over the distribution of the households in the relevant dimensions, including such characteristics as education, national origin, or religion. However, if the joint density function is sufficiently concentrated, the error

[20]The fact that fixed obligations and household workers do not affect the production decisions, that is, output supply and labor demand, is a direct consequence of our block recursive assumption.
[21]See the discussion in Yotopoulos (1967*a, b*) and in Lau and Yotopoulos (1971).

incurred by our approximation will be small. Alternatively, we can justify our present approach by appealing to the useful paradigm of a "representative household."

Thus, the macroeconomic output supply, labor demand, and labor supply functions are[22]

$$
\begin{array}{l}
\ln V_S{}^M \\
\ln L_D{}^M \\
\ln L_S{}^M
\end{array}
=
\begin{array}{l}
\ln(1 - \alpha_1{}^*) + \ln A^* + \ln n \\
\ln(-\alpha_1{}^*) + \ln A^* + \ln n \\
\ln \gamma_0{}^* + \gamma_2{}^* + \ln A^* + \ln n
\end{array}
\quad
\begin{array}{l}
\alpha_1{}^* \\
\alpha_1{}^* - 1 \\
\gamma_1{}^* + \gamma_2{}^* \alpha_1{}^*
\end{array}
\quad
\begin{array}{l}
-\alpha_1{}^* \\
-(\alpha_1{}^* - 1) \\
(\gamma_1{}^* + \gamma_3{}^*) - \gamma_2{}^* \alpha_1{}^*
\end{array}
\quad
\begin{array}{l}
\beta_2{}^* \\
\beta_2{}^* \\
\gamma_2{}^* \beta_2{}^*
\end{array}
\quad
\begin{array}{l}
\beta_1{}^* \\
\beta_1{}^* \\
\gamma_2{}^* \beta_1{}^*
\end{array}
\quad
\begin{array}{l}
0 \\
0 \\
\gamma_3{}^*
\end{array}
\quad
\begin{array}{l}
0 \\
0 \\
\gamma_4{}^*
\end{array}
\quad
\begin{array}{l}
0 \\
0 \\
(\gamma_5{}^* - \gamma_2{}^* - \gamma_3{}^*)
\end{array}
\quad
\begin{array}{l}
1 \\
\ln q_L{}' \\
\ln p_A \\
\ln K \\
\ln T \\
\ln O \\
\ln N_w \\
\ln N_f
\end{array}
$$

where the superscript M signifies that the variable refers to the macroeconomic or aggregate output supply, labor demand, or labor supply, and the independent variables $\ln K$, $\ln T$, $\ln O$, $\ln N_w$, and $\ln N_f$ are to be interpreted as the mean values of all the households in the agricultural sector.

Types of Macroeconomic Equilibria

We now turn our attention to examination of the nature of the various types of macroeconomic equilibria of the agricultural sector. We consider the macroeconomic equilibria of three institutional prototypes with respect to the agricultural sector: closed, regulated, and open. These terms will be defined presently; they refer to the agricultural sector's relationship vis-à-vis the rest of the national economy. Most actual agricultural sectors are, of course, a mixture of all three types.

Macroeconomic Equilibrium in a Closed Agricultural Sector

A *closed* agricultural sector is one that has no linkages with the rest of the national economy. The equilibrium prices and quantities of agricultural output and inputs are determined without reference to the other sectors. If, in addition, competitive markets prevail in the agricultural sector, the prices and quantities of agricultural output and inputs will be determined by the simultaneous equality of supply and demand functions of output and inputs.

[22]To the extent that there exist landless laborers, the number of households included in deriving the microeconomic labor supply function may be different from the number of households included in deriving the macroeconomic labor demand function. Even if this discrepancy occurs, our analysis is almost completely unaffected, except for a change in the constant term, as long as we maintain the hypothesis that the utility functions of the landed and landless laborers are identical despite differences in endowments.

Should data be available at the household level for the estimation of a microeconomic demand function for agricultural output, a macroeconomic demand function for the closed agricultural sector can be obtained by aggregating across the households. This macroeconomic demand function for agricultural output, together with the macroeconomic supply function of agricultural output and the macroeconomic demand and supply functions for labor, will comprise a simultaneous system of four equations, which jointly determine the equilibrium levels of the price and quantity of output and of labor. These four functions alone determine the behavior of the closed agricultural sector.

Unfortunately, consumption data on the agricultural households that are consistent with the production data are unavailable in our case. Consequently, in our illustrative model for India, it is not possible to study the full implications of a closed agricultural sector.

Macroeconomic Equilibrium in a Regulated Agricultural Sector

A *regulated* agricultural sector is a sector in which one or more of the markets are controlled by the government. The regulations can take various forms: price control of outputs (either price support or price ceiling), price control of inputs, compulsory purchases of outputs, or rationing of inputs. The distinguishing feature of a regulated agricultural sector is that at least one equilibrium price or quantity is not determined by the equality of supply and demand in its market. For example, in an agricultural sector in which the output price is a government purchase price (fixed regardless of the quantity supplied), the equilibrium quantity, assuming that there are no quota restrictions, is determined by the supply function, given the government purchase price. In this case, the demand function for agricultural output does not play a role in the determination of the equilibrium. Another example of regulation arises if fertilizers are sold by the government at a fixed (subsidized) price. At this price, however, the quantity supplied falls short of the quantity demanded. Consequently, some kind of nonmarket rationing mechanism is required. In this case, neither the price nor the quantity of fertilizers may have any relevance to the supply function of or the demand function for fertilizers.

Within the context of our illustrative model, several alternative specifications of regulations are possible. First, one can consider an agricultural sector that is closed with respect to the labor market (there is no possibility of migration) and regulated with respect to the output market (the price of output is determined by the government). In this case, given the government determined price of output, the equilibrium price and quantity of labor are determined by the equality of the supply and demand functions in the labor market, and the equilibrium quantity of output is then given by the supply function.[23] Second, one can consider an agricultural economy regulated in both the output and labor markets, with the government setting both the price of the output and the price of labor (for instance, setting a minimum wage). In this case, the equilibrium quantities of output and labor are determined from the output supply function and the labor demand functions alone. Third, one can also consider the symmetrical case of an economy that is closed with respect to the output market but regulated with respect to the labor market. This case is not of practical interest for our illustrative model, however, because the macroeconomic demand function for output is missing.

The first specification, that of an agricultural sector closed with respect to the labor market but regulated with respect to the output market, implies that the quantity of labor demanded must be equal to the quantity of labor supplied at the macroeconomic level;

$$L_D{}^M = L_S{}^M = L^M$$

In this process, the price of labor is also determined as that price which clears the labor market. The three endogenous variables under this specification, $V_S{}^M$, L^M, and q_L', may be solved simultaneously as functions of the exogenous variables: the price of output and the levels of fixed capital, land, fixed obligations, the numbers of working and of total family members. Rewriting the macroeconomic supply and demand functions in matrix form, with all the endogenous variables on the left-hand side, and bearing in mind the equilibrium condition above, we have

$$
\begin{bmatrix}
1 & 0 & -\alpha_1{}^* \\
0 & 1 & -(\alpha_1{}^* - 1) \\
-\gamma_2{}^* & 1 & -\gamma_1{}^*
\end{bmatrix}
\begin{bmatrix}
\ln V_S{}^M \\
\ln L^M \\
\ln q_L'
\end{bmatrix}
=
\begin{bmatrix}
\ln(1 - \alpha_1{}^* + \ln A^* + \ln n \\
\ln(-\alpha_1{}^*) + \ln A^* + \ln n \\
\ln \gamma_0{}^* - \gamma_2{}^* \ln(1 - \alpha_1{}^*) + \ln n
\end{bmatrix}
$$

$$
+
\begin{bmatrix}
-\alpha_1{}^* & \beta_1{}^* & \beta_2{}^* & 0 & 0 & 0 \\
-(\alpha_1{}^* - 1) & \beta_1{}^* & \beta_2{}^* & 0 & 0 & 0 \\
-(\gamma_1{}^* + \gamma_3{}^*) & 0 & 0 & \gamma_3{}^* & \gamma_1{}^* & (\gamma_5{}^* - \gamma_2{}^* - \gamma_3{}^*)
\end{bmatrix}
\begin{bmatrix}
1 \\
\ln p_A \\
\ln K \\
\ln T \\
\ln O \\
\ln N_w \\
\ln N_f
\end{bmatrix}
$$

The coefficients of the reduced form output supply, employment, and wage functions are presented in Table 15.7.[24]

An increase in the price of output leads to decreases in the equilibrium levels of aggregate output supplied and employment and an increase in the equilibrium wage rate. This result may be contrasted with the effects of an increase in the price of output at the microeconomic household level. There, an increase in the price of output leads to an increase in output supplied and labor demanded, but a decrease in the labor supplied. This decrease in the labor supply at the household level is responsible for the negative output and employment response at the macroeconomic level. The decrease in labor supply leads to an increase in the equilibrium wage rate, and the increase in the equilibrium wage rate causes a decline in both output supply and employment, which overwhelms the direct positive response of output supply and labor demand to an increase in the price of output.

An increase in the quantity of land, for example, through reclamation projects, leads to an increase in the equilibrium level of output supplied and the equilibrium wage rate, but a decrease in the equilibrium level of employment. The mechanism is similar to that of an increase in the price of output, except

---

[23]In practice, this case appears to be extremely likely.

[24]We note that if and only if $(-\gamma_1{}^* - \alpha_1{}^* \gamma_2{}^* + \alpha_1{}^* - 1) \neq 0$, the matrix on the left-hand side can be inverted to provide estimates of the reduced form output supply, employment, and wage functions. For our sample estimates of the coefficients, we have $(-\gamma_1{}^* - \alpha_1{}^* + \gamma_1{}^* + \alpha_1{}^* - 1) = -1.583 - 2.166 = -3.749$

Table 15.7 *Coefficients of the Reduced-Form Output Supply, Employment, and Wage Functions: Macroeconomic Analysis of Regulated Agriculture*

Endogenous Variables	Exogenous Variables						
	Intercept	$\ln p_A$	$\ln K$	$\ln T$	$\ln O$	$\ln N_w$	$\ln N_f$
$\ln V$	16.778	−0.154	−0.085	0.463	0.154	0.490	0.366
$\ln L$	10.713	−0.287	0.035	−0.190	0.285	0.910	0.680
$\ln q_L'$	5.445	0.646	−0.120	0.653	−0.132	−0.420	−0.314

Note: For variable definitions, see Appendix.
Source: Yotopoulos, P. A., and L. J. Lau (1974), "On Modeling the Agricultural Sector in Developing Economies: An Integrated Approach of Micro and Macroeconomics," *J.D.E.,* 1 (June), p. 117.

that the decline in equilibrium employment is compensated by the increase in land, and so the equilibrium output supplied shows a net increase.

An increase in fixed obligations, for example, agricultural taxation, shifts the microeconomic labor supply functions to the right. It does not affect the production sector at the microeconomic level. Consequently, at the macroeconomic level, it leads to increases in equilibrium output supplied and employment, and to a decrease in the equilibrium wage rate. The effects of increases in the numbers of working and of total family members can be similarly analyzed. The fact that the effects of changes in exogenous variables may be quite different between the micro- and macroeconomic models emphasizes the importance of general equilibrium considerations in the analysis and evaluation of policy changes.

The second specification, that of a completely regulated agricultural sector (in which the prices of inputs as well as output are determined by the government), implies that the output supply is determined by the macroeconomic output supply function, and the labor demand is determined by the macroeconomic labor demand function. Since all the variables entering these two functions are exogenous under the assumption of perfect regulation, the reduced form functions are given precisely by the macroeconomic output supply and labor demand functions themselves. Hence, no new computation or interpretation is needed.

Macroeconomic Equilibrium in an Open Agricultural Sector

An *open* agricultural sector is one that has linkages with the rest of the national economy. These linkages can operate through the out-

put market, the input market, or both. An agricultural sector is considered open if it is not completely closed or regulated in all markets. To take into account the effects of these linkages on the equilibrium of the agricultural sector, linkage equations can be specified. These equations typically consist of the demand functions of the nonagricultural sector for agricultural output and labor and the supply functions of manufactured inputs and consumption commodities to the agricultural sector. Generally speaking, one may consider these demand and supply functions as functions of the price of agricultural output and labor, the income level of the nonagricultural sector, the population of the nonagricultural sector, the prices of the intermediate inputs and consumption commodities supplied by the nonagricultural sector to the agricultural sector, and the quantities of imports and exports of each commodity that is specifically distinguished, including labor. Thus, for a typical linkage equation, one may write

$$D_i = g_i(p_A, q_L', Y_{na}, N_{na}, P_{na}, M)$$

where

Y_{na} = real nonagricultural income

N_{na} = nonagricultural population

p_{na} = prices of nonagricultural commodities (possibly a vector)

M = net imports of agricultural commodities (possibly a vector).

In the context of our illustrative model, we once again consider several alternative specifications. First, consider an agricultural economy that is open with respect to the output market and closed with respect to the labor market, that is, equilibrium of the output market is achieved by the equality of output supply and the sum of the demands for agricultural output of the agricultural and nonagricultural sectors, and equilibrium of the agricultural labor market is achieved by the equality of the labor supply and labor demand in the agricultural sector itself. In other words, the equilibrium conditions are

$$V_S{}^M = V_D{}^M + D_V$$
$$L_S{}^M = L_D{}^M$$

where D_V is the demand for agricultural output by the nonagricultural sector.

Second, consider an agricultural economy that is open with respect to both the output and the labor markets. The equilibrium conditions in this case are

$$V_S{}^M = V_D{}^M + D_V$$
$$L_S{}^M = L_D{}^M + D_L$$

where D_L is the demand for agricultural labor by the nonagricultural sector.

Third, consider the symmetrical case of an economy that is open with respect to the labor market and closed with respect to the output market. The equilibrium conditions in this case are

$$V_S{}^M = V_D{}^M$$
$$L_S{}^M = L_D{}^M + D_L$$

Because the macroeconomic demand function of agricultural output of the agricultural sector is not available, in principle, neither the first nor the second specifications can be implemented. And because data are not available for the estimation of a demand function for agricultural labor of the nonagricultural sector, the third specification cannot be implemented either. In the case of the first specification, however, one can circumvent the difficulty by directly specifying a macroeconomic demand function for agricultural output

of the whole economy. It can be written as

$$V_D{}^T = g(p_A, p_{na}, Y, N, M)$$

where $V_D{}^T$ is the total quantity of agricultural output demanded in the whole economy,[25] p_{na} is the price of nonagricultural commodities, Y is the real national income used as a proxy for the activity level, N is the total population, and M is the net imports of agricultural commodities. Imports and domestic output are not required to be perfect substitutes.

For this case, the output and labor markets must clear. Hence, we have

$$V_S{}^M = V_D{}^T = V^M$$

and

$$L_S{}^M = L_D{}^M = L^M$$

By imposing these equilibrium conditions on our system of four functions—output supply, output demand, labor demand, labor supply—the equilibrium values of the price and quantities of output and labor can be determined as functions of the exogenous variables: fixed capital, land, fixed obligations, the number of working family members, the number of total family members, the price of nonagricultural commodities, real national income, total population, and net imports of agricultural commodities.[26] With these functions, one can analyze the effects of various government policies.

For purposes of empirical estimation, we specify the total demand function for agricultural output as

$$\ln V_D{}^T = \ln \delta_0{}^* + \delta_1{}^* \ln p_A - \delta_1{}^* \ln p_{na}$$
$$+ \delta_2{}^* \ln Y + \delta_3{}^* \ln N + \delta_4{}^* \ln M$$
$$(27)$$

where zero-degree homogeneity in prices has been imposed. Given this specification, one can write the four equations in matrix form

$$
\begin{bmatrix}
1 & 0 & -\alpha_1{}^* & \alpha_1{}^* \\
0 & 1 & -(\alpha_1{}^*-1) & \alpha_1{}^*-1 \\
-\gamma_2{}^* & 1 & -\gamma_1{}^* & (\gamma_1{}^*+\gamma_3{}^*) \\
1 & 0 & 0 & -\delta_1{}^*
\end{bmatrix}
\begin{bmatrix}
\ln V \\ \ln L \\ \ln q_{L}' \\ \ln p_A
\end{bmatrix}
=
\begin{bmatrix}
\ln(1-\alpha_1{}^*) + A^* + \ln n \\
\ln(-\alpha_1{}^*) + A^* + \ln n \\
\ln \gamma_0{}^* - \gamma_2{}^* \ln (1-\alpha_1{}^*) + \ln n \\
\ln \delta_0{}^*
\end{bmatrix}
$$

$$
\begin{bmatrix}
\beta_1{}^* & \beta_2{}^* & 0 & 0 & 0 & 0 & 0 & 0 & 0 \\
\beta_1{}^* & \beta_2{}^* & 0 & 0 & 0 & 0 & 0 & 0 & 0 \\
0 & 0 & \gamma_3{}^* & \gamma_4{}^* & (\gamma_5{}^*-\gamma_2{}^*-\gamma_3{}^*) & 0 & 0 & 0 & 0 \\
0 & 0 & 0 & 0 & 0 & -\delta_1{}^* & \delta_2{}^* & \delta_3{}^* & \delta_4{}^*
\end{bmatrix}
\begin{bmatrix}
1 \\ \ln K \\ \ln T \\ \ln O \\ \ln N_w \\ \ln N_f \\ \ln p_{na} \\ \ln Y \\ \ln N \\ \ln M
\end{bmatrix}
$$

---

[25]The demand function must be zero degree homogeneous in p_A and p_{na}, as any consumer demand function should be, that is

$$\frac{g}{p_A} \frac{\partial g}{\partial p_A} + \frac{p_{na}}{g} \frac{\partial g}{\partial p_{na}} = 0$$

[26]Strictly speaking, real national income is not an exogenous variable. The total population variable should also be interpreted carefully. The impact of a given change in total population consists of two effects: a direct effect through the output demand function and an indirect effect through the induced

Table 15.8 *Coefficients of the Reduced-Form Output, Employment, Wage, and Price of Output Functions: Macroeconomic Analysis of Open Agriculture*

Endogenous Variables	Exogenous Variables									
	Intercept	$\ln K$	$\ln T$	$\ln O$	$\ln N_w$	$\ln N_f$	$\ln p_{na}$	$\ln Y$	$\ln N$	$\ln M$
$\ln V$	19.219	−0.111	0.606	0.202	0.642	0.479	−0.202	−0.384	0.067	0.008
$\ln L$	17.761	−0.014	0.075	0.374	1.192	0.889	−0.374	−0.714	0.125	0.015
$\ln q_L'$	−31.571	0.073	−0.398	−0.482	−1.534	−1.145	1.482	2.827	−0.494	−0.061
$\ln p_A$	−32.410	0.170	−0.928	−0.309	−0.984	−0.734	1.309	2.497	−0.436	−0.054

Note: For variable definitions, see Appendix.
Source: Yotopoulos, P. A., and L. J. Lau (1974), "On Modeling the Agricultural Sector in Developing Economies: An Integrated Approach of Micro and Macroeconomics," *J.D.E.*, 1 (June), p. 122.

The coefficients of the reduced form functions are reported in Table 15.8.[27]

The price of output for this model of an open and regulated agricultural sector is now endogenously determined. An increase in the quantity of land leads to increases in the equilibrium levels of output supplied and employment but to decreases in the equilibrium wage rate and the price of output. The mechanism may be understood as follows: other things being equal, an increase in the quantity of land leads to an increase in the output supplied. The increase in the supply of output in turn depresses the price of output. A decrease in the price of output leads to a decrease in employment; this decrease overwhelms the direct negative effect on employment of an increase in the quantity of land, resulting in an overall increase in employment. The effects of changes in the other variables that do not appear in the output demand function, such as fixed obligations and the numbers of working and total family members, may be traced in an analogous way.

The effects of changes in the levels of the exogenous variables included in the output demand function can be studied through hypothetical shifts of the demand functions. Consider an increase in net agricultural imports, for example, through Public Law 480 programs. By shifting the demand for domestic agricultural output to the left, other things being equal, a decrease in the price of output is induced. Consequently, the effects outlined in the analysis of Table 15.7 follow: the equilibrium levels of output supplied and employment increase, and the equilibrium wage rate decreases. One should exercise some care in analyzing the effect of an increase in total population: the total effect will consist of two parts, the direct effect of an increase in total population and the indirect effect through an induced increase in the agricultural labor force and the agricultural population, represented by the numbers of working and total family members.

Again, this model differs sharply from the previous ones as to the effects of various government policy variables included, such as capital, land, fixed obligations, and workers per household. These differences emanate from alternative assumptions about the price of output—being fixed by government policy in the regulated model, as opposed to being determined by supply and demand in the open model. The relevance of one or the other model depends on the institutional context of the specific economy. In any actual situation, it is important to know which variables are subject to direct control and which are to be determined as a result of market forces. In our opinion, the validity of any model linking

---

change of the family size and composition, which in turn affects the equilibrium through the labor supply function.

[27] The reduced form values for output, employment, the wage rate, and the price of output can only be obtained if the matrix on the left-hand side is nonsingular. The necessary and sufficient condition for singularity is

$-\alpha_1^*\gamma_3^* + \delta_1^*(\gamma_1^* + \alpha_1^*\gamma_2^* - \alpha_1^* + 1) = 0$

Some sufficient conditions are:
(1) $\alpha_1^* = \delta_1^* = 0$, that is, both the elasticity of the wage rate with respect to profit and the elasticity of demand with respect to price are equal to zero.
(2) $\delta_3^* = \delta_1^* = 0$, that is, the elasticities of labor supply with respect to fixed obligations and of output demand with respect to price are equal to zero.

changes in the agricultural sector to overall growth and development rests heavily on the skill with which such distinctions are made.[28]

Summary and Conclusions

The role of agriculture in economic development has been exhaustively studied from different viewpoints in the literature. It has often been approached from the point of view of the intersectoral transfer of resources, mainly agricultural surplus. Even more commonly, it has been viewed within the dualism model, based on surplus labor but supplemented by a set of dynamic laws leading to the break-out point and to the disappearance of dualism.

In this chapter, we have presented a synthesis that departs from previous approaches. The contributions of agriculture have been defined in terms of both intersectoral transfers of agricultural surplus arising from the production squeeze and increasing sectoral interdependence involving output, intermediate inputs, capital, and labor. The production squeeze portion of the agricultural surplus aspect has been made operational and applied with respect to Taiwan, 1952–1970. Even though the human capital flows arising from the expenditure squeeze have been neglected, the estimates presented have provided a dramatic example of how, in the early stages of development, flows out of agriculture may account for as much as 25 percent of per capita income, gradually decreasing in the process of growth.

The sectoral articulation approach has been based on input-output analysis and on sectoral linkages of three kinds: interindustry linkages, employment linkages, and income-generation linkages. When linkage coefficients are combined with the demand satisfied by the agricultural sector, we obtain measures of linkage potentials. From these measures, the full contribution of the agricultural sector in providing intermediate inputs and employment can be appreciated. This approach is especially relevant when the employment and income distribution aspects of economic development are emphasized.

Our earlier treatment of agriculture (in Part II) was based on partial analysis and microeconomic equilibrium. In the present chapter, we have extended that framework, first by incorporating sectoral resource flows and then by including sectoral interrelations. The next step has been to cast agriculture into a general equilibrium macroeconomic model. In this context, what previously were exogenous variables, namely, the prices of output and of the variable factors of production, as well as the endogenous equilibrium quantities of output and inputs, have been jointly determined in a system treating as exogenous variables the factors that determine the supply and demand curves of inputs and output. The supply of labor has served as the link between the consumption decisions of the family and the production decisions of the household. The supply of purchased inputs and the demand for agricultural output have become the linkage equations between agriculture and the rest of the economy. This framework is extremely appropriate for the treatment of sectoral articulation and of the interactions between agriculture and nonagriculture.

In preceding chapters, we have repeatedly emphasized the need to approach development within an integrated and general equilibrium framework rather than in terms of partial analysis. General equilibrium analysis is relatively scarce in development economics, but where it is introduced the results are substantially different from those obtained by partial equilibrium analysis. This was, for example, demonstrated in Chapter 7, with the study of the macroeconomics of efficiency, and it is a theme that will recur in Part V, on international trade, and in Chapter 21, on macroeconomic planning. The macroequilibrium model of this chapter further demonstrates this proposition. Although the data used have been crude and we wish to treat the results as merely illustrative, we can still see a dramatic change in parameters as we go from partial to general analysis and as the specification of the agricultural sector changes to reflect different degrees of openness. As expected, an increase in the price of output,

[28]For some alternative general equilibrium models of interdependence between agriculture and nonagriculture, see Zarembka (1972, especially Chapter 2), Kelley, Williamson, and Cheetham (1972), and Kelley and Williamson (1973). While these models are more suitable for dynamic analysis, they are far less suitable for empirical estimation. Thus far, their use has been limited to that of hypothetical simulation, which can always be challenged on grounds of lack of realism and relevance. See Higgins (1973) for one such challenge.

for example, leads to an increase in output supplied and labor demanded at the household level. The general equilibrium results obtained within an institutional framework of an agricultural sector closed with respect to the labor market are quite different from those obtained from a sector regulated with respect to the output market. An increase in the price of output leads to a decrease in the equilibrium levels of both output and employment. The results for the other institutional specifications are also different.

In view of this discussion, one can hardly overstate the need for careful specification of the institutional framework of the analysis and for constructing as general a system as possible, which could also account for the indirect effects of economic policies. Chapter 15 has presented an empirical method for doing precisely that.

Our analysis of the interdependencies between agriculture and nonagriculture is, however, not without its shortcomings. Most notably, the analysis has been overly static, and the treatment of the industrial sector has been cursory. In Chapter 16, we shall attempt to overcome these shortcomings.

Appendix

Estimates of Structural Equations of the General Equilibrium Model for the Household Sector

Joint Estimation of the Profit Function and the Labor Demand Function

$$\ln \Pi = \ln A^* + \sum_{i=1}^{4} \alpha_{0i}^* D_i + \alpha_1^* \ln q_L'$$
$$+ \beta_1^* \ln K + \beta_2^* \ln T \tag{1}$$

$$-\frac{q_L' L_D}{\Pi} = \alpha_1^* \tag{2}$$

There are two restrictions:

$$\alpha_1^* = \alpha_1^*; \beta_1^* + \beta_2^* = 1$$

The Zellner's (1962) method estimates, appearing in Table 15.9, are

$\ln A^* = \quad 4.415$	$\alpha_1^* = -1.166$
(0.194)	(0.376)
$\alpha_{01}^* = \quad 0.776$	$\beta_1^* = -0.224$
(0.377)	(0.153)
$\alpha_{02}^* = -1.133$	$\beta_2^* = \quad 1.224$
(0.497)	(0.153)
$\alpha_{03}^* = -0.310$	$\alpha_1^* = -1.166$
(0.238)	(0.376)

$$\alpha_{04}^* = -0.111$$
$$(0.383)$$

Variables are

Π = profit including interest on fixed capital, and land rent
D_i = regional dummies (WB, MAD, UP, MP)
K = interest on fixed capital
q_L' = money wage rate
T = land, average farm size
L_D = total labor days.

The intercepts of the two regressions are increased by $\ln n$ to account for macroequilibrium (n = 61,780,000 estimated number of operational holdings in India, 1953–1954). Data are from India, Government of: Ministry of Food and Agriculture (1957–1962), *Studies in the Economics of Farm Management*. Delhi. Reports for the year 1955–1956: West Bengal (WB), Madras (MAD), Uttar Pradesh (UP). Report for the year 1956–1957: Madhya Pradesh (MP).

Table 15.9 *Joint Estimation of Cobb-Douglas Profit Function and Labor-Demand Function*

Function	Para-meter	Single Equation Ordinary Least Squares	Estimated Coefficients		
				Zellner's Method with Restrictions	
			Unrestricted	One Restriction $\alpha_1{}^* = \alpha_1{}^*$	Two Restrictions $\alpha_1{}^* = \alpha_1{}^*$ $\beta_1{}^* + \beta_2{}^* = 1$
UOP Profit	ln A	4.888	4.440	4.470	4.415
Function		(0.499)	(0.441)	(0.300)	(0.194)
	$\alpha_1{}^*$	−2.368	−1.071	−1.156	−1.166
		(1.123)	(0.992)	(0.379)	(0.376)
	$\beta_1{}^*$	−0.573	−0.303	−0.263	−0.224
		(0.258)	(0.227)	(0.221)	(0.153)
	$\beta_2{}^*$	1.581	1.278	1.241	1.224
		(0.199)	(0.176)	(0.168)	(0.153)
Labor Demand	$\alpha_1{}^*$	−1.209	−1.209	−1.156	−1.166
Function		(0.412)	(0.412)	(0.379)	(0.376)

Notes: The estimating equations are

$$\ln \Pi^* = \ln A^* + \alpha_1{}^* \ln q_{L'} - \alpha_1{}^* \ln p_A + \beta_1{}^* \ln K + \beta_2{}^* \ln T$$
$$\ln L_D = \ln (-\alpha_1{}^*) + \ln A^* + (\alpha_1{}^* - 1) \ln q_{L'} - (\alpha_1{}^* - 1) \ln p_A + \beta_1{}^* \ln K + \beta_2{}^* \ln T$$

where

Π^* = profit (current revenue less current variable costs) in rupees per farm
$q_{L'}$ = money wage rate in rupees per day
p_A = the price of agricultural output
L = labor in days per year per farm
K = interest on fixed capital per farm
T = cultivable land in acres per farm.
Numbers in parentheses are asymptotic standard errors.

Source: Lau, L. J., and P. A. Yotopoulos (1972), "Profit, Supply and Factor Demand Functions," *A. J. A. E.,* 54 (February), p. 16.

Estimation of the Labor Supply Function

$$\ln L_S = \ln \gamma_0{}^* + \gamma_{01}{}^* D_1 + \gamma_{04}{}^* D_4$$
$$+ \gamma_1{}^* \ln \left(\frac{q_{L'}}{p_A} \right) + \gamma_2{}^* \ln \left(\frac{\Pi}{p_A N_f} \right)$$
$$+ \gamma_3{}^* \ln \left(\frac{O}{p_A N_f} \right)$$
$$+ \gamma_4{}^* \ln N_w + \gamma_5{}^* \ln N_f \tag{3}$$

The estimates are

$\ln \gamma_0{}^* = 6.522$ $\gamma_1{}^* = 0.417$
       (0.952)   (2.840)

$\gamma_{01}{}^* = -1.022$ $\gamma_2{}^* = -1.000$
       (1.256)

$\gamma_{04}{}^* = 0.996$ $\gamma_3{}^* = 1.495$
       (0.320)   (0.163)

              $\gamma_4{}^* = 1.576$
                   (0.971)

              $\gamma_5{}^* = 0.671$
                   (0.777)

The coefficient of $\gamma_2{}^*$ is estimated by non-linear methods, constraining its value between −1 and 0.
Variables are

L_S = family labor supply, net of hired in and hired out labor, in days
p_A = price of output
N_w = number of workers in household
N_f = total number of household family members
O = fixed obligations less nonfarm asset income.

The intercept of the regression is increased by ln n to account for macroequilibrium (n = 61,780,000 the estimated number of operational holdings as above). Data are from India, Government of: Ministry of Food and Agriculture (1957–1962), *Studies in the Economics of Farm Management.* Delhi.

Estimation of the Demand for Output Function

$$(\ln V_D - \ln N) = \ln \delta_0{}^* + \delta_1{}^*(\ln p_A - \ln p_C)$$
$$+ \delta_2{}^*(\ln Y - \ln N)$$
$$+ \delta_4{}^*(\ln M - \ln N) \qquad (4)$$

The estimates are

$$\ln \delta_0{}^* = -2.402 \qquad \delta_4{}^* = -0.027$$
$$(0.066) \qquad\qquad (0.060)$$

$$\delta_1{}^* = -0.652 \qquad \delta_3{}^* = (1 - \delta_2{}^* - \delta_4{}^*)$$
$$(0.233) \qquad\qquad = -0.217$$

$$\delta_2{}^* = 1.244$$
$$(0.376)$$

Variables are

$V_D =$ value of agricultural production minus exports in constant prices

$N =$ population; the coefficient is constrained to 1.0 to express the demand in per capita terms

$p_A =$ index of prices of agricultural output, 1959/60–1961/62 = 100

$p_C =$ index of wholesale prices of manufactures, 1959/60–1961/62 = 100

$Y =$ national output at factor cost in constant prices

$M =$ imports of agricultural commodities in constant prices.

Data are from

India, Government of:

Ministry of Food and Agriculture, *Agricultural Situation in India*, 27 (November 1972); and previous issues.

Ministry of Food and Agriculture, *Estimates of Area and Production of Principal Crops in India, 1968–69.*

Ministry of Commerce and Industry, *Annual Statement of the Foreign Trade of India*, various years.

Reserve Bank of India Bulletin, various years.

Directorate of Economics and Statistics, *Monthly Abstract of Statistics*, various issues.

Ministry of Food and Agriculture, *Bulletin on Food Statistics*, various years.

Planning Commission, Statistical and Survey Division, *Basic Statistics Relating to the Indian Economy*, various years.

U.N., *Yearbook of National Account Statistics*, various years.

Chapter 16
The Morphology of Growth

The preceding chapters in Part IV have described development in a closed economy within a disequilibrium framework, emphasizing change that is not uniform and not always smooth. The present chapter, by concentrating on the morphology of growth, addresses the grand themes in the process of developmental change: what regularities are observed in the process of development? Why do they occur? What happens if the regularities do not take place—perhaps as a result of deliberate policies to avoid them?

We begin our discussion with a bird's-eye view of the structural changes that occur as an economy grows. A subset of these structural changes, namely, those associated with the relationships between different sectors of the economy, is singled out for further study in the section on sectoral change. The "normal" patterns of sectoral change and the effects of observed deviations from these patterns are investigated from the viewpoint of balances, imbalances, and linkages.

One of the conclusions that will emerge from the analysis in this chapter is that the morphology of growth, more specifically the patterns that sectoral change will follow, depend to a large extent on international trade and the role it can play in mitigating some of the national constraints to development, such as country size or resource endowments. Chapter 16, therefore, leads into Part V and the study of development disequilibrium in an open economy.

Structural Change

As we have seen, common to many growth theories in different disciplines, ranging from biology and chemistry to economics and sociology, is the notion that the relation of parts to the whole (and between parts) is likely to change in the process of growth. Moreover, the character and magnitude of these changes are thought to be predictable and fundamental to the understanding of growth.[1]

Kuznets[2] and subsequently Hagen and Hawrylyshyn (1969), on the one hand, and Chenery and his associates,[3] on the other, succeeded in identifying a number of striking changes in structure that take place in the process of economic development. These changes have been identified from historical studies (mainly with data from DCs),[4] from analysis of international cross-sections at one point in time, or from the combination of cross-sections and time series.

In one of the most comprehensive of the international cross-section studies, Chenery, Elkington, and Sims (1970) utilized data from an impressively large sample of countries (more than 100) to identify and quantify a number of such changes. The changes they consider deal with aspects of the development process—accumulation, mobilization, and allocation—that can be observed as countries make the transition from income levels of $50 per capita to levels of $2,000 per capita. Eighteen of these indicators of structural change, as well as the values they "normally" assume at different levels of GNP per capita, are given in Table 16.1. These normal values were estimated by regressing each structural indicator, X_i, on income, Y, and population size, N, in the following nonlinear relationship:

$$X_i = \alpha + \beta_1 \log Y + \beta_2 (\log Y)^2 + \gamma \log N \quad (1)$$

and then plugging in the appropriate values of Y and an "average" population size of 10 million.

One can easily see that these normal structural changes vary, in both direction and magnitude, from one indicator to the other. They also vary in timing. Indeed, the nonlinearity of the model allows the authors to distinguish between structural changes that occur "early" in the process of development

and those that occur "late" in the following way. Early changes are defined as those in which 50 percent or more of the total change in structure takes place by the time GNP has reached $400 in per capita terms; late changes are defined as those in which less than 50 percent of the total change is completed by the time per capita GNP has reached $400. By referring to columns 7 and 8 of Table 16.1, the reader should be able to apply these definitions in such a way as to verify the timing classifications given in column 9.

Patterns of Sectoral Change

A type of structural change that is singled out for further study is the change in the sectoral composition of output.[5] In the process of development, as seen from Table 16.1, there occurs a dramatic decline of the proportion of GDP (and employment) generated by the primary sector. It is counterbalanced by a dramatic increase in the share of the industrial sector and by a modest increase in the share of the service sector. As noted in the table, most of these changes occur relatively "early" in the process of growth of income per capita and therefore have particular relevance to LDCs.

In Chapter 15, where the disproportionate relationship between agriculture and industry in the process of growth was first noted, several explanatory factors were suggested: the change in the composition of demand (of which the decline in the share of food is the most notable feature), population increases, or input substitution and factor cost changes that can tip the balance in favor of nonagriculture. These factors are certainly at play. Nonetheless, some of them are likely to be endogenously explained by other characteristics of a country or by systematic features inherent in its growth structure. A changing composition of domestic demand, for example, can be offset by a country's participation in foreign trade and the export of primary commodities. We will first explore the ultimate determinants of sectoral change in an attempt to discover any regularities that underlie the process of growth. On the basis of this de-

[1]See Boulding (1953).

[2]See Kuznets (1955a, 1957, 1958, 1959, 1961b, 1962, 1964, 1966, 1967).

[3]See Chenery (1960, 1964, 1969, 1970a, 1970b), Chenery, Elkington, and Sims (1970), Chenery, Shishido, and Watanabe (1962), Chenery and Taylor (1968), Chenery and Eckstein (1970), Landau (1971), S. Robinson (1971), Weisskoff (1969), Weisskopf (1972), Taylor (1969), U.N.: Statistical Office (1963).

[4]See Kuznets (1958, 1959, 1961b, 1962, 1966, 1967), Chenery, Shishido, and Watanabe (1962), and for financial structure, Goldsmith (1955, 1969).

[5]Conjectures on the nature of this relationship are quite old. However, systematic and quantitative work on the subject dates from A. G. B. Fisher (1939) and C. G. Clark (1940).

Table 16.1 *Quantitative Indicators of Structural Change in the Process of Economic Development*

Structural Indicator	Normal Value of Structural Indicator at Per Capita GDP Level of:						Proportion of Change Completed by Per Capita GDP of:		Timing Classification
	$50 (1)	$100 (2)	$200 (3)	$400 (4)	$800 (5)	$2,000 (6)	$200 (7)	$400 (8)	(9)
1. Gross National Saving as Percent of GNP	7.8	11.0	14.1	17.1	19.9	23.4	40	78	Early
2. Gross Domestic Investment as Percent of GDP	12.7	14.8	17.1	19.4	21.8	25.2	35	73	Early
3. Capital Inflow as Percent of GDP	4.9	3.8	3.0	2.4	2.0	1.8	61	93	Early
4. Government Revenue as Percent of GDP	12.2	14.2	17.0	20.6	25.1	32.4	24	42	Late
5. Primary and Secondary Enrollment Ratio	17.5	36.2	52.6	66.9	78.9	91.4	48	67	Early
6. Adult Literacy Ratio	15.3	36.5	55.2	71.5	85.4	100.0	47	66	Early
7. Food Consumption as Percent of Total Consumption	61.9	56.1	49.9	43.0	35.9	25.6	33	52	Neither[a]
8. Gross Product of Primary Sector as Percent of GDP	58.1	46.4	36.0	26.7	18.6	9.8	46	65	Early
9. Gross Product of Industry Sector as Percent of GDP	7.3	13.5	19.6	25.5	31.4	38.9	39	58	Early
10. Gross Product of Service Sector as Percent of GDP	29.9	34.6	37.9	39.9	40.5	39.3	85	100	Early
11. Exports as Percent of GDP	16.5	17.1	18.2	19.7	21.6	24.8	21	39	Late
12. Industry Exports as Percent of GDP	0.0	0.8	3.7	6.9	10.5	15.7	24	44	Late
13. Birth Rate	46.6	41.8	36.6	31.1	25.3	17.1	34	53	Neither[a]
14. Death Rate	20.5	15.2	11.4	9.3	8.9	10.9	93	114	Early
15. Urban Population as Percent of Total Population	6.9	20.0	33.8	45.5	55.3	65.1	49	68	Early
16. Primary Employment as Percent of Total Employment	84.2	74.0	57.4	43.9	29.0	7.1	35	52	Neither[a]
17. Industry Employment as Percent of Total Employment	6.5	9.9	15.3	23.4	31.1	40.5	26	50	Neither[a]
18. Service Employment as Percent of Total Employment	19.5	21.8	27.3	32.7	40.0	52.4	24	40	Late

Notes: See text for method of estimation.

[a]"Neither" indicates neither "early" or "late."

Source: Chenery, H. B., H. Elkington, and C. Sims (1970), "A Uniform Analysis of Development Patterns," Economic Development Report No. 148 (July), Project for Quantitative Research in Economic Development. Cambridge: Harvard Center for International Affairs, Table G, pp. 42–43.

termination, we will explain the changes in sectoral composition.

The Determinants of Sectoral Change

The first question that arises is whether the pattern of sectoral change—as revealed in the coefficient of structural indicators 8 to 10 in Table 16.1—is uniform for all countries or varies depending on the type of country. The operational approach to this question is to define the type of country on the basis of some quantifiable characteristics, which are then included in regression 1. The regression coefficients of the additional variables indicate the magnitude of the impact of each such variable on the sectoral composition of output.

Chenery and Taylor (1968) defined the type of country in terms of three variables: one that reflects a country's rate of resource mobilization for growth, I/GNP, that is, the share of capital formation in GNP; and two variables on trade that reflect a country's relative endowments of natural resources, E_p/GNP, the share of primary exports in GNP, and E_m/GNP, the share of manufacturing exports in GNP. The addition of these variables to equation 1 yields

$$X_i = \alpha + \beta_1 \log Y + \beta_2 (\log Y)^2 + \gamma N$$
$$+ \delta_1 \log \frac{I}{GNP} + \delta_2 \log \frac{E_p}{GNP}$$
$$+ \delta_3 \log \frac{E_m}{GNP} \tag{2}$$

Estimating the proportions of GNP originating in the primary sector, X_p; in industry, X_m, and in services, X_s, on the basis of pooled cross-section and time series data for 54 countries during the period 1950–1963 via equations 1 and 2, Chenery and Taylor obtained the results given in Table 16.2.

The pattern of sectoral change in the process of growth is reflected in the coefficient of income, β_1. The dramatic decline of agriculture's share and the rise of industry's share are portrayed by comparing the estimates of β_1 for primary and for industry obtained from equation 1 in Table 16.2. The value of β_1 for primary is 0.02, whereas that for industry is 1.50. The greater the difference between sectors with respect to this elasticity and therefore the expected growth rates, the greater should be the amount of sectoral change as income rises. Note, however, that the inclusion of the additional variables, as

in equation 2, raises the estimates of β_1 for primary and lowers that for industry, considerably reducing the amount of sectoral change. At the same time, from the estimates of β_2 it can be seen that as income increases the inclusion of the additional variables accentuates the rate of decline of the former but softens the decline of the latter. Judging by the (absolute) size and significance of their coefficients, the share of primary exports in GNP, E_p/GNP, is clearly the most important of the additional variables. This variable may be interpreted as reflecting the impact of natural resource endowments. Countries with substantial natural resource endowments, according to the neoclassical version of comparative advantage, would be expected to undergo less sectoral change, especially in the earlier phases of economic development. This is an important finding with potential policy implications. By emphasizing free trade and comparative advantage, countries with substantial endowments of natural resources may postpone or even cancel structural changes, which would otherwise be considered normal or perhaps even beneficial.

The type of country has so far been defined in terms of a set of characteristics. These may not be independent of each other but can have important interaction terms, which can be captured by splitting the sample on the basis of one or more of the characteristics and separately reestimating with respect to each subsample regression 2. If the results differ significantly (as determined from an analysis of covariance based on computing an F-ratio) from one subsample to another or relative to the total sample, it would indicate that the separation into subsamples is important and must be considered in interpreting the results.

To test for the significance of these interdependencies, Chenery and Taylor (1968) first divided their sample into two groups, large countries with populations of 15 million or more and small countries with populations of less than 15 million, and recomputed regressions 1 and 2 separately for each subsample. The results of this partition revealed startling differences between the two groups and as compared to Table 16.2. The estimates of the income elasticities, β_1, for the primary sector were substantially lower and for industry were substantially higher in large countries than in small countries, suggesting that small

Table 16.2 Empirical Estimates of Sectoral Patterns from Data for 54 Countries, 1950–1963

Sector	Estimating Equation	Intercept α	$\log Y$ β_1	$(\log Y)^2$ β_2	$\log N$ γ	$\log \dfrac{I}{GNP}$ δ_1	$\log \dfrac{E_p}{GNP}$ δ_2	$\log \dfrac{E_m}{GNP}$ δ_3	R^2
Primary X_p	(1)	-0.0981 (0.35)	0.0204 (0.12)	-0.0433 (0.01)	-0.0287 (0.01)				0.788
	(2)	-1.5470 (0.33)	0.4983 (0.01)	-0.0750 (0.01)	0.0657 (0.01)	0.0019 (0.02)	0.1880 (0.01)	-0.0584 (0.01)	0.866
Industry X_m	(1)	-7.0315 (0.33)	1.5024 (0.11)	-0.0970 (0.01)	0.0768 (0.01)				0.727
	(2)	-5.8453 (0.33)	1.2594 (0.11)	-0.0838 (0.01)	0.0264 (0.01)	0.1024 (0.02)	-0.1087 (0.01)	0.0573 (0.01)	0.794
Services X_s	(1)	-1.4783 (0.20)	0.1638 (0.07)	-0.0060 (0.01)	-0.0279 (0.01)				0.321
	(2)	-1.1874 (0.23)	0.0393 (0.08)	0.0038 (0.01)	-0.0513 (0.01)	-0.0144 (0.01)	-0.0452 (0.01)	-0.0026 (0.01)	0.359

Note: Numbers in parentheses are standard errors.
Source: Chenery, H. B., and L. Taylor (1968). "Development Patterns: Among Countries and Over Time," *R. E. Stat.*, 50 (November), Table 1, p. 393.

size also tends to exert a dampening influence on the degree of structural change. One explanation for this tendency for large countries to undergo more rapid industrialization may be that industrial technology is subject to greater economies of scale than technology in the primary sector, as was suggested in Chapter 9.

In order to further disentangle the interdependencies between country characteristics and their effect on sectoral change patterns, Chenery and Taylor then further divided their small country sample into "primary-oriented" countries with substantial natural resource endowments, those with high E_p/GNP ratios, and "industry-oriented" ones, those with small E_p/GNP but large E_m/GNP ratios. Small industry-oriented countries turn out to be like large countries, in that they have high income elasticities for industry but low (even negative) income elasticities for the primary sector. This suggests that such countries tend to undergo rapid industrialization relatively early in the process of development. On the other hand, by emphasizing primary exports, small primary-oriented countries tend not simply to delay or mitigate the normal sectoral change patterns but rather to reverse them for a certain period of time. Thus, for small primary-oriented countries, the income elasticity of the primary sector is positive and large, while that for industry is significantly negative.

Clearly, country size and trade policies have significant effects on the time path and nature of sectoral structure and change. Small countries that are open to trade and have factor endowments that give them comparative advantage in the primary sector are unlikely to undergo the type of structural changes normally associated with development. This finding raises questions on international trade and growth, which will be taken up again in Part V.

The Explanation of Sectoral Composition

What does all this mean? Does the apparent uniformity of the patterns of sectoral change indicate that the relationship between income and structure is a causal one? If it is causal, what is the direction of causality?[6] Or is the relationship only tautological, as suggested by

[6]If higher incomes cause industrialization and the relative decline of agriculture, how are higher incomes achieved? On the other hand, in what way does industrialization raise income?

Singer (1964, Chapter 5)? What explanation can be offered for the changes in sectoral patterns that emerge? Why do all sectors not grow at the same rate?

Scientific explanation presupposes the existence of a theoretical model. A number of models that propose to explain sectoral change have featured in the literature (Taylor 1969; Kelley 1969; S. R. Lewis and Soligo 1965). Most are unfortunately tautological, in that they consist of a series of accounting or definitional identities with no theoretical red thread running through them. Chenery's (1960) model still constitutes the best point of departure for studying what may eventually develop into a fully empirical model of sectoral change.

Chenery's model may be represented as follows:

$$Z_{it} = Y_{it} \tag{3}$$

$$Z_{it} = P_{it} + M_{it} \tag{4}$$

$$Y_{it} = D_{it} + W_{it} + E_{it} \tag{5}$$

where for a particular commodity, i, and time period, t, Z is total supply, Y is total demand, P is domestic output, M is imports, D is domestic final demand (private and government consumption plus private and government investment), W is intermediate demand, and E is exports. Equation 3 thus represents the equilibrium condition between supply and demand for commodity i at time t; supply is defined in equation 4 and demand in equation 5. Substituting equations 4 and 5 into equation 3 and rearranging terms, we obtain

$$P_{it} = D_{it} + W_{it} + E_{it} - M_{it} \tag{6}$$

Assume for any commodity, i, and time period, t, that imports are proportional to total demand, that is,

$$M_{it} = \mu_{it} Y_{it} \tag{7}$$

where μ_{it} is a given constant. Substituting equation 7 into equation 6, we have

$$P_{it} = (1 - \mu_{it})(D_{it} + W_{it} + E_{it}) \tag{8}$$

Considering two time periods, $t = 0$ and $t = 1$, we have

$$P_{i0} = (1 - \mu_{i0})(D_{i0} + W_{i0} + E_{i0}) \tag{8a}$$

$$P_{i1} = (1 - \mu_{i1})(D_{i1} + W_{i1} + E_{i1}) \tag{8b}$$

If from the base period, 0, all flow variables would grow by the same proportion, λ, so as to leave the structure unchanged, output in period 1, P_{i1}, could be expressed in terms of the base period values in the following way:

$$P_{i1} = \lambda P_{i0} = \lambda(1 - \mu_{i0})(D_{i0} + W_{i0} + E_{i0}) \quad (8c)$$

If P_{i0} and P_{i1} are the "normal" levels of output in sector i as computed from the normal shares, X_i, obtained from equation 1 or 2, that is, $P_{i0} = X_i Y_0 / V_{i0}$, where Y is GNP and V_i is the value added to gross production ratio in sector i, the change in structure, dX_i, relative to the structure that would have existed had there been no change in structure in time period 1, $X_{i1}{}^P$, can be expressed as equation $8b$ less equation $8c$:

$$
\begin{aligned}
dP_i &= \frac{(X_{i1} - X_{i1}{}^P)}{V_{i1}} Y_1 \\
&= (1 - \mu_{i0})[(D_{i1} - \lambda D_{i0}) + (W_{i1} - \lambda W_{i0}) \\
&\quad + (E_{i1} - \lambda E_{i0})] + (\mu_{i0} - \mu_{i1}) \\
&\quad (D_{i1} + W_{i1} + E_{i1}) \quad (9)
\end{aligned}
$$

Substituting for the last term in equation 9 from equations 3 and 5 and rearranging, we write

$$
\begin{aligned}
dP_i &= (1 - \mu_{i0})[(D_{i1} - \lambda D_{i0}) + (E_{i1} - \lambda E_{i0})] \\
&\quad + [(1 - \mu_{i0})(W_{i1} - \lambda W_{i0}] \\
&\quad + [(\mu_{i0} - \mu_{i1})Z_{i1}] \quad (9a)
\end{aligned}
$$

We thus express the deviation of actual output in sector i from proportional growth in three sets of terms in brackets: the first set represents the deviation of the actual increase in final demand for commodity i, domestic plus export, from proportional growth; the second set represents nonproportional increases in intermediate demand; the last set shows the effect of import substitution on commodity i and measures the difference between the growth in output with no change in the import ratio and the actual growth in supply.

Equation 9 becomes an operational method for "explaining" the sources of nonproportional change in output of any sector, i, derived from the foregoing analysis of normal patterns of sectoral change, given (1) data on GNP at different times ($t = 0$ and $t = 1$) and (2) estimates of the import propensity in the base year, μ_{i0}, and of the breakdown of aggregate demand into its various components, that is, by type of demand (D, W, or E) and by commodity ($i = 1, \ldots, n$). These latter estimates can be readily obtained from an I-O Table.

Utilizing a "representative" I-O Table and estimates of the changes in D and E obtained from other studies, Chenery (1960) followed such a procedure in arriving at separate explanations for the deviation of actual growth from proportional growth in 14 different sectors of manufacturing between income levels of U.S.$100 per capita and U.S.$600 per capita. Aggregating over all manufacturing sectors, he found that: (1) 22 percent of the nonproportional rise of the manufacturing sector is accounted for by the change in the structure of final demand (domestic and foreign); (2) an additional 10 percent of it is due to the indirect effects of that change in the structure of final demand, that is, to the change in interindustry demand derived from that change; (3) 50 percent is attributable to import substitution;[7] and (4) the remaining 18 percent is an unexplained residual caused by interaction between the various components as well as errors in measurement. This led Chenery to conclude that the traditional emphasis on changes in the composition of demand in explaining changes in sectoral composition is unjustified. An increase in a country's income with no change in its comparative advantage or other factors on the supply side would result in only about one-third of the normal increase in the manufacturing sector.

The problem of measuring the contribution of various factors to sectoral change is just a special case of the more general problem of quantifying the contribution of various factors of overall growth—an issue that has been discussed in Chapter 9. Clearly, the study of sectoral change has thus far explored a much narrower range of hypotheses than have been considered in connection with the explanations of overall growth. The roles of changing factor prices, technological change, human capital, and externalities, such as urbanization, on-the-job training, and organization, have thus far been completely overlooked. Moreover, as has already been

---

[7] Attributing more than half of the nonproportional increase in industry to the mysterious entity called "import substitution" is still unsatisfactory, unless import substitution can be explained. In subsequent work, Chenery (1969) has used CES production functions and attempted to probe deeper by explaining import substitution in terms of changes in factor prices which occur as income increases. However, since such a modification requires considerable change in the model and the way in which it is used, we shall not go into it here.

demonstrated, different types of countries are subject to different forms of structural transformation. Each type of structural change would then call for a different explanation. As a result, identification of the correct typology of structure for each country has been the main preoccupation of recent literature on the subject.

The Effects of Sectoral Change on Growth

The description of sectoral change, based as it is on correlation analysis, does not constitute theory that can lead to development prescriptions. The timid attempts to explain sectoral change we presented above come closer to constituting useful theory, although they too are largely based on equations that are tautological and devoid of behavioral content. We still need to formulate operational hypotheses that address the question of the effects a certain type of sectoral change may have on the rate of economic growth.

We approach this subject by linking the discussion of structural change with the long-standing controversy over whether development strategy should be balanced or unbalanced. We will proceed as follows: not unlike Chenery (1960), we will define the "normal" pattern of sectoral change in terms of the elasticity of a sector's share with respect to income. The next question is, what difference does it make whether or not a country follows the "normal" pattern? At this point, we will invoke the balanced and unbalanced growth hypotheses. Following the "normal" pattern must lead to higher rates of development if the former hypothesis is valid, and the converse if the latter is correct. Linking patterns of sectoral change to development strategies has been deliberately avoided by most contributors to the literature on structural change.[8]

[8]For example, in its attempt at describing and explaining the "normal" pattern of industrial growth, the U.N.: Statistical Office (1963, p. 29) said the following: " 'Normal' is an empirical concept derived from a systematic investigation of observed facts, and thus has no intrinsic normative value. . . . Even less could the model be used as a substitute for planning. . . ." Although the principals of the literature of structural change were exceedingly cautious, the onlookers were excessively rash. Papandreou (1962) suggested that Greek planners should see to it that Greece follow the "normal" pattern, in the sense that they should influence the allocation of resources among sectors so that the sectoral composition of output would cor-

Theories of Balanced and Unbalanced Growth

Assuming that insufficient capital formation acts as the major constraint on economic development, but emphasizing that capital formation is itself constrained more by an insufficient effective demand for investment than by an insufficient supply of savings, Nurkse (1953) advocated balanced growth. He argued that an investment in one industry (industry *A*) without an accompanying investment in other industries (industry *B*) will be self-defeating, since the investment in *A* will not be rewarded because of insufficient demand for *A*. Nurkse thus prescribed simultaneous expansion of each industry as a means of capturing the demand-creation aspects of investment. While an increase in output in one industry does not create its own demand, ". . . an increase in production over a wide range of consumables, so proportioned as to correspond with the pattern of consumers' preferences, does create its own demand" (Nurkse 1953, p. 12).

In contrast, Hirschman (1958) assumed that a shortage of decision-making ability (entrepreneurial talent) exercises the most important constraint on economic development. This assumption led him to advocate unbalanced development of industries that exert the strongest stimuli to investments in other industries. The voluminous literature on this controversy has demonstrated that even slightly different underlying sets of assumptions can yield considerably different sets of implications for the desired structure.[9]

---

respond to what would be expected on the basis of the "normal" pattern described by the results of Table 16.1 (for structural indicators 8, 9, and 10), given Greece's income and population size. Such a position would be defensible only if it could be shown that countries that follow the "normal" pattern enjoy more rapid growth than other countries. See Archibald (1964) and Nugent (1967*b*) for some pitfalls in such an approach. We will note later, however, that Papandreou's instinct might well prove correct.

[9]Scitovsky (1959) has demonstrated that, if economies of scale are present and important, unbalanced growth is likely to be more advantageous than balanced growth—even if all the other assumptions of balanced growth were realistic. Moreover, if the elasticities of substitution of consumers and producers are sufficiently high, a considerable degree of imbalance could be obtained even under assumptions not very dissimilar to those of balanced growth. If foreign trade is not subject to penalties in the form of deteriorating terms of trade (as envisaged by Nurkse, Prebisch, and others, which will be discussed in Chapter 18), imbalances in growth are not only possible but are also likely to be desirable from the point of view of comparative advantage.

Since it is difficult to determine whether development is constrained more by problems of insufficient demand generation, insufficient savings, insufficient decision-making capability, or some other factor, it is difficult to conduct direct tests of such hypotheses. Nevertheless, it is possible to test indirectly strategies of structural balance or imbalance by determining the extent to which conformity with any such strategy affects the rate of growth a country is able to achieve.

Tests of Balanced and Unbalanced Growth

The first timid step in the direction of testing hypotheses of balanced and unbalanced growth consisted of historical case studies, which have failed to settle anything. For example, Streeten (1959) cited the technological advances in the textile and iron industries in eighteenth-century England as instances of the success of unbalanced growth. Similarly, Ohlin (1959) found no evidence of balance in the successful development of other presently advanced countries. On the other hand, J. R. T. Hughes (1959) found that Western countries have followed a balanced growth path, which was the natural outcome of the "ceaseless ebb and flow of innovating and changing factor combinations."

A more general approach to the problem was suggested and applied by Chenery and Taylor (1968). These authors classified countries by the degree to which their actual sectoral composition deviated from the "normal" pattern obtained from the pooled cross-section and time series estimates of equation 2, taking their income level, population size, resource endowment, and so on, into consideration. The countries were then divided into three classifications—"low primary," "normal," or "high primary"—depending on whether or not the ratio of the primary share to the industry share was more than 0.15 below the norm, between 0.15 below the norm and 0.15 above the norm, or more than 0.15 above the norm. Then the growth rates of the three groups were compared, revealing no differences among them. This led the authors to conclude that "balance in this sense is neither necessary nor sufficient for rapid growth over the medium term,"

This procedure for testing is unfortunately quite arbitrary. A slightly different classification procedure might well give different re-

sults, as Demery and Demery (1973) have demonstrated.

For any version of balanced or unbalanced growth to become something more than a doctrine (to be followed by the believing faithful but dismissed by the disbelieving infidels), better tests must be constructed. The hypothesis must be formulated so that it is given the chance to be proven wrong. This requires the following: (1) that balance or imbalance be measured in such a way as to avoid recourse to arbitrary classification, as in the Chenery-Taylor approach; (2) that the extent to which individual countries do or do not comply with that balance or imbalance strategy be determined unambiguously; and (3) that it be determined whether or not countries that comply with a specific strategy are able to achieve higher rates of economic development than those that do not comply.

We start with the measurement of balance and imbalance. We propose a method for measuring balance or imbalance and then demonstrate its applicability by using it to test two different versions of the balanced growth strategy.[10] Admittedly, the definitions of balance we consider have been drawn from quite different types of literature and are taken out of their original contexts. Also, they are only two of a large number of alternative definitions. Nevertheless, since they are well known and quite simple to apply, they provide useful examples for demonstrating our methods and for deriving some potentially useful conclusions.

The "Normal" Pattern and the Measure of Imbalance

We will formulate the notion of balanced growth by combining elements of growth theory with principles of development economics. Solow and Samuelson (after von Neumann) formulate the notion of balanced growth by reference to the sectoral rates of growth. This formulation requires that

[10]Our presentation is based on Yotopoulos and Lau (1970). An earlier attempt to measure balance and imbalance was that of Swamy (1967). Swamy also provided some tests of balanced versus unbalanced growth, but his results are marred by his use of a statistically inappropriate measure of imbalance and incorrect data. For details, see Yotopoulos and Lau (1970). Shashua and Goldschmidt (1972) and incorrect index to replicate his results. See Yotopoulos Demery and Demery (1973) have gone back to Swamy's and Lau (1975).

. . . the output of each commodity increases or decreases by a constant percentage per unit of time, the mutual proportions in which commodities are produced remaining constant. The economy changes only in scale, but not in composition. (Solow and Samuelson 1953, p. 412.)

Nurske (1953) provides an alternative definition of balance that accounts for the income elasticity of demand. As we noted, the conceptual cornerstone of his doctrine of balanced growth is that supply creates its own demand, but this is so only if

. . . supply is properly distributed among different commodities in accordance with consumers' wants. An increase in consumable output must provide a balanced diet. Each industry must advance along an expansion path determined by the income elasticity of consumer demand for its [the sector's] product. (Nurkse 1953, pp. 250–251.)

The Nurksian concept of balance, therefore, allows for the fact that as the economy develops a certain amount of change in the sectoral composition of output is appropriate. The amount of change that is allowed for is that given by the sectoral differences in the income coefficients, in the case of Chenery, for example, the estimates of β_1 presented in Table 16.2.

Following Yotopoulos and Lau (1970), we combine elements of the two notions in order to define the criterion of balance (imbalance). Imbalance must be defined in terms of the dispersion around balance, and it must incorporate at least two elements: (1) the dispersion of sectoral growth rates around the overall rate of growth over a certain time period,[11] as follows from the Samuelson-Solow notion and (2) a sectoral weight that reflects the income elasticity of sectoral composition, as follows from the Nurkse-Chenery notion. A third element should also be introduced for the criterion to be conceptually sound: (3) the relative share of each sector within the

economy. A deviation of 100 percent in the growth rate of an industry that constitutes only 1 percent of national income would be less unbalancing than a 20 percent deviation of an industry that constitutes 50 percent of the national income. We therefore need to weight the individual sector variations around the average rate of growth by the relative importance of the sector.

What is an appropriate index of dispersion? The Pearson coefficient of variation is a natural choice for this measure. It is defined as the standard deviation divided by the mean. We thus define the index of imbalance as

$$V = \frac{1}{G} \sqrt{\sum_{i=1}^{u} w_i(g_i - \beta_i G)^2} \qquad (10)$$

where G is the average rate of growth of a country over a given period, g_i is the ith sector's rate of growth, β_i is Nurkse's notion of balance that corresponds to Chenery's income elasticity of sectoral composition, and w_i is the share of sector i with $\sum_{i=1}^{n} w_i = 1$.

An alternative index of imbalance, which applies to the manufacturing sector[12] alone, might be closer to Nurkse's conception of balanced growth as demand creating. We define

$$V_M = \frac{1}{G_M} \sqrt{\sum_{i=1}^{n} w_{iM}(g_{iM} - \beta_{iM}G_M)^2} \qquad (11)$$

where the subscript i refers to an individual subsector within the manufacturing sector, and the subscript M refers to the manufacturing sector as a whole.

From definitions 10 and 11, a high degree of dispersion of sectoral growth rates around the overall rate of growth (adjusted for the normal growth pattern and the relative importance of the sector) would define a high index of imbalance. In turn, a positive relationship between the index of imbalance and the observed rates of economic growth over a period of time would constitute rejection of the balanced-growth hypothesis. This will be our empirical test.

Empirical Results
We will report here only the results of the formal test of the balanced-growth hypothesis

[11]The theory on balanced-unbalanced growth fails to specify an applicable time interval for the test of the hypothesis. Our use of the 12-year period (1948–1960) is arbitrary and is dictated by data availability. One would expect that, at the limit, the application of a successful strategy of imbalance would be self-corrective, in the sense that by the end of a sufficient period of time it would reestablish a balanced equilibrium. Therefore, future researchers would do well to give serious consideration to the choice of time period in executing such tests.

[12]Actually, data permitting considerably greater disaggregation would probably be desirable.

Table 16.3 *Estimated Income Elasticities of Sectoral Composition*

Sectors	β_i
GLOBAL SECTORS	
1. Agriculture (0)	0.952
	(0.037)
2. Mining (1)	0.892
	(0.089)
3. Manufacturing (2–3)	1.044
	(0.030)
4. Construction (4)	1.035
	(0.026)
5. Electricity, coal, and water (5)	1.045
	(0.050)
6. Others (6, 8–9)	0.999
	(0.020)
MANUFACTURING SUBSECTORS	
1. Food, beverages, and tobacco (20–22)	0.821
	(0.248)
2. Textiles (23)	1.041
	(0.283)
3. Clothing and footwear (24)	1.046
	(0.245)
4. Wood products (25–26)	1.091
	(0.247)
5. Paper and paper products (27)	1.062
	(0.290)
6. Printing and publishing (28)	1.367
	(0.236)
7. Leather and leather products (29)	1.011
	(0.240)
8. Rubber products (30)	1.003
	(0.288)
9. Chemicals and petroleum (31–32)	1.077
	(0.236)
10. Nonmetallic mineral products (33)	1.107
	(0.218)
11. Basic metals (34)	1.157
	(0.164)
12. Metal products (35–38)	1.088
	(0.278)
13. Other manufacturing (39)	1.450
	(0.267)

Note: Elasticities are estimated from the equation $\ln X_i = a + \beta \ln Y$, where X_i is value added per capita for the industrial sector or subsector and Y is per capita GDP.

In parentheses under the coefficients are standard errors.

The sector number in parentheses refers to the International Standard Industrial Classification.

Source: Yotopoulos, P. A., and L. J. Lau (1970), "A Test for Balanced and Unbalanced Growth," *R. E. Stat.*, 52 (November), Table 1, p. 379.

conducted by Yotopoulos and Lau (1970). The two indexes of imbalance are computed for an international cross-section of 65 countries for V and 30 countries for V_M and for the periods 1948–1953, 1954–1958, and 1950–1960. The sources for the data on G, g_i, w_i, and G_M, g_{iM} and w_{iM} are described in the original article. The income elasticity of sectoral composition was computed from the international cross-section by regressing sectoral value added per capita on per capita income. The estimates appear in Table 16.3, which also describes the sectors, i, that have been defined for the purposes of the test. The six global sectors have been used for the estimation of the V index of imbalance. The 13 manufacturing subsectors refer to the estimation of the V_M index.

We utilize correlation analysis to test the existence of a relationship between the alternative indexes of imbalance and the rates of growth in GDP. The results, in Table 16.4, reveal that an inverse relationship exists between sectoral or subsectoral variability and the rate of growth. This finding appears consistently and uniformly for all periods for both the global sectors and the manufacturing subsectors. This evidence compels one to conclude that the higher the index of sectoral imbalance, the lower the overall rate of growth,

Table 16.4 *Tests of Balanced-Growth Hypothesis*

Correlation Coefficients	1948–1953	1954–1958	1950–1960
$r(G, V)$	−0.476	−0.423	−0.308
$r(G_M, V_M)$	−0.531	−0.528	−0.543
$R(Y, V)$	−0.403	−0.614	−0.680

Notes:
$r(G, V)$ is the correlation coefficient between the rate of growth and the index of imbalance for the global sectors.

$r(G_M, V_M)$ is the correlation coefficient between the rate of growth and the index of imbalance for the manufacturing subsectors.

$R(Y, V)$ is the rank correlation coefficient between GNP per capita (1958) and the index of imbalance, global sectors.

All coefficients are significantly different from zero at level $\geqq$ 5 percent on a one-tail test.

Source: Yotopoulos, P. A., and L. J. Lau (1970), "A Test for Balanced and Unbalanced Growth," *R. E. Stat.*, 52 (November), Table 2, p. 379.

thereby contradicting the unbalanced-growth hypothesis.[13]

Next, we investigate the relationship between the level of development, as indicated by GNP per capita, and the indexes of imbalance to see if richer countries are more or less unbalanced, in general, than poorer countries. If richer countries should turn out to follow more unbalanced growth paths than poorer ones, it would constitute evidence for an interesting "reversal" hypothesis along the lines that, although "imbalance may be bad for a country" in the early stages of development, countries generally grow in an unbalanced way after a certain level of development has been achieved.[14] This is tested by estimating Spearman rank-correlation coefficients between the three indexes of imbalance and the level of development as measured by GNP per capita for the year 1958. The results strongly suggest that developed countries have tended to grow in a more balanced fashion, which is consistent with our previous result, which indicated that countries with less imbalance grow faster. It is also consistent with the findings of Chenery, Elkington and Sims (1970) reported in Table 16.1 that most of the change in sectoral composition occurs "early" in the process of economic development.

By confirming the balanced-growth hypothesis, the evidence strongly suggests that the "normal" growth patterns described in the previous section may be useful not only for descriptive but also for prescriptive purposes, as Papandreou (1962) suggested. However, in arriving at this conclusion, we undoubtedly part company with the majority of researchers in this field. Moreover, as pointed out in footnote 13, this conclusion should be couched in the caveats that are appropriate when one deals with international cross-sections and relatively short periods. Also, in fairness to the proponents of unbalanced growth, it should be pointed out that we have made no effort to go behind the measure of imbalance to identify and evaluate the stimulus-response mechanism that imbalance is supposed to activate. This is the task of the rest of this chapter. In this manner, we will be able to separate desirable imbalances from undesirable ones, thereby formulating tests of somewhat more sophisticated versions of unbalanced growth strategy.

Hirschman's Imbalance Effects: Sectoral Linkages and Interindustry Linkages

The constraining factor in economic development according to Hirschman (1958) is the shortage of decision-making ability, particularly with respect to decisions to invest. An appropriate development strategy would then be to create strategic imbalances, which would induce easily made or even automatic investment decisions. Hirschman formulates his model in terms of "forward" and "backward" linkage effects. Forward linkages induce investment decisions by increasing the availability of a certain output for use at later stages of production, that is, by decreasing the cost of productive activities in "downstream" industries through pecuniary or nonpecuniary external economies. Backward linkages, on the other hand, stimulate demand at earlier stages in the production process, inducing positive investment decisions in industries that supply inputs to the industry in question. Hirschman first applies the distinction at an aggregate level by considering two "sectors," the government sector, which produces social overhead capital (SOC) and the private sector which engages in directly productive activities (DPA). He then applies the distinction at a later stage at a more disaggregated level.

In what follows, we first present the SOC-

[13]Demery and Demery (1973) suggest a slightly different formulation of this test, which may yield results more favorable to unbalanced growth. As we have seen, the relevant period in which growth should be balanced is not specified in most of the theories. In our formulation, the imbalances have been measured over at least a four-year period. Demery and Demery suggest that they should be measured over shorter periods (one year) and then the average of the annual imbalance indexes computed. In this way, growth that is unbalanced in the short run but balanced in the long run could be distinguished from growth patterns that are balanced in both the short and the long run. Because of economies of scale, it is particularly imbalances of the short-run variety that can be expected to be advantageous relative to balanced growth. However, the conclusions of these authors must be considered as tentative, since in part, at least, they may be due to the fact they also use the wrong index of imbalance, that is, the standard deviation unweighted by the nonidentical country means, G (Yotopoulos and Lau 1975).

[14]Swamy (1967) reported in favor of such a "reversal" hypothesis. In his case, the finding of a direct relationship between imbalance and the rate of growth was reversed by the result that countries, once past a certain level of development, tend to grow in a balanced way.

DPA imbalance sequence as an example of backward and forward linkages at the sectoral level. Next, we present a test of the linkage hypothesis that utilizes the tools of input-output analysis developed in an earlier chapter.

Imbalance through Social-Overhead-Capital— Directly-Productive-Activities

Hirschman has felicitously characterized development as a gigantic jigsaw puzzle. The choice of the efficient sequence for fitting that puzzle together depends on the "pressure" an individual piece in place exerts upon other pieces so that they, too, fall in place. Trial and error will soon lead to some simple rules of thumb: the time needed to fit each piece into place depends inversely on the number of contacts with pieces already in place; the larger the number of neighboring pieces already in place, the easier it is to fit the missing pieces, and so on (Hirschman 1958, pp. 81–82). The same principle of technical complementarity governs the choice of efficient development sequences: activities should be initiated in such a manner that increasing the production of A would lead to pressure for increasing the supply of B. This happens when B is the beneficiary of external economies (technical and pecuniary) emanating from A.

Investment in infrastructure is usually characterized by a certain degree of lumpiness and serves a variety of productive activities at the same time. Because of their lumpiness and the externalities they generate, which could make imputation of user cost cumbersome and the pricing principle uncertain, investment in infrastructure, SOC, is commonly provided by publicly regulated agencies, often at subsidized rates or free of charge, to the DPA that use it.

The relationship between SOC and DPA is one of complementarity. An efficient sequence of development would take full advantage of this complementarity. Investment in SOC has little direct effect on DPA, but indirectly, it invites DPA to come in by decreasing the costs of such activities, thus making them more profitable. For example, opening up the hinterland by road facilities induces agriculture and industry to establish there and to use the services of the new infrastructure. This is a case of forward linkage. The sequence may also go the other way, from DPA to SOC. Investments in the agricultural and industrial sectors of the hinterland may create sufficient pressure for decisions by the public or private sectors to build the required infrastructure and transport facilities. This is a case of forward linkage. The sequence may also go the other way, from DPA to SOC. Investments in the agricultural and industrial sectors of the hinterland may create sufficient pressure for decisions by the public or private sectors to build the required infrastructure and transport facilities. This is a case of backward linkage.

Figure 16.1 shows the minimum-cost combinations of DPA and SOC that produce quantities of output Q_1, Q_2, Q_3. Since SOC is not divisible, it can be produced only in discrete increments, S_1S_2, S_2S_3. Starting from position A, an excess of SOC cannot directly increase output. It can only lower the cost of DPA and lead to production of Q_1 at position A'. A surplus of DPA, on the other hand, cannot substitute for SOC, but it can directly increase final output by producing Q_2 at position B''. B is the minimum social cost position for output of Q_2. But poor countries may be too poor to afford the minimum cost strategy of balanced growth from A to B, because such a strategy would require large endowments of entrepreneurial skills—precisely the factor which in Hirschman's view is in shortest supply.

In a country plagued by deficiency of demand and high costs of production, a development-oriented government may do well to initiate the inducement mechanism by creating a surplus of SOC, from A to A'. This investment increases the demand for final output and decreases the costs of producing it. Increased profitability leads from A' to B— and the challenge-response sequence continues via BB' to C. On the other hand, in a country with deficiency of supply and a vigorous private sector, the stimulus should start by moving from A to B''. The shortage of SOC at this point decreases profit margins, and political pressure is brought to bear upon the public sector. This brings forth increased supply of SOC, with DPA costs decreasing and profitability increasing from B'' to B—and the challenge-response sequence continues via BC'' to C. Such aversive behavior (to use the language of behavioral psychologists) on the part of the government may explain the heavy investments in United States railroads in the antebellum period (Fishlow 1965a). Positive

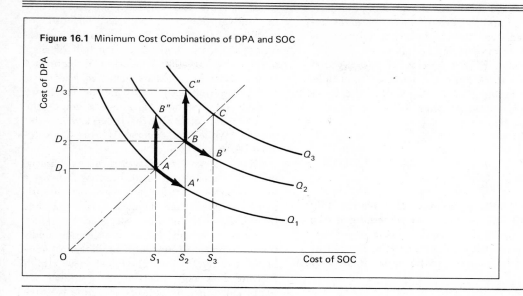

Figure 16.1 Minimum Cost Combinations of DPA and SOC

reinforcement of the private sector has been treated as the sequence to bring quick results in contemporary LDCs.

A Test of the Linkage Hypothesis

In the discussion of sectoral imbalance in the preceding section, linkage effects have been cast in general terms. One of Hirschman's most significant contributions, which has earned him the respect of academicians and planners alike, is that he has suggested ways to make the concepts of backward and forward linkage operational. He proceeded from there to suggest priority areas for investments by attaching different degrees of emphasis on backward and forward linkages in the development process.

The operational definition of Hirschman's linkages utilizes the measures of sectoral interdependence that were derived from input-output (I-O) Tables by Chenery and Watanabe (1958).[15] Specifically, backward linkage, L_{Bj}, for any industry, j, measures the contribution that intermediate inputs from other activities, i ($i = 1, \ldots, m$), make in the total value of production of industry j. The ratio of purchased inputs to the total value of production is

$$L_{Bj} = \frac{\sum_i X_{ij}}{X_j} = \sum_i a_{ij} \qquad (12)$$

[15]This section is based on an article by the authors. See Yotopoulos and Nugent (1973).

where X_{ij} represents the number of units of commodity i used in production of X_j units of commodity j. The higher the proportion of value added to gross production in any industry, the less backward linkage there is. Correspondingly, forward linkage, L_{Fi}, for any industry, i, measures the extent to which its output does not cater exclusively to final demand but rather to other industries, j ($j = 1, \ldots, n$). The ratio of interindustry demand to total demand for the output of the ith sector is

$$L_{Fi} = \frac{\sum_j X_{ij}}{Z_i} \qquad (13)$$

where Z_i is the sum of the interindustry demand for i, $\sum_j X_{ij}$, and the final demand for i, Y_i.

These linkages are direct measures that capture only part of the story, that is, only the first round of the backward or forward interactions between industries. In fact, however, an increase in sector j's output will require not only an increase in the outputs of the sectors producing inputs to sector j (given by the coefficients a_{ij} or their sum, which is the measure of backward linkage) but also increases in the outputs of the sectors contributing inputs to these sectors. Thus, additional increases in output of the different sectors are induced in the second, third, fourth, . . . rounds of this process. Eventually, as the process continues, the additional outputs induced approach zero, and the increases accumulated over all rounds of the process approach certain finite limits given by the column sum of the inverse of the Leontief $(I - A)$ matrix. Thus, we define a "total linkage" for sector j, L_{Tj}, as the sum of the direct and indirect linkages, that is, by

$$L_{Tj} = \sum_i a_{ij}{}^* \tag{14}$$

where

$$a_{ij}{}^* = (1 - a_{ij})^{-1}$$

This total linkage index captures not only backward linkages but also something in the way of forward linkages. This can perhaps best be seen by recalling that the inverse of the Leontief matrix can be approximated by

$$[I - A]^{-1} \simeq I + A + A^2 + A^3 + \cdots$$

The multiplication of A matrices to obtain A^2, A^3, and so on in this formula involves forward linkage to the extent that going backward ad infinitum in a closed system also captures forward aspects.

Chenery and Watanabe (1958) studied four countries (the United States, Japan, Italy, and Norway) that had I-O Tables reconcilable at a level of aggregation equal to 29×29. They computed backward and forward linkages for each of the 29 sectors for each country, and they concluded that the pattern of interdependence among sectors, defined in terms of linkages, was quite similar. Therefore, they proceeded to average the sectoral measures of backward and forward linkage for the four countries. Then, on the basis of whether each sector's measure of backward and/or forward linkage was above or below the four-country mean sectoral linkage of 0.425, they presented a four-way classification of each sector of production. The result of their classification procedure is reproduced in Table 16.5.

The sectors in category IV are the sectors with low backward as well as forward linkages that are relatively independent of other producers and provide a closer link between final users and the primary factors of production. They are characterized by a high proportion of value added to total production. Countries that emphasize these sectors in their development may be characterized as "inward-looking." The sectors in category II, with high backward and forward linkages, represent the

other extreme and appear most prominently in "outward-looking" countries. The ratio of purchased inputs to value added is in general higher than one, and more than half of their output goes to other producers. Categories I and III are intermediate between these extremes, in that either forward or backward linkage, but not both, is above average—the former being high and the latter low in category I, while the reverse is true in category III.

This categorization was used by Hirschman to assign priorities to different industries in the process of development. A "nonprimary" activity, that is, an industry that has high backward linkages, was said to induce attempts to supply its inputs through additional domestic production. Similarly, a "nonfinal" activity, that is, an industry with high forward linkages, was alleged to induce attempts to utilize its outputs as inputs to some new activities. Since derived demand may be considered to stimulate investment decisions to a greater degree than induced supply, Hirschman ranked category III ahead of category I in developmental priority. Hirschman's development strategy would, therefore, assign top priority to the sectors in category II that combine high backward and high forward linkage, second priority to the sectors in category III, third priority to those in category I, and lowest priority to those in category IV.

Linkages were empirically verified and measured in a number of historical and case studies of development.[16] Nevertheless, a general test of the linkage hypothesis has never been performed. The proposition that countries that conform to Hirschman's rank ordering of economic sectors have a better record of development than those that don't conform remains untested.

In the remainder of this chapter, we formulate the hypothesis of linkages in a manner that permits testing. First, we utilize the I-O Tables of a small number of countries that were available in order to measure "representative" sectoral linkages. Second, from an international cross-section of time series data, we establish the degree to which different countries have followed Hirschman's development strategy of imbalance. Third, we test

[16]See, for example, Rasmussen (1956), Fishlow (1965a), S. R. Pearson (1970), Roemer (1970), Hazari and Krishnamurty (1970), Acharya and Hazari (1971), and Lin (1973).

Table 16.5 *Linkage Typology for Inward- and Outward-Looking Countries*

		Low L_F			High L_F	
	III. FINAL MANUFACTURE			**II. INTERMEDIATE MANUFACTURE**		
		L_F	L_B		L_F	L_B
	Apparel	0.12	0.69	Iron and Steel	0.78	0.66
	Shipbuilding	0.14	0.58	Paper and Products	0.78	0.57
	Leather and Products	0.37	0.66	Petroleum Products	0.68	0.65
	Processed Foods	0.15	0.61	Nonferrous Metals	0.81	0.61
	Grain Mill Products	0.42	0.89	Chemicals	0.69	0.60
High L_B	Transport Equipment	0.20	0.60	Coal Products	0.67	0.63
	Machinery	0.28	0.51	Rubber Products	0.48	0.51
	Lumber and Wood Products	0.38	0.61	Textiles	0.57	0.69
	Nonmetallic Mineral			Printing and Publishing	0.46	0.49
	Products	0.30	0.47			
	Other Industry	0.20	0.43			
	IV. FINAL PRIMARY PRODUCTION			**I. INTERMEDIATE PRIMARY PRODUCTION**		
	Fishing	0.36	0.24	Agriculture and Forestry	0.72	0.31
	Transport	0.26	0.31	Coal Mining	0.87	0.23
Low L_B	Trade	0.17	0.16	Metal Mining	0.93	0.21
	Services	0.34	0.19	Petroleum and Natural Gas	0.97	0.15
				Nonmetallic Minerals	0.52	0.17
				Electric Power	0.59	0.27

Source: Chenery, H. B., and T. Watanabe (1958), "International Comparisons of the Structure of Production," *Econometrica*, 26 (October), Table III, p. 493.

two different versions of the linkage hypothesis with the same international cross-section of time series data.

Measurement of Linkages

Any cross-country comparison rests implicitly on the idea that there exist underlying systematic similarities among countries that make the comparison meaningful. Chenery and Watanabe demonstrated that there are international similarities among DCs, not only in the patterns of sectoral interdependence, as evidenced by the individual a_{ij} coefficients of the **A** matrices of different countries' I-O Tables, but also in the measure of sectoral linkages. Before proceeding, we must establish the existence of such similarities, more generally including those among LDCs, and measure the sectoral linkage effects for a sample of countries. Only then can we extrapolate for other countries and turn to the construction of the "Hirschman-compliance index" and to the test of the hypothesis.

From existing national I-O Tables, we have found 11 with industry classifications that were reconcilable without excessive aggrega-

tion. These 11 tables represent six DCs (Canada, Israel, Japan, Sweden, United Kingdom, and the United States) and five LDCs (Chile, Greece, Korea, Mexico, and Spain). We consolidated each I-O Table on a uniform basis at the 18 × 18 level, the sectors being defined in terms of the five global sectors (1, 2, 4, 5, and 6) and the 13 subsectors of manufacturing indicated in Table 16.3.

The differences in the Leontief coefficients of these countries, to the extent that they are not random, may reflect differences in income levels, country size, factor endowments, institutions, and presumably tastes. To what extent do these differences affect the linkage structure of each country? Chenery and Watanabe addressed this problem and found the patterns of interdependence and the structure of linkages in the four countries of their sample sufficiently similar to warrant the use of cross-country averages of linkages.[17] Our

[17] Their method of comparison consisted of triangularizing each country's I-O matrix. This amounts to establishing a hierarchy of sectors, leading from primary to finished products. To the extent that interindustry flows of each country lead to one-way interdependence (e.g., raw cotton-textiles-clothing), the

Table 16.6 *Sectoral Linkage Indexes and Comparison of Rankings: 18 × 18 I-O Tables, Developed Countries*

	Total L_T	Rank	Chenery-Watanabe-Hirschman Rank	Class	Forward L_F	Backward L_B
Food, Beverage Manufactures	2.43	1	7	III	0.223	0.743
Basic Metals	2.40	2	1	II	0.887	0.660
Textiles	2.34	3	4	II	0.671	0.615
Clothing	2.33	4	8	III	0.126	0.639
Paper	2.24	5	3	II	0.726	0.609
Metal Products and Machinery	2.21	6	9	III	0.413	0.550
Chemicals and Petroleum Refining	2.19	7	2	II	0.697	0.630
Wood, Furniture	2.09	8	5	II	0.564	0.576
Construction	2.09	9	10	III	0.374	0.536
Leather	2.08	10	6	II	0.584	0.555
Other Manufactures	2.02	11	17	IV	0.328	0.517
Rubber	1.99	12	13	I	0.586	0.496
Printing	1.99	13	14	I	0.564	0.482
Utilities	1.93	14	12	I	0.635	0.489
Minerals (nonmetallic)	1.91	15	11	I	0.767	0.478
Agriculture	1.81	16	16	I	0.623	0.405
Mining	1.70	17	15	I	0.715	0.385
Services	1.62	18	18	IV	0.438	0.303

Notes: For definition of linkages, see equations 12, 13, and 14 in the text.
Source: Yotopoulos, P. A., and J. B. Nugent (1973), "A Balanced-Growth Version of the Linkage Hypothesis: A Test," Q. J. E., 87 (May), Table 1, p. 162.

analysis of the linkages computed for each country in our 11-country sample confirms the Chenery-Watanabe result.[18] However, as Chenery and Watanabe have also pointed out, the similarity in linkages may result to a considerable degree from canceling out opposite deviations in the various coefficients of the same column or row. It is, therefore, more meaningful to test for similarities not in link-

ages but in the individual Leontief coefficients. If such similiarities exist, the linkage structure should also be similar and one should be able to extrapolate from the information of countries in the sample to countries for which no I-O Table is available.

First, we consolidate the 11 individual I-O Tables into two group aggregates, one for DCs and one for LDCs. Then we test the hypothesis that the a_{ij} coefficients are not significantly different between DCs and LDCs. The null hypothesis was rejected for some, but not all, sectors. We conclude that the structure of production—and hence also that of linkage—is identical for DCs and LDCs for some sectors, but specific to the level of development for others. Therefore, we formulate the following decision rule to guide our utilization of coefficients: (1) Use the average coefficient of all countries in the sample for all countries if, on the hypothesis that the average coefficient is the true coefficient, the average coefficient for the LDCs is different from that of the DCs at a probability level of

---

I-O matrix can be arranged in a triangular form having only zero elements on one side of the diagonal. The extent to which the economy actually departs from such one-way interdependence (with circular relations like coal-steel-mining equipment-coal) is indicated by the proportion of transactions that fall above the diagonal in the optimal arrangement. The test consists of ordering the sectors of each country in a triangular arrangement and testing the intercountry uniformity of this arrangement by computing Spearman rank-correlation coefficients among pairs of countries. See Chenery and Watanabe (1958, Table IV).

[18]Our procedure consisted of testing, by analysis of variance, the hypothesis that the sectoral linkages in the five LDCs are different from those in the six DCs of the sample. The hypothesis was rejected for each type of linkage.

less than 0.5. (2) Use different coefficients, that is, the average LDC coefficient for the LDCs and the average DC coefficient for the DCs, if the difference in sample means is significant at a probability level of 0.5 or more.

By utilizing the formulas specified in equations 12–14 and the above decision rules with respect to the I-O Tables, we compute separately for DCs and LDCs the sectoral linkage indexes, backward, forward, and total. The indexes for the 18 × 18 classification appear in Tables 16.6 and 16.7 for the DCs and LDCs respectively.

In general, these tables reveal considerable similarity in the structure of linkages between DCs and LDCs, although, not surprisingly, the indexes are generally higher in the DCs than in the LDCs. However, there are some individual industries with some striking differences. On the one hand, each of the indexes is considerably lower in the LDCs than in the DCs in agriculture, mining, utilities, and services. On the other hand, all the linkage

indexes are higher in the LDCs than in the DCs in the case of leather manufacturing, and at least one of the indexes is higher in wood and furniture, paper, metal products and machinery, nonmetallic mineral manufacturing (backward and forward); textiles, printing, and construction (backward); food and beverage manufacturing, basic metals, and other manufacturing (forward). Metal products and machinery deserve a special comment because of an unrealistically low forward linkage. Hirschman (1958, p. 107), who observed the same peculiarity, suggested that sales of these industries to other sectors are accounted for in I-O Tables as capital formation and are thus considered as final demand. The high backward linkage indexes for textiles, leather products, food and beverage manufactures, and construction might also appear surprising. We would argue, however, that the high linkages observed in these industries are realistic in view of the high domestically supplied input content typically found in these industries, particularly among LDCs. While several of

Table 16.7 *Sectoral Linkage Indexes and Comparison of Rankings: 18 × 18 I-O Tables, Less Developed Countries*

	Total L_T	Rank	Chenery-Watanabe-Hirschman Rank	Class	Forward L_F	Backward L_B
Leather	2.39	1	2	II	0.645	0.683
Basic Metals	2.36	2	3	II	0.980	0.632
Clothing	2.32	3	8	III	0.025	0.621
Textiles	2.24	4	5	II	0.590	0.621
Food, Beverage Manufactures	2.22	5	7	III	0.272	0.718
Paper	2.17	6	1	II	0.788	0.648
Chemicals and Petroleum Refining	2.13	7	4	II	0.599	0.637
Metal Products and Machinery	2.12	8	9	III	0.430	0.558
Wood, Furniture	2.07	9	6	II	0.582	0.620
Construction	2.04	10	10	III	0.093	0.543
Printing	1.98	11	14	IV	0.508	0.509
Other Manufactures	1.94	12	16	IV	0.362	0.505
Rubber	1.93	13	15	IV	0.453	0.481
Minerals (nonmetallic)	1.83	14	11	I	0.870	0.517
Agriculture	1.59	15	17	IV	0.502	0.368
Utilities	1.49	16	12	I	0.614	0.296
Mining	1.47	17	13	I	0.638	0.288
Services	1.41	18	18	IV	0.378	0.255

Notes: For definition of linkages, see equations 12, 13, and 14 in the text.
Source: Yotopoulos, P. A., and J. B. Nugent (1973), "A Balanced-Growth Version of the Linkage Hypothesis: A Test," *Q. J. E.*, 87 (May), Table 2, p. 163.

these high linkage sectors tend to be small, casual empiricism would point to the positive role of textiles in recent economic development in Korea, Hong Kong, and Taiwan and of the construction industry in the postwar development of Greece, Lebanon, and Singapore. Both of these industries have high total linkage indexes.

By utilizing our total linkage index, we obtain the unique cardinal orderings of all sectors, which also appear in Tables 16.6 and 16.7, for DCs and LDCs respectively. For purposes of comparison, we also supply the rankings that obtain if we rank sectors by the value of forward and backward linkages alone, following the Chenery-Watanabe-Hirschman ordinal ranking procedure. Although the sets of rankings are fairly consistent, there are some significant differences, particularly in the case of food and beverages, clothing, other manufacturing, minerals, and chemicals and petroleum in the DCs and of clothing, paper, other manufacturing, utilities, and mining in the LDCs. We would argue that our own total linkage index is superior to the Chenery-Watanabe-Hirschman categorization procedure in that: (1) it includes indirect as well as direct backward linkages; (2) it combines backward linkage effects with at least some forward linkage effects; and (3) it permits cardinal as opposed to only ordinal measurement. Therefore, it is our own total linkage index that will be utilized in subsequent testing.

The Hirschman-Compliance Index and the Extreme Version of the Linkage Hypothesis

The linkage hypothesis developed above predicts that countries that follow the Hirschman strategy of emphasizing high-linkage industries will in the long run be able to achieve higher overall rates of growth than countries that do not follow the Hirschman strategy. To test the linkage hypothesis, we need to devise an index that measures the extent to which a country follows the Hirschman strategy of emphasizing those industries with the highest linkage indexes as revealed by Tables 16.6 and 16.7.

A simple and yet adequate Hirschman-compliance index, ρ_{Hi}, is provided by the country-specific correlation coefficient between the sectoral total linkage indexes, L_{Tj}, and a country's sectoral rate of growth, g_{ij}. We thus define

$$\rho_{Hi} = \rho(L_{Tj}, g_{ij}) \qquad (15)$$

where i and j denote country and sector respectively. While in equation 15 we use the total linkage index, since it is more general, it is also possible to utilize only the direct backward or forward linkage indexes. Similarly, one could modify the Hirschman-compliance index in equation 15 to account for the relative importance of a sector in a country's economy, w_{ij}, and also for differences in income elasticity of sectoral composition, β_j, as in our previous discussion of balances and imbalances. Thus, we can define[19]

$$\rho_{Hi} = \rho(L_{Tj}\beta_j, g_{ij}w_{ij}) \qquad (16)$$

The sources of data for sectoral growth rates and sectoral weights are the same as those utilized in the test of balanced and unbalanced growth hypotheses, and the income elasticity of sectoral composition was given in Table 16.3. The Hirschman-compliance indexes computed from equations 15 and 16 are in some cases negative, reflecting the fact that a number of countries placed emphasis on the low-linkage sectors.

The test of the Hirschman hypothesis is to see if countries that complied with the Hirschman prescription by placing emphasis on the high-linkage sectors were able to achieve higher rates of growth than did countries that emphasized low-linkage sectors. The null hypothesis would be rejected by a significantly positive correlation between the overall country growth rates, G_i, and the Hirschman-compliance index, ρ_{Hi}.

The results reported in the left-hand portion of Table 16.8 fail to support this version of the linkage hypothesis. For the weighted version of the Hirschman-compliance index, that is, equation 16, the correlations are negative and insignificant, while for the simple index they are positive and insignificant.[20]

[19]Other combinations of the same weights were also tried, such as using only the sectoral importance weight or only the elasticity weight, applying one or both weights to the sectoral linkage index or to the sectoral rate of growth. No change in the results of the test was observed, despite the extreme sensitivity of the index to the weighting process.

[20]To test whether or not this version of the hypothesis might be operating with a lag, we computed Hirschman-compliance indexes for an earlier period (1948–1953) and related these new country-specific indexes to the overall growth rates in a subsequent period (1950–1960). Since we were able to compute Hirschman-compliance indexes for that earlier period for only 14 countries, the sample was unfortunately small. However, both equations 15 and 16

Table 16.8 *Correlation Coefficients (ρ) of the Overall Growth Rate (G$_i$) with the Hirschman-Compliance Indexes (ρ$_{Hi}$) and the Linkage-Balance Indexes (V$_{Li}$), 1950–1960*

Countries	Hirschman-Compliance Indexes (ρ$_{Hi}$)[a]		Linkage-Balance Indexes (V$_{Li}$)[b]	
	Equation 15	Equation 16	Equation 17	Equation 18
All Countries	0.17	−0.24	−0.31	−0.34
DCs Only	0.17	−0.06	−0.29	−0.32
LDCs Only	0.18	−0.23	−0.42	−0.37

Notes:
[a]The number of countries is 36: 16 DCs and 20 LDCs.
[b]The number of countries is 34: 15 DCs and 19 LDCs.
Source: Yotopoulos, P. A., and J. B. Nugent (1973), "A Balanced-Growth Version of the Linkage Hypothesis: A Test," *Q. J. E.,* 87 (May), Tables 3, 5, pp. 166, 170.

The Balanced-Growth Version of the Linkage Hypothesis

The preceding formulation of the Hirschman hypothesis is based on a rather extreme interpretation of the theory of unbalanced growth, in which there is no limit to the desirable degree of imbalance. The only constraint is that imbalance be in the right sectors, that is, those with high-linkage indexes. More realistically, however, a limit to the acceptable degree of imbalance seems desirable. Therefore, we propose a balanced-growth version of the linkage hypothesis.[21]

The degree of imbalance of an economy has been defined in equation 10 in terms of the coefficient of variation of the sectoral rates of growth from the overall rate of growth of an economy—appropriately weighted and

yielded negative rather than positive correlations, shedding additional doubt on the validity of this extreme version of Hirschman's hypothesis. As a further check on the validity of these generally negative results, we repeated some of the same experiments using either backward or forward linkage indexes in place of the total linkage indexes in computing the Hirschman-compliance indexes. However, the results were not very sensitive to such changes, yielding additional evidence negative to this formulation of Hirschman's hypothesis.

[21]While it is true that Hirschman's strategy of economic development was based upon his critique of the deficiencies of Nurkse's well-known theory of balanced growth (and he has therefore been widely regarded as an advocate of unbalanced growth), the massive literature on the balanced-unbalanced growth controversy has revealed many similarities between the two approaches. Both rely heavily on externalities and dynamic repercussions. Most balanced-growth strategies contain some elements of imbalance and most unbalanced-growth strategies contain some elements of balance. Therefore, it should not really be surprising that the linkage hypothesis could be formulated both as an unbalanced-growth strategy and as a balanced-growth strategy.

squared. Consider an optimum degree of imbalance that also reflects the sectoral linkage index. In this case, a sector, j, should grow at the overall growth rate, G, weighted by the linkage index, L_{Tj}. The coefficient of variation in the actual sectoral growth rates, g_{ij}, around the linkage-weighted overall growth rate therefore measures the degree of imbalance relative to linkage-balanced growth. Corresponding to the version of the imbalance index given by equation 10 is

$$V_{Li} = \frac{1}{G_i} \sqrt{\frac{1}{n} \sum_{i=1}^{n} w_{ij}(g_{ij} - L_{Tj}G_i)^2} \qquad (17)$$

or alternately

$$V_{Li} = \frac{1}{G_i} \sqrt{\frac{1}{n} \sum_{i=1}^{n} w_{ij}(g_{ij} - \beta_j L_{Tj}G_i)^2} \qquad (18)$$

where n is the number of sectors, w_{ij} and g_{ij} are the relative importance (the sectoral value added over GDP) and the growth rate of sector j in country i respectively, L_{Tj} is the total linkage index of sector j, G_i is the overall growth rate of country i, and β_j is the income elasticity of sectoral composition. The V_{Li} index is, of course, nothing more than a modified version of Pearson's coefficient of variation in which: (1) adjustment is made for differences among countries in the overall growth rate; (2) the variance is computed not in terms of the deviations in sectoral growth rates, g_{ij}, from the overall growth rate, G_i, but in terms of the deviations in g_{ij} from G_i weighted by the total linkage index, and in equation 18 also by the income elasticity of sectoral composition; and (3) the variances in sectoral growth rates from the linkage-weighted growth rates are in turn weighted by the relative importance of the sector, w_{ij}.

According to equation 17, country i's growth is linkage-balanced when each sectoral growth rate is proportional to that sector's total linkage index. However, since it is likely that country i's sectoral growth pattern will deviate from this proportionality rule to a different degree in different sectors, equation 17 appropriately weights these deviations by the relative importance of the sector. In the alternative measure of the degree of linkage-balance, equation 18, the sectoral growth rate is proportional both to the total linkage index and to the income elasticity of demand. As such, it might be said to combine elements of the structural change theories of Hirschman and Nurkse.

A high V_{Li} index suggests that a country has deviated from the optimum linkage-weighted growth proportions. Therefore, the balanced-growth version of the linkage hypothesis is supported by a negative correlation between the V_{Li} index and the overall rates of growth. The correlation results appear in the right-hand portion of Table 16.8. The coefficients are negative and significant for all countries in the 34-country sample with respect to both indexes of linkage-balance, thus providing support for the linkage-balance hypothesis.

In summary, on the basis of our indexes of sectoral linkage effects, a clear priority can be established for secondary production, especially manufacturing, over agriculture and services. Yet the record of growth of an international cross-section of countries does not support the Hirschman hypothesis in its extreme formulation—a result that merits the attention of policy makers. This in no way means that linkages are unimportant. Indeed, our alternative hypothesis, the balanced-growth linkage hypothesis, receives strong support from the same data.

Much of what Hirschman was trying to get at still remains difficult to operationalize. Our formulations of the linkage hypothesis are not the only ones possible, and we would not be surprised if alternative formulations yielded results that diverge from ours. Yet the concept of linkages is a powerful tool in the economics of development, and our results, although admittedly tentative, indicate that the linkage hypothesis merits further attention and empirical research.

Summary and Conclusions

Had neoclassical analysis been sufficient to fully determine the process of development, the study of structure per se would have been redundant. Within a state of development disequilibrium, however, such is not the case. Chapter 16, therefore, has been devoted to several aspects of structural change. First, we have outlined the most prominent types of structural change on the basis of different structural indicators. Second, we have concentrated more specifically on sectoral change—the change in the composition of sectoral output—and suggested typologies of different patterns of change in different types of countries. Third, we have attempted to develop the ingredients of a method that would explain the normal patterns of change and deviations from them. Finally, we have taken up what probably constitutes the most challenging aspect of structural change: the effects of sectoral change on the rate of economic development. Can a change in structure, that is, in the relationship between different sectors or subsectors of the economy, induce economic development? In a world of smooth adjustments and equilibrating processes, the answer would certainly have been negative. If and when investment opportunities could be found to exist, possible investment decisions would be made automatically. However, in a world where the ability to perceive effective opportunities and take investment decisions is in short supply, the shortage is remedied by forcing certain reaction patterns upon individuals. It is in this sense that changes in structure, which permeate the hypotheses of balanced and unbalanced growth and of linkages, are studied as disequilibrium phenomena in the process of development. Our tentative and admittedly rather unorthodox conclusion is that structural changes of appropriate direction and magnitude can accelerate development.

Empirical studies utilizing international cross-sections have identified a number of structural indicators, which assume different values at specific points of the development process. In this chapter, we have paid special attention to the indicators that describe the sectoral composition of output. The "normal" sectoral composition was determined from the overall sample. Analysis of variance was then used to measure the effects of specific characteristics on the "normal" sectoral composition.

In describing the changes in the sectoral composition of output that occur in the process of development, it has been found that small countries with substantial endowments of natural resources and relatively free trade policies maintain a considerably larger share for agriculture and considerably smaller share for industry. Thus, they undergo much less change in structure than either large countries or small countries with less substantial natural resource endowments. Moreover, these differences in patterns of different country types are above and beyond those that would be expected on the basis of their income, population size, and other characteristics. Further disaggregation for subsectoral composition has been used to identify industries or processes whose structural changes occur "early" as well as those that occur "late" in the process of development.

As far as the explanation of structural change is concerned, the results seem to be highly sensitive to differences in model specification and assumption. Probably supply as well as demand factors are involved. Demand factors would include foreign as well as domestic, and indirect as well as direct, demand. Supply factors would include import substitution and its determinants. Demographic changes, affecting both the supply and demand sides, may also be important.

The description of and the explanation for structural change, however, would imply nothing about development strategy. There would be no reason to believe that a per capita income of $2,000 could be achieved sooner if an LDC, for example, forced the metal products industry to assume the employment and output share values that are "normal" for a country with that per capita income. Instead of merely describing and explaining structural change, the hypotheses of balances, imbalances, and linkages purport to prescribe optimal policies with regard to sectoral structure.

We have defined imbalances in terms of the coefficient of variation of the sectoral growth rate from the appropriately weighted overall rate of growth—the weights being the "normal" growth elasticities of output and shares of output in GNP. Imbalance, then, is the deviation from the "normal" sectoral structure and reflects the fact that some sectors grow "too fast" and others "too slowly." We have found that balance rather than imbalance is associated with more rapid rates of growth. This finding is certainly contrary to some long-popular versions of the "big push."

Hirschman advocated another kind of imbalance based on linkages. As a prescription for rapid growth, he espoused the deliberate creation of tensions and imbalances. We have provided an operational formulation of the linkage hypothesis and presented an empirical test, which failed to support it. However, by redefining balance to include a sector's linkage coefficient along with its share in GNP and the normal growth elasticity of sectoral output, we have found evidence to support a modified version of the hypothesis, the linkage-balance hypothesis. This result reconciles the findings on normal growth patterns with the notion of linkage-induced growth.

Most of the hypotheses formulated in this chapter have assumed a closed economy or have at least ignored possible interactions with the rest of the world. As was noted in discussing the patterns of growth literature, country size, natural resource endowments, and trade policies may significantly affect structural change patterns. Indeed, small, open countries may postpone, cancel, or even reverse the types of structural change that larger and less open economies usually experience. To the extent that normal patterns of structural change induce rapid growth, distorted or unbalanced growth patterns shaped as a result of free trade policies may actually be inimical to growth. However, to the extent that countries with larger imbalance indexes are also able to increase their exports more rapidly and hence to achieve more rapid rates of growth, the results of some of the above tests could be biased.

This analysis leads directly into Part V. In Chapters 17 and 18, we will discuss the determinants and the effects of foreign trade. In Chapter 19, where we discuss economic integration, we will pay due attention to customs unions among LDCs with similar levels of development. Such schemes may make it possible for small LDCs to enjoy the advantages of openness and export-led growth without the disadvantages of freezing their sectoral composition of output and employment into patterns of underdevelopment.

Part V

Development Disequilibrium: International Trade and Growth

In evaluating the role of international trade in the process of development, one becomes acutely aware of the practical implications of the two contrasting views of development: one that examines development within a neoclassical equilibrium system, and one that approaches it as a series of successive disequilibria. The classical model originated with Adam Smith's "vent for surplus" theory and culminated with Marshall's view of trade as the "engine of growth." The "structuralist" approach to international trade, on the other hand, emphasizes distortions in the terms of trade and the asymmetry that exists in reaping the benefits of trade between the "center" and the "periphery."

Chapter 17 is devoted to the determination of both the level of exports and their composition. On the former topic, we shall present an empirical test using the export performance approach, the results of which suggest that both supply and demand factors must be integrated into the analysis. This conclusion points out the limitations of the more conventional market share approach, which concentrates exclusively on the demand factors. Still, our test may under-

estimate the effect of currency devaluations as a stimulant to trade and growth. This aspect is investigated separately by taking advantage of the historical experience of the period 1873–1894. The de facto devaluation of the silver standard countries will be found to have greatly improved their export performance and to have advanced their development. Finally, we shall examine alternative approaches to the determination of the commodity composition of exports, beginning with the classical and neoclassical models and ending with some modern theories.

Since the evidence seems inconsistent with the classical and neoclassical approaches, and yet tends to favor some of the modern theories, one may suggest that sectoral composition cannot be determined exclusively by natural endowments and environmental conditions but also by demand factors and allocative decisions about social overhead capital, which are more directly under government control. As a result, countries need not accept their commodity composition of exports as immutable but should instead be encouraged to consider the advantages and disadvantages of alternative commodity compositions.

Despite considerable openness to world trade and numerous technological and environmental changes, trade has not substantially contributed to either the equalization of factor prices or to the spread of development. Indeed, in Chapter 16, we came upon evidence to suggest that trade may mitigate, delay, or even cancel the structural changes that occur concomitantly with growth. Moreover, since the results of our test of the various versions of the sectoral balance hypothesis indicated that departures from balanced growth hinder development, this trade-induced distortion of the normal structural patterns may even have retarded economic growth. The failure in these respects of the classical and neoclassical paradigms calls for an investigation of the alleged backwash effects of international trade.

In Chapter 18, we consider two examples of such backwash effects, export instability and the deterioration of the terms of trade. With respect to the former example, although the instability of export earnings is generally higher for LDCs than for DCs, we conclude that its effects are not as demonstrably pernicious as the extant theorizing has generally assumed. Our empirical investigation of export instability, based on Friedman's permanent-income hypothesis, will suggest that instability, instead of hindering development, may in fact promote it. Similarly, with regard to the terms of trade, there seems little evidence to support the hypothesis that the terms of trade of the LDCs have been deteriorating steadily.

Historically, countries have erected tariff walls to protect themselves against real or imagined backwash effects of international trade. Tariff protection and the circumvention of the international division of labor, however, are by no means costless to a country, as our discussion in Chapter 7 has demonstrated. Chapter 19 deals with customs unions, which have appeared as international attempts to chart a middle course between the Scylla of unfettered free trade and the Charybdis of protectionism and autarky. We will extend the traditional partial analysis of the gains from participation in customs unions by also considering the effect of more homogeneous tariff rates in a general equilibrium setting. We suggest an alternative means of measuring the traditional trade-creation effects, and we develop a method for measuring the total effects, including dynamic effects excluded from the traditional measures. Our estimates suggest that the benefits of customs unions participation are considerably greater than has generally been assumed. Customs unions between DCs and LDCs would be likely to impose the same type of structural distortions on the normal growth patterns as free trade policy. However, participation in customs unions made up of partners with roughly similar levels of development would seem to offer a viable means for LDCs to obtain the engine-of-growth advantages of export trade without the disadvantages resulting from the inhibition of structural change.

Chapter 17

Trade Dependence and Export Composition

The role of international trade in the development process has received inordinate attention in the literature. Yet the empirical propositions that have been generated and meet with general agreement are relatively few. In general, they lie between two extremes, which we will characterize as the "classical" and "structuralist" positions. Starting with Adam Smith's "vent for surplus" theories of international trade, through Ricardo's trade statics of comparative advantage, and finally with Marshall's views that the causes of economic development must be sought in international trade, classical and neoclassical writers have generally considered trade as the "engine of growth." Structuralist views, on the other hand, draw on the experience of the twentieth century and generally emphasize the deterioration of the terms of trade for the LDCs and the asymmetrical effects of technological progress for the "center" and the "periphery." A

more moderate generalization would reverse D. H. Robertson's dictum and assign to development the role of being "an engine of trade."

The case study approach has been used extensively in empirical investigations of the interrelationships between international trade and development. It attempts to account for the domestic resource endowments, which vary among countries and correspondingly lead to varying trade opportunities. In this context, some of the cases studied, such as mineral exports from Liberia (Clower et al. 1966), revealed rapid export growth yet lack of spread effects to the rest of the economy and failure of general development.[1] In other cases, such as exports of natural rubber from Malaysia and Indonesia, a period of rapidly expanding

[1]Resnick (1970) argues that several Southeast Asian countries have historically suffered similar experiences.

313

export markets was followed by one of export contraction and stagnation. Finally, in other countries, such as Puerto Rico, Hong Kong, South Korea, Taiwan, and perhaps Thailand, exports increased rapidly through outward-oriented trade policies with simultaneous capital formation and high rates of economic growth.

In keeping with the general theme of this book, we will largely ignore the case study approach in favor of the selective treatment of policy problems that have a founding in theory and lend themselves to empirical analysis. We begin the chapter by considering the determination of the level of exports and their composition. Our treatment consists of three sections. First, we provide a critical comparison of the alternative approaches to determination of export growth. This discussion is supplemented by an empirical study of export performance of 38 LDCs in the postwar period. Next, we present a detailed examination of the relationship between exchange rate policies and export and income growth. The historical period for this analysis was chosen to remove some of the problems that commonly appear when one investigates the role of exchange rates within an export performance model. The final section is devoted to the discussion of the hypotheses that purport to explain the commodity composition of exports.

The Determinants of Export Growth

A country's participation in international trade is measured by trade dependence ratios. Trade dependence is expressed either in terms of foreign trade elasticities—the growth rate of imports or exports divided by the growth rate of GDP—or in terms of the share of the national product traded internationally. Trade dependence has commanded considerable attention among development economists because of the general observation that it varies systematically through time and with the level of development. It is found, for example, that over the past 100 years, the period 1953–1967 is especially characterized by a growth rate of trade in manufactures that is greater than the growth rate of world manufacturing output. During the same period, the majority of European countries and other DCs experienced foreign trade elasticities ranging between 1.5 and 2.0 (U.N. 1970). With regard to trade

dependence at different levels of development, it appears that over the long run, excluding petroleum exports,[2] the DCs have outstripped the LDCs in export growth performance.[3]

A model that considers the export performance of different countries must take into account a number of variables. The proportion of the national product traded internationally depends on the size of the country, as measured, for example, by population. The smaller the country, the more likely it is to have higher trade dependence, for it is expected to specialize in a limited range of (primarily) export products, while other requirements are covered by imports. Once we control for size, the more developed the country, the higher its trade dependence. This is because in DCs production is more concentrated in manufacturing, where economies of scale and income elasticities of demand are greater. The extent and nature of resource endowments, the proximity to world market centers, foreign aid, and invisible earnings can also offset the degree of trade dependence. In the broader context of political economy, tariff barriers may be determined endogenously by the size of the country and the level of development, with small and relatively developed countries

[2]The export performance of LDCs improves considerably when petroleum exports are included. The postwar record of both exports and GNP growth of most countries that discovered oil—such as Libya, Kuwait, Qatar, Iran, Saudi Arabia, and Venezuela—has been impressive. Indeed, there is probably no surer path to rapid export growth than the discovery and exploitation of petroleum resources. Still, there are many reasons to exclude petroleum resources from our analysis. Since the existence of oil is beyond any country's influence, there is little reason to develop a model to explain this type of success in exporting. Moreover, petroleum is a nonreproducible asset, and its export can be viewed as an exchange of one form of wealth for another rather than a net increase in wealth and welfare. Finally, the exploitation of oil requires a comprehensive array of specialized knowledge and skills that only a relatively small number of large international firms can provide. It seems appropriate, therefore, to treat petroleum exports as a special case.

[3]Nurkse (1961) showed: (1) that the share of LDCs in world exports fell from 33.8 percent in 1928 to 31.3 percent in 1957 and (2) that the LDC share in nonpetroleum exports fell even more abruptly from 32.2 percent to 24.4 percent during the same period. B. I. Cohen (1968), Lary (1968), and others have found the export performance of LDCs to be even poorer in the postwar period, and Balassa (1964) and others have used historical trends, income elasticities of demand, and so on, for individual products, to predict continued slow growth of exports for LDCs in the foreseeable future. Note, however, that Yates (1959), using an earlier base period, showed that the LDC share in world trade increased somewhat between 1913 and 1953.

imposing lower import tariffs. When import duties are reduced multilaterally through the participation in customs unions, however, tariff barriers must be treated as exogenous variables.

Our analysis of the determinants of export growth is organized around two approaches, the market share approach and the export performance approach.

The Market Share Approach
A country's market share is the ratio of its exports of a particular class to those for a region or even the world. The market share approach deals with the study of the factors that may change a country's export share. The factors usually considered invariably lie on the demand side, and among them are: (1) the commodity effect, that is, the extent to which a country's exports are concentrated on commodities for which demand is growing faster or slower than the average; (2) the regional market effect, that is, the extent to which exports may be going primarily to rapidly growing or to stagnant regions; and (3) the competitive effect, that is, the effect of changes in the prices of a country's exports relative to those of the region.

We will start with the competitive effect. We can define an exporting country's share in the total trade of commodity i by region j as $s_{ij} = q_{ij}/Q_{ij}$, where q_i is the individual country's exports of commodity i and Q_i is the total (regional) exports of commodity i. The demand for commodity i being a function of the price of the commodity, we can write

$$\frac{q_{ij}}{Q_{ij}} = f\left(\frac{p_{ij}}{P_{ij}}\right) \tag{1}$$

with p_{ij} and P_{ij} being the prices for commodity i in region j of the specific country and for that commodity in the region as a whole, respectively. By multiplying both sides of equation 1 by p_{ij}/P_{ij}, we obtain

$$\frac{p_{ij}q_{ij}}{P_{ij}Q_{ij}} = \frac{p_{ij}}{P_{ij}} f\left(\frac{p_{ij}}{P_{ij}}\right) \tag{2}$$

which indicates that a country's share of the value of exports of commodity i will remain constant, except as p_{ij}/P_{ij} changes. This is the constant share norm, and it suggests that deviations from the constant share are the result of the competitive effect, that is, changes in the country's price of commodity i relative to the regional average.

We return to the definition of the constant share in physical terms, which we rewrite

$$q_{ij} = s_{ij}Q_{ij} \tag{3}$$

By differentiating equation 3 with respect to time, we express as growth rates

$$\frac{dq_{ij}}{dt} = s_{ij}\frac{dQ_{ij}}{dt} + Q_{ij}\frac{ds_{ij}}{dt} \tag{4}$$

Thus, the growth rate of the country's exports is related to the product of its (constant) share and the rate of growth of the market for product i plus the product of the (constant) size of the market and the growth rate of the country's share. Defining

$$q = \sum_i \sum_j q_{ij}$$
$$s = \sum_i \sum_j s_{ij}$$

and

$$Q = \sum_i \sum_j Q_{ij}$$

the rate of growth of aggregate exports, dq/dt, is given by

$$\frac{dq}{dt} = \sum_i \sum_j s_{ij}\frac{dQ_{ij}}{dt} + \sum_i \sum_j Q_{ij}\frac{ds_{ij}}{dt} \tag{5}$$

By adding and subtracting terms, equation 5 can be reexpressed as

$$\frac{dq}{dt} = \left(s\frac{dQ}{dt}\right) + \left(\sum_i s_i\frac{dQ_i}{dt} - s\frac{dQ}{dt}\right)$$
$$+ \left(\sum_i \sum_j s_{ij}\frac{dQ_{ij}}{dt} - \sum_i s_i\frac{dQ_i}{dt}\right)$$
$$+ \left(\sum_i \sum_j Q_{ij}\frac{ds_{ij}}{dt}\right) \tag{6}$$

This formulation allows the overall growth in a country's export trade to be analyzed into four components that operate on the demand side. The first term of equation 6 accounts for the overall growth of world markets; the second term represents the commodity effect, that is, the influence of the world markets for the country's export bundle relative to total world exports; the third term accounts for the geographical market effect; and the last term is the change in the constant share which, by assumption, represents the competitive effect, that is, the role of the change in price.[4]

[4]This is the formulation and interpretation provided by J. D. Richardson (1971). See also Leamer and Stern (1970).

The market share approach is in principle neat and straightforward. Ideally, it should be applied as specified in equation 6, with aggregation taking place over each commodity, *i*, and the share being expressed in physical terms. In this manner, the changes in the share, as described in the fourth term of equation 6, are a function of prices, as in equation 2, and therefore represent the competitive effect.

Such simple application is not always feasible, however. Data on *q* and *Q* in physical terms are rarely available, but even if they are, the problem of aggregation of commodities arises. If commodities are not homogeneous, they are not comparable, and aggregation is not permissible. If, on the other hand, commodities are homogeneous, one would expect to observe perfect world markets with identical prices, and therefore, the last term of equation 6 must be interpreted as representing errors in measurement rather than the competitive effect as posited through changes in relative prices. Lack of data in quantity terms often makes it necessary to measure *q* and *Q* in value terms. In this case, the measurement of the competitive effect that is assumed to operate through changes in prices becomes distorted, and its interpretation is rendered ambiguous. Finally, the ordering of the terms in equation 6 is arbitrary. If one interchanges the second and third terms, calculating first the geographical market effect and then the commodity effect, the results of the calculations change (J. D. Richardson 1971). This sensitivity of the results to the ordering of the terms of equation 6, together with the data problems that arise in applications, may well account for the differences observed in the estimates of the four effects obtained by various authors.[5]

The fundamental defect of the market share approach is that it disregards the supply factors in the trade dependency of a country. Only the competitive effect, which incorporates prices, reflects the operation of both supply and demand conditions. However, the factors that explain the changes in these supply and demand conditions, and which are of major importance for policy purposes, remain

hidden behind the scaffolding of the model. The approach, as a result, becomes virtually powerless for policy purposes.

The Export Performance Approach

The export performance approach is complementary to the market share approach. By introducing to a market share equation, such as equation 6, additional variables to reflect supply factors and structural considerations, it becomes an analytically powerful tool that makes it possible to test alternative hypotheses and derive policy implications.

The estimation of the export performance approach is based on the utilization of international cross-sections of time series data, pioneered by the econometric work of Neisser and Modigliani (1953). In a comprehensive study, DeVries (1967) tried to explain the differences in export performance among countries, defined in terms of the percentage deviation of actual 1960–1963 exports from those that would have resulted if the country's market share had remained constant between 1950–1953 and 1960–1963. The explanatory variables included the initial share, the sectoral composition of GNP, the rate of inflation, and the change in the exchange rate relative to domestic prices. In subsequent applications, a geographic market variable was included, along with other variables, to account for the level of development and the degree to which the country or the region was affected by discriminatory import restrictions (Ooms 1966). Unfortunately, these applications have not been too successful in overcoming the principal weakness of the market share approach, the failure to get at the interesting analytic and policy issues lying behind the "competitive effect."

We formulate the export performance approach in a way that comes closer to providing interesting policy implications. We include supply as well as demand factors in our model and nontraditional structural factors as well as traditional relative price effects. We apply the model to an international cross-section of 38 LDCs[6] for the period 1949–1967.

Specifically, the variance in the logarithm of export growth, log $\dot{E}$, in the sample of 38 LDCs during the period 1949–1967 is expressed as a linear function of: (1) the change in the real exchange rate, that is, the change

[5]For a representative sample of such approaches, see Fleming and Tsiang (1956), Romanis (1961), Junz and Rhomberg (1965), GATT (1959, 1966), B. I. Cohen (1964, 1968). See also the surveys of McGeehan (1968) and Leamer and Stern (1970).

[6]The petroleum-exporting LDCs are excluded for reasons given in footnote 2.

in the domestic price of foreign exchange index relative to that of the domestic price index, $\log \dot{P}_{fe} - \log \dot{P}_d$; (2) the change in export prices, $\log \dot{P}_x$; (3) the growth in GDP, $\log \dot{GDP}$; (4) the growth in world demand for exports, expressed in terms of both geographic composition, $\log \dot{GEO}$, and commodity composition, $\log \dot{COMM}$; (5) the change in export tax rate, T_x, in licensing requirements on exports, L_x, and in foreign exchange surrender requirements on exports, S_x; (6) the participation in a regional trading arrangement, such as the European Economic Community (EEC), the European Free Trade Association (EFTA), the Central American Common Market (CACM), or the Latin American Free Trade Association (LAFTA); and (7) a dummy variable for recovery from the disruptive conditions that may have existed at the beginning of the time period on account of civil or other wars (WAR). The relationship may be expressed as

$$\begin{aligned}
\log \dot{E} = {} & a_1 + a_2(\log \dot{P}_{fe} - \log \dot{P}_d) + a_3 \log \dot{P}_x \\
& + a_4 \log \dot{GDP} + a_5 \log \dot{GEO} \\
& + a_6 \log \dot{COMM} + a_7 T_x + a_8 L_x \\
& + a_9 S_x + a_{10} EEC + a_{11} EFTA \\
& + a_{12} CACM + a_{13} LAFTA \\
& + a_{14} WAR \qquad\qquad (7)
\end{aligned}$$

where the dotted variables, $\dot{E}$, $\dot{P}_{fe}$, and so on, are defined in terms of $1 + g$, where g is the average annual growth rate, and the remaining (undotted) variables are defined in terms of absolute changes.

Note that the traditional relative price effects (on both the supply and demand sides) would be represented by the coefficients of $\log \dot{P}_x$ and $(\log \dot{P}_{fe} - \log \dot{P}_d)$. The effects of other demand factors would be represented by the coefficients of $\log \dot{GEO}$, $\log \dot{COMM}$, and the regional trading arrangement variables, while those of other supply factors would be reflected in the coefficients of T_x, L_x, S_x, $\log \dot{GDP}$, and WAR.

Some of the variables included in this export performance approach are thus common to the market share approach. In the export performance approach, however, greater consideration is given to supply factors, such as the influence of relative price changes on the composition of output, factors relating to aggregate supply, civil and other disturbances, and also to policy variables af-

fecting the relative profitability of export activities. Some of these variables, such as the relative price changes or the regional trading arrangement dummy variables, may exert their influence on both the supply and demand sides of the market. In the latter case, since each different arrangement might entail differing amounts of trade creation (in which the effects on exports would be positive) relative to trade diversion (in which the effects might be negligible or even negative), each of the four more important such arrangements established during the period have been distinguished.

The data used in fitting equation 7 for the sample of 38 LDCs for the period 1949–1967, the sources from which they were computed, and comments on data reliability and data compromises are presented in Nugent (1974). We turn directly to the results, given in Table 17.1. The regression results in column 1 show that most of the variables influenced exports in the expected direction, but the resulting coefficients are not always statistically significant. Since none of the rather crude proxies for restrictions on exports (the export tax rate, T_x, licensing requirements, L_x, and foreign exchange surrender requirements, S_x, were significant, these variables were dropped from the regressions reported in columns 2–4. Since the regression results shown in columns 1 and 2 indicate that the influences of the world export commodity index (COMM) as well as the EFTA and LAFTA dummy variables are all insignificant, these variables were omitted from the regressions reported in columns 3 and 4. Even on the basis of the remaining variables (some of which are significant only at the 10 percent level), the model can explain over 80 percent of the total variation in export performance among countries. Note also that the estimated coefficients are remarkably insensitive to these changes in specification.

Particularly significant at the 5 percent level are the variables for aggregate supply (GDP) and the real exchange rate, $\dot{P}_{fe}/\dot{P}_d$, as well as the dummy variable for participation in the CACM. As might be expected, the impact of customs union participation on export growth has varied considerably from case to case. The impact on LDC members of the EEC, EFTA, and LAFTA has been (at best) negligible, but participation in the CACM, where intraregional trade has grown

Table 17.1 *Regression Coefficients of Export Performance Equation: 38 Countries, 1949–1967*

Coefficients	(1)	(2)	(3)	(4)	(5)
log Constant	−5.089	−5.220	−4.806	2.048	0.922
$(\log \dot{P}_{fe} - \log \dot{P}_d)$	0.375 (0.160)	0.353 (0.170)	0.378 (0.160)	0.590 (0.232)	0.678 (0.256)
$\log \dot{P}_x$	0.480 (0.322)	0.470 (0.361)	0.544 (0.328)	0.919 (0.479)	0.501 (0.546)
$\log G\dot{D}P$	1.362 (0.233)	1.386 (0.244)	1.407 (0.227)		
$\log G\dot{E}O$	0.499 (0.236)	0.537 (0.272)	0.493 (0.250)	0.373 (0.371)	0.334 (0.398)
$\log CO\dot{M}M$	0.047 (0.240)	0.109 (0.268)			0.316 (0.400)
T_x	−0.018 (0.063)				−0.192 (0.090)
L_x	−0.006 (0.011)				−0.001 (0.018)
S_x	0.006 (0.009)				0.007 (0.015)
EEC	−0.032 (0.013)	−0.032 (0.015)	−0.035 (0.014)	−0.037 (0.022)	−0.030 (0.022)
EFTA	0.017 (0.018)	0.017 (0.021)			0.023 (0.029)
CACM	0.017 (0.009)	0.016 (0.008)	0.017 (0.008)	0.025 (0.012)	0.024 (0.012)
LAFTA	0.006 (0.008)	0.005 (0.009)			−0.002 (0.013)
WAR	0.026 (0.012)	0.024 (0.014)	0.024 (0.013)	0.054 (0.018)	0.047 (0.018)
R^2	0.824	0.822	0.812	0.571	0.666

Notes:

Dot indicates that the variable is defined in terms of $(1 + g)$, where g is the growth rate computed from 1949–1967 annual observations.

All figures in parentheses are standard errors of the regression coefficients under which they appear.

For definitions of variables, form of the estimating equations and interpretation of the results, see the text.

Source: Nugent, J. B. (1974), *Economic Integration in Central America: Empirical Investigations*. Baltimore: Johns Hopkins University Press, Tables 3 and 4, p. 58.

from a tiny fraction to more than 25 percent of total trade, seems to have increased the export growth rate of CACM members significantly.

While the export price variable, $\dot{P}_x$, is not significant at the 5 percent level, the coefficients of this variable are undoubtedly biased downward by the use of unit price indexes, which reflect changes not only in price but also in quality and composition, instead of true price indexes.

The regression results in columns 1–3 in Table 17.1 should be considered in light of methodological difficulties, inherent in this kind of study. Two such difficulties are particularly worthy of note: one concerning the relationship between GDP growth and export growth and the other concerning the effect of foreign exchange rates on export growth. In both cases, the source of the problem is the simultaneous equation bias.

Let us first consider the former case.[7] The

[7]For the examination of the relationship between exports and growth in GDP in a Harrod-Domar model, see Findlay (1972). In the simplest specification of the model, the paradoxical result arises that

results in columns 1–3 indicate that the growth of *GDP*, the proxy for aggregate supply, has been the single most important determinant of export performance among countries of the sample during the 1949–1967 period. Exports, however, as a major component of aggregate demand, constitute a large part of GDP in many LDCs. The model postulated by equation 7 does not account for this feedback of exports on growth. To do so would complicate the model, by bringing in additional variables that affect other components of GDP, and would require simultaneous equation estimation procedures. The deliberate omission of the accounting identity expressing the positive effect of exports on GDP imparts an upward bias of unknown magnitude to the estimates of the coefficient of the GDP variables, a_4. Thus, the true impact of the aggregate supply variable (for which GDP is the proxy) is probably smaller than the values indicated by our estimates. Since the value of this coefficient in itself may not be of particular interest, this shortcoming may not be important. Of greater concern, however, may be the distortion in the estimated coefficients of the other variables, which results from multicollinearity with the *GDP* variable.

As a crude attempt to determine the sensitivity of the results to the simultaneous equation bias and multicollinearity, we drop the *GDP* variable from the estimating equation, the results of which are given in columns 4 and 5 of Table 17.1. The omission of this catchall variable lowers the explained variance to about 60 percent of the total variance. Note, however, that in the estimation of the other coefficients, the omission of the *GDP* variable increases the absolute magnitude and significance of all remaining variables, with the exceptions of the geographic demand variable, *GEO*, and the *EEC* customs union dummy variable. Indeed, the results in column 5 show that the export tax rate variable, T_x, is significant when *GDP* is omitted. They also show that the impact of the commodity-weighted demand index *COMM* is increased when the *GDP* variable is excluded, although that variable is still not statistically significant. These findings reflect the mutual correlation

among all variables affecting exports directly and GDP indirectly. However, this approach to analyzing the various biases emanating from the failure of the model to include the feedback of exports on GDP is far from satisfactory. The true values of all coefficients and an accurate assessment of the explanatory power of the model could only be gained by specification of a more complete model, including additional equations for GDP and its other components.

The other area in which the simultaneous equation bias is evident is perhaps of more immediate concern, because it occurs in relation to the impact of a policy instrument, the price of foreign exchange, P_{fe}, on imports. We notice that, while the deflated exchange rate variable, $\dot{P}_{fe}/\dot{P}_d$, apparently has a significant positive effect on exports, the elasticity of exports with respect to the real exchange rate would seem to be fairly low. It is significant, however, that in this case the omitted relationship (the impact of export growth on the price of foreign exchange) is negative. That is, if the price of foreign exchange were allowed to move freely, rapid growth in exports would tend to lower the price of foreign exchange (measured in terms of units of domestic currency per United States dollar) while slow growth of exports would raise it. Even though in most countries P_{fe} is not free to fluctuate but is fixed by official policy, in the long run export performance does influence exchange rate policy. The poorer a country's export performance, the more it would be forced to devalue its currency, thereby raising its P_{fe}. The presence of negative simultaneous equation bias means that our estimate of a_2 in equation 7 is less than its true value. Similar studies, for example, DeVries (1967), which have included an exchange rate variable, have also suffered from this simultaneous equation bias. Furthermore, changes in monetary and fiscal policies and exchange reforms that commonly accompany a change in exchange rates can receive only incomplete consideration in such models.[8] This could also lead to unreliable estimates of the impact of exchange rate changes on export growth.

---

imports raise the rate of growth in GDP while exports lower it. However, when the import component of domestic investment and the import constraint from balance of payments deficits are introduced, the model reduces to the two-gap system.

[8]Indeed, in several instances, these changes have been designed to offset, neutralize, or compensate for the effects of devaluation or appreciation in countries included in our sample. It was partly as an attempt to account for these compensating or complementary changes in policy that we have included the variables L_x, S_x, and T_x pertaining to exchange restrictions on exports.

Larger and more complicated models could improve the measurement of the impact of devaluation. A simpler alternative, however, is to take advantage of historical data that may be amenable to more ordinary techniques of analysis. There is indeed an historical period in which, fortuitously, the possibility of bias arising from feedback mechanisms or policies of monetary, fiscal, and exchange reforms simultaneous to devaluations is practically eliminated. This was the period between 1873 and 1894, when the currencies of virtually all countries of the world were explicitly or implicitly committed to either the silver or the gold standard. In addition, this period was characterized by a more or less steady fall in the price of silver relative to gold, amounting to about 50 percent. This meant that silver standard countries devaluated relative to gold standard countries by approximately 50 percent over these two decades. The simultaneous equation bias is absent, in this case because the de facto devaluations by the silver standard countries relative to the gold standard countries derived entirely from changes in the relative supply and demand conditions for these two metals and were independent of the balance of payments position or export performance of any individual country. Another advantage of studying this period is that it was relatively free of war-caused distortions, tariff and quantitative restrictions, multiple exchange rates, and other complications that plague other empirical investigations of exchange rate policies. These advantages must ultimately be weighed against some special features of this period, which should be borne in mind when explaining the inter-country differences in export and income growth and when generalizing from the results obtained for 1873–1894 to other periods.[9]

An estimate of the impact of devaluation on export performance that is free of the simultaneous equation and other biases could

[9]Among the particular factors of importance during the 1873–1894 period whose effects were gradually realized are: (1) the opening of the Suez Canal in 1869; (2) the development of the steamboat; (3) the "opening-up," "peace making," and other effects associated with colonial penetration of many less developed areas of the world; and (4) the differences in supply and demand conditions for individual commodities. By and large, however, these were influences that might affect individual silver or gold standard countries relative to one another but not gold standard countries relative to silver standard countries as a whole.

be obtained by comparing the export performance of the devaluating silver standard countries with that of the gold standard countries between 1873 and 1894. Such a study was carried out by Nugent (1973), and shows that the value of exports of silver standard countries increased at a rate at least 1.5 percent per annum faster than that of gold standard countries—or four times as fast. Moreover, several gold standard LDCs were subject to substantial depressions during the period, at the same time that most silver standard countries were enjoying extremely rapid growth. The influence of devaluation may thus spread from exports to investment, income, and technology. There is no evidence, however, that the distribution of income was made more equal in the devaluating countries. If these results are representative of other periods, they would indicate that the downward bias in most estimates of the influence of devaluation, such as those we presented in Table 17.1, may be substantial.

Determinants of the Commodity Composition of Exports

We have seen that the quantity of aggregate exports can probably be increased by the adoption of outward-oriented policies, such as devaluation, subsidies to exports, liberal import policies, or at least export bonus schemes designed to offset the more obvious and pervasive disincentives to export development. The critics of such a development strategy, however, would argue that the problems LDCs face do not lie in the growth of aggregate exports alone but also in the commodity composition of output and trade.

In Chapter 16, we observed that open trade policies, small country size, and substantial natural resource endowments combine to delay or even reverse the normal changes in the sectoral composition of output that occur in the process of development. We also showed that deviations from the normal patterns of sectoral change lower the growth rate of GNP. Hence, in small, open, and primary-oriented LDCs, the structure-distorting effect of export growth may offset the classical engine-of-development effects of exports.

The argument over the effects of free trade policies on development is carried one step farther. It is argued that the commodity and geographic compositions of LDC exports tend to be highly concentrated, making for excessive dependence on a few commodities and countries. This results in increasing the risks of substantial fluctuations and of secular decline in the terms of trade.

Whether LDC exports are heavily concentrated, volatile, or subject to unfavorable long-run price changes are all questions that can be answered only by detailed empirical investigation. A considerable portion of the next chapter will be devoted to such issues. The harbinger of these analyses, however, is the study of the factors that determine the commodity composition of trade—which was largely considered as exogenous up to this point. A formal theory of long standing that explains trade patterns is the theory of comparative advantage. Of the many and not easily distinguishable expositions of this theory, two alternative operational versions have emerged and been subjected to empirical testing: the classical version, originating with Ricardo and more recently refined by Taussig, and the neoclassical version, associated with the names of Heckscher and Ohlin. A less formal but also testable approach has recently developed in the form of the product cycle hypotheses.

The Classical Theory of Comparative Costs

Consistent with his labor theory of value, Ricardo formulated the classical theory of comparative advantage in terms of output and one input, labor. He was, of course, not oblivious to the importance of capital in the world. The implicit assumption, however, is that labor and capital are employed in nearly the same proportions in all lines of production. As a result, changes in the relative quantities of output will produce no significant relative changes in factor prices. The prediction of this formulation of the theory of comparative advantage is that a country exports products with relatively low domestic labor requirements, that is, goods for which it has a high labor productivity (output per unit of labor) relative to other goods. Conversely, a country imports commodities in which its average labor productivity is relatively low.

In a one-factor production function, output, or value added, V, is determined by labor, L, and labor productivity A:

$$V = AL \qquad (8)$$

Labor productivity, $A = V/L$, is the exogenous factor that determines the composition of exports. In this form, the classical theory of comparative advantage was tested by MacDougall (1951), Stern (1962), and Balassa (1963), using trade and productivity data of the United States and the United Kingdom. For example, using cross-section data for the year 1950, Balassa obtained the following result for exports E:

$$\log \frac{E_{US}}{E_{UK}} = -1.761 + 1.594 \log \frac{\left(\dfrac{V}{L}\right)_{US}}{\left(\dfrac{V}{L}\right)_{UK}} \qquad (9)$$
$$\phantom{\log \frac{E_{US}}{E_{UK}} = -1.761 + } (0.328)$$

These results indicate that a 1 percent increase in the United States productivity ratio, $\left(\dfrac{V}{L}\right)_{US} \Big/ \left(\dfrac{V}{L}\right)_{UK}$, leads to an increase in its export share of approximately 1.6 percent.

Most interpretations of the classical version have granted that differences in productivity among countries could be offset by differences in factor costs. If United States labor productivity and wages are twice as high as in the United Kingdom, there must be no advantage for American exports. Balassa attempted to account for such effects by introducing additional explanatory variables. However, his results indicated that these influences were insignificant.

Although allowing for differences in wages among countries, the Ricardian model assumes away within-country, industry-specific wage differentials. But suppose that labor markets are not perfect, and thus, wages vary from industry to industry. If labor productivity does not differ from industry to industry, the relative wages rather than the relative productivities would determine the pattern of trade. Furthermore, one would predict that a country exports the commodities for which it has relatively low wage rates. This hypothesis was tested (Kravis 1956), and the converse was true. If anything, wages are higher in export industries than in other industries. A simple explanation of this result could lie in the misspecification of the labor variable. There could be skill differences between the export-producing and import-competing industries. If a country exports goods with higher skill requirements, it must also have higher wages in the export sector. The specification of the production function in terms of one variable, homogeneous labor, is in that case incorrect.

Alternatively, we can specify a two-factor model with capital, K, in addition to labor, L, of the Cobb-Douglass form and with constant returns to scale, as

$$V = AL^\alpha K^{1-\alpha} \qquad (10)$$

Labor productivity is now given by

$$\frac{V}{L} = A\left(\frac{K}{L}\right)^{1-\alpha} \qquad (11)$$

If perfect competition prevails in factor markets such that marginal productivities of K and L are equal to the respective factor prices, P_K and P_L, the marginal rate of substitution between capital and labor $(1 - \alpha)/\alpha$, is equal to the ratio of factor shares, $P_K K/P_L L$. Differences in V/L among countries no longer unambiguously reflect differences in technology but can also reflect differences in factor proportions. This leads to the neoclassical version of the theory of comparative advantage.

The Neoclassical Theory of Factor Endowments

The Heckscher-Ohlin version of the theory of comparative advantage admits of two factors, capital and labor. All countries face the same technological possibilities (summarized by the production function) for any given industry, although there are different factor intensities for different industries. In other words, A and $1 - \alpha$ are the same for all countries for an industry, but vary among industries. Furthermore, countries are characterized by different factor intensities, that is, there is not a perfect world market in factors of production. As a result, and contrary to the classical theory, in the neoclassical version factor price equalization in the world is eventually achieved not by international factor mobility but by commodity trade. This happens in a specific manner, which is termed the Heckscher-Ohlin theorem: a country that is well endowed with capital will export capital-intensive goods and correspondingly will import labor-intensive goods. The price of capital, therefore, will tend to rise in capital-abundant countries, and the price of labor will tend to fall.

This is the testable aspect of the neoclassical version of the hypothesis, which Ohlin (1933) submitted to a test with historical data. He divided the wheat-growing countries of Europe into two groups, the exporting countries, which also had low population densities, and the importing countries, which had high population densities. Contrary to the expectations of the Ricardian hypothesis, he found that the exporting countries had low wheat yields per acre, while the importing ones had high yields. This is precisely what the neoclassical theory would have predicted. In importing countries, where wheat is expensive and land is scarce, other factors of production are used abundantly per unit of land and produce high yields per acre. The converse happens in exporting countries with relatively cheap labor, which cultivate land extensively and obtain low yields per acre. This demonstrates the importance of relative factor prices and of factor proportions on the patterns of trade.

Leontief (1954, 1956, 1964) tested the implication of the neoclassical hypothesis that countries export commodities that use their relatively abundant factors intensively and import commodities that require relatively large quantities of their scarce factors. By utilizing data on the structure of the United States economy as revealed through the I-O Table, he estimated the capital and labor content of $1 million of American exports and also of $1 million of import competing goods. His computations produced the well-known Leontief paradox: import replacements demanded 30 percent more capital per worker than exports! The finding that the United States exports labor-intensive and imports capital-intensive commodities has been confirmed by subsequent studies (Baldwin 1971), and also the paradox has been replicated for other countries.

Several explanations of the Leontief paradox have been suggested, and some have been tested. The dominant explanation revolves around misspecification of the factors of production. Should one distinguish two categories of labor, skilled and unskilled, then the United States would be considered relatively better endowed in the former than other countries. If it is correct, as a number of studies have suggested, that American exports are skilled-labor-intensive, while imports are unskilled-labor-intensive, the Leontief paradox disappears (Baldwin 1971; Kenen 1965). Research and development, which is also complementary to skilled labor, is another important determinant of United States exports. This approach is also consistent with the predictions of the neoclassical theory (Keesing 1967). Similarly, another misspecification in Leontief's tests might be the omission of natural resources. With America's natural resources growing increasingly scarce, capital and labor might have become the abundant factors utilized intensively in exports. It has been found that the natural resource products embodied in a unit of United States exports are barely over half those contained in one unit of imports.

Despite the abundance of explanations, the Leontief paradox keeps cropping up, with respect to LDC exports as well. One might suppose that LDC exports are constrained not only by scarcity of human capital but also by small market size. Because of this latter constraint, one would expect LDCs to be more successful in exporting commodities that are not subject to substantial economies of scale. After controlling for these factors, however, a study (UNCTAD 1969) still found the exports of LDCs to be capital intensive. In this study, the imports of commodity i, M^i, of 18 DCs for the years 1960–1966 were distinguished by country of origin to form an index of the proportion of the total originating from LDCs. This was regressed on measures of human capital intensity, S, physical capital intensity, K, and scale, E, for industry, i, all obtained from United States and United Kingdom data. The following results were obtained

$$\log \frac{M^i_{LDC}}{M^i} = 7.04 - 2.72 \log S^i + 0.75 \log K^i$$
$$ (1.19) (0.42)$$
$$ - 0.29 \log E^i$$
$$ (0.10) (12)$$
$$\overline{R}^2 = 0.26$$

where the superscript denotes industry, i, and the dependent variable is the percent of imports of commodity, i, originating in LDCs. These results support the hypothesis that LDC exports of manufactures to developed countries are hindered by skill shortages and the small market size of the LDCs, but not by physical capital shortages. The Leontief paradox is again confirmed by the positive sign of the coefficient of K. However, the possibility that the result is only spurious remains, because each of the following factors could explain the relationship: (1) a positive correlation between the omitted natural resource intensity

and capital intensity; (2) a positive correlation between foreign investment (which might render the host country's factor endowment irrelevant) and capital intensity; and (3) the deliberate substitution of physical capital for the scarcer human capital.

The last point on the marginal rate of substitution brings us to an exotic explanation of the Leontief paradox suggested by Minhas (1963), which, a little earlier, provided the sperm for the development of the CES production function (Arrow, Chenery, Minhas, and Solow 1961). A crucial assumption of the Heckscher-Ohlin hypothesis is that all countries face the same technological possibilities for any given industry—which was defined above in the Cobb-Douglas case as the same constant term and the same exponent. The corollary to this is, given a common ratio of factor prices in two countries, one of the two commodities will be produced by labor-intensive methods, compared to the other. But in the C-D production function, the elasticity of substitution is equal to one. Should we admit the possibility of other values for the elasticity of substitution, the corollary is no longer valid. The possibility arises that, as the common ratio of factor prices in the two countries changes, a factor-intensity reversal occurs, that is, at one price ratio one commodity is produced by labor-intensive techniques, while at another price ratio the other is labor intensive.

Factor-intensity reversal is illustrated in Figure 17.1.[10] In 17.1*a*, we show the isoquants for the production of X_1 and X_2, which, *ex hypothesi*, are the same for two countries. The factor price ratios and the factor intensities of 17.1*a* are drawn in logarithmic terms in 17.1*b*. The factor-intensity reversal occurs as the common wage-interest ratio increases from B to D. At low values of P_L/P_K, as at points B and B', commodity X_1 is labor intensive and commodity X_2 is capital intensive. The reverse happens as labor becomes relatively more scarce and P_L/P_K increases to D and D'. At an intermediate factor price, as at C and C', X_1 and X_2 exhibit identical capital-labor ratios. The assumption of competitive labor markets implies that P_L/P_K is the same in all sectors within a country, but may vary among countries. Suppose that in one country the ratio of P_L/P_K is at B and in

----

[10]The illustration of the factor-intensity reversal draws on Caves and Jones (1973).

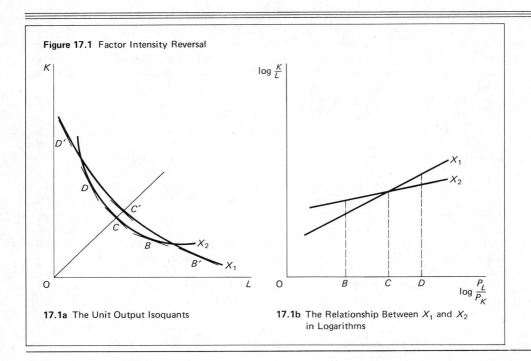

Figure 17.1 Factor Intensity Reversal

17.1a The Unit Output Isoquants

17.1b The Relationship Between X_1 and X_2 in Logarithms

another it is at D. If the labor-rich country were to export its labor-intensive commodity, it would export X_1. But so would the capital-rich country, if it were to export its capital-intensive commodity. Hence, when factor reversal occurs, one of the two countries is bound to reflect the Leontief paradox.

Factor-intensity reversals have been suggested as an explanation of the Japanese pattern of trade, which consists of labor-intensive imports (Naya 1967). Agriculture, a resource-intensive sector, is characterized by factor-intensity reversals in the factors of capital and labor. In Japan, for example, rice is cultivated by using large quantities of manual labor, in the United States, by using elaborate machinery. Indeed, agriculture in Japan is more labor intensive than any other sector of the economy, while agriculture in the United States is more capital intensive than any other sector. Leontief's paradox in the case of Japan is that a labor-intensive country exports goods that are more capital intensive than are her import replacements.[11]

[11]But the imports of Japan consist mainly of food that is natural-resource intensive. Had Japan been compelled to produce food locally, it would have been a labor-intensive operation. One can thus conjecture that Japan's imports would have been

After considering all these adjustments—more than two factors of production, the skill content of trade, the complementarity between human capital and research and development, as well as factor-intensity reversals in a CES production function with elasticity of substitution different from one—as well as others (such as the economies of scale and the role of tariffs), it would seem that the Heckscher-Ohlin theory can be rehabilitated. But this comes at the cost of greater complication, and even so, other important elements still remain unaccounted for in the model. For example, both the classical and neoclassical theories of comparative costs fail to incorporate dynamic elements of any kind and thus are unable to explain changes in trade patterns over time. Similarly, both theories concentrate on the production function, even though it is widely recognized that differences in demand preferences among countries are an important determinant of trade. The less elegant product cycle theory attempts to account for some of these factors that determine the commodity composition of exports.

more capital intensive than her exports if her lack of natural resources had not compelled her to import so much food.

Product Cycle Theories

Given the rather glaring shortcomings of comparative cost theories, the need for fresh theorizing in this important area should be obvious. Empirical testing will, of course, necessarily play its critical role in distinguishing promising approaches from unpromising ones. Before concluding this chapter, we shall note a few of the new directions in which the theory is going and indicate the ways empirical testing may be applied. Each new approach is designed to remove or at least mitigate one or more of the shortcomings in the traditional theories of comparative cost.

According to Lindner (1961), domestic demand and its determinants play an important and positive role in developing exports. In the face of a critical scarcity of information about market opportunities, which can be overcome more easily at the domestic than the foreign level, and because of learning-by-doing benefits and economies of scale, domestic demand for a product is considered a necessary condition for export development. Changes in trade patterns can, therefore, be explained by changes in domestic consumption patterns. If consumption patterns are determined by income, empirical tests would involve regressions of export patterns on the level of domestic income. However, since domestic demand is only a necessary and not a sufficient condition for trade, Linder's approach would presumably not exclude some role for comparative cost theories, particularly in the case of primary products.

One way domestic demand and factor proportions considerations can be combined is by relating changes in demand to changes in technology, and both changes in technology and the existing factor proportions to trade. This approach was taken by S. Hirsch (1967) in his version of a series of modern theories that have been characterized as "product cycle" theories.[12] In Hirsch's view, the market for every product undergoes a similar evolution, from its initiation with small demand, through a growth phase of rapid expansion, to its full development with a large mass market. In the first stage of a new product, large-scale production is not feasible, and the factor proportions are characterized by large doses of skilled labor combined with small amounts of capital and unskilled labor. In the second stage of the product cycle, capital intensity increases, but management and cost-control techniques and engineering skills for designing techniques for large-scale production are all vital. Finally, by the third stage when product standardization has taken place, large amounts of capital and unskilled labor are combined with small amounts of skilled labor. Standardization makes the locus of production highly sensitive to cost differences.

The small DCs with small highly skilled populations and moderate endowments of capital are ideal for production of commodities in the first stage of the cycle. The large DCs with large markets and large amounts of skilled labor and capital are well suited for making products in the second stage. Finally, LDCs with their vast quantities of unskilled labor provide appropriate factor proportions[13] for production of commodities in the third or "mature" phase.

Indeed, there is a certain correspondence between theory and reality, in terms of types of products in which different countries specialize. For example, certain LDCs have been able to export sizable quantities of certain standardized manufactures, such as textiles, cement, chemical fertilizers, and steel. Also, small DCs, such as Holland, Denmark, and Sweden, have done very well in engineering industries and machinery, where innovations are continuously taking place. Large DCs, such as the United States, Germany, and Japan, have been noted for the introduction of mass production techniques and capital-intensive processes with modern management techniques.

In an attempt to test the hypothesis, Hirsch examined six subdivisions of the electronics industry, in which the United States had an important position in world trade. He classified the stage in the product cycle of each of these commodities by the level and rate of growth of domestic value added in the industry during the period 1960–1963. On the other hand, the change in the United States trade position for each product was measured by the percentage change in the trade balance (exports minus imports) over the same period. One would expect on the basis of the hypothesis that the United States

[12]For other versions of product cycle, see Hufbauer (1966), Vernon (1966), Keesing (1967), and Wells (1969, 1972).

[13]This is particularly true if, as Vernon (1966) has argued, capital is mobile internationally.

would be enjoying an improving trade position in growth stage products whose value added was growing most rapidly, while suffering a deterioration in its trade position in the mature products subject to stagnating (mature) subdivisions. To distinguish his hypothesis from the traditional Heckscher-Ohlin hypothesis, Hirsch presented evidence indicating that the three "mature product" subdivisions were more capital intensive than the others. He thus concluded that the traditional hypothesis was contradicted. However, the positive relationship between growth rates and trade balance may not necessarily indicate causality going from growth rates to trade balance. The causality could conceivably go the other way. Indeed, Hirsch's test is inconclusive, for the positive outcome is consistent with many explanations other than the one posited. Larger samples and stronger tests, which discriminate more clearly between alternative versions of the product cycle, will be necessary.

The introduction of demand factors, as by Linder, and changes in the capital intensity parameter of the production function, as in the product cycle theories, do not exhaust the possibilities for constructing dynamic international trade theory. If the production of some commodities is associated with important learning-by-doing effects, differences in commodity composition and export performance among countries can also be attributed to deliberate government policies to encourage those industries in which learning-by-doing is substantial (Teubal 1973).

Summary and Conclusions

One aspect of trade dependence on which Chapter 17 has focused is the determination of a country's level of exports. There are two approaches to this topic. The first, the market share approach, considers the change in a country's exports relative to total regional or world trade. An operational formulation of this approach has led to the decomposition of the overall growth in a country's export trade into four components: the overall growth of world markets, the commodity effect as reflected by world demand for the specific bundle of exports the country produces, the geographical market effect that relates to the country's regional trade pattern, and the effect of a change in the prices of the country's exports relative to those of other countries. These effects operate entirely on the demand side.

We have therefore formulated as an alternative the export performance approach, which incorporates supply as well as demand factors and facilitates policy implications. This approach has been applied to study the rate of growth of exports in an international cross-section of 38 LDCs over the period 1949–1967. The most significant determinants of export growth were found to be the rate of growth of GDP, the rate of change in the real exchange rate deflated for the changes in the domestic price level, and participation in the Central American Common Market for the specific subset of member countries. The GDP effect operates on the supply side, the foreign exchange and CACM effects on both the demand and supply sides. This vindicates the use of the export performance approach, as opposed to the market share approach, which overlooks supply factors. In connection with the rate of exchange, it was found that while devaluation aids exports, the elasticity of exports with respect to the foreign exchange rate was quite low. This estimate, however, is biased downward by the simultaneous equation bias arising from negative long run effects of the rate of growth of exports on the price of foreign exchange. For this reason we have referred to a study of a particular historical period in which this simultaneous equation bias is largely absent. The results of that study indicate that the effects of devaluation are much more substantial and pervasive than they have generally been assumed to be.

These results support the view that, if exports and income do not grow rapidly enough as a result of the traditional spread effects and equilibrating mechanisms, LDCs can increase their exports and indirectly their income and output by adopting appropriate export-inducing policies. The structure of exports has been treated as an exogenous variable, however, and thus, these results do not account for the effects of exports on overall economic structure and indirectly on growth.

In the last part of this chapter, we referred to the determinants of the commodity composition of exports. We treated this topic first in terms of the classical theory of comparative costs, as developed by Ricardo, and then by the neoclassical theory of factor endowments, as developed by Heckscher and

Ohlin. While there is some support for the proposition that countries export products for which they have relatively high labor productivity, with productivity held constant, empirical studies have not generally supported the additional implication of the classical version of comparative cost theory that countries should export commodities they produce with relatively low labor cost. While the classical international equilibrating mechanisms are activated through international factor mobility, the competing neoclassical theory relies on commodity trade for achievement of trade equilibrium and for spreading internationally the effects of development. The neoclassical approach is founded on the Heckscher-Ohlin theorem, which states that a country well endowed with capital will export capital-intensive goods and import labor-intensive goods, and vice versa for a country with ample endowments of labor. This theory has been contradicted by the Leontief paradox, which despite numerous attempts to explain it away, still seems to be alive and well.

As noted in Chapter 16, participation of LDCs, especially small, natural-resource endowed ones, in international trade has meant exports of primary products and imports of manufactures. Changes in the structure of exports tend to come fairly "late" in the process of development. Dependence on trade, especially in small LDCs, tends to retard the normal and quite possibly desirable changes in the sectoral composition of output, lowering the growth rate of GDP. While the export composition of European and North American countries has changed significantly, that of LDCs has often remained remarkably constant. Syria and Iraq continue to export grains and fibers today just as they did in Roman times. Except for the dramatic rise of petroleum exports following the discovery of oil, Iraq continues to depend heavily on exports of dates just as it did in 2000 B.C.! It might turn out, after all, that the backwash effects of trade, which had been entirely overlooked in both the classical and neoclassical versions of comparative advantage, are as important as the spread effects, which were greatly emphasized. There is certainly a need for fresh theorizing to explain why some countries have achieved dramatic transformation in their trade structures while others have not. In this respect, the product cycle theories presented in the last section of the chapter offer a beginning.

Chapter 18

Export Instability and Terms of Trade

In the preceding chapter, we pointed to the possibility that the effects of trade can be either of the spreading or of the polarizing and "backwash" varieties. The former type was emphasized in our treatment of aggregate exports, while the latter was accented in discussing the composition of exports. The question of which will be dominant often leads to the examination of individual cases, generalization being rather difficult. In this chapter, we deal with two general hypotheses, which are amenable to empirical testing. Both are concerned with the price of exports, previously considered exogenous to the analysis.

The export instability hypothesis refers to export earnings, that is, the product of the volume of exports and the price of exports. It states that export earnings for LDCs are relatively unstable—whether because of wide fluctuations in export prices or in export volumes. Generally, it has been presumed that

the direct and indirect effects of this instability impose on LDCs substantial losses in welfare and slow down their rate of development. In order to curb these deleterious effects, special policies have been formulated at both the national and international levels. Such policies include schemes for trade restructuring, import substitution, diversification, buffer stocks, compensation, and international commodity agreements.

The second hypothesis is the terms of trade deterioration hypothesis, which, in contrast to the export instability hypothesis, assigns the pernicious effects of trade to secular changes in export prices.

On closer examination, it appears that the hypothesized relationship between economic development, on the one hand, and export instability and the terms of trade, on the other, is largely the product of casual empiricism and a priori rationalization. Recently, both the measurement of the phenomena under investigation and the analytical content of the hypotheses have been called into question. As we shall show, there seems little reason to believe that, in its most general form at least, either hypothesis holds.

Our study of export instability begins with the chain of reasoning that leads from instability to low levels of development. Partly, at least, it is the same argument that connects the deteriorating terms of trade with the LDCs. We then discuss the measurement of export instability, and in the process, we introduce a new index, the transitory index of export instability, based on the permanent-income hypothesis of consumption. We test for the effects of export instability on economic development and find that the results depend to a large extent on whether one adopts the conventional or the transitory index for measuring instability. We then proceed to an examination of the causes of instability. This discussion is closely related to our treatment of the determinants of the volume of exports, in the previous chapter, and of the price of exports measured by the terms of trade, in the concluding section of this chapter.

Our treatment of the terms of trade starts by addressing the problem of measurement. We then discuss the structural characteristics of LDCs, which have been alleged to account for the deterioration in their terms of trade. Finally, we present empirical evidence that casts grave doubts on the validity of the hypothesis.

Export Instability

The formulation of an operational export instability hypothesis is predicated on the construction of a chain of reasoning that goes from instability to development. The phenomenon must be defined in a way that is subject to measurement, and its effects must be quantified so as to afford tests of the a priori theorizing that instability is detrimental to economic development. Before we proceed to empirical investigation of export instability, we must provide the necessary conceptual framework and specify its predictions. We begin with the a priori reasoning, then go on to define alternative indexes of instability, finally using them in empirical tests that

purport to study the effects and the causes of instability.

A Priori Theorizing versus Empirical Evidence
The scenario that has been developed to explain why instability is a problem refers both to microeconomic behavioral considerations and to the effects instability may have on public policies for economic development.

Exports of LDCs are highly concentrated on a few primary products, which are subject to severely fluctuating supply conditions (mainly because of weather factors) and to vacillating demand in DCs. Under these circumstances, the prices of exportables vary more widely than those of other commodities. At the microeconomic level, we would expect the risk-averse subsistence farmers of LDCs to hedge against the "double risk on prices"[1] by shifting from the production of exportables to less profitable cash crops or even to low-productivity subsistence crops. This would be reflected in lower rates of growth of exports and income in LDCs than in DCs.

The pernicious effects of export instability would also be expected to permeate public policy and the macroeconomy. Since, in the short run, both demand and supply tend to be inelastic with respect to price, fluctuations in export prices are reflected in unstable export proceeds. In the presence of balance of payments constraints, shortfalls in export earnings would have to be compensated for by restrictions on imports. Since the fiscal authorities of LDCs rely rather heavily on tariffs and other taxes collected on traded commodities, for both administrative convenience and political feasibility, fluctuations in export earnings and hence in imports are also reflected in the form of fluctuating revenues for the government. Finally, confronted as they are by limitations on foreign borrowing, the fiscal authorities of most LDCs are forced to adopt procyclical instead of countercyclical expenditure policies, thereby exacerbating rather than smoothing the cyclical movements induced by the fluctuations of exports. Moreover, the restrictions imposed on imports during trough periods in export earnings force the import-using sectors to

[1]This is the risk that the price of the cash crop farmers sell might decrease while simultaneously the price of the subsistence crop farmers buy for their own consumption might increase. For further discussion, see Chapter 8.

operate at less than full capacity, thus creating cyclical unemployment for the work force. Cyclical movements in government expenditure are most sharply reflected in alternations between "stop" and "go" in executing investment projects, introducing costly delays and inefficiencies that in the long run reduce the rate of return and therefore impede new investments. Finally, the extreme fluctuations in capacity utilization, government spending, and income are formidable impediments to rational planning and to factor mobilization for developmental purposes.

The scenario we described represents the conventional theorizing on export instability. It goes from instability through the intermediate link of uncertainty to behavioral effects that are generally detrimental to economic development. Yet despite its plausibility on a priori grounds, this hypothesis on instability has fared extremely poorly when confronted with empirical evidence. Coppock's (1962) influential book, the first in a long series of empirical studies of the relationship between instability and development, dealt with the causes of instability and formulated policy prescriptions to reduce fluctuations in export proceeds, in spite of his consistent finding that the effects of instability on growth rates and other economic parameters are insignificant. So too, MacBean (1966) set out to confirm conventional theorizing on export instability, concluding his analysis with policy prescriptions for stabilizing export earnings. Yet his empirical investigation revealed no evidence that export instability had damaging economic effects on development for the countries in his sample. Instead, in one of the few definite results of the study, he found a positive and significant coefficient in a multiple regression of the rate of growth of investment on instability. Subsequent studies have turned up results that have been generally at variance with extant theorizing.

However, an alternative hypothesis concerning the effects of export instability, which is more consistent with the empirical evidence, can be readily formulated. The permanent-income hypothesis of consumption predicts that the unexpected and temporary component of income contributes to savings more than does the permanent and predictable component. Specifically, as noted in Chapter 10, it states that the marginal propensity to consume out of transitory income is lower than

that out of permanent income. (In the extreme case, the former is zero while the latter is close to one.) Therefore, where the transitory component of income is relatively larger, the savings and investment ratios and the rate of income growth should be larger. This would imply that policies to reduce export instability in LDCs would be detrimental to their growth. The permanent-income hypothesis thus yields a set of behavioral hypotheses contrary to the accepted dogma on export instability and suggests, as an obvious index of instability, the variance of the transitory component of income. In our empirical investigation, we will formulate and directly test this hypothesis.

The Measures of Instability

Measurement is often arbitrary. For most measuring operations, any yardstick will do as long as it is used accurately and consistently. It might appear, therefore, that any heuristic measure of export earnings fluctuations, first differences, for example, would be an adequate index of export instability.

On closer examination, this is not the case. When measurement is to lead to the test of hypotheses, one must make certain that the behavioral characteristics specified in the hypothesis under consideration are also adequately reflected in the index. The construction of an adequate index of instability must therefore have as a point of origin the a priori theorizing on export instability that must be tested. The preceding section identified two specific aspects of export instability that may lead to the detrimental effects on development that the theory predicts: first, the shortfall of earnings effect, and second, the uncertainty effect. Should one wish to test for the shortfall of earnings effect, the appropriate index of instability should measure only declines in export earnings. This approach converges to that of the foreign exchange constraint approach in the two-gap literature that will be discussed in Chapter 21; yet it is not the approach the literature on export instability has taken. Instead, the uncertainty effect has received exclusive attention, and a number of indexes for measuring it have been forged. To these, we will add the transitory index of export instability which, besides measuring uncertainty per se, pertains directly to the characteristics specified in the permanent-income hypothesis of consumption.

The Indexes of Export Instability

The statistical definition of uncertainty is straightforward. It refers to deviations from specified levels. When uncertainty refers to export earnings, a number of alternative indexes of instability can be constructed, depending on: (1) the level of export earnings from which the deviations are measured and (2) the specific way the deviations are measured.

The level of earnings taken as a point of reference for the measurement of export instability may be that of a single year, for example $t - 1$, or an average of a number of years. The average may be arbitrary, for example, of the three or five previous years (Reynolds 1963), or a moving average that takes into account not only previous but also future years (MacBean 1966).[2] Another type of average from which deviations can be measured is the linear or exponential trend (Massell 1964, 1970).[3]

Deviations, on the other hand, can be measured as the sum of absolute deviations or the sum of squared deviations, either corrected or uncorrected for the value of the mean. In the form of the sum of squared deviations, corrected for the value of the mean, the export instability index becomes identical with the Pearson coefficient of variation we used in Chapter 16 for the index of imbalance.

Despite the variety of instability indexes

used in empirical work, the choice of index has usually not affected the results significantly. Predictably, there exists a high correlation between the alternatives.[4] The index of instability we will use in our empirical application is the corrected for the mean sum of the squared deviations from the fitted exponential trend line, obtained by minimizing the sum of squared residuals. We thus define

$$I_E = \frac{1}{\log \overline{X}} \sqrt{\frac{\sum_{t=1}^{N} (\log X_t - \log \hat{X})^2}{N}} \qquad (1)$$

where N is the number of annual observations, $t = 1, \ldots, N$, and X is the export earnings, with $\overline{X}$ indicating the mean value and $\hat{X}$ the fitted value estimated as

$$\log X_t = a + bt + u_t \qquad (2)$$

The instability index of equation 1 is simply the standard deviation of the observed u_t. It is the index used by Massell (1970), and it is especially appropriate if people (or countries) tend to plan in terms of absolute growth rates rather than constant increments to GNP, for if so, expectations take a geometric form. Hence it is appropriate to measure uncertainty in terms of deviations from an exponential line.

The Transitory Index of Instability

An alternative way to define uncertainty is in terms of the permanent-income hypothesis, discussed in Chapter 10. Suppose income in general, and export earnings in particular, have two components, one permanent and one transitory. The latter component of income is the unforeseen and thus uncertain one. Uncertainty, therefore, can be measured by the variations in the transitory component of income. Variations in the permanent income, on the other hand, are expected and thus outside the ambit of uncertainty.

By adopting this framework, we are able to accomplish two things. First, we define an alternative index of instability, the transitory index, which is firmly grounded on economic theory, namely, the permanent-income hypothesis. Second, by drawing on the permanent-income hypothesis in our test of export instability, we arrive at results contrary to

---

[2]It is possible, of course, in forming the average from which deviations are measured to give different years' earnings declining weights as they become more distant from the present year. This is the approach used in International Monetary Fund (1966), where the average was defined in terms of the three previous years' earnings with weights of 0.50 for $t - 1$ and 0.25 each for $t - 2$ and $t - 3$.

[3]Coppock (1962) and Erb and Schiavo-Campo (1969), who otherwise utilize as an instability measure the variance of the log of one year's exports relative to the previous year's, define the trend of exports in a most restrictive way. The "log variance" index is

$$I = \text{antilog} \sqrt{\frac{1}{n-1} \sum_{t=1}^{n-1} \left(\log \frac{X_{t+1}}{X_t} - m \right)^2}$$

where

$$m = \frac{1}{n-1} \sum_{t=1}^{n-1} \log \frac{X_{t+1}}{X_t}$$

The m term, which is the trend line, unhappily turns out to depend only on the first and last observations:

$$m = \frac{1}{n-1} (\log X_2 - \log X_1 + \log X_3 - \log X_2$$

$$+ \cdots + \log X_n - \log X_{n-1}) = \frac{1}{n-1} (\log X_n - \log X_1)$$

[4]For a comparison of different indexes of instability, see Leith (1970) and Glezakos (1970).

the conventional wisdom, suggesting that in the final analysis export instability may not be detrimental to economic development.

We rewrite the permanent-income hypothesis, developed in Chapter 10, as[5]

$$C^P = K(r, w, u)Y^P \qquad (3)$$

$$Y = Y^P + Y^T \qquad (4)$$

$$C = C^P + C^T \qquad (5)$$

$$E(Y^T) = E(C^T) = 0 \qquad (6)$$

$$\rho(Y^P, Y^T) = \rho(C^P, C^T) = \rho(Y^T, C^T) = 0 \qquad (7)$$

where C, Y are actual measures of consumption and income and the superscripts P and T refer to the permanent and transitory components of these variables respectively. Equations 6 and 7 represent, as in our earlier exposition, the zero mean and the lack of correlation assumptions of the hypothesis. The marginal propensity to consume out of permanent income, K, is now a function of the interest rate, r, the ratio of nonhuman wealth to permanent income, w, and more importantly, of the parameter u, which this time represents uncertainty. We will formulate the export instability hypothesis with regard to the parameter u. Specifically, and following Friedman (1957, p. 235), suppose that the derivative $dK/du < 0$; because the greater the uncertainty, the greater is the need for reserves. It is not possible, however, to observe u directly. We use instability, to be defined as the variance in the transitory component of income, to measure uncertainty and thus u. The hypothesis therefore predicts that the marginal propensity to consume is negatively related to this measure of u.

To this point, we have a general hypothesis of consumption, not export instability. We need, therefore, to distinguish specifically between the export and domestic components of income, Y_E and Y_D respectively. Assigning time subscripts, and with this modification, the model given by equations 3–7 can be rewritten as

$$Y_{Dt} = Y_{Dt}^P + Y_{Dt}^T \qquad (8)$$

$$Y_{Et} = Y_{Et}^P + Y_{Et}^T \qquad (9)$$

$$C_t^P = K_D^P Y_{Dt}^P + K_E^P Y_{Et}^P \qquad (10)$$

$$C_t^T = K_D^T Y_{Dt} + K_E^T Y_{Et}^T \qquad (11)$$

$$C_t = C_t^P + C_t^T \qquad (12)$$

[5]The formulation of this model is generally similar to Knudsen's (1972).

If export earnings require relatively little in terms of intermediate inputs, these earnings for the most part represent payments to the primary factors of production and thus constitute domestic value added.[6] If so, estimates of domestic income, Y_{Dt}, can be obtained by subtracting export earnings, Y_{Et}, from GNP.

There are two problems in equations 8–12 that must be overcome before the system can be estimated: the number of unknowns and the unobservable variables. We have five equations with six unknowns (the four marginal propensities to consume and the two components of income). The system could be solved by adding one more equation, which would be simple enough if panel data existed as we suggested in Chapter 10.[7] Since such data are unavailable, we resort to the original assumption of Friedman, wherein the propensity to consume out of the transitory component of income is zero. This eliminates two propensities to consume, K_D^T and K_E^T, from the number of unknowns and eliminates the need for equation 10, thus reducing to four the number of unknowns and equations. The second problem, that of the unobservable variables, C_t^P, Y_{Dt}^P, and Y_{Et}^P, can be readily handled. As we noted in Chapter 10, several approaches exist for expressing these unobservable variables in terms of observable variables. Here we utilize the adaptive expectations model, and we note

$$C_t^P = K_D^P Y_{Dt}^P + K_E^P Y_{Et}^P \qquad (13)$$

$$Y_{Dt}^P = (1 + r_D)Y_{Dt-1}^P + \beta(Y_{Dt} - Y_{Dt-1}^P) \qquad (14)$$

where $0 \leq \beta \leq 1$

$$Y_{Et}^P = (1 + r_E)Y_{Et-1}^P + \alpha(Y_{Et} - Y_{Et-1}^P) \qquad (15)$$

where $0 \leq \alpha \leq 1$

$$C_t = C_t^P + v_t \qquad (16)$$

where r_D and r_E are the expected rates of growth of domestic and export income respectively, v_t is the error term in measured consumption, and α and β have the usual

[6]This admittedly strong assumption is not inappropriate for LDCs, which almost exclusively export primary products. Ideally, countries that export manufactures or host large expatriate firms, utilizing more intermediate inputs and foreign factors of production, should be excluded.

[7]This was done, in another context, by Holbrook and Stafford (1971).

interpretation as coefficients of adaptation, as in Chapter 8. If α and β have values of one, and $r_D = r_E = 0$, it would imply that permanent income equals actual income in year t. This explains the bounds for the values of α and β. In the ordinary adaptive expectations model, $Y_{Dt}{}^P$ and $Y_{Et}{}^P$ could never be greater than the highest observed past values of domestic and export income respectively.[8] To relax this restrictive assumption, we have modified the usual adaptive expectations model by allowing for a constant rate of growth in permanent domestic and export income, r_D and r_E.

The reduced form of the system of equations 13–16, expressed in distributed lags notation,[9] is

$$C_t - (\lambda_1 + \lambda_2)C_{t-1} + \lambda_1\lambda_2 C_{t-2}$$
$$= K_D{}^P\beta Y_{Dt} - K_D{}^P\beta\lambda_2 Y_{Dt-1} + K_E{}^P\alpha Y_{Et}$$
$$- K_E{}^P\alpha\lambda_1 Y_{Et-1} + v_t - (\lambda_1 + \lambda_2)v_{t-1}$$
$$+ (\lambda_1\lambda_2 v_{t-2}) \tag{17}$$

where $\lambda_1 = (1 - \beta)$ and $\lambda_2 = (1 - \alpha)$. Equation 17 consists exclusively of observable variables: domestic income, Y_{Dt}, export income, Y_{Et}, and consumption, C_t. Depending on the assumptions on v_t, several methods of estimating equation 16 are available.[10] In our empirical application, we employ the simplest assumption on the error terms, that is, that the v_t's are normally distributed, and we use maximum likelihood estimation techniques.

The permanent-income hypothesis as applied to domestic income and export earnings in equations 13–16 leads to two separate indexes of instability, one for the domestic and one for the export component, $I_D{}^T$ and $I_E{}^T$ respectively. We thus define

$$I_D{}^T = \frac{1}{N}\sqrt{\sum_{t=1}^{N}\left[\frac{(Y_{Dt} - Y_{Dt}{}^P)}{Y_{Dt}{}^P}\right]^2} \tag{18}$$

$$I_E{}^T = \frac{1}{N}\sqrt{\sum_{t=1}^{N}\left[\frac{(Y_{Et} - Y_{Et}{}^P)}{Y_{Et}{}^P}\right]^2} \tag{19}$$

where N is the number of years of observations.

Since the difference between measured income and permanent income is transitory income, the numerator term in these indexes is

an estimate of the variance of transitory income. The transitory indexes of domestic and export instability are then defined as the normalized variance of the transitory income component of domestic and export earnings respectively. Furthermore, the latter, the transitory index of export instability, is conceptually equivalent to the conventional index of export instability, defined in equation 1.

A further extension of the hypothesis is to specify that uncertainty has certain effects upon a number of dependent variables, the rate of growth or capital formation, for example, regardless of the specific source of uncertainty. In this case, we may define an average transitory index of income instability as

$$\bar{I}^T = aI_E{}^T + (1 - a)I_D{}^T \tag{20}$$

where the weight, a, represents the average ratio of exports to GDP for each country over the years of observation in our sample.

Results and Implications of
Measurement Procedures
Table 18.1 presents the instability indexes and related statistics computed for a sample of 38 LDCs over the period 1949–1967. Column 1 gives the conventional index of instability, I_E, which consists of the sum of squared deviations from an exponential trend and was defined in equation 1. Columns 2–4 give the transitory indexes of instability, $I_E{}^T$ in column 2 computed from equation 18, $I_D{}^T$ in column 3 computed from equation 17, and finally $\bar{I}^T$ in column 4 from equation 19. The rest of the table gives the values of the marginal propensity to consume out of export earnings, $K_E{}^P$, and out of domestic income, $K_D{}^P$,[11] the respective rates of growth of the permanent-income component of the two income sources, r_E and r_D, and the adaptation coefficients, α for permanent export income and β for permanent domestic income.

The conventional and transitory indexes of export instability, I_E and $I_E{}^T$, are not strictly comparable, for they are obtained from different data sources. Even if the data used in computing them were the same, the relationship between them would vary from

---

[8]For proof of this proposition, see Knudsen (1972, pp. 78–79).

[9]See also Chapter 8 and Griliches (1967).

[10]For details on estimation procedures, see Knudsen (1972, Chapter 6).

[11]We first ran estimates with $K_E{}^P$ and $K_D{}^P$ unconstrained, and this resulted in 16 countries having both marginal propensities to consume within the limits of 0.3 and 1.2. We reran the remaining 22 countries by constraining the marginal propensities to consume within those limits. The results appear in columns 5 and 6 of Table 18.1.

Table 18.1 *Comparison of Instability Indexes and Related Statistics, 38 Countries, 1949–1967*

Country	I_E (1)	$I_E{}^T$ (2)	$I_D{}^T$ (3)	I^T (4)	$K_E{}^P$ (5)	$K_D{}^P$ (6)	α (7)	β (8)	r_E (per-cent) (9)	r_D (per-cent) (10)
1. Argentina	3.39	2.299	0.675	0.855	0.350	0.750	0.7	1.0	4.5	3.0
2. Bolivia	12.69	0.956	0.550	0.641	0.961	0.796	1.0	1.0	0.4	2.3
3. Brazil	2.04	0.699	0.931	0.918	0.500	0.700	0.9	0.1	2.2	5.5
4. Ceylon	0.75	0.479	0.891	0.774	1.100	0.650	0.9	1.0	2.1	4.1
5. Chile	1.04	1.228	0.904	0.937	1.057	0.745	1.0	1.0	3.9	4.1
6. Colombia	1.52	1.307	1.079	1.121	0.822	0.693	0.0	1.0	3.3	4.9
7. Costa Rica	3.40	1.880	0.600	0.880	0.978	0.704	0.3	0.0	6.6	5.2
8. Cyprus	1.08	2.027	1.540	1.712	0.300	1.150	0.1	0.0	8.0	3.5
9. Dominican Republic	18.89	2.630	1.092	1.409	0.300	0.800	0.1	1.0	2.5	4.8
10. Ecuador	2.03	0.826	1.075	1.036	0.358	0.762	0.0	0.8	3.7	4.9
11. El Salvador	2.14	1.475	0.617	0.848	0.806	0.835	0.5	0.0	6.2	4.2
12. Greece	2.72	2.916	1.264	1.431	0.465	0.748	0.3	0.9	10.8	5.9
13. Guatemala	2.92	2.293	0.528	0.780	0.447	0.883	1.0	0.0	8.1	4.0
14. Haiti	3.27	4.002	0.451	0.994	0.350	0.950	0.0	0.6	2.0	1.7
15. Honduras	3.88	3.981	0.721	1.487	0.994	0.756	0.1	0.0	4.5	3.8
16. Iceland	1.52	1.942	1.553	1.735	0.975	0.447	0.6	0.0	7.4	3.1
17. India	1.46	1.840	0.867	0.923	0.900	0.750	0.0	1.0	2.5	3.9
18. Israel	2.16	4.044	1.826	2.194	0.452	0.728	1.0	0.9	18.6	8.0
19. Jamaica	2.99	2.018	1.433	1.613	0.300	0.850	1.0	1.0	9.5	5.2
20. Korea	3.01	4.729	1.177	1.376	0.300	0.850	0.5	0.6	22.9	5.0
21. Malaysia	1.59	1.703	1.363	1.379	0.300	0.700	0.0	1.0	3.2	5.7
22. Mexico	1.41	1.135	1.349	1.315	1.200	0.650	0.0	1.0	5.5	6.3
23. Morocco	1.75	0.790	1.085	1.005	1.000	0.600	0.9	0.3	3.0	2.7
24. Nicaragua	2.74	1.921	2.824	2.590	0.764	0.737	0.9	0.3	8.7	3.8
25. Pakistan	2.38	1.582	0.890	0.929	0.300	0.850	0.6	1.0	1.7	3.8
26. Panama	3.69	1.938	1.413	1.592	1.200	0.500	0.0	0.7	5.0	6.6
27. Paraguay	2.85	3.139	0.807	1.147	1.100	0.700	0.0	0.9	2.9	3.6
28. Peru	1.95	1.990	1.081	1.249	1.076	0.565	0.1	1.0	8.1	5.0
29. Philippines	1.79	2.434	1.290	1.422	1.150	0.700	0.2	1.0	5.3	5.6
30. Portugal	2.64	2.647	0.710	1.074	0.400	0.850	0.0	0.0	8.1	4.0
31. Spain	2.65	3.900	1.306	1.524	0.300	0.700	0.0	0.8	1.7	5.1
32. Sudan	3.77	2.050	1.179	1.325	1.100	0.700	0.7	0.0	4.2	4.0
33. Taiwan	4.14	3.985	1.617	1.963	0.350	0.650	0.0	1.0	13.8	7.3
34. Thailand	2.34	2.285	1.720	1.823	0.347	0.804	0.5	1.0	5.4	4.7
35. Tunisia	2.76	3.012	1.147	1.639	1.200	0.550	0.0	1.0	1.0	4.7
36. Turkey	3.15	2.178	1.294	1.351	0.478	0.723	0.4	1.0	4.2	5.5
37. UAR (Egypt)	3.74	2.797	1.120	1.427	0.500	0.750	0.2	0.4	4.5	4.3
38. Uruguay	4.25	0.749	0.531	0.559	0.803	0.734	1.0	1.0	2.1	1.0

Notes:
Column 1: estimated from equation 1.
Column 2: estimated from equation 18 × 100.
Column 3: estimated from equation 17 × 100.
Column 4: estimated from equation 19 × 100.
For definition of variables, see the text.
Sources: Value of consumption used for the fitting of the permanent income hypothesis from United Nations, unpublished data. Other data from Nugent, J. B. (1974), *Economic Integration in Central America: Empirical Investigations.* Baltimore: Johns Hopkins University Press, pp. 53–55.

country to country, depending on the value of the coefficient of adaptation, α. Only for $\alpha = 0$ the $I_E{}^T$ index reduces to I_E—and this is obviously not the case with the estimated values of α given in Table 18.1. Not surprisingly, then, the correlation coefficient between the two indexes is only 0.082 and is not statistically significant. The rank correlation coefficient between the instability indexes of the two transitory components of income, $I_D{}^T$ and $I_E{}^T$, is also low, 0.205. On the other hand, since $\bar{I}^T$ is a weighted average that includes $I_E{}^T$, the rank-correlation coefficient between $\bar{I}^T$ and $I_E{}^T$ is 0.423 and is statistically significant. We also observe that the income fluctuations in the domestic source of income are smaller than those in export income: the mean value of $I_D{}^T$ is 1.12 (standard deviation = 0.46) as compared to 2.21 for the mean of $I_E{}^T$ (standard deviation = 1.07). This general tendency may well reflect the greater risk that export trade involves because of the vagaries of tariff policies, currency restrictions, exchange rates, and the supply and demand conditions for traded commodities.

The transitory index of export instability was constructed by extending the permanent-income hypothesis to export earnings. The intermediate link between the measurement of the phenomenon and the empirical implications of export instability is uncertainty. We interpret the transitory index of instability, the dispersion of transitory income, as a measure of uncertainty. Moreover, the permanent-income hypothesis predicts that it is not only the level of income, absolute or relative, that determines savings but also the level

of uncertainty. A certain kind of uncertainty, which does not reduce the average rate of return to capital, reduces the propensity to consume by requiring reserves for emergencies (Friedman 1957, p. 235). The direct implication of the hypothesis is that the transitory indexes of export and domestic instability, as measures of uncertainty, should be negatively related to the (marginal) propensities to consume, $K_E{}^P$ and $K_D{}^P$.

To test this implication, we regress the marginal propensity to consume from Table 18.1 on the respective indexes of instability. Besides the regressions of the marginal propensity to consume out of export income and domestic income on the transitory export instability index and the transitory domestic instability index respectively, we also regress the weighted average propensity to consume, $\bar{K}$, on the average transitory index of instability, $\bar{I}^T$. The three regressions that appear in Table 18.2 have the expected negative sign and are significant, with the exception of the result of $K_D{}^P$, which is weak. This might indicate that the other determinants of the marginal propensity to consume that we have omitted, such as the rate of interest and the ratio of nonhuman wealth to permanent income, may be more crucial in determining the marginal propensity to consume out of domestic income than that out of export income. Regression 4 pools the data from the domestic and the export income components. It also has the predicted negative (and significant) coefficient. Finally, in regression 5, we modify the pooled regression 4 by allowing for a dummy variable that takes the value of

Table 18.2 *Instability and the Propensity to Consume: Regression Results for 38 Countries, 1949–1967*

$K_E{}^P = 0.924 - 10.544\ I_E{}^T$ $\qquad\qquad (-2.107)$	$r^2 = 0.110$ observations $= 38$	(1)
$K_D{}^P = 0.791 - 4.818\ I_D{}^T$ $\qquad\qquad (-1.078)$	$r^2 = 0.031$ observations $= 38$	(2)
$\bar{K} = 0.808 - 5.188\ \bar{I}^T$ $\qquad\qquad (-2.527)$	$r^2 = 0.151$ observations $= 38$	(3)
$K_{TOT} = 0.847 - 7.965\ I_{TOT}{}^T$ $\qquad\qquad (-2.767)$	$r^2 = 0.094$ observations $= 76$	(4)
$K_{TOT} = 0.905 - 9.669\ I_{TOT}{}^T - 0.060\ D$ $\qquad\qquad (-2.788) \qquad\quad (-0.884)$	$R^2 = 0.103$ observations $= 76$	(5)

Note: Numbers in parentheses are values of *t*-statistic. For definition of variables, see the text.
Source: Table 18.1.

one for domestic and zero for export instability. The results of the pooled regressions reveal that this distinction between the two sources of instability is not significant.

The results in Table 18.2 confirm the primary implications of the permanent-income hypothesis, suggesting that further investigation of export instability with this model can be fruitful. In the cross-section of countries studied, the effect of uncertainty is to reduce the propensity to consume out of permanent income. As a result, one may expect higher aggregate savings ratios in countries with greater income instability, since over the long run the transitory components of income tend to a mean of zero, and hence, average permanent income approaches average actual income.[12] Should this be correct, it must also be reflected on other facets of the process of development.

The Effects of Export Instability

We have developed and discussed two indexes for measuring export instability, the conventional one based on squared deviations from an exponential trend and the transitory one that relies on the dispersion of the transitory component of export earnings. By the use of regression analysis, we proceed to investigate the possibility of a systematic causal relationship between the indexes of instability, on the one hand, and the rates of growth of investment, income, and exports, on the other. In this way, we may shed some light on whether instability in export earnings hampers or aids economic development.

Instability and Capital Formation

The conventional hypothesis that considers instability a deterrent to economic development would certainly also predict a negative relationship between capital formation and the index of instability. To the extent that uncertainty, as measured by instability, increases risk or decreases the rate of return to investment, it must decrease the willingness to invest. Moreover, instability may also reduce the ability to invest, especially in countries where a foreign exchange gap exists. Export

[12]This may not be correct in the short run or when there is a systematic overestimation or underestimation of the transitory component of income. In such cases, actual savings out of measured income might not reflect the lower propensities to consume out of permanent income that might be observed for countries with higher levels of instability.

earnings shortfalls could lead directly to shortages of imported capital goods. While the permanent-income hypothesis does not deny the influence of these factors, it places more emphasis on the positive relationship between export instability and the propensity to save—and consequently between the index of instability and the rate of growth of investment.

In testing the implications of the two alternative instability hypotheses with respect to capital formation, we use as dependent variable $IGNP$, the average ratio of gross capital formation to GNP, for the period 1949–1967.[13] Using the exponential trend index, I_E, as the measure of export instability for the independent variable, we obtain the regression results given in regression 1 of Table 18.3. The relevant regression coefficient is negative but nonsignificant. When the independent variable is the transitory index of export instability, I_E^T, as in regression 2, the coefficient is positive but insignificant. The coefficient is also positive and becomes significant when $IGNP$ is regressed on I_D^T or $\bar{I}^T$ as in regression 3 or 4. Finally, regression 5 controls for the differences in GNP per capita ($GNPC$) among the countries of the sample, and the results are again as expected and significant.

Our empirical analysis leads to the conclusion that investment is not deterred by instability in income but is in fact stimulated by it. The lower propensities to consume measured under higher levels of instability have resulted in increased aggregate savings, which in turn have led to increased aggregate investment. Such results, incidentally, are not novel in the literature. MacBean (1966, pp. 111–112) regressed the rate of growth of net capital formation on his index of instability (which is the five-year moving average) and found a positive and significant coefficient. He was led to consider it as a peculiarity, because he had no analytical framework that was consistent with this result.

[13]Besides $IGNP$, we also experimented with the rate of growth of gross investment and, where data were available, with the yearly first differences in capital stock. The results were not substantially different. It must be noted that $IGNP$ does not account for the intercountry differences in capital-output ratios that may exist and that can be quite significant in certain cases. On the other hand, the growth rate of investment is an unsatisfactory measure of the growth rate in the capital stock, since in the short run the influence of different starting points may be quite important.

Table 18.3 *The Effects and Causes of Instability: Regression Results for 38 Countries, 1949–1967*

Regression

$IGNP = 15.770 - \underset{(-0.449)}{0.097\ I_E}$ $\quad r^2 = 0.006$ (1)

$IGNP = 13.692 + \underset{(1.258)}{80.082\ I_E{}^T}$ $\quad r^2 = 0.042$ (2)

$IGNP = 10.926 + \underset{(2.949)}{405.209\ I_D{}^T}$ $\quad r^2 = 0.195$ (3)

$IGNP = 9.026 + \underset{(3.649)}{499.030\ \bar{I}^T}$ $\quad r^2 = 0.270$ (4)

$IGNP = 8.554 + \underset{(2.903)}{298.199\ \bar{I}^T} + \underset{(6.027)}{0.007\ GNPC}$ $\quad R^2 = 0.642$ (5)

$I_D{}^T = 0.010 + \underset{(0.861)}{0.060\ I_E{}^T}$ $\quad r^2 = 0.020$ (6)

$RGDP = 4.933 - \underset{(-1.083)}{0.091\ I_E}$ $\quad r^2 = 0.005$ (7)

$RGDP = 3.448 + \underset{(2.245)}{54.005\ I_E{}^T}$ $\quad r^2 = 0.123$ (8)

$RGDP = 1.532 + \underset{(2.081)}{42.272\ I_E{}^T} + \underset{(4.067)}{194.469\ I_D{}^T}$ $\quad R^2 = 0.404$ (9)

$RGDP = 1.579 + \underset{(4.814)}{237.393\ \bar{I}^T}$ $\quad r^2 = 0.392$ (10)

$RGDPC = -0.473 + \underset{(4.038)}{199.157\ \bar{I}^T}$ $\quad r^2 = 0.312$ (11)

$\dot{E} = 5.753 - \underset{(-1.072)}{0.217 I_E}$ $\quad r^2 = 0.015$ (12)

$\dot{E} = 0.929 + \underset{(3.506)}{186.987\ I_E{}^T}$ $\quad r^2 = 0.255$ (13)

$I_E = -3.640 + \underset{(1.504)}{0.059\ CC} + \underset{(0.593)}{1.120\ I_{GEO}} + \underset{(0.599)}{0.915\ I_{COMM}}$ $\quad R^2 = 0.047$ (14)

$I_E{}^T = 0.023 - \underset{(-1.872)}{0.001\ CC} + \underset{(1.355)}{0.007\ I_{GEO}} + \underset{(1.513)}{0.009\ I_{COMM}}$ $\quad R^2 = 0.167$ (15)

Notes: For definition of variables, see the text. Numbers in parentheses are values of *t*-statistic.
Sources:
$IGNP$ is derived from data in United Nations (1969), *Yearbook of National Accounts Statistics*. New York; also United Nations unpublished data.
$RGDPC$ is $RGDP$ minus rate of growth of population from United Nations (1969), *Statistical Yearbook*. New York.
CC from Coppock, J. D. (1962), *International Economic Instability*. New York: McGraw-Hill.
Other data from Nugent, J. B. (1974), *Economic Integration in Central America: Empirical Investigations*. Baltimore: Johns Hopkins University Press; and from unpublished data provided by the United Nations.

Instability and Income

The overriding concern of the export instability hypothesis is the relationship between instability and economic growth. This can be investigated by using the rate of growth in GDP as the dependent variable.

A subsidiary and lower level hypothesis relates export instability to domestic economic instability. A shortfall in export proceeds decreases domestic consumer demand which, through the operation of the multiplier, leads to recession in the domestic production sector.

MacBean (1966, p. 65) investigated this hypothesis by regressing an index of instability of national income on his index of export instability. The results were not significantly different from zero. Similarly insignificant are the results we obtain by regressing our transitory index of domestic income instability on the index of export instability as in regression 6 of Table 18.3.

On the effect of export instability on the rate of growth, the results are negative but again statistically insignificant when the traditional index of instability is used as the independent variable in regression 7. Such results agree with Coppock's (1962, p. 106), although MacBean (1966, p. 122) found a positive and significant relation by regressing the capital-output ratio, interpreted as an index of productivity, on his instability index. (This finding he considered a statistical fluke.)

On the other hand, when the transitory instability indexes are used, as in regressions 8–11 of Table 18.3, a strong positive relationship with the rate of growth of GDP, *RGDP*, is consistently obtained. While regression 8 in Table 18.3 considers only export earnings instability, regressions 9 and 10 include the transitory component of domestic income as well. Similar results obtain in regression 11, where the rate of growth of GDP per capita, *RGDPC*, is used as the dependent variable. This suggests that the growth-enhancing effects of export instability arising through higher savings rates dominate over the growth-inhibiting effects. Their combined effect is higher rates of investment and income growth in countries with higher instability indexes.

Instability and Exports
According to the traditional hypothesis, in a world of imperfect capital markets where it pays to avoid risks, the greater the uncertainty or instability of export earnings, other things being equal, the lower the incentive to allocate resources in the export sector. On this basis, one would expect to find export instability lowering the rate of growth of exports. On the other hand, according to the permanent-income hypothesis, this effect could be offset by the positive effect of export and income instability on capital formation and aggregate capacity, including capacity to export.

To test for the effect of instability on exports, we regress the rate of export growth,

$\dot{E}$, on the two indexes of export instability. The results obtained with the conventional index of instability appear in regression 12 of Table 18.3 and are negative but insignificant. However, the results of equation 13, which employs the transitory index of export instability, are positive and significant.[14]

The Causes of Export Instability
Before any conclusions can be drawn about the importance of export instability and the extent to which it could, or should, be controlled or stimulated, it is necessary to identify the factors responsible for instability. Assuming for the moment that instability could be shown to be deleterious in its effects on development, as Prebisch (in U.N.: Department of Economic Affairs 1949, 1950) had suggested, is it also a natural and inevitable consequence of participation in international trade? Or does it emanate from factors within the control of LDCs?

The starting point for the discussion is the empirical observation that instability is greater in LDCs than in DCs. Almost all researchers agree on this point, and the results do not seem to be sensitive to the choice of the instability index. For example, Coppock (1962) found that for the period 1946–1958 the mean instability of LDCs is 23.0 (standard deviation = 12.8), and for DCs it is 17.6 (standard deviation = 7.1). Erb and Schiavo-Campo (1969), with Coppock's instability index, found that for the period 1954–1966 the mean instability for LDCs is 13.4 (standard deviation = 6.2), while for DCs it is 6.2 (standard deviation = 2.2). A *t*-test for these values suggests that the probability of drawing these means from the same random sample of instability indexes for DCs and LDCs is 0.025 and 0.005 for the Coppock and Erb and Schiavo–Campo results respectively. Similarly, MacBean (1966) found for the period 1946–1958 the average instability index of LDCs to be 23.1, compared to only 17.6 for the DCs, while Glezakos (1970) found the average export instability indexes to be 10.0 for the LDCs and 5.3 for the DCs.

Given these rather striking differences between DCs and LDCs, one might hypothesize that the degree of export instability is in-

---

[14]These results are not affected by the introduction of additional explanatory variables, such as those included in the export performance model presented in Chapter 17.

versely related to the level of development. Both Erb and Schiavo-Campo (1969) and Massell (1970) have examined this relationship, but surprisingly enough, they have obtained results tending to refute the hypothesis, especially when the level of development is measured by a more complex index that includes socioeconomic factors. The same authors find a negative relationship between instability and the size of an LDC. They interpret size in this case as a proxy for flexibility and the lack of trade dependence. Whatever the relationship between instability, on the one hand, and level of development or country size, on the other, it remains true that the latter are variables not easily amenable to policy control. It would seem more profitable, therefore, to formulate hypotheses of export instability in terms of more specific characteristics and factors.

The composition of exports would seem to be one factor worth exploring in the search for more specific explanations of export instability. A specific hypothesis is that primary products, which constitute 88 percent of the exports of LDCs,[15] are subject to greater export instability than manufactures, which compose the bulk of the DC exports. In general, however, this hypothesis has not been supported by empirical evidence, implying either that the specific primary products LDCs export are more unstable than primary products in general or that the explanation must be sought elsewhere (Coppock 1962; Massell 1964, 1970).[16]

Closely related to, but nevertheless distinct from, this hypothesis is the concentration hypothesis. According to this view, it is the lack of diversification, or rather the concentration on either a single commodity or no more than a very few commodities, that makes the LDCs highly vulnerable to export instability. The hypothesis has also been formulated with respect to the geographic destination of the country's exports. Again, it is thought that dependence on a single geographical market, for example, a colony's dependence on the market of its imperial master, makes the exporting country particu-

larly vulnerable to the fluctuations originating in one or more importing countries.

Hirschman's (1945) version of the Gini coefficient is commonly used as an index of concentration,

$$C = \sqrt{\sum_i Y_i^2} \qquad (21)$$

where Y_i represents the percentage (by value) of exports of commodity group i in total exports, in the case of the commodity concentration index, or the percentage (by value) of exports to country i in total exports, in the case of the geographic concentration index. One practical shortcoming of this index is that it may be sensitive to differing degrees of disaggregation among different types of commodities.

Plausible as it sounds, the connection between concentration and instability is certainly not a necessary one. For example, there may be nothing unstable about the concentration of exports on a single highly stable commodity (like crude petroleum a few years back) or on a single stable geographical market (like that of Germany, Japan, or the United States in the postwar period). Similarly, even if a country concentrated on unstable commodities or markets, diversification may not imply stability in the export values (or prices) if the different commodities with unstable export earnings are positively correlated one to the other.[17] It may hardly be surprising, then, that the results obtained thus far with respect to concentration indexes have been quite mixed—reflecting the sensitivity of the results to the countries and years included in the sample—although the balance of the evidence is probably favorable to the hypothesis.[18] However, even if one could obtain stronger results with concentration indexes or broad structural characteristics, it would be difficult to reach unambiguous interpretations, because all such measures combine the influences of so many different factors. They include influences on the supply and demand sides, some of domestic origin and others imposed externally.

To avoid the shortcomings of inapplicable

[15]International Monetary Fund and IBRD (1969, p. 1).

[16]Some of the more important primary products, such as coffee and sugar, are subject to international agreements that are specifically intended to stabilize exports. However, some doubts have been raised as to the success of these agreements.

[17]Brainard and Cooper (1968) have investigated the covariance in the price fluctuations of different export commodities.

[18]Massell (1970) obtained results quite favorable to both of these versions of the concentration hypothesis, but Coppock (1962), MacBean (1966), and Massell (1964) obtained much less favorable results.

generalization, on the one hand, and of ambiguity of interpretation on the other, we apply the export instability measures defined by equations 1 and 19 to the time series data for: (1) world imports of the particular commodity bundle exported by each individual country and (2) total imports of the geographical region to which each individual country exported. For this purpose, we use in equations 14 and 15 the variables COMM and GEO, defined in Chapter 17, to construct a commodity instability index, I_{COMM}, and a regional instability index, I_{GEO}, for the countries of our sample in the period 1949–1967. Because of the methods by which they have been computed, these indexes reflect not only the fluctuations in the world demand for the individual components of each country's export bundle but also the degree to which the fluctuations in the demand for different commodities offset or reinforce one another. Still, examination of indexes I_E, I_{COMM}, and I_{GEO} shows that the instability of LDC exports is generally greater than what would be expected on the basis of either the instability of world demand for the commodities they export or the instability of the imports of the geographic region to which they export. Indeed, an analysis of variance reveals that the mean of the I_E indexes (2.17) is statistically greater than the mean of I_{COMM} (1.02) and of I_{GEO} (1.04) at the 0.01 probability level. We would not, therefore, expect to explain much of the variance of the instability indexes with demand variables alone. The poor results of regressions 14 and 15 in Table 18.3 suggest that our attempt to include I_{COMM} and I_{GEO} together with the concentration index is equally futile with that of other researchers who had tried to explain instability with the CC variable alone.

We have so far attempted to trace the causes of export instability to demand factors external to the individual exporting LDCs. The destabilizing factors on the supply side, such as rainfall, strikes, revolutions, or natural catastrophes, are harder to document carefully and more difficult to quantify. Partly, however, such factors may be reflected in the instability of export prices relative to domestic prices, the index $I(P_x P_{fe}/P_d)$. Although the world price, P_x, is in almost every case entirely beyond the influence of the individual exporting LDC, domestic prices, P_d, and the exchange rate, P_{fe}, are certainly subject to a country's policy instruments. Still, our attempt to include in the regression the index of the instability of export prices relative to domestic prices did not improve the results. The only guarded conclusion that can be drawn from this analysis is that the supply side must be more carefully studied and included in the investigation.

Traditionally, national and international policies aiming at stabilization of export proceeds have dealt with stabilization of prices, mostly on the demand side of the market, through commodity agreements or buffer stocks.[19] To some extent, this emphasis may be due to the fact that it is easier to stabilize prices than quantities and to stabilize demand than supply. It may also have been motivated by the belief that fluctuations in export values are more closely related to fluctuations in export prices than in export volumes. The validity of this belief, of course, can be tested relatively easily.

Glezakos (1970) computed instability indexes separately for export volumes, I_V, and prices, I_P, for his sample of 36 LDCs and 18 DCs. He found that the instability indexes of export proceeds exceeded the instability indexes of export volumes and export prices for most countries, LDCs, and DCs alike. This implies that the fluctuations of export prices and quantities tend to reinforce rather than offset each other. He then examined the relationship between export values, volumes, and prices for each country in each of the following ways: (1) by computing the elasticities of export values, E, with respect to both volume, V, and price, P, from $E = AV^\beta P^\delta$ and (2) by computing the partial correlation between export values and alternatively export quantities or prices. In both cases, he found that the instability of export proceeds was better explained for most countries by fluctuations in export quantities than by fluctuations in export prices. These results suggest that international stabilization of prices would have less influence on the stability of export proceeds than domestic efforts to remove fluctuations in the quantities exported.[20]

---

[19]For discussions of the pros and cons of various such schemes, see MacBean (1966, Parts III and IV), Caine (1954), McKinnon (1967), Kravis (1968), G. Blau (1964), Nurkse (1958b). Porter (1964), G. H. Anderson (1970), and Meier (1963).

[20]Other drawbacks to any approach via price stabilization are derived from the difficulties of: (1) assuring that welfare would be improved by such

The Terms of Trade

Not unlike the case of export instability, the hypothesis of secular deterioration in the terms of trade of the LDCs was a combination of introspective rationalization and some weak empirical evidence. The works of some economists, especially in the early 1950s,[21] made the case that: (1) the structure of international trade led to declining terms of trade for LDCs relative to DCs, and (2) the deterioration in the terms of trade led to continued economic and social underdevelopment.

The latter part of the argument runs parallel to the link between instability and underdevelopment, as presented above, especially when the discussion on export instability concentrates on the pernicious effects of a shortfall of export earnings, rather than on the effects of uncertainty. Here we will limit our attention to the measurement of the terms of trade, to the hypothesized causes of the deterioration of the terms of trade, and to empirical evidence that has been brought to bear on the hypothesis. As is the case also with export instability, this evidence casts serious doubt on the validity of the hypothesis.

Alternative Measures of the Terms of Trade

An extremely simple and commonly applied measure of the terms of trade is an index of export prices, Px, relative to import prices, Pm, that is, Px/Pm. This index, known alternatively as the "net barter terms of trade" or the "commodity terms of trade," which we shall designate by N, consists of comparisons between a final period, $t = 1$, and an initial period, $t = 0$. The final period value of this index expressed in terms of the initial period is thus given by

$$N = \frac{\dfrac{Px_1}{Px_0}}{\dfrac{Pm_1}{Pm_0}} \quad (22)$$

An alternative yet equally simple measure of the terms of trade is the "gross barter terms of trade," G, which is defined in terms of the quantity or volume of imports, Qm, that can

be earned by the corresponding quantity or volume of exports, Qx. The gross barter terms are therefore given by

$$G = \frac{\dfrac{Qm_1}{Qm_0}}{\dfrac{Qx_1}{Qx_0}} \quad (23)$$

Indeed, as long as all trade is balanced in each period, that is, the value of imports is equal to the value of exports in each and every period, the index of the net barter or commodity terms of trade, N, will be identical with that of the gross barter terms of trade, G. However, when the values of imports and exports differ, the two indexes, G and N, will no longer be identical, the choice between them presumably depending on the use to which the measures are to be put and the nature of the compensating monetary movements. If, for example, the compensating monetary arrangements are seen to be either somehow dependent on changes in the prices of exports relative to imports, or supplementary to (or compensating for) simple changes in prices, the gross barter terms of trade, G, would be preferable to N. On the other hand, if one wanted to abstract price changes from unilateral transactions that were considered exogenously determined and therefore separately treated, the net barter terms of trade, N, would be a more appropriate measure.

If the purpose of the terms of trade index is to measure the capacity to import, some combination of N and G might be desired. For example, starting from the net barter terms of trade, N, one might want to correct for changes in the quantity of exports, Qx. The resulting measure of the terms of trade is known as the "income terms of trade," N_Y,

$$N_Y = \frac{\left(\dfrac{Px_1}{Px_0}\right)\left(\dfrac{Qx_1}{Qx_0}\right)}{\dfrac{Pm_1}{Pm_0}} \quad (24)$$

The use of the income terms of trade would be especially appropriate if the price of exports, Px, were a function of the quantity of exports, Qx, as might well be the case if the measure were applied to a country with a large share of the world market of the commodities it exports, or to a large group of countries such as the LDCs as a whole.

schemes (Massell 1969, 1970; Hueth and Schmitz 1972) and (2) designing a scheme that would adequately reflect all the factors involved.

[21] See U.N.: Department of Economic Affairs (1949, 1950), Singer (1950), W. A. Lewis (1954), and Prebisch (1959).

While each of the above measures of the terms of trade, N, G, and N_Y, pertain to the conditions of exchange between commodities, more relevant to the implications for development is what is happening to the conditions of exchange between resources. The conditions of exchange between one country's resources and another's can be characterized by correcting the net barter terms of trade, N, by appropriate productivity indexes. If productivity is defined in terms of the ratio of output to total inputs, Rx, the resulting index is defined as the "single factorial terms of trade," S,

$$S = \frac{\left(\dfrac{Px_1}{Px_0}\right)\left(\dfrac{Rx_1}{Rx_0}\right)}{\dfrac{Pm_1}{Pm_0}} = N\frac{Rx_1}{Rx_0} \qquad (25)$$

Such a correction would be particularly appropriate if the changes in the world price of the country's exports, Px, were compensated for or brought about by changes in productivity in the export sector.[22]

The practical application of the indexes of the terms of trade encounters a number of limitations that may distort the results of measurement. Among these limitations are the following:

1. The terms of trade measures reflect almost exclusively trade in commodities. Unilateral transactions and trade in invisibles are accounted for only in the gross barter terms of trade and the income terms of trade, and even in these instances only very imperfectly.

2. Since Px is usually measured at f.o.b. prices (excluding international transport cost) and Pm at c.i.f. prices (including international transport costs), all measures involving prices of imports and exports are subject to an unfortunate asymmetry with respect to transport costs. Thus, the terms of trade may reflect changes in international transport costs rather than real changes in the prices received for exports in different countries.

3. Changes in the quality of exports and imports are ignored.[23]

4. Even when the productivity adjustment is introduced, as in S, the index still does not account for changes in internal transport costs, such as those incurred in getting exports from the point of production to the point of export or imports from the point of entry to the point of consumption.

5. The factorial terms of trade become further complicated by the problems that attend the measurement of productivity. Partial productivity indexes are extremely restrictive, while total productivity indexes run into the problem of appropriately weighting inputs and output. Constructing the productivity index from sectoral data would be preferable, although even then it is difficult to confine the index to exports, since the individual sectors usually produce output both for the domestic and the foreign markets.

6. The weighting problem arises, in connection not only with the factorial terms of trade but also with the individual commodities or countries when aggregate indexes are involved. In connection with time trends, no single set of weights—generally those of the initial period as in the Laspeyres index, P_1Q_0/P_0Q_0, or of the final period as in the Paasche index, P_1Q_1/P_0Q_1—is entirely valid. The results may therefore be sensitive to the arbitrary choice of base period.

Explanations for the Deteriorating Terms of Trade of LDCs

The a priori theorizing on the deteriorating terms of trade has as a point of departure the observation that LDCs are largely exporters of primary commodities. The conclusion of the argument is that industrialization could forestall the deterioration of the terms of trade. Between the premises and the conclusion, the causes for the deterioration are usually described as follows:

1. The world's income elasticity of demand for manufactures is substantially higher than the income elasticity of demand for

---

[22]There also exist other terms of trade measures, such as the double factorial (it corrects S by multiplying the denominator of equation 25 by the index of productivity of imports), the real cost terms of trade, or the utility terms of trade. These are of more limited empirical applicability and will be ignored in the present discussion.

[23]Confining their attention to the prices of machinery exports of certain DCs, Kravis and Lipsey (1971, p. 23) have estimated that correction for quality changes would have lowered the growth in export prices and thus the terms of trade in developed countries by more than one-third.

primary products, which is fairly low. Indeed, world output and trade in manufactures grew fourfold between 1900–1960, while trade in primary products grew only by 50 percent (Maizels 1963, Chapter 4). Moreover, the threat of further substitution of manufactured synthetics for primary commodities tends to depress further the prices that LDC exporters of primary commodities can obtain.

2. Prebisch originated the argument that the structure of the agricultural and the manufacturing sectors differs—the former being characterized by competition, the latter by different degrees of monopoly. This is reflected in differences in price flexibility, with productivity gains in LDCs leading to lower prices for primary products and productivity gains in DCs leading to higher money wages. Although the structure of production in DCs and LDCs probably differs, the argument for deteriorating terms of trade can be correct if monopoly power in DC manufacturing is not only high but also increasing. However, there is no evidence that this is the case either internally or internationally. Indeed, if anything, there are reasons to suspect that the decline in colonialism and other privileged positions of individual DCs with respect to individual LDCs may have been accompanied by increasing competition in international markets, even if internally the industrial sectors of DCs may have remained quite monopolistic. This argument, therefore, seems incorrect, except to the extent that it reverts back to differences in the elasticities of demand.

3. Another argument is that technological change is biased against labor and natural resources and favors capital and skills. It must then work against primary production which, in LDCs at least, commonly involves relatively plentiful endowments of labor and natural resources. The evidence adduced in favor of this argument is mostly impressionistic. Furthermore, on conceptual grounds, there is no reason why technological change should in the long run be biased in any direction, except possibly in substituting cheaper inputs for more expensive ones.[24]

4. Among other possible explanations for the alleged deterioration in the terms of trade of primary products are some arguments that are not entirely consistent with the policy conclusions based on the hypothesis. For example, to the extent that internal as well as international transport costs inevitably creep into the price calculations, the seemingly greater rate of innovations in bulk transport (generally confined to primary products, which LDCs export) than in general cargo transport (used in LDC imports) may serve as a partial explanation for the alleged deterioration. If transport costs of primary commodities shipped in bulk have fallen relative to those of manufactured goods shipped as general cargo, the measured deterioration in the terms of trade of LDCs cannot support the policy conclusion that favors industrialization. This conclusion would be equally inappropriate if the relative increase in prices of manufactures was (because of the increasing sophistication of manufactured goods) due to the rising importance of selling costs in total costs of these products.

Since the change in the terms of trade of primary-producing countries seems to be the resultant of the many causes we have enumerated, the appropriate model for the test of the hypothesis must be rather complex and should involve both supply and demand factors in the way we developed the export instability model. Such a complete attempt at studying the terms of trade has not yet been made.[25] We proceed instead to present the sparse evidence that has been marshalled on the hypothesis.

The Evidence on the Terms of Trade
The original case for the deteriorating terms of trade was primarily presented in a series of papers by Raul Prebisch (U.N.: Department of Economic Affairs 1949, 1950; Prebisch 1959). It rested on the argument that, because the United Kingdom's net barter terms of trade, N, revealed an improvement over the period between 1875 and World War I,[26] the terms of trade of the LDCs must have deteriorated.

[24]For further discussion of the bias in technological change, see Chapter 9.

[25]For an early example of a quantitative model incorporating some of the many factors influencing the terms of trade, see Atallah (1958).

[26]The data for this observation were contained in Schlote (1938).

Even though the improvement in N for the United Kingdom may have been quite significant (probably around 30 percent for the 1875–1913 period), and may have continued (despite some fluctuations) into the 1930s and possibly beyond,[27] there would seem little reason to believe that the inverse of N for the United Kingdom would be indicative of N for the LDCs. Indeed, Kindleberger's (1956) indexes of N for other European countries show that the United Kingdom's terms of trade were not generally representative. Similarly, Morgan's (1959) time series for N of a number of primary-producing countries suggest that it would be difficult to generalize from the pattern of any single primary-producing country to all LDCs. Even in the simplest case, in which two countries trade exclusively with each other, it is still possible that N for both moves in the same direction—under appropriate conditions of supply and demand elasticities or transport costs. Indeed, Bhatia (1969) has demonstrated that this was the case for India and the United Kingdom, two countries that have traded extensively with each other for substantial periods of time.

The problem of choosing an appropriate time period arises once more in connection with the Prebisch evidence. For example, extensions of the calculations backward in time show that a remarkable deterioration in N of the United Kingdom took place in the 80 years prior to 1875 (Imlah 1958; C. G. Clark 1940). Similarly, the W. A. Lewis (1952) extension of the same calculations forward in time shows other sharp deteriorations in the N of the United Kingdom in the late 1930s and again in the late 1940s and early 1950s.

To these doubts about the validity of interpreting the improvement in British net barter terms of trade, N, between 1880 and 1913 as indicative of general deterioration in N of the LDCs during the same period should be added doubts about the degree to which the improvement in the British N was real and not just an artifact of the shortcomings in the measures of the terms of trade. For example, during the period under consideration, there is good reason to believe: (1) that manufactured goods may have undergone more significant qualitative improvements than primary products and (2) that international shipping rates were falling as a result of the opening of the Suez and Panama Canals or the development of steamboats and refrigerated cargo ships.

Since qualitative improvements are ignored and international transport costs enter the measurement of import prices only (because they are measured c.i.f., whereas exports are measured f.o.b.), these two factors would have led to an upward bias in N of the United Kingdom, suggesting that the measured improvement may have been more apparent than real.

Limitations of this sort on the validity of indirect inferences of terms of trade movements in the LDCs from those in the DCs lead us to endorse greater efforts to measure directly the terms of trade of LDCs. Unfortunately, direct measurement of the terms of trade of LDCs is rendered difficult by the absence of detailed historical data in all but a few such countries. Short time series are available for a larger number of LDCs,[28] but the sensitivity of any such calculations to the particular dates chosen for the starting and ending points would make any results less than definitive. Even longer-period results[29] may be unconvincing because of the problems in measurement we have already mentioned.

Despite their shortcomings, the general picture obtained from direct estimates of the terms of trade of LDCs is constancy or even some decline in N or in G. Because of the overall increase in world trade, however, deterioration in N or G is offset by rising export volumes so that the income terms of trade of LDCs, N_Y, have been increasing quite significantly. There is also some crude evidence of increasing labor productivity in the export sectors, indicating that the single factorial terms of trade, S, of LDCs may also have improved. With respect to almost any measure of the terms of trade, however, DCs seem to have been doing better than LDCs. Within this general picture there is, not surprisingly, considerable variation from country to country, depending on the individual countries' trade patterns.

The conclusion is that the evidence does not support the general thesis of deteriorating terms of trade for the LDCs. This is not to

---

[27]The evidence for this period is from Imlah (1958) and C. G. Clark (1940).

[28]See Wilson, Sinha, and Castree (1969) and UNCTAD (1971).

[29]For example, for India (Bhatia 1969; Appleyard 1968) and for Chile (U.N.: ECLA 1963).

say that unfavorable long-term movements in relative prices, in particular commodities and for individual LDCs, do not exist. Indeed, they do exist, and such movements are among the many factors a country should consider in deciding on the best allocation of its resources in alternative production activities.

Summary and Conclusions

In Chapter 17, we saw that by adopting appropriate policies LDC governments can achieve highly satisfactory export growth which, in turn, may have numerous static as well as dynamic influences that tend to raise the level of income and the rate of growth. In this sense, exports constitute an engine of growth.

Nevertheless, Chapters 16 and 17 discussed some disturbing features of export growth that should not be overlooked. Most theories that attempt to explain the composition of exports are static theories of comparative advantage. Since comparative advantages are unlikely to change substantially over time, these theories do not predict changes in the commodity composition of exports. Perhaps this is as it should be, because, for many LDCs at least, the composition of exports has remained remarkably constant, even over long periods of time. Most LDCs are exporters of primary products and importers of manufactures, and this is the way it has been for centuries.

In Chapter 16, we have shown that dependence on primary exports tends to retard, cancel, or even reverse the normal patterns of change in sectoral composition that are associated with development. Moreover, from our tests of various versions of the balanced-growth hypothesis, we found that the larger the departures from the "normal" pattern, the lower the growth rate of GNP.

Exports of primary products are also often embedded in a colonial or neoimperialist environment. In such an environment, the benefits of trade are unlikely to be retained by the indigenous population and may lead to the creation of a foreign enclave dualism, which hampers the spread effects of trade. Openness to trade often nips in the bud the development of an indigenous class of entrepreneurs and capitalists, and of local manufacturing (Resnick 1970), thereby increasing trade dependence and bringing "growth with-

out development." In other words, besides the stimulating effects of export growth, there are also some backwash effects. A full evaluation and analysis of these effects would lead us into detailed case studies and also into the treacherous world of political economy, which, because of the difficulty of testing, lies outside the scope of this book.

In this chapter, we have focused on two of the more operational and more general hypotheses concerning the backwash effects of trade—the hypotheses of export instability and of the deteriorating terms of trade.

With respect to export instability, policy implications depend crucially on the theory of the causes and effects of export instability one adopts. Conventional theorizing goes from instability through the intermediate link of uncertainty to behavioral effects that are in general detrimental to economic development. We have formulated an alternative hypothesis of export instability, based on the permanent-income hypothesis. Following that hypothesis, we have interpreted the unstable component of export earnings as unexpected and transitory income, which is associated with a lower (or zero in the extreme) marginal propensity to consume than the one out of permanent income.

We have measured instability by means of two indexes—a traditional one, the squared deviations from an exponential trend index, and the transitory one—and we have tested for the effects of instability on investment, exports, and income growth. The primary implication of the permanent-income hypothesis—that the effect of uncertainty, as measured by the transitory component of income, tends to decrease the marginal propensity to consume out of permanent income—has been confirmed by the results of the cross-section of 38 LDCs we studied. The conclusion that this would lead to higher savings ratios and thereby to higher levels of investment has also been confirmed. Moreover, this beneficial effect of instability on capital formation seems to have dominated any other negative effects on productivity and exports, so that higher export and income instability has been associated with higher rates of growth of GDP. In contrast to these strong results obtained with the use of the transitory index of export instability, utilization of the conventional index has generally led to negative and nonsignificant results. In view of the evidence, the rejection of the traditional theorizing, in which on a general basis instability is considered detrimental to development, would seem warranted. Indeed, instability—at least when measured as the dispersion of transitory income—may well have beneficial effects. This is a rather unorthodox conclusion that deserves further investigation and possibly the attention of policy makers.

We have also tried to explain the causes of export instability, unfortunately without much success. However, in view of the fact that export instability, that is, instability of export proceeds, is apparently more closely associated with instability of export quantities, which are mainly determined by domestic supply rather than foreign demand conditions, this failure is not critical.

Not unlike the case of export instability, the measurement of the terms of trade is subject to a number of alternative indexes, each one yielding different results and policy implications. A comprehensive study of the terms of trade, therefore, must go beyond questions of measurement to investigate the alleged causes of terms of trade deterioration —such factors as the differences in the world's income elasticity of demand for manufactures as compared to agricultural products, the market organization for the manufacturing and agricultural sectors that grants a greater degree of monopoly to the former, or the bias in technological change that works against labor and natural resources and thus against primary-producing countries. Such a

comprehensive study is not available. The evidence we reviewed, nevertheless, casts doubt on the hypothesis that the terms of trade of LDCs as a whole and for all periods are subject to secular deterioration.

We conclude, therefore, that while there is evidence of important backwash effects of trade dependence that tend to offset, or at least mitigate, the engine-of-growth benefits of trade, the traditional emphasis on export instability and terms of trade deterioration as the source of the problems seems misplaced. The export instability and terms of trade hypotheses emphasize what is wrong with individual commodities. Indeed, natural rubber or cocoa may be more subject to instability and terms of trade deterioration than soybeans or petroleum. Yet in our view, soybeans or even petroleum may not have brought much more development than rubber or cocoa. The real problem of the trade backwash effects is that the "normal" patterns of structural change are delayed or even reversed, and that structural distortions of this type are inimical to long-run economic development. Few LDCs, indeed, have been able to achieve a natural evolution of the structure of their exports permitting them to follow the normal patterns of sectoral change in the process of development. Usually, open trade policies and comparative advantage translate, for LDCs at least, into dependence on primary products today, tomorrow, and forever, thus inhibiting the normal patterns of sectoral articulation and change, which are conducive to development.

Chapter 19

Economic Integration with Special Reference to Customs Unions

In preceding chapters, we have seen the concern that many development theorists and policy makers have for the seeming inability of LDCs to reap the static and dynamic benefits of international trade to the same extent that DCs appear to do. By and large, export growth of the LDCs has lagged behind that of the DCs.[1] Even when exports have grown fairly rapidly, for example, by adopting trade liberalizing policies, fears have been expressed that export expansion is accompanied by an increasing concentration of exports, dependence on foreign markets, and vulnerability to destabilizing fluctuations in export proceeds and to terms of trade deterioration, all of which are alleged to impede development.

[1]According to B. I. Cohen and Sisler (1971), LDC exports grew at an average annual rate of 2.1 percent in the 1950s and 6.4 percent in the 1960s as compared to more than 7 and 9 percent for the DCs for the same periods respectively.

Moreover, when LDCs exploit their comparative advantage through free trade, it often distorts their productive structure in favor of primary sectors with low linkages to the rest of the economy, thus perpetuating existing structural dualisms and inhibiting the changes in sectoral compostion that are apparently conducive to development.

In Chapter 18, we saw that some of these backwash effects of trade may have been exaggerated. In Chapter 17, we saw that some LDCs have achieved remarkably high export growth rates, some even being successful in expanding nontraditional exports, changing their productive structures, and achieving satisfactory rates of income growth. Nevertheless, the structural distortions and the inhibition of normal changes in that structure that trade seems to bring deserve serious concern. For this and other reasons, most LDCs have opted for import substitution, based on substantial protection in the form of high nominal tariff rates and quantitative restrictions. Import substitution fundamentalism has been bought by LDCs partly because of lingering memories of the worldwide calamity that befell primary producers during the depression of the 1930s, partly in order to compensate for dualistic distortions (such as higher wage rates in industry than in agriculture),[2] partly as a consequence of universal government weakness in the face of the appeals of private interest groups, partly as a second-best policy to compensate for the dynamic externalities alleged to be associated with industrialization, and partly because of an ultimately noneconomic preference for industry. Quite often, the high nominal rates on finished goods are combined with low tariff rates on inputs, making for even higher effective tariff rates, that is, tariffs expressed in relation to domestic value added rather than to gross production.

Over time, however, the deleterious effects of these policies have become increasingly noticeable. This is not surprising, in view of our demonstration in Chapter 7 that attempts to circumvent the international division of labor are likely to impose allocative and dynamic inefficiencies on the countries employing them. In an effort to chart an optimal course between free trade, on the one hand, and protectionism and autarky, on the other, increasing attention has been devoted to regional trading arrangements as a means of having some of the benefits of international trade without some of its alleged drawbacks.

The variety of possible regional trading arrangements is great. Existing arrangements range in scope from a partial free trade area (total or partial elimination of tariffs on specified products originating from a partner country), through a customs union (elimination of tariffs on all commodities originating from a partner country plus adoption of an external tariff common to all partners on commodities originating from nonmember countries), to a complete common market (a

customs union with mobility of all factors of production among its members). Advocates of regional integration point out that there are still other possible institutional mechanisms of broader scope, such as harmonization of policies, regional planning, or monetary union, which could be adopted and could entail even greater advantages. Since these latter instruments of economic integration clearly lead beyond the domain of trade in particular, and economics in general, and since even full-fledged common markets do not seem politically feasible at the present time, we shall confine our attention in this chapter to the theoretical and empirical assessment of a form of integration that has already come into practice in several areas of the world—customs unions (CU). Another form of economic integration, coordination among countries of their monetary and fiscal policies, will be treated in Chapter 21.

The effects of CU participation can be divided into two categories: the fundamental effects of trade creation and trade diversion, treated in the first section of this chapter, and other nontraditional effects, treated in the second section. While the tools for measuring trade creation and trade diversion are fairly well developed, this is not the case with respect to the other effects. Since the nontraditional effects may be even more important than the trade creation and trade diversion effects, especially in CUs among LDCs, our treatment of the nontraditional effects includes an application of two somewhat more general methods for assessing the effects of CU participation.

Our results will indicate that the benefits of CU participation are much larger than have generally been assumed. The suggestion is that CU participation can provide a viable means of attaining the engine-of-growth benefits of export growth without the deleterious structural change-inhibiting effects of dependence on primary exports.

Fundamental Effects of Customs Unions: Trade Creation and Trade Diversion

Viner (1950) has provided the classical treatment of CUs within a partial equilibrium framework. Consider the domestic demand and supply curves, D_h and S_h respectively, shown in Figure 19.1. If one makes the small country assumption, the supply curves of po-

---

[2]Tariff protection is, of course, only a third-best policy in such a situation. Removal of the impediments to wage equalization is the best policy. If this cannot be done, direct subsidies to industrial employment is second best—since it offsets the distortions on production as well as on consumption. Only if neither of these policies can be adopted is the imposition of a protective tariff desirable in such circumstances (Bhagwati 1968).

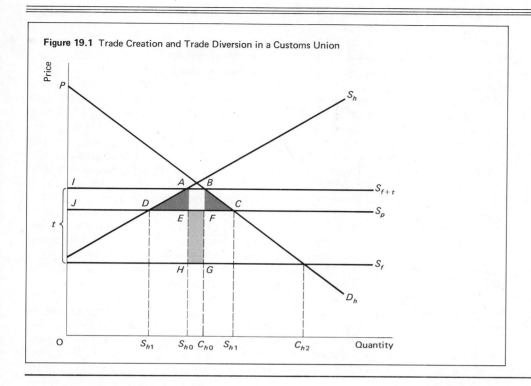

Figure 19.1 Trade Creation and Trade Diversion in a Customs Union

tential trading partners are perfectly elastic, S_p for the CU partner and S_f for the rest of the world in Figure 19.1. This diagram permits comparison of three alternative institutional arrangements: free trade, nondiscriminatory tariff restrictions, and CU. Under free trade, all of domestic demand, C_{h2}, will be imported from the rest of the world suppliers at the price, S_f. If, as seems more realistic, free trade does not prevail and a protective tariff (100 percent in our example) is imposed, the relevant foreign supply curve in domestic price terms is S_{f+t}. Supply and demand intersect at B, and C_{h0} will be consumed domestically, with S_{h0} being produced domestically and the remainder, $C_{h0} - S_{h0}$, imported from the rest of the world.

The formation of a CU changes the configuration of foreign prices. Since the CU partner is not subject to the tariff, the partner's supply curve, S_p, which is higher than S_f but lower than S_{f+t} in the diagram, now becomes the pertinent supply curve. The new equilibrium of supply and demand is at C. Consumption is thus increased to C_{h1}, of which S_{h1} is supplied by domestic producers and $C_{h1} - S_{h1}$ is supplied by the CU partner.

The move from point B to point C involves both production and consumption effects, which entail trade creation. The quantity $S_{h1}S_{h0}$ that was previously produced locally is now imported. Furthermore, there is a net increase in local consumption by $C_{h0}C_{h1}$.

However, since imports are no longer supplied by the lowest cost supplier and trade is diverted from the lowest cost supplier in the rest of the world to the higher cost CU partner supplier, there is also trade diversion. Specifically, pre-CU imports of $S_{h0}C_{h0}$ are obtained at the import price of S_f per unit, that is, at an opportunity cost of $S_{h0}C_{h0}GH$, but are sold to consumers for $S_{h0}C_{h0}BA$. The difference $ABGH$ represents the government tariff revenues. Once the imports $S_{h0}C_{h0}$ are diverted to the less efficient supplier elsewhere in the CU, the opportunity cost of the same amount of imports rises to $S_{h0}C_{h0}FE$ and no tariff revenue is collected.[3]

[3]The higher the pre-CU protective tariff, the smaller the post-CU trade diversion effect. If, in the example of Figure 19.1, the protective tariff raised the price of rest of the world supplies above the intersection of D_h and S_h, the post-CU trade diversion effect would be eliminated and the only change that remained would have been the trade creation effect.

Using traditional consumer surplus analysis, total consumer surplus in the pre-CU case (with the tariff) is measured by *PIB*, whereas post-CU it is the larger area, *PJC*. The difference or the change in consumers' surplus is measured by *IBCJ*. One part of the difference, *IADJ*, represents a transfer from producers to consumers,[4] and another part, *ABFE*, represents a transfer from government (tariff revenue) to consumers. (This latter redistribution is usually assumed to take the form of neutral consumption subsidies.) The remaining areas, triangles *DAE* and *BCF*, represent net welfare gains (as opposed to simple changes in distribution in favor of consumers), but these gains are offset by additional losses in government tariff revenue, *EFGH*. CU participation, therefore, brings trade creation gains of *DAE* plus *BCF* but also trade diversion losses of *EFGH*. The net effect cannot be predicted a priori. CU participation could raise welfare if the trade creation gains exceed the trade diversion losses, but it could lower welfare if the trade diversion losses exceed the trade creation gains. This indeterminacy on a priori grounds underlines the importance of empirical investigations.

Viner's analysis can be applied in principle at any level of aggregation, and therefore at the national as well as the individual commodity level. Being a form of partial equilibrium analysis, however, it is particularly inappropriate for analyzing the effects of the changes in relative prices resulting from CU formation. Indeed, Lipsey (1957, 1960) showed that Viner's analysis required the fairly unrealistic assumption that consumption would not be affected by changes in relative prices. This has led to reformulations of the analysis in general equilibrium terms.

Figure 7.2 provided a single-country two-commodity general equilibrium analysis of tariff protection. The effect of the CU in that context could be represented by introducing a new set of market opportunities with slopes intermediate between those of the free trade opportunities, $w_0, w_1, \ldots$, and those corresponding to tariff protection, $d_0, d_1, \ldots$. In the CU case, however, the country would have

to trade from its new point of productive efficiency according to terms of trade defined by the partner's supply price of the importable commodity. Since the partner's supply price is higher than that of the rest of the world, the relevant international terms of trade are in this case inferior to that of the nondiscriminatory tariff or free trade cases. If, as we have argued above, the potentially first-best position of free trade is unattainable for political or other reasons, the relevant comparison is between CU and the nondiscriminatory tariff case. Once again, CU participation can be the second-best arrangement (inferior to free trade but superior to the nondiscriminatory tariff alternative) as long as the net trade creation effects attributable to the use of less distorted prices for domestic producers and consumers exceed the trade diversion loses derived from trading internationally with the partner on less advantageous terms.

Even in such a model, all relative prices (of the partner, of the rest of the world, and of the country itself) are assumed to be given or at least exogenously determined. In a truly general equilibrium model, however, relative prices should be endogenously determined. By extending this analysis to at least two countries, but as Arndt (1968, 1969) and Kemp (1969) have argued, more appropriately to three or four countries, and introducing trade offer curves, the terms of trade and therefore relative prices become endogenous.

The more general and comprehensive the analysis, however, the more cumbersome and less operational it becomes. Everything depends on everything else. The benefits and costs of CU vis-à-vis nondiscriminatory tariff protection depend on a large number of different factors and parameters, whose magnitudes are difficult to estimate. It is not surprising, then, that most attempts at quantification of the benefits of CU participation have been based on the simpler partial equilibrium analysis of Viner.

The application of the Vinerian model of trade creation and trade diversion is based on measurement of the areas indicated in Figure 19.1—the size of the two shaded triangles, *ADE* and *BFC*, representing trade creation, relative to that of the cross-hatched rectangle representing trade diversion. Assuming that demand and supply curves can be adequately represented by straight lines, as in Figure 19.1, the welfare gains (or losses) of CU participa-

----

[4] Mishan (1968) has argued that, under competitive conditions, domestic producers should be indifferent between points on their supply curve, such as between points *D* and *A*, and therefore, that the area of *IADJ* is not a transfer from the producers to consumers but is rather a net gain to consumers.

tion can be estimated only if it is possible to measure the length of certain of the relevant sides and the slopes of the supply and demand curves. The former two areas can be measured if there exist estimates of $S_{f+t} - S_p$, which need be combined either with estimates of the slopes of the S_h and D_h curves or with measures of $S_{h0} - S_{h1}$ and $C_{h1} - C_{h0}$. Likewise, the area $EFGH$ can be estimated if it is possible to measure both $S_p - S_f$ and $C_{h0} - S_{h0}$.

The information on which estimates of the relevant areas are usually based is not always reliable. The magnitudes on the vertical axis, $S_{f+t} - S_p$ and $S_p - S_f$, are usually inferred from intercountry comparisons of preunion tariff rates. Since pre-CU tariff rates are not always set in such a way that S_{f+t} is equal to the marginal and average costs of domestic production, such estimates are generally inaccurate. A better alternative is to obtain direct information on the costs of production in the various countries for comparable qualities of output, but unfortunately, this information is seldom available. Similarly, estimation of the horizontal magnitudes is rendered difficult by differences in quality from country to country or one time period to another, the influence of other factors unrelated to CU on imports and consumption, and in the case of intermediate goods the absence of reliable and up-to-date information or interindustry transactions.[5] Some of these difficulties (e.g., the lack of product homogeneity) can be overcome by disaggregating sufficiently, but this increases the data requirements severely. As a result, careful detailed attempts to overcome these problems[6] are unfortunately the exception rather than the rule. More often, estimation of the welfare gains and losses of CU participation is based on crude estimates of the vertical magnitudes combined with assumptions of the slopes or elasticities of supply and demand.

To facilitate assessment of the actual bene-

fits of CU participation, Balassa (1967) proposed a relatively simpler estimation procedure, still based more or less explicitly on the Vinerian model. In the absence of the CU, assuming that income elasticities of the demand for imports (although not necessarily of imports themselves) would have remained constant, Balassa suggested that the dominance of trade creation over trade diversion, or vice versa, could be determined by whether the income elasticity of the demand for imports increased or decreased between the pre-CU and post-CU periods. This procedure amounts to direct estimation of the net horizontal magnitudes indicating the quantity of trade creation less trade diversion, but must be supplemented by estimates of the vertical magnitudes to arrive at estimates of the welfare gains or losses. The increase in productivity associated with the increase in the income elasticity of imports can be estimated in several ways, for example, from the average tariff rate indicating how much cheaper (in world prices) or more productive (for equal values) imports (or exports) are relative to domestic production of import substitutes or, alternatively, as the economies of scale that intra-CU producers may be able to exploit in satisfying the increase in regional demand.

Empirical applications of any of these methods have been limited by, among other things, the dearth of actual CUs. The CUs involving European countries, the European Economic Community (EEC) and the European Free Trade Association (EFTA), have received the most attention. The most comprehensive arrangements among LDCs are the Central American Common Market (CACM) and the East African Common Market (EACM). The usefulness of the latter case, however, is limited by the fact that there exist little data on the preunion period. Less comprehensive arrangements are presently in effect in Central Africa, West Africa, North Africa, Latin America, the Andean region (Latin America), the Caribbean, the Middle East, and Southeast Asia.

While the earlier assessments of the EEC and EFTA were based almost exclusively on the strict Vinerian model, for the reasons given above it is Balassa's income elasticity method that has been used much more extensively in recent years. In applying that method to the EEC, Balassa (1967) found an overall increase of 0.3 in the income elasticity of

---

[5]For examples of such studies, see Bentick (1963), Liesner (1958), Janssen (1961), Scitovsky (1958), Verdoorn and Meyer zu Schlochtern (1964), Duquesne de la Vinelle (1965), Lamfalussy (1961), and Waelbroeck (1964). In these studies, changes in quantity have been estimated by changes in shares of members' imports or exports in world markets. However, an increased trade share could be caused either by trade creation or trade diversion or both and hence it is not immediately translatable into welfare gains or losses.

[6]See J. Williamson and Bottrill (1971), Truman (1969), and Major and Hays (1970).

demand for total imports between the pre-union period (1953–1959) and the immediate postunion period (1959–1965).[7] While net trade diversion (evidenced by a rise in the intraunion import elasticity and a decline in the extraunion import elasticity) was observed in some commodities (e.g., chemicals and miscellaneous manufacturing), the overall effect was clearly that of net trade creation. Assuming that every 1 percent increase in the share of imports would raise productivity by 0.3,[8] Balassa arrived at 0.09 percent (0.3 × 0.3) as the best estimate of the annual contribution of the formation of the EEC to the growth rate of GNP among EEC members. Although not exactly negligible, and indeed somewhat larger than the earlier estimates, a contribution to the income growth rate of less than 0.1 percent per annum is still small. If such estimates are to be believed and if the effects of trade creation and trade diversion constitute most of the influence of CU participation, the potential benefits of CU participation would seem to be small indeed.

However, the Balassa and most other estimates of the trade creation effects refer explicitly to the EEC, an arrangement only involving DCs. The effects might be somewhat larger in the case of CUs among LDCs. Indeed, when the Balassa method was applied rather mechanically to the CACM, as in Wilford (1970), somewhat larger estimates of the increases in income elasticities of demand for imports were obtained. This would seem to suggest that the net gains of trade creation and trade diversion were larger in the CACM than in the EEC. Nevertheless, more detailed subsequent applications of the Balassa method to the CACM case by Willmore (1972) and Nugent (1974) yielded estimates of the same order of magnitude as those obtained for the EEC.

The General Effects of Customs Unions

The partial equilibrium Vinerian analysis, utilized in the previous section, of course, ignores a number of possibly significant effects of CU formation, including the effects on tariff structure, economies of scale, technological change, and various kinds of efficiency. These effects constitute the subject of the present section.

The Effects on Tariff Structure

The analysis based on Figure 19.1 assumed that the external tariff rate is unaffected by the CU. This will, in general, not be the case. As long as the preunion tariff rates of all CU members are not identical for every commodity, some external tariff rates must change as a result of the CU. Although the General Agreement on Tariffs and Trade (GATT) rules prohibit CUs from increasing the average external tariff rate relative to the average of preunion rates, many countries are not signatories to GATT, and even if they are, it is far from clear that such provisions are strictly enforced. When the external tariff rate is lowered, there will be additional trade creation effects, referred to as "external" trade creation. On the other hand, if the average of the external tariff rates is raised, "external trade suppression" will result. Naturally, since preunion tariff rates are likely to vary among countries, CU participation can bring about external trade creation in some CU members and external trade suppression in others. Furthermore, not only may CU participation affect the average tariff rate but it may also affect the whole structure of tariffs, including the nature and degree of the dispersion of individual tariff rates around their mean.

If an effect such as this on the dispersion of tariff rates around the mean exists, what is its significance? Intuitively put, the answer is quite simple. Assuming that some price distortions are regarded as necessary (e.g., to protect infant domestic industry), the more uniform the distortions, the smaller the number of relative prices distorted and the smaller the magnitude of the distortions.[9] The welfare cost of any set of price distortions, such as those from tariffs, may thus be expected to increase not only with the average rate of distortion (the average tariff rate) but also with the degree of dispersion of the distortions (tariff rates) among commodities.

---

[7]The overall rise in the income elasticity of demand for imports of 0.3 was composed of rises in the income elasticities of demand for extraregional imports and for intraregional imports amounting to 0.1 and 0.4 respectively.

[8]This estimate is from Walters (1963b) and is based on the experience of the United States in the early twentieth century.

[9]A formal argument to the same effect has been made by Bertrand (1972) and Bertrand and Vanek (1971). Intuitive arguments along the same lines emphasizing policy implications have been made by Little, Scitovsky, and Scott (1970) and Balassa and Associates (1971).

If CU participation is likely to affect the tariff structure in such a way as to make tariff rates more uniform among commodities (as will presently be argued), CU participation would have a positive effect on economic welfare, which should be recognized and measured.

It may be reasonable to suppose that any country's tariff structure is a result of both historical accidents and the political power of domestic producers relative to that of domestic consumers. If this is true, and if these factors vary significantly from country to country even within a common geographic region, it would follow that the structure of tariffs would vary considerably from one country to another. If so, it will be likely that intercountry comparisons of tariff rates would reveal cases in which one country has a high tariff rate on one commodity and a low one on another commodity, while in another country the reverse is true.

What effect would the adoption of a common external tariff among such countries have on their tariff structure? There is, of course, no single set of rules that potential CU partners must adopt to resolve their differences over individual preunion tariff rates and arrive at a common external tariff structure. However, the guideline followed by the EEC—to adopt the mean of the existing preunion rates as the common external tariff rate—seems to be a natural expedient, which has apparently also formed the basis of the common external tariff regime in the CACM. If preunion tariff rates differ among commodities and countries, as we have just suggested, and the tariff-averaging procedure for adopting the common external tariff rates is employed, as it apparently has been in both the EEC and

CACM, CU participation would have the effect of making tariff rates more uniform among commodities.

Let us illustrate this possibility with a simple hypothetical example. Suppose, as shown in Case I of Table 19.1, there are two countries, 1 and 2, and two commodities of equal importance, A and B. Assume further that the two countries have different tariffs on different commodities but the same average tariff rate of 20 percent. The effect of CU participation would then be to make the tariff rates more homogeneous than the preunion rates. (In fact, in this example, it would make them identical.) This need not be so, and indeed Case II of the same table illustrates a situation in which the tariff rates of one of the countries are made less uniform as a result of CU participation.

Since the tariff-homogenizing effect of CU participation (like most other effects) is not a logical necessity but only a possibility that depends on circumstances, our hypothesis of a tariff-homogenizing effect can be demonstrated only by empirical testing. Using the coefficient of variation (CV), that is, the standard deviation divided by the mean, as the measure of the degree of dispersion in tariff rates, our hypothesis would be confirmed if, and only if, postunion tariff rates were found to be more uniform than preunion tariff rates.

Following Nugent (1974), we have carried out such comparisons for two complete CUs, the European Economic Community (EEC) and the Central American Common Market (CACM), one partial CU, the Andean group (or Acuerdo de Cartagena), and finally one free trade area that is presently considering adoption of a common external tariff regime, the Arab Common Market (ACM).

Table 19.1 *Hypothetical Tariff Rates Before and After Adoption of Common External Tariff Regime*

	Preunion Tariff Rates (percent)			Common External Rates (percent)		
	Sector A	Sector B	Average	Sector A	Sector B	Average
			CASE I			
Country 1	40	0	20	20	20	20
Country 2	0	40	20	20	20	20
			CASE II			
Country 1	20	20	20	10	30	20
Country 2	0	40	20	10	30	20

Table 19.2 *Coefficients of Variation in Preunion and Postunion Tariff Rates in the European Economic Community (1,011 Manufactured Commodities)*

	Unweighted	Weighted by Share in EEC Imports	Weighted by Share in UK Imports
I. Preunion			
Benelux (Belgium, Netherlands, and Luxembourg)	0.793	0.585	0.571
France	0.608	0.496	0.487
Germany	0.767	0.562	0.507
Italy	0.548	0.393	0.400
II. Postunion: The Common External Rate	0.544	0.405	0.430

Source: Political and Economic Planning (PEP) (1959), *Tariffs and Trade in Western Europe.* London: Allen and Unwin.

To gain maximum comparability of commodities and their respective tariff rates between and among individual countries in the preunion period and with respect to those in the postunion period, the classification used has been as disaggregated as possible. As far as possible, we have attempted to find weights appropriate for representing the relative importance of each individual commodity in total imports. However, data limitations have made it possible to obtain satisfactory weights only in the EEC. In the other cases, the best that could be done was to test the sensitivity of the results to different sets of weights chosen arbitrarily. Specific tariffs have been converted to their ad valorem equivalents on the basis of prices implicit in the value and quantity figures from import statistics.[10] Since in the case of the ACM a common external tariff regime has not yet been established (although a number of alternative proposals exist), we had to make some assumptions about the likely features of a future regime. The assumptions about the tariff agreement are specified in footnote *c* of Table 19.5.

The results for the EEC, CACM, Acuerdo de Cartagena, and ACM are shown in Tables 19.2, 19.3, 19.4 and 19.5. In the case of the

[10]In the relatively few cases where such conversions could not be made, the particular commodities were excluded from the CV calculations. In the CACM, where this problem was most serious, two sets of calculations have been carried out: one with all commodities but including only the ad valorem tariffs that could be obtained directly or converted from specific tariffs on the basis of computed prices, and the other excluding those commodities for which it was not possible to convert specific tariffs to their ad valorem equivalents.

EEC, the reduction in the coefficient of variation resulting from customs union participation ranges from nil in the case of Italy to about 0.2 for Germany and the Benelux countries. In the case of the CACM, reduc-

Table 19.3 *Coefficients of Variation in Preunion and Postunion Tariff Rates in the Central American Common Market (654 Commodities)*

	All Commodities	Excluding Commodities with Specific Tariff Rates in Preunion Period
I. Preunion		
Costa Rica	0.819	0.800
El Salvador	0.537	0.456
Guatemala	0.584	0.583
Honduras	0.524	0.629
Nicaragua	0.510	0.509
II. Postunion: The Common External Rate	0.507	0.508

Sources:
Costa Rica: Ministerio de Economia y Hacienda (1961), *Arancel de Aduanas.* San Jose.
El Salvador: Ministerio de Hacienda (1959), *Tarifa de Aforos.* San Salvador.
Guatemala: Guatemala (1959), *Arancel de Aduanas, Republica de Guatemala.* Guatemala.
Honduras: Honduras (1955), *Arancel de Aduanas.* Tegucigalpa.
Nicaragua: Nicaragua (1955), "Codigo Arancelario de Importaciones," *La Gaceta.* Managua (July 1).
Central America: Secretaria Permanente del Tratado General de Integracion Economica Centroamericana (1965), *Arancel de Aduanas Centro Americano.* Guatemala City; and modifications of same in 1968.

Table 19.4 *Coefficients of Variation in Preagreement and Postagreement Tariff Rates in Countries of the Acuerdo de Cartagena (The Andean Group) (200 Commodities in the Metal and Machinery Sector)*

I. Preagreement Rates	
Bolivia	0.56
Chile	0.56
Colombia	0.59
Ecuador	0.45
Peru	0.44
II. Postagreement: The Common	
External Rate	0.22

Notes: For various reasons, certain products of the sector have not yet been accorded a common external tariff.

Source: Junta, Acuerdo de Cartagena, Lima, Peru.

tions in the coefficient of variation are limited to Costa Rica (0.3), Guatemala (0.1), and Honduras (0.1), and of about the same order of magnitude as in the EEC. The calculations for the Acuerdo de Cartagena group pertain to the only sector for which thus far a common external tariff regime has been adopted, the metal and machinery industries. Even within this specific sector, however, there are significant reductions in the coefficient of variation among tariff rates as a result of participation in the agreement. Indeed, in every country, the preunion coefficient of variation is at least twice that of the common external tariff regime, the absolute differences varying between 0.2 and 0.4. In connection with the ACM group, one observes a relatively high preunion dispersion of tariff rates, as compared with the other groups. It appears, therefore, that the coefficient of variation could be reduced to a greater extent in the ACM than in the other regions if a common external tariff regime along the lines of that assumed in Table 19.5 were adopted.

In summary, then, the reductions in the coefficient of variation attributable to CU participation seem to average about 0.1 in the EEC and CACM, but could be considerably higher, perhaps 0.3 in the Acuerdo de Cartagena, and 0.5 in the ACM. Naturally, one cannot easily make claims for generality on the basis of these few and rather crude computations. Indeed, one might speculate that because of their unusually low (preunion) tariff rates and rather similar tariff structures, Southeast Asian countries would not be likely

to enjoy comparable reductions in the coefficients of variation as a result of adopting a common external tariff rate.

The reader is referred to Chapter 7, especially to Tables 7.1 and 7.2, where we presented some simulation estimates of the production and consumption costs, respectively, of tariff rates of varying mean and variance from our three-commodity general equilibrium model of tariff distortions. We now confine our attention to what were thought to be the

Table 19.5 *Coefficients of Variation in Preunion and Hypothetical Postunion Tariff Rates in the Arab Common Market[a] (3,245 Commodities[b])*

I. Preunion	
Egypt	1.37
Iraq	1.81
Jordan	1.37
Syria	1.04
II. Postunion: The Common	
External Rate[c]	0.85

Notes:

[a] Some specific tariffs are in effect, but since reliable prices of imports (c.i.f.) for those commodities were available for the year 1961, it was possible to convert all specific tariffs to their ad valorem equivalent.

[b] Tariff rates of certain commodities for certain countries do not appear in the source used. Thus, the number of commodities varies somewhat in each case. Only for Jordan is it the full 3,245 commodities; in the other countries, the number of commodities were 3,244 for Egypt, 3,242 for Syria, 2,958 for Iraq, and 3,196 for the Arab Common Market.

[c] In the absence of an agreement as to how the contemplated common external tariff rate would be selected, the hypothetical set of common external rates used in these computations was arrived at from the existing (preunion) external rates by the following rules:

(1) In general, the common external tariff rate was the mean of the preunion rates with the following exceptions:

(2) Every rate higher or lower than the other three by at least 50 percent was deleted in computing the common external rate.

(3) Of the four rates, if one was higher and the other was lower than the middle two rates by at least 50 percent, both extreme rates were deleted in computing the average.

(4) If each of the rates differed from the next closest rate by at least 50 percent, or any two rates from any other two rates by at least 100 percent, the commodity was excluded from the scheme, on the grounds that agreement would be infeasible in such cases. In the few such cases which arose, the commodities were excluded both from the individual country (preunion) computations and from the (postunion) common external tariff computation.

Source: Council of Arab Economic Unity, General Secretariat, *Manual of the Tariff Rates Applied until 31 December 1968 in Each of the Countries of the Arab Common Market* (in Arabic). Cairo.

Table 19.6 *Welfare Costs of Protection for Alternative Average Tariff Rates and Coefficients of Variation*

Case	Tariff Rates (Percent)			Coefficient of Variation	Welfare Cost (Percent of National Income)
	Average	t_1	t_2		
A	20	20	20	0.87	4.09
	40	40	40	0.87	12.25
	60	60	60	0.87	21.91
B	20	10	30	1.15	5.79
	40	30	50	1.00	13.60
	60	40	80	1.05	24.89
C	20	0	40	1.73	10.65
	40	0	80	1.73	20.13
	60	0	100	1.73	31.90

Notes: The tariff rate on the exportable commodity X is assumed to be zero in all of these computations.

In the case of homogeneous tariff rates (case A), the computations of welfare cost are identical to those for the corresponding parameters obtained by Johnson (1965b). Indeed, this provides a check on the validity of the computations.

Source: Tables 7.1 and 7.2.

most realistic parameter values in these tables, namely, curvature coefficients of 1.5 (indicative of a fairly flat transformation curve), elasticities of substitution in consumption of 1.0, and average tariff rates of 20, 40, and 60 percent. Adding individual elements of the production cost calculations of Table 7.1 to the corresponding consumption costs of Table 7.2, we arrive at the estimates of total costs given in Table 19.6 for various assumptions about tariff rates. For each structure of tariff rates considered, there corresponds a particular coefficient of variation measuring the relative dispersion. The values of the coefficient of variation corresponding to the alternative sets of tariff rates are also given in Table 19.6. By comparing different coefficients of variation with different estimates of social cost for any given average tariff rate, one can isolate the effect of a change in that coefficient on welfare cost. Within the relevant range of parameter values, tariff rates, and coefficients of variation, an increase (decrease) in the coefficient of variation of the tariff distortions of 0.1 seems to raise (lower) the social cost of the distortions by slightly less than 1 percent of national income.

These calculations serve to indicate the order of magnitude of the social gains of CU participation engendered by the reduction in the degree of dispersion of tariffs likely to result from the adoption of a complete set of common external tariffs. Since we have seen from the calculations presented in Tables 19.2 to 19.5 that the reductions in the coefficient of variation of the tariff structures of actual CUs are generally at least 0.1 and could for certain prospective CUs run as high as 0.5, the welfare gain of this single effect of CU participation would seem to be at least 1 percent of GNP and could be considerably higher in some not unrealistic circumstances.

One must bear in mind that the validity of our results is limited on the grounds that: (1) the calculations account only for distortions imposed by tariffs; (2) tariffs may not be as great an impediment to foreign trade as quantitative restrictions; and (3) there exist various limitations on the method used for calculating the welfare cost of such distortions (which were reviewed in Chapter 7). Still, our analysis is general and can be applied to any type of distortion, including quantitative restrictions. In fact, as was shown in Chapter 7, it is always possible to translate quantitative restrictions into their tariff equivalents, enabling us to analyze the entire protective structure in common terms. Finally, our analysis would lead to specific provisions for removal, reduction, or at least standardization of quantitative restrictions, which in principle can be built into regional trade arrangements (and in fact are commonly a part of those arrangements).

Terms of Trade Effects

The Vinerian analysis also ignores the terms of trade effect. We have already seen that, although of considerable potential importance and relevance, terms of trade effects cannot be treated systematically, except by a full-fledged general equilibrium analysis. Such an analysis would involve the complete specification of the trade offer curves of each CU member and each relevant group of nonmembers—a task of considerable difficulty.

Theoretical analyses on the basis of three- or four-country general equilibrium models provided by Arndt (1968, 1969) or the n country models of Kemp (1969) have demonstrated that, once terms of trade effects are admitted, welfare of individual CU members, of the CU as a whole, and of the rest of the world will no longer generally coincide. Distributional effects between and among union partners, between and among nonunion countries, and between union members as a whole and nonunion members as a whole become possible and, in fact, probable. The welfare effects of a CU thus come to depend upon the particular CU, upon the particular country or countries inside or outside of the CU, and the circumstances of each.[11] Krauss (1972) has suggested that the distributional effects could justifiably be considered in even greater detail, such as at the level of producers of an individual commodity in an individual country or even at the level of the owners of an individual factor of production within that industry and country.

If the membership of the CU is large enough so that the members of the CU can collectively exercise some degree of monopsony power over their imports or monopoly power over their exports, CU participation can bring its members some terms of trade benefits (at the expense of the rest of the world). Although in such situations CU participation may not offer the only means of capitalizing on these benefits, it may constitute one of the most durable and effective means of doing so (Arndt 1968).

Dynamic Effects

If economies of scale are introduced, general equilibrium analysis becomes completely inoperable, except in special circumstances. In a partial equilibrium setting, economies of scale can be handled by imparting a downward slope to S_h and/or S_p in Figure 19.1. The net result is, however, simply to require consideration of a number of additional factors, such as the relative position of the average cost curve of union members, the elasticity of cost with respect to scale, and differences in average cost among CU members, making generalizations even more difficult. However, except in cases where no union members can compete with imports from the rest of the world at the preunion tariff rate, the benefits of CU participation are likely to be greater in the presence of economies of scale than without them.[12]

Closely related to economies of scale is the learning-by-doing effect. If (1) the attraction of a larger market, or a larger pool of resources as a result of CU participation, makes it possible to start local production in a certain industry earlier than it would have been possible without the CU and (2) efficiency increases with experience in production or investment, additional economies derived from the learning can and should be attributed to CU participation.

No matter how narrowly commodities or industries are defined, the level of aggregation in Viner- or Balassa-type analyses is bound to be excessive, causing some potential advantages of CU participation to be ignored. This is because, aside from economies of scale, learning-by-doing, and interindustry specialization, competition among different firms in the same industry may induce the individual firms to take advantage of economies derived from longer production runs and from reducing machine "down time" for conversion of equipment to different product lines and specifications, thus achieving greater specialization and efficiency within the industry.[13]

Also overlooked in the traditional model of CUs is the possible effect of increased competition on "X-efficiency." Whereas in the

---

[11]Vanek (1965), however, has argued that the analysis can be facilitated through the assumption that the CU adopts a "compensating common tariff," that is, a set of tariffs on different commodities that leaves the volume of trade and the terms of trade of the rest of the world unchanged. The analysis of the net as well as distributional effects can thereby be confined to the effects on the union partners alone.

[12]See Corden (1972) for a discussion of several alternative possibilities of CU benefits in the presence of economies of scale.

[13]These economies have received much attention in the work of Balassa (1965, 1971). See also Grubel's (1970) questions concerning the likelihood of such effects.

conventional analysis it is usually assumed that all firms, industries, or economies are operating in such a way that they are always on their production frontiers, the advocates of X-efficiency argue that they in fact tend to operate at points inside these frontiers. Through the greater competition that intra-regional trade would be likely to encourage, managerial personnel may be forced to face up to the competition by becoming technically more efficient in the sense of moving closer to their production frontiers, thereby raising the level of income and welfare.[14]

The traditional analysis also assumes that the quantity and quality of factors of production are given. However, increasing recognition has been given to the fact that factors of production are mobile internationally. Scarce factors, such as capital and skills, are particularly likely to move to areas where exports are increasing and the composition of trade is changing, bringing about changes in relative factor prices which, in turn, help induce additional factor flows. Thus, the supply of productive factors may be affected by CU participation through its effect on the level and composition of trade. There may be not only a net inflow of productive factors to the CU but also, particularly in the case of a common market, a redistribution in the supply of productive factors within the region to achieve greater efficiency in allocation. Admittedly, these effects may imply inequality in the distribution of the benefits of CUs among participating countries, which may create tensions that may ultimately constrain or even reverse the political commitment to economic integration.

Alternatively (but what may amount to the same thing), as Caves (1965b), Ranis and Fei (1961), and W. A. Lewis (1954) have pointed out, there may be surplus resources that can be used for producing commodities that can be exported to other members of the CU. If in a foreign exchange-constrained world, trade balances are improved as a result of CU participation (as has been sug-

gested by Resnick and Truman 1973, and various others), relaxation of the foreign exchange constraint can lead to increases in income and welfare. In each of these circumstances, even trade-diverting CUs can be beneficial, especially if the CU has a payments arrangement that conserves on foreign exchange.

Transport costs are also ignored in the traditional analysis. In some cases where internal exchanges are encumbered by large distances or physical obstacles, CU participation may encourage the exchange of commodities between contiguous portions of different countries, thereby economizing on transport costs.[15]

Being entirely static in its outlook, the traditional analysis ignores the possibility of dynamic externalities associated with CU—induced changes in income distribution or in industrial structure. It also ignores the possibilities that technological change might be induced by the increased trade.[16] Moreover, it assumes away the possibility that advantages could be derived from harmonization and coordination of policies among member countries resulting from CU participation. Since the external tariff rates of CUs are settled by negotiation at the regional level, usually on the basis of some rather general formulas for harmonizing preunion differences in tariff rates among countries, CU participation has the effect of freeing (or at least relieving to some extent) public officials from the constant harassment of local interest groups pressing for higher rates of effective protection. As Tullock (1967) has argued, this permits entrepreneurs to go back to what they should be doing: running their businesses rather than courting government officials.

Measurement

Few of these interesting but difficult to quantify effects are explicitly ruled out in Balassa's

---

[14]Leibenstein (1966) made a strong case for this view. Using a definition of X-efficiency in which X-efficiency is a function of managerial effort and the utility of managers is a function of income and leisure, Corden (1970) has shown that an increase in X-efficiency could take place only in rather special circumstances. However, these circumstances, involving some asymmetry in behavior between exporters and import competitors, may be quite realistic (J. Williamson 1971).

[15]For example, before the effective partition of Pakistan into Pakistan and Bangladesh, B. I. Cohen (1969) argued that a customs union between India and Pakistan would be beneficial in enabling both East and West Pakistan to take advantage of transport savings by trading with contiguous parts of India rather than with each other. On the other hand, where customs unions are formed between noncontiguous countries, transport costs might be increased rather than lowered.

[16]For advocacy of some of these more dynamic effects, see Cooper and Massell (1965), H. G. Johnson (1965a), Bhambri (1962), Balassa (1965, 1971), Mikesell (1965), and Kreinin (1964).

(1967) method of measuring the trade creation effects. Some of these effects may have been captured in the applications of the Balassa method to the EEC and CACM already mentioned. However, by deflating the percentage increase in imports by the percentage change in income (which is the definition of the elasticity of imports with respect to income), Balassa's method eliminates any effects of the income growth attributable to CU participation from the estimates of net trade creation. Since most of these factors would affect income directly or indirectly, it is extremely doubtful that those estimates have in fact captured much in the way of the more general effects of CUs.

If the Balassa method had been successful in including these more general effects, it would be clear from the magnitudes reported (adding about 0.1 percent per annum to the income growth rate) that their overall impact has been very small in both the EEC and CACM. In our judgment, however, such an assessment is at best premature and at worst wrong and misleading.

If the general as well as trade creation effects are negligible, one would not expect to find significant structural changes in the economies of CU participants in the period immediately following formation of the union. Yet in the experience of the CACM, rather remarkable changes have taken place since the establishment of the union. For example, while intraregional trade constituted less than 5 percent of total trade of Central America in the decade before establishment (in 1961) of the CACM, by 1968 it constituted 25 percent of total trade. During the same period, Central America's dependence on trade with a single extraregional country (the United States) decreased from about 60 percent of total trade to about 35 percent. Similarly, dependence on the three traditional exports—coffee, bananas, and cotton—decreased from about 80 percent to a little over 50 percent of total exports; at the same time, the share of manufactures in Central American exports increased from 1 percent to 20 percent of the total. The share of manufacturing in GDP increased from 11 to 17 percent in the region as a whole; also capital inflows from private as well as public sources jumped from $50 million per annum to more than $150 million per annum in recent years.[17]

[17]For more details, see Nugent (1974, Chapter 1).

Of course, some of these structural changes may merely be indicative of trade diversion and therefore may not signify real gains in trade and income. In order to reach a more careful assessment of the effects of the CACM in the growth of trade and income in the region, and in the process, to overcome the limitations of the more traditional estimation procedures, in the following paragraphs we shall demonstrate the application of two alternative means of evaluation: the export performance approach to the measurement of trade creation and income growth and the production function approach to the measurement of overall income growth.

Whereas the Balassa method assumes that the differences between preunion and postunion elasticities of imports with respect to income are due solely to the creation of the CU, the export performance approach to trade creation attempts to account for as many factors as possible (including CU participation) that may differ over time or between countries. In this way, the export performance approach more clearly distinguishes the CU effect from these other influences. While this approach captures only the effects of CU participation on trade, it should account for all such effects, including the indirect and dynamic effects. Moreover, the effect on trade can easily be converted to an effect on income, as in the Balassa approach.

Actually, the export performance approach has already been presented. The reader will recall from Chapters 17 and 18 our attempts to explain variations in export performance among a sample of 38 LDCs for the period 1949–1967. A fairly large number of explanatory variables (identified in Chapter 17) were utilized. Among these were a number of both demand and supply factors, including dummy variables for participation in various regional trading arrangements, such as the CACM, LAFTA, EEC, and EFTA. While, as was shown in Table 17.1, the effects of the dummy variables for LAFTA and EFTA were in all cases insignificant and that of the EEC (indicating the association status of Greece and Turkey) negative, the CACM dummy variable was consistently positive and significant in all different specifications of the estimating equations. Indeed, the results indicated that participation in the CACM has added about 2 percent to the annual growth rate of total exports in the Central American countries.

Multiplying this increase in the export growth rate by 0.276 (the regression coefficient obtained by regressing the growth rate of GDP on the export growth rate), we obtain as an estimate of the contribution of the direct and indirect effects of trade creation on income growth in the CACM, 0.0055 or 0.55 percent per annum. This is about five times as large as the estimates obtained by the modified Balassa approach.

An alternative and more direct quantitative assessment of the overall effect of CU participation on welfare and growth can be obtained by estimating an aggregate production function for CU members from time series data with dummy variables for the formation of the CU.

Assuming an aggregate production function of the Cobb-Douglas form and a "neutral" customs union, we obtain the following relationship for a country or group of countries that joins a CU during a specific period of time:

$$GNP = AK^{\alpha}L^{\beta}e^{\gamma_1 CU_1}e^{\gamma_2 CU_2} \qquad (1)$$

where K, L, CU_1, and CU_2 represent capital, labor, and two dummy variables for the commencement of the customs union. The two CU dummy variables, CU_1 and CU_2,[18] with coefficients γ_1 and γ_2 respectively, distinguish between the once-and-for-all effect, CU_1, representing a shift in the intercept, and the gradual or continuous effect, CU_2, representing a gradual drift in the elasticities after the formation of the union. Time series data could then be used to estimate this function —subject, of course, to all the usual problems of time series analysis, such as multicollinearity, simultaneous equation bias, and measurement errors. The coefficients obtained for α and β would be interpreted in the usual way, and the coefficients of the CU dummy variables, γ_1 and γ_2, would represent the percentage increases in total productivity attributable to the formation of the customs union via the once-and-for-all and gradual effects respectively.

To account for the effect of CU participation on resource formation (such as labor or capital), one could first estimate the direct effects of CU on these variables and then the indirect effect via the effect of these variables,

L and K, on GNP. For present purposes, we shall ignore the effect of CU on K and L in order to concentrate on estimating the direct effects of CU on GNP.[19]

Assuming constant returns to scale, an attempt has been made to mitigate the problems common to most empirical applications of this approach, namely, the lack of adequate employment data and multicollinearity among variables, by dividing equation 1 through by L, giving

$$\frac{GNP}{L} = Ae^{\gamma_1 CU_1}e^{\gamma_2 CU_2}\left(\frac{K}{L}\right)^{\alpha} \qquad (2)$$

Simultaneously with the institution of the CU, participating countries may have been affected by changes in their international terms of trade, the completion of transportation links, and perhaps other factors. Since each of these factors could have appeared without the CU, we have tried to distinguish their effect from that of the CU itself by adding three additional variables: a dummy variable, R, with an initial value of zero and additional 1.0s after the completion of each important link in the regional transport system; an index of the international terms of trade, TT, to account for the influence of world market conditions for exports and imports; and time, T, as a proxy for the various other factors affecting per capita income, which vary with time. The expanded and stochastic version of equation 2 is

$$\frac{GNP}{L} = A\left(\frac{K}{L}\right)^{\alpha}TT^{\beta}e^{\gamma_1 CU_1}e^{\gamma_2 CU_2}e^{\sigma R}e^{\delta T}V \qquad (3)$$

where V is a random disturbance. The log linear version of equation 3 is given by

$$\log\frac{GNP}{L} = \log A + E(u) + \alpha \log\frac{K}{L}$$
$$+ \gamma_1 CU_1 + \gamma_2 CU_2 + \beta \log TT$$
$$+ \sigma R + \delta T + u^* \qquad (4)$$

where $u = \log V$ and $u^* = u - E(u)$ so that $E(u^*)$ becomes zero.[20]

---

[18]CU_1 is defined by zeros for all years prior to CU and by one for postunion years, whereas CU_2 increases from one to 2, 3, 4 . . . in subsequent postunion years.

[19]The effects of the formation of the EEC and EFTA on foreign investment in Europe have been studied by Scaperlanda (1967), Scaperlanda and Mauer (1969), d'Arge (1969), and Schmitz (1970), while those on the CACM have been studied by Nugent (1974).

[20]The variable TT, in contrast to the dummy variables, CU, R, and T, is specified in double logarithmic form. This specification allows one to treat the exogenous external conditions like a factor of production, and permits one to interpret β as an elasticity which is invariant with respect to the values that the terms of trade indexes take.

This method has been applied with respect to CACM countries on the basis of time series data for the period 1950–1966 presented in Nugent (1974, Appendix A). Selected results obtained for the five individual countries of the CACM, as well as for the region as a whole, are shown in Table 19.7. In some cases, some variables have shown little influence on per capita income and have thus been eliminated from the equation with little loss in explanatory power. The remarkable fact is that without exception one or the other (or in some cases both) of the CU dummy variables was found to have had a fairly significant positive influence on per capita income. While because of the multicollinearity among explanatory variables,[21] the results were in some respects rather sensitive to changes in specification, the influence of the CU dummy variables was consistent, their coefficients being generally quite insensitive to such changes. Some of the results had very low Durbin-Watson (DW) coefficients, indicating autocorrelation among the residuals, and these equations were rerun using an autoregressive scheme.

The results indicate that increases in the capital-labor ratio had in all cases a highly significant effect on per capita income. The terms of trade indexes and the disembodied technological change were significant in some cases. Of immediate relevance, however, are the coefficients of the CU dummy variables. By taking the antilog of the coefficients of the CU variables in Table 19.7, the reader can easily determine the percentage increase in per capita income attributable to formation of the CACM in each and every country.

Thus, by referring to the results for the CACM as a whole, one can see that the one-shot increase in per capita income resulting from CACM participation has been 5.2 percent. Moreover, CACM countries have also benefited by an additional increase of 0.3 percent in the annual growth rate as a result of participation in the union. For some of the individual countries, the effect seems even larger.

The crudeness of this procedure can hardly be overstated. Some upward bias in the estimates may be possible, insofar as the

CU variables have picked up nonlinearities in the production functions. However, this overestimate is counterbalanced by the fact that no provision has been made for the probably positive effect of CU participation on resource formation. The relative consistency of the various results and the relative insensitivity of the estimates of γ_1 and γ_2 to changes in specification tend to lead to confidence that for an overall order of magnitude these estimates may be fairly accurate.

The results obtained for the CACM from the production function approach are thus quite consistent with those obtained from the export performance approach. Moreover, both sets of results suggest that the benefits of CU participation may be considerably greater than indicated by the traditional methods of estimating the trade creation gains alone.

Summary and Conclusions

In Chapter 19, we have presented a study in prescriptive economics that combines elements of Chapter 7, on the welfare cost of tariffs, and Chapter 17, on the export performance approach of international trade. The objective has been to identify the gains that can be obtained by a specific form of economic integration, the creation of customs unions.

The welfare gains of a CU have traditionally been analyzed in terms of the trade creation effects that result from trade with CU partners who are not subject to tariffs, and the trade diversion effects of shifting trade from the lowest cost supplier in the rest of the world to the higher cost CU partner supplier. Measurement of these welfare gains through a simple partial equilibrium model has yielded estimates of the contribution of CUs to the rate of growth of income that are of negligible magnitude.

We have expanded the analysis within the general equilibrium framework by explicitly considering the gains from making tariff rates more homogeneous, as discussed in Chapter 7. Indeed, in our study of four CUs (the EEC, the CACM, the Andean group, and the proposed Arab Common Market), we have found reductions of 0.1 to 0.5 in the coefficients of variation of tariff rates between preunion and postunion periods. By combining representative coefficients of variation with typical values of the parameters that enter the production costs and the consump-

---

[21]The correlations between log K/L and T were particularly strong, making it seldom possible to retain both variables in the selected results—one almost always overshadowed the other.

Table 19.7 Selected Estimates of the Production Function Approach to Measurement of the Effects of Customs Union Participation, Central American Common Market Countries

Country	Regression Results	$\bar{R}^2$	DW
Central America	$\log \dfrac{GNP}{L} = 1.52 + 0.614 \log \dfrac{K}{L} + 0.032 \log TT + 0.050\, CU_1 + 0.003\, CU_2 - 0.012\, R + 0.007\, T$ $(1.446) \quad (3.507) \quad (2.304) \quad (5.193) \quad (-3.121) \quad (1.023)$	0.964	1.75
	$\log \dfrac{GNP}{L} = 0.04 + 0.845 \log \dfrac{K}{L} + 0.045 \log TT + 0.022\, CU_1 + 0.002\, CU_2$ $(6.802) \quad (4.377) \quad (2.210) \quad (3.210)$	0.939	1.36
Costa Rica	$\log \dfrac{GNP}{L} = -0.40 + 0.978 \log \dfrac{K}{L} + 0.004 \log TT + 0.024\, CU_1 + 0.017\, CU_2 + 0.024\, R - 0.022\, T$ $(0.967) \quad (0.312) \quad (0.715) \quad (1.472) \quad (0.639) \quad (-0.793)$	0.868	2.32
	$\log \dfrac{GNP}{L} = 4.23 + 0.249 \log \dfrac{K}{L} + 0.018\, CU_2$ $(2.436) \quad (2.636)$	0.897	2.48
El Salvador	$\log \dfrac{GNP}{L} = 3.32 + 0.370 \log \dfrac{K}{L} + 0.010 \log TT + 0.026\, CU_1 + 0.024\, CU_2 - 0.015\, T$ $(0.393) \quad (1.044) \quad (1.744) \quad (2.026) \quad (-0.982)$	0.627	2.18
	$\log \dfrac{GNP}{L} = 1.52 + 0.631 \log \dfrac{K}{L} + 0.036 \log TT + 0.080\, CU_1$ $(2.383) \quad (2.532) \quad (2.236)$	0.531	1.16
	$\log \dfrac{GNP}{L} = 3.70 + 0.285 \log \dfrac{K}{L} + 0.052 \log TT + 0.020\, CU_2$ $(0.774) \quad (1.526) \quad (1.523)$	0.594	2.29

Guatemala

$$\log \frac{GNP}{L} = \begin{array}{c} 1.38 + 0.646 \log \frac{K}{L} + 0.027 \log TT - 0.011\, CU_1 + 0.019\, CU_2 - 0.011\, R + 0.005\, T \\ (2.238) \qquad (2.529) \qquad (-0.616) \qquad (2.815) \qquad (-0.621) \quad (1.291) \end{array}$$
0.926 2.42

$$\log \frac{GNP}{L} = \begin{array}{c} 0.59 + 0.771 \log \frac{K}{L} + 0.032 \log TT + 0.015\, CU_2 \\ (3.710) \qquad (4.083) \qquad (4.080) \end{array}$$
0.938 2.24

Honduras

$$\log \frac{GNP}{L} = \begin{array}{c} -10.07 + 2.548 \log \frac{K}{L} - 0.025 \log TT + 0.076\, CU_1 + 0.025\, CU_2 + 0.015\, R - 0.029\, T \\ (1.879) \qquad (-1.422) \qquad (1.128) \qquad (2.851) \qquad (0.469) \quad (-1.596) \end{array}$$
0.817 1.70

$$\log \frac{GNP}{L} = \begin{array}{c} 1.72 + 0.581 \log \frac{K}{L} + 0.013\, CU_2 \\ (3.415) \qquad (4.814) \end{array}$$
0.864 1.79

Nicaragua

$$\log \frac{GNP}{L} = \begin{array}{c} -9.42 + 2.449 \log \frac{K}{L} + 0.029 \log TT + 0.136\, CU_1 - 0.005\, CU_2 + 0.044\, R - 0.059\, T \\ (5.309) \qquad (1.905) \qquad (2.979) \qquad (-0.409) \qquad (1.672) \quad (-3.800) \end{array}$$
0.919 3.08

$$\log \frac{GNP}{L} = \begin{array}{c} -0.35 + 0.920 \log \frac{K}{L} + 0.055 \log TT + 0.032\, CU_1 \\ (7.655) \qquad (3.841) \qquad (1.857) \end{array}$$
0.882 1.95

Notes: Numbers in parentheses indicate t-values. For definition of variables, see the text.
Source: Nugent, J. B. (1974), *Economic Integration in Central America: Empirical Investigations*. Baltimore: Johns Hopkins University Press, p. 73.

tion costs of tariffs (analyzed in Chapter 7), we have therefore concluded that welfare gains of CU participation from this one effect alone could amount to at least 1 percent of GNP, even under assumptions that are not overly strong.

In an attempt to include some dynamic effects of CU participation, such as those of economies of scale, gains in efficiency, and utilization of surplus resources, we have studied the effects of the creation of the CACM for the individual member countries within an export performance approach framework and again via an aggregate production function approach. In each case, the variable representing the CU participation was found to have significant impact on GNP per capita. For the CACM as a whole, the effect of CU participation on per capita income has exceeded 5 percent. We conclude, therefore, that by joining a customs union of countries at similar levels of development and with similar economic structures, LDCs may be able to take advantage of some of the dynamic as well as static benefits of international trade, while largely avoiding some of the backwash effects of openness that were spelled out in previous chapters.

Part VI
Development Disequilibrium: Planning

The substantive content of planning depends, to a large extent, on considerations about the degree to and the efficiency with which the market mechanism accomplishes economic decision making. In an economy with unfettered market mechanisms, the content of planning might well be limited to the normal task of government budgeting. Where market imperfections are substantial and price distortions significant, planning may be used as a mechanism to correct for disequilibria. The alternative is, of course, to make the market mechanisms work better, but this may be more easily said than done. However, even where the market mechanisms are working relatively well, circumstances can arise—as has been demonstrated—in which development is not smooth, continuous, and automatic, and the optimum development path cannot be achieved simply by making marginal adjustments. In such circumstances, planning may be not only useful but indeed imperative. To appreciate the potential importance of planning, one need only realize that the selection of a particular growth path at one point in time inevitably forecloses alternatives available then, and perhaps at all future points in time.

Planning decisions often set off processes and changes that are irreversible and irrevocable.

The considerable attention planning has received in recent years has come none too soon. For many a country, however, there has been a short distance from the appreciation of the potential benefits of planning to what we defined as "planning fundamentalism," in Chapter 1. In their frenzy to plan, some countries have been driving hell-bent the wrong way, because the plans they have followed have not only been suboptimal but perhaps downright injurious. If a plan is not carefully checked for feasibility and internal consistency, it may lead to nothing but frustration and eventual disaffection with planning and planners. Moreover, if plans are to become more than irrelevant exercises and material for feeding the government printing presses, they must be translated into policy instruments that are effectuated in such a way that the plan objectives can be achieved.

Finally, the broad guidelines and goals of macroeconomic planning must be articulated in a series of well-coordinated and carefully designed and evaluated individual development projects, the "guts" of the development plan.

We begin in Chapter 20 at the micro level, with the selection of individual development projects. While project evaluation is grounded on the neoclassical tools of partial equilibrium and consumer surplus developed in Part II, in the context of project appraisal in LDCs it is necessary to relax many of the restrictive assumptions of that analysis. Chapter 20 begins with the strict neoclassical framework and then progressively relaxes assumptions to achieve greater realism. This culminates in some operational methods for selecting projects even when investments are risky and indivisible, and market prices are distorted by taxes, monopolies, tariffs, and other factors. In Chapter 21, we demonstrate general equilibrium methods for evaluating projects where externalities are involved.

In earlier parts of the book, we have not hesitated to spell out policy implications of our analysis whenever it seemed appropriate. At the macroeconomic level, however, any one policy change will undoubtedly affect many variables other than those it is specifically designed to influence. These secondary effects may require additional corrective or compensatory action. Development planners are normally concerned with a multiplicity of objectives and have a number of policy instruments at their disposal. There are considerable interdependencies among goals and policy instruments. Moreover, these interdependencies tend to strengthen as the time horizon of the planner increases. Policy decisions with regard to macroeconomic plans must, therefore, be treated within a general equilibrium context. Planners, however, cannot hide in ivory towers. They must be able to recognize short-run problems as they arise and be prepared to deal with them without losing sight of long-run objectives. If the short-run problems turn into crises, there will be no long run.

Chapter 21 is primarily devoted to macro-planning and quite appropriately utilizes general equilibrium methods. We first discuss criteria for evaluating macroeconomic plans—internal consistency, feasibility, and optimality. Then we present and demonstrate methods for testing plans and planning models with respect to these features. We close the chapter by treating a more universal problem of planning, the failure to link planning goals with the specific policy instruments that would provide for plan implementation. The methods developed allow us to quantify the potential benefits of policy planning and coordination within countries over time or between and among different countries. This is what planning is all about.

Chapter 20
Micro-Planning: Project Appraisal

The mobilization of resources and the achievement of technological change (reviewed in Part III), and the ability to bring about desirable structural changes both with respect to the domestic economy and the international economy (reviewed in Parts IV and V respectively), are of considerable consequence for development. Yet in the long run, the success of any such changes will be conditioned by the efficiency and effectiveness with which the mobilized resources and technical and structural changes are articulated in the form of project proposals and then allocated among alternative proposals. Project formulation is an activity that inevitably involves engineers as well as economists and is therefore beyond the scope of this book. Project evaluation, however, the process of selecting the individual development projects to be included in the development plan, is the subject of this chapter.

If markets and information about the present and the future were perfect and complete and there were no externalities, indivisibilities, and so on, projects could be selected simply on the basis of ordinary profit maximization. These conditions are patently unrealistic in LDCs, and as a result, market distortions, externalities, and disequilibria must be reflected in investment decision making. This calls for the use of a broader concept of social profitability, as opposed to private profit maximization. Yet, in a world of imperfect information and considerable complexity and interdependence, values of social parameters, such as shadow prices, which are necessary for computing social profitability, are not readily available. Project evaluators, therefore, need a set of guidelines to assist them in estimating the social costs and benefits of alternative projects under consideration.

Project appraisal focuses to a considerable

degree on questions of efficiency of the type dealt with in development statics, in Part II. Nevertheless, since it is usually new projects that are to be evaluated and therefore additional resources that must be mobilized, and future revenue and cost streams that need to be projected, some aspects of development dynamics, Parts III and IV, are also intimately involved. Projects may also have effects on structural factors, such as income distribution, the nature of dualism, the degree of sectoral articulation, and the structure of foreign trade. If so, these aspects must also be considered. Moreover, since the position of the project evaluator is intermediate between the manager, who would implement the project, and the central macroeconomic planner, who designs the overall environment within which individual projects are to be selected, project evaluators should make a conscious effort to avoid the introduction of unwanted inconsistencies between overall plan formulation and detailed implementation.

Simultaneous consideration of all these factors may require an analytic tool kit of such complexity as to be unworkable. It is desirable to make simplifications wherever they are appropriate. The determination of what simplifications can usefully be made will necessarily depend on the circumstances prevailing in the country under consideration. Therefore, there is no single rule of thumb, evaluative criterion, or procedure that can be relied on in all situations.

This chapter is divided into three sections. We begin with a presentation of the traditional two-commodity neoclassical model of investment decisions, including a discussion of the "present value" and "internal rate of return" criteria and decision rules that are derived from the model. In the next section, we relax the assumptions of the simplified model, one at a time, and consider the implications of these changes for project appraisal. In the third section, we present a detailed critical examination of two of the more operational methods that have been proposed for project evaluation under realistic circumstances. Other simpler but generally less valid criteria for project appraisal in LDCs are discussed in the Appendix. General equilibrium approaches to project evaluation will be demonstrated in Chapter 21.

In accord with the early notions of capital

fundamentalism, the criteria for project evaluation have historically focused on the allocation of investment. Most of the concepts and techniques developed, however, are also applicable to the allocation of scarce resources in general. We will emphasize this generality.

Simplified Neoclassical Models for Investment Decision Making

Although investment decisions obviously affect economic activities in many different periods, an analysis of investment criteria and decision rules is generally predicated on one or the other of two highly simplified two-period models. In one, there are two distinct periods of time—a present and a future. In the other, there are a present period and an indefinite future period (or an infinite number of future periods, in which consumption and income are to remain constant).[1]

Both of these simplified models are presented graphically in Figure 20.1. From this diagram, it can be seen how the individual or society maximizes utility, given the utility function (defined in terms of present consumption C_0 and future consumption C_1 and represented by the series of indifference curves U_0, U_1, U_2, . . .), the endowment in terms of present and future income potential, Y, the transformation function, PP, representing the productive opportunities for converting present consumption into future consumption, and vice versa, and the market opportunities for doing so given by the set of parallel lines M_0M_0, M_1M_1, M_2M_2. The interest rate, r, determines the slopes of the market opportunity curves, MM, which are given by $-(1 + r)$. The higher the interest rate, the steeper the downward slope of MM and the lower (in terms of the vertical axis C_1) will be the point of tangency to PP, which in the diagram is designated P^*. If the individual (or society) is able to take advantage of both productive and market opportunities, he will move from the endowed position, Y, along PP to P^*, where M_1M_1 is tangent to PP. He then follows that market opportunity line, M_1M_1 to the point of tangency with the highest attainable indifference curve, which in this case is U_2, at point C^*. Wealth, defined as the present discounted value of present and future consump-

[1] The analystical portions of this section depend heavily upon Hirshleifer (1970).

Figure 20.1 The Two–Period Optimization Model

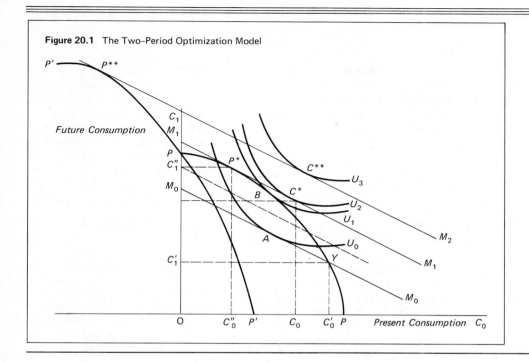

tion, is thus maximized at C^* with a value of $C_0^* + 1/(1 + r) C_1^*$. The optimum position requires a sacrifice in terms of present consumption out of endowed current income of C_0' $- C_0''$, which is invested in order to produce C_1'' of future consumption. $C_1'' - C_1^*$ of claims on future consumption is then exchanged for $C_0^* - C_0''$ of present consumption to bring the individual (or society) to C^*.

Note that, should the individual not be able to take advantage of the productive opportunities, PP, he would maximize utility by moving from his endowment point along his market opportunity line, $M_0 M_0$, to point A, where $M_0 M_0$ is tangent to the highest attainable indifference curve, U_0. Alternatively, if he is able to take advantage of his productive opportunities but not of the exchange or market opportunities, he will move from the endowment position, Y, along PP to the point of tangency with the highest attainable indifference curve, in this case U_1 at point B. Factor market imperfections, which may bend either PP or MM inward, will therefore lower wealth, defined as the present discounted value of attainable present and future consumption.

Present Value and Internal Rate of Return Criteria and Decision Rules

An investment *criterion* is most commonly a formula by which alternative investment opportunities or packages can be compared or ranked. A *decision rule* states, "invest in the project if . . . (some specific condition with respect to the investment criterion is satisfied); otherwise do not invest in it." Errors can be made in the choice of an investment criterion, a decision rule, or both.

The most comprehensive and general of the criteria and rules proposed for analyzing and prescribing investment decisions is that of *present value*. The present value criterion is given by the formula

$$V_0 = R_0 + \frac{R_1}{(1 + r_1)} + \frac{R_2}{(1 + r_1)(1 + r_2)} + \cdots$$

$$+ \frac{R_T}{(1 + r_1)(1 + r_2) \ldots (1 + r_T)} \quad (1)$$

where V_0 is the present value of the net returns stream, $R_0, R_1, \ldots, R_T$, over the finite time horizon, T, discounted by the expected interest rates, $r_1, r_2, \ldots, r_T$. When these interest rates are assumed to remain constant, equation 1 simplifies to

$$V_0 = R_0 + \frac{R_1}{(1+r)} + \frac{R_2}{(1+r)^2} + \cdots + \frac{R_T}{(1+r)^T} \tag{2}$$

In the special case in which $R_0 = 0$ and the net returns stream is constant ($R_1 = R_2 = \cdots = R_T = \overline{R}$) over an infinite time horizon, the criterion can be simplified even further to

$$V_0 = \frac{\overline{R}}{r} \tag{3}$$

or when $R_0 \neq 0$ to

$$V_0 = \frac{\overline{R}(1+r)}{r} \tag{3a}$$

If in addition to the simplifying assumptions allowing us to use equation 3a in place of equation 1, it can be assumed that the welfare goal is to maximize wealth (in the sense of present discounted value of future consumption) and that market opportunities, such as those given by the lines M_0M_0, M_1M_1, . . . exist, the maximization of V_0 would yield an optimum like that of C^* in Figure 20.1. Assuming that the present value criterion could be applied to each alternative combination of investment projects, the choice of that set of investment projects would locate a position, such as P^*, from which the individual could exchange his way to C^*. However, it is often not possible to evaluate all combinations of individual projects, and thus, the criterion is commonly applied to single projects. The decision rule in that case is to adopt the project if $V_0 > 0$. Naturally, such an application is valid only if the individual projects are independent of each other.

Another and rather similar criterion that has frequently been proposed is the *internal rate of return* or marginal efficiency of capital criterion. The internal rate of return, ρ, may be expressed as

$$0 = R_0 + \frac{R_1}{(1+\rho)} + \frac{R_2}{(1+\rho)^2} + \cdots + \frac{R_T}{(1+\rho)^T} \tag{4}$$

The net returns stream, $R_0, R_1, \ldots, R_T$, for the finite horizon, T, is common to both the present value and the internal rate of return criteria. However, instead of computing the present value V_0, given r, as in the present value criterion, the internal rate of return criterion solves for ρ (given a present value of zero). The decision rule usually employed with this criterion is to invest only if $\rho > r$.

Following I. Fisher (1930) it may be convenient to apply this criterion by comparing two alternative projects or by comparing net returns streams resulting from the project with those which would hold in the absence of the project. In other words, there will be two different returns streams to be compared, indicated by the superscripts A and B. One can then substitute the differences in the net returns streams, for example, $R_0^A - R_0^B$, $R_1^A - R_1^B$, and so on, in equation 4, yielding

$$0 = (R_0^A - R_0^B) + \frac{(R_1^A - R_1^B)}{(1+\rho)} + \frac{(R_2^A - R_2^B)}{(1+\rho)^2}$$
$$+ \cdots + \frac{(R_T^A - R_T^B)}{(1+\rho)^T} \tag{4a}$$

This version is known as the *rate of return over cost* criterion. Assuming that A requires a larger present sacrifice in consumption than B, that is, that $R_0^A - R_0^B$ is negative, the decision rule is then to invest in A if ρ, calculated from equation 4a, is greater than r; otherwise to invest in B.

Assuming perfect capital markets, that is, that there exist opportunities for converting present consumption into claims on future consumption and vice versa, wherein the price is not affected by the quantities exchanged (opportunities such as those represented by the straight lines MM in Figure 20.1), and considering only two periods, all of these decision rules give identical (and correct) decisions as to whether or not to invest. Each criterion involves a comparison of the point Y representing the endowment stream, C'_0, C'_1, with other points (presumably on PP), such as B or P^*. Since these other points with their net returns streams, R_0, R_1, are to the left of Y, it is presumed that R_0 would be negative and R_1 would be positive.[2] Even if these conditions should be fulfilled and therefore the various *decision rules* give identical results, the different *criteria* may not yield the same ranking of projects. For example, a small project may have a larger internal rate of return than a large project and therefore rank above the large project on the basis of this criterion, but because of its size advantage, the large project may have the larger

[2]If this is not in fact the case, there will be no $\rho > -1$ for which the simplified version of equation 4 would hold.

present value and therefore rank above the small project on the basis of the present value criterion.

Another situation in which the various decision rules give identical results is in equilibrium, where the level of investment in any project can be adjusted freely, and perfect competition prevails.[3] In such an equilibrium position, ρ is of course equal to r in every activity, and the present value of additional net investment will be zero. Both decision rules would indicate that no additional investment should be undertaken, the optimum position having already been attained. Furthermore, even if equilibrium does not obtain at a specific time, the existence of equilibrating mechanisms strong enough to ensure that the optimum is automatically attained obviates the need for any decision rule.

In more complicated and realistic situations, equivalence of the various decision rules breaks down. When this happens, the present value rule is generally correct in the sense that its application leads to the optimum point on the transformation surface; however, the use of the internal rate of return may be misleading. We can demonstrate this proposition with examples in which we maintain the assumptions of perfect capital markets and lack of externalities and we distinguish n periods.

First, to be consistent with equation 1, if interest rates are allowed to vary from one period to another, there is obviously no single r that can be compared to the value of ρ computed from equation 4.

Second, even with constant interest rates, but the need to choose between two mutually exclusive projects (A and B), the internal rate of return criterion can be misleading. For example, assume the following income streams over three time periods, 0, 1, and 2, for the two projects:

Project A: $R_0 = -10, R_1 = 20, R_2 = 10$
Project B: $R_0 = -10, R_1 = 0, R_2 = 40$

The internal rate of return, ρ, for project A, $\rho_A = 141.4$ percent, is greater than that for project B, $\rho_B = 100$ percent. At high interest rates (above 50 percent), project A would also have a higher present value, but at low interest rates, project B would have the higher

[3]Note that this was the context for which Keynes developed his concept of the marginal efficiency of capital (Ramsey 1970).

present value and would thus be the superior alternative. (Note, for example, that if $r = 0$, the present value of project B is 30 compared to only 20 for project A.) This example demonstrates that present value may not be a monotonic function of the interest rate. Thus, present value may be positive at some (low) interest rates, negative at other (higher) rates, and positive at other still higher interest rates, and so on.

Third, given the interest rate, the present value decision rule is unique and correct. However, the calculation of ρ, and subsequently $\rho - r$, will not be generally unique, and thus, the application of the internal rate of return rule may lead to ambiguity. This is the multiple roots problem. From Descartes' rule of signs, there will be as many positive solutions to ρ as there are changes in signs in the values of successive net returns, R. If we assume: (1) that R_0 is always negative; (2) that there is at least one subsequent R that is positive; and (3) that the final R is negative (e.g., because disposal costs exceed scrap value), there will always be a minimum of two positive solutions for ρ, and thus, ambiguity will almost always arise when the internal rate of return is utilized in such situations.

The Effects of Relaxing the Restrictive Assumptions of the Simplified Models

We have seen that the present value decision rule has more general validity than the alternatives. Furthermore, it is both simple to apply and objective in the sense that there is no need to know the relevant utility function, which in Figure 20.1 is summarized by the indifference curves, $U_0, U_1, \ldots$. However, the validity and the simplicity of the present value rule depends on a number of assumptions of the neoclassical intertemporal decision-making model. These crucial assumptions are: (1) that information is complete, that is, we know the streams $R_0, \ldots, R_T$; (2) that all markets, present and future, exist and are perfect; (3) that uncertainty is absent; (4) that there are no externalities or interdependencies among projects; and (5) that there are no distortions, thereby ensuring that market prices are identical to social opportunity costs for all commodities and resources.

In highly developed competitive market

economies, these assumptions are sometimes realistic enough that project evaluation can proceed by simply computing the present values. Given reliable estimates of future net returns streams, project appraisal becomes an extremely simple matter. In LDCs, however, where these assumptions are often violated, the ordinary present value rule becomes invalid unless it is modified. Since the necessary modification depends on which assumption is violated, we shall discuss each such assumption individually, considering alternative approaches to project evaluation.

Indivisibilities

The existence of indivisibilities implies that the returns streams of a project are not independent of its scale. This situation may be due to economies of scale in the utilization of technology or of other inputs. The relationship between scale and technology can be represented by a new transformation curve, such as $P'P'$ in Figure 20.1. This new technology is inferior within the northeast quadrant, but at higher levels of current sacrifice, that is, in the northwest quadrant to the left of point O, it becomes superior. If capital markets are still perfect, the optimal investment decision in this case would be to move from Y to P^{**} on the new transformation curve $P'P'$ rather than to P^* on the old or traditional transformation curve PP. This would afford the higher consumption standard given by C^{**} on U_3.

Indivisibilities may be relevant and important in many types of industrial investments. In electricity generation, for example, the choice of technique for small-scale production may lie between coal- and oil-based steam plants. For a larger scale, however, hydroelectric or atomic plants may be superior. Similarly, given the small size of the domestic market for industrial commodities in most LDCs, project evaluators are frequently asked to evaluate proposals for small-scale projects of an import substituting character. At first inspection, such projects may often appear to be economic. But under more careful scrutiny, such an investment bundle may turn out to be inferior to a smaller number of large-scale plants using different technologies, which can take advantage of economies of scale by exporting substantial portions of their output.

The decision-making calculus remains the same in the presence of indivisibilities. The present value criterion is correct in that it shows the larger investment to P^{**} to be superior to that which would lead to P^*. The consideration of indivisibilities thus places more of a burden on project formulation than on project evaluation. It suggests that, before proceeding to the evaluation of a project on the basis of the traditionally employed technology and scale, the project evaluator should seek assurances from engineers that all feasible technologies and scales have been considered.

Capital Market Imperfections

The existence of capital market imperfections, not unlike the existence of indivisibilities, complicates project evaluation and sometimes biases it in favor of small or large projects. Capital market imperfections appear in the form of differential rates of interest or as an absolute limitation on the amount of borrowing that can be undertaken.

Instead of a perfect capital market, we often observe a dual market with interest rates higher for borrowers than for lenders. In this case, we have two different sets of market opportunity lines, one with steeper slopes for borrowers and another with flatter slopes for lenders. These can be shown by using two different lines, $M_B M_B$ for borrowers, and $M_L M_L$ for lenders, in part a of Figure 20.2, instead of the single set MM in Figure 20.1. It is obvious from the geometry that there is no longer a unique productive optimum corresponding to P^* in Figure 20.1. The choice of a point in part a of Figure 20.2 that maximizes present value now depends upon the relevant range of PP within which tangency is to be achieved; and this, in turn, depends upon the position of the indifference curves, U_0, U_1, . . . , with respect to $M_B M_B$ and $M_L M_L$. If tangency with the highest indifference curve can be achieved by $M_B M_B$ somewhere between C and D, C will be the optimum production point with maximum present value. On the other hand, if that tangency can be achieved by $M_L M_L$ somewhere between A and B, B will be the optimum production point. If tangency with the highest indifference curve is attained between B and C, there will be no borrowing or lending and the production optimum will be attained at exactly the point of tangency.

Another form of imperfection, in which

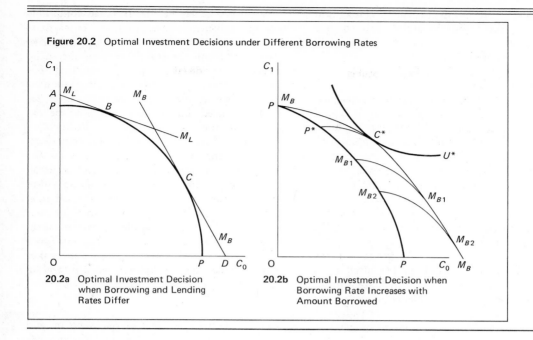

Figure 20.2 Optimal Investment Decisions under Different Borrowing Rates

20.2a Optimal Investment Decision when Borrowing and Lending Rates Differ

20.2b Optimal Investment Decision when Borrowing Rate Increases with Amount Borrowed

the rate of interest increases with the amount borrowed, is shown in part b of Figure 20.2. The market opportunity frontier indicated by $M_B M_B$ is the result of the superimposition of the envelope formed by the different borrowing curves, $P^* C^*$, $M_{B1} M_{B1}$, $M_{B2} M_{B2}$, and so on, on the productive opportunity frontier, PP. If tangency with the highest possible indifference curve, U^*, is obtained at C^* on $M_B M_B$, the relevant borrowing curve is $P^* C^*$, and the optimal investment decision will bring production to P^*. The computation of the present value in this case must involve the marginal rather than the average cost of borrowing, and the application of the criterion requires knowledge of the exact location of the indifference curve.

A third form that capital market imperfections may take appears as a limitation on the amount of borrowing and lending available. This situation could be handled by imposing side constraints on capital availability in the selection of projects.[4]

As far as possible, the objective of project appraisal should be to correct for market imperfections so that investment decisions are made within the context of perfect capital

markets. This may be advisable if the imperfections arise from monopoly power, government favoritism, or other genuine market distortions. Often, however, the imperfections are real and reflect differences in the opportunity cost of capital, including transactions costs. Up to a point, the latter may decrease with the amount of credit, for it is more costly to check credit ratings and supervise credit extension to a large number of small borrowers than to a small number of large and wealthy ones. In these cases, instead of eliminating differential interest rates, public policy could be geared to compensate for them through subsidies. If the cost of borrowing in one sector, for example, the public or the modern, is low or at least constant, while investment opportunities yielding high social returns go begging in another sector, for example, the private or the traditional, because of high interest rates or borrowing constraints, the appropriate solution may well be to divert credit from the former sector to the latter. With these policies, however, the public sector itself will soon reach the limit of the amount of capital that becomes available from domestic sources and foreign borrowing. There is no easy remedy for project appraisal when there are constraints to the amount of borrowing and lending. The social welfare function must then be explicitly specified, and the capital constraints must be included in a programming model, such as the one we will present in Chapter 21.

Risk and Uncertainty

Another assumption of the simplified neoclassical model, which is closely related to capital market imperfections, is that of certainty with regard to the net returns streams associated with particular investments. This assumption is highly unrealistic even for DCs, which enjoy the momentum of many years of relatively steady growth. It is even more dubious in LDCs, which may face a cloudy economic outlook and lack statistical services capable of sophisticated forecasting.

At best, the uncertain future net returns streams may be thought of in terms of a series of alternative values with known probabilities of occurrence. This is the situation of *risk*. At worst, not even these probabilities will be known. This is a situation of genuine *uncertainty*.

In the case of risk, the approach should generally be to specify the whole set of alternative net returns streams, attaching the appropriate probabilities to each occurrence (the probabilities over all alternatives summing to unity). Then one should compute the expected present value of the probability-weighted alternative outcomes. This approach would be valid only if the decision maker is not subject to risk aversion—which may well be the case for the public sector, which has a large portfolio of projects, a relatively long planning horizon, and a considerable capacity to borrow in the event of unexpected shortfalls.

If the decision makers are subject to risk aversion, two alternative approaches become relevant, representing a more substantial modification.

First, Hirshleifer (1970, Chapters 8 and 9) has demonstrated that the basic present value criterion or decision rule can be utilized under certain conditions. The conditions are: (1) that the markets in which the consumption alternatives of each and every time-state are exchanged are both perfect and complete and (2) that utility can be defined cardinally in terms of the various possible outcomes of varying risk and pay-off via the postulates of rational choice developed by Neumann and Morgenstern (1947) and generalized by Hirsh-

leifer (1970, Chapter 8).[5] If these conditions are not satisfied (and as soon as transactions costs are considered, it is difficult to believe they would be), the specification of the social welfare function will again be required. For this purpose, a full-fledged programming model, such as that presented in Chapter 21, could be used, but it would have to be extended to include risk-versus-return choices and an adequate number of future time periods.

A second and simpler approach to the problem of risk in the presence of risk aversion is that of portfolio analysis. Assuming either that the probability distributions of alternative outcomes of all projects are normal or that the utility function is quadratic in the mean, μ, and standard deviation, σ, the utility function, U, of the risk-averting decision maker can be measured by reference to μ and σ alone.[6]

$$U = \mu + A\sigma^2 \tag{5}$$

where A is the coefficient of risk aversion and is negative. The purpose of portfolio analysis is to maximize utility defined in equation 5 by taking advantage of complementarities and substitution among alternative projects as reflected in the covariance of their rates of return. The lower the positive correlation or the larger the negative correlation between the rates of return of the different investments, the more efficient the diversified portfolios relative to concentrated ones. However, information on μ's and σ's of all projects and on their covariance, which is necessary for this approach, is generally unavailable. In the context of evaluating development projects, therefore, its practical application is limited.

[5] The assumptions that underlie these conditions are as follows: (1) Alternative time streams of consumption may be ordinally ordered such that, if the stream C_A has one dated element that is larger than the corresponding element in the stream C_B, all other dated elements being the same, C_A is preferred to C_B. (2) If the same alternative consumption stream outcomes, C_A and C_B, are assigned the probabilities of occurrence, p and $1 - p$ respectively, there exists a certainty equivalent consumption stream, C_C, that is intermediate to C_A and C_B. (The converse of this relation is also assumed to hold.) (3) There is no complementarity among the alternative outcomes, that is the alternative consumption streams. Thus, if one is indifferent between the consumption stream C_A and C_B, one would also be indifferent between $pC_A + (1 - p)C_C$ and $pC_B + (1 - p)C_C$. (4) The certainty equivalent stream, C_C, corresponding to any alternative consumption streams, C_A and C_B, depends only upon the probabilities assigned to the alternatives and the consumption levels and not to any other factors in the decision-maker's environment.

[6] See Hirshleifer (1970, pp. 280–281).

Uncertainty, rather than risk, is probably a more realistic situation for LDCs, where more discontinuities may occur, and the importance of the unique event may become dominant. As Hirschman (1967) has argued, uncertainty concerning the outcome of investment projects may dominate all other characteristics of the projects. Since "all projects are problem-ridden," the success of a project is predicated on its ability to generate positive responses to the difficulties (usually unforeseen) with which it is confronted. Uncertainty arises in connection with a project because neither the problems nor the responses it will elicit can be assigned probabilities of occurrence. Unfortunately, no satisfactory approaches to uncertainty have been proposed.

The introduction of uncertainty must not evoke a defeatist attitude toward project appraisal. Although the characteristics of success may be uncertain, the ingredients of failure are not. To be successful, a project must first be undertaken, and to be undertaken, it must be politically and socially acceptable. Even if undertaken, it would be unsuccessful if it were discontinued before its full benefits were derived. It will be discontinued if it does not generate sufficient public enthusiasm and commitment on behalf of the management to overcome obstacles in implementation. It is thus imperative that a project and its inputs and outputs be defined broadly enough to include the political, social, and other effects that may be crucial to its long-run success.

Externalities

Until now it has been assumed that all the direct and indirect effects of the project accrue in the form of benefits and costs to the project activity itself. In other words, all effects are internalized, at least indirectly; there are no economic externalities.

Externalities[7] arise when there are nonmarket interdependencies, the existence of which conflicts with the basic assumption of Paretian equilibrium in which every economic influence of one person's (or firm's) activity on his well-being (or its profit) is transmitted through its impact on market prices, without recourse to any other form of compensation. The nonmarket interdependencies giving rise to externalities may be between one or more

consumers and other consumers,[8] between producers and consumers (through advertising, product promotion, and wage and salary determination), between consumers and producers,[9] or between and among different producers. Among these different types of externalities, the ones that affect various producers are generally thought to be most important and pervasive.

Externalities can be classified in various ways: for example, by their source, by the industry affected, or more importantly, by whether they are "technological" or "pecuniary."[10]

Externalities that are not accounted for may lead to incorrect decisions despite the application of the otherwise correct decision rules. As the following example will demonstrate, however, it is not always true that anything that can be classified as an externality must be accounted for in arriving at the optimal investment decisions.

Suppose there exists a project, project A, which by itself is not profitable and would therefore not be undertaken according to any appropriate decision rule. Assume that project A generates a pecuniary externality for another, otherwise unprofitable, project, project B, whereby the increase in present value of project B attributable to the existence of project A is more than sufficient to offset the original negative present value of project A. Should the recognition of this kind of externality be reflected in the investment decision

---

[7]This section has benefited greatly from the survey of externalities by Margolis and Vincent (1966).

[8]Leibenstein's (1950) "bandwagon effect," the increase in individual i's demand for a commodity attributable to individual j's consumption of the same commodity, and "snob effect," the decrease in i's consumption due to individual j's consumption, are examples of such interdependencies among consumers.

[9]Leibenstein's (1957b) wage-productivity relationship may be an example of such interdependencies between consumers and producers.

[10]Technological externalities pertain to situations in which the *output* of firm j is affected by changes in output or factor utilization in any other firm i. Pecuniary externalities pertain to cases in which the effect of firm i is on the *profits* of j as a result of changes in relative prices. Thus, pecuniary externalities arise from changes in the prices of inputs or outputs of firm j that are caused by the actions of firm i. Pecuniary externalities are usually defined broadly enough to include quality changes, price changes, changes in profits, or changes in risk and uncertainty. In the short run, changes in profitability attributable to pecuniary externalities may not affect allocation but only the distribution of income, and therefore may not seem relevant to efficiency and allocation considerations. In the long run, however, pecuniary externalities are likely to affect resource allocation and therefore should not be excluded.

rule? If the ordinary present value decision rule is invoked on a project-by-project basis, project *A* would not be undertaken, and therefore, project *B* would not be as profitable as it would be if project *A* were undertaken. If, on the other hand, the pecuniary externality arising from the effect of the existence of project *A* on the profitability of project *B* were considered, both projects would be undertaken. In order to account for the pecuniary externality, is the adjustment in the decision rule legitimate, in the sense that it leads to the optimal investment decision? The reader will probably be tempted to suggest that it is. However, the possibility cannot be ignored that there may be other projects (*C* and *D*) contemplated or already completed, with which project *B* is competitive and whose profitability would be diminished by the existence of projects *A* and *B*. If the investment decision rule were adjusted to include the negative effects of project *A* on projects *C* and *D* as well as the positive effect on project *B*, the present value calculations would certainly change.[11] These considerations are based exclusively on grounds of allocative efficiency. A further modification may be necessary if the income distributional effects of a project are substantial.[12] The most general and universally

accepted externalities that require modification of the ordinary investment decision rules are the public-good externalities. Use of a public good by one consumer does not limit the amount of it that can be used by another. Commonly, public goods are characterized by indivisibility and inappropriability. Indivisibilities imply that there are such significant economies of scale that marginal or incremental investments (as opposed to large indivisible ones) cannot be considered. (Of what good is a bridge that only crosses two-thirds of the river?) Inappropriability implies that the costs of implementing and administering a pricing scheme on such an investment are prohibitively high. (The cost of collecting tolls on the bridge might offset the revenue collected and also lead to traffic congestion.)

Arrow (1962) and Marglin (1963*a,b*) have called attention to related but somewhat more dynamic forms of externalities which, although more controversial, may also merit special consideration in project appraisal. According to Arrow, there is a "learning-by-doing" effect as a result of which the higher the level of investment today, the more will be learned and hence the higher the productivity of future investments. The private profitability of present investment does not fully reflect its social profitability, for individual investors cannot always capture the greater profitability of future investment. Marglin notes the same discrepancy between private and social profitability, but for a different reason. Assuming that individuals evaluate the consumption of future generations positively, and that savings and investment of all members of the present generation are equally productive in terms of raising the consumption of future generations, any individual will maximize his own welfare by minimizing his own sacrifice of present consumption, leaving it up to others to make that sacrifice. The problem, Marglin argues, is that in this situation there is no incentive or compulsion for anyone to make that sacrifice, and the stalemate of underinvestment and suboptimal welfare is thereby perpetuated. One way to handle this type of externality would be to utilize a deliberately low discount rate

[11]Young's (1928) example of the decision to build a subway system in London is illustrative of the problem. Project *A* per se—constructing and running the subway system—is unprofitable. If it would be possible through taxation or ownership to capture some of the pecuniary externalities generated by the existence of the subway system (for example, its effect on the profitability of newspaper stands, shops, and housing in close proximity to the subway lines), the combination of project *A* and these subsidiary activities would be profitable and would seem to be justified. However, what about the profitability of the newspaper stands, shops, and housing (either planned or existing) in locations distant from the subway lines? Should not the pecuniary diseconomies imposed upon these actual or potential investments also be considered?

[12]It has become quite conventional to exclude distributional effects on the grounds that: (1) it is the primary interest of society to increase the size of the pie, because, if so, it can always be sliced in such a way that everyone can obtain a larger slice than before and/or (2) since there is no way of comparing utilities of different individuals, the marginal utility of income is most easily assumed to be equal for every individual. We have already noted that income distribution can have effects on factor accumulation and hence on efficiency in the dynamic sense (e.g., through the income distribution effects on savings and investment). As a result, even on economic grounds alone, the issues of distribution and allocation are not as independent and separable as traditional economic analysis would imply. Distributional

objectives may quite properly be given explicit attention by planners and policy makers in the choice among alternative projects.

in present value computations. We shall return to this issue in the final section of this chapter.

There has been a general presumption that the existence of these types of external economies justifies both: (1) the expansion of the activity giving rise to the external economy and (2) the use of collective as opposed to market forms of organization. However, Baumol (1964) and Buchanan and Kafoglis (1963) have demonstrated that the former is not always true—particularly when there are other activities that may give rise to externalities reciprocal to the original external economy. Meanwhile, in regard to the latter issue, Buchanan (1962) and Buchanan and Tullock (1962) have demonstrated that when collective decisions are made democratically, collective organization will be superior to market organization only if people's political behavior is inconsistent with their market behavior, that is, they vote in the public interest but buy, sell, and invest in their private interest. If McKean's (1965) description of governmental activities and bargaining arising out of rivalries between different agencies is realistic, it would seem unlikely that there would be much difference between the outcomes obtained via competitive markets and those obtained by government or other collective organizations.

As market-oriented economists are eager to point out, the cause of many externalities is likely to lie in the incomplete specification of property rights. Favorite examples are depletion and pollution associated with intensive use of nonowned resources, such as rivers, oceans, and lakes. Regardless of the source of the externality, any one of several mechanisms may arise naturally so as to avoid the need for government intervention: bribes and legal action (Buchanan and Kafoglis 1963; Coase 1960), mergers, collusion, and monopolization (Stigler 1951; Davis and Whinston 1962). Moreover, such economists often argue that alleged externalities are not always valid on closer inspection. For example, it is often argued that the on-the-job training provided by industrial firms generates an externality, because the mobility of labor prevents the firms from fully capturing the benefits of the externality. The market-oriented economists contend that as long as labor markets are competitive and the costs of training can be calibrated, training costs would be deducted from wages during the period of training. However, labor markets may not be competitive, and enterprises may not be in a position to measure the costs and benefits of the externalities involved, let alone get another party to agree. Also, if capital markets are imperfect, it may be difficult for firms to buy out other firms and thus to effect an internalization of existing externalities. Furthermore, even if compensation through the legal system is technically feasible, it may be so time consuming, costly, and unpredictable that it is impractical. These considerations, particularly in the less sophisticated institutional context of LDCs, are likely to prevent us from assuming away the externalities—at least not without being flagrantly unrealistic. On the other hand, the exaggerated claims frequently made for externalities to justify virtually any departure from the ordinary investment decision rules may make it desirable to impose on claimants of externalities the burden of proving their existence and importance.

The following conclusions arise from the consideration of externalities in the context of project appraisal:

1. The existence of an externality should not be admitted without convincing evidence.
2. Once its existence has been demonstrated, one should determine its nature and type to see whether or not and to what extent it requires amendment of the ordinary decision rules.
3. The source of the externality should be identified to see whether or not it could be eliminated, thereby doing away with the need to amend the ordinary decision rules.
4. Genuine and important externalities that cannot easily be eliminated should be considered.
5. In considering an externality, its impact should be measured and then converted into the unit of account, usually present consumption.
6. When simple and ad hoc procedures are insufficient to fully capture all the interdependencies and externalities, a full-fledged general equilibrium programming approach may be necessary.

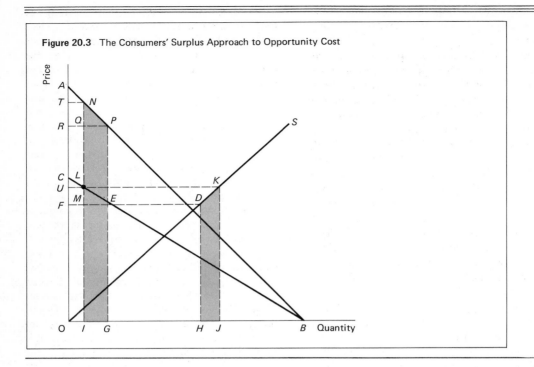

Figure 20.3 The Consumers' Surplus Approach to Opportunity Cost

Distortions

Price distortions are closely related to both capital market imperfections and externalities. Price distortions may be derived from a variety of different sources, such as tariffs, excise taxes, subsidies, barriers to mobility, and monopoly. In preceding chapters, we have seen good reasons to believe that such distortions are relatively more important in LDCs than in DCs. The welfare effects of distortions have been examined in Chapters 7 and 19. Here, we shall concentrate on how distortions can and should be treated in the context of project evaluation.

The primary effect of price distortions from any source is that they drive a wedge between market prices and costs. How should price-distorted inputs or outputs of projects be evaluated? The answers most frequently put forward to this question are "the market price *exclusive* of the distortion" and "the market price *inclusive* of the distortion." However, by once again utilizing the well-worn tool of consumer surplus analysis, which of course integrates the supply or production side of the market with the demand side from the point of view of revealed preference, it can

be demonstrated that neither of these answers is correct, except in extreme circumstances.

This can be seen by reference to Figure 20.3. Let us assume a straight line market demand curve (inclusive of the tax) of the private sector, given by *AB*, the corresponding net of tax demand curve being *CB*, and a straight line supply curve given by *OS*. Let us assume that initially the price including the tax is *OR* and excluding the tax is *OF*. This implies private sector demand of *OG* and domestic supply of *OH*. The excess supply of *OH − OG* or *GH* is allocated to the public sector. Suppose that as a result of implementation of the project under consideration, public sector demand would increase to *IJ*. The additional public sector demand is obviously *IG + HJ* and would raise the equilibrating net of tax price from *OF* to *OU*. At what opportunity cost do the increased inputs to the public sector come? The portion *IG* comes at an opportunity cost of *INPG*, consisting of *NQP* (the loss of consumers' surplus not offset by increased taxes), plus *MQPE* (the loss in tax revenue), plus *IMEG* (the additional net of tax loss in consumers' satisfaction). Meanwhile, the additional portion, *HJ*, comes at an opportunity cost of *HDKJ*, the accumulated supply price of the additional units of the commodity that are supplied. The total opportunity cost of *IG + HJ* is thus the sum of the two shaded trapezoids, *INPG* and *HDKJ*. The opportunity cost per unit is, therefore, in general neither the distorted price (between *OT* and *OR*) or the net price exclusive of the tax (between *OF* and *OU*), but rather is a weighted average of the two. The respective weights are the elasticities of net of tax demand and supply with respect to the net (tax excluded) price. The opportunity cost will be the distorted demand price (the net supply price) only when the price elasticity of supply (of demand) is zero.

Harberger (1964, 1968a,b) has demonstrated how this approach can be generalized: (1) to account for other distortions, such as those on the supply side of the market;[13] (2) to distinguish between different groups in terms of differing distortions they may face and different behavior they may reflect; and (3) to account for certain kinds of externalities so as to constitute a general equilibrium framework.[14] His approach has not specifically considered nontax distortions, such as quotas, but in certain situations such cases could be handled by way of equivalent tariffs (see Chapter 7).

The approach, which has been pictured in terms of a single period of time, can easily be extended to deal with *n* periods by discounting with the present value formulas presented above.

While Harberger (1971) has demonstrated that the consumers' surplus approach can deal with distortions in other markets or activities that may offset or reinforce distortion in the activity under consideration, he has also admitted that when the policy (removal or imposition of the distortion) affects the availability of resources, the terms of trade, or technology, such effects have to be handled on an ad hoc basis, because one can no longer be confident that the calculated opportunity cost prices are correct. Harberger (1968a, 1971) has advocated that such ad hoc amendments can be handled relatively easily by estimating the shadow prices of the few products or factors whose prices are generally distorted and of other factors or products that are both disturbed to a significant degree and significantly affected by the policies or projects under consideration. However, one can only suspect that the dearth of empirical applications[15] is testimony to the fact that it may not be as easy as Harberger makes it sound. Opening up the doors to shadow prices may be somewhat akin to inadvertently opening up Pandora's box. The shadow price of capital or rate of return will depend on the price of labor, which may itself be distorted and require calculation, and so on for other factors. Thus, if shadow prices are introduced, one may have to solve for a whole set of such prices simultaneously.

Practical Approaches to Project Evaluation

We have seen that the conventional investment decision rules apply to situations where all markets are perfect, information is complete, and externalities and distortions are absent. In LDCs, where these assumptions are unlikely to hold, project appraisal entails substantial modification of the conventional decision rules. Modifications, however, complicate the analysis considerably. For example, relaxing any of the assumptions frequently implies that the welfare function must be specified and brought to bear in the investment decision process. Similarly, where various prices are distorted, one may need to calculate a whole set of shadow prices simultaneously. While programming models and general equilibrium and dynamic extensions of consumer surplus analysis may offer considerable

---

[13]A nontax distortion, such as monopoly power, can quite realistically be treated as a privately imposed and collected excise tax.

[14]In general equilibrium terms, the change in welfare, ΔW, attributed to any specific distortion, such as a tax on commodity, j, T_j, which when imposed assumes the value, T_j^*, and when unimposed assumes a zero value, can be analyzed in two components. The first integral in the equation below represents the normal partial equilibrium magnitude, while the second captures the effects of the interdependence with other commodities, i, $(i \neq j)$ and which can be positive or negative:

$$\Delta W = \int_{T_j=0}^{T_j^*} T_j \frac{\partial x_j}{\partial T_j} \, dT_j + \int_{T_j=0}^{T_j^*} \sum_{i \neq j} T_i \frac{\partial x_i}{\partial T_j} \, dT_j$$

Application of this more general formula requires knowledge of the cross-elasticities of supply and demand with respect to price. Since this information is seldom readily accessible, the general equilibrium application is not very common.

[15]See, however, Fontaine (1969), Schydlowsky (1968), Wallace (1962), Dean and Collins (1967), Zusman, Melamed, and Katzir (1969), and several contained in Harberger (1974).

promise for coming to grips with these issues, their informational requirements are enormous and generally well beyond the data available in LDCs. Some cruder methods with modest data requirements have been advocated for making investment decisions in LDCs, such as incremental capital-output ratios, social marginal productivity, and the reinvestment rate criterion. These compromise analytical rigor and are of questionable validity, as will be pointed out in the Appendix to this chapter.

Two efforts deserve special attention as serious attempts to admit the complexities confronting "real world" investment decisions in LDCs without sacrificing operationalism or much analytical rigor. These are the studies commissioned by the Organization for Economic Cooperation and Development (OECD) referred to as Little and Mirrlees (1968) and the United Nations Industrial Development Organization (UNIDO 1972), referred to also as Dasgupta, Marglin, and Sen (1972).

Both studies provide practical guidelines for the evaluation of (especially industrial) projects in LDCs. The basic criterion is the discounted value of the benefits (measured as consumers' surplus in one and social value in the other) over the lifetime of the project. These benefits must be evaluated within the specific environment of LDCs, which both studies consider from similar angles.

For example, both studies assume that market imperfections and distortions arising from government intervention are sufficiently widespread to make market prices generally unreliable guides to social profitability. Both recognize the existence of certain political constraints, which may require LDC governments to retain suboptimal policies that may need to be considered in project evaluation. Both share the same analytical tool kit. Basically, they use marginal analysis in an essentially partial equilibrium setting. They justify these simplifications by arguing that most industrial projects are small, relative to the economy, and that interdependencies among projects are also small. (When there are significant interdependencies, for example, when individual industrial projects fit together as part of a complex, the interdependent projects should be treated collectively as one large project.) Both studies recognize similar limitations of their simplifications. Partial

equilibrium analysis, for example, cannot generally provide what is needed, that is, the consistent set of shadow prices for many, if not all, commodities and resources that would equate supplies and demands at optimal (or rather second-best) levels. Yet without the information and knowledge with which to specify and empirically estimate the complete simultaneous equation system that would be required for general equilibrium solutions, both studies are viewed as providing useful but imperfect starting points, together with rules of adjustment that could lead the user to the correct general equilibrium solutions by successive approximations.

Given these many similarities, it is not surprising that Dasgupta (1970) has been able to show that the two approaches are in fact identical in certain limiting circumstances. However, in such situations (excluding externalities, interdependence, and political constraints), Harberger's version of consumers' surplus would also give similar results. Even aside from these special circumstances, all these approaches call for an iterative process of tentative answers and repeated revision until a completely consistent set of prices equating supplies and demands is obtained. Since such a solution must be unique in most cases, given enough time and information to work everything out, each of the approaches would be presumed to give the same solutions.

However, the justification for developing practical criteria for resource allocation in the first place is precisely that time and information are likely to be deficient. Therefore, the fact that the OECD and UNIDO approaches would give identical results in these rather unlikely circumstances is hardly relevant or important. It is the differences in the way they start out to reach their conclusions that make each interesting and valuable. As we shall see, each is more convenient and appropriate than the other in certain situations. Before going on to a critical examination of their differences, we shall present each of them separately.

We start with the approach of the UNIDO manual, which, because consumption (or rather consumers' surplus) is taken as the numeraire whose present value is to be maximized, is most akin to the simple analytical model portrayed in Figure 20.3.

The UNIDO Manual

As UNIDO sees it, except for the invaluable tool of marginal analysis, much of the neoclassical theory underlying the conventional approaches to project analysis is insufficiently realistic to be of use in the context of the LDCs. The shortcomings of economic theory (and of existing markets) are most noticeable in regard to the intertemporal decisions relevant to project evaluation. In UNIDO's view, these shortcomings can be characterized in general terms by: (1) overemphasis on optimization of the best (as opposed to second- or third-best) variety; (2) underemphasis on considerations of equity and income distribution; and (3) unrealistic assumptions about certainty and learning patterns.

Actually, all these difficulties are interrelated. As opposed to an ideal world where the best alternative is feasible, LDCs have to operate within political constraints that result in suboptimal policies. The insufficiency of savings and investment, a central tenet of the UNIDO approach, is at least partly due to such political constraints. The distribution of income is another essential determinant of saving and investment behavior, and thus, it too needs to be considered. Yet it has been largely overlooked in traditional intertemporal analysis as a result of the insufficient attention to uncertainty. Similarly overlooked has been the contribution to both equity and productivity that a project can make through the provision of merit goods, such as better nutrition, health, or learning-by-doing. For these reasons, UNIDO feels that income distribution considerations, merit goods, and political constraints should all be brought explicitly into project appraisal.

Income distribution considerations and merit goods are treated as externalities and introduced as separate elements in the welfare (utility) function. For example, the income distribution may be influenced through pecuniary externalities. Better education, improved nutrition, or the introduction of the workers to modern work methods and new ways of living are examples of merit good externalities. These externalities should be considered over and above the basic component of the welfare function to be maximized, which is the time stream of aggregate consumption. Each of these additional elements would have to be weighted for its relative importance. Since it would be hard to obtain objective estimates of the relevant weights, UNIDO recommends that sensitivity analysis be employed with respect to several alternative sets of weights.

The political constraints are brought into the project appraisal by limiting the scope of the project evaluator. Project evaluators are in an intermediate position, with central planners above them and project managers below them. The former prescribe the present and future environments in which the project is born and will operate. The latter are responsible for the final microeconomic and managerial decisions for the projects selected. Efficient and consistent decisions can be reached only if the channels of communication and coordination among the three groups are unrestricted and felicitously utilized. However, the project evaluators are viewed as having little influence on the basic policy decisions of the central planners, which, therefore, must be translated into market prices, weights for externalities, or other signals on the basis of which the project managers can operate.

The job of the project evaluator, therefore, is neither exclusively one of allocating given resources among competing uses nor that of mobilizing resources. It is more properly a combination of the two, with fairly heavy emphasis on the former. As such, the primary criterion for assessing the value of the benefits of the project is the "consumers' willingness to pay." Because of this, the UNIDO approach relies heavily on consumers' surplus analysis. For example, by returning once again to Figure 20.3, the reader is reminded of the fact that the consumers' willingness to pay at a quantity IG is measured by the area of the trapezoid $INPG$, regardless of the taxes or other distortions included in the price consumers are willing to pay.

Since consumption is the basic component of the welfare function to be maximized, the evaluation of the costs of any input and of the benefits of any output of the project takes place with reference to its contribution to final demand. As a result, the consumers' surplus analysis can be applied directly. In measuring the value of intermediate goods, one needs to determine the value of the change in output flows of the consumer goods attributable to the change in availability of the intermediate goods. Since inputs are simply negative outputs, the same criterion can be utilized in assessing the values of both inputs and outputs. Thus, all commodities and resources that enter the project's evaluation and whose total availability is not affected by the project, whether they are items of final demand or intermediate demand, should be analyzed directly or indirectly at the *demand margin*, that is, at a price between *OR* and *OT* in Figure 20.3.

When the total availability of commodities produced as outputs or of resources used as inputs is changed as a result of the project's implementation, their value should be measured in terms of the opportunity cost of the resources used up in supplying the extra units. This is what UNIDO refers to as evaluation at the *supply margin*. For additional output of *HJ* in Figure 20.3, opportunity cost at the supply margin is measured by *HDKJ*. Take the example of skilled labor used as an input in the project under consideration, the total availability of which is increased (by training) as a result of the project. The appropriate measure of opportunity cost would be the direct cost of training (and perhaps relocating) the workers plus the opportunity cost of having decreased the amount of unskilled labor available to the rest of the economy.

There may be several commodity and resource markets in disequilibrium. In such cases, evaluations at the appropriate margin will not generally yield valid estimates of the opportunity costs or benefits. For example, if the commodity is subject to price control and rationing, and evaluation at the demand margin is appropriate, the market price would not be indicative of the willingness to pay. Perhaps the market price would represent the direct willingness to pay, but certainly not the ultimate willingness to pay. The market price would have to be adjusted upward to reflect this ultimate willingness to pay. But by how much? This is the task of shadow pricing, the rules of which must be determined by particular circumstances.

The three most important shadow prices to be estimated are those of foreign exchange, investment, and unskilled labor. All of these are referred to as "national parameters," parameters that could ideally be supplied by the central planners and that would apply to all projects. This is because they depend not on any individual project but rather on macroeconomic considerations and projected trends

in relative supplies and demands for the resources common to all projects. Central planners would presumably be in the best position to supply this information. The job of the project evaluators is to enter into a dialogue with the planners in order to help them reveal their preferences and other information at their disposal, which would make calculation of national parameters possible.

Calculation of these shadow prices is complicated by the fact that they do not depend entirely on objective phenomena that can be foreseen easily by the central planners. They depend, at least in part, on the subjective values attached to the elements that enter the welfare (utility) function. As has already been mentioned, these values cannot be estimated with any degree of precision but rather must be guessed at and then subjected to sensitivity analysis.

Let us take the price of foreign exchange first. If exports and imports do not compete with domestic production (implying that total exports and imports are given), evaluation should be at the demand margin. In this case, the shadow price of foreign exchange, P_{fe}, is basically a weighted average of the domestic market-clearing prices of the individual imports and exports, P_d, relative to their world prices, P_w, the weights, M_j, being the proportions of any additional unit of foreign exchange that would result in increased imports or reduced exports of commodity. j.[16] The domestic prices used, P_d, would be those that could clear the markets (in the absence of rationing) and would include tariffs and other excise taxes. P_w, being the c.i.f. price of imports or the f.o.b. price of exports, should naturally exclude excise taxes, import duties, and domestically imposed export taxes. The formula for the shadow price of foreign exchange would thus be

$$P_{fe} = \sum_j M_j \frac{P_{dj}}{P_{wj}} \tag{6}$$

However, if the consumer or capital goods to be imported or subtracted from exports compete with or substitute for domestic production, one should measure (via the supply

[16]Neither the current foreign exchange requirements nor those that would arise under optimal exchange rates are considered representative of the expected marginal use of foreign exchange. It is rather represented by the situation that would prevail under an exchange policy that is somewhere in between but closer to the optimum policy than the current one.

margin) the benefit in terms of the additional consumption that could be generated by freeing domestic resources from domestic production of these goods. Since the supply margin becomes relevant in such cases, excise taxes on domestic production should be deducted from the value of output derived from the freed resources.[17]

Consumption is the numeraire in the UNIDO approach, and thus, its shadow price is equal to unity. If one unit of investment (valued in terms of domestic currency), a dinar's worth, were equivalent in social terms to a dinar's worth of consumption, the shadow price of investment would also be unity.[18] However, this is not the case with the UNIDO approach. Although it is admitted that it would be better to allow fiscal policy to narrow the gap between actual and optimal savings and investment and also to achieve the desired degree of equity in income distribution, UNIDO feels that political constraints make it impossible for fiscal policy to achieve either objective. Therefore, it is argued, the insufficiency of capital formation and the inequity of income distribution in the real world make it imperative to consider the reinvestment and redistributive aspects of projects in choosing between the alternatives.

It is further assumed that the social rate of return in any period, t, on investment, r_t, and on consumption, i_t (which in equilibrium should be equal to the social discount rate), are different from each other but constant over time. It is also assumed that a portion, s, of the return on investment will be saved and reinvested. Thus, if investment in year one is one dinar, at the end of the year, $(1 - s)r$ would be consumed and sr would be invested. Accumulated investment in year 2 would thus be $1 + sr$, in year 3 it would be $(1 + sr)^2$, and in year t, it would be $(1 + sr)^{t-1}$. The

shadow price of investment, P_K, which in UNIDO terms is the relative value of such an income stream to that of a consumption stream, would be

$$P_K = \sum_{t=1}^{\infty} \frac{(1-s)r(1+sr)^{t-1}}{(1+i)^t}$$

$$= \frac{(1-s)r}{1+sr} \sum_{t=1}^{\infty} \left(\frac{1+sr}{1+i}\right)^t \qquad (7)$$

The term $\sum \left(\dfrac{1+sr}{1+i}\right)^t$ is of course a geometric sum, the value of which is $(1 + sr)/(i - sr)$. Substituting this simplified expression into equation 7, we obtain

$$P_K = \frac{(1-s)r}{i-sr} \qquad (8)$$

If the savings rate on profits is zero, the shadow price of capital is simply the ratio of r to i, which is, by assumption, greater than one. As the savings rate increases, P_K increases in value until eventually it becomes infinite.

If any of the parameters (i, r, or s) changes in value over time or between sectors, the relevant formula for calculating P_K becomes more complicated and, although still manageable, requires more information (UNIDO 1972, pp. 181–186, 194–198).

In addition to the inadequacy of savings and investment, it is possible that savings rates are higher for capitalists, s_p, than for workers, s_w, because of such factors as capital market imperfections or differences in tastes. The inadequacy of fiscal policy, constrained as it is by political realities, is also likely to be reflected in the excess of market wage rates, w, over the social cost of labor. While the shadow wage rate, P_L, in the case of unconstrained fiscal policy would simply be its opportunity cost (the marginal product of labor, mpl), in the constrained case it would be this opportunity cost plus an allowance for the social cost of the excess consumption generated by the income tranfer. The income transfer, $w - mpl$, reduces the consumption of profit earners by $(1 - s_p)(w - mpl)$ but raises it for wage earners by $(1 - s_w)(w - mpl)$. At the same time, it reduces investment of capitalists by $s_p(w - mpl)$ and raises that of workers by $s_w(w - mpl)$. In order to convert investment flows into the

[17]If the scarcity of imported capital goods constitutes the bottleneck to additional savings and investment, upward adjustments to account for the contribution of the additional foreign exchange to capital formation would have to be made. If foreign exchange is desired not only as a means to an end but as an end in itself (e.g., to enable the country to become more "independent"), it should be treated as a merit want with an appropriate subjective national parameter rather than as a shadow price.

[18]This would be the case in conventional consumers' surplus analysis, as the utilities of a dinar's worth of consumption and of investment are equal at the margin. Even if, allowing for capital market imperfections, they should not be valued equally, fiscal policy could be relied upon to restore this equality.

unit of account (consumption), one should multiply the investment flow by the shadow price of investment, P_K. The shadow price of labor is thus

$$P_L = mpl + (1 - s_p)(w - mpl)$$
$$- (1 - s_w)(w - mpl) + P_K s_p(w - mpl)$$
$$- P_K s_w(w - mpl) \qquad (9)$$

which simplifies to

$$P_L = mpl + (w - mpl)[(P_K - 1)s_p$$
$$+ (1 - P_K)s_w] \qquad (10)$$

Note that the shadow wage rate could in fact exceed the market wage rate if P_K is sufficiently large.[19]

The OECD Manual

The OECD also perceives that existing market prices are distorted and thus cannot be relied upon in evaluating a project's output. However, for a large class of commodities—those that are traded or could be traded at an optimal exchange rate—a usable set of estimates is readily available, namely, world prices (the c.i.f. prices of importables and the f.o.b. prices of exportables). World prices, even if distorted by the trade policies of other countries, represent the terms at which a country can (and should) exchange with the outside world and hence reflect its market opportunity costs.[20] The prices are converted from prices in foreign currency at the official (or any other single) exchange rate and constitute a convenient numeraire, particularly since they are likely to cover a broad range of commodities and services in the economy. In situations where the official exchange rate overvalues domestic currency, most "home" or "nontraded" commodities would presumably turn out to have opportunity costs lower than their market prices. (For this reason, the OECD and UNIDO approaches should give rather similar results as far as the

relative price of domestic goods to foreign exchange is concerned.)

If the country in question is able to exercise any monopsony power with respect to imports of a particular commodity, that is, if the quantity of imports affects the world price of the importable, a somewhat higher price might be used, such as the world price plus the domestically imposed tariff. This situation is not likely to arise in many LDCs, however, and therefore, for all practical purposes, importables can be evaluated at world prices converted to domestic currency by the official exchange rate plus (in the case of a project's inputs) any domestic transport and/or distribution costs necessary to bring the importable input to the site of the project in which it will be used. In the more likely possibility that the country exercises some monopoly power over certain exportable commodities, the marginal revenue and not the price (average revenue) should be used. Also, a slightly lower price might be used in the case of new exports, which may entail expenses on behalf of export promotion. Taxes are to be excluded, since one is implicitly working on the supply margin.

From this standpoint, the evaluation of tradeable goods would seem both simple and straightforward. However, even if their use is conceptually appropriate, practical application of world prices may involve errors and difficulties. For example, such factors as quality, delivery time, market conditions, and bargaining power may make it practically difficult to determine which world prices should be used. Even if these factors are meticulously dealt with, certain other adjustments may be necessary. Moreover, some uncomfortable qualitative judgments probably cannot be avoided in deciding which goods and services that are not presently traded might be traded under the regime of optimal exchange rates. Consequently, somewhat different results would be obtained if one subscribed to the more pessimistic UNIDO philosophy that appropriate exchange policies will not be adopted.

For commodities that would not be traded even at optimal exchange rates world prices cannot be used; prices have to be calculated. The basic calculation rules are:

1. That the prices of each commodity or resource should be the same in all its uses

---

[19]In Chapter 13, we took note (in connection with David's model of sequential search under uncertainty) of an additional factor, which should perhaps be included in the shadow price of labor: namely, any decreased output in agriculture resulting from excessive migration to the industrial sector as a result of hiring by the project.

[20]In other words, foreign and domestic goods compete with each other, and thus, evaluation at the supply margin is relevant as it is in the UNIDO approach.

unless there are real differences in transport and distribution costs.

2. That the prices arrived at should equate supply and demand (after considering the restructuring of demand that the government may wish to impose.

3. That the prices of nontradeable goods should reflect the contribution these goods make to the saving or earning of the numeraire, that is, foreign exchange.

The situation is complicated by the fact that the cost of an untraded service, such as construction, is composed of many other inputs, some of which may themselves be untraded, such as unskilled labor and local stones, whose values must also be computed. Complete calculations may reveal that the initial calculations or assumptions about prices will not equate supply and demand, thereby indicating the need for revisions. Fortunately, prices of many such nontraded inputs can be satisfactorily approximated by market prices net of taxes (because it is assumed that the supply margin is the relevant one), by world prices, or by zero (in the case of commodities with excess supply). Thus, there is every hope that the calculations can be kept within manageable limits.

Also, if detailed calculation of social cost is either infeasible or would have turned out to make little difference in the overall evaluation, one can resort to standard conversion factors to express a representative bundle of domestic goods into their equivalent value on the world market. Little and Mirrlees (1972b) suggest the use of a simple form of input-output analysis as a means of facilitating simultaneous equation solutions. Thus, OECD feels that complete shadow price calculations probably need to be done for only a small number of important commodities and services, such as construction, electricity, and transport. However, by brushing over (perhaps too quickly and lightly) the existence of domestic excess capacity,[21] limited access

to export markets, government policies in restraint of trade and the internal obstacles to trade and integration (such as the poor quality and high cost of transport and communication), all of which would make the use of world market prices inappropriate, OECD may have underestimated the extent to which more complicated calculations would be necessary.

The computation of the shadow price of home goods relative to that of tradeable commodities on the world market, that is, foreign exchange, which is the numeraire, substitutes for the need to compute a shadow price of foreign exchange. As in the UNIDO approach, however, shadow prices for labor and capital must also be computed.

Some types of skilled labor may be traded and can therefore be evaluated at world prices. Other nontraded types of skilled labor should be evaluated by a method that is almost identical to that of UNIDO. If the skilled labor is to be trained, the appropriate price should include the income forgone while in training, the marginal cost of the extra training, and a portion of the extra consumption (evaluated at world prices) that skilled laborers would demand over what they commanded before training. If the skilled labor cannot be trained, the appropriate price would be a wage rate that would divert the worker from alternative activities, that is, the opportunity cost evaluated at the demand margin.

Likewise, the shadow price of unskilled labor in industry, as in UNIDO,[22] is its opportunity cost (in the familiar two-sector surplus labor model the marginal productivity of labor in the agricultural sector) plus the social cost of the additional consumption (evaluated at world prices) and hence reduced present and future investment. Although the formula

---

[21]The direction and extent to which world prices should be modified when there is excess capacity in the domestic industry depends on the source or explanation of the excess capacity. For example, if the reason for the excess capacity is a constraint on demand and/or on imported raw materials for balance of payments purposes, it is not necessarily advisable to abandon world prices. Similarly, if the excess capacity is temporary but intentional as part of the

cost of taking advantage of economies of scale, the full cost, and not a lower marginal cost, of additional output should be charged.

[22]Despite substantial similarity between UNIDO and OECD with respect to the shadow price of unskilled labor, Sen (1972) has detected an inconsistency in the OECD formulation. The OECD authors, on the one hand, deny the existence of surplus labor but, on the other hand, accept a utility function that is determined by income alone. These two postulates are inconsistent because: (1) implicit in their utility function is an assumption that the marginal disutility of labor is zero and (2) as we discussed in Chapter 11, this is a necessary and sufficient condition for the existence of surplus labor.

provided and the parameters to be estimated are somewhat different than in the UNIDO approach, the social cost of the additional consumption again depends on the social rate of return to capital, r (which is termed the accounting rate of interest, because foreign exchange, convertible into investment, is the numeraire) relative to the consumption rate of interest, i (or social discount rate), and the difference in savings rates between profit earners and workers. The only substantive difference is that, while UNIDO is content to leave the determination of the consumption rate of interest, i, strictly to the arbitrary discretion of the decision makers (making it advisable for the unknowing analyst to experiment and conduct sensitivity analysis with several such values), OECD suggests how it might be estimated practically.[23]

Since investment in terms of foreign exchange is the numeraire, OECD does not formally introduce a shadow price of investment as does UNIDO, but the same parameters (r, i, s_p, s_w) determine the superiority of investment (and profits) to consumption (and wage income). As with UNIDO, the eventual convergence of r and i on the basis of gradual improvements in fiscal policy is expected.

The shadow wage rate, P_L, is not independent of the social rate of return or accounting rate of interest, r, since P_L depends partly on r and vice versa. However, it is thought practical to proceed to the estimation of P_L on the basis of an assumed value of r, since P_L may not be very sensitive to small changes in r. If the computed value of r is inconsistent with the assumed one, both P_L and r must be recomputed until convergence in the assumed and computed values of r is achieved. The accounting rate of interest is, in principle, the rate that equates the marginal project's present value to zero. However, since it may not be feasible to identify with any confidence—especially at the beginning of one's analysis and in the absence of a large stockpile of projects—which project is the marginal one whose present value is zero, certain more operational alternatives may have to be relied upon to provide useful starting

points. First, a lower bound on the appropriate estimates can be set equal to that which can be earned on international capital markets (the rate should be at least 6 percent).[24] Second, experience with past projects may provide a range of social rates of return from which the rate for the marginal project can be chosen. If market wage rates do not differ greatly from the shadow prices of labor, another possibility is the use of the average rate of return in the private sector. If public projects are more socially profitable than projects in the private sector and/or if problems on the tax side make it difficult to finance all the socially desirable investments, a rate somewhat above the average market rate should be used.[25]

A Critical Comparison and Evaluation of the UNIDO and OECD Approaches

Having presented each approach, at least in summary form, we are now in a position to point out some of the more obvious differences and to discuss some of the advantages of each one.

Choice of Numeraire

The first difference between the two approaches is in the choice of the numeraire. The UNIDO approach has the advantage of conforming rather closely to the conventional analytical model, in which consumption is the numeraire. But UNIDO also includes income distribution and merit goods in the objective function to be maximized. Rather unconventionally, the OECD's numeraire is government profits which, because the marginal propensity to save in the public sector is assumed to be unity, are convertible into investment and are expressed in terms of foreign exchange. Since the choice of numeraire is completely arbitrary, however, one cannot discriminate between the two methods on this basis alone.

Discount Rates

Since the numeraires to be discounted are different, and since capital market imperfections are assumed in both cases, the use of different discount rates is both expected and

---

[23]Specifically, it consists of the sum of: (1) an arbitrary allowance for impatience of 2 or 3 percent per annum; (2) between one-half and three-quarters of the annual growth rate of consumption per head in the modern (industrial) sector; and (3) between two and three times the annual growth rate of consumption per head in the traditional (agricultural) sector.

[24]The IBRD reportedly uses a gross rate of about 10 percent for this purpose, but this is a market rate unadjusted for departures of social from private benefits and costs. As reported by Halevi (1969), Israel has used a figure of 8 percent.

[25]Such an adjustment was also recommended by Harberger (1968a).

valid. With consumption as the numeraire, the UNIDO authors use the consumption rate of interest, i, as the discount rate. This, it will be recalled, is a "national parameter" set by the central planners to reflect social values. It is selected on the basis of expectations about how fast consumption will increase over time and how rapidly marginal utility will decline with the level of consumption. On the other hand, since OECD is discounting net returns or profit streams, it uses the more conventional (and presumably higher) accounting rate of interest, r.

While we have already seen that the existence of capital market imperfections or of externalities and the insufficient flexibility in fiscal policy can justify the use of different interest rates, UNIDO's use of a social discount rate substantially below the social rate of return or accounting rate of interest, r, would not seem justified.

If the purpose of using different rates were simply to reflect realistically the capital market imperfections that project evaluators are unable to ameliorate, interest rates to consumers would be generally significantly higher than to investors. As a result, the appropriate value of the consumption rate of interest, i, would be higher than that of the accounting rate, r. The main function of the discount rate in project appraisal, however, is to screen projects according to their social profitability (measured in terms of the numeraire). The present value, which serves as the investment criterion and decision rule in both approaches, increases as the discount rate decreases. Therefore, the lower the rate of discount, the higher the probability that the project will pass the test of "present value greater than zero," regardless of what is used as the numeraire.

Suppose it were true that investment is in some sense insufficient, and yet that the number of projects able to show positive present values at the accounting rate of interest, r, is too small to utilize all the available investable funds. This does not necessarily imply that the accounting rate of interest should be abandoned in favor of a social discount rate set sufficiently low to exhaust the investable resources. It could simply mean either that a larger list of public projects should be evaluated or that investable funds should be diverted from the less (socially) profitable public sector to the more (socially)

profitable private sector. An artificially low rate of interest would further distort the price of capital goods, making it low relative to the price of labor and foreign exchange. It is precisely this distortion that is largely responsible for the difficulties LDCs encounter in generating more industrial employment.

We conclude, first, that the concern of UNIDO and OECD for the inadequacy of investment may be somewhat exaggerated and, second, that even if investment were inadequate, it would not justify the use of discount rates substantially below the social rate of return, which in turn is not likely to be much below the average rate of return in the private sector.

This would leave as the rationale for UNIDO's use of a low discount rate only two arguments: the externality argument and the sweeping generalization that savings and investment behavior can be explained only in terms of income distribution and other nontraditional factors. In Chapter 10, we presented evidence to suggest that a good portion of savings and investment behavior can be explained without recourse to income distribution and, therefore, that argument does not seem well taken. While there may be some grounds for considering intergenerational externalities in those rich DCs that are in danger of running out of natural resources and polluting their environments beyond redemption, the argument seems far-fetched in LDCs whose futures would appear bright, at least relative to their present poverty. Given UNIDO's concern for emphasizing political constraints, what LDC government—capitalist, socialist, feudalist, military, civilian, or religious—feels sufficiently secure or well off to deliberately deemphasize the material welfare of the present generation in favor of that of future generations?

Role and Importance of Project Evaluators
As we have already seen, policy makers are depicted as having to cope with nonoptimal policies, especially in the short run, by both UNIDO and OECD. However, the tightness of the constraints is assumed to be qualitatively greater by UNIDO than by OECD. For example, UNIDO sees the project evaluators as so powerless and/or unwilling to influence policy decisions that they refuse to take a position on policy choices, such as that between devaluation and the rationing of im-

ported goods. OECD, on the other hand, assumes more optimistically that in the long run the project evaluator will be able to have an influence on policy and that more rational policies will eventually be forthcoming; for example, devaluation will be favored over import licensing. Moreover, should there be some doubt about whether or not the more rational policies will be invoked, OECD feels that there may be good reason for evaluating projects on the basis of assumptions about more consistent and rational policies.[26]

Another way of comparing the role of project evaluators in the OECD and UNIDO approaches is to distinguish the directions in which they are urged to coordinate. UNIDO stresses the importance of obtaining coordination and cooperation between project evaluators and central planners. By insisting that policy recommendations reflect economic realities, OECD emphasizes the importance of coordination between project evaluators and project managers. Coordination in both directions is, of course, imperative if planning is going to be reflected in appropriate decisions by both project evaluators and managers. If, in fact, the optimal policies advocated by the evaluators cannot be imposed for political reasons, the effects of the evaluation will unfortunately be irrelevant and misguided (UNIDO 1972; Dasgupta 1972; Sen 1972; Little and Mirrlees 1972a). By the same token, however, if UNIDO's project evaluators were able to predict policies correctly and to derive an appropriate set of projects from their criteria, and yet if these criteria (including the weights attached to income and locational distribution preferences and merit wants) cannot be translated into market prices (or some other suitable set of incentives upon which the project managers can operate), the results are likely to fall well short of the second best that is aimed for in their approach.[27]

In our opinion, UNIDO's heavy emphasis on the political straitjacket within which project evaluators and central planners must operate has some important disadvantages. No matter how satisfactory the manuals or guidelines that project evaluators may have at their disposal, it is essential that they be well-trained professional economists. The task of being able to predict the time path of government policies (whatever economists think they should be), which the UNIDO approach would impose on the project evaluator, however, would seem to require the skills of a political scientist, not an economist. Unless both types of professionals are to be represented on the project evaluation team, UNIDO's attempt to distinguish and defend their approach from that of OECD would have the undesirable consequence of requiring economists to operate in an area in which they are at a distinct disadvantage relative to others. This difficulty seems particularly relevant now and in the near future, while central planners are still unprepared to supply project evaluators with policy forecasts and while LDCs will still be relying heavily for their project evaluation teams on foreign or newly repatriated technicians unfamiliar with the domestic political scene. The other side of the coin gives smaller emphasis to an economist's area of comparative advantage in explaining to policy makers (and planners) what policies should be adopted and ignores the possibility that some of these political constraints are endogenous, that is, are affected by the project.

Project Financing
In the OECD approach, the way a project is financed can be ignored (except in the special case in which foreign assistance is available but tied to particular projects). For UNIDO, on the other hand, the importance of income distribution, both as an end in itself and as an influence on the rate of capital formation,

---

[26]For example, external donors are unlikely to be interested in supporting "hothouse" industries, and may insist that rational criteria be reflected at least in project appraisal, if not in the actual policies adopted. Second, commitments toward regional integration with neighboring countries may dictate that new industries be evaluated with world criteria even if "irrational" policies are presently followed.

[27]Sen (1972) has cited the case that project evaluators choose a less efficient location in a backward region for a specific project in order to provide employment opportunities for the people in the region because of the merit good weight attached to this in the

welfare function of the central planners. However, if in the implementation stage the project managers choose to import the (presumably more efficient) workers from a more advanced region of the country, the result could well be that both efficiency and the merit goods aspect are sacrificed. This is because project managers operate on the basis of a different criterion (generally profit maximization) than do project evaluators. Sen gives little indication that the UNIDO authors have appreciated the general significance of this point.

makes it imperative that financing of the projects be carefully studied.

Choices of Margin

In our view, the most fundamental difference between OECD and UNIDO is in the margin (demand or supply) used to measure opportunity costs. We have seen in Figure 20.3 that in general the appropriate measure will not be one or the other of these margins, but rather a weighted average of the two. Unfortunately, this means that the measurement of opportunity cost will depend upon the elasticities of supply and demand, which are difficult to obtain. The use of either of the extreme values eliminates the need for measurement of these magnitudes but is valid only in special circumstances. Specifically, the use of the demand margin is appropriate only when the elasticity of supply with respect to price is zero. Meanwhile, the use of the supply margin is appropriate when the elasticity of demand with respect to price is zero. Thus, the UNIDO and OECD approaches, in avoiding the need to measure elasticities of supply and demand, amount to special cases of the more general method provided by Harberger (1971). Both advocate using the supply margin in some cases and the demand margin in others, but they differ as to which one is to be used more frequently. Since most goods are likely to be traded at optimal exchange rates and, therefore, since most projects change the reserves of foreign exchange available for other projects, the OECD emphasis on evaluation at the supply margin seems reasonable. On the other hand, UNIDO's acceptance of the "what the consumer will pay" principle and its assumption of domestic supply rigidities give heavy weight to measurement at the demand margin.[28]

We have to conclude that it is highly unlikely that either approach will be more appropriate, convenient, or reliable in all situations. While in specific circumstances it may be possible to argue rather convincingly for one approach or the other, in general it would seem wise to utilize both simultaneously. Once the underlying project data necessary for computing social benefits and costs via either approach are obtained, the additional effort required to compute them with respect to the other approach is likely to be marginal. Comparison of the present value computations obtained by alternative approaches will generally provide much additional information about the project. For example, if both methods give similar results, there is additional reason for confidence in the conclusion. Alternatively, if the results differ significantly, one would have reason to be suspicious about the validity of either conclusion and, at the same time, would be able, by successive recalculations under differing assumptions, to trace the overall differences in outcomes to specific differences in assumptions or parameter values, such as the choice of the social discount rate, the assumptions with respect to political constraints, or the choice of the appropriate margin for evaluation.

Summary and Conclusions

The purpose of project appraisal is to provide the connecting link between the overall objectives of the macroeconomic plan (which will be discussed in Chapter 21) and plan implementation in the form of a set of specific development projects.

We have developed a simplified neoclassical model for intertemporal decision making. From this model, we have derived several alternative criteria and decision rules. The present value criterion and decision rules were shown to be generally superior to the alternatives. If all assumptions of the neoclassical model—perfect markets, complete information, certainty, and no indivisibilities, externalities, or distortions—are valid, ordinary present value computations on the basis of market prices provide a simple, yet perfectly valid, way of deciding on whether or not an individual project should be included in the development plan.

In the second section of the chapter, we have discussed the realism of these assumptions and examined the implications for project appraisal should these assumptions not be

[28]Admittedly, the choice of margin is not independent of assumptions about the nature of the policy constraints. Indeed, the theoretical work of Diamond and Mirrlees (1971), A. B. Atkinson and Stiglitz (1972), Dasgupta and Stiglitz (1974) has demonstrated that the choice of margin depends also on the nature of the constraints. For example, where a disequilibrium exchange rate is retained and reinforced by exchange rationing, shadow pricing from the demand margin is appropriate. However, even in such situations, the use of prices based on one or the other margin exclusively, without weights being attached according to the elasticities of supply and demand and other parameters, is justified only under very special conditions.

fulfilled. Indeed, we have found that many of the assumptions are highly unrealistic in the LDC context, suggesting that ordinary present value computations are inadequate as criteria or decision rules for project appraisal. While some of the assumptions (e.g., those of certainty and the absence of indivisibilities) can generally be relaxed with only very slight modification in the analysis, the relaxation of other assumptions (e.g., market imperfections, externalities, and distortions) requires more substantial changes. With regard to capital market imperfections, externalities, and distortions, each of which could be caused by many different factors, we have found it important to determine which particular factor best explains the imperfection, and why it is not corrected or adjusted for by ordinary market forces. Only then can a proper judgement be made as to how any such factor that is considered important in particular circumstances can best be incorporated into project appraisal.

The most commonly used practical rules for project appraisal, such as ICORs, SMP, or reinvestment rates, will be critically reviewed in the appendix. While these rules conserve on information—a very scarce resource for project appraisal in LDCs—they are valid only in circumstances that virtually never prevail. These traditional criteria are far too naive; yet more comprehensive criteria and decision rules tend to be nonoperational.

The final section of the chapter provided detailed outlines of the OECD and UNIDO approaches to project appraisal. While both have definite shortcomings, they represent commendable attempts to strike a felicitous balance between analytical rigor and practicality in dealing with some highly complex issues. Indeed, project appraisal calls upon many of the analytical tools and deals with many different issues of development economics that have been treated in other parts of this book.

The particular circumstances pertaining to the type of project to be evaluated, and to the type of country in which it is to be evaluated, will go a long way in determining which specific approach should be followed in the micro-planning of project appraisal. However, because there is considerable merit in both approaches, and yet the costs of utilizing one approach after having followed the other are likely to be small, we recommend that both be used simultaneously. This would allow project evaluators to double-check their computations and identify the specific source of any differences in evaluations that may be observed from one approach to the other. The most important shadow prices that have to be computed by either approach are those for labor, capital, and foreign exchange. The choice of the social discount rate is also of great importance in project appraisal.

Appendix

A Critical Review of Conventional Criteria for Project Appraisal

Capital-Output Ratios

Assuming that capital is the only scarce factor of production, the cost of an individual project relative to the output it generates could presumably be captured by the capital-output ratio, K/O, or in incremental terms by the ICOR, $\Delta K/\Delta O = I/\Delta O$.[29] Even if data on capital stock are not available for any sector

or country, data for the change in stock or net investment are likely to be available, and thus, the use of one or the other of these criteria is generally easy. The use of these criteria as decision rules requires that K/O and/or ICOR calculations be carried out for each project (or sector), which would then be ranked according to their K/O or ICORs,

[29]One reason for the popularity of capital-output ratios and ICORs is undoubtedly the central role played by capital scarcity and hence the ICOR in Domar's growth model. This well-known model was derived from the following identities:

$$\Delta Y_p = \frac{I}{ICOR} \tag{1n}$$

where I is net investment and ΔY_p is the change in productive capacity,

$$\Delta Y = \Delta I \frac{1}{\alpha} \tag{2n}$$

where α is the marginal and average propensity to save, and Y is the change in spending (or in the demand for output), and

$$\Delta Y_p = \Delta Y \tag{3n}$$

which is the equilibrium condition.

Substituting equations 1n and 2n into equation 3n and rearranging terms, the dynamic equilibrium condition can be reexpressed as

$$\frac{\Delta I}{I} = \frac{\Delta S}{S} = \frac{\Delta Y}{Y} = \frac{\alpha}{ICOR}$$

Note that according to this formulation the rate of growth in income is determined by only two parameters—the savings ratio and the ICOR. Since the growth rate is inversely related to the ICOR, reductions in the ICOR for any economy can immediately be converted into higher growth rates of national income.

and the available investment funds would be allocated to projects starting from the top of the list (those with lowest K/Os or ICORs), working down it until all such funds were expended.

This criterion involves a number of serious limitations. First, it excludes the cost of all inputs other than that of capital.[30] Second, it neglects the time-phasing of benefits and costs of the project. This is indeed a serious limitation, and in this respect, the ICOR criterion is vastly inferior to the present value and internal rate of return criteria. Indeed, investments requiring large ICORs are often those with greater durability and lesser depreciation than those with smaller ICORs. Similarly, investments with low ICORs may require long maturation periods before they become productive, whereas those with high ICORs may mature quickly. Third, measurements of ICORs can often be misleading, in the sense that they hide changes in the utilization of resources that may exist for reasons completely independent of the relative merits of alternative investment projects. Fourth, as with the present value criterion, the use of the capital-output ratios, or ICORs as investment decision rules, normally ignores indirect costs and benefits of the projects and precludes consideration of externalities and interdependencies among different projects.

While one extremely important justification for the use of ICORs as investment criteria is certainly their greater degree of operationalism, their use has sometimes been justified on the ground that ICORs are inversely related to the rate of return to capital, r, which can be defined as $\Delta R/\Delta K$, where R is net revenue. Dividing numerator and denominator by ΔO, we obtain

$$r = \frac{\dfrac{\Delta K}{\Delta O}}{\dfrac{\Delta R}{\Delta O}} = \frac{\dfrac{\Delta R}{\Delta O}}{ICOR} \qquad (1)$$

where $\Delta R/\Delta O$ is the share of returns to capital in additional revenue or value added. This formula shows, however, that differences in ICORs from project to project or sector to sector provide satisfactory measures of the corresponding differences in the rates of return

to capital only if the ratios $\Delta R/\Delta O$, representing the incremental factor share of capital in value added, remain constant. National accounts statistics and other data suggest that the $\Delta R/\Delta O$ ratios vary considerably between sectors and projects, limiting the usefulness of ICOR as an inverse measure of the rate of return on capital.

Some of the limitations of capital-output ratios and ICORs would be mitigated if one could be assured that these ratios are stable over time. Gianaris (1970) has provided evidence for a number of countries suggesting that ICORs are indeed relatively stable in some sectors (manufacturing, transport, electricity, and services) but not in others (agriculture, mining, and public administration).

An empirical generality that has received considerable attention in recent years is the negative relationship between ICORs and the rate of growth.[31] In footnote 29, we demonstrated how such a relationship can be derived from the Domar growth model. That the relationship may simply be tautological can be seen by reexpressing the definition of ICOR as

$$ICOR = \frac{\Delta K}{\Delta O} = \frac{\dfrac{\Delta K}{K}}{\dfrac{\Delta O}{O}} \frac{K}{O} \qquad (2)$$

Thus, given an average capital-output ratio, the ICOR is inversely related to the rate of growth of output.[32]

From the "two-gap model" they have developed, Chenery and Strout (1966) and Strout (1969) argue that growth in GNP, ΔO, is constrained both by shortages in capital formation, I, and by shortages in foreign exchange, which limit the growth of raw material and intermediate goods imports, ΔM_v,

$$\Delta O = \frac{1}{ICOR} I + b \, \Delta M_v \qquad (3)$$

Assuming: (1) that imports of consumer goods, M_c, can be ignored; (2) that imports of investment goods, M_i, are proportionate to the level of investment; and (3) that the rate

---

[30]While it has been suggested that such an omission may be justified on the grounds of "surplus labor," Sen (1960) has pointed out that, even if surplus labor exists, the wage bill imposes a legitimate social cost to the extent that it generates additional consumption.

[31]See Walters (1966), Vanek and Studenmund (1968), Chenery and Strout (1966), Strout (1969), and Archibald (1964).

[32]Vanek and Studenmund (1968) note that this inverse relationship between ICOR and the rate of growth has most often been obtained empirically with the use of gross ICORs instead of net ICORs, and they argue that the relationship may be explained by the fact that at higher rates of growth smaller proportions of additional national income will be required for maintenance and replacement.

of growth of investment tends to be constant, we can write

$$\Delta M = \Delta M_i + \Delta M_c + \Delta M_v \tag{4}$$

$$\Delta M_i = c\Delta I \tag{5}$$

$$\Delta I = dI \tag{6}$$

$$\Delta M_v = \Delta M - cdI \tag{7}$$

Substituting equation 7 into equation 3, we obtain

$$\Delta O = \left(\frac{1}{ICOR} - bcd\right)I + b\,\Delta M \tag{8}$$

Dividing equation 8 through by I, we obtain

$$\Delta O/I = \left(\frac{1}{ICOR} - bcd\right) + b\frac{\Delta M}{I} \tag{9}$$

One can add to the expression for the marginal productivity of investment, (1/gross ICOR), a term for the rate of growth in GNP, $\Delta O/O$, to take account of any of the interactions between gross ICORs and the rate of growth, and another term, O/P, to account for the empirical generality observed by Kuznets (1960), that ICORs tend to rise with the level of per capita income, reflecting among other things the rising importance of social overhead capital as income rises. Thus, Strout (1969) expresses the inverse of the gross ICOR as

$$\Delta O/I = \left(\frac{1}{ICOR} - bcd\right) + b\frac{\Delta M}{I} + e\frac{\Delta O}{O}$$
$$+ f\frac{O}{P} \tag{10}$$

Using international cross-section data for 32 LDCs over each of two different five-year periods, Strout obtained estimates of the parameters b and e that were significantly positive and of f that was significantly negative, thereby confirming each of his a priori expectations. Strout argues that the relaxation of the foreign exchange constraint either by export promotion or foreign assistance plays a critical role in stimulating growth and improving capital productivity. Improvements in capital productivity (decreases in ICOR) might then be taken as indicators of development potential and/or performance. Somewhat akin to this conception is that of Leibenstein (1957), who interpreted the inverse relationship between the ICORs and the rate of growth in income as evidence in support of his "critical minimum effort" or "big push" hypothesis. Only rapid rates of growth gen-

erated by a big push lead to successful and sustained growth and improvements in factor productivity.

Social Marginal Productivity

In proposing the use of the social marginal productivity (SMP) criterion, Chenery (1953) has tried to relax some of the more unrealistic assumptions in the ICOR and ordinary unmodified present value criteria. In contrast to these other investment criteria, the SMP criterion allows one to consider the scarcity of resources other than capital, and also to consider indirect and direct effects and those affecting social as well as private profitability. For example, the SMP calculation for any project usually includes not only the increase in output (net of the opportunity cost of the resources utilized) resulting from the project but also the increased output attributable to the external economies derived from the project, such as the social evaluation in terms of national income of the improvement in the balance of payments position attributable to the project. Warning against excessive reliance on market prices, Chenery (1955, 1958) and others proposed and pioneered the use of linear and nonlinear programming methods to compute the social opportunity cost, "shadow" or "accounting" prices in evaluating the indirect welfare effects in terms of various other resources, including capital, foreign exchange, and skilled labor. Comparing the application of the ICOR and SMP criteria in evaluating a number of different investment projects in several Mediterranean countries, Chenery demonstrated that the two criteria can yield quite different rankings and investment decision rules, thereby emphasizing the importance of carrying out the more sophisticated SMP calculations. Chenery (1959), Hirschman (1958), and others have demonstrated that the programming approach to SMP also accounts for interdependencies between different investment projects. Moreover, Chenery's simulations (discussed in the following chapter) indicate that failure to coordinate investments particularly in regard to their time-phasing can lead to substantial losses in productivity.

The Reinvestment Rate Criterion

The SMP criterion has been severely criticized by Leibenstein (1957b) and Sen (1957) on the grounds that it is too static. They have conceded that successful determination of

SMP would maximize income and output in the short run, but have argued that only by the most fortunate of coincidences would SMP also maximize income and growth in the long run. Assuming that capital is the only scarce resource, Leibenstein proposed that the correct criterion for long-run development is to maximize the rate of reinvestment per unit of capital. Since it is assumed that the reinvestment rate will be higher the greater the share of capital in value added, Leibenstein's criterion would tend to favor allocation of investment to capital-intensive activities, probably increasing unemployment in the short run. Moes (1957) pointed out that there is little reason to believe that Leibenstein's reinvestment rate criterion would be very different from ordinary profit maximization nor can one see why profit-maximizing entrepreneurs would ever want to employ capital-intensive techniques, especially if labor becomes relatively cheaper as a result of increasing unemployment. The problem of feeding the unemployed may impose real social costs on society, thereby lowering the realizable reinvestment rate in macro terms (Neisser 1956). The real mechanism behind Leibenstein's criterion is income redistribution. The necessity of raising income inequality farther to achieve a higher investment ratio seems a hard pill to swallow for most LDCs. Even if such redistribution were necessary, however, it would seem worthwhile to investigate the possibility that there might be more efficient ways of achieving redistribution without having to resort to investment criteria.

Although Leibenstein's criticism of ICOR and SMP criteria for being too static and short-sighted is appropriate, it should be obvious to the reader that maximization of the rate of growth is as simplistic and deficient a goal as that of short-term maximization of output.[33] Present value or internal rate of return calculations are much superior, in that both present and future benefits and costs are evaluated and weighted appropriately.

Other Approaches to the Shadow Price of Foreign Exchange

The exchange rate tends to be one of the most distorted prices in LDCs, because among other reasons its adjustment often entails an exces-

sive cost in political terms (R. N. Cooper 1971). Therefore, determination of the shadow price of foreign exchange has received somewhat more attention in the context of LDCs than have other shadow prices. Krueger (1966) and Bruno (1967) have suggested that the shadow price of foreign exchange be computed as a simple average of the direct and indirect domestic resource costs (computed with input-output analysis) of saving one unit of foreign exchange via import substitution, on the one hand, and exports, on the other.

To avoid penalizing industries that use domestic inputs whose prices are distorted by tariffs, Balassa and Schydlowsky (1968) recommend the use of effective protective rates in which nontraded tradeable goods are evaluated at free trade prices. Although in principle the calculations could be carried out in terms of implicit exchange rates, as in S. R. Lewis (1968), the Balassa-Schydlowsky modifications and their practical applications are limited to trade restrictions in the form of tariffs. For practical purposes, both the Krueger-Bruno and Balassa-Schydlowsky approaches assume that the input-output coefficients used in the calculations are not affected by changes in regime, that is, from one of exchange control to one of free trade at an equilibrium exchange rate. However, neither approach gives much of a clue as to exactly how to select from the whole range of domestic resource costs per unit of foreign exchange or effective protective rates the particular rate that should be used for the shadow price of foreign exchange.

Among other practical approaches that have been suggested for obtaining an "equilibrium" exchange rate or a "shadow price" of foreign exchange are several varieties of parity rates. These involve comparisons of the current exchange rate relative to an index of internal and/or external prices relative to that of another country, or another period in which an appropriate exchange rate (deflated by the appropriate corresponding price index) is assumed to prevail. Practical problems with this approach include: (1) the difficulty of demonstrating that the base year or country in fact did have an appropriate exchange rate; (2) the numerous problems concerned with the choice of weights attached to prices of individual items in arriving at an overall deflator; and (3) insufficiency of satisfactory data.

---

[33]A more formal comparison of SMP and reinvestment rate criteria, which comes to the same conclusion, is provided by Marglin (1968).

Chapter 21
Planning for Economic Development

Planning, at least in name, is widespread in both DCs and LDCs. Ministries of planning, central planning boards, economic plans, and planners abound all over the world. The scope of planning, however, varies considerably from one country to another.

At one extreme, planning may consist only of the normal task of government budgeting, the management of public enterprises, and the rational time-phasing of certain public services, such as national defense expenditure, public utilities, and public education. At the other extreme, planning consists of preparing detailed blueprints of the future economic structure and implementing them through direct or indirect manipulations of government instruments. While in the former case market prices play a large role, in the latter they are less important relative to nonprice allocation by fiat or decree. In between these two extremes, there are several varieties of planning.

For example, in some countries, planning means providing "reasonable forecasts" of the supplies and demands of a number of goods and services and their aggregates such as industrial production, GNP, employment. Once these forecasts are made, it is hoped that they will be broadly accepted to help form people's expectations, thus becoming self-fulfilling prophecies.[1] This is the notion behind "indicative planning," which is being used extensively in France and the Netherlands. In other cases, planning represents an attempt to bring factors other than market prices into the economic calculus by which scarce resources are allocated among competing uses.

Which type of planning should most profitably be practiced in each country is largely a normative question beyond the com-

[1] For analysis of how the forecast can affect behavior, see Grunberg and Modigliani (1964) and Simon (1954).

petence of the professional economist. In the short run, the appropriate type of planning presumably depends on such considerations as the degree to which the market mechanism pervades economic decisions or the extent of market imperfections and price distortions and their causes. In the long run, a country's approach to planning will be determined by the political, social, and philosophical judgments of its people.

Why Plan?

The problem with development is that its path may not be as smooth or automatic as the dominant paradigm of neoclassical economics would have it. It is not necessarily true, especially in a world with imperfect markets and incomplete adjustments, that, after an early rough ascent, development trickles down and spreads among individuals and sectors of an economy. The backwash effects of growth are important, and development must be studied as a system in disequilibrium. It is apposite to conclude this book with a chapter on planning—the attempt to correct for imperfections and for the breakdown of automatic adjustment mechanisms.

The free market has been shown to provide for an optimal allocation of resources at a particular point in time under the following conditions: (1) there is perfect competition in all product and factor markets; (2) technical and price efficiency prevails; (3) consumers and producers alike have immediate and complete access to information about their productive and market opportunities; (4) there are no externalities in production or consumption; and (5) a system of lump-sum taxes and subsidies can be designed to account for any differences that arise between the efficient and the desired distribution of resources. Furthermore, for the free market to yield an optimal allocation of resources over time, these same conditions must prevail with respect to present and future production and allocation decisions.[2]

Clearly, neither the static nor the dynamic conditions are easily met in the real world, especially in LDCs. Market forces, therefore, cannot be entirely relied upon for spreading economic development; planning becomes an imperative. As a result, most LDCs

have felt justified in their attempts to supplement or substitute for free market forces through planning. By planning their economies, they have hoped to avoid the obvious defects of the market economy (which are thought to be at least partially responsible for the existing disequilibrium and for underdevelopment) and at the same time to mobilize additional resources, marshall existing resources more efficiently, bring interdependencies and externalities into the decision-making calculus, change expectations, and reduce inequalities and uncertainties.

Unfortunately, a good deal of this has been wishful thinking. Planning procedures, too, have suffered from obvious defects; important factors have been overlooked; inconsistencies have been introduced. As a number of market-oriented economists have noted,[3] proper planning requires heavy doses of the very inputs that are generally extremely scarce in LDCs—such as information and the skilled practitioners who are able to process and analyze it. Therefore, planning may not be particularly well suited to the factor proportions of LDCs. Moreover, in terms of the ultimate test of performance, there does not seem to be any clear-cut evidence that growth rates of income or income per capita are positively correlated with the resources expended in planning.

However, improvements in macro-planning are being made and further refinements are well within the realm of possibility. In this chapter, we attempt to demonstrate some methods for improving the quality of economic plans and their implementation.

We begin by considering various criteria for evaluating a development plan, and we demonstrate with reference to specific development plans and types of planning models how these criteria can be applied. Next, we demonstrate methods by which a planning model (and the plan based upon it) can be tested. Finally, we present methods for linking the goals of development plans with the policy instruments available, and we demonstrate how these methods can be applied.

Criteria for Planning

As experience with planning has accumulated, there has been an increasing tendency to substitute formal procedures and models for

---

[2]For a more detailed exposition of these conditions and what happens when they are not fulfilled, see Chapter 20.

[3]For example, see H. G. Johnson (1958).

intuitive judgments about priority areas, broad developmental strategies, and so on. Likewise, development plans, and the planning models on which they are based, have been subjected to increasingly formal criteria in their evaluations. The purpose of the increased formality and sophistication of these models and of the criteria used for evaluating them has, of course, been to overcome the shortcomings of past attempts at planning.

The type of planning model used and the criteria employed in its evaluation naturally depend to a large extent on the scope and nature of planning. In some cases, it may be sufficient that the plan (or the planning model) be internally consistent. In other cases, it will be necessary to test the plan for feasibility and optimality.

Consistency tests are demonstrated in the case of Ecuador's First Development Plan with respect to an input-output (I-O) model, and in the case of external assistance planning in Central America with reference to a two-gap model. Feasibility and optimality tests are demonstrated with respect to a linear programming (LP) model of the Greek economy.

A Consistency Test with an Input–Output Model

We refer again to the I-O model for the Ecuadorian economy presented in Chapter 4. Table 4.2 represents the interindustry transactions for Ecuador, 1963. By adding together (for simplicity) the imported and domestic interindustry inputs that were given separately in that table, we reduce the number of rows from 18 to 9.[4] Likewise, we add the domestic services to imports (given in column 10) to the ordinary service inputs of columns 7–9. In this way, the 10 × 10 interindustry transactions table (Table 4.2) is reduced to a 9 × 9 table that does not distinguish between imported and domestic intermediate goods. We further aggregate the 9 × 9 table into three sectors, primary (sectors 1–3), industry (sectors 4 and 5), and services (sectors 6–9). The resulting 3 × 3 aggregate interindustry transactions table for Ecuador

---

[4]We adopt this procedure here only to facilitate demonstration of the method. In most cases, it is extremely important to keep the domestic and imported input components separate. In this way, they can be of considerable use in checking for internal consistency with respect to the foreign exchange constraint.

appears in Table 21.1. This table will form the basis for judging the consistency of the projections of components of final demand for the period 1963–1973 (expressed in 1963 prices) that were made in Ecuador's First National Development Plan. These projections appear in Table 21.2.

From the 3 × 3 interindustry transactions table given in Table 21.1, the I-O matrix of coefficients a_{ij} can be computed: $a_{ij} = X_{ij}/X_j$, as was shown in our discussion of I-O analysis in Chapter 4. The subtraction of the resulting 3 × 3 I-O matrix, $\mathbf{A}$, from the 3 × 3 identity matrix, $\mathbf{I}$, yields a 3 × 3 Leontief matrix, $\mathbf{I} - \mathbf{A}$. The inverse of this matrix $(\mathbf{I} - \mathbf{A})^{-1}$ is presented in Table 21.3.

Multiplying the column vector of sectoral changes in final demand from column 9 of Table 21.2 by the 3 × 3 inverse matrix of Table 21.3, we obtain the vector of sectoral increments in gross production implied by the plan's projected increases in final demands between 1963 and 1973. These required increases in gross production, shown in column 1 of Table 21.4, are not directly comparable to the plan's output projections, because the latter were given in terms of value added. Therefore, from Table 21.1, we compute the value-added coefficients by dividing the value added in any sector, j, V_j, by the corresponding gross production in that sector, X_j. For example we divide value added of the primary sector (which from column 1 of Table 21.1 is 6,154) by the value of gross production of the primary sector, 8,829, and similarly for the other sectors. Under the assumption that the calculated value added and input-ouput coefficients would remain constant throughout the plan period, 1963–1973, we obtain the required increases in value added shown in column 2 of Table 21.4.

However, the realism of the assumption of constant value added and input-output coefficients is subject to challenge, and therefore, one needs a method for "updating" or forecasting changes in the original $\mathbf{A}$ matrix of I-O coefficients. One method that is commonly used for this purpose is the so-called RAS method pioneered by Stone and Brown (1962). This method consists of premultiplying the original matrix, $\mathbf{A}$, by the diagonal matrix, $\mathbf{R}$, of the expected price indexes in the plan year and postmultiplying the $\mathbf{A}$ matrix by another diagonal matrix, $\mathbf{S}$, of indexes of resource use per unit of output. The new updated matrix

Table 21.1 *Aggregate Interindustry Transactions Table for Ecuador, 1963 (in Millions of Sucres at Current Consumer Prices)*

	Primary (1)	Industry (2)	Services (3)	Inter-industry Demand (4)	Private Con-sumption (5)	Fixed Invest-ment (6)	Changes in Stocks (7)	Govern-ment Con-sumption (8)	Exports (9)	Subsidies Less Indirect Taxes (10)	Imports (11)	Domestic Services to Imports (12)	Final Demand (13)
Sector of Origin													
Primary	347	1,586	11	1,944	4,740		209	205	2,178	−128			6,885
Industry	433	2,524	722	3,679	4,185	2,142	156	524	492	−215			5,140
Services	1,895	1,596	472	3,963	3,425			462	354	−320	319		3,630
Interindustry Inputs	2,675	5,706	1,205	9,586	12,350	2,148	305	1,191	3,024	−663	2,150		15,655
Value Added	6,154	3,113	6,388							−861		455	
Gross Production	8,829	8,819	7,593								746		

Source: Table 4.2.

Table 21.2 *Projections for Increases in Components of Final Demand, 1963–1973, Ecuador Development Plan (in Millions of Sucres at Current Consumer Prices)*

Sector of Origin	Sector of Destination								
	Private Consumption (1)	Fixed Investment (2)	Exports (3)	Changes in Stocks (4)	Government Consumption (5)	Subsidies Less Indirect Taxes (6)	Imports (7)	Domestic Services to Imports (8)	Final Demand (9)
Primary	2,483		850	200	150	100	−31		3,614
Industry	2,729	4,099	550	300	400	300	2,500		5,278
Services	3,009		50	0	450	200	700	500	3,109
Total	8,221	4,099	1,450	500	1,000	600	3,169	500	12,001

Note: The disaggregation of private consumption for the three sectors was based on the figures given in Table 21.1 and the relative rates of increase of consumption from the classes given in the *Memorias of the Banco Central del Ecuador* (years 1950 and 1964).

Sources:

Private consumption was estimated from data in the *Plan General de Desarrollo Económico y Social del Ecuador.* Quito: Junta Nacional de Planificación y Coordinación Económica, 1963.

Investment, exports, government consumption and imports were estimated from the projections of the *Plan General de Desarrollo Económico y Social del Ecuador.* Quito: Junta Nacional de Planificación y Coordinación Económica, 1963; and *Programa de Desarrollo Agropecuario: Metas y Perspectivas.* Quito: Junta Nacional de Planificación y Coordinación Económica, 1964.

Table 21.3 *Inverse of the 3×3 Leontief Matrix Derived from the Interindustry Transactions Table for Ecuador, 1963*

	Primary	Industry	Services
Primary	1.06152	0.27487	0.02949
Industry	0.10804	1.46578	0.14876
Services	0.26375	0.34569	1.10171

Source: Table 21.1.

of I-O coefficients, $\overline{\mathbf{A}}$, is therefore given by

$$\overline{\mathbf{A}} = \mathbf{RAS}$$

Usually, it is wise to supplement this rather mechanical procedure with other methods and information on an ad hoc basis. For example, by referring to the original more disaggregated interindustry transactions table—in this case the 10 × 10 table given in Table 4.2—one can adjust for expected changes in subsector composition within any sector by multiplying all elements of a subsector column by an index of expected subsector size in the plan year and then recomputing the **A** matrix.[5]

[5]For example, suppose that the subsectors (agriculture, livestock, and mining) of industry 1, "primary" in the 3 × 3 classification of Table 21.1, are expected to change in the following way: agriculture to increase by 10 percent relative to the base period, livestock

Also, engineers or economists may be able to predict some of the more obvious changes in individual coefficients on the basis of the experience of other countries. Over a period of as long as a decade, two of the most predictable changes in input-output relationships are the increased use of agricultural and industrial inputs by the agricultural sector. Indeed, changes in the coefficients a_{11} and a_{21} were projected in the Agricultural Plan itself. Therefore, we have utilized the plan's projected changes in this respect in arriving at the revised estimates of the required increases in value added (implied by the final demand projections) given in column 3 of Table 21.4. These increased value-added requirements are converted into the sectoral investment requirements of column 7 by multiplying them by the incremental capital-value-added ratios given in column 6, taken directly from the plan.

Are these value added and investment requirements consistent with the value-added projections and investment allocations of the plan shown in columns 4 and 8 respectively?

to increase by 25 percent, and mining to fall by 10 percent. This could be achieved by multiplying the figures in column 1, agriculture, of Table 4.2 by 1.1, those in column 2, livestock, by 1.25, and those in column 3, mining, by 0.9, then reaggregating to the single sector "primary" and recomputing the I-O coefficients for that sector.

Table 21.4 *Consistency of Value Added, Investment, and Final Demand Projections of Ecuador's Development Plan, 1963–1973*

	Required Increase in Gross Production (1)	Required Increase in Value Added (2)	Required Increase in Value Added[a] (3)	Planned Increase in Value Added (4)	Value Added Discrepancy Column 4 — Column 3 (5)
Primary	5,379	3,749	4,052	4,627	575
Industry	8,589	3,032	3,132	3,030	−102
Services	6,203	5,219	5,219	4,915	−304

Note:

[a]Using the changes in the agricultural input coefficients postulated by the Agricultural Plan (*Programma de Desarrollo Agropecuario: Metas y Perspectivas.* Quito: Junta Nacional de Planificación y Coordinación Económica, 1964).

Source: Tables 21.2 and 21.3.

This question can be answered by referring to the calculated discrepancies shown in columns 5 and 9 for value added and investment respectively. The largest discrepancies, amounting to about 12 percent in relative terms, are in the agricultural sector. However, since these discrepancies are positive, that is, they represent an overexpansion or overinvestment in the sector, they should not constitute cause for alarm. Indeed, the expansion of this sector would presumably allow for greater exports to pay for additional imports of industrial goods to offset the expected deficit in industrial value added and at the same time to narrow the rather alarming balance of trade deficit for 1973 that was forecast by the plan. The one possibly serious inconsistency is in the services sector, where a relatively high capital-output ratio makes the absolute magnitude of the investment discrepancy rather large —indicating a lingering underestimate of the social overhead capital requirements implied by Ecuador's plan targets. Since the percentage errors are in all cases relatively small, however, and since all the capital-output ratios used in the plan estimates were considerably higher than those observed historically, we may conclude that the plan targets and projections have been remarkably consistent, even though I-O analysis was not, in fact, employed.

A Consistency Test with a Two-Gap Model

Another type of model that can be employed to test for internal consistency of some aspects of a development plan is the so-called gap model. Gap models focus on the consistency, or rather inconsistency, of plan projections in respect to certain resource requirements. Although not usually referred to as a form of gap model, manpower planning models have attempted to compute the manpower gaps in plans both with respect to overall manpower requirements and with respect to specific kinds of skills.[6] Most gap models, however, focus on two scarce resources, capital and foreign exchange, the shortages in which are seen as imposing effective constraints on economic development.[7]

After a brief critical exposition of the logic of two-gap models, we proceed to an application of the model to external assistance planning in Central America.

The Logic and Empirical Relevance of Two-Gap Models

While the notion of a capital constraint can hardly be challenged, the notion of a foreign exchange constraint independent of the capital constraint (which can, of course, be seen as a constraint on the country's ability to borrow externally) requires some explanation and some rather special assumptions.

To illustrate the model and indicate its relation to neoclassical trade theory of the type developed in Chapter 7, we follow Lal

[6]For examples of such studies (which are usually based on I-O methods), see Harbison and Myers (1965) and Parnes (1962); for an evaluation, see Hollister (1967). Indeed, applications of this sort may be particularly important because of the long lead times required to bring such investments to fruition.

[7]For examples, see Chenery and Bruno (1962), McKinnon (1964), Chenery and Strout (1966), Vanek (1967), and UNCTAD (1968).

Table 21.4   *Continued*

Planned Capital to Value Added Ratios (6)	Required Investment Implied by Final Demand (7)	Planned Investment (8)	Investment Discrepancy Column 8 — Column 7 (9)	Investment Discrepancy (Percent) (10)
1.6287	6,600	7,536	936	12.4
2.8977	9,085	8,780	−295	− 3.3
5.9495	31,051	29,242	−1,809	− 6.2

(1972) in utilizing a two-period two-commodity model. While somewhat less restrictive formulations are possible,[8] this version highlights the characteristics of the model.

Let us assume that there are two goods: an exportable, X, and an importable, M. To make the model fit the conditions of most LDCs, we assume that X is food and M is manufactures that are composed of both intermediate and capital goods. To fit the conditions of the two-gap model, we assume that M cannot easily be produced locally (e.g., because of insufficient local markets, excessive transport costs to external markets, and inadequate technical skills), or if it were produced locally, it would require a large input of imported M per unit of output. Hence, M is typically imported. Production of one unit of X requires an input of a_{xx} units of X, made up of raw materials and labor (paid in terms of food) and also af a_{mx} units of M, consisting of fertilizers, tractors, and tools. While it may be possible to have negative import substitution in production of X (i.e., a_{mx} could be raised relative to a_{xx}), it is assumed that positive import substitution (an increase in a_{xx}) relative to a_{mx} is impossible, because import substitution has already been pushed to the limit of practicality. Since M cannot be consumed, consumption must take the form of X. That X which is not consumed domestically can be exported or used as an input in producing X, but for reasons given above, it cannot be used to produce M domestically. Similarly, foreign (developed) countries are

not able to transform X into M on an economic basis. They use X only for consumption, and their consumption of food is (after a point) subject to elasticities of demand with respect to income of zero and with respect to price of unity. At a particular point in time, therefore, there is a maximum amount of export proceeds, which means (in the absence of capital inflows) that the capacity to import is fixed. Although X can be saved and invested to increase the productive capacity of X in subsequent periods, after a point additional savings have no effect on future output of X, that is, the transformation function between present and future consumption becomes horizontal.

These assumptions are embodied in Figure 21.1. The series of parallel kinked output isoquants, Q_0, Q_1, Q_2, Q_3, reflect the limited degree and nature of substitution between the two inputs, X and M, in the production of X.[9] Note that the angle of the ray OD is determined by the input of M per unit of X, a_{mx}. Let us assume that initially the quantity of X not consumed domestically (i.e., saved), is OX_1. From X_1 in the horizontal axis, the country can trade for M along the foreign offer curve, X_1AT, to the point of tangency with the highest possible output isoquant, Q_1. At the optimum, then, the country trades $X_1 - X_2$ of X for OM_1 of M. The remaining savings of X, that is, OX_2, and of M, that is, OM_1, can then be utilized for producing out-

[8]See, for example, Nelson (1970).

[9]These isoquants touch the M axis because of the assumption that M can be substituted indefinitely for X without affecting the marginal rate of substitution.

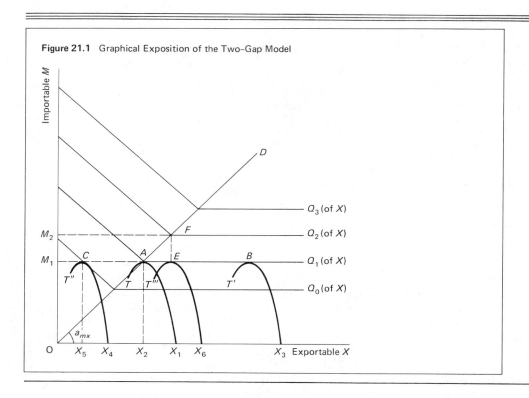

Figure 21.1 Graphical Exposition of the Two-Gap Model

put of Q_1 in the next period. In this range of savings, an increase in savings (in terms of X), for example, to OX_3, does not allow the economy to attain a higher output isoquant, because the foreign exchange constraint is binding (imports cannot exceed OM_1).[10] A higher isoquant (e.g., Q_2) can be reached only if more foreign exchange is made available, so that with savings of OX_6, from which OM_1 of imports can be earned, as at point E, and the foreign assistance supplement of $M_2 - M_1$, imports can reach OM_2 at point F. In such a situation, the growth rates of output and consumption are, therefore, constrained by the shortage of foreign exchange and not by insufficient savings.

These conclusions hold only with respect to specific ranges of the parameters, such as the level of savings. For example, if the original level of savings were only OX_4, an increase in savings to OX_1 would not be redundant, and thus, the foreign exchange constraint would not be binding.

[10]With savings in excess of OX_1 redundant, point A indicates the most likely "equilibrium" position; *ex post* savings will not exceed OX_1 unless, of course, the marginal utility of present consumption is zero.

While the model is undoubtedly unrealistic for some LDCs, it may be realistic for others, for example, when the returns to additional traditional exports may be very small and the costs of additional import substitution very high. Quibbling about assumptions is, however, not likely to resolve the issue of whether or not two-gap models are useful.

Diwan (1968) and Diwan and Marwah (1973) have attempted to test the empirical relevance of the model by estimating production functions (or time derivatives thereof) that include imports as an independent variable along with the ordinary factors of production, capital, labor, and resources. Generally, their results show that labor is redundant (as in the surplus labor hypothesis) and that capital and foreign exchange are the relevant constraints. These results would seem to support the usefulness of the two-gap model formulations. However, since their estimates are based on single equation methods and since there are surely positive effects going the other way, from income to imports, the elasticities of output with respect to imports are biased upward. Without knowledge of the magnitude of this bias, it cannot be asserted with confidence that the true elasticity is greater than zero.[11] Even if growth is constrained by foreign exchange or imports, one need not adhere to the further assumption of the two-gap models that domestic tax and allocation policies are powerless to bring about change.[12]

The uses of two-gap models include forecasting the order of magnitude of foreign assistance that would be required to achieve different target rates of growth, and also planning an efficient allocation of foreign assistance among recipients.[13] Next, we provide an application of the model in such a context.

Application of the Model to External Assistance Planning in Central America

Assuming one or more alternative target rates of growth of GNP, the two-gap model can be applied to foreign assistance planning in the following steps: First, with respect to the savings-investment gap:

1. Compute the investment requirements for achieving the target rate of growth (on the basis of actual, assumed, or forecasted incremental capital-output ratios).
2. Estimate the expected flow of savings consistent with past behavioral patterns and future projections.[14]
3. Calculate the net savings-investment gap by subtracting the estimates of step 2 from those of step 1.

Next, with respect to the foreign exchange gap, the following steps apply:

4. Compute the import requirements for achieving the target rate of growth (on the basis of historical or forecasted average or marginal imported input requirements).
5. Estimate the expected demand for exports and other sources of foreign exchange.
6. Calculate the foreign exchange gap by subtracting the estimates of step 5 from those of step 4.

[11]For criticism of two-gap models, see Fei and Ranis (1968), Bruton (1969), and Behrman (1971).

[12]For example, in our chapter on exports, we presented fairly strong evidence that exchange rate and tax policies can increase the values of exports and hence the capacity to import.

[13]It was in this context that the gap models were originally developed and applied, for example, by AID and subsequently by UNCTAD (1968).

[14]This may not be so easy as it sounds, because the redundancy of some *ex ante* savings means that the *ex ante* marginal propensity to save cannot be obtained simply by regressing savings on income (Behrman 1971).

Ex post the two gaps will, of course, be identical, the residual *F* being defined as net foreign investment. The above computations refer to *ex ante* relationships. The results of such computations, therefore, may be used for checking the consistency between the trade projections and the savings-investment projections. If one gap is found to be considerably greater than the other, it helps to indicate priorities for policy planning and suggests the extent to which *ex ante* plans will not be fulfilled and why. By repeating such calculations for different target rates of growth and different countries, donor agencies may be able to compare the marginal productivity of external assistance at different levels of aid among a number of aid-receiving countries. Chenery and Strout (1966) and others have suggested that the marginal productivity of external assistance will be greater when the two (*ex ante*) gaps are close together, because only in such situations will one dollar of foreign aid serve to relax both constraints simultaneously.[15]

We proceed now to a simple application of the model for estimating foreign assistance requirements for Central America between 1968 and 1972.[16] While the model is clearly of the two-gap variety, our interpretation of the results differs considerably from the standard one.

In 1967, the five countries of Central America (Costa Rica, El Salvador, Guatemala, Honduras, and Nicaragua) had total population of 13.6 million, which was increasing at about 3.5 percent per annum, and gross regional product of $4,000 million at 1962 prices, which was increasing at about 5 percent per annum, implying that per capita income was about $288 and growing at a rate of 1.5 percent per annum. We desire to estimate (via the two-gap model) the resource costs of raising the growth rate of per capita income to 2.5 percent per annum by 1972.[17] It was assumed, perhaps optimistically, that the population growth rate could be cut to 3 percent per annum by 1972. This would mean that

[15]If technical skills are in shorter supply than capital, however, foreign aid that is more closely linked to provision of technical assistance can be more effective than capital-linked foreign assistance.

[16]This application can be found in greater detail in Nugent (1967c).

[17]This rate of growth is the hemispheric target set by the Organization of American States for the period under investigation.

Table 21.5 *Foreign Exchange and Savings Gap Projections for Central America 1968–1972 under Different Assumptions (in Millions of U.S. Dollars)*

Item	Row Computations	1967	1968	1969	1970	1971	1972
I. TARGET VALUES OF GROSS DOMESTIC PRODUCT							
1. Gross Domestic Product	GDP_5	3,930	4,126	4,332	4,459	4,776	5,015
2. Gross Domestic Product	$GDP_{5.5}$	3,930	4,146	4,374	4,615	4,869	5,137
II. FOREIGN EXCHANGE GAP PROJECTIONS							
3. Exports	E_A	705	729	755	781	810	839
4. Exports	E_B	705	737	771	810	852	900
5. Net Factor Income Inflow	NFY	−48	−52	−57	−63	−70	−78
6. Private Capital Inflow	P_A	72	82	93	105	117	129
7. Private Capital Inflow	P_B	72	87	104	124	146	169
8. Imports	M_5	836	891	950	1,014	1,081	1,153
9. Imports	$M_{5.5}$	836	905	978	1,058	1,145	1,239
10. Foreign Exchange Gap	FEG_{A5} $(3+5+6-8)$	−107	−132	−159	−191	−224	−263
11. Foreign Exchange Gap	$FEG_{A5.5}$ $(3+5+6-9)$	−107	−146	−187	−235	−288	−349
12. Foreign Exchange Gap	FEG_{B5} $(4+5+7-8)$	−107	−119	−132	−143	−150	−162
13. Foreign Exchange Gap	$FEG_{B5.5}$ $(4+5+7-9)$	−107	−133	−160	−187	−214	−248
III. SAVINGS GAP PROJECTIONS							
14. Depreciation	D_5 (0.0526) (Row 2)		217	228	239	251	264
15. Depreciation	$D_{5.5}$ (0.0526) (Row 3)		218	230	243	256	270
16. Private Domestic Savings	S_5		162	170	178	186	193
17. Private Domestic Savings	$S_{5.5}$		163	172	181	190	198
18. Private Capital Inflow	P_A	72	82	93	105	117	129
19. Private Capital Inflow	P_B	72	87	104	124	146	169
20. Government Savings	G	75	81	88	94	105	120
21. Investment Required	I_5	600	642	687	735	786	841
22. Investment Required	$I_{5.5}$	600	648	700	756	816	881
23. Savings Gap	SG_{A5} $(14+16+18+20-21)$	−107	−100	−108	−115	−127	−135
24. Savings Gap	$SG_{A5.5}$ $(15+17+18+20-22)$	−107	−104	−117	−133	−148	−164
25. Savings Gap	SG_{B5} $(14+16+19+20-21)$	−107	−95	−97	−96	−98	−95
26. Savings Gap	$SG_{B5.5}$ $(15+17+19+20-22)$	−107	−99	−106	−114	−119	−124
IV. INCREASE IN LARGEST GAP REQUIRED TO RAISE TARGET GDP GROWTH RATE FROM 5 TO 5.5 PERCENT PER ANNUM							
27. Increase in FEG_A	$(11-10)$		13	28	44	64	86
28. Increase in FEG_B	$(13-12)$		13	28	44	64	86
29. $FEG_{B5.0} - FEG_{A5.0}$	$(13-10)$		1	1	−4	−14	−15

Source: Nugent, J. B. (1967c), "Foreign Assistance Planning: A Semi-Quantitative Approach to Development Planning in Central America," Los Angeles, University of Southern California (mimeo).

the growth rate of gross regional product would have to be increased from 5 percent to 5.5 percent if the target growth rate of per capita income of 2.5 percent per annum was to be achieved. The alternative target values for GDP for the 1967–1972 period are given in section I (rows 1 and 2) of Table 21.5.

Section II of the table is devoted to the various projections required for computing the alternative values of the foreign exchange gap. Since exports have historically constituted the most important determinant of income growth in the short run, we begin with the export projections. Two sets of export projections,[18] one pessimistic, E_A, and one optimistic, E_B, are presented in rows 3 and 4. Two alternative sets of projections are also presented for private capital inflows, P_A and P_B, in rows 6 and 7. A single set of net factor income and transfer projections, NFY, is presented in row 5. Two different sets of import projections are presented: (1) computed on the basis of the 5 percent target growth rate of GDP, M_5, given in row 8; and (2), computed on the basis of the 5.5 percent target growth rate, $M_{5.5}$, given in row 9.[19] These projections are utilized in calculating the foreign exchange gap projections (FEG) for each of the two growth rate and export and capital inflow assumptions. The results are given in rows 10–13.

Likewise, in section III of the table, we present the projections needed for computing the savings-investment gaps. Projections of depreciation allowances under the alternative income growth rate assumptions are given in rows 14 and 15. Similarly, those for private domestic savings are given in rows 16 and 17. Government savings are projected in row 20. Investment requirements for each different growth-rate assumption (in each case computed by multiplying the expected change in output by the forecasted incremental capital-output ratio) are given in rows 21 and 22.

The foreign capital inflow projections presented in rows 6 and 7 are, of course, also applicable to savings and are repeated in rows 18 and 19. The resulting forecasts of the savings gap during the years 1968–1972 are presented in rows 23–26.

In every case, the *ex ante* foreign exchange gap is larger than the *ex ante* savings gap. Since both gaps would have to be covered for the assumed growth targets to be achieved, the size of the foreign exchange gap indicates the amount of external assistance that would be required to meet the growth targets in the face of the standard two-gap model assumptions. While the magnitudes of these gaps are in both cases smaller under the more optimistic export and private capital inflow projections, E_B and P_B, than under the more pessimistic projections, E_A and P_A, as shown in rows 27 and 28, the increased external assistance required to raise the GDP growth rate of the region from 5 percent per annum to 5.5 percent per annum is the same in each case. If the external assistance itself could be assumed to be used so that it would raise the export and capital inflow projections from those of case A to those of case B, then the relevant comparison would be between FEG_{A5} and $FEG_{B5.5}$. This result is given in row 29, indicating that slightly higher levels of external assistance in the initial years of the period would substantially reduce the external assistance required in subsequent years.

The opening between the two gaps can be closed in different ways. In providing the foreign assistance required to cover the larger gap, FEG, domestic consumption may be allowed to increase, thereby increasing the size of SG. Alternatively, additional efforts might be made internally, that is, in the plan, to narrow FEG by devaluation, tariffs, and so on, on the import side or by subsidies to exports, devaluation, or export promotion on the export side. This is perhaps the most important function of gap models—they call attention to the need for adjustments to *ex ante* imbalances and provide a convenient setting for weighing the policy alternatives.

An Application of Feasibility and Optimality Tests in a Linear Programming Model

Linear programming (LP) models are potentially more general than either the I-O or the two-gap models we have considered. Economy-

---

[18]These include exports both of merchandise and of services (tourism). For three of the most important exports, coffee, sugar, and cotton, it was assumed that Central America could do no better than retain its share in world trade because of international agreements and cost considerations. Bananas, meat, and other exports were expected to grow more rapidly than world imports of these commodities.

[19]Since the import growth rate was historically found to increase more than in proportion to the growth rate of GDP, these assumed target rates of growth of GDP imply annual growth rates of imports of 6.3, 8, and 10 percent respectively.

wide LP models can be specified to include both the intersectoral consistency analysis of I-O and consistency in terms of resource requirements of the two-gap models. At the same time, they permit consideration of alternative choices, such as the choice between different production techniques, different location of economic activities, different patterns of specialization in production and exchange, and different approaches to relaxing the constraints on development imposed by scarce resources.

The reader is referred to Chapter 4 for the properties of LP production functions and the duality properties of LP problems and solutions. Here, we demonstrate how an economywide LP model can be used for testing not only the consistency of a plan but also its feasibility and optimality. Because of its relative simplicity and small size, we utilize the LP model developed by Nugent (1966) for the Greek economy.[20] In this section, we describe the model, outline the methods of estimation, summarize the results, and derive some implications. In the next section, we demonstrate how such a model might be tested.

A Brief Description of the Model
The model is designed to answer the following question: given the technology of the Greek economy in 1961 and the values of various other exogenously determined parameters and variables, starting from the actual activity levels of 1954 (of domestic production, exports, idle capacity, if any, for each of 15 commodity sectors of the economy and 3 labor-training sectors) what endogenously determined activity levels could and should have been obtained at the optimum in Greece by 1961? The scarce resources specified in the model are capital, foreign exchange, and three different categories of skilled labor. Since only one target year (1961) is specified, the model is only semidynamic; nevertheless, considerable effort is made to overcome the most glaring weaknesses in semidynamic models with short planning horizons.

[20]Among the LP models of similar or greater sophistication and scope to which the interested reader may wish to refer are Chenery and Kretschmer (1956), Chenery (1958, 1969), Manne (1963, 1973), Frisch (1960, 1962), Sandee (1960), Eckaus and Parikh (1968), D. A. Kendrick (1967), Kendrick and Taylor (1969), Chenery and Uzawa (1958), Chenery et al. (1971), Adelman and Sparrow (1966), and Westphal (1971).

The model consists of the following equations and inequalities: 15 balance equations (one for each of the 15 commodity sectors in the model), supply constraints on each of the three different capital goods specified in the model, one constraint on the availability of foreign exchange, a large number of upper and lower bounds on particular production, import, and export activities, and the welfare criterion of national income maximization in the target year, 1961.

For each of the constraints, there is at least one but more often a number of different activities that serve to relax the constraint. Thus, total demand for each commodity can be met either by domestic production or by imports; labor skills can be supplied from the existing stock of such skills, from imports of skilled personnel, or by appropriate kinds of education; capital can be supplied from the accumulated stock of capital or from domestic savings generated by current income or from foreign savings; the foreign exchange constraint can be relaxed by additional exports of particular commodities or by import substitution. Some effort was made to approximate nonlinearities in production and exports by introducing a series of linear step functions.

The Balance Inequalities
The economy has been divided into 15 productive sectors. Supply and demand conditions are given for each commodity sector as follows:

$$\Sigma_r X_{ir} + M_i - \sum_h E_{ih} - \sum_j \sum_r a_{ijr} X_{jr}$$

$$- h_j \sum_j \sum_r b_{ijr} X_{jr} - c_i Z \geqq C_i + G_i$$

$$+ \Delta S_i - h_j \sum_j b_{ij} X_{j1954} \qquad \text{(1) to (15)}$$

for each i, $i = 1, 2, \ldots, 15$,

where

$M_i =$ imports of commodity i in 1961

$E_{ih} =$ exports of commodity i at price h in 1961

$a_{ijr} =$ input of commodity i per unit of domestic production in sector j by technique r in 1961

$h_j =$ linear approximation to that proportion of investment in sector j during the period

1954–1961 that would be required in 1961, assuming a one-year lag and that the level of output in sector j would grow at an exponential rate during the periods 1954–1961 and 1961–1962.

b_{ijr} = input of capital goods i per unit of output in sector j by technique r

c_i = marginal propensity to consume commodity i

Z = income generated by the model for 1961 above the actual 1961 level

$C_i + G_i + \Delta S_i$ = given final demand of commodity i in 1961

C_i = private consumption of commodity i in 1961

G_i = public consumption of commodity i in 1961

ΔS_i = changes in stocks of commodity i in 1961

X_{j1954} = gross production in sector j in 1954

Verbally, for each of the 15 sectors distinguished in the model, the system of inequalities given by 1 to 15 says that

Production + imports − exports − interindustry demand − investment demand − endogenous portion of private consumption $\geqq$ exogenous portion of private consumption + government consumption + changes in stocks.[21]

All the endogenous variables have been placed on the left-hand side of the inequalities, while the exogenous variables have been placed on the right-hand side. The supply and demand relations are stated as inequalities rather than equalities, on the assumption that all these commodities could be disposed of at practically no private or social cost.

Resource Constraints

All activities and resource requirements have thus far been defined in terms of absolute levels of output in the target year, 1961. However, net investment requirements for physical and human capital must be defined in terms of changes in output instead of levels of output. Thus, if net investment requirements

[21]The last term on the right-hand side of the equation will be explained immediately.

in sector j could be computed by multiplying the incremental capital-output ratio in sector j, k_j, by the change in output in sector j, ΔX_j, between the target year (1961) and the initial condition (1954), $\Delta X_j = X_j^{1961} - X_j^{1954}$, the same requirement $k_j X_j$ could be reexpressed as $k_j X_j^{1961} - k_j X_j^{1954}$. Since the latter term is exogenous, it can be brought over to the right-hand side of the inequality. This maintains consistency with the rest of the model by expressing the constraint in terms of activity levels. Furthermore, since investment in the target year is limited to that required to provide the increase in productive capacity desired in the year 1961 alone (or, since we assume a one-year maturation period, the increase in productive capacity in the year 1962 alone), the investment actually required in the target year is only a fairly small fraction, h_j, of the investment outlays taking place between 1954 and 1961. Assuming that output and investment in sector j grow exponentially at a constant rate, g_j, we define

$$I_j^{1961} = h_j \sum_{t=1954}^{t=1961} I_{jt} \simeq h_j^*(1 + g_j)k_j X_j^{1954}$$

Allowing for exogenous supplies of domestic saving, S_A, and of foreign saving, F, for an exogenous demand for inventories, ΔS, for endogenously determined increases in savings generated by income increases, sZ, and finally providing that any excess capacity in the target year, W, also requires investment, the aggregate savings constraint becomes

$$\sum_j I_j = h_j \sum_j \sum_r k_{jr} X_{jr} + h_j \sum_j k_j W_j - sZ$$
$$\leqq S_A + F - \sum_i \Delta S_i$$
$$+ h_j \sum_j k_j X_{j1954} \qquad (16)$$

Since the overall incremental capital-output ratios, k_j, can be broken down into their individual investment goods components (machinery, transport equipment, and construction), the investment requirements of individual capital goods are treated in the same way as the overall investment requirements. This explains the presence of the term $h_j \sum_j \sum_r b_{ijr} X_{jr}$ in the balance equations 1 to 15.

Similarly, the demand for skilled labor of any type k in 1961 is obtained by multiplying the activity levels, X_{jr}, in 1961 by the assumed amount of skilled labor of type k required per unit of X_{jr}, n_{kjr}, for that year. The supply of skilled labor of any type k is given by: (1) the total labor force—both employed and unemployed, U—at the beginning of the period (1954) net of emigration, D, retirements, R, and any increase in frictional unemployment, H over the period; and (2) by the net additions to the skilled workers of class k (during the 1954–1961 period) that education of level m creates, $P_{km}X_m$, where P_{km} is the net number of skilled laborers of skill class k added to the labor force in the period 1954–1961 per unit of education expenditure of type m in the year 1961, assuming that education grows at a constant exponential rate. Thus, the skilled labor constraints can be expressed as

$$\sum_{j}\sum_{r} \overset{1961}{\underset{kjr}{n}} X_j - P_{km}X_m \leqq \sum_{j} \overset{1954}{\underset{kj}{n}} X_{j1954}$$
$$+ U_{k1954} - D_k - R_k - H_k$$

for each $k = A, B, C$ and $m = H, S, T$
$$\text{(17) to (19)}$$

The skill classes A, B, and C are defined to match with the three different educational sectors specified, higher, H, secondary, S, and technical T.

A foreign exchange constraint is imposed, requiring that the current account deficit, $M - E$, be limited to the expected availability of foreign investment, F. Imports are specified as activities requiring inputs of foreign exchange and domestic services (transport, commercial margins) and yielding outputs of the commodities imported. Similarly, exports require inputs of the commodities exported and supply outputs of foreign exchange. The foreign exchange constraint may thus be specified as

$$\sum_{j} f_j M_j + \sum_{j}\sum_{h} f_{jh} E_{jh} \leqq F \qquad (20)$$

where f_j = input (+) or output (−) of foreign exchange per unit of imports or exports respectively.

Other Constraints

Because plant and equipment already installed in one sector cannot easily be transferred for use in another sector, we impose a constraint requiring that capital stock existing in any sector in 1954 will either be used in the same sector in 1961 or will wear out or remain idle.

By making the convenient and probably quite realistic assumption that capacity was fully utilized in 1954, this constraint can be stated as

$$\sum_{r} X_{jr} + W_j \geqq (1 - d_j)^{\tau} X_{j1954}$$

for each $j = 1, 2, \ldots, 15$ \qquad (21) to (36)

where d_j = annual depreciation rate in sector j.

The remaining equations of the model express upper and lower bounds on particular variables of the model. These restrictions are imposed to avoid the extremes of the proportionality assumptions underlying any linear programming model, thereby achieving greater realism. By introducing more than one variable for production, imports and exports in every sector with upper and sometimes lower bounds on each (indicated by a bar over the variable), we can approximate nonproportional or even nonlinear functions with a series of proportional ones.

Since relative to that of the rest of the world the Greek market is extremely small, we have assumed that imports (with certain exceptions) are obtainable from abroad without limit and without change in price. Restrictions are imposed on imports only in those commodity sectors in which the commodities are not generally transportable (electricity, construction, services)

$$M_j \leqq \overline{M}_j \qquad (37) \text{ to } (52)$$

On the other hand, for most of the commodities that Greece exports (or might export in the future), it seems reasonable to assume that additional amounts could be exported only by lowering prices and/or by increasing domestic or foreign expenditures in order to increase quality or penetrate new markets. Thus, we specify various alternate export activities in any sector j, E_{jh}, $h = 1, 2, 3$, such that additional exports earn lower amounts of foreign exchange per unit. Each individual export activity specified in this way is subject to an upper bound, $\overline{E}_{jh}$

$$E_{jh} \leqq \overline{E}_{jh} \qquad (53) \text{ to } (98)$$

for each j, $j = 1, 2, \ldots, 15$ and h, $h = 1, 2, 3$

Considering the breadth of each of the 15 sectors defined (agriculture, mining, tobacco, textiles, clothing, miscellaneous manu-

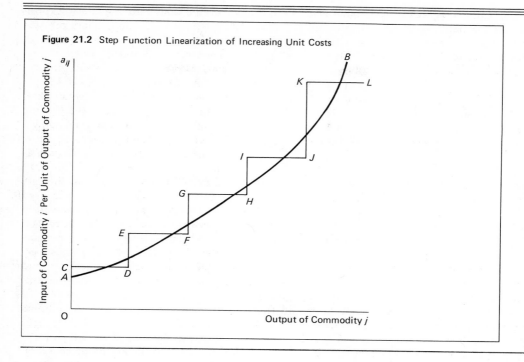

Figure 21.2 Step Function Linearization of Increasing Unit Costs

facturing, chemicals, metallurgy, construction materials, transport equipment, utilities, petroleum refining, construction, services, and tourism), decreasing returns to further specialization would seem more likely than increasing returns.[22] As the market for the more suitable subsectors within any such sector becomes saturated, further domestic production in the sector requires a shift in the subsector product mix from the more advantageous to the less advantageous subsectors. As a result, production in any sector j by technique r, X_{jr}, above certain specified levels, $\overline{X}_{jr}$, is assumed to involve increasing inputs of certain resources, for example, capital, skilled labor, and utilities per unit of output

$$X_{jr} \leqq \overline{X}_{jr}$$

for each j, $j = 1, 2, \ldots, 15$ and

$$r = 1, 2, 3 \qquad \qquad (99) \text{ to } (144)$$

Suppose the true relation between the input per unit of output j, a_{ij}, and output of j

is given by the curve AB in Figure 21.2. This curve can, as shown, be approximated by the series of jagged steps CD, DE, EF, ... By specifying a large number of steps with small increments, the approximation to the curve can be made sufficiently close. Each separate step in this approximation would be defined as a different activity, X_{jr}, each with its own set of input coefficients a_{ijr}[23]

Finally, we impose the following nonnegativity constraints

$$X_{jr} \geqq 0, M_j \geqq 0, E_{jh} \geqq 0, W_j \geqq 0, Z \geqq 0$$

The Objective Function

If there exists a feasible solution to the set of constraints given by equations 1 to 144 plus the nonnegativity constraints, it is likely that there will be an infinite number of feasible solutions. Therefore, a criterion is needed to select an optimal solution from all the feasible ones. The criterion utilized should reflect the goals of the development plan. The Greek government's development plans and related

[22]If increasing returns seem evident and important in some sectors, integer programming methods are usually employed. This greatly increases the computational cost and thus should be avoided, if it is realistic to do so. For examples of the application of mixed-integer programming methods, see Stoutjesdijk and Westphal (1973).

[23]For an alternative procedure that requires fewer constraints to achieve satisfactory linear approximations to nonlinear relationships, see the grid linearization procedure utilized by Duloy and Norton (1973, especially pp. 314–316).

policy statements have generally emphasized maximization of national income. Therefore, we specify that national income in the target year (1961) should be maximized. This is equivalent to specifying

$$Z = \text{maximum (or } -Z = \text{minimum)} \qquad (145)$$

Alternative goals, such as maximizing employment or minimizing the capital or foreign exchange costs, could also be represented.

Estimating the Parameters of the Model
The largest number of coefficients of the LP model that have to be estimated are the I-O coefficients, a_{ijr}, for each alternative commodity input i, sector j, and technique r. While in principle, estimates of these parameters can be obtained from engineering studies, such data are seldom available. In the case under discussion, the I-O coefficients for the basic domestic production variable in each sector have been computed from an interindustry transactions table of the Greek economy provided by Geronymakis (1965) by the same methods illustrated with respect to Ecuador, in Chapter 4. Since the entries of that table pertain to the year 1954, the coefficients had to be adjusted on the basis of I-O Tables for other countries, direct data on indirect taxes, tourism, and agriculture, or actual or assumed changes in subsector composition, technology, and prices. On the basis of engineering studies of the planned investment projects in that sector, the coefficients for the second and subsequent production alternatives in each sector were interpolated from the first set in the sector.

Incremental capital-output ratios, k, have been estimated from historical data on investment, I, and output, X, in each sector, j, obtained from the National Accounts of Greece (Government of Greece, Ministry of Coordination 1961, 1963). The overall capital-output ratios, k_j, have then been broken down into requirements of individual capital goods i per unit of output j, b_{ij}, on the basis of disaggregated data of capital stock and investment in each sector obtained from an industrial survey (Government of Greece, National Statistical Service 1961).

The stock-flow adjustment coefficient, h (measuring the proportion of investment in the target year 1961 to total investment between 1954 and 1961), was estimated to be 0.19 on

the basis of the ability of the linear expression, $h(1 + g)^8 - 1$, to approximate the true proportion, $g(1 + g)^8$, for reasonable values of g, that is, between 0.03 and 0.15.[24]

The marginal and average coefficients expressing the requirements of skill class k per unit of production in sector j by technique r, n_{kjr}, were obtained for the year 1960, along with projections for 1970, from manpower studies of the Greek economy (Haniotis 1967; Government of Greece, Ministry of Coordination 1962). Since the projections for 1970 were based primarily on past trends, the rate of change between 1960 and 1970 was used to interpolate the 1960 coefficients backward to 1954 and forward to 1961. The estimation procedures and data sources for the remaining exogenous variables and coefficients pertaining to the skilled labor constraints and educational activities—nonfrictional unemployment, U, emigration, D, retirements, R, frictional unemployment, H, and the outputs and inputs of skill class k per unit of output of educational section m, P_{km}—are too detailed for the brief summarized presentation given here. Suffice it to say that all were based on conventional methods of estimation and commonly published data.[25]

The foreign exchange coefficients of the import and export activities in inequality 20 were estimated as follows. The input of foreign exchange, f_j, for each import activity, M_j, was estimated as $1 - s_j - t_j$, where s_j is the input of transport and commercial enterprises in getting the M_j from the ports (at c.i.f. prices) to the consumers, and t_j is the nominal tariff rate for commodity j. The foreign exchange coefficient, f_{jh}, of the first export activity in any sector j, E_{jh}, where $h = 1$, was estimated as $1 - e_j$, where e_j is the export tax rate on E_j. The upper bounds on export activity h of sector j and the average foreign exchange earnings per unit of export of activity h, $h \neq 1$, have been estimated from time series data on exports and prices of different countries and from other special studies.

Since Suits (1964, Chapter 2) has found that the income elasticities of consumer demand computed from time series analysis agree rather closely with those computed by Kevork

[24]These computations are given in Nugent (1966, Table 4.16).
[25]See Nugent (1966, Tables 4.23, 4.32) for the details.

(1962) from cross-section data published by the National Statistical Service of Greece (1961), both cross-section and time series data have been employed in arriving at the estimates of the marginal propensities to consume commodity i, c_i, appearing in inequalities 1–15.

Some Results

Having obtained empirical estimates of all parameters and exogenous variables in the system of equalities and inequalities given by 1–145, the model is fully operational. Since that system is of the form

$$\min \mathbf{C'} \, \mathbf{X}$$

$$\mathbf{D'X} \geqq \mathbf{B} \qquad \mathbf{X} \geqq 0$$

the system constitutes a primal problem formulation of a standard LP problem. Computer programs that quickly and inexpensively solve for the optimal values of X even in very large problems of this sort are generally available. Moreover, as was pointed out in Chapter 4, for every primal problem there is a corresponding dual problem of the form

$$\max \mathbf{B'} \, \mathbf{P}$$

$$\mathbf{D'} \, \mathbf{P} \leqq \mathbf{C} \qquad \mathbf{P} \geqq 0$$

According to the duality theorem of LP, if there exists an optimal solution to the primal, there also exists an optimal solution to the dual, such that

$$\min \mathbf{C'} \, \mathbf{X} = \max \mathbf{B'} \, \mathbf{P}$$

Thus, if there exists a feasible and optimal solution to 1–145 consisting of the optimal values of all activities—domestic production of commodity j by technique r, X_{jr}, imports of j, M_j, exports of j at price h, E_{jh}, idle capacity in j, W_j, national income above that which was actually attained in the target year 1961, Z, and so on—there also exists a set of shadow prices, P, corresponding to the various commodity, resource, and other constraints specified in the model, which can also be obtained from the computer results, which are potentially extremely powerful. However, many ad hoc assumptions of unknown validity are necessary in order to make an economy-wide LP model operational. For this reason, it is desirable to apply sensitivity analysis to identify those parameters and assumptions, to which the results are highly sensitive and which must thus be precisely specified and accurately measured.

Sensitivity analysis was applied rather extensively in the case of the Greek model, yielding a large number of alternative sets of optimal solutions to the primal as well as dual problems under different sets of parameter values and assumptions. For present purposes, we have chosen from the large number of alternative solutions and variables solved for six different sets of solutions to the most important variables. From these, we have computed the arithmetic means of each variable. The results for the solutions to the primal problem variables are given in the first three columns of Table 21.6. For purposes of comparison, the actual (observed) values of these variables for the same year (1961) are given in the last three columns. Compared to the LP planning model solutions, the reader can easily see that the actual Greek economy significantly underproduced in almost all sectors except metallurgy. In this sector, actual production overshot the optimal levels of production. Although the LP solutions reveal higher export levels in agriculture and in one or two other industries, in most sectors production increases would seem to be motivated more by import substitution than export expansion. The overall results imply that the growth rate in GNP could have been raised by some 2 or 3 percent per annum above the actual growth rate of 5 or 6 percent per annum if resources had been more efficiently and fully utilized.

While it might be easy to think of political and other constraints, the omission of which from the model might be responsible for the high output levels obtained in the LP solutions, the interesting case of the metallurgy sector, in which actual production exceeded optimal production significantly, deserves special consideration. The metallurgy sector in Greece is dominated by two enterprises, the integrated steel complex near Athens and the alumina-aluminum complex near Delphi. The fact that the steel industry manages to survive by virtue of prohibitive tariffs and "anti-dumping" restrictions and the alumina-aluminum complex (a large electricity user) by virtue of a heavily subsidized price of electricity gives one some justification for believing this result of the LP model.

Since the shadow prices (resulting from the optimal solution to the dual problem) are defined relative to the objective function, which in the process of carrying out the sen-

Table 21.6 *Domestic Production, Imports and Exports by Sector in Greece in the Year 1961: Linear Programming Solutions and Actual Values Compared*

	Optimal Activities[a,b]			Actual[a]		
	Production	Imports	Exports	Production	Imports	Exports
1. Agriculture	61,044	397	2,132	49,360	4,123	1,962
2. Mining	2,627	198	632	2,080	301	632
3. Tobacco Processing	2,853	1	1,763	2,594	1	2,307
4. Textiles	9,225	1,393	599	8,319	1,529	1,164
5. Clothing	12,515	10	10	10,364	59	10
6. Miscellaneous Manufacturing	14,191	2,007	58	11,486	4,826	56
7. Chemicals	10,224	242	212	6,591	1,713	212
8. Metallurgy	1,404	2,070	16	2,047	2,070	16
9. Construction Materials	2,246	171	31	1,756	171	30
10. Transport Equipment	3,081	1,307	27	1,226	2,690	26
11. Electricity, Gas, Water	3,540	50	—	2,761	50	—
12. Petroleum Refining	1,946	702	—	1,512	702	—
13. Construction	16,863	0	—	12,800	77	—
14. Services	49,003	1,326	0	42,279	1,326	—
15. Tourism	2,052	358	2,052	2,052	358	2,052
16. Technical Education	111	—	—	70	—	—
17. Secondary Education	534	—	—	318	—	—
18. Higher Education	337	—	15	140	—	—

Notes:
[a]All values are in millions of drachmas at 1954 prices.
[b]Arithmetic mean of six different optimal solutions.
Source: Nugent, J. B. (1966), *Programming the Optimal Development of the Greek Economy 1954–1961.* Athens: Center of Planning and Economic Research, Tables 5.12, 5.15.

sitivity analysis was varied from one LP run to the next, the shadow prices of the different solutions have been standardized in terms of the price of clothing—a commodity whose market price would seem to be close to its social opportunity cost. The arithmetic means of the resulting shadow prices (standardized in terms of the shadow price of clothing) are given in Table 21.7. These results reveal that market prices undervalue services, electricity, and foreign exchange but overvalue labor-intensive activities, such as education and labor skills, agriculture, tobacco processing, textiles, construction, tourism, and miscellaneous manufactures. The shadow price of capital (or the shadow rate of interest) would seem to be about double the official interest rate offered by the authorized financial institutions.

One might conclude from the high shadow price for electricity of Table 21.7 that the electricity producer (which in Greece is the Public Power Corporation) underprices electricity to a considerable extent. Why should electricity production be so expensive (in the social sense) in Greece? First, since water for power is extremely limited, imported coal or petroleum, both of which require scarce foreign exchange, must serve as the power source. Second, power is a very capital-intensive, labor-extensive activity in a country in which capital is relatively scarce and labor relatively abundant. Third, by virtue of its public nonprofit status, the Public Power Corporation receives a large subsidy in the form of government credit at 5 or 6 percent interest and need not generate even a "normal" profit to stay in business. On the demand

Table 21.7 *Optimal Shadow Prices of Commodities and Resources*

Commodity or Resource	Relative Shadow Prices
1. Agriculture	0.816
2. Mining	1.006
3. Tobacco Processing	0.654
4. Textiles	0.887
5. Clothing	1.000
6. Miscellaneous Manufacturing	0.890
7. Chemicals	1.072
8. Metallurgy	1.030
9. Construction Materials	0.950
10. Transport Equipment	1.046
11. Electricity, Gas, Water	2.374
12. Petroleum Refining	1.086
13. Construction	0.783
14. Services	1.462
15. Tourism	0.814
16. Labor-Skill Category C	0.027
17. Labor-Skill Category B	0.031
18. Labor-Skill Category A	0.135
19. Labor-Unskilled	
20. Capital	0.282
21. Foreign Exchange	1.200

Note: Shadow prices have been standardized in terms of the shadow price of clothing.

Source: Nugent, J. B. (1966), *Programming the Optimal Development of the Greek Economy 1954–1961.* Athens: Center of Planning and Economic Research, Tables 5.11, 5.19.

side, increased income and output would seem to require substantial increases in electricity both for final consumers and for enterprises.

A potentially important use of the shadow prices of an LP model, such as the one presented here, is for project appraisal. In Chapter 20, we noted the various complexities of project appraisal which cannot be handled satisfactorily by the more traditional evaluation procedures. Among these are externalities and linkages among projects, risk, and price distortions of various sorts. Yet each of these aspects can easily be incorporated in a programming model—indeed, the externalities, linkages, and price distortions have been treated in the model under consideration. Moreover, the fact that the model is economywide gives it a genuine general equilibrium character—a feature that was lacking in the other approaches reviewed in Chapter 20. Any individual project (or group

of projects) could be evaluated simply by computing the present value with respect to: (1) the projected quantities of the project's inputs and outputs and (2) the shadow prices presented in Table 21.7. If present value of the project (estimated on the basis of the shadow prices) is positive, the project should be undertaken. Otherwise, it should be omitted from the plan.

Because important policy implications can be drawn from both the primal and the dual solutions, LP models are directly applicable to: (1) the planning done by central planners who dictate detailed production and investment behavior and (2) the planning done by planners who in a world of decentralized decision making are content to influence the prices, which in turn help direct the optimal product mix in the economy. By comparing the model's results with actual plan prescriptions or forecasts, one can determine whether or not the plan is feasible, and if it is feasible, whether it is optimal.

The Testing of Planning Models

In the preceding section, we have demonstrated several means of testing economic plans with reference to criteria of consistency, feasibility, and optimality. In each case, we have utilized a specific planning model. The purpose of any planning model is to provide an operationally meaningful framework for relating the instruments of planning and policy to the goals of planning, that is, the phenomena to be planned.

However, just as the market mechanism can provide efficient and optimal allocations of resources over time only under certain conditions, so too planning models provide solutions with the desired properties of consistency, feasibility, efficiency, and optimality only if certain assumptions are fulfilled. These assumptions involve identifying the constraints realistically, specifying the correct form of the relationships between economic activities and scarce resources, accurate and unbiased estimation of the various parameters the values of which describe these relationships, and so on. Since these necessary conditions are not easy to fulfill, the validity of any planning model is open to challenge. The fact that certain or all of the assumptions of a planning model may be somewhat unrealistic does not imply that the model must necessarily be discarded. To the contrary, as with any hypothesis, the relevant test of a planning model is: are the assumptions sufficiently realistic that one can have confidence that its implications are at least as valid as those that could be derived from the most relevant alternative (another planning model, a simple rule of thumb derived from past experience, intuition, or no model at all)?

In the case of planning models that satisfy only the criteria of consistency and feasibility, such as I-O models, two-gap models, and econometric models, the testing methods are fairly straightforward. Tests are of two general types: direct tests, which refer to various methods to check the realism of the assumptions directly, and indirect tests, which involve determining how well the model works (predicts) relative to other possible models.

For example, in the case of I-O models relating output levels in different sectors, X, to the sectoral final demands, B, such as $(I - A) X = B$, direct testing might involve estimating more general production functions (such as CES functions) in different sectors to see whether or not the assumptions (e.g., that inputs are strictly proportional to outputs and that the elasticity of substitution among the different inputs is zero) are reasonably realistic. Indirect testing of I-O models usually consists of seeing whether or not the sectoral outputs, X, can be predicted more accurately by the I-O model, that is, by computing $(I - A)^{-1}B$, than by other available models (naive or serious). Because planning models are much larger in size, contain many more variables, and serve more functions than models containing individual hypotheses, it is relatively more difficult to arrive at clear-cut conclusions about the adequacy or realism of planning models. But it is only a matter of degree.

In the case of planning models that yield solutions satisfying the properties of efficiency and optimality, such as LP models, testing is considerably more complicated. While direct tests can usually be applied in ways similar to those outlined for I-O models, indirect testing is much more difficult, because such models provide prescriptions that may or may not have any correspondence to the actual values of the variables prescribed. Some analysts have been deterred from testing such models on the grounds of humility, their belief that the models they have developed are

satisfactory only for demonstration purposes. Others, however, have concluded that such models cannot and should not be tested.[26] We hasten to point out, though, that unless such models can be tested, the proposition that a properly designed planning model (which would satisfy all the desirable criteria outlined in the previous section) can be a useful tool in economic planning would be operationally meaningless! In the remainder of this section, we shall attempt to demonstrate that it is at least feasible to test such a proposition empirically.

An Empirical Test of the Validity of the Greek LP Model

Our demonstration[27] pertains to the same LP model of the Greek economy, the specification and results of which were summarized in the previous section. As we have seen, the assumptions upon which the model is based are not, and have not been, satisfied historically in Greece. Undoubtedly, the Greek economy is far more complicated and flexible than even the most sophisticated programming models would have it. On the other hand, no one would deny that there are in Greece, as in most LDCs, obvious manifestations of misallocation of resources—widespread unemployment and underemployment, persistent and lopsided deficits in the balance of trade—and also obvious departures from the conditions under which a free market can guarantee an efficient allocation of resources. Therefore, neither the historical path of development nor the "optimal" path calculated from and prescribed by the LP model for the same historical period represent the truly optimal path. Neither, therefore, can be used as a fixed standard by which to judge the other.

If we had observations on the true optimum as well as the calculated optimum and the actual activity levels or prices for each sector, testing the model would indeed be a simple and straightforward procedure. The problem is that the solution values of the true social optimum are unobserved. For any sector, the true optimum could lie between the calculated optimum and the actual, or it could be above or below both of them. Therefore, the model can be tested only indirectly by reference to comparisons of the *calculated*

---

[26]See, for example, Chenery (1957).
[27]This example is based on Nugent (1970).

optimal and *actual* solutions. Such comparisons from the solutions presented in Tables 21.6 and 21.7 could, in principle, be carried out with respect to production, import, and export levels for each of the 18 commodity sectors and/or with respect to each of the shadow prices corresponding to each of the 21 different commodity and resource constraints specified in the LP model. Primarily for simplicity, however, we have restricted our attention to the first twelve sectors.[28] For each sector, we have made three different kinds of optimal-actual comparisons: two based on production levels and one based on prices. The results of each of these comparisons are given in Table 21.8. In the first column (labeled *OAPR*) are the optimal-actual domestic production ratios for each sector, computed by dividing the mean of the "optimal" production levels from column 1 of Table 21.6 by the actual production levels from column 4. These ratios have been multiplied by a factor of 100. In the second column (labeled *OAPD*) are the absolute differences, in millions of drachmas, between these same optimal and actual production levels. Finally, in the third column (labeled *OSPMPR*), we present the ratios of the standardized shadow prices to the actual market prices for each of the 12 sectors, multiplied by a factor of 1,000.

The more closely the calculated optimum approximates the true optimum, the more justifiable it would be to ascribe the deviations between the calculated optimum and the actual to "market imperfections" rather than to "errors and omissions in the model." On the other hand, the more closely the actual market activity levels and prices approximate the truly optimal ones, the more the deviations between the calculated optimum and actual could be attributed to "errors and omissions in the model." It is the converse of these propositions that provides the means with which to test the validity of the LP model's prescription relative to actual achievements. Thus, if the variation in the sectoral deviations of the LP optimal from the actual (or

[28]The other sectors were excluded from the present analysis for the following reasons. First, several of them (tourism, technical, secondary, and higher education) were extremely small relative to the other sectors; second, in several cases (especially construction and services) substitution by imports is impossible and hence optimal-actual comparisons are much less interesting; and third, for these sectors, it was extremely difficult to obtain estimates of the measures of the various alternative hypotheses considered.

Table 21.8 *The Dependent Variables: Optimal-Actual Comparisons of Domestic Production and Prices for 1961*

Sector	OAPR	OAPD	OSPMPR
1. Agriculture	124	11,684	816
2. Mining	126	547	1,006
3. Tobacco Processing	110	259	654
4. Textiles	111	906	887
5. Clothing	121	2,151	1,000
6. Miscellaneous Manufacturing	124	2,705	890
7. Chemicals	155	3,633	1,072
8. Metallurgy	69	−643	1,030
9. Construction Materials	128	490	950
10. Transport Equipment	251	1,855	1,046
11. Electricity, Gas, Water	128	779	2,347
12. Petroleum Refining	129	434	1,086

Notes: The variables are defined as follows:

$OAPR$ = the optimal to actual ratio of domestic production × 100

$OAPD$ = the absolute difference between optimal and actual domestic production levels, in millions of drachmas

$OSPMPR$ = the ratios of the standardized shadow prices to market prices × 1000.

Source: Tables 21.6 and 21.7.

"market") solution could be "explained" by the indexes of market imperfections, it would imply that the true optimum was nearer to the LP optimal than to the actual solution. A strong relationship between the variation in the sectoral indexes of "errors and omissions in the model" and the optimal-actual comparisons would imply that the true optimum was more closely approximated by the actual market values than by the LP model's optimal solutions.

In testing the LP model vis-à-vis the market model, we can use any one of the three optimal-actual comparisons of Table 21.8 as the dependent variable to be explained by two alternative sets of hypotheses—hypotheses related to certain observed or supposed defects in the market and hypotheses pertaining to observed or supposed defects in the model.

Several kinds of market imperfections are considered—monopoly power (*RORD*), managerial backwardness (*MB*), inertia (*INER*),

price discrimination (W) among consuming sectors with respect to interest rates (IR) and electricity rates (ER), investment licensing ($ILIC$), degree of government participation and subsidization (P_I/P_T), and the effective rate of protection (ERP). On the other hand, several kinds of defects (mostly omissions) of the model are also considered: land requirements (LR), forward linkages (FL), economies of scale ($SCALE$), factor substitution ($SUBS$), and the secondary planning goals of geographic dispersion of economic activity (GD) away from its historic concentration in the Athens-Piraeus area.[29]

In order to implement quantitative tests with respect to such variables, we have had to quantify each of the indicators of market imperfections and of errors and omissions in the model sector by sector. We have also had to consider the indirect as well as the direct effects of these factors.

Let us consider a particular kind of market imperfection—monopoly power. First, we have had to obtain a comparable set of measures of monopoly power (defined in terms of the above normal rate of return) for each sector of the economy. In the absence of decreasing costs, two effects of monopoly relative to the competitive case are likely: increased prices and lower production. The effect of monopoly in any sector, however, will generally not be limited to that sector. Lower output will imply lower demand for the inputs purchased from other industries and hence lower levels of output in other sectors. Similarly, higher prices of its output will be passed on to other sectors as higher prices of inputs to these sectors. There can, of course, be compensating adjustments reflecting both supply and demand factors. However, it should be possible, at least crudely, to incorporate indirect effects by using the inverted Leontief matrix $(I - A)^{-1}$ which has already been utilized in the empirical application of the model. Specifically, in the case of quantity effects from the demand side, the total effects, $\overline{X}$, have been arrived at by postmultiplying the inverse of the Leontief matrix $(I - A)^{-1}$ by the column vector, X, of absolute amounts by which each output would be reduced as the direct result of monopoly power:

$$(I - A)^{-1} X = \overline{X} \tag{146}$$

Similarly, to obtain the total price effects of monopoly power, $\overline{Y}$, we must premultiply the inverted Leontief matrix by the row vector index of direct price effects, Y:

$$Y(I - A)^{-1} = \overline{Y} \tag{147}$$

Given the relatively sparse density of the Leontief matrix typical of Greece as well as of most other LDCs, one would expect the direct effects to dominate the indirect effects in most industries. Therefore, to lessen the danger of attributing meaningful conclusions to spurious correlations, we have imposed the following rule throughout: the indirect effects as calculated by multiplication with the $(I - A)^{-1}$ matrix should not be included, unless the direct effects of the particular market defect or omission in the model were first found to be related sufficiently strongly to the variation in the optimal-actual indexes.[30]

The sector-by-sector measures of market imperfections are given in Table 21.9 and those of omissions from the model in Table 21.10. Because the methods of estimation and the detailed nature of these measures are well beyond the scope of the present work, the reader is referred to the original work for these matters. The measures are admittedly rather crude and the way the effects have been "predicted" somewhat naive. However, our present purpose is merely to offer a demonstration of how an LP planning model could be tested. We do not claim that the model utilized has been successfully tested.

To demonstrate the significance of each member of the alternative sets of hypotheses, X, from Tables 21.9 and 21.10 in explaining variations in the calculated optimal-actual ratios, Y, of Table 21.8, we use the following linear regression model:

$$Y_i = a + bXj$$

for each $i = OSPMPR$, $OAPR$, $OAPD$, and $j = RORD$, $MB \cdots SUBS$ \qquad (148)

The complete set of results of the simple linear regressions is presented in Nugent (1970, Tables 4–7). However, since the results were found to be fairly insensitive to the particular choice of optimal-actual comparison

---

[29]Naturally, these are not intended to form a complete catalogue of the important considerations omitted from the model, but only examples of some of the more easily measured ones.

[30]The criterion used is that the regression coefficient must have the expected sign and be of at least the size of its standard error.

Table 21.9 *Measures of Market Defects and Government Intervention by Sector*

Sector	ROR	RORD	MB	INER	IR	ER	WIR	WER	ILIC	PI/PT	ERP
1. Agriculture	7.6	−1.6	110	1.3	2.0	0.68	11.6	7	37.0	41.1	56.1
2. Mining	20.0	10.3	100	2.0	1.5	0.61	9.5	0	2.6	9.3	22.7
3. Tobacco Processing	13.7	4.2	40	1.1	0.0	0.61	0.0	0	2.7	0.0	321.8
4. Textiles	6.5	−3.1	50	1.4	1.9	0.61	3.9	0	30.0	1.4	145.9
5. Clothing	10.2	0.6	90	1.5	2.4	0.61	2.4	0	24.5	0.1	231.9
6. Miscellaneous Manufacturing	12.6	2.9	70	1.8	3.2	0.61	8.2	0	15.8	0.1	49.9
7. Chemicals	7.0	−2.8	60	1.8	1.8	0.61	5.0	0	22.8	1.0	77.4
8. Metallurgy	12.3	2.4	20	2.3	3.0	0.41	5.6	−544	4.2	0.5	9.9
9. Construction Materials	9.5	−0.2	80	1.7	2.7	0.61	10.3	0	24.2	0.2	86.8
10. Transport Equipment	4.9	−5.1	120	3.0	2.2	0.61	3.4	0	6.4	0.7	10.3
11. Electricity, Gas, Water	3.5	−5.6	30	2.4	−3.0	0.61	−107.7	0	15.0	85.3	40.0
12. Petroleum Refining	8.6	−2.1	10	20.7	2.0	0.61	4.0	0	2.4	68.8	104.8

Note: The variables are defined in the text.
Source: Nugent, J. B. (1970), "Linear Programming Models for National Planning: Demonstration of a Testing Procedure," *Econometrica*, 38 (November), Table II, p. 840.

used as the dependent variable, for brevity we shall confine our attention to the results with respect to the optimal shadow price—market price ratios OSPMPR given in the third column of Table 21.8. The results obtained by regressing OSPMPR on each of the measures of market imperfections or errors in the model are given in Tables 21.11 and 21.12.

The sign of the regression coefficient expected is presented before the name of the variable in Table 21.11. When the regression coefficient has the expected sign and is larger than its standard error, we postmultiply it by the inverted Leontief matrix $(I − A)^{-1}$ as in equation 147, to obtain a measure of the total effects (direct plus indirect) of the indexes in question and then regress *OSPMPR* on the new variable.

The results show that there are four (or possibly five) different indexes of market im-

Table 21.10 *Measures of Errors and Omissions in the Linear Programming Model by Sector*

Sector	LR	FL	GD	SCALE	SUBS
1. Agriculture	3	37	8	1,000	39.75
2. Mining	20	65	1	1,000	12.75
3. Tobacco Processing	5	68	4	800	46.50
4. Textiles	5	71	5	970	29.00
5. Clothing	41	0	1	1,098	22.00
6. Miscellaneous Manufacturing	5	57	3	1,150	29.70
7. Chemicals	1	55	4	1,072	20.00
8. Metallurgy	3	97	6	553	15.30
9. Construction Materials	4	66	7	1,311	40.50
10. Transport Equipment	3	0	2	1,281	70.50
11. Electricity, Gas, Water	30	53	7	1,500	5.40
12. Petroleum Refining	1	83	10	1,072	9.00

Note: The variables are defined in the text.
Source: Nugent, J. B. (1970), "Linear Programming Models for National Planning: Demonstration of a Testing Procedure," *Econometrica*, 38 (November), Table III, p. 845.

Table 21.11 *Linear Regressions of Shadow to Market Price Ratios (OSPMPR) on Various Independent Variables*

Expected Effect		Variable	Constant	Regression Coefficient	Standard Error of Regression Coefficient	R^2	Accepted for Further Investigation
		MARKET IMPERFECTIONS					
−	ROR	Monopoly Power	1,496.91	44.26	26.78	0.441	*
−	MB	Managerial Backwardness	1,299.51	3.57	3.59	0.300	
−	INER	Inertia	1,050.67	0.05	0.25	0.063	
−	WIR	Weighted Cost of Capital	1,022.34	−12.39	1.29	0.939	*
−	WER	Weighted Electricity Rate	1,071.35	−0.08	0.08	0.252	?
−	ILIC	Investment Licensing	1,105.47	−2.42	11.25	0.068	
+	PI/TI	Government Investment	894.18	9.98	3.16	0.706	*
−	ERP	Effective Rate of Protection	1,218.68	1.57	1.34	0.347	*
		OMISSIONS FROM MODEL					
−	LR	Land Requirements	907.02	15.92	9.09	0.485	
+	FL	Forward Linkage	1,094.68	−0.50	4.60	0.034	
?	GD	Geographic Dispersion	1,019.48	9.16	44.03	0.065	
+	SCALE	Economies of Scale	−47.44	1.04	0.45	0.593	*
+	SUBS	Elasticity of Substitution	1,376.99	−10.91	6.43	0.472	
		ADJUSTED VARIABLES					
−	PC1		1,193.00	−4,815.54	555.72	0.940	*
−	PC2		874.36	−5,263.84	891.38	0.882	*
	$PC1X = PC1 \times (\mathbf{I} - \mathbf{A})^{-1}$		1,264.49	−44.11	4.59	0.950	*
+	$SCALEX = SCALE \times (\mathbf{I} - \mathbf{A})^{-1}$		440.25	0.74	0.85	0.237	

Note: The variables are defined in the text. The regressions are of the form given by equation 148 in the text.
Source: Nugent, J. B. (1970), "Linear Programming Models for National Planning: Demonstration of a Testing Procedure," *Econometrica*, 38 (November), Table IV, p. 849.

perfections and government interference—
ROR, WIR, PI/PT, ERP, and possibly *WER*
—which meet the criterion that the regression coefficients are of the correct sign and are at least as large as the standard error. Of the five indicators of errors and omissions of the model, only one (the economies of scale indicator, *SCALE*), passes this test. Note also that, when postmultiplied by $(\mathbf{I} - \mathbf{A})^{-1}$ to reflect the total (direct plus indirect) effects, *SCALEX,* the economies of scale index becomes less significant rather than more significant as an explanatory variable. Its R^2 is somewhat less than one-third that of *PC1,* which is the sum of the direct price effects of monopoly, *ROR,*[31] discrimination pricing of

capital, *WIR,* discriminatory pricing of electricity rates, *WER,* one-tenth of the effective tariff rate, *ERP,* and the proportion of total investment that is undertaken or subsidized by the government, *PI/PT,* or of *PC1X,* which is the *total* price effect of monopoly estimated by postmultiplying *PC1* by the $(\mathbf{I} - \mathbf{A})^{-1}$ matrix as in equation 147. *PC2* is identical to *PC1,* except that it does not include the *PI/PT* variable. The multiple regressions of Table 21.12 aslo show that when *PC1* or *PC1X* are included along with *SCALE* the economies of scale variable becomes quite insignificant.[32]

Although the results found in Table 21.12 lead one to the tentative conclusion that cer-

---

[31]The price effect of monopoly was computed from the output effect as follows: The output effect of monopoly was estimated by multiplying the "excess" profit rate, *RORD* in Table 21.9, by the 1961 stock of capital multiplied by the output-capital ratio for each sector. Given the actual level of output in 1961 and also the absolute loss in output caused by monopoly power, the percentage change in output is

immediately obtainable. Assuming an elasticity of demand of unity, this percentage of output lost is identical to the percentage increase in price.

[32]This was the only case in which an indicator of "errors and omissions of the model" explained a significant portion of the variance in one of the dependent variables.

Table 21.12 *Multiple Regressions Using Shadow to Market Price Ratios (OSPMPR)*

$$OSPMPR = 1{,}195.08 - 38.58\ ROR - 1.32\ ERP, \qquad R^2 = 0.119$$
$$\phantom{OSPMPR = 1{,}195.08 - }(27.41) \qquad (1.29)$$

$$OSPMPR = 944.43 + 0.22\ SCALE - 4{,}466.23\ PC1, \qquad R^2 = 0.871$$
$$(0.22) \qquad\qquad (658.13)$$

$$OSPMPR = 1{,}058.55 + 0.18\ SCALE - 41.48\ PC1X, \qquad R^2 = 0.889$$
$$(0.21) \qquad\qquad (5.57)$$

Note: The variables are defined in the text.
Source: Nugent, J. B. (1970), "Linear Programming Models for National Planning: Demonstration of a Testing Procedure," *Econometrica*, 38 (November), Table VII, p. 852.

tain kinds of market imperfections and forms of government interference have brought about significant departures from optimal resource allocation in Greece in the recent past, these results do not allow us to discriminate between an interpretation that stresses imperfect behavior resulting from free market forces and an alternative one that places most of the blame on misguided government intervention. A number of economists familiar with the Greek scene[33] have pointed to various ways Greek public policy has tended to reinforce market imperfections and to ways monopolists in turn have often exerted considerable influence over public policy. Interdependencies of this kind—between government intervention and market imperfections—would provide an explanation for the relatively high correlation between the independent variables discussed above.

Since the above regressions are strictly linear, we cannot reject the hypothesis that errors and omissions of the model may have been nonlinearly related to the optimal-actual ratios of Table 21.8. Neither can we dismiss the possibility that other simplifications in the model, which are responsible for its nonstochastic and largely static characteristics, might turn out to be more important than market imperfections in explaining variations in the optimal-actual ratios. In addition, one hardly need mention the perils of estimating regression coefficients with only 12 observations or using measures as crude as those utilized here. The outcome of the tests, therefore, could be swamped by measurement error, estimation error, and other errors. Another consideration that limits the power of

the tests of the LP model demonstrated here is that the model is not compared with an alternative model, since none had existed. Without such a test, however, even if it could be concluded that the LP model performs better than the actual economy, the possibility that an alternative model might outperform the LP model in terms of cost effectiveness cannot be ruled out. On the other hand, even if a more complete and rigorous series of tests that would reverse the present findings could be performed, it would not necessarily follow that planning by LP models should be abandoned. The outcome of the tests point out the specific aspects of the model that should be handled most carefully. Almost all the defects of simple LP models can be overcome at some cost.

If one could be reasonably well satisfied from the outcome of the regressions and the more informal intuitive reasoning that one or more particular market defects were responsible for the optimal-actual deviations, these defects could, at least in principle, be imposed on the LP model and utilized for further testing. For example, if monopoly power were the culprit, one could impose monopolistic price and output determination on the model by appropriate restrictions in the dual solution for the monopolistic sectors. If the revised monopoly-laden LP model produced an optimal solution very similar to the observed "market" solution, a higher order test would have been achieved.

The Theory of Economic Policy and Policy Planning

Perhaps the greatest shortcoming in planning to date has not been internal inconsistency, infeasibility, or suboptimality of the plans per

[33]See, for example, Ellis, Psilos, Westebbe, and Nicolaou (1962), Papandreou (1962), and Coutsoumaris (1963).

se but rather the failure to link planning goals with practical and specific policy instruments, the utilization of which would ensure fulfillment of the planning goals. In this section, we explore approaches to economic policy determination and lay the groundwork for a more satisfactory linking of policy instruments to planning goals.

This book thus far has dealt almost exclusively with economic models that attempt to explain various important economic variables (endogenous to the economic system) in terms of exogenous variables. Among the exogenous variables commonly used to explain the economic ones are variables, such as weather or geographic position, over which a country has little control. But there are also social variables (literacy rates, newspaper circulation, etc.), and most importantly policy variables, over which the country may have considerable control, but which are considered exogenous to the economic system itself. The inclusion of policy variables provides the analyst with the opportunity to trace and quantify their impact on the economic variables with which he is concerned.

Two considerations deserve special mention in connection with the inclusion of policy variables. First, while it may be quite realistic to assume that policy variables are exogenous in the short run, the longer the time horizon of the analysis, the less realistic such an assumption is. Second, regardless of the direction of behavioral responses in the real world, one can for analytical purposes change or reverse the directions at will. Thus, the theory of economic policy involves an intentional reversal of the direction of determination from that of economic analysis. While *economic analysis* (in its simplest form at least) considers policy variables as given or exogenously determined, and the economic variables as the endogenous ones to be explained, in the theory of *economic policy* the endogenous variables to be determined are the policy variables (called "instruments"), and the economic variables are "given" or exogenously determined (called "targets" or "goals").

Assume a linear economic model of the following form:

$$(I - A)Y = BX + EZ \qquad (149)$$

where Y is a vector of the endogenous economic variables or targets, X is a vector of

policy variables or instruments, Z is a vector of other predetermined variables, and A, B, and E are matrices of coefficients. The (reduced form) solution to this system is

$$Y = (I = A)^{-1}BX + (I - A)^{-1}EZ \qquad (150)$$

The coefficients of the matrix $(I - A)^{-1}B$ are known as the impact multipliers. Any individual coefficient of this matrix indicates the effect of a unit change in a particular policy instrument x_j in X on the corresponding economic variable y_j in Y. Such impact multipliers can be static or dynamic, depending on whether or not the time period during which x_j is changed is the same as that during which y_i is affected. If the original model involves lagged endogenous variables among the other predetermined variables included in Z, there will generally be intertemporal effects of the policy variables. Sometimes reference is made to the "steady-state" or "long-term" multipliers. These refer to the total effect that a unit change in the exogenous variable, x_j, would have on the endogenous variable, y_i, after all repercussions had been felt, that is, after y_i had assumed its new equilibrium level. Generally speaking, these long-term multipliers are irrelevant to practical policy decisions, because inevitably there are intervening disturbances that prevent the new equilibrium position from being achieved.[34]

The solution to the *policy model* derived from the *economic model* given by equation 150 is thus

$$X = B^{-1}(I - A)Y - B^{-1}EZ \qquad (151)$$

The "target" variables, y_i, included in Y can be either "fixed" or "flexible." Examples of fixed targets are "GNP should be 100 million pesos" or "GNP should increase by 6 percent per annum." Examples of flexible targets are "income should be maximized" or "the employment rate should be as low as possible." Whether or not the targets are fixed or flexible, they can differ in number. Cases of single fixed targets are rather rare in development planning; more commonly, there will be multiple fixed targets.

[34]The long-term multipliers must be computed by solving difference equations of the order corresponding to the total number of periods by which the lagged endogenous variables are lagged in the system. These can be difficult to compute in large systems with long lags. However, these values may be approximated by simulating the behavior of y_i over a sufficiently long period given an initial change in x_j.

The use of fixed targets is limited by the fact that the number of targets and instruments must be identical if a unique policy solution is to be attained. If the number of instruments is less than that of targets, there will normally be no solution. To obtain a feasible solution in such cases, one must either dispose of targets or add instruments until equality between the numbers of instruments and targets is achieved (Tinbergen 1952). Moreover, the approach permits the policy instruments to take on any values whatsoever, regardless of political, social, and administrative conditions governing their use.

The use of flexible targets obviates the need for mechanical counts of variables and allows the policy maker to retain all the relevant targets without having to introduce false or unimportant policy instruments. It also allows one to place limitations of various kinds on the flexibility of policies to reflect the political and administrative realities. However, not all specifications of the flexible target policy models represent a clear improvement over the fixed target approach. For example, the most common flexible target approach is that of Theil (1964, 1965), in which a quadratic welfare function in terms of both targets and instruments is specified. Since the specified objective is to minimize the sum of the weighted squares of deviations of instruments and targets from desired levels (the fixed target values), Theil's flexible target approach converges on the fixed target approach. Moreover, this specification has the unfortunate characeristic of treating as equally undesirable positive and negative deviations from the fixed targets. In general, asymmetric preferences would seem more realistic, that is, people prefer more income to less income.[35]

Some of the shortcomings of Theil's quadratic objective function can be overcome by specifying a somewhat more general objective function, that is, a complete multitarget social welfare function, each different goal being weighted by its relative importance from the point of view of the decision makers.[36] It is certainly possible to interview the policy makers in depth, to examine their written and

oral pronouncements in detail, or to study past decisions in respect to the circumstances in which they were made (as if to derive the policy makers' "revealed preferences"). It is highly doubtful, nevertheless, that this approach will yield for the model builder any particular welfare specification that the policy makers would be willing to maintain regardless of the consequences. The policy maker is not only likely to be unable to reveal all the subtleties of his welfare function but he is unlikely to want to reveal them, even if he could, in fear that the model builder might subsequently show him that rationally he should do something he really does not want to do.

Therefore, it would seem preferable that policy models be used in such a way as to provide policy makers with more useful and comprehensive information upon which decisions can be made, without requiring full disclosure of their preference functions. The information made available to the policy maker should include not only the relation of individual targets to individual instruments or the substitutability of one instrument for another (as has become customary), but also the possibility trade-offs between each of his different instruments. In short, the policy maker should be provided with a complete set (a whole matrix as it were) of possibility trade-offs, which would allow him to study the implications of all the available alternatives in terms of different combinations of target satisfaction and instrument manipulation. Knowing the possibility trade-offs between instruments and targets, among instruments themselves, and between and among the different targets, the policy maker would then be able to select the policy package that equates the demonstrated possibility trade-offs with his own subjective desirability trade-offs.[37]

With fairly simple econometric models, the possibilities for substitution among alternative instruments to achieve a unit increase in any given target are likely to be quite limited in the short run. In the longer run, however, with a dynamic model in which both the target variables, Y, and the policy instruments, X, have time subscripts denoting each calendar year in the plan period, there will be many more possibilities for substitution

---

[35]The approach does have an advantage in that with no extra difficulty certain types of uncertainties can be incorporated into the model by invoking the certainty equivalence theorem (which is a property of quadratic functions only).

[36]See, for example, Fox, Sengupta, and Thorbecke (1966).

[37]For a simple discussion of these points, see Goldberger (1965).

among policy instruments, between instruments and targets, or among targets. Normally, most macroeconomic models involve some lagged targets (particularly with respect to savings and investment decisions) and, in fact, specifications involving multiple or distributed lags are increasingly common. Therefore, the longer the planning horizon, the greater the likelihood that the possibility trade-offs among instruments and targets can be utilized to achieve the desired (fixed) targets within the relevant economic, technical, administrative, and political constraints. Indeed, this principle would seem to come to the core of planning—through planning a decision maker attempts to take the fullest possible advantage of the intratemporal as well as intertemporal possibility trade-offs.

A Linear Programming Approach to Policy Planning

We have found that linear programming is an approach with which policy makers can become comfortable. Furthermore, the use of a simple linear programming procedure can greatly facilitate the computations. This procedure can be outlined as follows:

First, we arbitrarily choose one of the targets in **Y,** for example, GDP, as the single flexible target to be maximized

$$GDP = \text{maximum} \qquad (152)$$

Second, we set appropriate constraints on each of the other welfare targets: consumption, C, investment, I, the balance of payments, BP, and government savings, SG.

$$C \geqq C_{\min} \qquad (153)$$

$$I \geqq I_{\min} \qquad (154)$$

$$BP \geqq BP_{\min} \qquad (155)$$

$$SG \geqq SG_{\min} \qquad (156)$$

Third, we include the trade-offs between the instruments, X, and targets, Y, specified in the model. These can be obtained from the complete reduced form solutions to a macroeconometric model of the form of equation 149 above.

Fourth, we impose upper and lower bounds on each of the policy instruments to represent political constraints on policy changes, thereby ruling out very large and very sudden changes in policy,

$$X_{\min} \leqq X \leqq X_{\max} \qquad (157)$$

Since all the variables can be scaled (and the constraints and equations changed accordingly), one can add nonnegativity constraints on each of the target and instrument variables. This gives to the system of equations and inequalities represented by 152–157 the form of an LP model, which will have both primal and dual formulations and solutions. From the primal solution, we can obtain the optimal policy package, X, as well as the maximum welfare attainable (in this case, GDP), given the constraints. From the dual solution, we obtain the shadow prices, P, representing the cost in terms of welfare of tightening each particular constraint by one unit. The way our system has been formulated, it is the shadow prices that provide both the trade-offs between each limitation on each policy instrument and the welfare target, GDP, and the trade-offs between each other welfare target (C, I, BP, and SG) and GDP. Since all the shadow prices are relative prices and are relative to the same standard (in this case, GDP), ratios of the different shadow prices of the different constraints can also be calculated. Thus, a whole matrix of all the possible trade-offs between each policy instrument and welfare target, and policy instruments and welfare targets with one another respectively can easily be obtained. These trade-offs are the possibility trade-offs. With knowledge about the possibility trade-offs, the policy maker can choose the optimal policy mix by matching the possibility trade-offs with his (undeclared) desirability trade-offs.

The linear programming approach to policy planning has certain definite shortcomings. In the first place, it has not specifically treated the problem of risk. Note, for example, that the economic model, given in structural form by equation 149 and in reduced form by equation 150, and therefore the policy model derived from it (equation 151), were defined in nonstochastic terms. This was, of course, simply for convenience of exposition. Nevertheless, the admission of error terms in equations 149 and 150 raises a question about how these errors should be treated in the linear programming solutions. The normal procedure consists of two steps: (1) equations 150 and then 149 are estimated in such a way as to preserve the independence and other properties of the error terms by two-stage least squares and (2) these results in nonstochastic form are used to solve for the optimal policy solutions. Additive errors can be incorporated in the LP model by changing the right-hand sides, as in parametric programming, but for more ad hoc simulation and sensitivity analysis, this leaves the problem of multiplicative errors, that is, errors in the policy multiplier coefficients contained in the **B** matrix in our formulation.

A general problem is that this procedure is based on incremental analysis and pertains to discrete periods of time. This limits the model's ability to achieve much in the way of "fine tuning" of policy choices. For this reason, many analysts are now turning to control theory approaches to policy choices (Intriligator 1971).

In order to give the reader some empirical feel for the LP approach we shall briefly sketch a specific application[38] to intertemporal policy planning and present a sample of tentative results.

Intertemporal Coordination of Economic Policies

Using a macroeconometric model for Ecuador, with target variables gross domestic product, GDP, private consumption, C, investment, I, government savings, SG, and the balance of payments, BP, and with policy instruments government spending, G, the stock of high-powered money, RM, the import tax rate, Tn/N, and the other tax rate, To/GDP, Nugent and DePrano (1967) applied the LP approach to intertemporal policy planning.

The application proceeded in the following way: (1) GDP was maximized; (2) lower and upper bounds were imposed on the secondary target variables as in equations 152–156 and on the policy instruments as in equation 157; (3) impact multipliers taken from the reduced form estimates of the macroeconometric model were used as the basis of the relationships between the policy instruments and the target variables; (4) optimal solutions were computed for each of three years in the plan horizon in two alternative situations—one, in which the solutions for each year were computed sequentially one year at a time, and the other, in which the solutions for all three years were computed simultaneously; and (5) the two alternative solutions were compared and the difference between them was attributed to intertemporal coordination of policies.

[38]For other applications of the method, the reader is referred to Chenery (1959) and Nugent (1974).

The results obtained from the primal solution indicated that intertemporal coordination of policy would make no improvement in GDP in the first two years of the plan, but in the third year, the improvement could be very sizable (almost 15 percent of GDP). The higher GDP in the third year is achieved through a whole series of policy substitutions that take advantage of the additional flexibility offered by the intertemporal as well as the intratemporal possibility trade-offs.

The results obtained from the dual solution indicate the shadow prices of the respective constraints or the relative possibility trade-offs between and among the various targets and policy instruments. By sensitivity analysis, it was revealed that the results depend to a large extent on the relative tightness of the SG and BP constraints.

Therefore, it seems wise to consider two different sets of shadow prices (possibility trade-offs), the choice between them being dependent on which constraint is thought to be more binding in particular circumstances. For illustrative purposes, we present in Table 21.13 these two alternative sets of shadow prices with respect to a single year rather than all three years together. Referring, for example, to the set pertaining to the case where the constraints on G and SG are not binding (but that on BP is) shown in part A of the table, one can see that the policy maker could trade off one Ecuadorean sucre of deterioration in the balance of payments, BP, for 1.75 sucres of gain in GDP, or a 0.75 sucre gain in consumption, C. Similarly, a relaxation of the constraint (an upper bound) on the import tax rate equivalent to one sucre would allow C to rise by 0.67 sucres.

The results of the dual solutions under the two alternative conditions, that is, simultaneous solution of all three years and sequential year-by-year solutions, are consistent with those of the primal problems, in that with intertemporal coordination the shadow prices are more homogeneous than those for a single year, indicated in Table 21.13. Thus, there are more possibilities for trade-offs, and the trade-offs are more balanced.

Summary and Conclusions

The conditions under which unfettered market forces can provide for an optimal allocation of resources at a particular point in time are exigent: perfect competition and complete in-

Table 21.13 *Target and Instrument Trade-Off Ratios, Ecuador*

Effect on	A. Trade-off Ratios When *G* and *SG Are Not* Binding							B. Trade-off Ratios When *G* and *SG Are* Binding						
	Ease Constraints by One Unit (sucre)							Ease Constraints by One Unit (sucre)						
	C	*SG*	*BP*	*G*	$\frac{Tn}{N}$	$\frac{To}{GDP}$	*RM*	*C*	*SG*	*BP*	*G*	$\frac{Tn}{N}$	$\frac{To}{GDP}$	*RM*
GDP	.00023	..	1.75349	..	1.54493	0.00009	0.00042	..	0.27981	..	0.45637	..	0.83976	0.31602
C		..	0.75520	..	0.66530	0.37989	1.81456		..	..	..	..	..	..
SG			..	..	..	..	..			..	..	1.63100	3.00119	1.12941
BP				..	0.88106	0.00005	0.00024				..	..	..	..
G					..	..	..						1.84009	0.69247
Tn/N						0.00006	0.00027							0.37632
To/GDP							4.77656							
RM														

Notes: The variables are defined in the text. . . indicates trade-off insignificantly different than zero.
Source: Nugent, J. B., and M. E. DePrano (1967), "The Effects of Long-Run and Short-Run Planning Goals on Economic Policy Instruments." Paper presented to the Econometric Society, Washington, D.C. (December).

formation, perfect technical and price efficiency, lack of externalities, and the availability of a system of lump-sum taxes and subsidies that can reconcile the efficient with the desired distribution of resources. Optimal allocation over time becomes even more difficult, because the above conditions must also be met with respect to future decisions. Since the choice of a growth path in the present forecloses development alternatives for the future, intertemporal optimality becomes especially difficult. Macroeconomic planning proposes to identify the optimal time path for economic development.

National development plans may be the product of formal economic modeling or the informal result of a combination of administrative experience and political expediency. In either case, a plan that is not internally consistent is bound to remain an empty monument of serendipity. Testing for the consistency of the projected time path of economic development is relatively simple, as we demonstrated in the case of Ecuador by using the I-O model.

The two-gap models, focusing on shortages of capital and foreign exchange, have commanded considerable attention in the literature. While this two-factor focus can often be overly restrictive from the point of view of overall growth and development, two-gap models can almost always be useful in highlighting the *ex ante* imbalances present in alternative states of the world and in pointing to alternative kinds of policy solutions. More particularly, such models can be useful in soliciting and allocating foreign assistance. We presented a consistency test within the two-gap model framework for the five countries of Central America. By making foreign trade projections and savings-investment projections, we have found the foreign exchange constraint more binding than the savings-investment constraint. By comparing the gap under alternative growth target rates, the usual approach draws conclusions about the marginal productivity of foreign assistance. Alternatively, the same results can be viewed as signifying that additional efforts should be expended internally to bring the two gaps closer together.

Linear programming techniques are well suited to comprehensive planning—centralized or decentralized. We have presented an LP model of the Greek economy, emphasizing its construction and its application to national development planning. Our results suggest that the Greek economy underachieved, with respect to its potential, in the period 1954–1961. The subsequent dynamism of the economy in the 1960s has tended to confirm this finding. Although testing of LP models is not the common practice, we have presented a technique to test the LP planning model of Greece. In this procedure, we observe the deviations between the LP optimal solution and the one actually obtained by the country for each sector. If these deviations can be explained by various indexes of market imperfections, the implication is that the LP optimum is closer to the true optimum than is the market solution. If, on the other hand, these deviations are explained by factors that have been omitted from the model, it is likely that the market solution lies closer to the true optimum than the model solution. Our conclusion favors the former case for Greece, which suggests that the underachievement of the economy was most likely caused by the conjoint forces of market distortions and misguided government policies.

The more common failure of planning is not the internal inconsistency of the plan, its infeasibility, or its suboptimality. Instead, it is that it affords too few degrees of freedom to the policy maker for implementation. We have closed this chapter by looking into economic policy in a way that reverses the procedure employed in economic analysis, which attempts to explain various important economic variables, endogenous to the system, in terms of exogenous variables. Among the latter are also policy variables, such as tax rates, investment credits, and so on. In the theory of economic policy, the endogenous and exogenous variables are reversed. "Policy instruments" are endogenously determined on the basis of economic variables that are set exogenously as the "targets." We have illustrated the process of planning policy with an example of an approach using linear programming. It refers to policy coordination in Ecuador under a three-year planning horizon. The approach culminates in deriving a whole matrix of possibility trade-offs between each policy instrument and each welfare goal. The policy maker can then compare these possibility trade-offs with political desirability trade-offs and thereby set the subsequent course of economic policy. In this light, the role of the economic planner is best characterized as being "the psychiatrist of the collective will." By revealing trade-offs, he encourages the soul-searching that will allow policy makers to decide what are the politically acceptable choices among competing economic goals.

The preceding chapters have given numerous indications that development is not a smooth process that spreads automatically. The theory of takeoff into self-sustained growth is more a dream than a practical schema. Rather, we have found development to be a process that from time to time or place to place may benefit from skillfully designed and carefully metered and timed jolts to stimulate dynamic disequilibria, to lead the economy over the various bumps, barriers, and constraints it will confront. To some extent, the path to development may be rendered somewhat smoother and easier by removing the sources of market imperfections and improving information and its availability. In other portions of this book, we have given much attention to identifying such possibilities and measuring the potential gains derived from them.

We believe, however, that some such efforts will be resisted and that those which do come to fruition will be insufficient to transform the LDCs into DCs within a reasonable period of time. Planning will therefore be imperative. It is most suitable then to conclude the book on the somewhat optimistic note that the means are available for making plans internally consistent, feasible, and optimal. Also, we seem to have theoretically satisfying as well as practical methods for ensuring their successful implementation by linking planning goals to policy instruments, on the one hand, and macroeconomic plans with an efficient combination of carefully evaluated development projects, on the other. In other words, tools—perhaps not the best ones—are available. What is needed is better understanding of the underlying behavioral processes. This reminder may hopefully bring our readers back to the task to which this book is devoted—the formulation and testing of operational hypotheses about the development process.

Chapter 22
Postscript

The beginning of the 1970s has marked a watershed—if not for economic development, certainly for development economics.

While output has traditionally been considered the jugular of development, and growth its manifestation, the battlecries have recently become more complicated and more shrill: "Output, employment, and income distribution," "Development from below," "Income with redistribution." This change may not amount to much for economic development as a goal. It may, nevertheless, herald a revolution for development economics.

Economic development has always had a "humane face." As a normative goal, it is supposed to lead to the realization of the potential of human personality. An absolute necessity for this realization is to take care of basic human needs. These needs can be translated into income terms and imply the elimination of poverty. Another requirement is a job—both as a means of earning income and, perhaps as a self-rewarding aim: having a useful task to perform, whether in paid employment, self-improvement, or subsistence activities, is crucial for maintaining an individual's dignity, self-respect—and sanity. The goal of development has always been triadic, its components being output, employment, and income distribution (Seers 1973).

Development economics, on the other hand, has gone almost exclusively for the jugular—the growth in output—not so much in an act of a willful abrogation of other goals as in an expression of confidence that all facets of the goal of development are the joint products of a single process of development. This article of faith was incorporated in the leading neoclassical paradigm of trade and development upon which we have dwelled at length. This paradigm envisioned development as a gradual, continu-

429

ous, harmonious, and cumulative process, with significant spread and trickling-down effects. An important hypothesis derived from the neoclassical paradigm is that after an initial "rough ascent," growth is smooth, balanced, and all-encompassing from the point of view of the distribution of benefits. Trade, specialization, factor mobilization, and technological change were all thought to be complementary processes, which would raise the aggregate level of welfare and then insure that the gains in welfare were spread among individuals in a society, and even from one society to another. In our view, this hypothesis is possibly false and in any event unsupported by empirical evidence. The respectable rates of growth in GNP that many LDCs achieved in the 1950s and especially in the 1960s have apparently had little or no effect on the large numbers of people who live in abject poverty.

Cracks in the armor of the neoclassical paradigm began to be observed in the 1950s. Why are large numbers of persons employed in agriculture beyond the point that would be justified by the marginal productivity rule of profit maximization? Why do different groups have different propensities to save and invest? How can different technologies be employed side by side in the same country? Why have some countries not been able to achieve development in the face of dramatic increases in their exports? Why do LDCs seem to have greater difficulty in taking advantage of the benefits of international trade than DCs? Why do societies in which capital is cheap and labor expensive tend to export labor-intensive and import capital-intensive commodities?

Neoclassical economics has not taken these contradictions lying down. Several lines of defense have been developed. Economic theory was right, but economic policies were wrong—for example, in subsidizing the use of capital-intensive technology in LDCs. The observed paradoxes were optical illusions or the products of errors in measurement—for example, with labor surplus or the Leontief paradox. Endless epicycles were added to the theory to patch it up—for example, with the permanent-income hypothesis. The aberrations were the result of temporary accidents or disequilibria that would be overcome by vigorously pursuing the dictates of free market policies—such as in the case of trade liberalization, migration from the rural to the urban sector, or investment in the human agent. In the long run, dualism and disequilibria are bound to be phased out via the traditional adjustment mechanisms and the classical sources of accumulation and growth are bound to be reactivated—as exemplified by the theories of dual development.

The development economics of the 1960s provided a reassuring and conservative answer to the challenges raised by economic development in the 1950s. As we have pointed out throughout this book, however, these exercises in equilibrium dynamics have been off the mark in a number of respects. Most notably, the adjustment mechanisms, such as education, migration, and industrialization, have not only failed to eliminate dualism, income inequality, and other forms of disequilibrium but in many instances have even exacerbated them.

We have provided a review of the troops as we enter a period that brings both a reorientation in economic development and perhaps a revolt in development economics against its leading paradigm. For as Senator Hubert Humphrey perceptively remarked in introducing in the United States Congress the 1973 foreign aid bill, there is ". . . a veritable intellectual revolt among scholars of development who are turning against the long-held view that growth alone is the answer that will trickle benefits to the poor majority."

It is still too early to tell precisely what this revolt against the ruling paradigm will entail. It is our opinion that as a minimum the development economics of the 1970s and beyond is likely to give much less attention to smooth adjustment mechanisms, harmonies of interest, and spread effects and more emphasis to disequilibria, backwash effects, and conflicts of interest. There may even emerge a new paradigm, representing a radical departure from the neoclassical paradigm.

Bibliography and Authors' Index

The bibliography lists alphabetically by author and by year of publication all works referred to in the text. The only exception is the statistical material that is not readily identifiable by the name of an author and for which full reference has been given in the Table or Figure where it was used. Such references are not repeated in the bibliography.

The bibliography serves also as an Authors' Index. Following each citation, there is a list of the pages in the text on which the citation appears. This index, therefore, identifies authors by the references to their works also, rather than by the reference to their name alone.

Second authors are also included in the alphabetical listing, with reference made to the first author's name under which the full bibliographical and index information appears.

The following is a list of titles of journals and names of organizations with their abbre-viated forms as they appear in the bibliography.

A.E.R.	American Economic Review
A.J.A.E.	American Journal of Agricultural Economics
E.D.C.C.	Economic Development and Cultural Change
E.J.	Economic Journal
F.R.I.S.	Food Research Institute Studies
IBRD	International Bank for Reconstruction and Development (World Bank)
J.D.E.	Journal of Development Economics
J.D.S.	Journal of Development Studies
J.E.L.	Journal of Economic Literature
J.F.E.	Journal of Farm Economics
J.P.E.	Journal of Political Economy
M.I.T.	Massachusetts Institute of Technology
N.B.E.R.	National Bureau of Economic Research

OECD   Organization of Economic Cooperation and Development
O.E.P.   *Oxford Economic Papers*
Q.J.E.   *Quarterly Journal of Economics*
R.E.S.   *Review of Economic Studies*
R.E.Stat.   *Review of Economics and Statistics*
U.N.   United Nations
U.N.: ECAFE   United Nations Economic Commission for Asia and the Far East
U.N.: ECLA   United Nations Economic Commission for Latin America
UNESCO   United Nations Educational, Social and Cultural Organization
UNCTAD   United Nations Conference on Trade and Development
UNIDO   United Nations Industrial Development Organization
U.N.: FAO   United Nations Food and Agriculture Organization

ABRAMOVITZ, M. **1956.** "Resources and Output Trends in the United States Since 1870." *A.E.R.*, 46 (May), 5–23. **154**

ACHARYA, S. N., and B. R. HAZARI **1971.** "Linkages and Imports: A Comparative Study of India and Pakistan. *J.D.S.*, 8 (October), 107–115. **302n.**

ACKLEY, G. **1961.** *Macroeconomic Theory.* New York: Macmillan. **168n.**

ADELMAN, I., M. GEIER, and C. T. MORRIS **1969.** "Instruments and Goals in Economic Development." *A.E.R.*, 59 (May), 409–426. **36**

ADELMAN, I., and C. T. MORRIS **1965.** "A Factor Analysis of the Interrelationship between Social and Political Variables and Per Capita Gross National Product." *Q.J.E.*, 79 (November), 555–578. **33, 35, 37**
1967. *Society, Politics, and Economic Development.* Baltimore: Johns Hopkins University Press. **32n., 33–36, 37, 38**
1968a. "Performance Criteria for Evaluating Economic Development Potential: An Operational Approach." *Q.J.E.*, 82 (May), 260–280. **36**
1968b. "An Econometric Model of Socio-Economic and Political Change in Underdeveloped Countries." *A.E.R.*, 58 (December), 1184–1218. **36, 37, 38**
1970. "Factor Analysis and Gross National Product: A Reply." *Q.J.E.*, 84 (November), 651–662. **34, 37**
1971. "Analysis-of-Variance Techniques for the Study of Economic Development." *J.D.S.*, 8 (October), 91–105. **33**
1973. *Economic Growth and Social Equity in Developing Countries.* Stanford: Stanford University Press. **7n., 238, 239, 248n., 251–253**

ADELMAN, I., and F. T. SPARROW **1966.** "Experiments with Linear and Piece-wise Linear Dynamic Programming Models." In I. Adelman and E. Thorbecke, eds., *The Theory and Design of Economic Development.* Baltimore: Johns Hopkins Press. **408n.**

AGASSI, J. **See** Klappholtz, K., and J. Agassi

AHLUWALIA, M. S. **1974.** "Income Inequality: Some Dimensions of the Problem. In H. B. Chenery, *et al.*, eds., *Redistribution with Growth.* London: Oxford University Press, 4–37. **238, 239, 241, 249**

AHLUWALIA, M. S., and H. B. CHENERY **1974.** "A Model of Distribution and Growth." In H. B. Chenery, *et al.*, *Redistribution with Growth.* London: Oxford University Press, 209–235. **238**

AIGNER, D. J., and A. J. HEINS **1967.** "On the Determinants of Income Equality." *A.E.R.*, 57 (March), 175–184. **193, 250**

AITCHISON, J., and J. A. BROWN **1957.** *The Lognormal Distribution.* Cambridge: Cambridge University Press. **243**

AKBAR, M. A. **See** Nugent, J. B., and M. A. Akbar.

ALCHIAN, A. A. **1959a.** "Costs and Output." In M. Abramovitz, ed., *The Allocation of Economic Resources.* Stanford: Stanford University Press, 23–40. **64**
1959b. "Private Property and the Relative Cost of Tenure." In P. D. Bradley, ed., *The Public Stake in Union Power.* Charlottesville: University of Virginia Press, 350–371. **76**
1970. "Information Costs, Pricing and Resource Unemployment." In E. S. Phelps *et al.*, eds., *Microeconomic Foundations of Employment and Inflation Theory.* New York: Norton, 27–52. **231**

ALONZO, R. P. **1969.** "Welfare Effects of Monopoly Positions in the Philippines." Unpublished M.A. thesis, University of the Philippines. **109n., 110n.**

AL-SAMARRIE, A., and H. P. MILLER **1967.** "State Differentials in Income Concentration." *A.E.R.*, 57 (March), 59–72. **193, 250**

ANDERSON, G. H. **1970.** "Income Stabilization for Primary Producers: An Empirical Evaluation of the Bauer-Paish Proposal." *South African Journal of Economics*, 38 (March), 35–49. **340n.**

ANDERSON, J. E. **1970.** "General Equilibrium and the Effective Rate of Protection." *J.P.E.*, 78 (July), 717–724. **113n.**

ANDO, A., and F. MODIGLIANI **1963.** "The 'Life Cycle' Hypothesis of Saving: Aggregate Implications and Tests." *A.E.R.*, 53 (March), 55–84. **177n., 178**
1964. "The 'Life Cycle' Hypothesis of Saving: A Correction." *A.E.R.*, 54 (March), 111–113. **177n.**
See also Modigliani, F., and A. Ando.

ANDREWS, W. H. **See** Marschak, J., and W. H. Andrews.

ANSCHEL, K. R. **See** Kao, C. H. C., K. R. Anschel, and C. K. Eicher.

APPLEYARD, D. R. **1968.** "Terms of Trade and Economic Development: A Case Study of India." *A.E.R.*, 58 (May), 188–199. **344n.**

ARCHIBALD, G. C. **1964.** *Industrialization and Capital Requirements in Greece.* Athens: Center of Planning and Economic Research. **293n., 394n.**

1966. "Refutation or Comparison?" *British Journal for the Philosophy of Science*, 17 (May), 279–296. **24, 25n., 26n.**

ARNDT, S. W. **1968.** "On Discriminatory vs. Non-Preferential Tariff Policies." *E.J.*, 78 (December), 971–979. **350, 357**

1969. "Customs Unions and the Theory of Tariffs." *A.E.R.*, 59 (March), 108–118. **350, 357**

ARROW, K. J. **1951.** *Social Choice and Individual Values.* New York: Wiley. **37**

1962. "The Economic Implications of Learning by Doing." *R.E.S.*, 29 (June), 155–173. **378**

1965. *Aspects of the Theory of Risk-bearing.* Helsinki: Yrjö Jahnssonin Säätiö. **246, 247**

ARROW, K. J., H. B. CHENERY, B. S. MINHAS, and R. M. SOLOW **1961.** "Capital-Labor Substitution and Economic Efficiency." *R.E.Stat.*, 43 (August), 225–250. **52, 151, 323**

ARROW, K. J., and M. KURZ **1970.** *Public Investment, the Rate of Return and Optimal Fiscal Policy.* Baltimore: Johns Hopkins University Press. **246**

ASHENFELTER, O., and J. D. MOONEY **1968.** "Graduate Education, Ability and Earnings." *R.E.Stat.*, 50 (February), 78–86. **195n.**

ATALLAH, M. K. **1958.** *The Long-Term Movement of the Terms of Trade between Agricultural and Industrial Products.* Rotterdam: Netherlands Economic Institute. **343n.**

ATKINSON, A. B. **1970.** "On the Measurement of Inequality." *Journal of Economic Theory*, 2 (September), 244–263. **244, 246**

ATKINSON, A. B., and J. E. STIGLITZ **1972.** "The Structure of Indirect Taxation and Economic Efficiency." *Journal of Public Economics*, 1, 97–119. **391n.**

BAILEY, D., and C. SCHOTTA **1972.** "Private and Social Rates of Return to Education of Academicians." *A.E.R.*, 62 (March), 19–31. **188n.**

BAILEY, M. J. **1956.** "The Welfare Cost of Inflationary Finance." *J.P.E.*, 64 (April), 93–110. **171n.**

BAIN, J. S. **1951.** "Relation of Profit Rate to Industry Concentration: American Manufacturing, 1936–1940." *Q.J.E.*, 65 (August), 293–324. **109n.**

BALASSA, B. **1963.** "An Empirical Demonstration of Classical Comparative Cost Theory." *R.E.Stat.*, 45 (August), 231–238. **321**

1964. *Trade Prospects for Developing Countries.* Homewood, Ill.: Irwin. **314n.**

1965. *Economic Development and Integration.*

Mexico City: Centro de Estudios Monetarios Latinoamericanos. **357n., 358n.**

1967. "Trade Creation and Trade Diversion in the European Common Market." *E.J.*, 77 (March), 1–21. **351–352, 359**

1971. "Regional Integration and Trade Liberalization in Latin America." *Journal of Common Market Studies*, 10 (September), 58–77. **357n., 358n.**

BALASSA, B. A., and ASSOCIATES **1971.** *The Structure of Protection in Developing Countries.* Baltimore: Johns Hopkins University Press. **14, 112, 122, 352**

BALASSA, B. A., and D. SCHYDLOWSKY **1968.** "Effective Tariffs, Domestic Cost of Foreign Exchange, and the Equilibrium Exchange Rate." *J.P.E.*, 76 (May), 348–360. **396**

BALDWIN, R. E. **1971.** "Determinants of the Commodity Structure of U.S. Trade." *A.E.R.*, 61 (March), 126–146. **322**

See also Meier, G. M., and R. E. Baldwin.

BALOGH, T. **1967.** "The Economics of Educational Planning: Sense and Nonsense." In K. Martin and J. Knapp, eds., *The Teaching of Development Economics.* Chicago: Aldine, 85–105. **195**

BARAN, P. A. **1952.** "On the Political Economy of Backwardness." *Manchester School of Economic and Social Studies*, 20 (January), 66–84. **13**

1957. *The Political Economy of Growth.* New York: Monthly Review Press. **7n., 8**

BARAN, P. A., and E. J. HOBSBAWM **1961.** "The Stages of Economic Growth: A Review." *Kyklos*, 14, No. 2, 234–242. **7n.**

BARAN, P. A., and P. M. SWEEZY **1966.** *Monopoly Capital.* New York and London: Modern Reader Paperbacks. **77**

BARKER, R. **1966.** "The Response of Production to a Change in Rice Price." *Philippine Economic Journal*, 5, 260–276. **137n.**

BAUMOL, W. J. **1964.** "External Economics and Second Order Optimality Conditions." *A.E.R.*, 54 (June), 358–372. **379**

BECKER, G. S. **1962.** "Investment in Human Capital: A Theoretical Analysis." *J.P.E.*, 70 (October, Supplement), 9–49. **184n.**

1964. *Human Capital.* New York: N.B.E.R. **184n., 191n., 195n.**

1965. "A Theory of the Allocation of Time." *E.J.*, 75 (September), 493–517. **196**

BECKERMAN, W. **1973.** "Economic and Social Costs of Modernization and Development." Paper presented at the Rehovat Conference on Economic Growth in Developing Countries, Israel (September 5–11). **9n.**

BECKMAN, M. J., and R. SATO **1969.** "Aggregate Production Functions and Types of Technical Progress: A Statistical Analysis." *A.E.R.*, 59 (March), 88–101. **147n.**

BEHRMAN, J. R. **1966.** "The Price Elasticity of the Marketed Surplus of a Subsistence Crop." *J.F.E.*, 48 (November), 875–893. **141**
1968. *Supply Response in Underdeveloped Agriculture.* Amsterdam: North Holland. **137n., 140, 141**
1971. "Review Article: UNCTAD Secretariat. Trade Prospects and Capital Needs of Developing Countries." *International Economic Review*, 12 (October), 519–525. **405n.**

BELL, F. W. **1968.** "The Effect of Monopoly Profits and Wages on Prices and Consumers' Surplus in American Manufacturing." *Western Economic Journal*, 6 (June), 233–241. **109n., 122**

BENNETT, R. L. **1967.** "Surplus Agricultural Labor and Development—Facts and Theories: Comment." *A.E.R.*, 57 (March), 194–202. **73n.**

BENTICK, B. L. **1963.** "Estimating Trade Creation and Trade Diversion." *E.J.*, 73 (June), 219–225. **351**

BERG, E. J. **1961.** "Backward-Sloping Labor Supply Functions in Dual Economies—The Africa Case." *Q.J.E.*, 75 (August), 468–492. **131n.**

BERGSMAN, J. **1974.** "Commercial Policy, Allocative Efficiency, and 'X-Efficiency.'" *Q.J.E.*, 88 (August), 409–433. **122**

BERGSMAN, J., and P. MALAH **1970.** "The Structure of Protection in Brazil." In J. Bergsman, ed., *Brazil: Industrialization and Trade Policies.* Oxford: Oxford University Press. **118n.**

BERINGER, C. **1963.** "Real Effects of Foreign Surplus Disposal in Underdeveloped Economies: Comment." *Q.J.E.*, 77 (May), 317–323. **136**

BERRY, R. A., and S. R. SOLIGO **1968.** "Rural-Urban Migration, Agricultural Output and the Supply Price of Labour in a Labour-Surplus Economy." *O.E.P.*, 20 (July), 230–249. **211**

BERTRAND, T. J. **1972.** "Decision Rules for Effective Protection in Less Developed Economies." *A.E.R.*, 62 (September), 743–746. **352n.**

BERTRAND, T. J., and J. VANEK **1971.** "The Theory of Tariffs, Taxes and Subsidies: Some Aspects of the Second Best." *A.E.R.*, 61 (December), 925–931. **352n.**

BHAGWATI, J. N. **1965.** "On the Equivalence of Tariffs and Quotas." In R. E. Baldwin *et al.*, eds., *Trade, Growth and the Balance of Payments.* Chicago: Rand McNally. **119n.**
1968. "The Theory and Practice of Commercial Policy: Departures from Unified Exchange Rates." *Special Papers in International Economics*, No. 8, International Finance Section, Princeton University. **348n.**

BHAGWATI, J. N., and T. N. SRINIVASAN **1974.** "On Reanalyzing the Harris-Todaro Model: Policy Rankings in the Case of Sector-Specific Sticky Wages." *A.E.R.*, 64 (June), 502–508. **229**

BHAMBRI, R. S. **1962.** "Customs Unions and Underdeveloped Countries." *Economia Internazionale*, 15 (May), 235–258. **358n.**

BHATIA, B. M. **1969.** "Terms of Trade and Economic Development: A Case Study of India—1861–1939." *Indian Economic Journal*, 16 (April), 414–433. **344**

BICANIC, R. **1962.** "The Threshold of Economic Growth." *Kyklos*, 15, No. 1, 7–28. **31n.**

BLAU, G. **1964.** "International Commodity Arrangements." In C. K. Eicher and L. Witt, eds., *Agriculture in Economic Development.* New York: McGraw-Hill, 322–339. **340n.**

BLAU, P. M., and O. D. DUNCAN **1967.** *The American Occupational Structure.* New York: Wiley. **195n.**

BLAUG, M. **1967.** "The Private and Social Returns on Investment in Education: Some Results for Great Britain." *Journal of Human Resources*, 2 (Summer), 330–346. **188n.**

BODKIN, R. G. **1959.** "Windfall Income and Consumption." *A.E.R.*, 49 (September), 602–614. **176n.**
1963. "Windfall Income and Consumption: Comment." *A.E.R.*, 53 (June), 445–447. **176n.**

BOEKE, J. H. **1953.** *Economics and Economic Policy of Dual Societies.* New York: Institute of Pacific Relations. **253–254**

BOTTOMLEY, A. **1964.** "The Structure of Interest Rates in Underdeveloped Rural Areas." *J.F.E.*, 46 (May), 313–322. **255**
1966. "Monopolistic Rent Determination in Underdeveloped Rural Areas." *Kyklos*, 19, No. 1, 106–118. **110n.**

BOTTRILL, A. **See** Williamson, J. G., and A. Bottrill.

BOULDING, K. E. **1953.** "Toward a General Theory of Growth." *Canadian Journal of Economics and Political Science*, 19 (August), 326–340. **15, 287n.**

BOWLES, S. **1970.** "Migration as Investment: Empirical Tests of the Human Investment Approach to Geographical Mobility." *R.E.Stat.*, 52 (November), 356–362. **226**
1972. "Schooling and Inequality from Generation to Generation." *J.P.E.*, 80 (May, Supplement), S219–S251. **187, 195n., 196**

BRADY, D. S., and R. D. FRIEDMAN **1947.** "Savings and the Income Distribution." Conference on Research in Income and Wealth, *Studies in Income and Wealth*, 10. New York: N.B.E.R., 247–265. **173**

BRAINARD, W., and R. N. COOPER **1968.** "Uncertainty and Diversification in International Trade." *F.R.I.S.*, 8, No. 3, 257–285. **339n.**

BRAITHWAITE, R. **1953.** *Scientific Explanation.* Cambridge: Cambridge University Press. **19–20, 23n., 28–29**

BRONFENBRENNER, M. **1953.** "The High Cost of Economic Development." *Land Economics*, 29 (May), 93–104; (August), 209–221. **7**
1966. "Paul Baran: An Appreciation." *J.P.E.*, 74 (February), 69–71. **11**

1971. *Income Distribution Theory.* Chicago: Aldine. **247n.**

BROOKINS, O. T. **1970.** "Factor Analysis and Gross National Product: A Comment." *Q.J.E.,* 84 (November), 648–650. **37**

BROWN, J. A. **See** Aitchison, J., and J. A. Brown.

BROWN, M. **1966.** *On the Theory and Measurement of Technological Change.* Cambridge: Cambridge University Press, **149n., 154n.**

BROWN, M., and J. POPKIN **1962.** "A Measure of Technological Change and Return to Scale." *R.E.Stat.,* 44 (November), 402–411. **148n.**

BROWN, R. W. **1965.** *Social Psychology.* New York: Free Press. **39n.**

BROWNING, H. L. **1971.** "Migrant Selectivity and the Growth of Large Cities in Developing Societies." In National Academy of Sciences, *Rapid Population Growth,* 2 (Research Papers). Baltimore: Johns Hopkins University Press. **227**

BRUMBERG, R. **See** Modigliani, F., and R. Brumberg.

BRUNO, M. **1967.** "The Optimal Selection of Export-Promoting and Import-Substituting Projects." In U.N., *Planning the External Sector: Techniques, Problems and Policies,* ST/TAO/91/Series C. New York: U.N., 88–135. **396** **See also** Chenery, H. B., and M. Bruno.

BRUTON, H. J. **1969.** "The Two-Gap Approach to Aid and Development: Comment." *A.E.R.,* 59 (June), 439–446. **402n.**

BUCHANAN, J. M. **1962.** "Politics, Policy and Pigovian Margins." *Economica,* 29 (February), 17–28. **379**

BUCHANAN, J. M., and M. Z. KAFOGLIS. **1963.** "A Note on Public Goods Supply." *A.E.R.,* 53 (June), 403–414. **379**

BUCHANAN, J. M., and G. C. TULLOCK **1962.** *The Calculus of Consent.* Ann Arbor: University of Michigan Press. **379**

BUTLER, A., and G. DEMOPOULOS **1974.** "The Labor Force Continuum and the Analysis of Labor Market Behavior." State University of New York at Buffalo, Department of Economics, Discussion Paper #298 (February, mimeo). **202n.**

CABEZON, P. **1969.** "An Evaluation of Commercial Policy in the Chilean Economy." Unpublished Ph.D. Dissertation, University of Wisconsin. **112**

CAGAN, P. **1956.** "The Monetary Dynamics of Hyper-Inflation." In M. Friedman, ed., *Studies in the Quantity Theory of Money.* Chicago: University of Chicago Press, 25–117. **138**

CAINE, S. **1954.** "Instability of Primary Product Prices: A Protest and a Proposal." *E.J.,* 64 (September), 610–614. **340n.**

CARNOY, M. **1972.** "The Political Economy of Education." In T. J. LaBelle, ed., *Education and Development: Latin America and the Caribbean.* Latin American Studies Series 18. Los Angeles: University of California Press, 177–215. **195**

CARNOY, M., and D. MARENBACH **1975.** "The Rate of Return to Schooling in the United States." *Journal of Human Resources* (forthcoming). **193**

CARTER, H. O., and H. Q. HARTLEY **1958.** "A Variance Formula for Marginal Productivity Estimates Using the Cobb-Douglas Function." *Econometrica,* 26 (April), 306–313. **83n.**

CASTREE, J. R. **See** Wilson, T., R. P. Sinha, and J. R. Castree.

CAVES, R. E. **1965a.** *American Industry: Structure, Conduct, Performance.* Englewood Cliffs, N.J.: Prentice-Hall. **260** **1965b.** "Vent-for-Surplus Models of Trade and Growth." In R. E. Baldwin et al., eds., *Trade, Growth and the Balance of Payments.* Chicago: Rand McNally. **260, 358**

CAVES, R. E., and R. W. Jones **1973.** *World Trade and Payments.* Boston: Little, Brown. **323n.**

CHAMPERNOWNE, D. G. **1974.** "A Comparison of Measures of Inequality of Income Distribution." *E.J.,* 84 (December), 787–816. **244**

CHEETHAM, R. **See** Kelley, A. C., J. G. Williamson, and R. Cheetham.

CHENERY, H. B. **1952.** "Overcapacity and the Acceleration Principle." *Econometrica,* 20 (January), 1–28. **181** **1953.** "The Application of Investment Criteria." *Q.J.E.,* 67 (February), 76–96. **12, 395** **1955.** "The Role of Industrialization in Development Programs." *A.E.R.,* 45 (May), 40–57. **395.** **1957.** "Tests of Interindustry Models of Growth." Stanford Project for Quantitative Research in Economic Development, Stanford University (mimeo). **416n.** **1958.** "Development Policies and Programmes." *Economic Bulletin for Latin America,* 3 (March), 51–77. **395, 408n.** **1959.** "The Interdependence of Investment Decisions." In M. Abramovitz et al., *The Allocation of Economic Resources.* Stanford: Stanford University Press, 82–120. **395, 425** **1960.** "Patterns of Industrial Growth." *A.E.R.,* 50 (September), 624–654. **14, 150n., 260, 287n., 291–293** **1964.** "The Effect of Resources on Economic Growth." In K. Berrill, ed., *Economic Development with Special Reference to East Asia.* New York: St. Martin's, 19–52. **287n.** **1969.** "The Process of Industrialization." Economic Development Report No. 146, Project for Quantitative Research in Economic Development. Cambridge: Harvard Center for International Affairs. **287n., 292n., 408n.** **1970a.** "The Normal Developing Economy." Economic Development Report No. 162, Project for Quantitative Research in Economic Development. Cambridge: Harvard Center for International Affairs. **287n.**

1970b. "Alternative Patterns of Development." Economic Development Report No. 163, Project for Quantitative Research in Economic Development. Cambridge: Harvard Center for International Affairs. **287n.**

See also Ahluwalia, M. S., and H. B. Chenery; Arrow, K. J., H. B. Chenery, B. S. Minhas, and R. M. Solow.

CHENERY, H. B., ed. **1971.** *Studies in Development Planning.* Cambridge: Harvard University Press. **408n.**

CHENERY, H. B., et al. **1974.** *Redistribution with Growth.* London: Oxford University Press. **7n., 240–241**

CHENERY, H. B., and M. BRUNO **1962.** "Development Alternatives in an Open Economy: The Case of Israel." *E.J.,* 72 (March), 79–103. **402n.**

CHENERY, H. B., and P. G. CLARK **1959.** *Interindustry Economics.* New York: Wiley. **57n., 265**

CHENERY, H. B., and P. ECKSTEIN **1970.** "Development Alternatives for Latin America." *J.P.E.,* 78 (July, Supplement), 966–1006. **176n.**

CHENERY, H. B., H. ELKINGTON, and C. SIMS **1970.** "A Uniform Analysis of Development Patterns." Economic Development Report No. 148, Project for Quantitative Research in Economic Development. Cambridge: Harvard Center for International Affairs. **287**

CHENERY, H. B., and K. S. KRETSCHMER **1956.** "Resource Allocation for Economic Development." *Econometrica,* 24 (October), 365–399. **408n.**

CHENERY, H. B., S. SHISHIDO, and T. WATANABE **1962.** "The Pattern of Japanese Growth, 1914–1954." *Econometrica,* 30 (January), 98–139. **287n.**

CHENERY, H. B., and A. M. STROUT **1966.** "Foreign Assistance and Economic Development." *A.E.R.,* 56 (September), 679–733. **394, 402n., 405**

CHENERY, H. B., and L. J. TAYLOR **1968.** "Development Patterns: Among Countries and Over Time." *R.E.Stat.,* 50 (November), 391–416. **150n., 260, 287n., 289, 294**

CHENERY, H. B., and H. UZAWA **1958.** "Nonlinear Programming in Economic Development." In K. J. Arrow, L. Hurwicz, and H. Uzawa, eds., *Studies in Linear and Non-linear Programming.* Stanford: Stanford University Press, 203–229. **408n.**

CHENERY, H. B., and T. WATANABE **1958.** "International Comparisons of the Structure of Production." *Econometrica,* 26 (October), 487–521. **299, 300, 302n.**

CHILD, F., and C. STORM **1956–1957.** "Self-ratings and TAT: Their Relationships to Each Other and to Childhood Background." *Journal of Personality,* 25 (September), 96–114. **39n.**

CHILTON, C. H. **1950.** "Six-Tenths Factor Applies to Complete Plant Cost." *Chemical Engineering,* 57 (April), 112–114. **150, 153**

CHISWICK, B. R. **1968.** "The Average Level of Schooling and the Intra-regional Inequality of Income: A Clarification." *A.E.R.,* 58 (June), 495–500. **193n., 250**

CHO, Y. S. **1963.** *Disguised Unemployment in Underdeveloped Areas, with Special Reference to South Korean Agriculture.* Berkeley and Los Angeles: University of Californa Press. **212n.**

1966. "An Estimate of Technical and Tradition-Directed Underemployment: Methodological Considerations." *Indian Economic Journal,* 13 (January), 523–540. **212n.**

CHRISTENSEN, L., D. W. JORGENSON, and L. J. LAU **1973.** "Transcendental Logarithmic Production Frontiers." *R.E.Stat.,* 55 (February), 28–45. **64n.**

CLAGUE, C. K. **1969.** "Capital-Labor Substitution in Manufacturing in Underdeveloped Countries." *Econometrica,* 37 (July), 520–537. **151**

CLARK, C. G. **1940.** *The Conditions of Economic Progress.* London: Macmillan. **287n., 344**

CLARK, J. M. **1917.** "Business Acceleration and the Law of Demand: A Technical Factor in Economic Cycles." *J.P.E.,* 25 (March), 217–235. **180**

CLARK, P. G. **See** Chenery, H. B., and P. G. Clark.

CLOWER, R. W., et al. **1966.** *Growth Without Development: An Economic Survey of Liberia.* Evanston, Ill.: Northwestern University Press. **313**

COASE, R. H. **1960.** "The Problem of Social Cost." *Journal of Law and Economics,* 3 (October), 1–44. **379**

COATS, A. W. **1969.** "Is There a 'Structure of Scientific Revolutions' in Economics?" *Kyklos,* 22, No. 2, 289–294. **19**

COHEN, B. I. **1964.** "The Stagnation of Indian Exports, 1951–1961." *Q.J.E.,* 78 (November), 604–620. **316n.**

1968. "The Less Developed Countries' Exports of Primary Products." *E.J.,* 78 (June), 334–343. **314n., 316n.**

1969. "Optimal International Development of India and Pakistan." Paper presented to the International Economic Association Conference on Economic Development in South Asia, Kandy, Sri Lanka (mimeo). **358n.**

COHEN, B. I., and D. G. SISLER **1971.** "Exports of Developing Countries in the 1960's." *R.E.Stat.,* 53 (November), 354–361. **347n.**

COHEN, M. R., and E. NAGEL **1938.** *An Introduction to Logic and Scientific Method.* New York: Harcourt Brace. **18n.**

COLLINS, N. R. **See** Dean, G. W., and N. R. Collins.

CONRAD, A. H., and J. R. MEYER **1964.** *The Economics of Slavery.* Chicago: Aldine. **22**

COOPER, C. A., and B. F. MASSELL **1965.** "Toward a General Theory of Customs Unions for Developing Countries." *J.P.E.*, 73 (October), 461–476. **358n.**

COOPER, R. N. **1971.** "Currency Devaluation in Developing Countries." Essays in International Finance, No. 86 (June). Princeton University: Department of Economics. **396**
See also Brainard, W., and R. N. Cooper

COPPOCK, J. D. **1962.** *International Economic Instability.* New York: McGraw-Hill. **330, 331n., 338, 339**

CORDEN, W. M. **1970.** The Efficiency Effects of Trade and Protection. In I. A. McDougall and R. H. Snape, eds., *Studies in International Economics.* Amsterdam: North Holland. **358n.** **1972.** "Economies of Scale and Customs Union Theory." *J.P.E.*, 80 (May), 465–475. **357n.**

COUTSOUMARIS, G. **1963.** *The Morphology of Greek Industry.* Athens: Center of Planning and Economic Research. **421n.**

COWNIE, J. **See** Johnston, B. F., and J. Cownie

CURRIE, J. M., J. A. MURPHY, and A. SCHMITZ **1971.** "The Concept of Economic Surplus and Its Use in Economic Analysis." *E.J.*, 81 (December), 741–799. **107n.**

DALLOUL, R. A. **1969.** "A Study on the Determinants of Long-Run and Short-Run Savings Propensities in Developing Countries." UNCTAD (May) (mimeo). **176n.**

DANDEKAR, V. M. **1962.** "Economic Theory and Agrarian Reform." *O.E.P.*, 14 (February), 69–80. **211**

DANTWALA, M. L. **1963.** "International Planning to Combat the Scourge of Hunger Throughout the World." *Annals of Collective Economy*, 34 (January), 71–95. **136**

d'ARGE, R. **1969.** "Note on Customs Unions and Direct Foreign Investment." *E.J.*, 79 (June), 324–333. **360n.**

DASGUPTA, P. **1970.** "An Analysis of Two Approaches to Project Evaluation in Developing Countries." UNIDO, *Industrialization and Productivity*, Bulletin 15, 5–15. New York: U.N. **382**
1972. "A Comparative Analysis of the UNIDO Guidelines and the OECD Manual. *Bulletin of the Oxford Institute of Economics and Statistics*, 34 (February), 33–51. **390**

DASGUPTA, P., S. A. MARGLIN, and A. K. SEN **1972.** *Guidelines for Project Evaluation.* New York: UNIDO, 1D/Ser.H/2. **382**

DASGUPTA, P., and J. E. STIGLITZ **1974.** "Benefit-Cost Analysis and Trade Policies." *J.P.E.*, 82 (January), 1–33. **391n.**

DAVID, P. A. **1973.** "Fortune, Risk and the Microeconomics of Migration." In P. A. David and M. W. Reder, eds., *Nations and Households in Economic Growth: Essays in Honor of Moses Abramovitz.* New York: Academic Press, 21–88. **227, 231, 386n.**

DAVID, P. A., and T. van de KLUNDERT **1965.** "Biased Efficiency Growth and Capital-Labor Substitution in the United States, 1899–1960." *A.E.R.*, 55 (June), 357–394. **160, 161**

DAVIS, O. A., and A. WHINSTON **1962.** "Externalities, Welfare and the Theory of Games." *J.P.E.*, 70 (June), 241–262. **379**

DAY, R. H. **1967.** "Comment on Yotopoulos' Measuring Capital Services." *J.F.E.*, 49 (May), 491–495. **67n.**

DEAN, G. W., and N. R. COLLINS **1967.** *World Trade in Fresh Oranges: An Analysis of the Effect of European Economic Community Tariff Policies.* Berkeley: California Agricultural Experiment Station (Giannini Foundation, Monograph 18). **381n.**

DEMERY, D., and L. DEMERY **1973.** "Cross-Section Evidence for Balanced and Unbalanced Growth." *R.E.Stat.*, 55 (November), 459–464. **294**

DEMOPOULOS, G. **See** Butler, A., and G. Demopoulos

DePRANO, M. E., and J. B. NUGENT **1966.** *A Global Financial Model of Ecuador.* Quito: Junta Nacional de Planificación. **409**
1968. "Individual Educational Subsidies as a Remedy for the School Dropout Problem: A Procedure for Estimating Costs" (mimeo). **189–191, 194–195**
1969. "Economies as an Antitrust Defense: Comment." *A.E.R.*, 59 (December), 947–953. **120–122**
See also Nugent, J. B., and M. E. DePrano.

DESAI, M., and D. MAZUMDAR **1970.** "A Test of the Hypothesis of Disguised Unemployment." *Economica*, 37 (February), 39–53. **211**

DeVANY, A. **1970.** "Time in the Budget of the Consumer: The Theory of Consumer Demand and Labour Supply under a Time Constraint." Provisional Paper No. 36, Center for Naval Analyses (June). **196**

DeVRIES, B. A. **1967.** *Export Experience of Developing Countries.* Washington: IBRD **316**

DHRYMES, P. J. **1970.** *Econometrics: Statistical Foundations and Applications.* New York: Harper and Row. **33n.**

DHRYMES, P. J., and M. KURZ **1964.** "Technology and Scale in Electricity Generation." *Econometrica*, 32 (July), 287–315. **150n.**

DIAMOND, P. A., and J. A. MIRRLEES **1971.** "Optimal Taxation and Public Production." *A.E.R.*, 61, Part I (March), 8–27; Part II (June), 261–278. **391n.**

DILLON, J. L. **See** Heady, E. O., and J. L. Dillon.

DIWAN, R. K. **1968.** "A Test of the Two-Gap Theory of Economic Development." *J.D.S.*, 4 (July), 529–537. **404**

DIWAN, R. K., and K. MARWAH 1973. "Two Empirical Tests of the Trade Gap Theory of Economic Development." Paper presented to the Econometric Society, New York (December) (mimeo). **404**

DOMAR, E. 1962. "On Total Productivity and All That." *J.P.E.*, 70 (December), 597–608. **154n.**

DOYLE, C. J. 1974. "Productivity, Technical Change and the Peasant Producer: A Profile of the African Cultivator." *F.R.I.S.*, 13, No. 1, 61–76. **142n.**

DRÈZE, J. See Zellner, A., J. Kmenta, and J. Drèze.

DUCROS, B. See Marchal, J., and B. Ducros.

DUESENBERRY, J. 1949. *Income, Saving and the Theory of Consumer Behavior.* Cambridge: Harvard University Press. **173**

DULOY, J. H., and R. D. NORTON 1973. "CHAC, A Programming Model of Mexican Agriculture." In L. M. Goreux and A. S. Manne, eds., *Multi-Level Planning: Case Studies in Mexico.* Amsterdam: North Holland, 291–337. **411n.**

DUNCAN, O. D. See Blau, P. M., and O. D. Duncan

DUQUESNE de la VINELLE, L. 1965. "La Creation du Commerce Attributable au Marché Commun et son Incidence sur le Valeur de Produit National de la Communauté." *Informations Statistiques*, No. 4 (1965), 61–70 and No. 3 (1966), 5–31. **351n.**

EARLEY, J. S. 1957. "The Impact of Some New Developments in Economic Theory: Exposition and Evaluation—Discussion." *A.E.R.*, 47 (May), 828–838. **77**

ECKAUS, R. S. 1955. "The Factor Proportions Problem in Underdeveloped Areas." *A.E.R.*, 45 (September), 539–565. **255**

ECKAUS, R. S., and K. S. PARIKH 1968. *Planning for Growth: Multi-sectoral Intertemporal Models Applied to India.* Cambridge: M.I.T. Press. **408n.**

ECKSTEIN, P. See Chenery, H. B., and P. Eckstein.

EHRLICH, P., and A. EHRLICH 1970. *Population, Resources, Environment.* San Francisco: Freeman. **8**

EICHER, C. K. See Kao, C. H. C., K. R. Anschel, and C. K. Eicher

EISNER, R., and M. I. NADIRI 1968. "Investment Behavior and the Neo-Classical Theory." *R.E.Stat.*, 50 (August), 369–382. **180n.**

EISNER, R., and R. H. STROTZ 1963. "Determinants of Business Investment." In Commission on Money and Credit, *Impacts of Monetary Policy.* Englewood Cliffs, N.J.: Prentice-Hall. **180n.**

ELDRIDGE, H. T. 1965. "Primary, Secondary and Return Migration in the U.S., 1955–1960." *Demography*, 2, 444–455. **236**

ELKINGTON, H. See Chenery, H. B., H. Elkington, and C. Sims.

ELLIS, H. S., D. D. PSILOS, R. M. WESTEBBE, and C. NICOLAOU 1962. *Industrial Capital in Greek Development.* Athens: Center of Planning and Economic Research. **421n.**

ERB, G. F., and S. SCHIAVO-CAMPO 1969. "Export Instability, Level of Development and Economic Size of Less Developed Countries." *Bulletin of the Oxford University Institute of Economics and Statistics*, 31 (November), 263–283. **331n., 338, 339**

ETHERINGTON, D. M. 1973. *Smallholder Tea Production in Kenya: An Econometric Study.* Nairobi: East African Literature Bureau. **78**

EVANS, H. D. 1970. "A Programming Model of Trade and Protection." In I. A. McDougall and R. H. Snape, eds., *Studies in International Economics.* Amsterdam: North Holland, 19–34. **112**

——— 1971. "Effects of Protection in a General Equilibrium Framework." *R.E.Stat.*, 53 (May), 147–156. **112**

——— 1972. *A General Equilibrium Analysis of Protection.* Amsterdam: North Holland. **112**

EZEKIEL, H. 1967. "Monetary Expansion and Economic Development." *International Monetary Fund Staff Papers*, 14 (March), 80–86. **171** See also Mathur, P. N., and H. Ezekiel.

FALCON, W. P. 1964. "Farmer Response to Price in a Subsistence Economy: The Case of West Pakistan." *A.E.R.*, 54 (May), 580–591. **131, 137n.**

FARRELL, M. J. 1957. "The Measurement of Productive Efficiency." *Journal of the Royal Statistical Society* (Series A), 120, Part 3, 253–381. **72**

FEI, J. C. H., and G. RANIS 1964. *Development of the Labor Surplus Economy: Theory and Policy.* Homewood, Ill.: Irwin. **206, 230n., 256, 261**

——— 1968. "Foreign Assistance and Economic Development: Comment." *A.E.R.*, 58 (September), 897–912. **405n.**

——— 1972. "Less Developed Country Innovation Analysis and the Technology Gap." In G. Ranis, ed., *The Gap Between Rich and Poor Nations.* London: Macmillan. **256** See also Paauw, D. S., and J. C. H. Fei; Ranis, G., and J. C. H. Fei.

FERGUSON, C. E. 1969. *The Neoclassical Theory of Production and Distribution.* Cambridge: Cambridge University Press. **160**

FERGUSON, C. E., and E. J. NELL 1972. "Review Article on Two Books on the Theory of Income Distribution." *J.E.L.*, 10 (June), 437–453. **247n.**

FINDLAY, R. 1972. "Some Theoretical Notes on the Trade-Growth Nexus." In G. Ranis, ed., *The Gap Between Rich and Poor Nations.* London: Macmillan, 270–280. **318n.**

FISHER, A. G. B. **1939.** "Production, Primary, Secondary and Tertiary." *Economic Record*, 15 (June), 24–38. **287n.**

FISHER, F. M. **1963.** "A Theoretical Analysis of the Impact of Food Surplus Disposal on Agricultural Production in Recipient Countries." *J.F.E.*, 45 (November), 863–875. **136**

FISHER, I. **1930.** *The Theory of Interest.* New York: Macmillan. **372**

FISHLOW, A. **1965a.** *American Railroads and the Transformation of the Ante-Bellum Economy.* Cambridge: Harvard University Press. **298**

1965b. "Empty Economic Stages?" *E.J.*, 75 (April), 112–125. **31**

1972. "Brazilian Size Distribution of Income." *A.E.R.*, 62 (May), 391–402. **249, 250–252**

FLEMING, J. M., and S. C. TSIANG **1956.** "Changes in Competitive Strength and Export Shares of Major Industrial Countries." *International Monetary Fund Staff Papers*, 5 (August), 218–248. **316n.**

FLETCHER, L. B. **See** Lu, Y. C., and L. B. Fletcher; Mubyarto and L. B. Fletcher.

FOGEL, W. A. **1966.** "The Effect of Low Educational Attainment on Incomes: A Comparative Study of Selected Ethnic Groups." *Journal of Human Resources*, 1 (Fall), 22–40. **191n.**

FONTAINE, E. R. **1969.** *El Precio Sombra de las Divisas en la Evaluación Social de Proyectos.* Santiago, Chile: Universidad Católica de Chile. **381n.**

FOX, K. A., J. K. SENGUPTA, and E. THORBECKE **1966.** *The Theory of Quantitative Economic Policy with Applications to Economic Growth and Stabilization.* Chicago: Rand McNally. **423n.**

FREEDMAN, D. S. **1970.** "The Role of the Consumption of Modern Durables in Economic Development." *E.D.C.C.*, 19 (October), 25–48. **260**

FRIEDMAN, M. **1953.** "The Methodology of Positive Economics." In M. Friedman, ed., *Essays in Positive Economics.* Chicago: University of Chicago Press, 3–43. **18, 21**

1957. *A Theory of the Consumption Function.* Princeton: N.B.E.R. **173–174, 175n., 176n., 332, 335**

1962. *Price Theory: A Provisional Text.* Chicago: Aldine. **135, 165n.**

FRIEDMAN, M., and L. J. SAVAGE **1948.** "The Utility Analysis of Choices Involving Risk." *J.P.E.*, 56 (August), 279–304. **130**

FRIEDMAN, R. D. **See** Brady, D. S., and R. D. Friedman.

FRIEND, I., and I. B. KRAVIS **1957.** "Consumption Patterns of Permanent Income." *A.E.R.*, 48 (May), 536–555. **175n.**

FRIEND, I., and P. TAUBMAN **1966.** "The Aggregate Propensity to Save: Some Concepts and Their Application to International Data." *R.E.Stat.*, 48 (May), 113–123. **175**

FRISCH, R. **1960.** *Planning for India: Selected Explorations in Methodology.* Bombay: Asia Publishing House. **408n.**

1962. "Preface to the Oslo Channel Model—A Survey of Types of Economic Forecasting and Programming." In R. C. Geary, ed., *Europe's Future in Figures.* Amsterdam: North Holland, 248–286. **408n.**

FURNIVALL, J. S. **1948.** *Colonial Policy and Practice.* Cambridge: Cambridge University Press. **254**

FURTADO, C. **1967.** *Development and Underdevelopment.* Berkeley and Los Angeles: University of California Press. **255**

GALENSON, W., and H. LEIBENSTEIN **1955.** "Investment Criteria, Productivity and Economic Development." *Q.J.E.*, 69 (August), 343–370. **12**

GASTWIRTH, J. L. **1972.** "The Estimation of the Lorenz Curve and the Gini Index." *R.E.Stat.*, 54 (August), 306–316. **242**

GENERAL AGREEMENT ON TARIFFS AND TRADE (GATT) **1959.** "Contracting Parties to the General Agreement on Tariffs and Trade. *International Trade, 1957–1958.* Geneva. **316n.**

1966. "Note on the Export Performance of Less-Developed Countries." *International Trade, 1965.* Geneva, 23–32. **316n.**

GEERTZ, C. **1963.** *Agricultural Involution.* Berkeley and Los Angeles: University of California Press. **254**

GEIER, M. **See** Adelman, I., M. Geier, and C. T. Morris.

GEISEL, M. S. **See** Zellner, A., and M. S. Geisel.

GEORGESCU-ROEGEN, N. **1960.** "Economic Theory and Agrarian Reforms." *O.E.P.*, 12 (February), 1–40. **211**

1969. "Process in Farming Versus Process in Manufacturing: A Problem of Balanced Development." In U. Papi and C. Numm, eds., *Economic Problems of Agriculture in Industrial Societies.* London: Macmillan, 497–528. **261**

1970. "The Economics of Production." *A.E.R.*, 60 (May), 1–9. **64**

GERONYMAKIS, S. **1965.** *The Structural Interdependence of the Greek Economy in 1954.* Athens: University Press. **412**

GERSCHENKRON, A. **1962.** *Economic Backwardness in Historical Perspective.* Cambridge: Belknap Press. **39, 40**

GIANARIS, N. V. **1970.** "International Differences in Capital-Output Ratios." *A.E.R.*, 60 (June), 465–477. **394**

GLEZAKOS, C. **1970.** "Export Instability and Economic Development: A Statistical Verification." Unpublished Ph.D. Dissertation, University of Southern California (August). **340**

GOLDBERGER, A. S. **1964.** *Econometric Theory.* New York: Wiley. **78n.**

1965. "The Economist's Role in Policy Formation." In P. A. Yotopoulos, ed., *Economic*

Analysis and Economic Policy. Athens: Center of Planning and Economic Research, 15–29. **423n.**

1968. *Topics in Regression Analysis.* New York: Macmillan. **68n.**

GOLDENWEISER, A. A. **1936.** "Loose Ends of a Theory of the Individual: Pattern and Involution in Primitive Society." In R. H. Lowie, ed., *Essays in Anthropology.* Berkeley and Los Angeles: University of California Press, 99–104. **254n.**

GOLDSCHMIDT, Y. **See** Shashua, L., and Y. Goldschmidt.

GOLDSMITH, R. W. **1955.** "Financial Structure and Economic Growth in Advanced Countries: An Experiment in Comparative Financial Morphology." In M. Abramovitz, ed., *Capital Formation and Economic Growth.* New York: N.B.E.R., 113–160. **287n.**

1969. *Financial Structure and Development.* New Haven: Yale University Press. **287n.**

GRAYBILL, R. A. **See** Mood, A. M., and R. A. Graybill.

GREECE, GOVERNMENT OF: Ministry of Coordination **1961, 1963.** *National Accounts of Greece.* Athens. **412**

1962. *The Demand for Skilled Personnel in Relation to Economic Development.* Athens. **412**

GREECE, GOVERNMENT OF: National Statistical Service **1961.** *1961 Annual Industrial Survey.* Athens. **412, 413**

GRIFFIN, K. **1969.** *Underdevelopment in Spanish America.* London: Allan & Unwin. **226**

GRILICHES, Z. **1957.** "Specification Bias in Estimates of Production Functions." *J.F.E.,* 39 (February), 8–20. **68n., 78n., 80**

1967. "Distributed Lags: A Survey." *Econometrica,* 35 (January), 16–49. **138n., 333n.**

GRUBEL, H. G. **1970.** "The Theory of Intra-Industry Trade." In I. A. McDougall and R. H. Snape, eds., *Studies in International Economics.* Amsterdam: North Holland. **357n.**

GRUNBERG, E., and F. MODIGLIANI **1964.** "The Predictability of Social Events." *J.P.E.,* 62 (December), 465–478. **397n.**

GUGLER, J. **1969.** "On the Theory of Rural-Urban Migration: The Case of Sub-Saharan Africa." In J. A. Jackson, ed., *Sociological Studies Two: Migration.* Cambridge: Cambridge University Press, 134–155. **229**

GUPTA, K. L. **1970.** "Personal Saving in Developing Nations: Further Evidence." *Economic Review,* 46 (June), 243–249. **175**

GURLEY, J. G. **1971.** "The State of Political Economics." *A.E.R.,* 61 (May), 53–68. **7, 8**

HAAVELMO, T. **1960.** *A Study in the Theory of Investment.* Chicago: University of Chicago Press. **156**

HAGEN, E. E. **1962.** *On the Theory of Social Change.* Homewood, Ill.: Dorsey Press. **39**

1968. *The Economics of Development.* Homewood, Ill.: Irwin. **239n.**

HAGEN, E. E., and O. HAWRYLYSHYN **1969.** "Analysis of World Income and Growth 1955–1965." *E.D.C.C.,* 18 (October, Supplement), 1–96. **287**

HALDI, J., and D. WHITCOMB **1967.** "Economies of Scale in Industrial Plants." *J.P.E.,* 75 (August), 373–385. **153**

HALEVI, N. **1969.** "Economic Policy Discussion and Research in Israel." *A.E.R.,* 59 (September, Supplement), 74–118. **388n.**

HAMILTON, C. H. **1965.** "Practical and Mathematical Considerations in the Formulation and Selection of Migration Rates." *Demography,* 2, 429–443. **236**

HANIOTIS, G. **1967.** *The Industrial Sector of the Greek Economy 1960–70.* Athens: Ministry of Coordination. **412**

HANOCH, G. **1965.** "Personal Earnings and Investment in Schooling." Unpublished Ph.D. Dissertation, University of Chicago (December). **189, 191n.**

HANSEN, B. **1966.** "Marginal Productivity Wage Theory and Subsistence Wage Theory in Egyptian Agriculture." *J.D.S.,* 2 (July), 367–399. **216**

HANSEN, W. L., B. A. WEISBROD, and W. J. SCANLON **1970.** "Schooling and Earnings of Low Achievers." *A.E.R.,* 60 (June), 409–418. **195n.**

HAQ, M. **1973.** "The Crisis in Development Strategies." In C. K. Wilber, ed., *The Political Economy of Development and Underdevelopment.* New York: Random House, 367–372. **257n.**

HARBERGER, A. C. **1954.** "Monopoly and Resource Allocation." *A.E.R.,* 44 (May), 77–87. **108n., 109**

1959. "Using the Resources at Hand More Effectively." *A.E.R.,* 49 (May), 134–146. **108n., 110n.**

1964. "The Measurement of Waste." *A.E.R.,* 54 (May), 58–76. **381**

1968a. "On Measuring the Social Opportunity Cost of Public Funds." *The Discount Rate in Public Investment Evaluation.* Denver: Western Agricultural Economics Research Council, Report No. 17 (December), 1–24. **381, 388n.**

1968b. "Survey of Literature on Cost-Benefit Analysis for Industrial Project Evaluation." UNIDO, *Evaluation of Industrial Projects.* Project Formation and Evaluation Series, Vol. 1, ID/SER.H/1, New York: U.N. 229–246. **381**

1971. "Three Basic Postulates for Applied Welfare Economics: An Interpretive Essay." *J.E.L.,* 9 (September), 785–797. **381, 391**

1974. *Project Evaluation: Collected Papers.* Chicago: Markham. **381n.**

HARBISON, F., and C. A. MYERS, eds. **1965.** *Manpower and Education: Country Studies in Development.* New York: McGraw-Hill. **402n.**

HARMON, H. H. **1960.** *Modern Factor Analysis.* Chicago: University of Chicago Press. **32n.**

HARRIS, J. R., and M. P. TODARO **1969.** "Wages, Industrial Employment and Labor Productivity: The Kenyan Experience." *Eastern Africa Economic Review,* 1 (June), 29–46. **229n.** **1970.** "Migration, Unemployment and Development: A Two-Sector Analysis." *A.E.R.,* 70 (March), 126–142. **227n.**

HARRISON, B. **1974.** "Ghetto Economic Development: A Survey." *J.E.L.,* 12 (March), 1–37. **235, 238n., 256**
See also Vietorisz, T., and B. Harrison.

HARTLEY, H. Q. **See** Carter, H. O., and H. Q. Hartley.

HAWRYLYSHYN, O. **See** Hagen, E. E., and O. Hawrylyshyn.

HAYAMI, Y., and V. W. RUTTAN **1971.** *Agricultural Development: An International Perspective.* Baltimore: Johns Hopkins University Press. **260n., 261**

HAYS, S. **See** Major, R. L., and S. Hays.

HAZARI, B. R., and J. KRISHNAMURTY **1970.** "Employment Implications of India's Industrialization: Analysis in an Input-Output Framework." *R.E.Stat.,* 52 (May), 181–186. **300n.**
See also Acharya, S. N., and B. R. Hazari.

HEADY, E. O., and J. L. DILLON **1961.** *Agricultural Production Functions.* Ames: Iowa State University Press. **68n.**
See also Srivistava, U. K., and E. O. Heady.

HEINS, A. J. **See** Aigner, D. J., and A. J. Heins.

HELMER, O., and N. RESCHER **1959.** "On the Epistemology of the Inexact Sciences." *Management Science,* 6 (October), 25–52. **27**

HERRICK, B. **1965.** *Urban Migration and Economic Migration in Chile.* Cambridge: M.I.T. Press. **226**

HICKS, J. R. **1946.** *Value and Capital.* 2nd ed. Oxford: Clarendon Press. **134, 138**

HIGGINS, B. **1956.** "The 'Dualistic Theory' of Underdeveloped Areas." *E.D.C.C.,* 4 (January), 99–115. **254n.**
1973. "Book Review of Dualistic Economic Development: Theory and History." *J.E.L.,* 11 (December), 1378–1380. **281**

HIRSCH, S. **1967.** *Location of Industry and International Competitiveness.* Oxford: Clarendon Press. **325**

HIRSCH, W. Z., and E. W. SEGELHORST **1965.** "Incremental Income Benefits of Public Education." *R.E.Stat.,* 47 (November), 392–399. **191n.**

HIRSCHMAN, A. O. **1945.** *National Power and the Structure of Foreign Trade.* Berkeley and Los Angeles: University of California Press. **339**
1958. *The Strategy of Economic Development.* New Haven: Yale University Press. **293, 297–300, 303, 395**
1967. *Development Projects Observed.* Washington, D.C.: The Brookings Institution. **40–41, 377**
1970. *Exit, Voice and Loyalty.* Cambridge: Harvard University Press. **77, 234**

HIRSHLEIFER, J. **1970.** *Investment, Interest and Capital.* Englewood Cliffs, N.J.: Prentice-Hall. **370n., 376**

HOBSBAWN, E. J. **See** Baran, P. A., and E. J. Hobsbawn.

HOCH, I. **1955.** "Estimation of Production Function Parameters and Testing for Efficiency." *Econometrica,* 23 (July), 325–326. **78**
1962. "Estimation of Production Function Parameters Combining Time-Series and Cross-Section Data." *Econometrica,* 30 (January), 34–53. **78, 85**

HOFFMAN, R. F. **See** Sato, R., and R. F. Hoffman.

HOLBROOK, R., and F. STAFFORD **1971.** "The Propensity to Consume Separate Types of Income: A Generalized Permanent Income Hypothesis." *Econometrica,* 39 (January), 1–21. **175, 176, 332n.**

HOLLISTER, R. **1967.** *A Technical Evaluation of the First Stage of the Mediterranean Regional Project.* Paris: OECD. **402n.**

HOOLEY, R. W. **1967.** "The Measurement of Capital Formation in Underdeveloped Countries." *R.E.Stat.,* 49 (May), 199–208. **169**

HOPPER, W. D. **1965.** "Allocation Efficiency in a Traditional Indian Agriculture." *J.F.E.,* 47 (August), 611–624. **81n.**

HOROWITZ, G. **1974.** "Wage Determination in a Labor Surplus Economy: The Case of India." *E.D.C.C.,* 22 (July), 662–672. **226**

HORST, P. **1965.** *Factor Analysis of Data Matrices.* New York: Holt, Rinehart and Winston. **32n.**

HOSELITZ, B. F. **1960.** "Theories of Stages of Economic Growth." In B. F. Hoselitz, ed., *Theories of Economic Growth.* New York: Free Press, 193–238. **29n.**

HOUTHAKKER, H. S. **1958.** "The Permanent Income Hypothesis." *A.E.R.,* 49 (June), 396–404. **175n.**
1961. "An International Comparison of Personal Savings." *Bulletin of the International Statistical Institute,* 38, 55–69. **175**
1965. "On Some Determinants of Saving in Developed and Underdeveloped Countries." In E. A. G. Robinson, ed., *Problems in Economic Development.* New York: Macmillan. **171**

HOYLE, F. **1957.** *The Black Cloud.* New York: Harper and Row. **23n.**

HUETH, D. and A. SCHMITZ **1972.** "International Trade in Intermediate and Final Goods: Some Welfare Implications of Destabilized Prices." *Q.J.E.,* 86 (August), 351–365. **341n.**

HUFBAUER, G. C. **1966.** *Synthetic Materials and the Theory of International Trade.* London: Duckworth. **325n.**

HUGHES, J. R. T. **1959.** "Foreign Trade and Balanced Growth: The Historical Framework." *A.E.R.,* 49 (May), 330–353. **294**

HUGHES, R. B. **1961.** "Interregional Income Differences: Self-perpetuation." *Southern Economic Journal,* 28 (July), 41–45. **226n.**

HUMPHREY, D. B. **1969.** "Measuring the Effective Rate of Protection: Direct and Indirect Effects." *J.P.E.,* 77 (September) 834–844. **118n.**

HUNT, S. N. J. **1963.** "Income Determinants for College Graduates and the Return to Educational Investment." *Yale Economic Essays,* 3 (Fall), 305–357. **189n.**

HUNTER, J. **See** Jorgenson, D. W., J. Hunter, and M. I. Nadiri.

HUTCHISON, T. W. **1938.** *The Significance and Basic Postulates of Economic Theory.* London: Macmillan. **23n.**
1960. "Methodological Prescriptions in Economics: A Reply." *Economica,* 27 (May), 158–160. **23n.**

HYMER, S., and S. RESNICK **1969.** "A Model of an Agrarian Economy with Nonagricultural Activities." *A.E.R.,* 59 (September), 493–506. **137n., 260**

IMLAH, A. H. **1958.** *Economic Elements in the Pax Britannica.* Cambridge: Harvard University Press. **344**

INDIA, GOVERNMENT OF: Ministry of Food and Agriculture **1957–1962.** *Studies in the Economics of Farm Management.* Delhi. Reports for the year 1955–1956: Madras, Punjab, Uttar Pradesh, West Bengal; Report for the year 1956–1957: Madhya Pradesh. **73, 93**

INTERNATIONAL LABOR OFFICE **1959.** "The International Standardization of Labor Statistics." *I.L.O. Studies,* New Series No. 53, Geneva. **203**

INTERNATIONAL MONETARY FUND **1966.** *Compensatory Financing of Export Fluctuations.* Washington, D.C.: International Monetary Fund. **331n.**

INTERNATIONAL MONETARY FUND and IBRD **1969.** *The Problem of Stabilization of Prices of Primary Products.* Washington, D.C.: International Monetary Fund. **339n.**

INTRILIGATOR, M. D. **1971.** *Mathematical Optimization of Economic Theory.* Englewood Cliffs, N.J.: Prentice-Hall. **425**

ISHIKAWA, S. **1967.** *Economic Development in Asian Perspective.* Tokyo: Kinokuniya Bookstore. **261**

ISLAM, N. **1964.** "Concepts and Measurement of Unemployment and Underemployment in Developing Economies." *International Labor Review,* 89 (March), 240–256. **212n.**

JACKSON, D. A. **See** Turner, H. A., and D. A. Jackson.

JANSSEN, L. H. **1961.** *Free Trade, Protection and Customs Union.* Leiden: Kroese. **351n.**

JOHANSEN, L. **1961.** "A Method for Separating the Effects of Capital Accumulation and Shifts in Production Functions upon Growth in Labor Productivity." *E.J.,* 71 (December), 775–782. **157–158**

JOHNSON, H. G. **1958.** "Planning and the Market in Economic Development." *Pakistan Economic Journal,* 8 (June), 44–55. **398n.**
1965a. "An Economic Theory of Protectionism, Tariff Bargaining and the Formation of Customs Unions." *J.P.E.,* 73 (June), 256–283. **358n.**
1965b. "The Costs of Protection and Self-Sufficiency." *Q.J.E.,* 79 (August), 356–372. **112, 114, 116, 117, 356**
1973. "Some Micro-economic Reflections on Income and Wealth Inequalities." *The Annals of the American Academy of Political and Social Science,* **409** (September), 53–60. **248n.**

JOHNSON, P. R. **1968.** "Discussion: A Test of the Hypothesis of Economic Rationality in a Less Developed Economy." *A.J.A.E.,* 50 (May), 398–399. **88n.**
1969. "On Testing Competing Hypotheses: Economic Rationality Versus Traditional Behavior—Reply." *A.J.A.E.,* 51 (February) 208–209. **88n.**

JOHNSON, T. **1970.** "Returns from Investment in Human Capital." *A.E.R.,* 60 (September), 546–560. **191n.**

JOHNSTON, B. F., and J. COWNIE **1969.** "The Seed-Fertilizer Revolution and Labor Force Absorption." *A.E.R.,* 59 (September), 569–582. **102, 233n.**

JOHNSTON, J. **1963.** *Econometric Methods.* New York: McGraw-Hill. **84**

JONES, R. W. **See** Caves, R. E., and R. W. Jones.

JONES, W. O. **1960.** "Economic Man in Africa." *F.R.I.S.,* 1, No. 2, 107–134. **142n.**

JORGENSON, D. W. **1961.** "The Development of a Dual Economy." *E.J.,* 71 (June), 309–334. **206, 211, 230n.**
1967. "The Role of Agriculture in Economic Development: Classical versus Neoclassical Models of Growth." In C. R. Wharton, Jr., ed., *Subsistence Agriculture and Economic Development.* Chicago: Aldine, 320–348. **230n.**
1969. "Testing Alternative Theories of the Development of a Dual Economy." In I. Adelman and E. Thorbecke, eds., *The Theory and Design of Economic Development.* Baltimore: Johns Hopkins University Press, 45–60. **230n.**
1971. "Econometric Studies of Investment Behavior: A Survey." *J.E.L.,* 9 (December), 1111–1147. **180n, 181**
See also Christensen, L., D. W. Jorgenson, and L. J. Lau.

JORGENSON, D. W., J. HUNTER, and M. I. NADIRI **1970.** "A Comparison of Alternative Econometric Models of Quarterly Investment Behavior." *Econometrica,* 38 (March), 187–212. **180n., 181**

JORGENSON, D. W., and L. J. LAU **1969.** "An Economic Theory of Agricultural Household Behavior." Paper presented at the Far Eastern Meeting of the Econometric Society, Tokyo (June, mimeo). **206, 271**

1974. "The Duality of Technology and Economic Behavior." *R.E.S.*, 41 (April), 181–200. **96**

JORGENSON, D. W., and C. D. SIEBERT **1968a.** "A Comparison of Alternative Theories of Corporate Investment Behavior. *A.E.R.*, 58 (September), 681–712. **180, 181**

1968b. "Optimal Capital Accumulation and Corporate Investment Behavior." *J.P.E.*, 76 (November–December), 1123–1151. **181**

JORGENSON, D. W., and J. A. STEPHENSON **1967.** "Investment Behavior in U. S. Manufacturing, 1947–1960." *Econometrica*, 35 (April), 169–220. **180n., 181n.**

JOSHI, V. **1972.** "The Rationale and Relevance of the Little-Mirrlees Criterion." *Oxford University Institute of Economics and Statistics Bulletin*, 34 (February), 3–32.

JUNZ, H. B., and R. R. RHOMBERG **1965.** "Prices and Export Performance of Industrial Countries, 1953–1963." *International Monetary Fund Staff Papers*, 12 (July), 224–269. **316n.**

KAFOGLIS, M. Z. **See** Buchanan, J. M., and M. Z. Kafoglis.

KALDOR, N. **1934.** "The Equilibrium of the Firm." *E.J.*, 44 (March), 60–76. **78**

1955. *An Expenditure Tax.* London: Allan & Unwin. **12**

KAMERSCHEN, D. R. **1966.** "An Estimation of the Welfare Losses from Monopoly in the American Economy." *Western Economic Journal*, 4 (Summer), 221–236. **109**

KAO, C. H. C., K. R. ANSCHEL, and C. K. EICHER **1964.** "Disguised Unemployment in Agriculture: A Survey." In C. K. Eicher and L. W. Witt, eds., *Agriculture in Economic Development.* New York: McGraw-Hill. **212n., 230n.**

KARPOFF, P. **See** Weisbrod, B. A., and P. Karpoff.

KATZIR, I. **See** Zusman, P., A. Melamed, and I. Katzir.

KEESING, D. B. **1965.** "Population and Industrial Development: Some Evidence from Trade Patterns." *A.E.R.*, 58 (June), 448–455. **150n.**

1967. "The Impact of Research and Development on United States Trade." *J.P.E.*, 75 (February), 38–48. **325n.**

1974. "Income Distribution from Outward-Looking Development Policies." *Pakistan Development Review*, 13 (Summer), 188–204. **249**

KELLEY, A. C. **1969.** "Demand Patterns, Demographic Change and Economic Growth." *Q.J.E.*, 83 (February), 110–126. **291**

KELLEY, A. C., and J. G. WILLIAMSON **1968.** "Household Saving Behavior in the Developing Economies: The Indonesian Case." *E.D.C.C.*, 16 (April), 385–403. **174–175**

1973. "Modeling Economic Development and General Equilibrium Histories." *A.E.R.*, 63 (May), 450–459. **281n.**

KELLEY, A. C., J. G. WILLIAMSON, and R. CHEETHAM **1972.** *Dualistic Economic Development.* Chicago: University of Chicago Press. **230n., 256, 281n.**

KEMP, M. C. **1969.** *A Contribution to the General Equilibrium Theory of Preferential Trading.* Amsterdam: North Holland. **350, 357**

KENDRICK, D. A. **1967.** *Programming Investment in the Process Industries.* Cambridge: M.I.T. Press. **408n.**

KENDRICK, D. A., and L. J. TAYLOR **1969.** "A Dynamic Nonlinear Planning Model for Korea." In I. Adelman, ed., *Practical Approaches to Developmental Planning: Korea's Second Five Year Plan.* Baltimore: Johns Hopkins University Press, 213–237. **408n.**

KENDRICK, J. W. **1961.** *Productivity Trends in the United States.* Princeton: Princeton University Press. **154**

KENDRICK, J. W., and R. SATO **1963.** "Factor Prices, Productivity and Economic Growth." *A.E.R.*, 53 (December), 974–1003. **161**

KENEN, P. B. **1965.** "Nature, Capital and Trade," *J.P.E.*, 73 (October), 437–460. **322**

KENNEDY, C., and A. P. THIRLWALL **1972.** "Surveys in Applied Economics: Technical Progress." *E.J.*, 82 (March), 11–72. **144, 156**

KEVORK, C. **1962.** *Model of Urban Consumption in Greece and Some International Comparisons.* Athens: Bank of Greece, Monograph Series No. 9 (in Greek). **412–413**

KEYNES, J. M. **1936.** *The General Theory of Employment, Interest and Money.* New York: Harcourt, Brace and World. **168, 172**

KHATKHATE, D. R. **1962.** "Some Notes on the Real Effect of Foreign Surplus Disposal in Underdeveloped Economies." *Q.J.E.*, 76 (May), 186–196. **136**

KINDLEBERGER, C. P. **1956.** *The Terms of Trade: A European Case Study.* New York: Wiley. **344**

1968. *International Economics.* Homewood, Ill.: Irwin. **119n.**

KLAPPHOLZ, K., and J. AGASSI **1959.** "Methodological Prescriptions in Economics." *Economica*, 26 (February), 60–74. **23n.**

1960. "A Rejoinder." *Economica*, 27 (May), 160–161. **23n.**

KLEIN, L. R. **1953.** *A Textbook of Econometrics.* Evanston, Ill.: Row, Peterson. **91**

KMENTA, J. **See** Zellner, A., J. Kmenta, and J. Drèze.

KNUDSEN, O. K. **1972.** "A Permanent Income Theory of Export Instability." Ph.D. Dissertation, Stanford University. **176n., 332n., 333n.**

KOREAN DEVELOPMENT ASSOCIATION 1967. *Effective Protective Rates for Korean Industries.* Seoul. **118n.**

KOYCK, L. M. **1954.** *Distributed Lags and Investment Analysis.* Amsterdam: North Holland. **139n.**

KRAUSS, M. B. **1972.** "Recent Developments in Customs Union Theory: An Interpretive Survey." *J.E.L.,* 10 (June), 413–436. **357**

KRAVIS, I. B. **1956.** "Wages and Foreign Trade." *R.E.Stat.,* 38 (February), 14–30. **321**

1960. "International Differences in the Distribution of Income." *R.E.Stat.,* 42 (November), 406–416. **248n.**

1968. "International Commodity Agreements to Promote Aid and Efficiency: The Case of Coffee. *Canadian Journal of Economics,* 1 (May), 295–317. **340n.**

1973. "A World of Unequal Incomes." In S. Weintraub, ed., *Income Inequality, The Annals of the American Academy of Political and Social Science,* 409 (September), 61–80. **248n.** **See also** Friend, I., and I. B. Kravis.

KRAVIS, I. B., and R. E. LIPSEY **1971.** *Price Competitiveness in World Trade.* New York: N.B.E.R. **342n.**

KREININ, M. E. **1961.** "Windfall Income and Consumption." *A.E.R.,* 51 (June), 388–390. **176n.**

1964. "On the Dynamic Effects of a Customs Union." *J.P.E.,* 72 (April), 193–195. **358n.**

KRETSCHMER, K. S. **See** Chenery, H. B., and K. S. Kretschmer.

KRISHNA, R. **1963.** "Farm Supply Response in India-Pakistan: A Case Study of the Punjab Region." *E.J.,* 73 (September), 477–487. **140**

1965. "The Marketable Surplus Function for a Subsistence Crop." *Economic Weekly,* 17 (February), 309–320. **141**

1967. "Agricultural Price Policy and Economic Development." In H. M. Southworth and B. F. Johnston, eds., *Agricultural Development and Economic Growth.* Ithaca: Cornell University Press, 497–540. **140n.**

1973. "Unemployment in India." *Indian Journal of Agricultural Economics,* 28 (January), 1–23. **201**

KRISHNAMURTY, J. **See** Hazari, B. R., and J. Krishnamurty.

KRISHNAMURTY, K. **1968.** "International Comparisons of Domestic Savings Rates—A Review." Economics Department (January, mimeo). **171**

KRUEGER, A. O. **1966.** "Some Economic Costs of Exchange Control: The Turkish Case." *J.P.E.,* 74 (October), 466–480. **396**

1974. "The Political Economy of the Rent-Seeking Society." *A.E.R.,* 64 (June), 291–303. **238**

KUH, E. **See** Meyer, J. R., and E. Kuh.

KUHN, T. S. **1962.** *The Structure of Scientific Revolutions.* Chicago: University of Chicago Press. **19**

KURZ, M. **See** Arrow, K. J., and M. Kurz; Dhrymes, P. J., and M. Kurz.

KUZNETS, S. **1955a.** "International Differences in Capital Formation and Financing." In M. Abramovitz, ed., *Capital Formation and Economic Growth.* New York: Princeton University Press, N.B.E.R., 19–106. **287n.**

1955b. "Economic Growth and Income Inequality." *A.E.R.,* 45 (March), 1–28. **238, 248n.**

1957. "Quantitative Aspects of the Economic Growth of Nations: Part 2, Industrial Distribution of National Product and Labor Force." *E.D.C.C.,* 5 (July, Supplement), 1–111. **287n.**

1958. "Quantitative Aspects of the Economic Growth of Nations: Part 3, Industrial Distribution of Income and Labor Force by States, United States, 1919–1921 to 1955." *E.D.C.C.,* 6 (July, Supplement), 1–128. **287n.**

1959. "Quantitative Aspects of the Economic Growth of Nations: Part 4, Distribution of National Income by Factor Shares." *E.D.C.C.,* 7 (April, Supplement), 1–100. **287n.**

1960. "Quantitative Aspects of the Economic Growth of Nations: Part 5, Capital Formation Proportions: International Comparisons for Recent Years." *E.D.C.C.,* 8 (July, Supplement), 1–96. **173, 395**

1961a. *Capital in the American Economy.* Princeton: Princeton University Press. **181**

1961b. "Quantitative Aspects of the Economic Growth of Nations: Part 6, Long-term Trends in Capital Formation Proportions." *E.D.C.C.,* 9 (July, Supplement), 1–124. **287n.**

1962. "Quantitative Aspects of the Economic Growth of Nations: Part 7, The Share and Structure of Consumption." *E.D.C.C.,* 10 (January, Supplement), 1–92. **287n.**

1963a. "Notes on the Take-off." In W. W. Rostow, ed., *The Economics of Take-off into Sustained Growth* (Proceedings of the Conference of the International Economic Association). London: Macmillan, 22–43. **31**

1963b. "Quantitative Aspects of the Economic Growth of Nations: Part 8, Distribution of Income by Size." *E.D.C.C.,* 11 (January), 1–80. **244, 248, 249, 249n.**

1964. "Quantitative Aspects of the Economic Growth of Nations: Part 9, Level and Structure of Foreign Trade: Comparisons for Recent Years." *E.D.C.C.,* 13 (October, Supplement), 1–106. **287n.**

1966. *Modern Economic Growth: Rate, Structure and Spread.* New Haven: Yale University Press. **239n., 248n., 260, 287n.**

1967. "Quantitative Aspects of the Economic Growth of Nations: Part 10, Level and Structure of Foreign Trade: Long Term Trends." *E.D.C.C.,* 15 (January, Supplement), 1–140. **287n.**

1972. "Problems in Comparing Recent Growth Rates for Developed and Less Developed Countries." *E.D.C.C.*, 20 (January), 185–209. **5**

LAGE, G. M. **1967.** "The Welfare Cost of Trade Restrictions: A Linear Programming Analysis." Unpublished Ph.D. Dissertation, University of Minnesota. **112**

1970. "A Linear Programming Analysis of Tariff Protection." *Western Economic Journal*, 8 (June), 167–185. **112**

LAL, D. **1972.** "The Foreign Exchange Bottleneck Revisited: A Geometric Note." *E.D.C.C.*, 20 (July), 722–730. **402–403**

LAMFALUSSY, A. **1961.** "Europe's Progress: Due to Common Market?" *Lloyds Bank Review*, No. 62 (October), 1–16. **351n.**

LAMPMAN, R. J. **1962.** *The Share of Top Wealth-holders in National Wealth.* Princeton: Princeton University Press. **248n.**

LANDAU, L. **1969.** "Brazilian Saving: A Note." Harvard University Project for Quantitative Research in Economic Development. Report No. 137. **173**

1971. "Saving Functions for Latin America: Differences in Savings Ratios among Latin American Countries." In H. B. Chenery, ed., *Studies in Development Planning.* Cambridge: Harvard University Press, 299–321. **170, 287**

LANDSBERGER, M. **1970.** "The Life-Cycle Hypothesis: A Reinterpretation and Empirical Test." *A.E.R.*, 60 (March), 175–183. **178**

LANSING, J. B., and E. MUELLER **1967.** *The Geographic Mobility of Labor.* Ann Arbor: Survey Research Center, University of Michigan. **226n.**

LARY, H. B. **1968.** *Imports of Manufactures from Less Developed Countries.* New York: N.B.E.R. **314n.**

LAU, L. J. **1969.** "Applications of Profit Functions." Stanford: Center for Research in Economic Growth, Memos No. 86A and 86B (mimeo). **96n., 271n., 272n.**

See also Christensen, L., D. W. Jorgenson, and L. J. Lau; Yotopoulos, P. A., and L. J. Lau; Yotopoulos, P. A., L. J. Lau, and K. Somel.

LAU, L. J., and P. A. YOTOPOULOS **1971.** "A Test for Relative Efficiency and Application to Indian Agriculture." *A.E.R.*, 61 (March), 94–109. **73n., 88, 93n., 97, 98n., 100n., 101, 271n., 275n.**

1972. "Profit, Supply and Factor Demand Functions." *A.J.A.E.*, 54 (February), 11–18. **271n., 272n.**

LAVE, L. B. **1966.** *Technological Change: Its Conception and Measurement.* Englewood Cliffs, N.J.: Prentice-Hall. **154n., 158**

LAWRENCE, R. **1968.** "Protection in the Central American Common Market in 1966." Agency for International Development, Regional Office for Central America, Panama, Guatemala (November, mimeo). **118n.**

LEAMER, E. E., and R. M. STERN **1970.** *Quantitative International Economics.* Boston: Allyn and Bacon. **315n.**

LEE, T. H. **1971.** *Intersectoral Capital Flows in the Economic Development of Taiwan, 1895–1960.* Ithaca: Cornell University Press. **261, 262, 264**

LEFEBER, L. **1968.** "Planning in a Surplus Labor Economy." *A.E.R.*, 58 (June), 343–373. **234**

LEFF, N. H. **1969.** "Dependency Rates and Savings Rates." *A.E.R.*, 59 (December), 886–896. **179**

LEIBENSTEIN, H. **1950.** "Bandwagon, Snob and Veblen Effects in the Theory of Consumers' Demand." *Q.J.E.*, 64 (May), 183–207. **377n.**

1957. *Economic Backwardness and Economic Growth.* New York: Wiley. **40, 377n., 395**

1966. "Allocative Efficiency versus X-Efficiency." *A.E.R.*, 56 (June), 392–415. **108n., 358n., 395**

See also Galenson, W., and H. Leibenstein.

LEITH, J. C. **1970.** "The Decline in World Export Instability: A Comment." *Bulletin of the Oxford University Institute of Economics and Statistics*, 32 (August), 267–272. **331n.**

LEONTIEF, W. W. **1954.** "Domestic Production and Foreign Trade: The American Capital Position Re-examined." *Economia Internazionale*, 7 (February), 9–38. **322**

1956. "Factor Proportions and the Structure of American Trade: Further Theoretical and Empirical Analysis." *R.E.Stat.*, 38 (November), 386–407. **322**

1964. "An International Comparison of Factor Costs and Factor Use." *A.E.R.*, 54 (June), 335–345. **322**

LeVINE, R. A. **1966.** *Dreams and Deeds: Achievement Motivation in Nigeria.* Chicago: University of Chicago Press. **39n.**

LEWIS, S. R., JR. **1968.** "Effects of Trade Policy on Domestic Relative Prices: Pakistan, 1951–64." *A.E.R.*, 58 (March), 60–78. **396**

1969. "Domestic Saving and Foreign Assistance When Foreign Exchange is Undervalued." Williams College: Center for Development Economics, Research Memo No. 34. **169**

LEWIS, S. R., JR., and S. R. SOLIGO **1965.** "Growth and Structural Change in Pakistan's Manufacturing Industry, 1954–1964." *The Pakistan Development Review*, 5 (Spring), 94–139. **291**

LEWIS, W. A. **1952.** "World Production, Prices and Trade, 1870–1960." *Manchester School of Economic and Social Studies*, 20 (May), 105–138. **344**

1954. "Economic Development with Unlimited Supplies of Labour." *Manchester School of Economic and Social Studies*, 22 (May), 139–191. **13, 206, 230n., 260, 341n., 358**

1955. *The Theory of Economic Growth.* London: Allan & Unwin. **12**

LIANOS, T. P. **1969.** "A Comment on a Traditional Behavior Model." *A.J.A.E.*, 51 (November), 937. **88**
1971. "The Relative Share of Labor in United States Agriculture, 1949–1968." *A.J.A.E.*, 53 (August), 411–422. **161**

LIESNER, H. H. **1958.** "The European Common Market and British Industry." *E.J.*, 68 (June), 302–316. **351n.**

LIN, W. L. **1973.** "Economic Interactions in Taiwan: A Study of Sectoral Flows and Linkages. Ph.D. Dissertation, Stanford University. **261, 262, 264, 267, 300n.**

LINDER, S. B. **1961.** *An Essay on Trade and Transformation.* Uppsala: Almquist and Wiksells. **325**

LINDSAY, C. M. **1971.** "Measuring Human Capital Returns." *J.P.E.*, 79 (November), 1195–1215. **195**

LIPSEY, R. E. **See** Kravis, I. B., and R. E. Lipsey.

LIPSEY, R. G. **1957.** "The Theory of Customs Union: Trade Diversion and Welfare." *Economica*, 24 (February), 40–56. **350**
1960. "The Theory of Customs Union: A General Survey." *E.J.*, 70 (September), 496–513. **350**

LITTLE, I. M. D., and J. A. MIRRLEES **1968.** *Manual of Industrial Project Analysis in Developing Countries, Vol. II, Social Cost-Benefit Analysis.* Paris: Development Centre, OECD. **382**
1972a. "A Reply to Some Criticisms of the OECD Manual." *Oxford University Institute of Economics and Statistics Bulletin*, 34, (February), 153–168. **390**
1972b. "Further Reflections on the OECD Manual of Project Analysis in Developing Countries" (mimeo). **387**

LITTLE, I. M. D., T. SCITOVSKY, and M. SCOTT **1970.** *Industry and Trade in Some Developing Countries.* London: Oxford University Press. **14, 112n., 352n.**

LONG, C. D. **1962.** "Comment: Labor Force Participation of Married Women." In *Aspects of Labor Economics, A Conference of the Universities—N.B.E.R.* Princeton: Princeton University Press. **226n.**

LU, Y. C., and L. B. FLETCHER **1968.** "A Generalization of the CES Production Function." *R.E.Stat.*, 50 (November), 449–452. **64**

LUCAS, R. E. **See** Thurow, L. C., and R. E. Lucas.

MACARIO, S. **1964.** "Protectionism and Industrialization in Latin America." *Economic Bulletin for Latin America*, 9 (March), 61–101. **112n.**

MacBEAN, A. I. **1966.** *Export Instability and Economic Development.* Cambridge: Harvard University Press. **176n.**

MacDOUGALL, G. D. A. **1951.** "British and American Exports: A Study Suggested by the Theory of Comparative Costs." *E.J.*, 61 (December), 697–724. **321**

MACHLUP, F. **1946.** "Marginal Analysis and Empirical Research." *A.E.R.*, 36 (September), 519–554. **102**
1955. "The Problem of Verification in Economics." *Southern Economic Journal*, 22 (July), 1–21. **21**

MACK, R. P. **1954.** "Factor Markets versus Product Markets—Discussion." *A.E.R.*, 44 (May), 88–89. **109n.**

MAIZELS, A. **1963.** *Industrial Growth and World Trade.* Cambridge: Cambridge University Press. **343**

MAJOR, R. L., and S. HAYS **1970.** "Another Look at the Common Market." *National Institute Economic Review*, No. 54 (November), 29–43. **321n.**

MALAH, P. **See** Bergsman, J., and P. Malah.

MANDELBAUM, K. **1945.** *The Industrialization of Backward Areas.* New York: Kelley and Millman. **206n.**

MANGAHAS, M., A. E. RECTO, and V. W. RUTTAN **1966.** "Market Relationships for Rice and Corn in the Philippines." *Philippine Economic Journal*, 5, 1–27. **141**

MANN, J. S. **1967.** "The Impact of Public Law 480 Imports on Prices and Domestic Supply of Cereals in India." *J.F.E.*, 49 (February), 131–146. **135n.**

MANNE, A. S. **1963.** "Key Sectors of the Mexican Economy, 1960–1970." In A. S. Manne and H. M. Markowitz, eds., *Studies in Process Analysis.* New York: Wiley, 379–400. **408n.**
1973. "Economic Alternatives for Mexico: A Quantitative Analysis." In L. Goreux and A. S. Manne, eds., *Multi-level Planning: Case Studies in Mexico.* Amsterdam: North Holland. **408n.**

MANNE, A. S., ed. **1967.** *Investments for Capacity Expansion: Size, Location and Time Phasing.* Cambridge: M.I.T. Press. **153**

MANSFIELD, E. **1968.** *Industrial Research and Technological Innovation.* New York: Norton. **144**

MARCHAL, J. and B. DUCROS, eds. **1968.** *The Distribution of National Income.* New York: Macmillan. **247n.**

MARENBACH, D. **See** Carnoy, M., and D. Marenbach.

MARGENAU, H. **1935.** "Methodology of Modern Physics." *Philosophy of Science*, 2 (April), 48–72; (July), 164–187. **18n.**

MARGLIN, S. A. **1963a.** "The Social Rate of Discount and the Optimal Rate of Investment." *Q.J.E.*, 77 (February), 95–111. **378**
1963b. "The Opportunity Costs of Public Investments. *Q.J.E.*, 77 (May), 274–289. **378**
1965. "Insurance for Innovators." In D. Hapgood, ed., *Policies for Promoting Agricultural Development.* Cambridge: M.I.T. (Report of a Conference on Productivity and Innovation in

Agriculture in the Underdeveloped Countries), 257–260 (mimeo). **130n.**

1968. "The Rate of Interest and the Value of Capital with Unlimited Supplies of Labour." UNIDO. *Evaluation of Industrial Projects*, Project Formation and Evaluation Series, Vol. 1, ID/SER.H/1. New York: U.N. **396**

See also Dasgupta, P., S. A. Marglin, and A. K. Sen.

MARGOLIS, J., and P. E. VINCENT 1966. "External Economic Effects—An Analysis and Survey with Special Reference to Water Resources Projects." Stanford University: Institute in Engineering-Economic Systems (September). **377n.**

MARSCHAK, J., and W. H. ANDREWS 1944. "Random Simultaneous Equations and the Theory of Production." *Econometrica*, 12 (July), 143–205. **78, 84**

MARSHALL, A. 1920. *Industry and Trade*. London: Macmillan. **9**

1952. *Principles of Economics*. 8th ed. London: Macmillan. **131n.**

MARTINA, A. 1966. "A Discussion of the Concept of Disguised Unemployment in Traditional Agriculture with Specific Emphasis to Africa South of the Sahara." *The South African Journal of Economics*, 34 (December), 305–321. **212n.**

MARTY, A. 1967. "Growth and the Welfare Cost of Inflationary Finance." *J.P.E.*, 75 (February), 71–76. **171n.**

MARWAH, K. **See** Diwan, R. K., and K. Marwah.

MASSELL, B. F. 1960. "Capital Formation and Technological Change in United States Manufacturing." *R.E.Stat.*, 42 (May), 182–188. **155n.**

1964. "Export Concentration and Fluctuations in Export Earnings: A Cross-Section Analysis." *A.E.R.*, 54 (March), 47–63. **331, 339**

1967a. "Elimination of Management Bias from Production Functions Fitted to Cross-Section Data: A Model and an Application to African Agriculture." *Econometrica*, 35 (July), 205–215. **78, 81n.**

1967b. "Farm Management in Peasant Agriculture: An Empirical Study." *F.R.I.S.*, 7, No. 2, 205–215. **80, 81n.**

1969. "Price Stabilization and Welfare." *Q.J.E.*, 83 (May), 284–298. **341n.**

1970. "Export Instability and Economic Structure." *A.E.R.*, 60 (September), 618–630. **331, 339, 341n.**

See also Cooper, C. A., and B. F. Massell.

MASTERS, S. H. 1969. "The Effect of Family Income on Children's Education: Some Findings on Inequality of Opportunity." *Journal of Human Resources*, 4 (Spring), 158–175. **195n.**

MATHUR, A. 1964. "The Anatomy of Disguised Unemployment." *O.E.P.*, 16 (July), 161–193. **212n.**

MATHUR, P. N., and H. EZEKIEL 1961. "Marketable Surplus of Food and Price Fluctuations in a Developing Economy." *Kyklos*, 14, No. 3, 396–408. **136**

MAUER, L. J. **See** Scaperlanda, A. E., and L. J. Mauer.

MAYER, T. 1966. "The Propensity to Consume Permanent Income." *A.E.R.*, 56 (December), 1158–1177. **175**

MAZUMDAR, D. **See** Desai, M., and D. Mazumdar.

McARTHUR, C. C. 1953. "The Effects of Need Achievement on the Content of TAT Stories: A Re-Evaluation." *Journal of Abnormal and Social Psychology*, 48, No. 4, 532–536. **39n.**

McCLELLAND, D. C. 1961. *The Achieving Society*. Princeton: Van Nostrand. **39**

McCLELLAND, D. C., and D. G. WINTER 1969. *Motivating Economic Achievement*. New York: Free Press. **39n.**

McFADDEN, D. L. 1970. "Cost, Revenue, and Profit Functions." Berkeley: University of California, Department of Economics (mimeo). **95, 96n., 272n.**

McGEEHAN, J. M. 1968. "Competitiveness: A Survey of Recent Literature." *E.J.*, 78 (June), 243–262. **316n.**

McKEAN, R. N. 1965. "The Unseen Hand in Government." *A.E.R.*, 55 (June), 496–506. **379**

McKINNON, R. I. 1964. "Foreign Exchange Constraints in Economic Development and Efficient Aid Allocation." *E.J.*, 74 (June), 388–409. **402**

1967. "Futures Markets, Buffer Stocks and Income Stability for Primary Producers." *J.P.E.*, 75 (December), 844–861. **340n.**

1973. *Money and Capital in Economic Development*. Washington: Brookings Institution. **8n., 176, 256**

MEIER, G. M. 1963. *International Trade and Development*. New York: Harper and Row. **340n.**

MEIER, G. M., and R. E. BALDWIN 1957. *Economic Development: Theory, History, Policy*. New York: Wiley. **9n., 11**

MELAMED, A. **See** Zusman, P., A. Melamed, and I. Katzir.

MELITZ, J. 1965. "Friedman and Machlup on the Significance of Testing Economic Assumptions." *J.P.E.*, 73 (February), 37–60. **21**

MEYER, J. R., and E. KUH 1957. *The Investment Decision: An Empirical Analysis*. Cambridge: Harvard University Press. **180n.**

See also Conrad, A. H., and J. R. Meyer.

MEYER zu SCHLOCHTERN, F. J. M. **See** Verdoon, P. J., and F. J. M. Meyer zu Schlochtern.

MIKESELL, R. F. 1965. "The Theory of Common Markets as Applied to Regional Arrangements among Developing Countries." In R. F. Harrod and D. Hague, eds., *International Trade Theory in a Developing World.* New York: St. Martin's Press, 205–229. **358n.**

MIKESELL, R. F., and J. E. ZINSER **1973.** "The Nature of the Savings Function in Developing Countries: A Survey of the Theoretical and Empirical Literature." *J.E.L.,* 11 (March), 1–26. **168n., 172**

MIKLIUS, W. **See** Yotopoulos, P. A., and W. Miklius.

MILLER, H. P. **1965.** "Lifetime Income and Economic Growth." *A.E.R.,* 55 (September), 834–844. **189n., 191n.**
See also Al-Samarrie, A., and H. P. Miller.

MILLIKAN, M. F., and W. W. ROSTOW **1957.** *A Proposal: Key to an Effective Foreign Policy.* New York: Harper and Row. **12**

MINCER, J. **1962.** "On-the-Job Training: Costs, Returns and Some Implications." *J.P.E.,* 70 (October, Supplement), 50–79. **186**

MINHAS, B. S. **1963.** *An International Comparison of Factor Costs and Factor Use.* Amsterdam: North Holland. **323**
See also Arrow, K. J., H. B. Chenery, B. S. Minhas, and R. M. Solow.

MIRRLEES, J. A. **See** Diamond, P. A., and J. A. Mirrlees; Little, I. M. D., and J. A. Mirrlees.

MISHAN, E. J. **1968.** "What Is Producer's Surplus?" *A.E.R.,* 58 (December), 1269–1282. **109n., 350n.**

MODIGLIANI, F. **1947.** "Fluctuations in the Saving Ratio." *Social Research,* 14 (December), 413–420. **173**
1966. "The Life Cycle Hypothesis of Saving, the Demand for Wealth and the Supply of Capital." *Social Research,* 33 (June), 160–217. **177n.**
1967. "Tests of the Long-Run Determinants of the Saving Ratio Based on International Comparisons" (mimeo). **177n.**
See also Ando, A., and F. Modigliani; Grunberg, E., and F. Modigliani; Nelsser, H., and F. Modigliani.

MODIGLIANI, F., and A. ANDO **1957.** "Test of the Life Cycle Hypothesis of Saving." *Bulletin of Oxford University Institute of Economics and Statistics,* 19 (May), 99–124. **177n.**

MODIGLIANI, F., and R. BRUMBERG **1955.** "Utility Analysis and the Consumption Function: An Interpretation of Cross-Section Data." In K. Kurihara, ed., *Post-Keynesian Economics.* London: Allan and Unwin, 388–436. **177n.**

MOES, J. **1957.** "Investment Criteria, Productivity and Economic Development: Comment." *Q.J.E.,* 71 (February), 161–164. **396**

MOOD, A. M., and R. A. GRAYBILL **1963.** *Introduction to the Theory of Statistics.* 2nd ed. New York: McGraw-Hill. **78n.**

MOONEY, J. D. **See** Ashenfelter, O., and J. D. Mooney.

MOORE, F. T. **1959.** "Economies of Scale: Some Statistical Evidence." *Q.J.E.,* 73 (May), 232–245. **150, 153**

MORGAN, T. **1959.** "The Long-Run Terms of Trade between Agriculture and Manufacturing." *E.D.C.C.,* 8 (October), 1–23. **344**

MORGENSTERN, O. **See** Neumann, J. V., and O. Morgenstern.

MORRIS, C. T. **See** Adelman, I., M. Geier, and C. T. Morris.

MUBYARTO, and L. B. FLETCHER **1966.** "The Marketable Surplus of Rice in Indonesia: A Study in Java-Madura." *International Studies in Economics,* Monograph No. 4. Ames: Iowa State University. **138**

MUELLER, E. **See** Lansing, J. B., and E. Mueller.

MUJUMDAR, N. A. **1961.** *Some Problems of Underemployment.* Bombay: Popular Book Depot. **212**

MUNDLAK, Y. **1961.** "Empirical Production Function Free of Management Bias." *J.F.E.,* 43 (February), 44–56. **68, 78, 80**
1964. *An Economic Analysis of Established Family Farms in Israel, 1953–1958.* Jerusalem: The Falk Project for Economic Research in Israel. **80**

MURPHY, J. A. **See** Currie, J. M., J. A. Murphy, and A. Schmitz.

MUSHKIN, S. J. **1962.** "Health as an Investment." *J.P.E.,* 70 (October, Supplement), 129–157. **186**

MUTH, R. F. **1971.** "Migration: Chicken or Egg?" *Southern Economic Journal,* 37 (January), 295–306. **236**

MYERS, C. A. **See** Harbison, F., and C. A. Myers, eds.

MYERS, R. G. **1972.** *Emigration and Education.* New York: McKay. **234n.**

MYINT, H. **1954.** "An Interpretation of Economic Backwardness." *Oxford Economic Papers,* 6 (June), 132–163. **253**
1964. *The Economics of the Developing Countries.* London: Hutchinson. **211, 255**

MYRDAL, G. **1957.** *Economic Theory and Underdeveloped Regions.* London: Duckworth. **226n.**
1968. *Asian Drama: An Inquiry into the Poverty of Nations.* New York: Twentieth Century Fund. **254**

NADIRI, M. I. **1970.** "Some Approaches to the Theory and Measurement of Total Factor Productivity: A Survey." *J.E.L.,* 8 (December), 1137–1177. **144, 156**
See also Eisner, R., and M. I. Nadiri; Jorgenson, D. W., J. Hunter, and M. I. Nadiri.

NADIRI, M. I., and S. ROSEN **1969.** "Interrelated Factor Demand Functions." *A.E.R.,* 59 (September), 457–471. **64**
1973. *A Disequilibrium Model of Demand for Factors of Production.* New York: N.B.E.R. **142n.**

NAGEL, E. **See** Cohen, M. R., and E. Nagel.

NAKAJIMA, C. **1969.** "Subsistence and Commercial Family Farms: Some Theoretical Models of Subjective Equilibrium." In C. R. Wharton, ed., *Subsistence Agriculture and Economic Development.* Chicago: Aldine, 165–185. **206**

NAYA, S. **1967**. "National Resources, Factor Mix and Factor Reversal in International Trade." *A.E.R.*, 57 (May), 561–570. **324**

NEISSER, H. **1956**. "Investment Criteria, Productivity and Economic Development: Comment." *Q.J.E.*, 70 (November), 644–646. **396**

NEISSER, H., and F. MODIGLIANI. **1953**. *National Incomes and International Trade.* Urbana: University of Illinois Press. **316**

NELL, E. J. **See** Ferguson, C. E., and E. J. Nell.

NELSON, R. R. **1964**. "Aggregate Production Functions and Medium Range Growth Projections. *A.E.R.*, 54 (September), 575–606. **159**
1965. "The CES Production Function and Economic Growth Projections." *R.E.Stat.*, 57 (August), 326–328. **156**
1968. "A Diffusion Model of International Productivity Differences in Manufacturing Industry." *A.E.R.*, 58 (December), 1219–1248. **255**
1970. "The Effective Exchange Rate: Employment and Growth in a Foreign Exchange-Constrained Economy." *J.P.E.*, 78 (May), 546–564. **403**
1973. "Recent Exercises in Growth Accounting: New Understanding or Dead End?" *A.E.R.*, 63 (June), 462–468. **149**

NELSON, R. R., and S. G. WINTER **1974**. "Neoclassical Vs. Evolutionary Theories of Economic Growth: Critique and Prospectus." *E.J.*, 84 (December), 886–905. **163n.**

NERLOVE, M. **1956**. "Estimates of the Elasticity of Supply of Selected Agricultural Commodities." *J.F.E.*, 38 (May), 496–512. **140n.**
1958. *The Dynamics of Supply: Estimation of Farmers' Response to Price.* Baltimore: Johns Hopkins University Press. **137n., 138–140**
1965. *Estimation and Identification of Cobb-Douglas Production Functions.* Chicago: Rand McNally. **150**

NEUMANN, J. V., and O. MORGENSTERN **1947**. *The Theory of Games and Economic Behaviour.* Princeton: Princeton University Press. **376**

NICHOLLS, W. H. **1960**. *Southern Tradition and Regional Progress.* Chapel Hill: University of North Carolina Press. **211**
1963. "An 'Agricultural Surplus' as a Factor in Economic Development." *J.P.E.*, 71 (February), 1–29. **260**

NICOLAOU, C. **See** Ellis, H. S., D. D. Psilos, R. M. Westebbe, and C. Nicolaou.

NORTON, R. D. **See** Duloy, J. H., and R. D. Norton.

NOWSHIRVANI, V. F. **1967a**. "A Note on the Fixed-Cash Requirement Theory of Marketed Surplus in Subsistence Agriculture." *Kyklos*, 20, No. 3, 772–773. **136n.**
1967b. "A Note on the Elasticity of the Marketable Surplus of a Subsistence Crop: A Comment." *Indian Journal of Agricultural Economics*, 22 (January), 110–114. **141n.**
1967c. "Allocation Efficiency in a Traditional Indian Agriculture: A Comment." *J.F.E.*, 49 (February), 218–221. **84**

NUGENT, J. B. **1966**. *Programming the Optimal Development of the Greek Economy 1954–1961.* Athens: Center of Planning and Economic Research. **408, 412, 415**
1967a. "The Construction and Use of Input-Output Tables in Determining the Consistency of Ecuador's First Development Plan." *Planificación*, 4 (Spring), 23–37. **57–59**
1967b. "Economic Thought, Investment Criteria, and Development Strategies in Greece: A Postwar Survey." *E.D.C.C.*, 15 (April), 331–335. **293n.**
1967c. "Foreign Assistance Planning: A Semi-Quantitative Approach to Development Planning in Central America." Los Angeles: University of Southern California (mimeo). **405n.**
1968. "La Estructura Arancelária y el Costo de Protección en America Central." *El Trimestre Económico*, 35 (October), 751–766. **118**
1970. "Linear Programming Models for National Planning: Demonstration of a Testing Procedure." *Econometrica*, 38 (November), 831–855. **416, 418–421**
1973. "Exchange Rate Movements and Economic Development in the Late Nineteenth Century." *J.P.E.*, 81 (September), 1110–1135. **320**
1974. *Economic Integration in Central America: Empirical Investigations.* Baltimore: Johns Hopkins University Press. **318, 352, 353, 359n., 360n., 425n.**
See also DePrano, M. E., and J. B. Nugent; Yotopoulos, P. A., and J. B. Nugent.

NUGENT, J. B., and M. A. AKBAR **1970**. "The Welfare Cost of Tariffs When the Tariff Structure Is Inhomogeneous." Los Angeles: University of Southern California (mimeo). **112, 118**

NUGENT, J. B., and M. E. DePRANO **1967**. "The Effects of Long-Run and Short-Run Planning Goals on Economic Policy Instruments." Paper presented to the Econometric Society, Washington, D.C. (December). **425**

NURKSE, R. **1953**. *Problems of Capital Formation in Underdeveloped Countries.* New York: Oxford University Press. **12, 168, 173, 206n., 211, 260, 295**
1958. "Trade Fluctuations and Buffer Policies of Low-Income Countries." *Kyklos*, 11, No. 2, 141–154. **340n.**
1961. "Patterns of Trade and Development." In G. Haberler and R. M. Stern, eds., *Equilibrium and Growth in World Economy.* Cambridge: Harvard University Press, 282–304. **40, 314n.**

OECD **1970**. *National Accounts of Less Developed Countries, 1959–1968.* Paris. **169**

OHKAWA, K., and H. ROSOVSKY **1960.** "The Role of Agriculture in Modern Japanese Development." *E.D.C.C.*, 9 (October), 43–67. **261**
1968. "Postwar Japanese Growth in Historical Perspective: A Second Look." In L. Klein and K. Ohkawa, eds., *Economic Growth: The Japanese Experience Since the Meiji Era.* Homewood, Ill.: Irwin, 3–34. **226**

OHLIN, B. G. **1933.** *Interregional and International Trade.* Cambridge: Harvard University Press. **322**
1959. "Balanced Economic Growth in History." *A.E.R.*, 49 (May), 338–353. **294**

OLSON, E. **See** Tolley, G. S., and E. Olson.

ONER, A. **1968.** "The Test of the Permanent Income Hypothesis." Unpublished M.A. Thesis, University of Southern California (January). **176**

OOMS, V. D. **1966.** "Regionalization and Export Performance: A Study of Primary Commodities." Unpublished Ph.D. Dissertation, Yale University. **316**

ORCUTT, G. H. **1952.** "Toward Partial Redirection of Econometrics." *R.E.Stat.*, 34 (August), 195–200. **22**

OSHIMA, H. T. **1962.** "The International Comparison of Size Distribution of Family Incomes, with Special Reference to Asia." *R.E.Stat.*, 44 (November), 439–445. **248n.**

OSTHEIMER, J. M. **1967.** "The Achievement Motive Among the Chagga of Tanzania." Ph.D. Dissertation, Yale University. **39n.**

OWEN, W. F. **1966.** "The Double Developmental Squeeze on Agriculture." *A.E.R.*, 56 (March), 43–70. **135n., 260, 261**

PAAUW, D. S., and J. C. H. FEI **1973.** *The Transition in Open Dualistic Economies: Theory and Southeast Asian Experience.* New Haven: Yale University Press. **230n.**

PAGLIN, M. **1965.** " 'Surplus' Agricultural Labor and Development—Facts and Theories." *A.E.R.*, 55 (September), 815–834. **73n.**

PAPANDREOU, A. G. **1958.** *Economics as a Science.* Chicago: Lippincott. **21**
1962. *A Strategy for Greek Economic Development.* Athens: Center of Planning and Economic Research. **14, 293n., 297, 421n.**
1972. *Paternalistic Capitalism.* Minneapolis: University of Minnesota Press. **77**

PARIKH, K. S. **See** Eckaus, R. S., and K. S. Parikh.

PARNES, H. S. **1962.** *Forecasting Educational Needs for Economic and Social Development.* Paris: OECD. **402n.**

PAUKERT, F. **1973.** "Income Distribution at Different Levels of Development: A Survey of Evidence." *International Labour Review*, 108 (September), 97–125. **248n.**

PEARSON, K. **1937.** *The Grammar of Science.* London: Dent. **18**

PEARSON, S. R. **1970.** *Petroleum and the Ni-gerian Economy.* Stanford, Calif.: Stanford University Press. **300n.**
1971. "The Economic Imperialism of the Royal Niger Company." *F.R.I.S.*, 10, No. 1, 69–88. **110n.**

PEN, J. **1971.** *Income Distribution: Facts, Theories, Policies.* New York: Praeger. **234n., 242n., 247n.**

PEPELASIS, A. A., and P. A. YOTOPOULOS **1962.** *Surplus Labor in Greek Agriculture, 1953–1960.* Athens: Center of Planning and Economic Research. **83, 203, 212**

PETERSON, W. C. **1965.** "Investment and the Threshold of Economic Growth." *Kyklos*, 18, No. 1, 132–138. **31n.**

PHELPS, E. S. *et al.* **1970.** *Microeconomic Foundations of Employment and Inflation Theory.* New York: Norton. **11n., 231**

PLEASE, S. **1967.** "Savings Through Taxation—Mirage or Reality." *Finance and Development*, 4 (March), 1–10. **170**
1970. "The Please Effect Revisited." Economics Department Working Paper, No. 82 (July, mimeo). **170**

POPKIN, J. **See** Brown, M., and J. Popkin.

POPPER, K. R. **1959.** *The Logic of Scientific Discovery.* New York: Harper and Row. **23**

PORTER, R. C. **1964.** "The Optimal Price Problem in Buffer Fund Stabilization." *O.E.P.*, 16 (November), 423–430. **340n.**

POWER, J. H. **1966.** "Import Substitution as an Industrialization Strategy." *The Philippines Economic Journal*, 5, No. 2, 167–204. **118n.**

PRATT, J. W. **1965.** "Bayesian Interpretation of Standard Inference Statements." *The Journal of the Royal Statistical Society*, Series B, 27, No. 2, 169–192. **25n.**

PREBISCH, R. **1959.** "Commercial Policy in the Underdeveloped Countries." *A.E.R.*, 49 (May), 251–273. **14, 341n., 343**

PRYOR, F. L. **1972.** "The Size of Production Establishments in Manufacturing." *E.J.*, 82 (June), 547–566. **150**
1973. "Simulation of the Impact of Social and Economic Institutions on the Size Distribution of Income and Wealth." *A.E.R.*, 63 (March), 50–72. **248n.**

PSACHAROPOULOS, G. **1971.** "On Some Positive Aspects of the Economics of the Brain Drain." *Minerva*, 9 (April), 231–242. **191, 192–193**

PSILOS, D. D. **See** Ellis, H. S., D. D. Psilos, R. M. Westebbe, and C. Nicolaou.

RAHMAN, M. A. **1968.** "Foreign Capital and Domestic Savings: A Test of Haavelmo's Hypothesis with Cross-Country Data." *R.E.Stat.*, 50 (February), 137–138. **176n.**

RAMSEY, J. B. **1970.** "The Marginal Efficiency of Capital, the Internal Rate of Return and Net Present Value: An Analysis of Investment Criteria." *J.P.E.*, 78 (September), 1017–1027. **373**

RANADIVE, K. R. **1965.** "The Equality of Incomes in India." *Bulletin of the Oxford University Institute of Economics and Statistics*, 27 (May), 119–134. **244, 245**

RANIS, G., and J. C. H. FEI **1961.** "A Theory of Economic Development." *A.E.R.*, 51 (September), 533–565. **230n., 358**
See also Fei, J. C. H., and G. Ranis.

RASMUSSEN, P. N. **1956.** *Studies in Intersectoral Relations.* Amsterdam: North Holland. **300n.**

RAVENSTEIN, E. G. **1889.** "The Laws of Migration." *Journal of the Royal Statistical Society*, 52 (June), 241–301. **227**

RAYNER, A. C. **1970.** "The Use of Multivariate Analysis in Development Theory: A Critique of the Approach Adopted by Adelman and Morris." *Q.J.E.*, 84 (November), 639–647. **34, 38**

RECTO, A. E. See Mangahas, M., A. E. Recto, and V. W. Ruttan.

REES, A. **1963.** "The Effects of Unions on Resource Allocation." *Journal of Law and Economics*, 6 (October), 69–78. **109**

REICHENBACH, H. **1958.** *The Rise of Scientific Philosophy.* Berkeley and Los Angeles: University of California Press. **18**

RESCHER, N. See Helmer, O., and N. Rescher.

RESNICK, S. A. **1970.** "The Decline of Rural Industry under Export Expansion: A Comparison among Burma, Philippines and Thailand, 1870–1938." *Journal of Economic History*, 30 (March), 51–73. **254n., 313, 345**

RESNICK, S. A., and E. M. TRUMAN **1973.** "An Empirical Examination of Bilateral Trade in Western Europe." *Journal of International Economics*, 3 (November), 305–336. **358**
See also Hymer, S., and S. Resnick.

REYNOLDS, C. W. **1963.** "Domestic Consequences of Export Instability." *A.E.R.*, 63 (May), 93–102. **331**

RHOMBERG, R. R. See Junz, H. B., and R. R. Rhomberg.

RICHARDSON, J. D. **1971.** "Constant-Market Shares Analysis of Export Growth." *Journal of International Economics*, 1 (May), 227–239. **315n., 316**

ROBBINS, L. C. **1935.** *Essay on the Nature and Significance of Economic Science.* London: Macmillan. **20**

ROBINSON, J. **1933.** *Monopolistic Competition and General Equilibrium Theory.* London: Macmillan. **121**
1960. "The Theory of Distribution." In J. Robinson, ed., *Collected Economic Papers*, Vol. 2. London: Blackwell, 145–158. **247n.**

ROBINSON, S. **1971.** "Sources of Growth in Less Developed Countries: A Cross-Section Study." *Q.J.E.*, 85 (August), 391–408. **287n.**
1972. "Theories of Economic Growth and Development: Methodology and Content." *E.D.C.C.*, 21 (October), 54–67. **260n.**

ROBINSON, W. C. **1969.** "Types of Disguised Rural Unemployment and Some Policy Implications." *O.E.P.*, 21 (November), 373–386. **212n.**

ROEMER, M. **1970.** *Fishing for Growth: Export-Led Development in Peru, 1950–1967.* Cambridge: Harvard University Press. **300n.**

ROMANIS, A. **1961.** "Relative Growth of Exports of Manufactures of United States and Other Industrial Countries." *International Monetary Fund Staff Papers*, 8 (May), 241–273. **316n.**

ROSEN, S. See Nadiri, M. I., and S. Rosen.

ROSENBERG, R. **1970.** "The Effects of the Social Security System on Income Redistribution in the Philippines." Unpublished Ph.D. Dissertation, University of Wisconsin. **249**

ROSENSTEIN-RODAN, P. N. **1957.** "Disguised Unemployment and Underemployment in Agriculture." *Monthly Bulletin of Agricultural Economics and Statistics—FAO*, 6 (July–August), 1–10. **206n., 212n.**
1961. "Notes on the Theory of the 'Big Push.'" In H. S. Ellis, ed., *Economic Development for Latin America.* New York: St. Martin's Press, 57–81. **40**

ROSOVSKY, H. See Ohkawa, K., and H. Rosovsky.

ROSTOW, W. W. **1961.** *Stages of Economic Growth: A Non-Communist Manifesto.* Cambridge: Cambridge University Press. **29n., 30–31**
1962. *The Process of Economic Growth.* New York: Norton. **29–31**
See also Millikan, M. F., and W. W. Rostow.

RUTTAN, V. W. **1968.** *Growth Stage Theories, Dual Economy Models and Agricultural Development Policy.* Guelph: University of Guelph, Department of Agricultural Economics. **260, 261**
See also Hayami, Y., and V. W. Ruttan; Mangahas, M. A., A. E. Recto, and V. W. Ruttan.

SADIE, J. L. **1960.** "The Social Anthropology of Economic Underdevelopment." *E.J.*, 70 (June), 294–303. **253n.**

SAHOTA, G. S. **1968a.** "An Economic Analysis of Internal Migration in Brazil." *J.P.E.*, 76 (March), 218–245. **226**
1968b. "Efficiency of Resource Allocation in Indian Agriculture." *A.J.A.E.*, 50 (August) 584–605. **73n.**

SAMUELSON, P. A. **1958.** "Aspects of Public Expenditure Theories." *R.E.Stat.*, 40 (November), 332–338. **256**
1963. "Discussion—Problems of Methodology." *A.E.R.*, 53 (May), 231–236. **21**
See also Solow, R. M., and P. A. Samuelson.

SANCHEZ, N. **1972.** "Economics of Sugar Quotas: An Econometric Analysis." Unpublished Ph.D. Dissertation, University of Southern California. **142, 150**

SANDEE, J. **1960.** *A Long-Term Planning Model for India.* Bombay: Asia Publishing House. **408n.**

SATO, R., and R. F. HOFFMAN **1968.** "Production Functions with Variable Elasticity of Factor Substitution: Some Analysis and Testing." *R.E.Stat.,* 50 (November), 453–460. **64n.** See also Kendrick, J. W., and R. Sato.

SAVAGE, L. J. See Friedman, M., and L. J. Savage.

SCANLON, W. J. See Hansen, W. L., B. A. Weisbrod, and W. J. Scanlon.

SCAPERLANDA, A. E. **1967.** "The EEC and US Foreign Investment: Some Empirical Evidence." *E.J.,* 77 (March), 22–26. **360n.**

SCAPERLANDA, A. E., and L. J. MAUER **1969.** "The Determinants of U.S. Direct Investment in the EEC." *A.E.R.,* 59 (September), 558–568. **360n.**

SCHATZ, S. P. **1965.** "Achievement and Economic Growth: A Critique." *Q.J.E.,* 79 (May), 234–241; "Rejoinder." Same issue, 246–247. **39n.**

SCHERER, F. M. **1973.** "The Determinants of Industrial Plant Sizes in Six Nations." *R.E.Stat.,* 55 (May), 135–145. **150n.**

SCHIAVO-CAMPO, S. See Erb, G. F., and S. Schiavo-Campo.

SCHLOTE, W. **1938.** "Entwicklang und Strukturwandlungen des Englischen Aussenhandels von 1700 bis zur Gegenwart." *Probleme der Weltwirtschaft,* 62 (Jena). **343n.**

SCHMITZ, A. **1970.** "The Impact of Trade Blocs on Foreign Direct Investment." *E.J.,* 80 (September), 724–731. **360** See also Currie, J. M., J. A. Murphy, and A. Schmitz; Hueth, D., and A. Schmitz.

SCHULTZ, T. P. **1968.** "Secular Equalization and Cyclical Behavior of Income Distribution." *R.E.Stat.,* 50 (May), 259–267. **248n.** **1971.** "Rural-Urban Migration in Colombia." *R.E.Stat.,* 53 (May), 157–163. **226**

SCHULTZ, T. W. **1960a.** "Capital Formation by Education." *J.P.E.,* 68 (December), 571–583. **184n.** **1960b.** "The Value of U.S. Farm Surplusses to Underdeveloped Countries." *J.F.E.,* 42 (December), 1019–1030. **136** **1961.** "Investment in Human Capital." *A.E.R.,* 51 (March), 1–17. **184n.** **1962.** "Reflections on Investment in Man." *J.P.E.,* 70 (October, Supplement), 1–8. **184n.** **1964.** *Transforming Traditional Agriculture.* New Haven: Yale University Press. **81n.**

SCHUMPETER, J. A. **1934.** *The Theory of Economic Development.* Cambridge: Harvard University Press. **8, 109**

SCHWARTZMAN, D. **1959.** "The Effect of Monopoly on Price." *J.P.E.,* 67 (August), 352–362. **109** **1961.** "The Effect of Monopoly: A Correction." *J.P.E.,* 69 (October), 494. **109**

SCHYDLOWSKY, D. M. **1968.** "On the Choice of a Shadow Price of Foreign Exchange." Economic Development Report No. 108, Development Advisory Service. Cambridge: Harvard University Press. **381n.** See also Balassa, B. A., and D. M. Schydlowsky.

SCITOVSKY, T. **1958.** *Economic Theory and Western European Integration.* Stanford, Calif.: Stanford University Press. **351n.** **1959.** "Growth—Balanced or Unbalanced?" In M. Abramovitz, ed., *The Allocation of Economic Resources.* Stanford, Calif.: Stanford University Press, 207–217. **293n.** See also Little, I. M. D., T. Scitovsky, and M. Scott.

SCOTT, A. **1970.** "The Brain Drain—Is a Human Capital Approach Justified?" In W. L. Hansen, ed., *Education, Income and Human Capital* (Studies in Income and Wealth, Vol. 35). New York: N.B.E.R. **234n.**

SCOTT, M. See Little, I. M. D., T. Scitovsky, and M. Scott.

SEGELHORST, E. W. See Hirsch, W. Z., and E. W. Segelhorst.

SEN, A. K. **1957.** "Some Notes on the Choice of Capital-Intensity in Development Planning." *Q.J.E.,* 71 (November), 561–584. **395** **1960.** *Choice of Techniques.* Oxford: Blackwell. **394n.** **1964.** "Size of Holdings and Productivity." *The Economic Weekly,* 16 (February), 323–326. **73n.** **1966a.** "Education, Vintage and Learning by Doing." *Journal of Human Resources,* 1 (Fall), 3–21. **195n.** **1966b.** "Peasants and Dualism With or Without Surplus Labor." *J.P.E.,* 74 (October), 425–450. **206–210, 212n.** **1972.** "Control Areas and Accounting Prices: An Approach to Economic Evaluation." *E.J.,* 82 (March, Supplement), 486–501. **387n., 390** See also Dasgupta, P., S. A. Marglin, and A. K. Sen.

SENGUPTA, J. K. See Fox, K. A., J. K. Sengupta, and E. Thorbecke.

SHASHUA, L., and Y. GOLDSCHMIDT **1972.** "The Merits of Balanced Growth Reconsidered." *R.E.Stat.,* 54 (August), 337–339. **294n.**

SHAW, E. S. **1973.** *Financial Deepening in Economic Development.* New York: Oxford University Press. **8n.**

SHEPHARD, R. W. **1953.** *Cost and Production Functions.* Princeton: Princeton University Press. **95, 272**

SHISHIDO, S. See Chenery, H. B., S. Shishido, and T. Watanabe.

SIDHU, S. S. **1974.** "Relative Efficiency in Wheat Production in the Indian Punjab." *A.E.R.,* 64 (September), 742–751. **102**

SIEBERT, C. D. See Jorgenson, D. W., and C. D. Siebert.

SILBERSTON, A. **1972.** "Economies of Scale in Theory and Practice." *E.J.*, 82 (March, Supplement), 369–391. **150n., 152–153**

SIMMONS, J. **1972.** "Formal and Informal Education: The Relative Benefits for African Workers" (mimeo). **186n.**

SIMON, H. A. **1954.** "Bandwagon and Underdog Effects and the Possibility of Election Predictions." *Public Opinion Quarterly*, 18 (Fall), 245–253. **397n.**

SIMS, C. See Chenery, H. B., H. Elkington, and C. Sims.

SINGER, H. W. **1950.** "The Distribution of Gains between Investing and Borrowing Countries." *A.E.R.*, 40 (May), 473–485. **255, 341n.**
1964. *International Development: Growth and Change.* New York: McGraw-Hill. **291**

SINGH, S. K. **1970.** "Rural-Urban Wage Differential." Washington IBRD, Working Paper No. 70-14, Basic Research Center (mimeo). **226**
1972. "The Determinants of Aggregate Savings." In S. K. Singh, ed., *Development Economics: Theory and Findings.* Lexington, Mass.: Heath. **171, 173, 175**

SINHA, R. P. See Wilson, T., R. P. Sinha, and J. R. Castree.

SISLER, D. G. See Cohen, B. I., and D. G. Sisler.

SJAASTAD, L. A. **1962.** "The Costs and Returns of Human Migration." *J.P.E.*, 70 (October, Supplement), 80–93. **226**

SMITH, A. **1937.** *The Wealth of Nations.* New York: Kelley (Modern Library edition). **131**

SOLIGO, S. R. See Berry, R. A., and S. R. Soligo; Lewis, S. R., Jr., and S. R. Soligo.

SOLOW, R. M. **1957.** "Technical Change and the Aggregate Production Function." *R.E.Stat.*, 39 (August), 312–320. **154–155**
1967. "Technical Change and the Aggregate Production Function." In M. Brown, ed., *The Theory and Empirical Analysis of Production.* New York: N.B.E.R. 25–50. **159**
See also Arrow, K. J., H. B. Chenery, B. S. Minhas, and R. W. Solow.

SOLOW, R. M., and P. A. SAMUELSON **1953.** "Balanced Growth Under Constant Returns to Scale." *Econometrica*, 21 (July), 412–424. **295**

SOLTOW, L. **1965.** *Toward Income Equality in Norway.* Madison: University of Wisconsin Press. **248n.**
1968. "Long-run Changes in British Income Inequality." *Economic History Review*, 32 (April), 17–29. **248n.**

SOMEL, K. See Yotopoulos, P. A., L. J. Lau, and K. Somel.

SRINIVASAN, T. N. **1972.** "The State of Development Economics." (August, mimeo). **3n.**
See also Bhagwati, J. N., and T. N. Srinivasan.

SRIVASTAVA, U. K., and E. O. HEADY, **1973.** "Technological Change and Relative Factor Shares in Indian Agriculture: An Empirical

Analysis." Ames: Iowa State University (mimeo). **162**

STAAF, R. J. See Tullock, G. C., and R. J. Staaf.

STAFFORD, F. See Holbrook, R., and F. Stafford.

STEPHENSON, J. A. See Jorgenson, D. W., and J. A. Stephenson.

STERN, R. M. **1962.** "British and American Productivity and Comparative Costs in International Trade." *O.E.P.*, 14 (October), 275–296. **321**
See also Leamer, E. E., and R. M. Stern.

STIGLER, G. J. **1951.** "The Division of Labor Is Limited by the Extent of the Market." *J.P.E.*, 59 (June), 185–193. **379**
1956. "The Statistics of Monopoly and Merger." *J.P.E.*, 64 (February), 33–40. **109**
1958. "The Economies of Scale." *Journal of Law and Economics*, 1 (June), 54–71. **150n.**
1962. "Information in the Labor Market." *J.P.E.*, 70 (October, Supplement), 94–105. **184n., 186, 230**

STIGLITZ, J. E. **1969.** "Rural-Urban Migration, Surplus Labor and the Relationship between Urban and Rural Wages." *Eastern Africa Economic Review*, 1 (December), 1–27. **210–211**
1974. "Alternative Theories of Wage Determination and Unemployment in LDCs: The Labor Turnover Model." *Q.J.E.*, 58 (May), 194–227. **226n.**
See also Atkinson, A. B., and J. E. Stiglitz; Dasgupta, P., and J. E. Stiglitz.

STONE, R. **1954.** "Linear Expenditure Systems and Demand Analysis: An Application to the Pattern of British Demand." *E.J.*, 64 (September), 511–527. **32n.**

STONE, R., and J. A. C. BROWN **1962.** "A Long-Term Growth Model for the British Economy." In R. C. Geary, ed., *Europe's Future in Figures.* Amsterdam: North Holland, 287–310. **399**

STORM, C. See Child, F., and C. Storm.

STOUTJESDIJK, E., and L. E. WESTPHAL **1973.** *Industrial Planning with Economies of Scale.* Amsterdam: North Holland. **411n.**

STREETEN, P. **1959.** "Unbalanced Growth." *O.E.P.*, 11 (June), 167–190. **294**

STROTZ, R. H. See Eisner, R., and R. H. Strotz.

STROUT, A. M. **1969.** "Korea's Use of Foreign and Domestic Resources: A Cross-Country Comparison." In I. Adelman, ed., *Practical Approaches to Development Planning: Korea's Second Five-Year Plan.* Baltimore: Johns Hopkins University Press, 277–288. **394n.**
See also Chenery, H. B., and A. M. Strout.

STUDENMUND, A. H. See Vanek, J., and A. H. Studenmund.

SUITS, D. B. **1963.** "The Determinants of Consumer Expenditure: A Review of Present Knowledge." In D. B. Suits, ed., *Impacts of*

Monetary Policy. Englewood Cliffs, N.J.: Prentice-Hall. **391**

1964. *An Econometric Model of the Greek Economy.* Athens: Center of Planning and Economic Research. **412**

SUN, I. S. **1966.** "Trade Policies and Economic Development in Taiwan." In T. Morgan and N. Spoelstra, eds., *Economic Interdependence in Southeast Asia.* Madison: University of Wisconsin Press, 99–123. **118n.**

SWAMY, D. C. **1967.** "Statistical Evidence of Balanced and Unbalanced Growth." *R.E.Stat.,* 49 (August), 288–303. **294n., 297n.**

TAEUBER, K. E., and A. F. TAEUBER **1965.** *Negroes in Cities.* Chicago: Aldine. **226n.**

TASKIER, C. E. **1961.** *Input-Output Bibliography, 1955–60.* New York: U.N. (ST/STAT/7). **57**

TAUBMAN, P. **See** Friend, I., and P. Taubman.

TAYLOR, L. J. **1969.** "Development Patterns: A Simulation Study." *Q.J.E.,* 83 (May), 220–241. **287n., 291**

See also Chenery, H. B., and L. J. Taylor; Kendrick, D. A., and L. J. Taylor.

TEUBAL, M. **1973.** "Comparative Advantage and Technological Change: The Learning by Doing Case." *Journal of International Economics,* 3 (May), 161–177. **326**

THEIL, H. **1957.** "Specification Errors and the Estimation of Economic Relationships." *Review of International Statistical Institute,* 25, No. 1–3, 41–51. **78n., 80**

1964. *Optimal Decision Rules for Government and Industry.* Amsterdam: North Holland. **423**

1965. "Linear Decision Rules for Macrodynamic Policy Problems." In B. G. Hickman, ed., *Quantitative Planning of Economic Policy.* Washington, D.C.: Brookings Institution. **423**

1967. *Economics and Information Theory.* Amsterdam: North Holland. **244**

THIRLWALL, A. P. **See** Kennedy, C., and A. P. Thirlwall.

THORBECKE, E. **See** Fox, K. A., J. K. Sengupta, and E. Thorbecke.

THUROW, L. C. **1969.** *Poverty and Discrimination.* Washington, D.C.: Brookings Institution. **231**

THUROW, L. C., and R. E. LUCAS **1972.** "The American Distribution of Income: A Structural Problem." U.S. Congress, Joint Economic Committee. **193n., 231, 233, 234**

THURSTONE, L. L. **1961.** *Multiple Factor Analysis.* Chicago: University of Chicago Press. **32n.**

THWEATT, W. O. **1968.** "Investment and Per Capita Consumption During the Threshold of Economic Growth." *E.D.C.C.,* 16 (January), 175–187. **31n.**

TIEBOUT, C. M. **1956.** "A Pure Theory of Local Expenditure." *J.P.E.,* 64 (October), 416–424. **256**

TINBERGEN, J. **1952.** *On the Theory of Economic Policy.* Amsterdam: North Holland. **423**

TODARO, M. P. **1969.** "A Model of Labor Migration and Urban Unemployment in Less Developed Countries." *A.E.R.,* 59 (March), 138–148. **227**

1971. "Income Expectations, Rural-Urban Migration and Employment in Africa." *International Labor Review,* 104 (November), 387–413. **224, 229**

See also Harris, J. R., and M. P. Todaro.

TOLLEY, G. S., and E. OLSON **1971.** "The Interdependence between Income and Education." *J.P.E.,* 79 (May), 460–480. **196**

TRUMAN, E. M. **1969.** "The European Economic Community: Trade Creation and Trade Diversion." *Yale Economic Essays,* 9 (Spring), 201–257. **351n.**

See also Resnick, S. A., and E. M. Truman.

TSIANG, S. C. **See** Fleming, J. M., and S. C. Tsiang.

TULLOCK, G. C. **1967.** "The Welfare Costs of Tariffs, Monopolies and Theft." *Western Economic Journal,* 5 (June), 224–232. **110, 358**

TULLOCK, G. C., and R. J. STAAF **1973.** "Education and Equality." In S. Weintraub, ed., *Income Inequality, The Annals of the American Academy of Political and Social Science,* 409 (September), 125–134. **193n.**

See also Buchanan, J. M., and G. C. Tullock.

TURNER, H. A., and D. A. JACKSON **1970.** "On the Determination of the General Wage Level—A World Analysis." *E.J.,* 80 (December), 827–849. **226**

TURNHAM, D. J. **1971.** *The Employment Problem in Less-Developed Countries: A Review of Evidence.* Paris: OECD, Development Center. **6, 199, 200, 201, 203, 204, 205**

U.N. **1963.** *A Study of Industrial Growth.* New York. **150n., 293n.**

1970. "Trade Dependence in European Countries, 1958 to 1967." *Economic Bulletin for Europe,* 21, No. 1, 43–65. New York. **314**

UNCTAD **1968.** *Trade Prospects and Capital Needs of Developing Countries.* TD/34/Supp.1/Rev. 1. New York. **402n.**

1969. *Trade in Manufactures of Developing Countries, 1968 Review.* TD/B/C.2/51/Rev. 1. New York. **323**

1971. "The Terms of Trade" (mimeo). **344n.**

U.N.: DEPARTMENT OF ECONOMIC AFFAIRS **1949.** *Relatives Prices of Exports and Imports of Underdeveloped Countries.* Sales No. 49. II. B.3 New York. **341n., 343**

1950. *The Economic Development of Latin America and Its Principal Problems.* E/CN.12/89/Rev. 1. New York. **341n., 343**

U.N.: DEPARTMENT OF ECONOMIC AND SOCIAL AFFAIRS **1969.** *Growth of the World's Urban and Rural Population, 1920–2000.* ST/SOA/Service A/44, New York. **224, 225**

1972. *Input-Output Bibliography, 1966–1970.* Vol. I. Authors; Vol. II. Countries; Vol. III.

Subjects. Series M. No. 55 ST/STAT/SER.M/ 55. New York. **57**

U.N.: ECAFE **1960.** *Programming Techniques for Economic Development with Special References to Asia and the Far East.* Development Programming Techniques Series, No. 1. New York. **12**

U.N.: ECLA **1963.** *Economic Bulletin for Latin America,* 8 (March), 103–109. **343n.**
1966. "The Process of Industrialization in Latin America." U.N. document, ST/ECLA/ Conf. 23/L2/Add. 2, Statistical Annex (January, mimeo). **12n.**

U.N.: FAO **1957.** *The State of Food and Agriculture, 1957.* Rome. **259n.**

UNIDO **1967.** "Industrial Excess Capacity and Its Utilization for Export." UNIDO/IPPD/1, (October, mimeo). **12n.**
1972. *Guidelines for Project Evaluation,* ID/ Ser.H/2. New York. **382, 383–386, 388–391**

U.N.: STATISTICAL OFFICE. **1967.** *Input-Output Bibliography, 1963–1966.* Statistical Papers, Series M, No. 46. New York. **57**

UPPAL, J. S. **1969.** "Measurement of Disguised Unemployment in an Underdeveloped Economy —An Economic Approach." *The Asian Economic Review,* 11 (August), 405–411. **216n.**

UZAWA, H. **See** Chenery, H. B., and H. Uzawa.

VANDERKAMP, J. **1971.** "Migration Flows, Their Determinants and the Effects of Return Migration." *J.P.E.,* 79 (September), 1012–1031. **236**
1972. "Return Migration: Its Significance and Behavior." *Western Economic Journal,* 10 (December), 460–466. **236**

Van de KLUNDERT, T. **See** David, P. A., and T. van de Klundert.

VANEK, J. **1965.** *General Equilibrium of International Discrimination.* Cambridge: Harvard University Press. **357n.**
1967. *Estimating Resource Needs for Economic Development.* New York: McGraw-Hill. **402n.**
1971. "Tariffs, Economic Welfare and Development Potential." *E.J.,* 81 (December), 904–913. **123**
See also Bertrand, T. J., and J. Vanek.

VANEK, J., and A. H. STUDENMUND **1968.** "Towards a Better Understanding of the Incremental Capital-Output Ratio." *Q.J.E.,* **82** (August), 452–464. **394n.**

VERDOON, P. J., and F. J. M. MEYER ZU SCHLOCHTERN **1964.** "Trade Creation and Trade Diversion in the Common Market." In *Integration Européene et Realité Economique.* Brussels: College of Europe. **351n.**

VERNON, R. **1966.** "International Investments and International Trade in the Product Cycle." *Q.J.E.,* 80 (May), 190–207. **77n., 325n.**

VIETORISZ, T., and B. HARRISON **1973.** "Labor Market Segmentation: Positive Feedback and Divergent Development." *A.E.R.,* 63 (May), 366–376. **256**

VINCENT, P. E. **See** Margolis, J., and P. E. Vincent.

VINER, J. **1950.** *The Customs Union Issue.* New York: Carnegie Endowment for International Peace. **348**

WAELBROECK, J. **1964.** "Le Commerce de la Communauté Européene avec les Pays Tiers." In *Integration Européene et Realité Economique.* Brussels: College of Europe, 139–164. **351n.**

WALLACE, T. D. **1962.** "Measures of Social Costs of Agricultural Programs." *J.F.E.,* 44 (May), 580–594. **381n.**

WALTERS, A. A. **1963a.** "Production and Cost Functions: An Econometric Survey." *Econometrica,* 31 (January), 1–66. **84**
1963b. "A Note on Economies of Scale." *R.E.Stat.,* 45 (November), 425–427. **352n.**
1966. "Incremental Capital-Output Ratios." *E.J.,* 76 (December), 818–822. **394n.**

WATANABE, T. **1965.** "Economic Aspects of Dualism in the Industrial Development of Japan." *E.D.C.C.,* 13 (April), 293–312. **255**
See also Chenery, H. B., S. Shishido, and T. Watanabe; Chenery, H. B., and T. Watanabe.

WEINTRAUB, S. **1958.** *An Approach to the Theory of Income Distribution.* Philadelphia: Chilton. **247n.**

WEISBROD, B. A. **1961.** "The Valuation of Human Capital." *J.P.E.,* 69 (October), 425– 436. **187n.**
1962. "Education and Investment in Human Capital." *J.P.E.,* 70 (October, Supplement), 106– 123. **187n.**
1964. *External Benefits of Public Education.* Princeton: Princeton University, Department of Economics, Industrial Relations Section. **187n.**
See also Hansen, W. L., B. A. Weisbrod, and W. J. Scanlon.

WEISBROD, B. A., and P. KARPOFF **1968.** "Monetary Returns to College Education, Student Ability and College Quality." *R.E.Stat.,* 50 (November), 491–497. **195n.**

WEISS, R. D. **1970.** "The Effect of Education on the Earnings of Blacks and Whites." *R.E.Stat.,* 52 (May), 150–159. **191**

WEISSKOFF, R. **1969.** "Demand Elasticities for a Developing Economy: An International Comparison of Consumption Patterns." Economic Development Report No. 125, Project for Quantitative Research in Economic Development. Cambridge: Harvard Center for International Affairs. **287n.**
1970. "Income Distribution and Economic Growth in Puerto Rico, Argentina and Mexico." *Review of Income and Wealth,* 16 (December), 303–332. **248n., 249, 250**

WEISSKOPF, T. E. **1972.** "An Econometric Test of Alternative Constraints on the Growth of

Underdeveloped Countries." *R.E.Stat.*, 54 (February), 67–78. **287n.**

WELLISZ, S. **1968.** "Dual Economies, Disguised Unemployment and the Unlimited Supply of Labor." *Economica*, 35 (February), 22–51. **212n.**

WELLS, L. T., Jr. **1969.** "Test of a Product Cycle Model of International Trade: United States Exports of Consumers' Durables." *Q.J.E.*, 83 (February), 152–162. **325n.**

1972. "International Trade: The Product Life Cycle Approach." In L. T. Wells, Jr., ed., *The Product Life Cycle and International Trade.* Boston: Harvard University, Graduate School of Business Administration, 3–33. **77n., 325n.**

WERTHEIMER, R. F., II **1970.** *The Monetary Rewards of Migration within the U.S.* Washington, D.C.: The Urban Institute. **226n.**

WESTEBBE, R. M. **See** Ellis, H. S., D. D. Psilos, R. M. Westebbe, and C. Nicolaou.

WESTPHAL, L. E. **1971.** *Planning Investments with Economies of Scale.* Amsterdam: North Holland. **408n.**

See also Stoutjesdijk, E., and L. E. Westphal.

WHINSTON, A. **See** Davis, O. A., and A. Whinston.

WHITCOMB, D. **See** Haldi, J., and D. Whitcomb.

WILBER, C. K., ed. **1973.** *The Political Economy of Development and Underdevelopment.* New York: Random House. **257n.**

WILFORD, W. T. **1970.** "Trade Creation in the Central American Common Market." *Western Economic Journal*, 8 (March), 61–69. **352**

WILLIAMSON, J. **1971.** "Trade and Economic Growth." In J. Pinder, ed., *The Economics of Europe.* London: Knight, 19–45. **358n.**

WILLIAMSON, J., and A. BOTTRILL **1971.** "The Impact of Customs Unions on Trade in Manufactures." *Oxford Economic Papers*, 23 (November), 323–351. **351n.**

WILLIAMSON, J. G. **1965.** "Regional Inequality and the Process of National Development: A Description of Patterns." *E.D.C.C.*, 13 (July), 1–84. **248n.**

1968. "Personal Saving in Developing Nations: An Intertemporal Cross-Section from Asia." *Economic Record*, 44 (June), 194–210. **171, 174, 175, 176**

See also Kelley, A. C., and J. G. Williamson; Kelley, A. C., J. G. Williamson, and R. Cheetham.

WILLIAMSON, O. E. **1968.** "Economies as an Antitrust Defense: The Welfare Tradeoffs." *A.E.R.*, 58 (March), 18–36. **120**

WILLMORE, L. N. **1972.** "Trade Creation, Trade Diversion and Effective Protection in the Central American Common Market" (mimeo). **352**

WILSON, T., R. P. SINHA, and J. R. CASTREE **1969.** "The Income Terms of Trade of Developed and Developing Countries." *E.J.*, 79 (December), 813–832. **344**

WINTER, D. G. **See** McClelland, D. C., and D. G. Winter.

WINTER, S. G. **See** Nelson, R. R., and S. G. Winter.

WINSTON, G. C. **1971.** "Capital Utilization in Economic Development." *E.J.*, 81 (March), 36–60. **12n.**

WISDOM, J. D. **1952.** *Foundations of Inference in Natural Science.* London: Methuen. **23n.**

WISE, J., and P. A. YOTOPOULOS **1969.** "The Empirical Content of Economic Rationality: A Test for a Less Developed Economy." *J.P.E.*, 77 (November), 976–1004. **88–93**

See also Yotopoulos, P. A., and J. Wise.

WITTE, A. D. **1970.** "Employment in the Manufacturing Sector of Developing Economies: A Study of Mexico, Peru and Venezuela." Ph.D. Dissertation, North Carolina State University. **151**

1971. "Alternative Estimates of Capital-Labor Substitution in Manufacturing in Developing Economies: Comments on Professor Clague." *Econometrica*, 39 (November), 1053–1054. **151**

WOLF, C., Jr. **1964.** "Savings, Regressions, Self Help and Development Performance." RAND mimeo. **176n.**

WORCESTER, D. A., Jr. **1969.** "Innovations in the Calculation of Welfare Loss to Monopoly." *Western Economic Journal*, 7 (September), 234–243. **109n.**

YATES, P. L. **1959.** *Forty Years of Foreign Trade.* London: Allan & Unwin. **314n.**

YOTOPOULOS, P. A. **1964.** *The Elasticity of the Labor Supply Curve: A Theory and an Evaluation for Greek Agriculture.* Athens: Center of Planning and Economic Research. **83, 203**

1967a. *Allocative Efficiency in Economic Development: A Cross Section Analysis of Epirus Farming.* Athens: Center of Planning and Economic Research. **66n., 67, 68n., 82, 84n., 100n., 101, 180n., 213, 275n.**

1967b. "From Stock to Flow Capital Inputs for Agricultural Production Functions: A Microanalytic Approach." *J.F.E.*, 49 (May), 476–491. **67n., 100n., 101, 156, 275n.**

1968. "On the Efficiency of Resource Utilization in Subsistence Agriculture." *F.R.I.S.*, 8, No. 2, 125–135. **82**

See also Lau, L. J., and P. A. Yotopoulos; Pepelasis, A. A., and P. A. Yotopoulos; Wise, J., and P. A. Yotopoulos.

YOTOPOULOS, P. A., and L. J. LAU **1970.** "A Test for Balanced and Unbalanced Growth." *R.E.Stat.*, 52 (November), 376–384. **294n., 295–297**

1973. "A Test for Relative Efficiency: Some Further Results." *A.E.R.*, 63 (March), 214–223. **100n.**

1974. "On Modeling the Agricultural Sector in

Developing Economies: An Integrated Approach of Micro and Macroeconomics." *J.D.E.*, 1 (June), 105–127. **73n., 102, 206, 271n., 273n.**

1975. "The Balanced-Unbalanced Growth Controversy Revisited." *R.E.Stat.* (forthcoming). **297n.**

YOTOPOULOS, P. A., L. J. LAU, and K. SOMEL 1970. "Labor Intensity and Relative Efficiency in Indian Agriculture." *F.R.I.S.*, 9, No. 1, 43–55. **69, 73n.**

YOTOPOULOS, P. A., and W. MIKLIUS 1970. "A Framework for Studying Technological Change and the Impact on the Manpower Situation in Hawaii." Honolulu, Hawaii: Economic Research Center (mimeo). **158**

YOTOPOULOS, P. A., and J. B. NUGENT 1973. "A Balanced-Growth Version of the Linkage Hypothesis: A Test." *Q.J.E.*, 87 (May), 157–171. **299n.**

YOTOPOULOS, P. A., and J. WISE 1969a. "On Testing Competing Hypotheses: Economic Rationality Versus Traditional Behavior—A Further Development." *A.J.A.E.*, 51 (February), 203–209. **88n.**

1969b. "On Testing Competing Hypotheses: Economic Rationality Versus Traditional Behavior: Rejoinder." *A.J.A.E.*, 51 (February), 209–210. **88n.**

1969c. "Epilegomena on Traditional Behavior Models." *A.J.A.E.*, 51 (November), 938–939. **88n.**

YOUNG, A. 1928. "Increasing Returns and Economic Progress." *E.J.*, 38 (December), 527–542. **378n.**

ZAREMBKA, P. 1972. *Toward a Theory of Economic Development.* San Francisco: Holden Day. **211, 212, 227, 256, 281n.**

ZELLNER, A. 1962. "An Efficient Method of Estimating Seemingly Unrelated Regressions and Tests for Aggregation Bias." *Journal of the American Statistical Association*, 57 (June), 348–368. **273, 283**

ZELLNER, A., and M. S. GEISEL 1970. "Analysis of Distributed Lag Models with Applications to Consumption Function Estimation." *Econometrica*, 38 (November), 865–888. **175**

ZELLNER, A., J. KMENTA, and J. DRÈZE 1966. "Specification and Estimation of Cobb-Douglas Production Function Models." *Econometrica*, 34 (October), 784–795. **85n.**

ZEMAN, M. 1955. "A Quantitative Analysis of White-Non-White Income Differentials in the U.S. in 1939." Unpublished Ph.D. Dissertation, University of Chicago. **191n.**

ZINSER, J. E. **See** Mikesell, R. F., and J. E. Zinser.

ZUSMAN, P., A. MELAMED, and I. KATZIR 1969. *Possible Trade and Welfare Effects of EEC Tariff and "Reference Price" Policy on the European-Mediterranean Market for Winter Oranges.* Berkeley: California Agricultural Experiment Station, Giannini Foundation, Monograph 24. **381n.**

Index